BOYS AND GIRLS

The Development of Gender Roles

BOYS AND GIRLS
The Development of Gender Roles

Carole R. Beal

*University of Massachusetts
at Amherst*

McGraw-Hill, Inc.
New York   St. Louis   San Francisco   Auckland   Bogotá   Caracas
Lisbon   London   Madrid   Mexico City   Milan   Montreal   New Delhi
San Juan   Singapore   Sydney   Tokyo   Toronto

BOYS AND GIRLS: The Development of Gender Roles

This book is printed on acid-free paper.

1 2 3 4 5 6 7 8 9 0   AGM   AGM   9 0 9 8 7 6 5 4 3

ISBN 0-07-004533-X

This book was set in Garamond by Better Graphics, Inc.
The editors were Jane Vaicunas and Fred H. Burns;
the design was done by Circa '86;
the production supervisor was Paula Keller.
The photo editor was Jennifer Atkins.
Arcata Graphics/Martinsburg was printer and binder.

Permission to reprint excerpts from Ann Landers in Chapters 3, 10, and 13 is gratefully acknowledged.

Permission to reprint "Ask Beth" from *The Boston Globe*, November 10, 1992, page 73, is gratefully acknowledged.

CHAPTER OPENING PHOTO CREDITS
Chapter 1: Susie Fitzhugh/Stock, Boston; *Chapter 2:* Rita Nannini/Photo Researchers;
Chapter 3: John Coletti/Picture Cube; *Chapter 4:* Renee Lynn/Photo Researchers;
Chapter 5: Michael Siluk/Image Works; *Chapter 6:* David M. Grossman;
Chapter 7: Susan Woog Wagner/Photo Researchers; *Chapter 8:* Elizabeth Crews;
Chapter 9: Carol Palmer/Picture Cube; *Chapter 10:* Margaret Miller/Photo Researchers;
Chapter 11: Paul Conklin/Monkmeyer; *Chapter 12:* Lynne Jaeger Weinstein/Woodfin
Camp & Associates; *Chapter 13:* Elizabeth Glasgow/Monkmeyer; *Chapter 14:* Elizabeth
Crews.

Library of Congress Cataloging-in-Publication Data

Beal, Carole R.
   Boys and girls: the development of gender roles / Carole R. Beal.
      p.   cm.
   Includes bibliographical references and indexes.
   ISBN 0-07-004533-X
   1. Sex role in children.   2. Sex differences (Psychology) in
children.   3. Psychosexual development.   I. Title.
BF723.S42B435   1994
155.43—dc20   93-6422

Carole R. Beal is Associate Professor of Psychology at
the University of Massachusetts at Amherst. She graduated
summa cum laude from the University of California at
San Diego in 1977, where she was elected to Phi Beta Kappa.
She received her Ph.D. from Stanford University in 1983 and
then joined the faculty of Dartmouth College, where she
taught several courses in gender role development.
She has published many articles on children's cognitive
development and in 1988 won a National Academy
of Education Spencer Fellowship to conduct research
on children's writing skills.

To M. Allan Beal, in memory

CONTENTS

Preface · xvii
Acknowledgments · xxi

1 Introduction · 2
The "Cory Incident" · 3
Gender Roles and Stereotypes · 3
Gender Roles as Socially Determined · 4
From Roles to Stereotypes · 5
Learning Gender · 6
Punctuated Socialization · 8
Targeted Learning · 8
Developmental "Windows of Opportunity" · 9
Decreased Emphasis on Parents · 9
Asymmetric Socialization · 10
Gender Self-Defines · 11
Organization of This Book · 11

2 Biological Beginnings · 14
Conception: Chromosomal Sex · 16
Sex Determination · 16
Abnormalities of Sex Chromosomes · 17
Male Vulnerability · 18
Prenatal Development: Gonadal Sex · 20
Masculine Development · 20
Feminine Development · 21
Genital Sex: Ambiguous Sexual Differentiation · 22
"Masculinized" Females · 22
Feminized Males · 23
Gender as a Dichotomy · 25
Sex Assignment within a Critical Period · 25
Inconsistent Sex of Rearing · 26
Counterexamples · 27
Summary · 29

3 Boys and Girls: The First Year · 30

Is It a Boy or a Girl? · 32

    The Preference for Boys · 32

    Sex Selection · 36

    Does It Matter? · 39

Characteristics of Boy and Girl Babies · 40

    Physical Development · 40

    Perceptual Abilities · 40

    Activity Level · 41

Creating Differences · 42

    Gender Clues · 42

    The Eye of the Beholder · 44

Getting to Know You: Parents' Behavior with Sons and Daughters · 45

    Mothers and Daughters · 45

    Fathers and Sons · 48

Summary · 48

4 Theories of Gender Role Development: The Psychoanalytic Perspective · 50

Framework of the Theory · 52

The Psychosexual Stages · 53

    The Oral Stage (0 to 1 Year) · 53

    The Anal Stage (1 to 3 Years) · 54

    The Genital Stage (3 to 6 Years) · 55

Contributions of the Theory · 59

    A Foundation for the Future · 59

    Clinical Insights · 60

Weaknesses of the Theory · 63

    Status as a Theory · 63

    Evidence for the Theory · 64

Summary · 66

5 Theories of Gender Role Development: Social Learning · 68

Components of Social Learning Theory · 70

    Reinforcement · 70

    Role Models · 70

    Representativeness · 71

Boys and Girls: Differential Reinforcements · 71

    Play · 72

    Independence and Compliance · 74

    Achievement · 76

    Other Cultures · 78

  Role Models in the Family · 80

    Employed Mothers · 80

    Absent Fathers · 81

    Gay and Lesbian Parents · 84

    Siblings · 85

  Evaluation of the Social Learning Approach · 87

    Comparison with Psychoanalytic Theory · 87

    Strengths and Weaknesses of the Social Learning Approach · 88

6 Theories of Gender Role Development: Cognitive-Developmental
Approaches · 90

  Theorists and Schemas · 92

    Major Theorists · 92

    Gender Schemas · 92

  Gender Identity · 93

    Infancy · 94

    Early Gender Identity · 94

    The Toddler Period: Using Gender Labels · 95

    The Preschool Period · 97

    Gender Identity: Effects on Behavior · 100

  Gender as an Organizing Principle · 102

    Reasoning about Others · 102

    Memory Effects · 103

    Exaggerated Stereotyping · 105

    In-Group, Out-Group · 106

    Self-Regulation of Behavior · 107

  The Possibilities for Change · 110

    Direct Intervention · 111

    Raising Gender-Aschematic Children · 111

  Summary · 112

    Comparisons with Other Theories · 113

    *Strengths and Weaknesses of the Cognitive-Developmental
Perspective* · 113

7 Beyond the Family: The Power of Peers · 116

  Separate Worlds: Gender Segregation in Play · 118

    Toddlers and Preschoolers: Pulling Apart · 118

    Middle Childhood: "Border Work" · 121

Boys' and Girls' Friendships · 122
   The Structure of Play Groups · 122
   Sex Differences in Favorite Games · 125
   The Language of Friendship · 126
Separate Worlds: Implications for Mixed-Sex Interaction · 128
Asymmetry in Peer Socialization · 130
The Possibilities for Change · 131
Summary · 133

8 Beyond the Family: Schools and the Hidden Curriculum · 134
Interactions with Teachers · 136
   Compliant Girls, Rambunctious Boys · 136
   Instruction · 137
   What about Male Teachers? · 139
   Why are Boys and Girls Treated Differently? · 140
The Effects of Differential Treatment · 144
   Academic Self-Confidence · 144
Peer Relations in School · 150
   Why Are You Taking That? · 150
   "Just Ignore It" · 151
The Possibilities for Change · 152
   Teachers as Agents of Change · 152
   Reorganizing the Classroom · 153
   Teacher Training · 154
Summary · 154

9 Beyond the Family: Media Messages · 156
Television: The Universal Curriculum · 157
   What Do Children See on TV? · 158
   The Impact of TV on Children's Gender Stereotypes · 163
The Power of Words · 169
   Children's Books · 169
   The Effects of Sexist Language · 173
Summary · 175

10 Personality Characteristics of Boys and Girls · 176
What Is a Gender Difference? · 178
   Example: Gender Differences in Height · 178
Aggression · 187
   Patterns of Aggression in Boys and Girls · 187

Theories of Aggressive Behavior · 189
Aggression: The Bottom Line · 197
Prosocial Behavior · 198
Altruism · 198
Nurturance · 200
Prosocial Behavior: The Bottom Line · 204
Moral Reasoning · 204
Cognitive Theories of Morality: Fairness and Justice · 205
The Voice of Care · 206
Moral Reasoning: The Bottom Line · 208
Stereotypes: A Kernel of Truth? · 209
Summary · 210

11 Intellectual Characteristics of Boys and Girls · 212
Cognitive Abilities of Boys and Girls · 214
Verbal Skills · 214
Spatial Ability · 215
Mathematical Reasoning · 217
Theories of Cognitive Abilities · 219
Hemispheric Organization: Sex Differences in the Brain? · 219
Tradeoffs: Specialization versus Collaboration? · 220
The Socialization of Cognitive Abilities · 223
Verbal Abilities · 223
Spatial Abilities · 225
Mathematics · 227
Does It Matter? · 230
Interpreting Gender Differences · 232
Summary · 234

12 Growing Up: The Transition to Adult Roles · 236
Puberty: Physical Changes · 238
Female Development · 238
Male Development · 242
Cognitive Development · 243
The "Flight into Femininity" · 244
Media Messages · 244
Timing of Puberty: The Interaction of Biology and Cognition · 245
Family Influences · 247
Peers · 249
Same-Gender Friendships · 249

Dating and Sexual Relationships · 252
Sexual Activity · 254
School · 257
School Structure · 258
Class Participation · 258
The Role of Culture: Rites of Passage · 259
Male Rites · 260
Female Rites · 260
Female Circumcision · 260
Benefits? · 261
Summary · 261
Pay Now, Pay Later? · 262

13 Gender Identity Disturbance in Childhood · 264
Diagnosing Gender Identity Disturbance · 266
Diagnostic Criteria · 266
Gender Identity versus Gender Role · 268
Childhood Gender Disturbance: "Failed" Socialization? · 269
Gender Lessons: Mixed Messages? · 269
Does Failed Socialization Explain Gender Disturbance? · 272
The Question of Intervention · 273
Adult Outcomes · 273
Transsexualism · 273
Treatment Programs · 274
Do Gender-Disturbed Children Need Therapy? · 275
Summary · 278

14 Conclusions · 280
Gender Role Learning · 282
Beyond Parents · 282
Punctuated Socialization · 282
The Role of Biology · 283
Are Gender Roles Good or Bad? · 283
Benefits · 283
Costs · 284
What If? · 284
The Possibilities for Change · 285
Changing the Message · 285
Nonsexist Child Rearing? · 286
Just a Matter of Time · 287

References · 289
Indexes
Author Index · 343
Subject Index · 350

P R E F A C E

As infants, boys and girls are so similar to one another that their sex is easily mistaken by the casual observer. Yet by adolescence they have developed different behaviors, styles of dress and speech, interests and skills, and ways of relating to parents and peers, as well as different dreams and hopes for the future. The goal of this book is to describe the processes through which this happens, that is, how children learn to be boys and girls.

Most people find the topic of gender role development to be quite interesting. I think this is because gender issues touch everyone's lives directly—after all, everyone grew up as a boy or girl and has some personal experience to draw upon—and people often have quite strong feelings about why the sexes are the way they are and whether gender roles can or should be changed. Some people assume that males and females are simply born with particular characteristics and that as a result of biological predispositions little boys will inevitably want to bash one another over the head with pretend swords while girls will cuddle their baby dolls in the kitchen corner of the preschool. Others are equally convinced that biology has nothing to do with it and that children are molded and shaped by how they are treated by their parents, as well as by imitating what they see in the society around them. As the result of numerous research projects conducted over the last quarter-century or so, we are now beginning to move beyond this simple nature-versus-nurture dichotomy. In fact, as we will see throughout the book, biological and socialization forces interact to shape children's development as a male or female.

Saying that both biology and socialization are involved in children's development is not particularly profound; any introductory child development textbook will make the same point! Yet in the specific area of gender roles these issues have often been highly controversial, eliciting heated arguments about the roles of nature and nurture from professional researchers as well as parents, educators, religious leaders, politicians, and media figures. My own view, which you will see woven throughout the book, is that in no area of child development will we find that biology is a sufficient explanation for the behavioral differences between the sexes. In fact, in most cases there is considerable evidence that gender roles are learned, beginning very early in the life span. In other words, biology is not destiny, and the fact that we can observe differences in how boys and girls behave does not mean that those differences are inevitable or unchangeable. Throughout the book you will see examples of situations in which the behaviors that are considered "normal" can be eliminated or reversed. These findings suggest that children in future generations may grow up free of some of the limitations that are currently imposed by traditional gender role expectations. At the same time, the prevalence with which gender distinctions are made across cultures, the tenacity with which people cling to traditional ideas about masculinity and feminity, and the surprising eagerness with which children learn the male and female roles considered appropriate in their culture all suggest that gender roles are serving important social and psychological functions, both for individuals and for societies. Those of us who would like to see a reduction in stereotyping must take this into account, and so one of the goals of the book will be to consider how gender roles serve to support children's development in terms of helping them establish a personal identity and acquire the skills that they will need to fit into the society as adult men and women.

Organization and coverage

The book is organized to follow the sequence of a child's development from the time of conception through adolescence, as I have found that the chronological approach is easiest for most students to follow.

We begin with an introduction to the area of gender role studies and child development in Chapter 1, and a discussion of what makes a developing child male or female in biological terms in Chapter 2.

A complete chapter on gender issues during the first year of life is included, reflecting the growing interest in developmental psychology in infant development (Chapter 3).

We also consider the major theories of gender role development, reviewing and evaluating the key claims and evidence for each (Chapters 4, 5, and 6). The influence of the family is considered in these chapters, including separate discussions of the role of mothers, fathers, gay and lesbian parents, single parents, and siblings.

The book moves beyond the traditional focus on the family to examine other influences such as teachers, peers, children's literature, and television. Some of this material, reviewed in Chapters 7, 8 and 9, is often otherwise not easily accessible to students. It will become clear that although parents are certainly important they are hardly the entire story in gender role socialization. In fact, their voices can sometimes be drowned out by the proliferation of stereotyped messages from these other sources.

In Chapters 10 and 11 we look at some of the consequences of growing up as a boy or girl for children's personality characteristics, their cognitive and intellectual abilities.

A complete chapter on adolescence is included (Chapter 12), in which the experiences of boys and girls as they move into the adult male or female role are reviewed.

Finally, we consider the issue of childhood gender identity disturbance, a disorder in which a very young child believes that he or she is really the other sex (Chapter 13). Although extremely rare, the existence of such children raises important questions about the process of gender role learning and the role of culture, questions that are addressed again in our conclusions (Chapter 14).

Special features

There are several unique features to the book.

First, we focus on *both* sexes, boys as well as girls. There are many excellent books that discuss the unique aspects of feminine development, as well as several books on the adult male gender role, yet none includes a thorough coverage of both. Considering both male and female development allows us to see that gender role stereotyping negatively affects both sexes; in fact, boys may even be more strongly affected than girls. This may be a surprise to some students, as the discrimination faced by girls and women in our culture as well as most cultures around the world is ongoing and easily perceived. Yet discrimination comes in many forms, and it will become clear that the costs to boys in terms of restricted choices are also high, at least early in development.

Second, the book helps students to evaluate the sometimes exaggerated claims in the popular media about gender differences. One of the most difficult ideas for students to grasp is the notion that group differences do not mean that individuals are necessarily different. For example, the fact that American boys are on average more aggressive than girls does not mean that any one boy will be more aggressive than any particular girl. A true understanding of this concept ordinarily requires some statistical training that is not always yet possessed by students. Chapters 10 and 11 help students with this abstract concept by walking them through a concrete example of a gender difference (in height) and showing them specific examples of group versus individual characteristics.

Third, as much as possible I have tried to consider how gender interacts with social class and ethnicity to shape children's development. However, it must be acknowledged that in many areas a detailed consideration of these issues is not yet possible. Fortunately, this is changing rapidly, as researchers are increasingly moving beyond the traditional focus on white middle class children who live near universities. In some cases I have drawn on studies of British and European children where researchers have examined issues of social class, ethnicity and culture.

Carole R. Beal

ACKNOWLEDGMENTS

This is my chance to thank the many people who have helped me with this project, which initially grew out of my experiences developing and teaching a class on gender role development. I owe a great deal to the Dartmouth College students who took the class over the years; many of the examples, anecdotes, and concerns sprinkled throughout the book can be traced back to a particular discussion on a spring afternoon, a perceptive question by a student, or a truly thoughtful term paper for the class. Their tolerance for ambiguity and their willingness to question long-held assumptions about gender development—theirs and mine—has been inspiring. In addition, when I first began teaching in this area, several people were kind enough to send materials to help me get started, including Sandra Bem at Cornell University, Gail Hornstein at Mount Holyoke College, and Bonnie Strickland at the University of Massachusetts at Amherst. Their generosity was gratefully appreciated at the time and is still remembered.

A second group to whom I owe thanks includes the people who helped with the preparation of the book. Among my colleagues at Dartmouth College, Bill Morris and Rogers Elliott shared their developmental journal collections for which I am deeply thankful as they saved me numerous treks to the library, as I am to Hilda Sokol for her expertise in biology, Christopher Strenta for help with issues regarding standardized testing, Patrick Nickoletti for sharing his expertise on dominance hierarchies, and Jennifer Kleck for her help with tracking down references and sources. Wendy Lehnert and Mark Snyder, along with Jenny and Peter Foord, generously provided me with many examples of the delights of raising boys and girls, as well as comments on the manuscript. I must thank Jane Vaicunas, Renee Leonard and Beth Kaufman at McGraw-Hill for their interest in the project and their assistance with its development. I would also like to thank the following reviewers of the manuscript for their perceptive comments and helpful suggestions: Dr. Bruce Carter, Syracuse University; Beverly Fagot, University of Oregon; Mykol Hamilton, Centre College; Aletha Huston, University of Kansas; Paul Jose, Loyola University of Chicago; Campbell Leaper, University of California, Santa Cruz; Carol Nagy Jacklin, University of Southern California; Michele Paludi, Hunter College; Sharon Presley, California State University, Northridge; and Pamela Reid, City University of New York.

Third, I must acknowledge those debts that have a much longer history, long enough so at this point mere thanks alone cannot possibly repay them, although it's at least a start to mention them here. These include my deep intellectual debt to John Flavell at Stanford and the friendship of Gary Bonitatibus of Keene State College, Barbara Bautz at Bridgewater State College, and Andrew Garrod at Dartmouth College. Many thanks also go to my parents and family for never once saying, "But why on earth would you want to do something like that?" And as always, my greatest debt is to Paul R. Cohen; he can collect anytime.

Carole R. Beal

BOYS AND GIRLS

The Development of Gender Roles

CHAPTER 1

INTRODUCTION

THE "CORY INCIDENT"

Some years ago I was interviewing 9-year-old students about stories as part of a project on children's writing. I had just finished one interview and was making some quick notes when the next child came into the office. I looked up, and an odd thing happened: I could not tell whether the child was a boy or a girl. The usual cues were not there: The child's hair was trimmed in a sort of pudding-bowl style, not really long but not definitively short either. The child was dressed in a gender-neutral outfit of jeans, sneakers, and a loose t-shirt, like most of the children at the school. The name on the interview permission slip was "Cory," which did not clarify matters much as it could be either a boy's or girl's name. Still puzzled, I began the interview and found myself becoming increasingly frustrated at not knowing Cory's sex. I quickly realized how many unconscious assumptions I usually made about boys and girls; for example, that a girl would probably like a particular story about a horse and be willing to answer a few extra questions about it, or that a boy would probably start to get restless after a certain point and I would have to work a bit harder to keep his attention. After the interview, I went out to watch the class on the playground at recess. Sometimes Cory played with the boys, other times with the girls, and when the class was called to come inside, Cory stood in line between a girl and a boy; no clues there. There seemed to be no way to tell from Cory's behavior whether Cory was a boy or girl, and to this day I don't know the answer.

GENDER ROLES AND STEREOTYPES

It is unusual to encounter a child like Cory. Most young children have an appearance, style of dress, ways of walking and talking, favorite games and interests, and preferred playmates that are distinctly male or female. In other words, most children indicate clearly that they have learned the gender role for their sex. By *gender role* we mean the behaviors that are expected of males and females within a particular society, including dress and appearance, work and leisure activities, obligations within the family, skills, and social behavior. Part of the process of development for young children is to learn to be male or female, to master the behaviors that are expected for their sex, just as they learn to speak a particular language. This book is designed to show how gender role learning takes place in development, that is, how boys learn to be boys and girls to be girls.

■ Gender Roles as Socially Determined

As languages vary around the world, so do gender roles; thus, children have to figure out what it means to be a boy or girl within a particular society. No human culture that we know of has raised boys and girls identically; every society makes some distinctions between male and female roles, and this is reflected in how young children are treated. Some of the distinctions between male and female gender roles probably originate in biological differences between the sexes, namely, that women bear and nurse infants and toddlers, and so certain kinds of activities may be more conveniently performed by women, such as work that can be continually interrupted and does not require long travel. Yet the particular divisions that are made between male and female roles vary considerably over time and across cultures, indicating that gender distinctions are at least in part social constructions (Hare-Mustin & Maracek, 1990; Riger, 1992; Unger & Crawford, 1992). Men's work at one point may be women's in another. For example, most typists were male when the typewriter first became available; then women gradually came to dominate the secretarial field; now men are increasingly returning to clerical work that involves more technical equipment and specialized subjects, such as producing company newsletters with computer publishing software. Other distinctions between males and females also vary considerably; for example, in India many men wear skirts while women wear a tunic and pants, and men often walk about holding hands with one another, a practice that most men in the United States would be very careful to avoid. Gender boundaries are often more flexible that they appear on the surface, again showing that they are customs that can be modified when necessary rather than biological imperatives. Girls may do boys' tasks such as watching cattle or mowing the lawn if no boys of the right age are available in the family or neighborhood; a boy will be told to take care of the younger children if there is no older sister in the family to take on the job; and women who have spent decades in complete seclusion within their own courtyards often emerge when they become widows and manage the family rice fields in place of their husband (Wiser, Wiser, & Wadley, 1989). This sort of flexibility with regard to how males and females are expected to behave tells us that gender roles are socially determined and, consequently, that they must be learned by young children.

What are *our* gender role expectations? In the United States there have certainly been considerable changes in gender roles over the last three decades. Men now feel freer to devote time to their families, and most women work outside the home. Yet increased flexibility in gender roles does not mean that distinctions between males and females have disappeared or that we now treat boys and girls identically while they are growing up. Our gender role expectations for children are still strong: We expect boys to dress in pants and shirts, play outdoors, ride bikes, get dirty, find their way when they get lost, and hold back their tears when they fall off their bikes. We expect girls to dress in skirts (at least sometimes), play close to home, stay neat and tidy, be nice to other children, and to be pretty. One of the goals of this book is to illustrate how these expectations about male and female behavior are still prevalent despite several decades of societal change and how such expectations still influence children's development.

◼ From Roles to Stereotypes

Of course these images of pretty girls and rough-and-tumble boys are often unrealistic exaggerations. Yet there is general agreement about what typical boys and girls are like, and these expectations can easily become prescriptive: If most boys like football, then boys *should* like football, and a particular boy who detests it will probably feel the need at some point to pretend that he is interested in the sport or come up with a plausible excuse. In other words, shared assumptions about the sexes become *stereotypes* that influence how we perceive others, leading us to assume they will behave in the ways that they expect and unconsciously overlooking their unique characteristics as individuals.

Stereotypes are pervasive in social interaction; we have stereotypic expectations about people based on many factors, including age, ethnicity, social class, the types of work we do, and so on. Yet of all our personal characteristics, gender stands out as most important and most prevalent. Others notice first if we are male or female before they see whether we are young or old, whether we are dressed nicely or in worn clothes, or whether we look friendly or distant. We divide the social world into males and females, and we expect different things of the sexes, as I realized when I interviewed Cory. Gender distinctions can even be made in areas of behavior that are clearly trivial: At a fabric store recently I overheard a man asking a clerk where the men's buttons were displayed. She pointed to the racks of hundreds of buttons nearby, but he protested, "No, those are for *women*; where are the men's?" Of course, buttons are not really different for men and women, but it is not surprising that someone who has grown up in a world in which many distinctions are made on the basis of gender, from jobs to family roles to which side one's shirt buttons are sewn on, would assume that the buttons themselves are also male or female.

Gender stereotypes have several functions. First, they guide our behavior so that we fit into the expected roles, which can facilitate many forms of interaction because each participant shares similar assumptions. For example, when two people approach a door, it is convenient for them to share unconscious expectations about who will pass through first; it might be quite tedious to negotiate this anew with every doorway that is encountered during the day. Second, gender stereotypes help shape children's development, leading children to master the skills that will be required as adults, whether they are weaving or tailoring, caring for babies or running a stall at the local market, deferring to others or leading them, and so on. If development is in part the process of socializing children so that they will fit smoothly into their culture as a well-functioning adult man or woman, then gender role learning is an important and necessary part of this process. In fact, a child who does not seem to be mastering the gender role behaviors considered appropriate for his or her sex attracts attention and concern, as we will see in Chapter 13.

Stereotypic expectations about males and females have drawbacks as well as advantages. First, gender distinctions tend to become exaggerated; we think of being male or female as an either-or proposition, even though in actuality there is considerable flexibility and overlap in male and female behavior. We also think of gender categories as polar opposites; for example, if boys are clever, then girls are silly, if boys are tough and mean, then girls are soft and nice, and if boys are bad at reading, then girls are good at reading—even though in reality there is always considerable overlap, with plenty of clever girls and silly boys. Even the way we refer to boys and girls illustrates this tendency: We speak of "the opposite sex." (Boys and girls actually have so much in common that most researchers now prefer the phrase "the other sex," which does not imply that a particular characteristic will be found in only one sex and not the other.)

A second drawback to gender roles is that the developmental options for children of each sex become restricted, restrictions that come in both explicit and subtle forms. Twenty-five years ago it was impossible for a girl at my junior high school to sign up for auto shop, although girls were allowed to take graphic arts one summer as a special concession. Girls who would like to participate in high school or college athletic programs still have fewer options; a girl with the talent to become a female Larry Bird might attend a high school that does not support a women's basketball team although it fields men's teams in three different sports. Even when explicit distinctions between boys and girls have diminished they still exist in more subtle form. A boy can now legally enroll in home economics or early childhood education classes, but might feel uncomfortable as one of only a few males in the class, with his every comment attracting attention and every absence from class noted (Tavris & Wade, 1984). One college student told me that at parties girls would abandon him once they heard of his relatively low-paying career plans to be an elementary school teacher in favor of men who were economics or government majors. During the childhood and adolescence years such subtle pressures can be as much of a restriction as legal barriers.

With gender distinctions being so prevalent in the social world, it is not suprising that most children get the picture very early, making Cory the rare exception that tells us something important about the typical case. Developmental psychologists have studied how children learn gender roles, with the goal of pinpointing the processes by which they become boys or girls, why the learning appears so complete and effortless, and why the signs of gender role behavior appear so early in development. Parents are often startled when masculine or feminine characteristics appear in their very young offspring, especially when the parents themselves have tried to avoid obvious gender stereotyping in the home: The mother who is a high-powered academic researcher finds that her tiny daughter loves her frilly nighties and flirts with male visitors; parents who refuse to let their son have a toy gun see that he pretends to shoot with anything he can get his hands on, such as a stick or an empty cardboard paper towel roll (Shapiro, 1990). The goal of this book is to examine how this happens in children's development, with an emphasis on three themes.

LEARNING GENDER

The first theme of this book is that children *learn* to be boys and girls during development. When boys and girls are growing up, different behaviors are expected of them, they have different experiences, and they behave differently. Students sometimes find it hard to believe that being a boy or girl still makes much difference since gender distinctions are actually minimized in most western cultures, particularly in the United States in recent decades. Yet as we will see in subsequent chapters, most U.S. parents still have preferences for boys, and boys and girls continue to have quite different experiences in the home and classroom. In most areas of the world boys and girls are treated very differently from birth, and distinctions are made between boys and girls because children will have to fit into an adult world that is organized by gender.

What about biology? Focusing on the socialization process does not exclude the possibility that differences in male and female behavior might also reflect biology. Developmentalists reject the old "nature versus nurture" debate as simplistic and favor instead the view that biology and socialization interact. Children are born with a complex biological heritage that may well be expressed somewhat differently for the two sexes, but they always develop within a social environment. We cannot raise young children in isolation to see whether the behavior of boys and girls differs—it would not be ethical to do so. Furthermore, studies of children who actually have been isolated by abusive or deranged parents suggest that even if they managed to survive, their behavior would be so altered that it would be impossible to conclude anything about typical children. If the social environment in which children are raised is tinted with pink or blue, as all societies have been, then this will in turn influence children's development. Thus, in a fundamental sense we can never know precisely how much biology determines our behavior, since it never works independently of a social developmental context.

Studies of animal behavior offer us some insights into biological processes, but their relevance to human development is unfortunately often limited. For example, studies of other species, such as rodents, show that maternal behavior is regulated by hormones produced during pregnancy and after labor, and, as we will see in Chapter 10, it is possible that similar hormonal systems may be in place to facilitate nurturing behavior in new human mothers. However, it is also clear that social factors and the meaning of the experience for the new parent are tremendously important, since new fathers show the same emotional responses and nurturing behaviors as new mothers. The link between evolutionary theories and children's behavior in the contemporary world is also often tenuous. As one researcher mused, "Why would you evolve to want to play with a truck?" (Gorman, 1992, p. 42). The interactionist perspective thus acknowledges that biology is important without assuming that it is all-important or all-explaining, and tries to identify the specific environmental influences that shape children's emerging behavior.

Developmental psychologists have been able to discover many ways that socialization —meaning the influence of parents, peers, teachers, and the media—contributes to behavioral differences between boys and girls. We can observe, control, and alter the social environment and examine the effects on children's behavior, showing that they notice, learn, and internalize what is expected for their sex. In fact, much of the research described in the following chapters focuses on the social environment surrounding children, incorporating biological explanations if they are sufficiently detailed or if the data on social influences do not seem sufficiently strong to explain the behavioral differences. For example, we will see in Chapter 10 that higher rates of aggression in boys may well be related to androgen hormone levels. However, rates of aggression vary considerably across cultures, with girls in some societies being more aggressive than U.S. boys. In addition, boys and girls learn quickly that their aggressive acts will elicit quite different responses from those around them, and they see many more role models of male than female aggression. Thus, an explanation of sex differences in aggression that does not consider both biological and socialization factors is doomed to failure. The emphasis on both factors has led to the use of the term *sex* often being reserved for biological characteristics such as our chromosomes, hormone levels, and reproductive organs, while *gender* is used for more socially determined characteristics, such as the ways that males and females dress, behave, and interact with others. We may find in the future that some of the latter behaviors have a biological etiology, but at this point we do not know which or to what extent biology is involved. Thus, the term *gender* will be used in this book to refer to children's acquisition of social behaviors that vary for boys and girls.

PUNCTUATED SOCIALIZATION

A second theme of this book is that gender role learning is more fine-grained than coarse, meaning that only particular types of behavior are affected and that the learning occurs at specific points in the child's development and as the result of information from specific sources. Learning to be a boy or a girl seems to be more like walking along a path and periodically coming to a flashing sign that directs you to chose one direction over another than it is like walking along a path with a gentle but consistent slope that gradually and inexorably moves you in one direction. Learning can occur very quickly in response to particular salient experiences. How many times does a little boy need to pick up a Barbie doll to figure out from others' reactions that maybe he'd better find something else to play with? A junior high school girl who asks a question in algebra and hears a boy mutter behind her, "Is she a brain or something?" may not open her mouth in class again right through college.

The view of gender role development as punctuated has been evolving since Maccoby and Jacklin (1974) published the first comprehensive survey of resarch on boys' and girls' development and sex differences in children's behavior. On the basis of studies available at the time, they concluded that there was surprisingly little evidence that parents treated sons and daughters differently, a point that has been echoed in more recent reviews of parents' behavior (Lytton & Romney, 1991). However, other researchers immediately began to suggest that differential treatment of boys and girls did exist and to look for the particular forms that gender socialization might take (J. H. Block, 1983; Huston, 1983). Twenty years later, with additional research to draw upon, it now seems that the learning process is more finely focused in terms of the specific behaviors that are targeted and the times in development when the learning occurs.

■ Targeted Learning

While parents are important influences, not everything they do is relevant to the issue of gender socialization. Parents teach, discipline, and express affection to children of both sexes, with differential treatment of boys and girls being apparent only in particular areas, such as their reactions to children's sex-typed play. Also, parents are not equivalent; in fact, it seems that fathers play an especially important role in signaling the types of play that children should avoid; for example, dolls are not okay for boys. It is only relatively recently that researchers have observed fathers' influence on children; most initial studies focused on mothers, who were more often available to participate in research projects than fathers. The influence of parents was underestimated because mothers made fewer distinctions between boys and girls than fathers.

Developmental "Windows of Opportunity"

Gender lessons do not have to be hammered into children's heads year after year. Rather, ideas about what boys and girls should do seem to be learned quickly at particular times, often during transitional points in development when new abilities first emerge. For example, considerable learning occurs during the toddler period when children first start to make bids for autonomy and begin to talk and again during early adolescence when romantic relationships begin to develop. In addition, much of the learning about gender roles occurs much earlier in the life span than previously realized. Children form most of their ideas about what the sexes are like during the toddler period, that is, from about 1½ to 3 years. Most parents do not really start to think about gender issues until the child enters preschool or kindergarten, but by that point little in the way of overt socialization is necessary since children have already altered their behavior and learned to think of themselves as a boy or girl. Few parents have to tell their little boys not to wear pink pants to first grade.

Decreased Emphasis on Parents

In the last 20 years it has also become clear that parents are not the entire story in gender role socialization. In fact, they may even be relatively unimportant when compared to other factors, such as the child's own need to feel like a boy or girl and the influence of other children. As we will see in Chapters 6 and 7, children have their own ideas about what boys and girls should do, and they quickly figure out that if they want to fit in with their peers, they need to adhere to those expectations. For example, boys often engage in pranks with other boys as part of a mutual effort to convince themselves that they *are* boys, such as leaving newspaper-wrapped dog feces on a neighbor's porch, setting it alight, ringing the doorbell, and retreating to watch the neighbor stomp out the flaming parcel and then track the contents back into the house (G. Fine, 1986). Peers are powerful influences, and parents can sometimes be quite startled to find out what their child has been up to with other children!

There is also much evidence that gender stereotypes are still easy to find in the larger culture, including schools and the media, and that these factors also influence children's development. One of the most popular children's movie characters in the late 1980s was Ariel, the little mermaid who gave up her voice to win legs and the love of a prince. (Is it any wonder that girls remain silent while boys dominate classroom discussion when a song in the film includes such lines as, "She who holds her tongue will get her man"?) When all these factors are considered, there is strong evidence that the social environment beyond parents shapes children's behavior as boys and girls, and that children are willing and even eager to learn these lessons.

▌Asymmetric Socialization

The amount, timing, and intensity of socialization processes are not necessarily the same for the sexes, so considering boys and girls together can present a misleading picture. Boys receive earlier and more intense socialization than girls, who have it relatively easy in terms of learning the female gender role. Many female role models are available because most children are cared for by their mothers or other female caregivers, and most preschool and elementary school teachers are female. Mothers, fathers, peers, and teachers all expect a similar sort of behavior from girls, giving them a consistent message. In addition, girls are able to cross gender role boundaries with relative freedom until adolescence or even later, and most girls take advantage of this freedom: About two-thirds of U.S. women report that they were tomboys as children, and tomboys are often popular with their peers. This is not to deny that females face considerable discrimination both while growing up and as adults; only that from a developmental perspective girls do not need to be as careful as boys to avoid the clothing, toys, games, and activities typically associated with the other sex.

By comparison, the socialization of boys into the male role begins early, and the social costs of deviating from the expected roles are also higher for boys in terms of peer rejection and parental disapproval. Imagine a girl who is wearing a toy holster, bandana, and cowboy hat and who is running around the backyard on a stick pretending to chase cattle, versus a boy who is wearing a flowered hat, ropes of pearls, and lipstick and who is pretending to cook dinner on a toy stove. Students in my classes usually respond with smiles of mild amusement in the first case, but horrified groans in the second, reactions that are consistent with studies showing that effeminate behavior in boys elicits much more negative reactions than does masculine behavior in girls (Feinman, 1981; C. Martin, 1990). Boys also face a more difficult developmental task in learning the masculine gender role, because male role models are less accessible to young children, and as we will see, the messages from adults are not consistent: Mothers and teachers would like boys to behave one way—masculine, yes, but also neat, well-mannered, and considerate—while fathers and male peers encourage other types of behavior, including rough physical play and independence, meaning that the little boy is faced with figuring out whether he should be like Cary Grant or Hulk Hogan. While gender role expectations have become more flexible in recent decades, most of the changes have come in our expectations about what girls can or should do. Girls can now safely be ambitious, competitive and sports-inclined, but relatively few adults are equally supportive of boys' being gentle, interested in fashion, and eager to sign up for ballet classes.

The stronger emphasis on boys probably reflects the lingering societal belief that boys are more important. In most cultures, including the United States, boys are preferred, particularly as firstborn children. When families are poor, male children will be given more food and medical care, and the hopes of the family for the future are more often attached to the sons than the daughters. Parents surely love both their sons and daughters, but it is often the case that parents' plans for, expectations of, and investment in the two sexes are different and that their behavior at times reflects these differences. One grandmother in a poor village in India commented when a little girl toddled dangerously near a steep step in the garden, "Let her, she is only a girl" (Wiser et al., 1989). If boys are viewed as more important because they are future men, with the greater potential earning power and social status associated with the male role in most cultures, then it is in some sense not surprising that adults give them more attention, focus more socialization efforts on them, and express more concern that they become appropriately socialized into the expected behavior patterns. Of course, this is unfair to girls, who at times almost get lost in development. For example, we will see later that girls become nearly invisible in the classroom while boys receive most of the instruction and attention from teachers. However, it is important to keep in mind that asymmetric socialization is unfair to boys, too, because they are channeled early into a narrow set of behavioral options that may or may not match their individual talents and interests.

GENDER SELF-DEFINES

A third theme is that being male or female is important not only in our interactions with others but also as a central part of our self-concept. Most young children become very upset if you make a mistake about their sex. Going back to the Cory incident, you might have wondered why I didn't just ask the teacher or a classmate, "Hey, is Cory a boy or a girl?" But just imagine how chagrined and inadequate you would feel if you heard that someone had to ask what sex you were and how much teasing you might receive! Most of us feel that we would be fundamentally different people if we had been born the other sex, and from a developmental perspective this feeling would be accurate, since our experiences while growing up would have been quite different. Gender becomes a core part of our personal identity very early in development; as we will see in Chapter 6, we start to think of ourselves as male or female almost as soon as we have any sort of self-awareness, and our sense of being male or female then guides our interests and behavior and how we present ourselves to the world. Thus, children are not simply passive pupils in the process of learning to be male or female; mastering gender role behaviors becomes part of the process of figuring out who they are.

These three themes emphasize the importance of children's gender in development, with experiences, options, and pressures being different for the two sexes. In the following chapters we will examine in more detail how children learn to be boys and girls, the processes through which this learning occurs, the sources of influence and gender role information, and the possibilities for change.

ORGANIZATION OF THIS BOOK

The chapters are organized to follow the sequence of a child's development, starting with the development of a boy or girl during the prenatal period in Chapter 2, following by a review of parents' preferences for and differential treatment of boy and girl babies during the first year of life in Chapter 3.

Three chapters follow in which the influence of the family on boys and girls is examined from three theoretical perspectives, presented in more-or-less historical order. A century ago, Freud emphasized the potential importance of parents as male and female role models and argued that children might become masculine or feminine by trying to be like the same-sex parent. The second perspective, social learning theory, extended Freud's emphasis on role models but proposed a different mechanism for learning; namely, boys' and girls' behavior elicits different responses from the social environment which in turn alters their behavior accordingly. The third theoretical perspective, cognitive developmental theory, built on social learning theory by suggesting that children's own ideas about males and females are important and that the motivation for learning from role models comes from their need to establish a clear self-concept.

The next three chapters move us beyond the family to introduce sources of gender role information that become more influential as children move out into the larger world, including the influence of peers, school systems, and the media. Then we will examine some of the results of gender role development that are apparent by middle childhood, including boys' and girls' personality characteristics and cognitive abilities. This will be followed by an overview of some of the new issues that arise when children enter adolescence. Finally, we will consider the case of gender identity disturbance, in which a child believes that he or she is the other sex, and evaluate whether this reflects an as yet unidentified biological influence or a case of "failed" socialization.

BIOLOGICAL BEGINNINGS

"It's a boy!" "It's a girl!" When an infant is born, one of the first things we do is to look to see its sex. We usually make this assessment based on its genitals, assuming that a baby with a penis and scrotum is a male and that one with a clitoris and vagina is a female. Yet the birth of an infant with recognizably male or female genitals is only one milestone in an extended process of development as a boy or girl. Several events have occurred much earlier in prenatal development that will eventually result in the birth of a boy or girl baby. These events include the conception of an infant with male or female sex chromosomes and the development of a male or female system of internal reproductive organs, that is, testes in males and ovaries in females. The testes and ovaries also produce sex hormones in varying amounts that affect the developing fetus. The infant's biological sex is indicated by all these factors: chromosomes, reproductive organs, sex hormone levels, and the external genitals (Baker, 1980).

In the following sections we look at the process of conception and development of an infant that is male or female. In most cases the various indexes of sex are consistent with one another, and there is no uncertainty at birth about whether a baby is a boy or girl; for example, a boy who is genetically male will usually have testes, higher levels of male sex hormones such as testosterone, and a penis and scrotum. However, biological development is not always perfect, and sometimes the different aspects of biological sex are not consistent with one another. Thus we might have a baby who is genetically a boy and has testes inside the abdominal cavity but at birth has genitalia that resemble those of a girl. There are several ways that such inconsistencies can occur in development; although such cases are rare, they reveal a great deal about the nature of the processes that produce a boy or girl baby, and they allow us to look at the potential role of socialization: If you have a baby who is male in one way but female in another, should you raise the baby as a boy or

15

girl? We will review several such cases and examine how the gender of rearing influences the baby's development.

CONCEPTION: CHROMOSOMAL SEX

One measure of biological sex is determined when the baby is first conceived. Humans have 23 pairs of chromosomes in each cell, with one of these pairs being the *sex chromosomes*. In females this pair is composed of two X chromosomes (XX), while in males it is composed of an X and Y (XY). The egg and sperm cells are exceptions to the 23-pairs-per-cell rule; if they were like other cells in the body, the fertilized egg would have 46 pairs, twice the necessary number, and would not survive. Thus, the egg and sperm each have only 23 individual chromosomes, yielding 23 pairs when they combine at conception. Because the egg and sperm cells each have only half the necessary genetic information, it is only when their chromosomes are combined that the sex of the offspring is determined.

As we will see in the next chapter, throughout history parents have waited anxiously for the birth of the infant and hoped that it will be a son. Women have been divorced or even killed for not producing the desired male heir; Anne Boleyn's "failure" to produce a living son led Henry the Eighth to have her beheaded. Yet the child's sex is decided by the father, not the mother! The father's sperm cells can contain either X or Y chromosomes, while the mother's egg cells contain only X chromosomes. Thus, if an X sperm fertilizes the egg, the baby will be a girl (X from the mother, X from the father), while if a Y sperm fertilizes the egg, the baby will be a boy (X from the mother, Y from the father).

■ Sex Determination

Ordinarily, we have no reason to check our chromosomes to see whether we are XX or XY, but in some cases we might want to know whether a person is genetically male or female, for example, for purposes of athletic competition at the international level. Since the Y chromosome gives males greater average height and muscle strength, a man competing in a women's event could have an unfair advantage, although we should keep in mind that some women are taller and stronger than many men. In the ancient Greek Olympics, sex testing was simple: The athletes had to walk into the arena naked and were not admitted if they did not have a penis (Turnbull, 1988)! Until the mid-1960s female athletes in international competitions had to undergo a physical examination before the event, to verify that they were female, or walk nude in front of a group of doctors who would evaluate whether they looked feminine enough to be considered women. Because many women athletes found these methods invasive and degrading (one described the physical exam as amounting to a crude grope) and because external appearance can be ambiguous, international athletic organizations turned to more direct methods for establishing the sex of competitors by relying on tests of their sex chromosomes (Turnbull, 1988; Vines, 1992).

The "Two X's" Test

One technique, used until recently, assessed whether a woman had two normal X chromosomes. In most female cells only one of the X chromosomes is actually active, while the other one bunches up and can be seen clearly in a microscope if a dye is applied to the cell. This second inactive X chromosome is called the *Barr body*, and does not appear in male cells. Cells for the two X's test can be obtained from a gentle scraping of tissue on the inside of the mouth (a "buccal smear"). When this technique was introduced for international athletic events in the 1960s, two Soviet women who competed in the shotput and hurdling events quickly retired, raising speculation that they were actually men and knew they would not be able to pass the two X's test (Turnbull, 1988).

The "Y" Test

The problem with looking for the Barr body is that failing the test, that is, not having two X chromosomes, is not the same thing as having a Y chromosome. Yet without the Y there would be little masculinizing effect on the individual and, hence, no particular physical advantage in terms of height or muscular bulk. Thus, a preferred method is to examine the chromosomes with a more powerful microscope and look directly for the Y chromosome. This is done when the chromosomes within a cell have duplicated themselves just before cell division. Photographs of the chromosomes are taken and arranged into a *karyotype* in which each pair is identified, including the sex chromosomes. This is a relatively expensive, time-consuming process which requires a highly trained technician, so it would not be done on a routine basis; it only becomes necessary for situations such as athletic competitions. However, it can also be done during pregnancy by drawing samples of the amniotic fluid surrounding the developing fetus. The fluid contains discarded cells that can be cultured and examined, revealing the sex of the fetus several months before birth as well as possible abnormalities of other chromosomes. (The implications of knowing the sex of the offspring *before* birth as the result of an amniocentesis test will be considered in the next chapter.)

■ Abnormalities of Sex Chromosomes

Biological processes are not always perfect, and sex chromosomes, like other chromosomes, can become damaged as the result of exposure to radiation, drugs, or infections. They can also be deleted or randomly altered in the process of duplication when new cells are produced. Often these chromosomal defects are life-threatening, and the embryo containing the damaged genes is spontaneously aborted long before the woman realizes she has conceived, but genetic errors are not always lethal. In fact, errors on the sex chromosomes are relatively minor by comparison to other types of genetic abnormalities, although there is some increased risk of mental retardation in the offspring. One of the sex chromosomes may be damaged, or there may be an extra X or Y, or an X may be missing altogether. Human cells seem to need to have at least one X chromosome for the organism to survive; no people with the pattern YY or Y0 (meaning only one chromosome, a Y) have ever been observed. One estimate is that as many as 1:400 people may have a minor abnormality of the sex chromosomes, often without ever realizing it (Berch & Bender, 1987). In fact, some men even have two X chromosomes, with one of the X chromosomes carrying the bits of genetic information usually found on the Y chromosome, suggesting that at some point in development there may have been an exchange of small pieces of genetic material (Mittwoch, 1988).

Chromosomal Abnormalities Affecting Females

About 1 in 1000 women has an extra X chromosome (XXX pattern, or *Trisomy X*). Often this has little effect on development and may never be discovered; in other cases it is linked to slightly lower intelligence and an increased risk of speech problems. About 1 in 10,000 women suffers from *Turner's syndrome,* in which the cells have only one chromosome, an X (X0 pattern). Sometimes a segment of a second X chromosome is present, while at other times the second chromosome is missing altogether and could in theory have been either an X or a Y (Unger & Crawford, 1992). One consequence of Turner's syndrome is very short height; women with Turner's syndrome are usually less than 5 feet tall as adults. One woman recalled being teased to tears by her elementary school classmates for being so short and said that it still hurt her feelings to hear people shout "midget mama!" when they saw her. Women with Turner's syndrome usually lack ovaries, so they cannot ovulate or produce enough sex hormones at puberty to develop a mature female contour. Their general intelligence is not usually affected, although they may have difficulties with spatial reasoning and direction and with some cognitive processes, such as interpreting others' facial expressions (McCauley, Kay, Ito, & Treder, 1987). Some of these problems can be treated if the diagnosis is made early enough; for example, supplemental hormones can be given at puberty to help the girl's breasts to develop. A number of researchers have been attempting to treat Turner's syndrome girls with human growth hormone, which can now be synthetically produced, to try to increase their height by several inches, at least enough so that they will be in the normal range for children of their age.

Sex Chromosome Abnormalities Affecting Males

Like females, males may have an extra X chromosome. The XXY pattern is called *Klinefelter's syndrome* and occurs in about 1 of 1000 males. The extra X chromosome has some feminizing effects on the man; his penis and testes may be relatively small, and most men with Klinefelter's syndrome are sterile. As with other sex chromosomal abnormalities, there is also a risk of lower intelligence. Males can also have an extra Y chromosome (XYY), a combination that occurs in about 1 of 700 males. The extra Y chromosome seems to contribute to increased height and, again, slightly lower intelligence. In the past, XYY males were thought to be overrepresented in prison populations, leading to the theory that a propensity toward violent behavior might be associated with an extra Y chromosome. Careful studies have failed to confirm this theory. The reduced intelligence associated with XYY seems to be the primary reason for the slightly higher rates of incarceration for this group, and many XYY men in the general population are not incarcerated and may never realize they have an extra chromosome. In addition, when the criminal records of a group of XYY males were examined in more detail, it was discovered that the men had been convicted primarily for burglary and embezzlement, rather than for crimes involving physical aggression (Price & Whatmore, 1967; Unger & Crawford, 1992).

■ Male Vulnerability

We think of males as being the stronger sex and females as the weaker. Yet from the developmental perspective the reverse is true: Males are more likely to suffer from birth defects and various developmental problems. Some developmental problems occur more often in males because they are at greater risk of being affected by genetic damage. A male has one X chromosome, and if that chromosome contains damaged genetic material, he does not have another that can compensate. Defective genetic material causes more male than female fetuses to be spontaneously aborted. About 120 males for every 100 females are thought to be conceived, but by birth the sex ratio has fallen to about 105 males to 100 females, suggesting that more male conceptions have been lost during the pregnancy (Serr & Ismajovich, 1963).

If the defective gene is not immediately life-threatening to a male embryo, other functions may still be affected. The X chromosome carries genetic instructions that influence the development of many characteristics, such as color vision, blood clotting, and muscle function. If the genes that control these characteristics are defective, they may be passed on to the offspring and will be expressed more often in males because there is no second healthy X chromosome to "cover" for the defective one. For example, if a male baby has an X chromosome from his mother that contains defective genetic material, he may have hemophilia (a disorder in which the blood does not clot) or color blindness. A female baby with the same defective X chromosome from the mother would probably have a healthy X chromosome from the father to compensate. She could be healthy herself but, in turn, pass along the defective gene to her own offspring.

In addition to suffering more from sex-linked genetic abnormalities, males are more vulnerable to birth defects and developmental problems, including a higher rate of problems during the pregnancy, delivery complications, neurological damage, infections in the first year of life, mental retardation, learning disabilities, and delayed rate of development (Zachau-Christiansen & Ross, 1975). Some of these problems may be due to the fact that male infants are about half a pound larger at birth, which increases the risk of a difficult delivery and potential birth trauma to the infant. Other causes of the higher rate of developmental problems in boys are not known. One theory suggests that some of the risks for males may occur because the mother's immune system could react to the foreign genetic material that is present on the Y chromosome when she is pregnant with a male fetus (Gualtieri & Hicks, 1985). All the cells in her body contain X chromosomes, so embryonic cells with Y chromosomes could be mistakenly recognized as foreign invaders. Toxemia, a condition involving high blood pressure, water retention, and poor kidney function, is more common in women who are pregnant with a boy than a girl; researchers have suggested that toxemia might involve an immune system reaction. In addition, the more male children a woman has conceived in the past, the less likely it is that a boy will be born in the future, suggesting that some women become sensitized to the Y chromosome during earlier pregnancies, alerting the immune system to attack a subsequent male embryo. This theory is still highly controversial, however; there is little direct evidence that the maternal immune system reacts differently to male than female fetuses, and there may well be other explanations for greater male vulnerability.

Clearly, the genetic definition of masculinity and femininity is not always a straightforward matter of males being XY and females being XX. As we have seen, men and women can have different patterns of sex chromosomes yet, for the most part, appear to be perfectly normal. Many individuals may never even realize that they are not perfect XXs or XYs because other indications of sex, such as their internal reproductive systems and their genitalia, are unaffected. The sex chromosomes are only the beginning of the story of masculine and feminine development, triggering a chain of events during the prenatal period that leads to the birth of a boy or girl baby.

PRENATAL DEVELOPMENT: GONADAL SEX

By about the sixth week after conception the embryo contains a cluster of cells that form a *gonad*, a ridge of tissue that is sexually undifferentiated; that is, it is not clearly male or female. The embryo also contains two systems of internal ducts: (1) the Wolffian ducts that will become the vas deferens and seminal vesicles in the male and (2) the Mullerian ducts that will become the fallopian tubes and uterus in the female. Thus, the embryo is neither clearly male or female; rather, it has the potential to develop either masculine or feminine reproductive organs and genitals. The determining factor is the presence of sex hormones at the particular critical times when these organs are being formed in the developing body. These sex hormones are produced in the embryo following instructions from the sex chromosomes in the cells. Thus, if a Y chromosome is present, it will signal the embryo to develop along the masculine pathway, while if it is absent, the female pathway will be followed.

■ Masculine Development

As far as we currently know, the Y chromosome does little but carry instructions that influence the development of the individual into the male form, although it may also include a gene for hairy ears and seems to contribute to increased height (Unger & Crawford, 1992). The genes on the Y chromosome trigger the production of a substance called *H-Y antigen*, which signals the gonadal tissue to develop into testes. The particular genetic sequence on the Y chromosome responsible for these signals has been isolated by researchers, who are currently investigating whether a similar "sex determining region" must also be present on the X chromosome for testes to be formed in the offspring. That is, the X and Y chromosomes may actually work together to signal the development of a male fetus (*Science News*, 1990b; Unger & Crawford, 1992).

If the Y chromosome is present, or at least the relevant genetic material ordinarily found on the Y chromosome, the embryo will develop testes, which will begin to produce male sex hormones, called *androgens*. Many people are familiar with one type of androgen, testosterone, but several androgen hormones are involved in this process. First, testosterone leads to the development of the male internal duct system (the Wolffian ducts), the "plumbing" that will later produce and transport sperm in the mature man. Second, a variant of testosterone, di-hydro-testosterone, causes the external genitalia to develop into a penis and scrotum. The outer folds of genital tissue fuse together to form the scrotum, and the upper nub of tissue elongates into the penis. Late in the pregnancy the testes drop from inside the abdominal cavity into the scrotum. In some cases a boy is born with an empty scrotum because the testes have not yet descended; most will move relatively quickly into position, but this can be surgically accomplished if necessary.

Finally, another hormone is produced that inhibits the development of the female duct system (Mullerian inhibiting factor). Recall that both sets of ducts are present to start, so one set must be signaled to stop developing, or the male will have fallopian tubes as well as vas deferens! Bits of tissue corresponding to the degenerated female Mullerian ducts can sometimes be seen in the male abdominal cavity. Thus, for the male fetus two hormones act to promote the growth of the male internal reproductive organs and the external genitals, while a third hormone acts to stop the development of the female system.

■ Feminine Development

The process of development in the female embryo seems simpler, but this impression may be misleading because female development has not attracted as much research interest. It is known that in the absence of the Y chromosome the gonadal tissue will develop into ovaries; it seems to take a bit longer for this differentiation to occur than for the testes to form in the male. The Mullerian duct system develops into the fallopian tubes, the uterus, and the upper part of the vagina, and the male duct system gradually degenerates. The folds of genital tissue remain open, forming the vagina and labia, and the upper nub forms the clitoris. The ovaries descend, but unlike the testes they remain within the abdominal cavity. Note that the external genitalia develop out of the same original tissue; so the penis and clitoris are analogous structures.

The process of female development has sometimes been described as the "default," since without a Y chromosome the baby will develop along the female pathway. This view represents female development as relatively passive, implying that something must be actively added for masculine development to occur but that nothing extra is necessary for feminine development (Fausto-Sterling, 1985). However, this view may simply reflect the fact that more studies have been done to identify the precise genetic and hormonal mechanisms that are necessary to direct development into the male path. Active instructions from the X chromosome may be equally necessary for the gonad to develop into ovaries and for the male internal duct system to be inhibited in female fetuses.

The popular view of female development as passive while male development as active is also found in descriptions of the process of conception in textbooks and medical research articles (E. Martin, 1991). In her review of such articles Martin found that sperm ejaculated by the male were often described as active warriors, battling their way through a hostile vagina and fallopian tubes and assaulting the egg's outer surface, with the "victor" achieving fertilization. Sperm were described as "strong, with efficiently powered tails that move with a whiplashlike motion, propelling the sperm forward, burrowing and penetrating." One article even referred to the sperm "harpooning" the egg's surface with a filament of protein—never mentioning that the sperm came from sea urchins and that human sperm do nothing of the sort! In contrast, the egg was portrayed as passive, drifting gently along the fallopian tubes in hopes of meeting a sperm. More recent research suggests a very different picture, one in which both the male and female systems work interactively. Female orgasm reduces the acidity of the vagina, making it more hospitable to sperm. During the woman's fertile period strands of mucus are produced on the cervix that serve as conduits for sperm, helping them move into the uterus and fallopian tubes. The egg does not merely drift along; once it is released from the ovary, the fallopian tubes gently sweep the area, catching the egg and guiding it into the tube where tiny hairs push it along toward the uterus. When sperm are encountered, the surface of the egg changes to help sperm penetrate; it does not merely wait to be pierced.

The traditional depictions of conception and prenatal development are an example of our tendency to think of maleness and femaleness as polar opposites; if the male is active, then the female is passive. In reality, the processes that lead to the birth of a boy or girl appear to be far from passive, and male and female processes interact to facilitate development.

GENITAL SEX: AMBIGUOUS SEXUAL DIFFERENTIATION

Imagine that you are in the delivery room and your new baby has just been born. Things have gone smoothly, and catching your breath, you turn to find out if the infant is a boy or girl. But the expected announcement, "It's a boy," or "It's a girl," is not immediately forthcoming because no one is quite sure. The first glance at the infant's genitals has shown them to be ambiguous. There may be a nubbin of tissue that could be an extremely small penis or an elongated clitoris. There might be folds of tissue that look something like female labia, but they may be partially fused together and contain testes like a male scrotum.

In other cases a baby may be born with normal-appearing male or female genitals but with internal reproductive organs that correspond to the other sex, for example, a baby with a female vulva but internal testes. Thse infants, along with those whose external genitalia are ambiguous, are called *pseudo-hermaphrodites*. The term *hermaphrodite* is reserved for individuals who have both an ovary and a testis; only about 60 such incidents have ever been verified (Tavris & Wade, 1984). In general there are two forms of pseudo-hermaphroditism: A genetically female infant can become masculinized, and a genetically male infant, femininized. These rare cases have helped us understand the role of sex hormones in prenatal development and the importance of socialization, that is, whether the baby is raised as a boy or girl. In this section we explore how such cases occur and what happens to the children as they grow up. Most of the cases described below are taken from the research of Money and his colleagues who have studied such children over the years (Money & Ehrhardt, 1972; Money & Tucker, 1975). As we will see, in most instances biology yields to socialization.

■ "Masculinized" Females

How could a genetically female baby be born looking like a boy? Recall that in males the Y chromosome signals the gonad to become testes, which then produce androgen hormones, which in turn cause the formation of a penis and scrotum. If the androgen is not produced by the fetus's own body but is administered from another source, the effects are pretty much the same even if the fetus is female! A female can be exposed to androgen in one of two ways. First, the adrenal glands in the developing fetus are defective and produce too much progesterone hormone, which can have androgenlike effects when it is processed by the body. The defective functioning of the adrenal glands can occur either as a congenital problem (congenital adrenal hyperplasia, or CAH) or as the result of a tumor. Second, the mother may have been given high levels of progesterone in an attempt to maintain the pregnancy during a high risk of a miscarriage, although this treatment is rarely used today.

When exposed to androgen or androgenlike substances, the female fetus's tissues react accordingly, with the clitoris becoming longer than normal, almost like a small penis, and the labia fusing like a scrotum. Generally, the internal organs continue on to become female; the ovaries have usually already been formed, and the fallopian tubes, uterus and upper vagina develop as usual because there are no testes to produce the Mullerian inhibiting factor. Thus, the end result is a female infant whose external genitalia have been masculinized but who usually still has female internal reproductive organs. At birth, the infant's genitals might be masculinized but still recognizably female, perhaps with labia that are partly fused or, depending on the timing and amount of hormone exposure, the infant might look like a boy.

Most of these infants are now correctly identified as females at birth because the CAH syndrome is well recognized and the potential masculinizing effect can be anticipated during the pregnancy. Surgery to reduce the extra clitoral tissue, separate the labia, and open the vagina may be necessary. Reports from adult CAH women who had this surgery as infants or children indicate that sexual responsiveness can be preserved. Since CAH girls usually have intact ovaries, they produce hormones at puberty and are usually fertile. Despite their masculinized appearance at birth, these girls are clearly female; they are raised as girls and grow up thinking of themselves as girls. Many were tomboys as children, and reports have indicated that they became interested in dating, their appearance, and romantic relationships later than other girls, but as adult women most married and had children (Ehrhardt & Baker, 1974; Ehrhardt & Meyer-Bahlburg, 1981; Hurtig & Rosenthal, 1987; Money & Ehrhardt, 1972; Money & Matthews, 1982).

A female who was exposed to a very high level of androgen during prenatal development may have been born looking so much like a boy that she was labeled and raised as a boy. Although in such cases the baby's scrotum would not contain testes, it could be assumed that the testicles had not yet completely descended from the abdominal cavity and there would be no reason to suspect that the baby actually had ovaries. The first signs that something was amiss might not have been noticed until puberty when the ovaries began to produce estrogren, the boy's breasts started to develop, and he might even have menstruated through his penis. A medical workup would reveal that the boy was actually a genetic female. Money and his colleagues at Johns Hopkins University studied several of these cases and found that, for the most part, having been raised as boys, these children had formed such a strong male identity that they never really considered that they might be female in any way (Money & Ehrhardt, 1972). One pubescent boy came in to his doctor and complained about his breast development, and when his internal ovaries were discovered, he simply assumed that he had some "female apparatus in there by mistake" (Money & Tucker, 1975, p. 60). He was unambiguously male in terms of his conception of self, his behavior, and how he was accepted by others.

These cases reveal the importance of socialization in shaping gender identity and role behavior. If a genetic female has a masculine appearance at birth, in one situation she might be raised as a girl, while in the other she might be raised as a boy. The cases described above suggested that as long as it is clearly established early in development whether the child will be considered a boy or girl, children seem to accept the gender of rearing, even though their chromosomes or hormones during prenatal development might have been more characteristic of the other sex. Further support for this possibility is found in studies of male infants who have been "feminized" during prenatal development.

■ Feminized Males

As we have seen, in prenatal development the Y chromosome signals the formation of testes and the production of androgen. The cells in the target genital tissues of the developing fetus have receptors that ordinarily receive and react to the androgen hormones, causing the formation of the penis and scrotum. But suppose the cells do not have these androgen receptors. The tissues may be literally bathed in androgen but will remain unaffected. The effect is rather like someone who is deaf; you can yell as loud as you can, but without auditory nerves, the person will not receive and respond to your signal. Similarly, a genetic male may be insensitive to androgen; his testes produce it, but it has no effect on his body. Without the masculinizing effect of androgen, his external genitalia develop along the female pathway; the clitoris remains relatively small, the labia do not fuse, and the testes do not descend. At birth, the genetic boy looks like a girl and often would be identified and raised as a girl. As with masculinized females the first indication that something is wrong might not become apparent until puberty. The girl will probably develop breasts—because the internal testes produce a small amount of estrogen as well as androgen at puberty—but she would not begin to menstruate, and a physical examination and chromosome study may eventually determine that the girl is a genetic male.

Studies of the development of feminized males show that, having been raised as girls, they think of themselves as girls, behave as girls, and are accepted as such by others. They may eventually need minor surgery to lengthen the upper vagina and to remove the internal testes (which can often become malignant if left in the body). They will also need to take supplemental estrogen to replace the estrogen that had been produced by the testes and that is not supplied by ovaries. Studies have indicated that most girls eventually married and reported normal orgasmic sex lives. They were infertile, lacking ovaries, fallopian tubes, and uterus, but many became mothers by adopting children.

Oddly enough, there can even be some advantages to being a feminized male! Some reports mention that feminized males grow up to be unusually attractive women because they tend to be tall and slim, which fits the western cultural ideal for the female body (Unger & Crawford, 1992). There can also be disadvantages, particularly for participation in athletic events for which sex determination tests are required. Some reports suggest that as many as 1 of 500 female athletes at the international level are feminized males, but a woman who has the XY chromosome pattern may have difficulty being allowed to compete in major women's events even though she has no special physical advantage over other women (Vines, 1992). She may produce androgen, but her body does not react to it, so she does not have additional muscle strength, and having been raised as a girl, she has no advantage in terms of self-confidence or childhood experiences with sports. It has also been pointed out that, in contrast to other women athletes who might gain an unfair competitive advantage by using illegal sex-steroids, a feminized male cannot because her body will not respond to the drugs. Several athletic organizations have decided that XY women would be allowed to compete in many major international events as females, but the International Olympic Committee still requires a chromosome test to "prove" femininity.

In some cases the feminization of a male fetus will be only partially accomplished, and the infant may be born with a recognizable penis that is not much larger than a clitoris, and perhaps with partially fused labia that begin to suggest a scrotum. If the parents desperately want a son, they might insist on raising the child as a boy. However, there are definite disadvantages to doing so. Surgery can be undertaken to repair the child's scrotum and insert artificial testicles or to reposition the testes if they have remained inside the abdominal cavity. But surgical attempts to create a functional penis of sufficient size to permit urination and to sustain sexual intercourse are still not completely satisfactory. Although a tube can be constructed from abdominal tissue, a prothesis is needed to create an erection. The urinary opening must be left in place under the newly constructed penis, as must the penile stub if sexual responsiveness is to be preserved. As the child reaches puberty, the other disadvantages of androgen insensitivity become apparent. Without responsiveness to androgen, the boy will never grow a beard or the muscular contour of a mature male; as a result, he will always appear quite childlike even in middle age. On the other hand, although raising the child as a girl seems to produce a better outcome in adulthood, it also means that she will have the societal disadvantages of being female.

GENDER AS A DICHOTOMY

We saw in the previous chapter that gender distinctions are central to social interaction. Because gender is defined as an exclusive, dichotomous category, we must fit people into either the role of male or female; we cannot imagine someone as neuter, as I realized when I interviewed Cory, the undifferentiated fourth-grader described in the previous chapter. When the baby is born with a clearly defined penis or clitoris, the assignment to one gender role is smooth; we see a penis and announce, "It's a boy!" or a clitoris and say, "It's a girl!" Generally, there is no uncertainty and the child is automatically slotted into one or the other role; we can easily overlook how important the sex of the child really is to parents and others who interact with the baby. However, if the infant's sex is not immediately clear, there is strong internal and social pressure to make a decision about its gender quickly, both on the part of parents and medical personnel involved in the case (S. J. Kessler, 1990). It is very hard for parents to interact with their baby without being able to think of it as clearly either a boy or girl. Imagine how you would feel if you were told by your obstetrician or nurse, "I think you have a boy, or no, maybe you have a girl," or if you had to fill out the birth certificate without marking down the baby's sex, or if you announced to your family and friends that your new baby was a boy but then a few days or weeks later had to explain that it was "really" a girl (S. J. Kessler, 1990, p. 10). When there is uncertainty about the infant's sex, tests to evaluate the infant's chromosomes and ability to respond to androgen can sometimes take weeks or months, and it is difficult for doctors and the parents to avoid making a tentative gender assignment, for example, by referring to the baby's "underdeveloped penis" rather than an "overdeveloped clitoris," or vice versa (S. J. Kessler, 1990). These examples show that the process of socialization into the male or female gender role has already started and that it is important for people to be able to construct an image of the infant as either a boy or a girl. Problems can be created if this decision is not made at an early point in the child's development, because uncertainty about gender affects the parents' behavior toward the child as well as the child's developing sense of self.

■ Sex Assignment within a Critical Period

Once a decision has been made about the baby's gender, that is, parents have given the baby a name, announced it as a boy or girl, and started to think of it in terms of having a son or daughter, it is recommended that the decision not be changed unless it is unavoidable. Uncertainty about the baby's "true" sex creates difficulties for parents—and for the child. In developmental terms there is a *critical period* during which the child's sense of self as male or female is being formed, meaning that during this period the learning is rapid and has long-term effects on the child's development. If the child's gender is reassigned after this critical period, serious emotional problems can develop. In one instance, a masculinized girl was labeled a boy at birth and raised as a boy, but as a result of his condition, he entered puberty at about 6 years, at which point it was recognized that he was a genetic female. The family pediatrician recommended that the parents let the boy's hair grow long, give him a girl's name, and dress him in girl's clothes—with disastrous results: Within the year the child had developed a stutter, was failing in school, and had no friends (Money & Ehrhardt, 1972). Sex reassignments have been more successful if they occur before the child is 2 or 3 years old, before the child begins to refer to himself or herself as a boy or girl. Recent studies indicate that aspects of gender identity may even be established before the child begins to use language, which again would imply that decisions about an infant's sex should be made as soon as possible; this issue will be discussed further in Chapter 6.

■ Inconsistent Sex of Rearing

Emotional problems can also develop if lingering uncertainty over whether a child is "really" a boy or girl affects the child's feelings about himself or herself. In one case the parents of a partially masculinized girl did not consider corrective surgery or treatment, believing for religious reasons that she should live as God had made her. She was born with a penis, she was listed as a boy on her birth certificate, but she was given a girl's name and dressed as a girl. The experience of growing up as neither clearly a boy or a girl was so traumatic that the child became mute, refusing to talk about her problem. She was completely rejected by other children because she seemed to be so awkward and masculine in appearance. A sympathetic school nurse eventually obtained treatment for her, and she indicated that she wanted to be a boy. After a confrontation with the parents, the child was reassigned to the male sex; the ovaries were removed, and at puberty he was given supplemental androgen to promote beard growth and muscle development. As an adolescent he had become poised enough to give a talk about his experience to a large audience at a medical conference (Money & Ehrhardt, 1972; Money & Tucker, 1975). In another case the mother of a masculinized girl was told to give the baby a boy's name but warned that she "might have to change it later." The boy appeared very feminine, had emotional problems, was rejected by his peers, and eventually indicated that he wanted to be a girl. After changing to the female role and receiving corrective surgery, she seemed much happier and more confident. As an adolescent, she had gained enough strength and confidence to charge a male relative with sexual assault after he tried to rape her. His excuse was that he was only trying to help her prove she was really female (Money & Ehrhardt, 1972; Money & Tucker, 1975).

Both cases show a similar pattern: the child's sex was never clearly established and the lingering uncertainty about whether the child was "really" a boy or girl created serious emotional difficulties. In a world in which gender distinctions are prevalent, from the clothes we wear to the names we are given to the restroom we use at school, to feel that you do not know where you fit in can be difficult. Note also that when the sex of rearing is ambivalent, the child may eventually indicate a preference to be the other sex. Since gender is defined as an either-or category, if you are not terribly happy, you may feel that your best option is to try to join the other group, and in the cases described above, both children gained strength and confidence from moving from one role to the other. The emotional improvement probably stems from making a clear commitment to one role, rather than from the new role being somehow more "natural" for the person. In the two cases discussed above, both children were genetically female, but one eventually decided that she would be happiest as a woman, the other as a man. Thus, we cannot conclude that the best or only option is for our gender identity to match our sex chromosomes. For most people the various components of masculinity and femininity happen to be consistent, but a match of chromosomes, reproductive organs, and gender identity does not seem to be required. What does seem to be necessary is that the individual should be conceptualized as clearly a male or female in others' minds, as well as in his or her own mind.

■ Counterexamples

The cases discussed so far suggest that the gender of rearing is the primary factor that determines whether we feel male or female and that, without gender being clearly established, it is difficult for others to know how to relate to the child. However, these claims are challenged by two additional examples, to be discussed below.

"Penis-at-Twelve"

Imagine that you are a girl looking forward to puberty when you will begin to turn into a grown-up woman. But then imagine that instead of developing breasts and hips and beginning to menstruate, you find that you are growing a penis! This apparent transformation from a girl to a boy at puberty can occur as the result of a particular type of androgen insensitivity. Recall that for a male fetus several types of androgen hormones are involved in the process of masculine development: Testosterone stimulates the development of the internal male duct system, Mullerian inhibiting factor prevents the female organs from developing, and di-hydro-testosterone causes the formation of the penis and scrotum. Suppose that, due to an inherited genetic defect, the body cannot produce one of these types of androgen, di-hydro-testosterone, because it lacks one of the enzymes necessary for its production (5 *alpha-reductase deficiency*). The fetus will develop internally as a male as the result of testosterone but will have external genitalia that do not become completely masculinized because there is no di-hydro-testosterone. At birth, the penis might look like a large clitoris, the labia might not be fused, and the testes might remain in the body, and so the infant would usually be labeled and raised as a girl. However, at puberty the testes produce large amounts of testosterone which causes the clitoris to grow into a small penis, the beard to develop, and the voice to deepen—in effect, changing the girl into a boy.

Although 5 alpha-reductase deficiency is relatively rare, several dozen affected men have been studied from a village in the mountains of the Dominican Republic. The village was relatively isolated, and the syndrome had occurred often enough in the small population that the term *penis-at-twelve* had been coined to refer to the affected children. They had been raised as girls, but then when their bodies became more masculine at puberty, most began to live as men, marrying women and behaving as adult males (Imperato-McGinley, Guerro, Gautier, & Peterson, 1974; Imperato-McGinley, Peterson, Gautier, & Sturla,

1979; Peterson, Imperato-McGinley, Gautier, & Sturla, 1977). A similar pattern was found in a community in New Guinea, in which the 5 alpha-reductase deficiency was again relatively common. As in the Dominican Republic village, most of the individuals eventually shifted to the male role as adults. Some did try to remain females but changed to the male role after they could not find husbands who would accept a prospective spouse who had a penis (Herdt & Davidson, 1988).

If the gender in which we are raised is such an important factor in development and if it is difficult for people to tolerate ambiguity in gender identity, we would not have expected these individuals to make the transition from being female to being male, which most were able to do successfully. On the other hand, while they were raised as girls, there are some indications that the syndrome was clearly recognized in the communities, and their genitals at birth were not completely like those of normal females. Thus, they may not have been treated as "real" girls by others, and they seemed to realize relatively early that they were not "real" girls. In other words, their childhood socialization may have been somewhat ambivalent, and as we have already seen, uncertainty about gender often seems to lead the individual to decide to move into the other gender role. The social advantages of being male in these particular cultures may also have provided some additional motivation for becoming men, even though they were sometimes laughed at or considered "inferior" men.

A Last Example

At this point it should be clear that being male or female is not a simple matter of chromosomes, hormones, or even our reproductive organs, but that it depends as well on whether we are raised as boys or girls. While there is some flexibility in gender assignments in development, there is also a strong need for a clear decision to be made; we do not tolerate gender ambiguity easily and find it difficult to relate to others when it is not clear whether they are male or female. As a result there is considerable social pressure to make a clear decision about the gender of a pseudo-hermaphroditic infant, and often the most straightforward decision seems to be to raise the infant as a female. This decision is often based on the belief that it is an unacceptable option to raise a boy with a penis that is "too small," that is, one that is noticeably different from his male peers' genitals and that will not sustain sexual intercourse. But because gender roles are asymmetric, with the male role often being considered more important, the relative advantages of being a male or female in the culture also become an issue. A boy with a tiny or malformed penis still has the social benefits of the male gender role. These considerations may be relevant to one now-famous case of gender reassignment, described next.

In the 1960s, parents of twin boys brought their babies in for a routine circumcision, but the result was unfortunately far from routine; the electric cauterizing device used for the circumcision operation malfunctioned, burned the first baby's penis, and destroyed most of the tissue (Money & Ehrhardt, 1972). After receiving considerable counseling and medical advice, the parents decided to raise the baby as a girl. When she was 17 months old, she had surgery to remove her testicles and to construct female genitals. She was given a girl's name, and her mother began dressing her in pink and letting her hair grow long. She was taught to sit down to urinate and, unlike her twin brother, soon insisted on coming inside to use the bathroom. She initially seemed to adjust well to the female role, playing with dolls, being ladylike, and helping her mother with housework. However, signs of potential problems began to appear when she was a teenager. She had often been teased by other children who called her "cavewoman," and she would only draw male figures, her reason being they were easier than females. Drawing has sometimes been taken to indicate whether the child feels masculine or feminine, although it is not considered to be a highly reliable measure (Farylo & Paludi, 1985). When she was interviewed by a group of psychiatrists at age 13 she seemed unhappy and said that boys had a better life than girls (M. Diamond, 1982). It is not particularly unusual for teenage girls to think that it would be better to be a boy, but her unhappiness apparently persisted, and recent reports indicate that as an adult she has returned to the male role, living as a man (Unger & Crawford, 1992).

This case might suggest that there are the limits to the power of socialization to determine our status as male or female. Because this baby had male chromosomes, prenatal hormones, and unambiguous genitals before the circumcision accident, perhaps he was male in some fundamental sense that could not be completely altered by the experience of growing up as a girl. On the other hand, the relative advantages and disadvantages of the male and female roles might also have been a factor. As a woman she was unable to bear children, had to take supplemental estrogens to maintain her feminine appearance, and was not considered particularly attractive. These factors combined with the ongoing discrimination faced by women in our culture might have made the female role less appealing (Unger & Crawford, 1992). In addition, as we have seen, when someone is uncertain or unhappy in one gender role there is only one other choice because we construct gender as a dichotomy. Other cultures have provided blended or alternative roles for both males and females. We will come back to this issue in Chapter 13 when we consider childhood gender identity disturbance.

SUMMARY

We have examined several definitions of what it means to develop as a male or female, including biological aspects of sex such as our chromosomes, the influence of sex hormones during prenatal development, and our reproductive organs and genitals. While these components are usually consistent within the same individual, this is not always the case. The examples of masculinized females and feminized males suggest that the gender assigned to the child at birth and the experience of growing up as a boy or girl are as important in development as the infant's physical characteristics. In the next chapter we will begin to examine the process of gender socialization, focusing on parents' preferences for a child of a particular sex and their behavior toward the male or female baby in its first year of life.

3

BOYS AND GIRLS: THE FIRST YEAR

Images of infants are almost invariably tinted with pink or blue: A new father leaves the delivery room and goes out to buy a hockey stick for his baby son (Macfarlane, 1977). In a children's shop a woman lingers for a moment and wistfully fingers a pink infant dress with smocking, while nearby a man purchasing a gift looks doubtfully at the blue and pink crib blankets and decides to stick to pale yellow. On an airplane flight to Europe a pregnant woman introduces herself and then pats her stomach and says, "And this is Heather" (Rothman, 1986). A new grandmother gushes over a tiny baby girl but later says privately to her son, "So, do you think you and Maryann will try again next year for a boy?" In a rural Asian village a midwife stands by the laboring mother with a bucket of water ready to drown the newborn if it is a girl, and on a Polynesian island a baby girl is decorated with shells and displayed proudly to relatives and neighbors while a boy is left naked and considered no cause for celebration.

Clearly, the sex of the baby is a salient feature from the earliest moments of life, both in its parents' eyes and to the social world into which it is born. The deep interest in the infant's sex reflects the fact that gender is one of the main ways to determine where an individual belongs in the culture. In cultures with clear divisions in the roles played by men and women, the announcement of the infant's sex at birth can in effect be a capsule description of his or her entire future. A girl born in a wealthy Moslem family in northern India knows that she will help care for her younger siblings during childhood, have her marriage arranged by her parents in early adolescence, and then spend her adult life almost entirely in seclusion within her own household. A boy in a western African tribe knows that he will spend his childhood with the women and children of the village and at puberty will be circumcised and then join the company of adult men. In contemporary western cultures there is currently considerably more gender role flexibility; a man can become a nursery school teacher or stay home with his new baby for a year without becoming a complete societal outcast, and it is conceivable that in the United States a woman could become President. Yet when the infant is first born, these variations are hard to anticipate, and people tend to rely on gender stereotypes when imagining the baby's future.

The goal of this chapter is to examine the earliest beginnings of the process of socializing children into gender roles. Since the baby's place in the surrounding society depends at least in part on its gender, it is not surprising that this process begins during infancy. It can even be argued that socialization begins well before the infant is conceived, in the sense that parents often have preferences for a boy or a girl, preferences that reflect the family's economic, religious, and emotional needs for a child of a particular gender in the context of a particular society. In the first part of this chapter we examine why parents have such preferences. The asymmetry of gender roles will become clear, in that for the most part parents have traditionally preferred to have male children, at least as their firstborn. Next we review the physical and behavioral characteristics of male and female infants at birth and through the first year of life. Male and female infants are not physically or behaviorally very different, but they are nevertheless viewed differently by parents, an illustration of our tendency to view the sexes as polar opposites. Finally, we examine the evidence for differential treatment of boys and girls by their parents during the first year of life.

IS IT A BOY OR A GIRL?

■ The Preference for Boys

Throughout history and across cultures parents have generally wanted at least one son. This preference is most evident when people are asked about their first child or if they expect to have only one child. When U.S. college students in the 1950s were asked, "If you could have only one child, which sex would you prefer?" 90 percent of the men and 66 percent of the women said they would prefer a boy. In 1970 the results for men were the same, and an even higher percentage of women (78 percentage) preferred a boy (Williamson, 1976). In the early 1990s the preference for sons had declined somewhat among women but had increased among men (Hamilton, 1991b; Pooler, 1991). Even people who initially say that they would not care will usually select a boy in a forced-choice situation. When mothers who are expecting their first child are asked whether they hope to have a boy or a girl, most say it doesn't matter as long as it's healthy. Yet after the baby is born, 93 percent of mothers of boys say they are happy with its sex, compared to 56 percent of mothers of girls (Oakley, 1980). Families with several girls tend to be larger and have shorter intervals between the children than those with a firstborn boy, as if parents who have daughters "keep trying" for a boy. The preference for boys is consistently stronger among men than women. The father of baseball player Pete Rose wanted a son so much that his wife dressed their second daughter in a boy's clothes and cut the girl's hair like a boy's. She was relieved when Pete was subsequently born and said, "I don't even want to think about how many girls I would have had to have before we stopped" (King, 1990). One man even designed a prenuptial agreement providing financial incentives to his bride for bearing children and offering extra "premium incentives" for sons (Zack, 1991, p. 16). (She refused to sign.)

Although parents want sons, they want daughters too—after their "son quota" has been filled. United States parents would typically like to have at least one child of each sex,

Doonesbury

BY GARRY TRUDEAU

a firstborn boy and a girl. If they plan to have three children, they generally would prefer two older boys followed by a girl. Parents who have very large families have little preference because the odds are high that they already have several of each sex. One study of poor families in Appalachia showed that the parents did not have any gender preferences, which was not surprising given that they had an average of nine children each. On the other hand I remember seeing a newspaper account several years ago about a rabbi and his spouse who celebrated the arrival of their twelfth child, who was *finally* a boy—their first 11 children were daughters.

An abstract preference is one thing, but once the baby is born, does it actually matter? In fact, there is evidence that one possibility is valued more than the other, at least with the delivery of a first infant. Transcripts of new parents' conversations in the delivery room show that references to its sex are embedded within the flow of excited comments about the baby's health and appearance. One mother said, "A girl. Oh I'm sorry darling," to her husband, whereupon the exasperated doctor said, "I'm not putting her back . . . What are you sorry about?" (Macfarlane, 1977, p. 67). In some cases parents are so sure that they will have a boy, they actually misperceive the infant's sex. One father looked at his new daughter, shouted, "It's a boy," and then sheepishly realized that he'd "gotten his things sorted out wrong" (Macfarlane, 1977, p. 108). The television news announcer Tom Brokaw "heard" the delivery room nurse say, "Congratulations, you have a healthy boy," after the birth of his first child. He called friends and relatives with the news and only later discovered that the baby was actually a girl.

Other people are also interested in the new baby's sex, specifically, if it is a boy. Admittedly, the question, "Is it a boy or a girl?" reflects the need to find out how to refer to the baby; referring to the baby as "it" for very long, rather than "he" or "she," seems rather unfriendly. But the pronoun problem does not account for the particular patterns in exactly how people ask about the baby's sex. In one study expectant parents were recruited in childbirth preparation classes to make notes about what people asked when they heard about the birth (Intons-Peterson & Reddel, 1984). After the baby had been delivered, the new parent (usually the father) called relatives and friends and said, "The baby is here," or "We've just had the baby." Questions from 273 people were recorded verbatim. *Eighty* percent of the first questions were about the sex of the infant; the remainder were questions about the health of mother and the infant ("Are they OK?") and about the labor ("How bad was it?"). In addition, the order in which people asked about "boy" versus "girl" suggested a particular interest in knowing if the infant was male. Of those who asked first about the infant's sex, 52 percent asked, "Is it a boy or a girl?" while 12 percent asked, "Is it a girl or a boy?" An additional 35 percent of the respondents (most of them men) asked, "Is it a boy?" without mentioning "girl" at all. Only one person asked, "Is it a girl?"

In many other countries the desire for sons is much stronger than in the United States for two reasons (Hammer, 1970). First, there are frequently strong religious traditions that lead parents to want sons. Women in Moslem countries can be divorced if they do not bear boys, and an ancient Hindu prayer for expectant parents pleads, "The birth of a girl, grant it elsewhere, here grant a son" (Kakar, 1978). Second, economic factors also increase the value of sons over daughters. Boys will work for the family and will often bring in a dowry when they marry. (Dowry is the money or property brought into the marriage by the bride; it is usually paid by her parents.) Once married, boys will produce offspring to continue the family line and support the parents when they are old. In contrast, daughters cost more than sons to raise but then marry, work, and produce children for another family. The prohibitive expense of providing a dowry for daughters when they marry is a significant negative factor among poor families. In economically developing countries, such as India, Korea, and Turkey, poor women will use family planning services after they have had several sons, but in poorer countries women are more likely to do so after the birth of several daughters, because the family cannot risk the additional expense of providing more dowries. One 10-year-old girl in India was sold by her parents to a visiting Saudi Arabian man for about $4000—selling her gained the impoverished family a sum equal to about 6 years' wages and spared them the cost of her dowry (*Boston Globe*, 1991f). Having sons is more important for women in other cultures than in the United States; where there is no social security system and women cannot work outside the home, a woman must depend on her sons for support if she is widowed or divorced.

Daughter Preference

There have been several cultures in which parents have preferred daughters, including groups in Sumatra, Tahiti, New Guinea, the Tiwi who live on islands off Northern Australia, a small Native American tribe in Peru, the Garo in Assam, India, and the Tolowa Native American tribe in the northwestern United States (Williamson, 1976). However, the parental preference for female children in these cultures did not reflect a more egalitarian view of gender roles. In these societies property was passed through the maternal line of the family, and women were highly productive economically, providing most of the family's support. A man would therefore want to have many daughters so he could prosper through their labor. Women were also considered property that could be traded; for example, a man could exchange one of his sisters for a wife. Women were also used to pay debts, to consolidate alliances with other families through marriage, and to bring a *bride-price* to the husband when they were married. (Bride-price is a sum of money or goods paid by the husband to the bride's parents to compensate them for the cost of her upbringing and the loss of her future labor; it is the reverse of a dowry system.) As these societies came in contact with western culture, the economic factors that made girls prized quickly changed and the preference for daughters declined.

Why Does the Preference for Boys Persist?

The preference for boys is rooted in religious traditions and economic circumstances that have endured for centuries. In many cultures these influences may still be at work, but most no longer seem to apply in contemporary western cultures. Elderly parents now receive benefits from Social Security programs and pension plans and daughters, not sons, are most likely to care for them when they become incapacitated. Relatively few U.S. families now work in such labor-intensive settings as farming, and technological advances have somewhat reduced the importance of sheer physical strength; clearing a field of embedded stones can now be done with a backhoe almost as easily by a daughter as a son. Some economists have suggested that in industrialized countries children are now economic liabilities because they require expensive training and maintenance and do not make financial contributions, whereas in the past they were cheap sources of labor and were capital assets to the family. If this is true, then sons should no longer hold an advantage in economic terms. Yet parents still seem to feel that boys are a better investment for the family and that daughters are more expensive to raise. Whenever families have to pay for services for children (private education, special lessons, computer camps, and so on) parents spend more on boys than on girls (*New York Times*, 1989). One advertisement for a small private college was actually based on the assumption that parents would ordinarily limit their spending on a girl's education: Its slogan was, "If you think a state school is the best you can do for your daughter . . . consider us."

There are other more emotional reasons for the continuing preference for sons among western parents. One is to carry on the family name. A letter to Ann Landers illustrates how important this can be in some families:

Dear Ann Landers,
I am writing this letter from the hospital. A nurse has promised to mail it. I need to know if I am justified in being upset. Three days ago I gave birth to my fourth daughter. My mother-in-law came to see me and the new baby within three hours of the birth. She patted my hand and said, "Don't be upset because it wasn't a boy. You can try again, dear. You know we are depending on you to make sure the family name is carried on." I said, "Look, Mother, I am 38 years old and have had four children and three miscarriages in seven years. Please don't depend on me to do any more." I then got a lecture on "tradition, family pride and a 'wife's obligation.'" I couldn't believe it. After all, they aren't exactly the Kennedys or the Rockefellers. My husband sat there like a bump on the log. He didn't say a word. Was I wrong to answer her back and to be hurt because he didn't speak up for me?

Ann Landers: Consider the source. Anyone who would come to the hospital three hours after a birth has oatmeal where her brains belong.

The emotional reasons may explain the one exception among U.S. couples for the male preference: adoption. Most couples who adopt say they will take a child of either sex, but those who do express a preference say they would rather have a girl. Raising a son of unknown parents is perceived as riskier, and there is a reluctance to have the family name and property pass on to future generations through a son who is a biological outsider. In other countries, such as Japan, this reluctance does not hold; once a child has been formally adopted, he or she is considered a "true" child of the family (Kadushin, & Seidl, 1971; Williamson, 1976).

In addition to the feeling that boys provide family continuity over the generations, they seem to play a special role with the father and strengthen the father's commitment to the family. In England, fathers stayed significantly longer in the delivery room and held their new baby more when it was a son (C. Lewis, 1986). In Israel, among kibbutz families fathers had longer visits with sons than daughters at the infant house (Gewirtz & Gewirtz, 1968). In India, sons are considered to be the keystone of a marriage, binding the parents together. United States fathers spend half an hour a day more with firstborn sons than firstborn daughters, and when the father has a demanding job, he is more likely to set aside time to spend with a son than a daughter (Kotelchuck, 1976). United States parents with sons are also more likely to remain married: An analysis of the 1980 census data showed that among couples with one child, those with a daughter were more likely to divorce than those with a son. For couples with two children, those with two daughters were most likely to divorce, while those with two sons were least likely to end their marriage. Some mothers may therefore express a preference for a son because they sense it will be beneficial to the marriage (L. Hoffman, 1977).

Clearly, new parents are not indifferent to the sex of their offspring, at least when it comes to firstborn or secondborn children. Most parents want sons, a preference that is rooted in religious and economic traditions and that continues to persist today. In the next section we look at parents' interest in and attempts to try to act on their preferences.

■ Sex Selection

At Conception

Parents have often tried to ensure the conception and birth of an infant of the desired sex. The ancient Greeks believed that the woman should lie on her right side after intercourse for a boy, her left side for a girl, and that the man should tie a string very tightly around his left testicle to shut down the production of "girl" semen and increase the chances of having a boy from the right testicle. In Italy the man would bite his wife's right ear for a boy, her left for a girl. In the United States a man would traditionally hang his trousers to the right side of the bed for a boy, the left for a girl. In cultures as diverse as Polynesia and Scandinavia the wife would keep a small boy in her room or dress up as a boy herself the day before intercourse to encourage a male conception, while in old Germany a woodsman would take an axe into the bed if he wanted a son. In the nineteenth century U.S. husbands were told that after intercourse, in hopes of "impressing" masculinity upon the fetus, they should read aloud to their wives from biographies of important men. The common themes running through these folk methods illustrate the asymmetry of gender roles: Extra effort is required if the parents want a son, and "right" is associated with masculinity; right has positive associations, while left has negative connotations (Brooks-Gunn & Matthews, 1979; Shettles & Rorvik, 1984).

More recent methods for conceiving a child of the desired sex have been based on a theory of sperm selection. As we saw in Chapter 2, the sex of the offspring is determined by the father's sperm. Because the father typically produces equal numbers of X and Y sperm, the ratio of conceptions should be fifty-fifty, but in fact, considerably more males are conceived. This discrepancy has led some researchers to suggest that the X sperm might be slightly larger and slower than the Y sperm. If the X's lag behind, they would be less likely to reach and fertilize the egg, thus leading to fewer female conceptions. One method based on the idea that X sperm are slow but hardy, while the Y sperm are fast but fragile, claims to increase the chances of conceiving a child of the desired sex to 75 percent (Shettles & Rorvik, 1984). It was rumored to have been used in 1982 by Charles, prince of Wales, and his bride Diana to ensure that their first child, the future heir to the British throne, would be a boy. The general method is as follows: If the parents want to conceive a boy, they should have intercourse close to the time of ovulation, so the faster Y sperm will reach the newly released egg first. In addition, several steps can be taken to purportedly increase the mobility of the Y sperm. The mother should use a baking-soda douche and have multiple orgasms to increase the alkaline secretions of the vaginal environment which is usually somewhat acidic and hostile to sperm. The father should drink several cups of strong coffee to give the sperm an extra "boost." Conversely, if the parents want to have a girl, intercourse should be timed 2 to 4 days before ovulation, so the faster Y sperm arrive and die while the slower X's will arrive just in time to meet the newly ovulated egg. In addition, the mother should use a vinegar douche to increase vaginal acidity and favor the hardier X sperm. One woman commented that "having to sit and watch the clock while the baking soda is dissolving and hubby is forcing down black coffee is enough to try anyone's patience! But we kept telling ourselves: what do you get for nothing? It's worth a bit of extra effort and sacrifice" (Shettles & Rorvik, 1984, p. 120).

Another method for selective conception involves separating the X and Y sperm with centrifuges or filters to catch the larger Xs, although this is hardly practical for most parents since it requires specialized laboratory equipment. There is also evidence that factors such as heat or stress can kill the more fragile Y sperm. Men who would like to have a son should avoid sitting in hot tubs or wearing scuba-diving wet suits for long periods, because these activities can raise the body temperature enough to damage sperm. They might also want to avoid space travel. According to Air Force mythology, fighter pilots have more daughters than sons; and a recent study provided confirmation: Astronauts and fighter pilots, who were exposed to high gravitational forces, had 62 percent daughters, while commercial and transport pilots had equal numbers of sons and daughters. It should be stressed here that methods for sex selection at the time of conception have not been clearly demonstrated to be completely reliable. Their popularity endures because even if they don't work, parents are satisfied with the outcome about half the time anyway.

Sex Selection after Conception

If there are economic or political pressures to restrict family size, parents may resort to selective abortion or infanticide to ensure that they will have at least one son. There have always been folk methods of determining the sex of the fetus during pregnancy (Brooks-Gunn & Matthews, 1979). For example, it was thought that if the pregnant mother has a rosy complexion and carries the baby high, it will be a boy, while if she is pale and carrying low, it will be a girl. Another quite dangerous method is for the pregnant mother to spit into a glass of drain cleaner; supposedly if it turns blue, she will have a boy (it could also

GEECH®

by Jerry Bittle

explode in her face). While none of these folk methods is reliable, medical techniques can determine fetal sex. A sonogram, or ultrasound exam, can show the outline of the fetus's genitals if it is in the right position. Prenatal testing for various genetic disorders, such as amniocentesis and chorionic villus sampling, reveal the sex of the fetus when its chromosomes are analyzed. These tests would not be done solely to determine sex because of their small associated risk of miscarriage, but most (80 percent) women who undergo amniocentesis for genetic screening purposes also ask about the sex of the fetus (Rothman, 1986). It is now quite common for friends and even salespeople to ask expectant parents if they are going to have a boy or a girl on the assumption that the fetal sex is known.

Once the sex of the fetus is known, it becomes possible for parents to select the sex of their offspring after conception by termininating the pregnancy. There is little evidence that parents systematically use abortion for sex selection in the United States, although it does occur on occasion (Rothman, 1986). Selective abortion on the basis of sex does occur on a wider scale in such countries as India and China where there are severe economic or political pressures to limit family size and where having sons is critical for the economic survival of the family (Kishwar, 1987). One clinic in Bombay advertised that parents should spend $39 on amniocentesis to save $3900 on a dowry later, while an analysis of 8000 aborted fetuses in 6 Bombay clinics revealed that 7999 were female. India is one of the few countries in the world in which men now outnumber women. If the pregnancy is not terminated, parents may resort to infanticide, the practice of killing the newborn baby or allowing it to die of neglect. Infanticide has occurred throughout human history whenever parents cannot provide for all the children they produce; in general, girls are at greater risk. When resources are limited, parents will give food and medical care to boy babies first. In one state in India, rural parents brought both their sons and daughters to village clinics for free immunizations against childhood diseases, but when the government subsidies for the program ended and parents had to pay a small fee for the vaccines, only sons were brought in. In some poor and underdeveloped countries, girl infants die at twice the rate of boys (Kishwar, 1987). A Chinese couple was recently jailed for abandoning their newborn daughter. At the birth the doctor had mistakenly recorded the baby as a boy on the birth certificate. When the parents got home and discovered the error, they took the baby back to the hospital and left her there, refusing to raise her (*Boston Globe*, 1991c).

■ Does It Matter?

Women students often say that their parents never hinted that they were not the "right" gender. They are no doubt right; parents do want daughters—just not at the exclusion of sons. Once a child has been born and becomes part of the family, an abstract preference for the other gender may be forgotten and parents may genuinely say they didn't care one way or another. In addition, while growing up, children typically think that their parents like girls better because girls are "nicer" than boys, and do not realize their parents value boys for their potential contributions as adults more than for their current behavior (Hartley, Hardesty, & Gorfein, 1962).

Although most parents are truly happy with their baby regardless of its sex, being born the "wrong" sex does occasionally have long-term consequences for the child's development. Dissatisfaction with the child's gender can create serious problems in dysfunctional families. One study of emotionally disturbed children found that some of them had been rejected by their parents because they were not the desired sex (Sloman, 1948). One troubled mother had wanted a son to replace one who had died, while another had only wanted a girl because she was convinced that a boy would grow up to be a criminal. Being the less preferred sex can also be a predictor of child abuse (H. Martin, 1976). In one Massachusetts case a father who was accused of killing his 3-month-old daughter told a friend, "I think I have a personality problem with the baby. I think boys are the way to go. Girls are a problem" (Langer, 1989, p. 31). In successful abuse prevention programs a delivery room nurse monitors the parents' reactions to the birth of their baby. Certain reactions are indications of possible problems in the future, including visible disappointment with the baby's sex. One mother who wanted a boy had planned to breast-feed, but when she gave birth to a daughter, she seemed disgruntled and immediately announced that she would bottle-feed the baby instead (Gray, Cutler, Dean, & Kempe, 1976, p. 383). In one program in Colorado new parents who showed such reactions were offered support services which helped reduce the incidence of abuse during the baby's first year.

Data from a longitudinal study in Sweden suggest that even among well-adjusted families, gender preferences may still influence parent-child interactions (Stattin & Klackenberg-Larsson, 1991). Parents visiting a large clinic for prenatal care during the late 1950s were enrolled in the study and as part of their initial interview, they were asked if they hoped for a boy or girl. Twenty years later, parents who had had consistent preferences (i.e., mother and father both wanted a boy or a girl) were identified, and data from their families were analyzed to learn if parents' initial disappointment or satisfaction with the child's gender had influenced the child's development. Immediately after the birth the parents were generally delighted with their child, but parents whose preference had been met gave higher ratings of pleasure with the child's sex than those who were disappointed. While the child was growing up, parents reported more conflicts and problems with children whose sex had not been preferred, particularly girls whose parents had hoped for a boy. When the children were interviewed as adults, women whose parents had originally wanted a boy reported less positive relationships with their fathers and said that their parents had not spent as much time with them as opposed to women whose parents had wanted a girl. In contrast, men whose parents had originally wanted a girl reported comfortable relationships with their parents and comparatively little childhood difficulty.

These findings should be interpreted with caution; in general, the parents were very happy with their children regardless of their initial preferences, and the effects observed in the study were quite modest. On the other hand, given parents' general reluctance to admit anything negative about their families, the relatively egalitarian nature of Swedish society, and the 20-year span of the observations, the fact that parents' initial preferences had any observable effect at all on the child's development was striking.

Although most parents are genuinely content with an infant of either sex, the evidence of parental preferences shows that gender is usually a highly salient feature of the infant even before it is born. Yet when male and female infants are compared in terms of their physical and behavioral development, their genitals are about the only things that are observably different about them. As we will see in the next section, the sexes are remarkably similar as infants.

CHARACTERISTICS OF BOY AND GIRL BABIES

■ Physical Development

When babies are first born, the physical differences between boys and girls are minimal. Newborn males weigh a bit more (about 5 percent) and are a bit longer on average than females (Freeman, Graves, & Thompson, 1970; Mednick, Hocevar, Baker, & Teasdale, 1983; Tanner, 1962). However, the difference is so small that it does not tell us much about the characteristics of individual babies; there are certainly plenty of delicate boys and hefty girls born, as a visit to a newborn nursery will quickly demonstrate. Although boys are slightly larger on average, girls' physical development is a bit ahead of boys' (Doyle & Paludi, 1991). Girls' skeletal maturation, as measured by the hardness of the wrist bones, is several weeks ahead of boys' at birth although this difference is gone by the end of the first year. Metabolic rates are the same at birth. As we saw in the last chapter, boys are more likely to be born with birth defects and developmental problems, but healthy boys and girls receive similar scores when their reflexes and neurological responses are assessed at birth (Rosenblith & DeLucia, 1963). The nervous system also develops after birth at the same rate for the sexes; boys and girls grasp, sit up, crawl, and walk at the same average ages (Bayley, 1965; Maccoby & Jacklin, 1974).

■ Perceptual Abilities

Male and female infants also come into the world with pretty much the same systems for interacting with the world: hearing, taste, sense of smell, and visual behavior are found to be similar in almost all studies and to develop at similar rates (Fagan, 1979; Maccoby & Jacklin, 1974). In early studies of tactile sensitivity there were hints that girls might be more sensitive, but the effects were not reliably observed, so at this point there is no clear evidence showing that female infants actually are more sensitive (R. Bell & Costello, 1964; Lipsitt & Levy, 1959). Most studies also find that boys and girls perform similarly on tests of infant memory and learning, although in one study girls could remember the location of a hidden object over longer delays than boys of the same age, suggesting that the girls' memory span was developing a bit ahead of boys' (A. Diamond, 1985).

■ Activity Level *t̬*

Many parents are convinced that boys are harder to care for, and studies have shown that in the first few weeks of life male infants do cry a bit more, have more disturbed sleep, and are more active on average than females (Ashton, 1971; M. Davis, 1991; Eaton & Enns, 1986; Freudigman & Thoman, 1991; P. Klein, 1984; Korner, 1969; Moss, 1967; Osofsky & O'Connell, 1977; M. Rosenthal, 1983). These differences were illustrated in a study comparing female and uncircumcised male newborns who had been carefully matched on body weight, length of labor, and use of medication in labor, all factors that could affect their sleep and motor behavior patterns (S. Phillips, King, & DuBois, 1978). The babies were observed for a total of 8 hours during their first 2 days of life, with the observers unaware of the infants' sex. The observers recorded such behaviors as yawning, mouthing, crying, head turns, arm and hand waves, muscle jerks and startles, kicks, and facial grimaces and found that male infants had slightly higher scores on all activity measures and were awake more of the time.

Sex differences in activity and irritability have not been observed in all studies, suggesting that the effects may depend on the particular sample of babies being studied (Eaton & Enns, 1986). Certainly, there is a great deal of overlap; many female babies scream themselves hoarse, while many male babies sleep sweetly through the night. The sex differences that have been observed in carefully controlled studies can easily become exaggerated in parents' minds as the result of factors related to the birth process. Even in uncomplicated deliveries, male infants take longer to be born, for unknown reasons. Mothers having their first child spend almost 100 minutes longer in labor with a son than a daughter, and this difference is still found after infant weight is taken into account (Jacklin & Maccoby, 1982; Zachau-Christiansen & Ross, 1975). Longer labors are correlated with other factors, such as delivery complications, birth trauma, and exposure to pain medication, which can increase the infant's irritability and contribute to sleep problems for up to 6 months after the delivery (Aleksandrowicz & Aleksandrowicz, 1974; Friedman & Neff, 1987; Kraemer, Korner, & Thoman, 1972; Stechler, 1964; Thoman, Leiderman, & Olson, 1972). In one study of male babies, those who had experienced traumatic deliveries were more active after birth (R. Bell, 1960).

A second factor that can affect male infants is *circumcision*, the removal of the foreskin of the penis. The operation is typically done without pain relief, so it is not surprising that some male babies would be a bit fussy (Richards, Bernal, & Brackbill, 1976)! Brackbill (1975) found that among 4-day-old babies, females and uncircumcised males were equally likely to be soothed by listening to white noise, while boys who had been circumcised a day or two earlier remained awake longer and cried more. Other sex differences in sensitivity and irritability have not been consistently replicated in European samples where circumcision is not performed routinely on newborn boys (Desor, Maller, & Turner, 1973; Dubignon, Campbell, Curtis, & Parrington, 1969; Nisbett & Gurwitz, 1970). Not all the sex difference in activity level can be attributed to circumcision, but it probably contributes to the stereotype that boy babies are more active and fussy than girls.

The general picture of infants, then, is one of similarity rather than difference. Boys and girls look and act about the same, or rather, the range of physical and behavioral characteristics is equally wide for both sexes. In fact, the sexes are so physically similar that adults cannot reliably tell if a baby is a boy or a girl (T. Bower, 1989; Langlois, Ritter, Roggman, & Vaughn, 1991; Shakin, Shakin, & Sternglanz, 1985).

CREATING DIFFERENCES

New parents are faced with a dilemma: On the one hand, the baby's gender is its most important social characteristic, but on the other hand, male and female babies are so similar that their sex cannot be easily distinguished by the casual observer. The solution is to "construct" the baby's gender by providing clues that signal to others whether it is male or female; such clues include the baby's name, clothing, and the surrounding environment.

◼ Gender Clues

Names

Gender distinctions are made even with the first step of naming the baby. First names are highly sex-typed, with a few such exceptions as Robin, Leslie, and Chris. The range of boys' names is fairly restricted; most parents choose old standards such as John, Robert, Mark, Richard, Paul, and Steven. Girls have a wider selection of first names, and more marked trends exist in feminine names; there is currently a bumper crop of "Jennifers" and "Heathers" in elementary schools. Girls are more likely to be named for television characters ("Krystle") or to be given unusual or frivolous names ("Star," "Moonbeam," or my all-time favorite: "Sin"). We know one family with the surname "Barr" in which the son was named a sedate "Aaron" while the daughter suffered through life with the first name "Candy." These patterns again suggest that parents view sons as a more serious matter than daughters.

Clothing

Parents are usually careful to dress the baby so that its gender is clearly indicated to others; otherwise, embarrassing mistakes can occur. On a winter's walk several years ago we ran into our neighbors with their new baby, who was wearing a light-powder-blue snowsuit. When my husband innocently referred to the baby as "pretty," the mother froze and said very distinctly, "He is a boy." Many infant clothes are highly sex-typed, and studies of infants observed in shopping malls or other public areas reveal that girls are often dressed in pink and yellow, while boys are dressed in blue and red (Shakin et al., 1985). Gender distinctions are indicated in other ways as well; girl babies are more likely to wear jewelry, girls are given pink pacifiers while boys receive blue ones, and infant researchers find that parents will even sometimes bring their newborn daughters into the laboratory with ribbon bows taped to their bare scalps (Pomerleau, Bolduc, Malcuit, & Cossette, 1990). When parents have twins, triplets, or quadruplets, they emphasize the gender differences between the babies by dressing them in sex-typed outfits (Goshen-Gottstein, 1981). Even disposable diapers are now marketed with a blue "extra-protection-up-front" or a pink "protection-down-low" lining, although for centuries parents have somehow managed to cope with unisex diapers. Parents sometimes rationalize their choice of gender-typed clothing by saying that it is hard to find baby clothes, such as snowsuits, that are not pink or blue. However, neutral pants and t-shirts *are* available, and it would be perfectly acceptable to dress a baby girl in light blue, but parents rarely do so. This suggests that they are actually choosing clothing to convey the baby's gender (Shakin et al., 1985).

The Physical Environment

Parents also create different physical environments for boys and girls. Studies of babies' rooms have found that pink, yellow, flowers, ruffles, and lace are used exclusively in girls' rooms, while boys' rooms are usually blue or red, with transportation (i.e., race cars) or outer space themes (Pomerleau et al., 1990; Rheingold & Cook, 1975). When we bought our first house, we had no trouble guessing the sex of the three children who had previously lived there: Two bedrooms were blue with handpainted *Star Wars* motifs, the third was pink with a Hollie Hobbie mural, and the children's shared bathroom had a gender-neutral cartoon mural of animals from *The Jungle Book*.

Parents also provide different types of toys and play objects to boy and girl babies. Mothers buy a wider variety of toys for boys, including more trucks and cars, tools, sports equipment, balls, gardening and beach toys (i.e., toy shovels), and construction toys. Girls have more dolls, toy kitchen appliances and utensils, toy furniture, jewelry, and musical toys (Bradbard, 1985; Pomerleau et al., 1990). Some of the gender typing of toys is no doubt due to the fact that toys are marketed according to the child's gender. Catalogs and toy stores have different sections for boys' and girls' toys, with dolls, doll houses, crafts, and domestic toys in one area, while transportation toys, construction toys, and sports items are in another area (Schwartz & Markham, 1985). Salespeople immediately ask parents or gift givers whether the toy is for a boy or a girl and direct people to the corresponding section of the store.

The process of constructing a gender-typed environment can now begin even *before* birth. Parents who know the sex of the fetus through prenatal tests refer to the fetus as "he" or "she," select the baby's name, and choose toys and nursery decorations in advance according to the baby's gender. The pregnant woman can now even wear a t-shirt with the slogan, "It's a boy/girl" (Rothman, 1986). Thus, gender distinctions are now even more likely to be emphasized than in the past, when parents did not know until the birth whether they would have a son or daughter. This tends to make gender even more salient than it would otherwise have been; if the only thing you know about your future child is that it is a girl, your daydreams and expectations for the future are going to be heavily based on stereotypes rather than on the child's individual characteristics.

Does It Matter?

It is clear that parents create different environments for boy and girl babies, but some of these differences seem trivial; from the infant's point of view, does it really matter if the crib blanket is pale yellow with tiny rosebuds or blue with comets and satellites? In fact, there are reasons to be concerned about the heavy emphasis on gender early in infancy. For instance, distinctions in the infant's environment may have longer-term consequences for his or her development. Researchers have suggested that boys and girls learn different skills through the types of toys that are typically provided to them in early childhood, for example, that boys have more opportunity to explore spatial relations through construction and transportation toys. We will consider this possibility in more detail in Chapter 11.

■ The Eye of the Beholder

Items like lace-trimmed blouses and blue pacifiers also matter because knowing the infant's sex changes how people perceive and interact with the baby. The baby will be perceived as a delicate rosebud or a miniature Rambo depending on whether adults think it is a boy or a girl—an example of how we think of gender as a dichotomy and exaggerate differences between the sexes. Rubin, Provenzano, and Luria (1974) found that parents' views of their baby during its first 24 hours of life varied according to its sex. Parents rated daughters as more delicate, finely featured, and softer than sons, who were viewed as strong, hardy, firm, and well coordinated. Other studies have found a similar "eye of the beholder" effect when the same baby is shown dressed as a boy to some viewers and dressed as a girl to others. This "Baby X" method shows clearly that adults are influenced by their own gender stereotypes, rather than responding to subtle differences in the appearance, size, or behavior of infant boys and girls, because the baby's behavior is the same in both cases (Stern & Karraker, 1989). The eye of the beholder effect has also been demonstrated before the baby has even been born: Expectant mothers who knew via amniocentesis that they were carrying boys described the fetus's movements as "vigorous," "a saga of earthquakes," "very strong," and "calm but strong," ("the John Wayne fetus"). Mothers of girls described the movements as "very gentle," "not terribly active," "lively but not excessively energetic," and "moderate, reassuring but not violent." Pregnant women who did not know the sex of the fetus described the movements as "lively, vigorous, strong" but their descriptions were not found to be related to the infant's sex, and studies of fetal movements before birth have found no evidence that males are more active; thus, the different perceptions seem to reflect gender stereotypes (Eaton & Enns, 1986; Rothman, 1986).

While boys tend to be perceived as strong and vigorous, it seems to be especially important for girls to be viewed as small and delicate. Parents underestimated the size and weight of their newborn daughters relative to sons, although the babies in the sample were the same average weight and the girls were actually slightly longer (Rubin et al., 1974). An obstetric nurse who recorded comments about the baby offered by visitors found that mothers were not pleased when the baby's size was described in gender-atypical terms, for example, "look at his delicate little fingers," or "good heavens, she's an absolute dumpling". One new mother burst into tears when a visitor referred to her baby daughter as "big." When a granddaughter of John Wayne was born several years ago, she was an average-sized infant at 7½ pounds, but the hospital press officer described her as a "very nice, petite baby."

Effects on Interaction

Adults not only describe the baby in terms of gender stereotypes, they also behave differently toward it when they think it is a boy or a girl. Choosing toys according to the infant's perceived sex, they hand a doll to the baby if they think is a girl, and a plastic football or hammer to a boy. They talk more to the infant if they believe it is a girl and bounce, toss, and roughhouse with the baby if they think it is a boy (N. Bell & Carver, 1980; Culp, Cook, & Housley, 1983; J. Meyer & Sobieszek, 1972; Seavey, Katz, & Zalk, 1975; Sidorowicz & Lunney, 1980; C. Smith & Lloyd, 1978; Sobieszek, 1978). Using the Baby X technique, Condry and Condry (1976) found that adults interpreted a baby's emotional expression differently if they thought it was a girl. They watched a videotape of a 9-month-old baby reacting to an attractive teddy bear, a startling jack-in-the-box, and a loud, unpleasant buzzer. Some were told they were watching "Dana," while others viewed "David," although it was the same baby in both cases. The viewers thought that both Dana and David reacted with pleasure to the teddy bear and fear to the loud buzzer, but they interpreted the baby's startled reaction to the jack-in-the-box as anger in the case of David and fear in the case of Dana. Similarly, J. M. Haviland (1977) found that adults interpreted emotional expressions in babies according to gender, with infants labeled as boys seen as being angry and upset more often than when the same babies were labeled as girls.

In general, the more experience viewers have had with infants, the less likely they are to show the eye of the beholder effect. Thus, young children and college students are more likely to be influenced by gender stereotypes when they play with a baby than are experienced parents, and men tend to be influenced by a gender label more than women, who often have had more contact with infants (Haugh, Hoffman, & Cowan, 1980). Stereotypes most often come into play when we are on unfamiliar ground, and gender stereotypes are particularly powerful (Rubin et al., 1974). The perfectly ordinary behavior of any baby can easily be interpreted in terms of gender; if a baby fusses a great deal, it is easy to say, "Oh well, he's a boy," or "She's a real prima donna." Gender supports many inferences about the baby's probable characteristics and behavior. Even though these initial inferences have a very high probability of being wrong, they reassure the viewer who is faced with an unfamiliar small baby. The drawback is that, as we have seen, once the baby is perceived as a boy or girl, the process of social interaction will be altered accordingly.

GETTING TO KNOW YOU: PARENTS' BEHAVIOR WITH SONS AND DAUGHTERS

We have seen so far that parents are generally not neutral with respect to the gender of their baby; often, they do have a preference for a boy or girl. Once the baby is born, or even before, they create a world in which the baby's gender is clearly signaled to others, and their behavior reflects their stereotyped beliefs about girls and boys, namely, that girls are delicate and fearful while boys are strong and sturdy. In the next section, we look at how these beliefs influence parents' patterns of interaction with their new baby over the first year of life. Several studies have found that parents generally behave quite similarly to infant sons and daughters; after all, the primary caregiving activities of bathing, diapering, and feeding the baby do not depend on its sex (Belsky, Gilstrap, & Rovine, 1984; N. Fox, Kimmerly, & Schafer, 1991; Huston, 1983; Lamb, 1977; Maccoby & Jacklin, 1974; Osofsky & Danzger, 1974; Pederson, 1980; P. K. Smith & Daglish, 1977). However, in several specific areas, particularly patterns of play and social interaction, parents have been found to relate differently to sons and daughters. These differences are particularly apparent when we look at how mothers and fathers interact with sons and daughters.

■ Mothers and Daughters

In comparison to sons, mothers are especially likely to enfold their baby girls into a warm, emotionally responsive social embrace. Mothers look more at their daughters than sons, and they hold their daughters closer, touch them more frequently, and cuddle them more often than their sons (Belsky, 1980; Goldberg & Lewis, 1969; Robin, 1982; Rosenthal, 1983). Mothers are also more emotionally expressive with their daughters than sons; they smile more at girls, talk to them more, show them a wider range of emotional expressions, and are more likely to respond to the little girl when she babbles or smiles at them (Cherry & Lewis, 1976; Clarke-Stewart, 1973, 1980; Frisch, 1977; Goldberg & Lewis, 1969; P. Klein, 1984; Malatesta, Culver, Tesman, & Shepard, 1989; Moss, 1967; Thoman, Leiderman, & Olson, 1972). Mothers are highly sensitive to a daughter's expressions of pain or discomfort, often mirroring the baby's expression themselves for a moment, while they tend to ignore such expressions in a son. If the girl has a difficult disposition, mothers will increase their level of affection, holding and comfort, but they back off with a boy who is similarly fussy and resistant (J. J. Haviland & Malatesta, 1981; Maccoby, Snow, & Jacklin, 1984). Some of these patterns have also been observed when mothers interact with an unfamiliar baby whom they believe to be a girl; this suggests that the mothers' behavior is due at least in part to stereotyped expectations about girls as more delicate, sociable, and emotional.

There are some important exceptions to these patterns in mothers' behavior with their infants: First, some studies have found that mothers talk to and hold sons more in the first few weeks of life, possibly because an infant who is very fussy after birth may be more likely to be a boy. By about 2 to 3 months, this pattern reverses, and we see daughters receive more cuddling and verbal contact with mothers. Second, mothers' warmth and expressiveness may be limited primarily to a firstborn daughter; one study found that mothers spent significantly less time interacting with a second daughter although they gave equal attention to the first and second sons in the family (Jacobs & Moss, 1976). Third, there have been studies showing the reverse pattern (Landerholm & Scriven, 1981; Parke & Sawin, 1980). For example, in Greece, where parents have a strong preference for boys, mothers were found to talk more with sons (Berko-Gleason, 1989). African-American mothers have also been observed to show as much or more affection to newborn boys than they do to girls, which is consistent with the finding that African-Americans are generally less gender-stereotyped than whites (Bakeman & Brown, 1977; Brown et al., 1975; S. Walker, 1982).

In contrast to the warm, expressive pattern of interaction with daughters, mothers seem to allow boys more independence, particularly when a male infant becomes a bit fussy or seems to resist her overtures by looking away or crying (J. J. Haviland & Malatesta, 1981; Malatesta et. al., 1989; Tronick & Cohn, 1989). There is some evidence that early in development more boys than girls may find social interaction a bit stressful. For example, in the first few days of life boys engage in less eye contact on average than girls and look away sooner (J. J. Haviland & Malatesta, 1981; Hittleman & Dickes, 1979; Rosenthal, 1983). Eye contact is arousing; if someone stares into your eyes for more than a few seconds, you will probably start to feel uneasy and look away; thus, the sex difference in eye contact suggests that more boys find social interaction to be somewhat overstimulating very early in development. Field (1979) also found that premature boys seemed more stressed by social interaction than girls. She measured babies' reactions to their own mother either silently nodding or talking with the baby. Premature boys were significantly more likely than girls to look away from the mother when she was talking, although there were no sex differences among full-term infants.

We can make sense of these patterns as follows: When groups of very young male and female babies are compared, there will be a range of maturity and temperamental style in both groups, but more boys may find social contact more difficult to handle when they are only a few weeks or months old. If the mother has a very stimulating social style, always swooping in to pick the baby up, showing exaggerated and rapidly changing facial expressions, and speaking constantly, the baby may be easily overwhelmed and try to signal this by looking away, fussing, or even crying. Although this may be somewhat more likely to occur with a boy than a girl, mothers then interpret these signals differently according to the baby's gender: If it is a boy, they back off, letting him have a few moments to collect himself. With a girl, they step up their efforts, perhaps shifting their expression to match the baby's frown, following the baby's averted gaze, and crooning, "What's the matter, sweetie?" In effect, they let the son direct the pattern of interaction, giving him more control in the social interchange. With girls, mothers work to create and sustain an ongoing, mutual exchange. Thus, even in the first few months of life we see girls subtly being encouraged to be sociable and responsive to others, while boys are allowed to be independent.

Social Responsiveness

The effects of these subtle tutorials are apparent by the end of the first year of life. Daughters smile more in response to their mother's smile, and if the mother momentarily turns away, a daughter is more likely to approach and touch her as if seeking to regain her attention (Clarke-Stewart, 1973; R. Klein & Durfee, 1978; Parke & Sawin, 1980; Wasserman & Lewis, 1985; Yang & Moss, 1978). In one study mothers were observed playing with their 6- to 12-month-old infants during a 5-minute "warm-up" period before the start of another experiment. Daughters were more responsive to their mother's overtures and more likely to make social bids of their own, such as looking at the mother and smiling, vocalizing, holding out a toy, and reaching out to touch her (Gunnar & Donahue, 1980). Girls are also more willing to interact with an intrusive stranger than boys, who tend to pull away and resist her overtures (Fagot & Kavanagh, 1990).

Responses to Stress

All this sounds as though little girls are trained to be dependent, but this is not quite the right interpretation, because the kind of supportive, responsive relationship fostered with girls helps develop their sense of self and their independence. In fact, having a responsive, warm caregiver enhances babies' confidence, their belief that the world is a predictable, secure place, and the expectation that when they need help and support from the caregiver they will get it. As a result, some studies have found that girls handle potentially stressful situations a bit better than boys of the same age. For example, when babies are separated from their mother by a clear plastic barrier, boys show more distress and will make greater efforts to try to reach her than girls (M. Bell, 1991; Corter, 1973; Corter & Bow, 1976; Corter, Rheingold, & Eckerman, 1972; Goldberg & Lewis, 1969; Jacklin, Maccoby, & Dick, 1973). Another example is babies' reactions to a potentially frightening toy: a large toy monkey with cymbals that clap loudly and eyes that flash on and off. Girls who were shown how to turn the toy on and off themselves—by pressing a control panel on in their high chair tray—lost their fear and began laughing and smiling as they turned the toy on and off, while more boys continued to be a bit frightened of it (Gunnar, 1980; Gunnar, Leighton, & Peleaux, 1984; Gunnar-VonGnechten, 1978). Thus, although parents encourage independence more in boys than girls during the first year, the end result is not necessarily that more boys are ready to go out and conquer the world by their first birthday. In fact, a large longitudinal study of infants' development found that girls were more resilient when the home environment was less than optimal, with unpredictable routines, few toys, and not much play and interaction (Bee, Mitchell, Barnard, Eyres, & Hammond, 1984). Out of a stereotyped belief that he is study and resilient and that boys need to learn to cope with challenges and stand on their own two feet, a parent might leave a little boy alone a bit too much, overlook his need for support in new situations, or miss his signals that he needs cuddling and attention more than the parent would for a girl.

■ Fathers and Sons

Like mothers, fathers generally behave quite similarly to sons and daughters and respond to their infant's individual needs and behavior (Lamb, 1977; Palkovitz, 1984; Snow, Jacklin, & Maccoby, 1983). However, they do show a special pattern of interaction with sons in two ways: First, as we saw at the start of the chapter, fathers have been found to spend significantly more time with sons than daughters, by talking to and playing with them more (Clarke-Stewart, 1980; Parke, 1981; Power, 1981; Rebelsky & Hanks, 1971; Weinraub & Frankel, 1977). Second, fathers cultivate a rough-and-tumble style of play with sons, which is physically stimulating, active, and unpredictable. My favorite example is a mild-mannered physicist whom I saw tossing his laughing, shrieking-with-delight son about 5 feet over his head one day while shouting, "Devil baby from hell!" Babies will often hunch their shoulders, lift their eyebrows, grin, and babble when their father comes home; they anticipate an exciting bout of play, and boys will sometimes desert their mother in favor of playing with their father (Clarke-Stewart, 1980). It is possible that male babies simply enjoy this sort of play more than females, which would in turn encourage fathers to treat them differently. However, when fathers are the primary caregivers, they tend to include daughters in rough play as well as sons, which suggests that gender stereotypes about sturdy boys and delicate girls, rather than the baby's reactions, usually lead fathers to roughhouse with their sons (Field, 1978; Lamb, Frodi, Hwang, Frodi, & Steinberg, 1982; Pruett, 1987). Also, fathers' propensity for rough play varies considerably by culture. Fathers observed in Germany, India, Malaysia, and Fiji, the !Kung Bushmen in Botswana, and the Aka Pygmies were found to spend quite a bit of time playing with their babies, but there was less bouncing, tossing, and roughhousing than U.S. fathers display (Parke, Grossmann, & Tinsley, 1981; Roopnarine, Talukder, Jain, Joshi, & Srivastav, 1990; West & Konner, 1981).

SUMMARY

Right from the start, a baby's sex is its most salient characteristic. Often, the first piece of information parents receive about their baby is whether it is a boy or girl, and this information immediately begins to alter how they and others perceive and interact with it.

SUMMARY

In this chapter we have seen examples of several of our developmental themes: First, the asymmetry of gender roles is apparent in the findings that boys are often preferred by parents and that boys are pushed to be more independent than girls even in the first few months of life. Second, our tendency to create and exaggerate differences between the sexes is apparent in how we create distinct environments for boys and girls and perceive them in terms of being small and delicate versus rough and sturdy, even though male and female babies are so similar that average adults cannot tell them apart. Third, the interaction of biology and socialization is apparent in the social development of infants during the first year. Although male babies may be a bit fussy early in life, parents are more willing to back off with boys and let them have their own way, while they step up their social overtures to girls who behave the same way. Thus, any initial behavioral differences that exist between the sexes become exaggerated through socialization.

Given the different preferences for, perceptions of, and interactions with boys and girls during infancy, we should not be particularly surprised to find that they act differently by their first birthday. Yet there is considerably more to come; differential treatment and parents' concern with appropriate gender role behavior become much more apparent as children move out of infancy into the toddler and preschool stages (Culp et al., 1983; Fagot, 1978; Pederson, 1980). Thus, gender role socialization intensifies as children's capabilities expand. Most parents would not be terribly concerned if their 16-month-old son pulled on a pink-sequined tutu, danced around the living room, and fluttered his hands, but they probably would be by the time he was 6 or 7 years old. In the next three chapters we will look at three theories of how parents and other family members shape the child's development as a boy or girl, beginning with the psychoanalytic approach of Freud. Although this theory was proposed a century ago, it provided an important foundation for much of modern psychology, particularly with its emphasis on parents as role models and its recognition of how children try to interpret the world around them as part of the process of becoming a boy or girl.

4

THEORIES OF GENDER ROLE DEVELOPMENT: THE PSYCHOANALYTIC PERSPECTIVE

I know that as a child I wanted for a long time to be a boy, that I envied Brandt because he could stand near a tree and pee, that in charades I played a prince, that I loved to wear pants and was happy in my gym suit, also that at the age of 12 I cut my hair off to my neckline, thus being the curly-haired prince again. (Quinn, 1987, p. 170).

Karen Horney, a psychoanalyst working early in this century, wrote this in her diary as she recalled how being a boy can seem more attractive to children than being a girl and how, from a child's perspective, becoming a boy or girl is simply a matter of wearing the right things, cutting one's hair, and copying others of the desired sex. Horney was a student and colleague of Sigmund Freud, the man whose theory of gender role learning is introduced in this chapter. Most people would share Horney's commonsense view that children become male or female by imitating those of the same sex; for example, boys help their father wash the car, fix flat bike tires, and play football, while girls learn to use makeup, frost cakes, and plan holiday parties by watching their mothers. Yet this straightforward view does not answer some important questions: How do children know whom they should imitate in the first place? What motivates them to adopt certain people as role models? And why do girls like Karen Horney so often want to be like boys, while boys rarely want to be girls?

The psychoanalytic theory of Sigmund Freud and his colleagues represents an effort to answer these questions over a century ago. The oldest son in a large family, Freud was born in 1856 in a small town not far from Vienna. Freud's parents favored him and expected great things of him. Even when young, Freud was a high achiever. For fun, he and a friend taught themselves Spanish so that they could read *Don Quixote* in the original language. During high school he became interested in science, with his first science project being an attempt to locate the testes of an eel (P. H. Miller, 1989). He went on to medical school and hoped to become a medical researcher, but he did not have the private income that at the time was necessary for such a career, and he faced considerable discrimination in the scientific community because he was Jewish. Instead, he set up a private practice as a physician specializing in the disorders of the nervous system and working with patients who had emotional and physical problems that often seemed interrelated (Krull, 1986; P. H. Miller, 1989). Freud's personal life was conventional, reflecting the morals of the Victorian period in Europe: When he finished medical school, he married Martha Bernays, with whom he had six children.

Freud devoted his practice and his career to understanding the inner workings of the human personality, its problems, and its development in infancy and childhood. In this chapter, we first look at Freud's view of the personality as a system of powerful forces that are both conscious and unconscious and how we learn during development to regulate these forces and turn them to productive use. Next, we examine Freud's ideas about child development, in particular, how children go from being helpless infants to being mature, self-managed adults and how, as part of this process, they come to identify with the parent of the same sex and adopt the male or female gender role. Then we consider the positive contributions of Freud's work as well as a critique of his ideas.

FRAMEWORK OF THE THEORY

Let us start with an overview of Freud's view of the human personality. He viewed the personality as being what he called a "dynamic system" of psychological energy termed the *libido*. The libido originates through our basic inborn drives, such as hunger or pain, as well as through direct physical stimulation of sensitive areas of the body, such as the mouth, anal area, and genital region. At birth, the libido is represented in a psychological structure termed the *id*. The id is illustrated by the young infant who cries furiously when hungry, cold, or wet, demanding that its needs be satisfied immediately. Of course, we cannot remain as babies forever, and the major task of development, according to Freud, is to gradually learn to control and shape the energy of the libido in order to become well-functioning members of the society. Freud saw the process of taming the libido in the infant and turning it to productive use in the adult as analogous to the evolution of human society from its origins in so-called primitive societies to what he viewed as the more civilized, industrial cultures of nineteenth-century Europe (P. H. Miller, 1989; J. H. Williams, 1987).

If the major task of early development is to get the libido under control, we have a problem, because its powerful urges never simply disappear; rather, it continues to express itself urgently, making us want things that may not be appropriate, such as eating three pieces of chocolate cake for lunch, drinking too much, having affairs with inappropriate people, or taking items that do not belong to us. It operates in a part of our personality that is unconsicous, so that we can find ourselves doing things, or wanting things, without quite realizing why. Although we cannot make the libido go away, we can learn to manage it through various strategies that divert it to more productive uses, distract ourselves to other goals, discharge it through other more appropriate activities, and so on. (This is why the personality is termed a "dynamic" or "hydraulic" system, meaning that we cannot make the energy within the system go away but we can reroute it to different locations.)

You may have had the experience of becoming very angry with someone whom it was not safe to argue, for example, a boss, teacher or parent, and then going home and finding yourself cleaning the entire house, tackling a pile of work on your desk, or going to the library and tracking down a long list of references that you had been meaning to get to; your anger has been unconsciously transformed or redirected into the energy to accomplish an unpleasant task. Another strategy is to ignore, or "repress," something that would be unpleasant to think about or deal with directly. This can lead us to behave in odd ways, for example, by repeatedly "forgetting" to attend a class that we do not really enjoy or "just happening" to mention to a dorm resident whom we dislike that we saw her boyfriend sitting in the campus coffeehouse with a gorgeous redhead the day before. Freud first recognized the power of the id and the unconscious mind when he worked with patients who suffered from physical problems that did not seem to have an organic cause, such as tremors and paralyzed limbs. He found that in many cases the patients' physical problems started at a point in their lives when there had been some emotional crisis or trauma. He reasoned that when a life event was too painful to confront directly, the unconscious mind would try to transform the feelings into another more acceptable form, often into symptoms of physical illness.

As we grow up, the id remains part of our unconscious personality and continues to influence our behavior, but we find many more ways to keep it under control and put its energy to productive use. The process of development is thus rather like learning to channel a surging, churning river (the libido) that is pouring down from the mountains (the id) and threatening everything in its path; while we cannot make the water disappear, we can divert it into new structures, such as irrigation corridors, dams, sluices, canals, and waterfalls and use it for productive purposes. Similarly, to channel our libido, we need to construct several new psychological structures, the ego and the superego. However, just as it takes time and the guidance of an engineer to build structures of concrete and rock, it takes children several years to build these new psychological structures, and they accomplish these tasks with the help of their parents. As part of the process, children also learn to become male or female. Freud proposed that this aspect of development occurred in distinct stages, as we will see in the next section.

THE PSYCHOSEXUAL STAGES

Freud proposed that the libido became focused on, or, as he put it, "cathected to," different parts of the body at different developmental stages, depending on the child's age and the challenges that were confronting the child at that particular point.

■ The Oral Stage (0 to 1 Year)

As anyone who has looked closely at an infant quickly realizes, one of the infant's primary ways of interacting with the world is through its mouth. Infants mouth and suck on objects, babble and engage in vocal play, and obtain nourishment through sucking, and the libido is thus focused on the oral cavity in the first year of life. During infancy, the id's urges are generally satisfied: The infant cries and the parent comes to feed, change, or cuddle it, so there is little frustration or buildup of unpleasant feelings. However, this pleasant time soon ends as the child becomes a toddler.

■ The Anal Stage (1 to 3 Years)

As most parents discover, the toddler period is often a frustrating time. Children become more independent, and they find that not all their desires are instantly gratified: The cookie before dinner is denied, the bedtime imposed, and the toy purchase refused at the grocery store. One of the major developmental tasks for toddlers is to learn to control their elimination, and toilet training is often one of the first settings in which parents become less accommodating to the child's wishes and in which the child's libido is frustrated. As a result of the parents' efforts to train toileting skills, the child becomes much more aware of his or her anal area and of how the postponement of urination and defecation can lead to uncomfortable physical feelings. The id has no way to cope with these discomforts and frustations; all it can do is make demands for satisfaction, which is one reason why we often see 2-year-olds having tantrums at the supermarket.

The Emergence of the Ego

Recall that the libido was originally contained in the id, the basic psychological structure of the infant. As a result of the increasing frustration of the toddler period, a new psychological structure—the ego—develops and functions as an intermediary between the id and the demands of the outside world; it acts as the problem-solving part of our personality. The ego uses various strategies to deal with psychological discomfort. The ego often proposes a delay of gratification, for example, telling the child to hold on for a few minutes in order to get to the potty rather than to wet his or her pants. While the id is unable to consider anything beyond its immediate goal of sensory satisfaction, the ego can consider the consequences of various actions—for example, that it will be uncomfortable to be wet and that the parent will be angry to discover the soggy diaper—and take steps to avoid them.

   While the id is an innate structure Freud thought that parents, especially the mother, played an important role in the construction of the ego. If the parents were too indulgent, instantly satisfying the child's every wish, there would be little frustration and hence no motivation to move on to the next stage of development. That is, Freud assumed that moderate levels of stress were necessary to promote development; after all, if our child-hoods were perfectly happy in every way, we would never have a reason to grow up! On the other hand, if the parents were too demanding and strict, the child might be completely overwhelmed with anxiety, which may also impede the emergence of the ego; if we feel we can never do anything right, we may give up trying. The delicate balancing act between discipline and gratification can be seen in such ordinary interactions as feeding. Freud thought that the mother should feed the infant in response to its signals and should do so sufficiently often to make it feel secure and comfortable rather than feeding it on a rigid schedule which might lead to frustration. On the other hand, she should not go overboard in the attempt to anticipate the infant's every need, because there would be no motivation to construct the ego under conditions of perfect contentment.

■ The Genital Stage (3 to 6 Years)

The Emergence of the Superego

Although the ego helps the toddler cope with some of the frustrations confronting him or her, it is not enough. The ego's solutions to the id's demands are often pragmatic, short-term, and weak, which is why children often give in to their impulses by grabbing handfuls of cookies even when they know better. This becomes an increasing problem as children move into the preschool stage and become even more autonomous and less often under their parents' direct supervision and control. Some broader, more powerful means of self-control must be instilled in the child at this point—a sense of right and wrong, or conscience, that will guide the child even when he or she is alone and help the child resist the temptations of the id. Freud termed this third structure the *superego*. If the id is like the infant screaming for satisfaction, the superego is like the demanding parent, insisting that its high standards be maintained. The ego is still a necessary part of the personality; it negotiates between the id and superego and proposes compromises to help children cope with conflicts between what they would like to do and what they know they should do instead.

The development of the superego leads us back to the issue of gender role learning, because Freud proposed that it develops through the child's imitation of and identification with the parent and through adopting the parent's values and standards for behavior to become appropriately masculine or feminine. However, this raises several questions: First, how do children know which parent they should try to be like, the mother or the father? Second, what motivates this process? We saw above that parents are instrumental in helping the child's ego emerge through creating the appropriate blend of frustration and support, but we still need to explain what leads the superego to emerge. The answers to these questions are found in what Freud termed the *oedipal crisis*.

The Oedipal Crisis

Freud observed that as children gain more motor control in the preschool period, they often explore their own bodies and discover the pleasant sensations produced by masturbation; as a result, the libido now becomes focused on the genitals. According to Freud, when children first begin to become aware of the pleasurable sensations in their genital region, they initially associate these feelings with the mother. After all, in most cases (at least in Freud's time) the mother has been the source of other pleasurable experiences, such as being fed, changed, and cared for, so it would be natural to link these new pleasurable feelings with her as well. Because their awareness of their genitals has been heightened, children notice that boys and girls are not the same—boys have a penis while girls do not—and this knowledge provokes an emotional crisis, a crisis that is only finally resolved when children identify with the same-sex parent, meaning that the child looks to the parent as a role model, imitates him or her, and internalizes the parent's values, behaviors, and ideals as his or her own. Thus, the oedipal crisis provides the motivation for the emergence of the superego and explains gender role learning in terms of the child's identification with the same-sex parent.

Up to this point the path of development has been similar for boys and girls, but it diverges here because of the inescapable fact that boys have a penis while girls do not; thus, the challenges presented to the sexes are necessarily different. Boys and girls are both initially close to their mother, but she does not have a penis, so boys must break away from her and identify with their father. Girls must somehow come to terms with the discovery that they lack a penis and identify with their mother, even though mother does not have a penis either. In the following sections we go through the oedipal stage that Freud proposed for boys and then turn to female development.

Male development: Castration fear. The little boy's attachment to his mother becomes increasingly sexualized as he enters the genital stage. He enjoys cuddling with her, and may even stroke her breasts or rub his penis against her (S. Stein, 1983). Associating the newly discovered pleasurable feelings of his penis with his mother, he cannot help noticing that she shares a special relationship with his father, and he begins to feel jealous and to view his father as a rival for his mother's attention and affection. This developmental stage is named after the ancient Greek Oedipus, the mythic hero who grew up in an adoptive family, unwittingly killed his biological father, returned to his natal home as an adult, and married his own mother.

During the oedipal phase the boy notices—perhaps while bathing with a sister, playing with girls in the neighborhood, or by following his mother into the bathroom— that girls do not have a penis. Although the boy might have seen female genitals before, the observation now has a special impact because he has become much more aware of his own genitals as the result of his experiments with masturbation; that is, we might say the subject is already on his mind. His recognition of the anatomical difference between the sexes provokes an emotional crisis: He reasons that the little girl must have had a penis and lost it through castration. (Children were often threatened with castration as punishment for masturbation in Freud's time, so this line of reasoning would have appeared more plausible than it does today.) The boy becomes afraid that he, too, might be castrated, perhaps by his father in retribution for the boy's attachment to his mother. The boy is faced with a terrible conflict: While he wants an intimate relationship with his mother, he definitely does not want to risk losing his penis, which he views as obviously superior to the girl's genitals. He resolves this conflict by aligning himself with his father and thus avoids parental anger and the potential threat to his penis. Although he must distance himself from his mother, he consoles himself by reasoning that if he strives to become a man like his father, he can both keep his penis and eventually have a woman of his own when he grows up.

One of Freud's most famous cases, Little Hans, provides an illustration of the oedipal conflict. Hans was a 5-year-old boy whom Freud analyzed through correspondence with the boy's father, a doctor, who described Hans's fears and symptoms. Hans had developed a phobia about horses biting him and then falling down in the street; the fear became so intense he would not leave the house. He was especially afraid of horses that had black faces or wore bridles. Freud's analysis revealed a deeper meaning: The horse in the phobia symbolized Hans's father, who had a mustache (black face) and wore glasses (bridle). Hans had been masturbating and fantasizing about sexual contact with his mother, and his fear of being bitten by a horse represented his worry that his father would castrate him in retribution. Although Hans feared his father, he also loved him and worried that his father would die or leave the family, a fear that was symbolized by the horse falling down after biting him. Hans's phobia was an extreme case, but Freud felt that all boys experienced a similar if less intense conflict as part of the normal process of development.

The intensity of castration fear provides enough motivation for the boy to break his strong attachment to his mother and turn to his father as a role model. As the boy identifies with his father, he internalizes his father's adult values which form the basis of his superego and his male identity. He may develop fantasies or play themes about his father and try to be like him. One boy described proudly to his preschool teacher an elaborate fantasy of how he and his father had dug big holes in the driveway and urinated into them together, a story that the boy's father heard with astonishment (S. Stein, 1983)! If he does not have a father at home, he may invent a fantasy father or even adopt a superhero, such as Batman, as his role model. As the boy identifies with his father and pledges allegiance to the world of men, he starts to view girls and women as inferior due to their lack of a penis. In addition, he infers that the girl must be jealous of him, as he is unable to imagine how she can be satisfied with her own genitals in comparison, and he assumes that she must be angry and bitter. His dread of her anger and resentment, coupled with his view of her as an inferior creature, makes it impossible for him ever to relate to her on an equal footing. Thus Freud traced the origins of male dominance within the culture back to the reasoning of children in the preschool stage about the differences between males and females.

Female development: Penis envy. Freud found it relatively straightforward to account for the development of male identity in boys because the fear of being castrated was strong enough to motivate the boy to identify with his father. In contrast, Freud found it more difficult to explain the development of feminine identity in girls. They obviously could not be motivated to be like their mothers through castration fear because they lacked a penis to begin with—they had nothing to lose. He suggested instead that the girl's development was motivated by penis envy.

According to Freud, girls also notice the anatomical differences between the sexes and experience a psychological crisis at the realization that they do not have a penis. However, while the boy responds to this discovery with fear and horror, the girl reacts with outrage that she does not have a penis and envy of those who do. At first, she may try to deny the fact that she does not have a penis. One girl walked about with her old baby bottle stuck between her thighs, the nipple pointing outward. She might claim that she has a penis inside her tummy that will eventually come out, especially if she has been told that babies come from mothers' tummies. Eventually, reality sets in, and the girl realizes that she does not and will never have a penis. She becomes angry with her mother for not providing her with a penis. (She assumes that her mother is responsible for this state of affairs, because mother has provided everything else—food, warmth, comfort—thus far in her life.) Her anger becomes even more bitter when she notices that her mother has an intense and special relationship with someone who does have a penis, namely, father. If she has a brother, she suspects that her mother loves him more. She feels contempt for herself, her mother, and other females, especially when she realizes they do not have a penis either; one little girl pulled frantically at her mother's pubic hair in the shower while desperately looking for a penis (S. Stein, 1983). Her anger and disappointment become internalized, leading to a lifetime of self-hatred for being feminine. Freud thought that girls would eventually assume a subordinate social role, feeling resentful and envious of males but recognizing that it is the appropriate place for them given their lack of a penis.

While the boy can resolve the oedipal crisis by identifying with the same-sex parent, the road is rockier for the girl because her mother is a less attractive role model; if her mother also lacks a penis, why should the girl ever try to be like her? Freud proposed that the girl initially would go through a phase of rejecting her mother and redirecting her affections to her father in hopes of obtaining a penis from him. During this phase the girl may become flirtatious and affectionate with her father, being "Daddy's little sweetheart," insisting that her father put her to bed in the evening or kissing her father good night while pointedly ignoring her mother. Eventually, however, she gives up, identifies with her mother as a role model, and adopts the feminine role. However, the girl's identification with her mother is always somewhat ambivalent, and so she does not incorporate her mother's attributes as thoroughly as the boy takes on those of his father. Thus, Freud concluded that the girl's superego—her conscience—does not become as fully developed as the boy's and that as a result women did not have as clear and firm a grasp of values and moral guidelines as men. (We will come back to the issue of gender differences in morality in Chapter 10.)

The ambivalence of feminine development also explains why many girls try to be tomboys; they initially reject the mother as a role model and continue the quest to be masculine through dressing and acting as much like a boy as they can or, in extreme cases, by pursuing a career and rejecting marriage, motherhood, and feminine sexuality as an adult. Freud suggested that for many women the complete acceptance of the feminine identity would only really come through giving birth, when the act of pushing a physical form out of the vagina, preferably a male child, would provide the woman with the symbolic experience of having a penis of her own. Freud thought that the mother-son relationship was the most pure and perfect of all human bonds because it is unencumbered by rivalry or envy on the mother's part. The son is a part of her, a part that has a penis, and through him she can at last enjoy the experiences of masculine activity and accomplishment which she has been denied for herself. One of Freud's followers, Erikson, noticed that girls' block play seemed to express an awareness of their future role as mothers. While boys tended to make tall buildings and towers, girls made quiet interior scenes, often enclosed by low walls with elaborate gates. Erikson interpreted girls' scenes as evidence of their awareness of their "inner space," the space that would be filled when they became mothers (Erikson, 1963). However, other researchers have not observed such consistent differences in children's block play (Reynolds, 1989).

Freud's account of feminine development clearly turns on the assumption that the penis and the masculine role are perceived as superior by the girl; in the theory, even the most uniquely feminine of accomplishments—giving birth—is viewed as an expression of the woman's wish to be male. However, he himself was never really satisfied with his explanation of feminine development, and several of his female colleagues and students subsequently tried to provide a more balanced explanation within the overall context of the psychosexual stages. Helene Deutsch reformulated the notion of penis envy as an instance of a more general human tendency for people to want what others have, rather than an emotion experienced only by girls, and placed greater emphasis on the role of the mother in the oedipal complex for the girl. In Deutsch's view the girl does not angrily turn away from her mother but uses her as a model to compare herself continually with while establishing her own independence. Karen Horney, the colleague whose diary entry was quoted at the start of the chapter, acknowledged that girls often envied boys but proposed that boys are deeply envious of the feminine breasts and women's capacities to give birth and to nurse.

She suggested that boys denigrated girls in an attempt to deny female superiority in such matters rather than for their lack of a penis. Similarly, Clara Thompson also challenged the central concept of penis envy. She agreed with Freud that girls might well envy boys but pointed out that girls did not necessarily want to have an actual penis. Rather, they could simply envy the social advantages and freedoms that come with being male (J. H. Williams, 1987).

To summarize: Freud proposed that children learn to become male or female by identifying with the parent of the same sex, meaning that the child adopts the mother or father as a role model, imitates the parent, internalizes his or her values, and tries to be like him or her in all ways. As a result of this identification, children acquire a superego to help guide their behavior as well as a masculine or feminine identity. The motivation for identifying with the same-sex parent comes from children's need to resolve the oedipal crisis, which is triggered by the discovery that boys have a penis while girls do not. The boy fears being castrated by his father, gives up his attachment to his mother, and adopts his father as a role model, while the girl becomes filled with envy, tries first to obtain a penis by becoming daddy's little girl, and then eventually accepts her mother as a role model. Freud thus embedded the process of gender role learning within a more general description of how the child grows up to become eventually autonomous from the parent by relying on the ego and superego to cope with the frustrations of everyday life and the demands of the libido.

Now that we have outlined the theory and seen how gender role learning fits within the broader context of the psychosexual stages, let us turn to an evaluation of the theory. This is particularly important given that Freud proposed these ideas so long ago; we now have much more information about children's development and can assess whether the concepts of penis envy, castration fear, and identification are valid. We can also step back and look at some of the contributions of the theory, including clinical insights into difficulties experienced by males and females. In the next section we look at the strengths and weaknesses of Freud's account of gender role learning.

CONTRIBUTIONS OF THE THEORY

◼ A Foundation for the Future

Freud's work, although in many ways superseded by contemporary theories, has provided a valuable foundation for some of the concepts that we will see in subsequent chapters. For example, one of his major contributions was the notion of developmental stages. In suggesting that children had common experiences and concerns at different ages and that their development might have an orderly and predictable sequence, Freud paved the way for Piaget and other researchers in developmental psychology early in this century and beyond. Although others had made a similar point, Freud's theory also gave credence to the idea that early experiences could have long-lasting influences on personality development, in particular, the idea that poor parent-child relationships could lead to anxiety, insecurity, or rebelliousness in the child (P. H. Miller, 1989).

More specifically, Freud's theory emphasized the role of learning in the development of gender. He did not assume that children were born with a male or female identity; rather, he suggested that these roles were learned through the process of identification with the parent, and in fact, his work foreshadowed several major elements of contemporary theories of gender role learning. These include his emphasis on the importance of role models and learning by imitation, which we will see in Chapter 5, covering social learning theory. He also introduced the idea that learning depends on the child's state. For example, in his discussion of how the discovery of the anatomical differences prompts the oedipal crisis, he acknowledged that most children probably would already have seen nude children of the other sex, for example, their own siblings, but he suggested that this information would have little impact until they became more aware of their own genital sensations. The idea of the child's changing receptiveness and resistance to learning at different times in development will reappear in Chapter 6 when we examine cognitive developmental theory. Thus, his work provided an important foundation for our general understanding of children's development and, specifically, their acquisition of gender roles.

■ Clinical Insights

Freud's work also suggested insights into the different sorts of emotional problems that males and females might be prone to experience as a function of their different developmental experiences early in life. Although evidence from clinical cases—that is, people who are undergoing treatment for emotional and psychological problems—cannot really be used to evaluate a theory of typical development, several clinical issues of interest to contemporary researchers can be traced back to Freud's analysis of the differing relations between boys and girls and their mothers. Several of these issues are reviewed next.

Mothers and Sons

In the theory of the psychosexual stages Freud emphasized that the boy needs to separate from his mother in order to identify with the father and to experience healthy personality development. He predicted that if the emotional bond with the mother was extremely close or if the father was not present to suggest the threat of castration, the little boy might find it hard to establish his independence, and contemporary researchers have found some evidence consistent with these predictions. For example, some emotionally troubled mothers relate to their sons more as a "male" than as a "child" by rubbing the little boy's tummy in a sensual manner while whispering in his ear, laughing and flirting with a child (e.g., "Don't you be so sexy!"), and passionately kissing the child on the mouth (Sroufe & Ward, 1980). This type of behavior is directed almost exclusively to sons, while the mothers are often cold and hostile toward their daughters. It is considered inappropriate not so much because of its sexual overtones but because the boy is being used to meet the mother's emotional needs at the expense of his own, which interferes with the development of his own personality. When researchers observed the sons of these mothers, the boys were found to have more trouble with self-control than other boys and were less able to pay sustained attention to a difficult task (Jacobvitz & Sroufe, 1987; Sroufe, Jacobvitz, Mangelsdorf, DeAngelo, & Ward, 1985). This would be consistent with Freud's prediction that a boy whose mother keeps him emotionally entangled with her will have trouble establishing a clear sense of self and the ability to set his own goals and guide his own behavior.

Similar patterns have been observed in other cultures in which close bonds between mothers and children are more common than in western countries. In many nonindustrialized cultures women breast-feed their children for several years, sleep with them at night, and keep them nearby while working, and there are often postpartum taboos on sexual intercourse between the father and mother for the child's first 2 years of life to reduce the physical demands of closely spaced pregnancy on the mother. In such cultures sons may have very little contact with adult men until middle childhood or adolescence. For example, in certain areas of India Hindu mothers have especially close, indulgent relationships with their little boys, feeding them by hand and responding quickly to their slightest needs, and the boys live within the women's courtyard of the household and see their fathers relatively rarely (Kakar, 1978). Freud's theory would predict that in such cases sons will face a greater struggle to identify with the father and to become autonomous. Whiting and Edwards (1988) in a review of family patterns in several cultures noted that very close mother-son relations in infancy and preschool were associated with high levels of mother-son conflict during middle childhood, as the son struggled to establish his independence. They suggest that these struggles extend into adulthood and contribute to more tense relations between husbands and wives, with more efforts at male dominance. In some cultures "rites of passage" for boys at puberty help the son break free of his emotional attachment to his mother and join the society of adult men. Such rituals are more severe and dramatic in cultures where sons spend their childhood exclusively with women; this suggests that boys need a stronger impetus and more support from older males to break away from their mothers (Raphael, 1988).

Effects on Male Sexuality. In extreme cases overly intimate mother-son relationships can lead to male sexual adjustment problems in adulthood. If the boy's sexuality has been aroused by a woman who is an inappropriate target for such feelings, namely, his mother, and if no father is present to suggest the threat of castration (thus making him "give up" his mother), the boy's later sexual feelings can be associated with guilt and anxiety. Sudhir Kakar, a psychoanalytic researcher in India, described one patient whose mother, a widow, had still allowed her son to breast-feed when he was 8 years old. As she sat in the family courtyard sipping tea and talking with her friends, he would lift her blouse and suckle her breasts, over the protests of her friends, and she continued to give him his bath, dress him, and have him sleep in her bed into his adolescence. As an adult, he felt overwhelming guilt when he had sex with his wife, due to the inappropriate association of sexuality with his mother (Kakar, 1991). Young women sometimes fall into the habit of acting in a motherly manner toward their boyfriends, reminding them of homework assignments, packing their lunch, choosing their clothes, and so on. This can eventually undermine the relationship because although being taken care of has its own appeal, it tends not to be associated with sexual attraction.

Mothers and Daughters

Freud also foresaw potential problems with issues of separation for daughters. In the first place, because the mother is the appropriate role model for the girl, the girl has less incentive to develop her autonomy. Second, the mother is often less forceful about pushing the daughter to develop her independence because she views the baby girl as an extension of herself due to their physical similarity. This close bond offers support but can also make it difficult for the daughter to establish her own personality, making her too vulnerable to the opinions of others and unsure of who she really is and what she wants for herself (Chodorow, 1978). One college woman said of her relationship with her mother, "I would experience something and then I'd relate it all to her and she would synthesize and digest it for me, and then I'd get the final word on what really happened." Another said, "I would fall into relationships and just kind of subsume myself in what that person expected. I never developed a sense of who I was and what I needed" (Belenky, Clinchy, Goldberger, & Tarule, 1986, pp. 125–126; Gilligan, 1982). This is less likely to occur with a boy because the son is physically different from the mother, and she finds it relatively easy to view him as a separate individual and to give him an earlier push towards autonomy. On the other hand, while the mother's behavior increases his sense of independence, his autonomy comes at the cost of decreased intimacy. As an adult, he has learned that he does not need to be close to his mother or other females, and he may even be angry with his mother and later with other women for pushing him away.

Some evidence consistent with these predictions from Freud's theory has been found in projective studies of men's and women's perspectives on relationships. In these experiments people are shown a picture—for example, a couple sitting on a bench by a river or a husband-and-wife trapeze team—and are asked to tell a story about the picture. The idea is that the issues of personal concern to the storyteller will be unconsciously projected into his or her story. Men more often mentioned themes of danger and problems in the relationship; for example, that the couple on the bench was watching her former fiancé drown in the river and gloating over the life insurance she would collect from his death or that the acrobat husband, tired of his wife, would intentionally drop her from the trapeze or fling her into the wall. Women were more likely to talk about themes of trust, support, and safety in relationships, for example, by mentioning that there was a net below the trapeze artists to keep them safe if one should fall (Pollak & Gilligan, 1982, 1983, 1985). Of course, it is difficult to know how to interpret these patterns; men may simply be more interested in stories with dramatic events, and the types of stories they create do not necessarily express unconscious anger over their mother's rejection (Benton et al., 1983; Weiner et al., 1983). Some of these differences probably reflect the influence of culture as much as early childhood experiences. Japanese men as well as women have been found to talk much more than U.S. persons about how the self is connected to others, for example, their place in the family and how what happens to them will affect those around them (DeAngelis, 1992). Even so, Freud's emphasis on the importance of early relationships with the mother provided the foundation for understanding why males and females often have different concerns about relationships, focusing on the benefits of intimacy and trust or the dangers of separation and rejection.

Girls' feelings of inferiority. One assumption of Freud's theory is that while the girl eventually identifies with her mother, she does so with reluctance, internalizing the feelings of contempt for females, including her mother, and directing them against herself. Freud observed several patterns in the personality and behavior of adult women that he thought could be traced back to their early feelings of genital deprivation and inferiority. First, women were often narcissistic, meaning that they were absorbed with themselves, had a strong need to be loved, and needed to have that love continually affirmed in order to compensate for their early feelings of deprivation. Second, women tend to focus on their appearance and their physical attractiveness, in order to make up for the fundamental lack of a penis. A third characteristic observed by Freud was shame, reflecting the woman's efforts to hide her inferior nature from the view of others. As we will see in later chapters, girls are in fact more likely to acknowledge their feelings of inferiority, to worry more about what others think of them and about their appearance, and to feel shame and to blame themselves when they do not do well, for example, on school assignments. Although we find other explanations for these patterns, Freud did recognize that it seemed to be harder for girls to establish a positive self-concept. Some feminist scholars have argued that while much of the theory appears biased against females—for example, the notion of penis envy seems based on the unwarranted assumption that one organ is superior to another—Freud at least tried to offer an explanation for how girls come to accept their subordinate position within a society and to feel that they are inferior (Kofman, 1985; J. Mitchell, 1974).

WEAKNESSES OF THE THEORY

Although psychoanalytic theory did provide a critical foundation for subsequent theories as well as perceptive insights into the potential clinical concerns of males and females, when we view it in light of current research methods and in the context of contemporary culture, we find that it has serious limitations as an explanation for gender role development. Several of these limitations are reviewed next.

■ Status as a Theory

A major limitation of Freud's ideas is that they do not meet the criteria now considered necessary for a scientific theory. Key mechanisms and assumptions, such as penis envy, castration fear, and children's sensual feelings for the parent, can never be directly tested because they are proposed to derive from the unconscious part of the human personality. The unconscious does not have to follow logical rules, so all possible findings can be interpreted as evidence to support the theory, and if everything can be made to fit the theory, it can never be disconfirmed. Suppose you are a woman and buy a shiny, new, bright red sports car, and when you show it to your best friend, she nods sagely and says that she always knew you resented being a girl and that the car obviously is a symbolic expression of penis envy. If you disagree, she can retort that you are merely repressing your true ongoing desire to be masculine. Thus, nothing you say can be a convincing denial because it can all be interpreted to be consistent with the theory. This is a problem because if a theory seems to explain absolutely everything after the fact, it is necessarily so vague that it doesn't really explain or predict anything very well.

Example: The Case of Dora

The resistance of the theory to challenge is illustrated in one of Freud's most famous cases, that of Dora. Dora was an adolescent girl whose parents had sent her to Freud when they suspected her of suicidal tendencies and for treatment of an unexplained lingering cough and vaginal discharge. She described to Freud that her father was having an affair with his best friend's wife, Frau K., and that she herself had been propositioned several times by the husband, Herr K. On one occasion, while watching a parade at Herr K.'s home, he had caught Dora in the dark hallway and forced a kiss on her. When she told her father of his friend's sexual advances, he said he did not believe her, and she suspected that he did not want to force the issue out of fear that his own affair would be revealed. If we look at the situation by contemporary standards, Dora had been abused by a family friend and then betrayed by her father, a situation that could certainly create considerable emotional distress in a teenage girl. Yet Freud insisted that, despite her denials, the real problem involved her being sexually attracted to her father, inappropriately jealous of Frau K., and also attracted to Herr K. but not wanting to admit it. He interpreted her cough as an indication of the sexual arousal he assumed she must have felt at Herr K.'s kiss and as a symbolic expression of her knowledge that her father and his mistress, Frau K., engaged in oral sex. When Dora failed to return for her sessions out of frustration at being misunderstood, Freud interpreted this as a sign that she had begun to be attracted to him as well and was afraid of her feelings for him! Thus, nothing Dora said or did, including walking away from her treatment, could challenge Freud's interpretation of her case because he took all her objections as indirect evidence for the conclusion that she denied.

■ Evidence for the Theory

In addition to the problem that all evidence can be interpreted after the fact to support the theory, it appears now that for some of the cases there may have been little evidence to begin with. For example, in the case of Little Hans described earlier, the boy's phobia of horses was diagnosed by Freud as an example of castration fear. Yet when questioned as an adult, Hans recalled that his fear of horses actually started when he was on summer holiday and had been frightened by a horse; he was unused to animals and had been warned repeatedly by family friends that horses could bite, which could have contributed to his excessive fear (Goleman, 1990). (Of course, this could be explained in terms of the boy repressing the real reason for his fear!) Scholars who subsequently reviewed the original case notes realized that much of the "evidence" for Hans' castration fear actually came from the boy's father, a close friend of Freud's, who imposed his own interpretation on the little boy's comments (Wolpe & Rachman, 1960). Similar questions have been raised about other cases. Freud's colleagues at the time considered that he had special insights that allowed him to see what others could not and could thus legitimately select or revise his material to fit his interpretations and to present the theory in its most clear form. Despite his brilliance as a theorist, we would now consider that "to accord such a privilege to anyone is to violate the spirit of science" (Wolpe & Rachman, 1960, p. 147).

There are other difficulties with the sources of evidence Freud considered in building the theory. First, Freud derived his ideas about children's development primarily from working with adults who recalled their childhoods during the process of therapy. We now know that our memories of early childhood are often highly selective and distorted, and unfortunately Freud had no way to verify the accuracy of the recollections; for example, if a male patient described his mother as excessively warm and clinging Freud would have had no way to tell whether the description was accurate or an unconscious distortion over time. Second, the theory was based on the experiences of patients who were undergoing treatment for serious psychological and emotional disturbances rather than from a group of more-or-less healthy adults. Freud felt that the conflicts and problems reported by his patients were simply more extreme examples of those experienced by all children and that working with troubled individuals in fact allowed him greater access to the often-mysterious workings of the human personality. Contemporary researchers, on the other hand, would argue that a theory of normative development should not be derived from a clinical population whose experiences are probably not typical.

Oedipal Stage

The evidence for the oedipal stage is particularly weak, casting doubt on its critical role in the process of gender role development. The hypothesized sequence of development, particularly the critical oedipal stage, simply does not fit with our current knowledge about children's gender role development. According to Freud, children should not begin to search for role models of male or female behavior until the oedipal stage, that is, until the preschool years. Yet as we will see in the next chapter more recent research has shown that toddlers have already acquired considerable knowledge about gender roles and have begun to behave appropriately for their own gender.

Penis envy, castration fear? In addition, there is little evidence that toddlers and preschoolers are aware of the anatomical differences between the sexes or that children with this knowledge actually experience castration fear or a deep envy of male anatomy (Bem, 1989). Tavris and Wade (1984) give the example of a little girl who, after seeing her male cousin's genitals in the bath, said to her mother, "Mommy, isn't it a blessing he doesn't have it on his face?" It is difficult to test for the existence of castration fear directly; if you were a parent, would you let your little boy be questioned about how he would feel if his penis was cut off? In any case a child's failure to report castration fear could always be interpreted as a sign that the fear had been repressed. Despite these difficulties, projective techniques have been used to try to elicit any unconscious fears that children might have about castration; in one instance children were told a story about a monkey who was very fond of his long beautiful tail. The story stopped with the line, "and then something different happened," and the child's task was to finish the story. Most of the children's stories involved the monkey losing his beloved tail, which was taken as an expression of castration fear. Clearly, though, children might make the tail the theme of their stories not because of their castration fear but because it had been emphasized in the first part of the story. In addition, there was no evidence that children viewed the tail as a phallic symbol; they would probably have told similar stories about the loss of any body part.

Attraction to the parent. Another key part of the theory is the notion that children would associate their early sexual feelings with the parent as part of the oedipal stage, but there is little evidence that this occurs. Freud initially derived this part of his theory from the recollections of women patients who reported that they had had as children sexual relationships with their fathers. Although at first he took these reports to be true, they occurred so frequently that he decided that his patients' memories must have been fantasies reflecting their childhood desires, because it was hard for him to accept that so many girls were victims of incest. More recent research, coupled with a growing awareness of the high incidence of the sexual abuse of children, suggests that many of the women's reports of sexual contact as children with adults were probably true (Masson, 1984). In fact, many of Freud's patients may have been seeking help precisely because they had been sexually abused as children, a traumatic experience that often leads to emotional and psychological problems later in life. The explanatory power of the oedipal crisis is considerably weakened if there is no evidence that the child desires the parent.

Identification. Finally, Freud's proposed mechanism for the acquisition of gender roles was identification, the process through which the child internalized the standards of the same-sex parent and adopted him or her as a role model for gender behavior. If the mother was an especially feminine model or if the father was extremely masculine, the child should be more strongly sex-typed as a result. Yet it turns out that there is little correspondence between the sex typing of parents and that of their children; for example, very "macho" fathers rarely have the most Rambo-like sons (Maccoby, 1980). The process of identification might explain how children acquire the general characteristics of male and female roles, but it does not seem to explain variations in masculinity or femininity at the level of the individual child.

SUMMARY

In this chapter we have outlined an early theory of gender role learning: Freud's proposal that children learn the male or female role through identification with the same-sex parent. Freud suggested that children develop through stages in which they confront developmental tasks such as toilet training and separating from the parent. In these stages the personality's psychic energy, the libido, becomes associated with areas of the body that form the core of the developmental tasks, including the oral cavity in infancy, the anal area in the toddler phase, and the genital region in the preschool period. While the path of development for boys and girls is similar in infancy and the toddler period, boys and girls experience the genital stage differently as a consequence of the fact that the sexes are anatomically different. They discover that boys have a penis, while girls do not, and their efforts to make sense of this discovery alter their relationships with the parents. Boys, feeling guilty about their sensual feelings for their mother, fear that their father might castrate them, and they abandon their mother in order to identify with their father. Through this process they internalize his ideals, values, and behaviors and acquire a masculine identity. In contrast, girls feel angry at the fact that they have apparently been deprived of a penis, turn to their father, eventually realize that the quest is hopeless, and accept their mother as a role model, often with lingering ambivalence. The theory thus provides answers to several of the questions posed at the start of the chapter: The motivation to learn gender roles comes from children's discovery of the anatomical differences between the sexes—boys by fear of losing what they have, girls by envy and anger over what they lack—and this process begins early in life through their association with the developmental tasks of toilet training, separation from parents, self-exploration, and masturbation that typically arise during the toddler and preschool stages. In addition, the asymmetry of gender roles, that is, why many girls would like to be boys, can in Freud's view be traced to the assumption that children of both sexes would view the penis as the superior organ.

Although Freud's ideas were innovations at the time and paved the way for important advances in the field of psychology, we have also seen that as a theory of gender role development it has several serious limitations. It does not meet the criteria for a scientific theory, in that it cannot be challenged by inconsistent evidence, and evidence for several of its critical assumptions is lacking; there is little indication that children are really aware of the genital differences or that this awareness prompts fear or envy of the sort that Freud suggested. Thus, researchers have continued to search for explanations for children's acquisition of gender roles. In the next two chapters we look at two major contemporary theoretical approaches: In Chapter 5 we look at how the family environment shapes children's behavior, and in Chapter 6 we consider the importance of the child's own ideas about being a boy or girl.

5

THEORIES OF GENDER ROLE DEVELOPMENT: SOCIAL LEARNING

I always go through the drawer and get an outfit, even knickers and that, I like them to match. She has to wear it even if she doesn't like it.

I like him to look like a little boy, with dungarees and little shirt with checks. I ask him what he wants. He gets quite upset so I'd let him wear it. (McGuire, 1991, p. 158)

These quotes from mothers of 2-year-olds illustrate how a simple daily event, helping the child get dressed in the morning, is often handled differently for boys and girls. When disagreements occur, the first mother overrides her daughter's choice, while the second mother is more likely to give in when her son expresses a preference. Stereotypes about gender roles often lead parents to react differently to the same behavior in a boy and a girl, for example, in this case the belief that girls should look nice, and that boys should be allowed to assert themselves. This is similar to the eye of the beholder effect that we discussed in Chapter 3; recall that people will perceive the same infant as either delicate and fearful or strong and angry depending on whether they think it is a boy or girl.

The idea that a child's behavior will elicit different reactions according to gender is one of the key components of social learning theory. As we saw in Chapter 4, psychoanalytic theory proposed that children learn gender roles by imitating the same-sex parent, in order to resolve the oedipal crisis. Social learning theory also suggests that children learn gender roles through imitation of role models but proposes a different motivation; namely, children's behavior is shaped by the reactions of others. In general, children will receive social rewards for doing gender-typical things, which encourages them to repeat those behaviors.

In this chapter we begin by reviewing the components of social learning theory, including reinforcement and role models. Then we review evidence showing that boys and girls are treated differently in several important behavior areas. We next consider the influence of role models in the family, including siblings, mothers and fathers, and how their presence or absence influences children's development. Finally, the strengths and weaknesses of the social learning approach are considered.

COMPONENTS OF SOCIAL LEARNING THEORY

■ Reinforcement

According to social learning theory, children's behavior is shaped by its consequences. Therefore, if boys and girls receive different reactions to the same behavior, they will begin to act differently over time. It is easy to see that a girl who puts on a pink dress and receives a smile and compliment from her father might want to wear the dress again. But children's behavior can also be shaped by reactions that are negative or neutral in tone as well as by warm, approving comments. The boy whose father says angrily, "What have you got on, nail polish?" will probably not play with his mother's cosmetics again, especially if he has found that other actions bring more positive responses. Of course, to a young child, any attention is better than none at all, so behaviors that are ignored or overlooked are especially likely to fade away over time. As we will see, reactions to a behavior are not only different for the sexes; they tend to come more quickly and clearly to boys than to girls, particularly when it comes to avoiding other-gender behavior. Remarks about feminine behavior in boys tend to be especially sharp and immediate: "Mom, look, Jeff's wearing your slip. Jeff's a fag! Jeff's a fag!" The resulting learning can occur very quickly; a boy does not have to try something several times and in several different settings to figure out that people do not want him to do it.

According to social learning theory, children do not have to experience reinforcements directly to learn; they can also learn by observation, watching what is going on around them and how different people act. When the day-care teacher says, "You look so pretty today," to a little girl who has just arrived wearing a new dress, every other child at the center has filed away a bit of information about who does and does not wear dresses. Children also can anticipate future reactions to behaviors; as Mischel (1966) put it, a man does not have to actually wear a dress in public to know how others will react. One reason we sometimes are surprised at how much children know about gender roles is that we underestimate their ability to learn by observation and inference.

■ Role Models

Children do more than observe others; they also try to copy others of the same sex. Imitation of role models is a powerful way to learn, and children do try to copy those whom they admire and would like to resemble. An advertising campaign encouraged boys to drink Michael Jordan's favorite juice drink and, "Be like Mike," suggesting that they might acquire his basketball prowess by copying his beverage choices. The *absence* of role models of a particular gender is also significant: One woman remembered that when she was in high school, her father had encouraged her to be an engineer, but that she never took him seriously because she did not see any girls in the advanced math classes, there were no women math teachers at her school, and she did not know any women in the profession.

■ Representativeness

Even if the girl described above had met a woman engineer, she might have felt that the woman was too unusual to be a desirable role model, not someone she would like to emulate. Children need some reassurance that a particular role model is appropriate, and early studies of imitation did not show clearly that boys and girls would copy a model of the same sex (Barkley, Ullman, Otto, & Brecht, 1977; Maccoby & Jacklin, 1974). More recent studies have shown that children will copy a new behavior if they see several people of the same sex demonstrate it (Bussey & Bandura, 1984; Bussey & Perry, 1982; Perry & Bussey, 1979). In one study children saw three men and three women perform a novel action sequence that was slightly different for the sexes: Each man chose a green "thinking cap" from a pile of hats on a table, walked across the room toward the boxes while saying, "Left, right, left, right," found the sticker and said, "A stickeroo," and slapped it on the wall with his hand and said, "Weto-smacko." Each woman chose a blue cap, marched across the room saying, "March, march, march," found the sticker and said "Bingo," and said, "Lickit, stickit," as she pasted the sticker on the wall. It is safe to assume that the children had probably never seen anything quite like this before! When children were invited to choose a thinking cap and to search for the sticker in the boxes, boys imitated more male behaviors and girls imitated more female behaviors, confirming that children would imitate as long as they had some evidence that what the models were doing was typical for their gender.

To review, social learning theory includes two components, first, the idea that differential treatment shapes children's behavior and, second, that children learn new behaviors by observing and imitating role models of the same sex. In the next sections we consider these components in turn, beginning with evidence that boys and girls are treated differently in several specific areas and that, as a result, they learn to behave differently. Then, we turn to consider the influence of role models within the family, including mothers, fathers, and siblings.

BOYS AND GIRLS: DIFFERENTIAL REINFORCEMENTS

As we mentioned in Chapter 1, several reviews of parents' behavior have concluded that for the most part boys and girls are treated quite similarly (Lytton & Romney, 1991; Maccoby & Jacklin, 1974). Parents are typically equally affectionate to both sons and daughters, want them both to be well behaved, to do well in school, and so on. It now seems that differential treatment of the sexes is targeted to specific times in development, most notably during the toddler period and early adolescence, and is most visible in specific areas of behavior, such as play, independence, and achievement orientation (J. H. Block, 1983; Fagot & Hagan, 1991; Huston, 1983). Parents' treatment of sons and daughters in these areas is reviewed next.

■ Play

By the time boys and girls are about a year old, they like to play with different toys; girls will often choose a doll or stuffed animal, while boys will go for the blocks and trucks (Jacklin, Maccoby, & Dick, 1973). Although it is striking that differences appear at such a young age, it becomes more understandable when we remember that they have been given different toys during their first year of life. Toy preferences also appear to be shaped by parents' reactions to children's play with different types of toys. When toddlers from working- and middle-class families were observed in their homes, the researchers found that 1-year-old boys and girls did not seem to have much preference themselves; their play often included dolls, puppets, and soft toys (feminine activities) as well as trucks, cars, and blocks (masculine activities). However, parents began to react more favorably to gender-typical play during the second year, affecting the children's choices. Aspects of the differential treatment were even starting to appear for boys when they were only 12 months old; thus, 1-year-old boys received more positive reactions than girls for playing with transportation and building toys, an example of asymmetric socialization. Parents tolerated some cross-gender play, but their positive reactions to such play declined steadily from about 18 months on and declined faster for boys than girls (Eisenberg, Wolchik, Hernandez, & Pasternack, 1985; Fagot, 1978; Fagot & Hagan, 1991; Fagot & Leinbach, 1989).

Most of the shaping of children's toy preferences occurs during the toddler period, a time in development when the child's capabilities are expanding dramatically. Toddlers are learning to talk, are forming a concept of self, and are becoming much more independent than they were as babies. Fagot and her colleagues, who have studied parents' behavior toward toddlers in the home, suggest that parents are most likely to provide differential reinforcements to boys and girls when children are first acquiring new behaviors. In other words, if your child is just starting out on a new journey, you want to step in quickly and provide a clear message about the direction that he or she should take, and at this early stage in development a tiny push may be all that is required to get the child on the "right track," that is, playing with toys that are considered gender-appropriate (Fagot & Hagan, 1991).

By the time children are about 4 to 5 years old, their play is usually so gender-typed that parents have little need to monitor it. Yet parents' ongoing concern can be elicited if the child seems to deviate from the expected type of behavior. Langlois and Downs (1980) deliberately manipulated preschool children's play in order to observe the parents' reactions. While the parents were being interviewed in another room, the child was placed in a playroom containing stereotypical girls' toys, such as a toy stove with pots and pans, and boys' toys, such as a toy gas station with trucks and cars. The child was directed to play with either gender-typical toys or gender-atypical toys. For example, a boy would be given the kitchen set and told, "Please play with these the way that girls do for a little while." The parent's reaction was monitored when he or she came into the room and saw the child. In general girls received a more consistent, tolerant message than boys: Both mothers and fathers reacted positively when they saw girls playing with the kitchen set and showed only mildly negative responses for play with the gas station. In contrast, boys got inconsistent messages: Their mothers were generally positive to both feminine and masculine play, often sitting down and joining in regardless of the type of toy. On the other hand, fathers reacted positively to boys' play with masculine toys and very negatively to play with feminine toys, including frowns, sarcastic comments, and even picking the boy up and physically moving him away from the kitchen set! Other studies have also found that fathers are more likely to react negatively to cross-gender play in children, especially sons (Jacklin, DiPietro, & Maccoby, 1984; Langlois & Downs, 1980; Maccoby, 1980; Margolin & Patterson, 1975; Price-Bonham & Skeen, 1982; Siegal, 1987; Tauber, 1979).

Other research also suggests that parents are concerned about the gender appropriateness of children's toys. Parents bring home different types of toys for boys and girls, a choice made easier by the sex-typed packaging of toys and their arrangement into girls' and boys' sections in toy stores (P. K. Smith & Daglish, 1977). When playing with their child at home, parents tend to reach first for gender-typical toys even when the child actually owns masculine, feminine, and neutral toys (Eisenberg et al., 1985; Schau, Kahn, Diepold, & Cherry, 1980). They also play less enthusiastically with gender-atypical toys. In one study, parents were given a series of boxes which contained boys' and girls' toys, such as trucks, baby dolls, blocks, and a kitchen set. The parents' job was to open each box and get the child to play with the toy for several minutes, but the parents showed considerably less interest and excitement when introducing the gender-atypical toys, and the children were more likely to reject them. One father in the study opened a box containing trucks, said, "Oh, they must have boys in this study," closed the box and went back to playing dolls with his daughter (Caldera, Huston, & O'Brien, 1989). Interestingly, parents do not really react differently to the type of play shown by boys and girls, as long as the toy itself seems gender-appropriate; once a little girl is holding a Barbie doll, it does not matter very much whether she pretends Barbie is a princess or a race-car driver, and a boy can sit quietly putting tiny dolls into a toy dump truck while singing to himself without worrying his parents (Eisenberg et al., 1985).

It is clearly important to parents that their children, especially boys, play in a gender-appropriate manner. As we have seen in this section, parents react differently to boys and girls as soon as children start to engage in independent play, that is, in the second year of life. In response, children's preferences for particular toys and games shift into sex-typed patterns almost immediately. In fact, after the toddler period, parents have relatively little need to monitor children's play, since the lesson has already been learned. Recall that in the Langlois and Downs (1980) study, the children had to be deliberately instructed to play with other-gender toys in order to study the parents' reactions.

Cathy, Copyright Cathy Guisewite. Reprinted with permission of Universal Press Syndicate. All rights reserved.

■ Independence and Compliance

By the time boys and girls are 2 years old, other striking differences in their behavior appear: A little girl will often gather toys and bring them back to sit near her parent's chair, while a little boy is more likely to wander all over the room to play, poke his fingers in the electric wall outlets, and try to open forbidden cupboards (Brooks & Lewis, 1974). Parents are well aware of these differences. Kronsberg, Schmaling, and Fagot (1985) gave parents short descriptions of child behavior, for example, a child who is approaching a cabinet that contains cleaning supplies, and asked them to describe what they would do. Parents of boys reported that they would intervene faster to prevent potential trouble than parents of a girl, as if raising a boy had taught them to expect the worst. At a lunch we attended recently with several mothers of young children, one announced firmly, "I don't care what the experts say—boys are much harder to raise!" The others agreed and one even offered (jokingly, we assume) to trade hers in for a girl. No one took her up on the deal! Can several million parents be wrong? No, boys are less obedient and more independent— but researchers have found that this is not merely because "boys will be boys"; rather, parents provide a program of "independence training" to sons beginning in the toddler period.

Toddlers

Toward the end of the first year, when children are beginning to crawl and walk, parents begin to encourage boys to move out into the world. When a child first toddles a few steps and falls down, the mother's reaction differs according to gender: The mother of one boy gave him a quick hug and then tossed a toy across the room and encouraged him to fetch it, while the mother of a girl also hugged her daughter but then handed her a toy while continuing to cuddle her, keeping her close (Brooks-Gunn & Matthews, 1979). Parents respond positively when their 2-year-old daughters follow them around the house but negatively when boys do the same thing, and they leave sons alone to play more often than daughters (Fagot, 1974, 1978). Daughters are *expected* to be closer to their parents: In one study women read descriptions of a 3-year-old child, labeled either "Mary" or "Bobby," and rated the child's emotional attachment to the mother. "Mary" was more often expected to follow her mother around the house, to recognize when her mother was upset, to understand what her mother wanted, and to stop misbehaving when the mother said "no" without having to be told twice. "Bobby" could be more independent while still being considered appropriately bonded to his mother; in fact, parents worry more about a boy who is too compliant than a girl (Goff, 1991; Kuczynski & Kochanska, 1990). Some of these patterns have also been observed in primates; rhesus monkey mothers tend to reject their sons earlier than their daughters and force the males to establish their own independence (Stevenson-Hinde & Simpson, 1981).

The result of this independence training is that boys are more likely than girls to get into trouble and to test parents' limits. Parents have to chastise sons more often for naughty behavior such as playing with electric wall sockets and other forbidden objects (Bellinger & Berko-Gleason, 1982; Cherry & Lewis, 1976; Minton, Kagan, & Levine, 1971). Sons are also less likely to obey when they are told to stop doing something, while daughters are more likely to back off when they hear, "No, leave that alone," or "Don't touch that!" (Minton et al., 1971; Snow, Jacklin, & Maccoby, 1983). One reason boys keep misbehaving may be that it retains the adult's attention. Recall that boys are generally left to play independently; one sure way to bring a parent running from the next room is to begin to play with the controls on the stereo, to open cupboard doors and rummage around inside, or, in the example of the humor columnist Dave Barry, to insert peanut butter into the video recorder and press the fast-forward button. Another reason that boys test limits is that mothers are more likely to yield out of the belief that boys need to learn to assert themselves. Going back to the two mothers quoted at the start of the chapter, the mother of the boy explained that she let him choose his clothes because she did not want to "break his spirit" by being too controlling. Yet by yielding when he became upset, she increased the probability that he would expect his own way in the future, whereas a girl is encouraged to rely on her mother longer.

School-Aged Children

Once children start school, they are out of the house for extended periods, away from parents' supervision, and they spend additional time with their peers. At this stage, parents grant boys much more independence than girls of the same age. The girls are likely to be picked up directly after school or at the mall; required to play at home rather than out in the neighborhood; forbidden to go on their own to parks, libraries, and other community centers; and "grounded" as punishment (L. Hoffman, 1977; Huston, 1983; Jurich, Bollman, & Moxley, 1976; Newson & Newson, 1986). One couple even allegedly chained their daughter to a pipe in their city apartment for several months to keep her from becoming involved with drugs and "the fast life out on the street" (Faison, 1991). At the other extreme, parents of sons are more likely than parents of daughters to report that at times they do not know where their child is (Newson & Newson, 1986). These gender effects are amplified across social class: Working-class girls are the most restricted, while upper-class boys are given the most independence. One 8-year-old boy even took airplane shuttles by himself from Boston, where he attended boarding school, to his home in New York each week (*Boston Globe*, 1992e).

Why do parents chaperone girls more carefully? For one thing, they believe that boys are more competent and better able to take care of themselves than girls of the same age. Parents judge that boys will be able to accomplish tasks at earlier ages than girls, such as crossing the street alone, tying their shoes, and riding the bus, even though girls are actually more mature and less impulsive on average than their male peers (Brooks-Gunn & Matthews, 1979; Callard, 1968; L. Hoffman, 1977). Parents think that daughters are in need of extra protection, being more fragile, easily frightened, and physically vulnerable, even though girls are more physically resilient throughout childhood (L. Hoffman, 1977; Kuebli & Krieger, 1991). Parents also worry about a daughter's vulnerability to sexual assault. Girls are more likely than boys to be warned not to talk to strangers or get into cars with people they don't know (Newson & Newson, 1986). While these concerns are legitimate, they also apply to boys, who are hardly immune from approaches by pedophiles. In fact, some researchers estimate that as many as one in six boys will be sexually abused; clearly, boys need these warnings too (Hunter, 1990).

As a result of their greater independence, boys have more opportunity to develop their self-confidence, particularly the belief that they can cope with failure and handle unexpected problems (J. H. Block, 1973, 1983). A boy who misses the bus home after a school soccer game can exercise his resourcefulness by examining the bus map for an alternative route, asking for a ride from a friend's parent, borrowing a bike, or even hitchhiking. Girls have fewer opportunities to build this sense of self-efficacy, particularly when it comes to physical skills. Often the result is a little girl who says, "I can't," and waits for someone to help her over the fence, pump up the flat bike tire, or turn on the computer (Brooks-Gunn & Matthews, 1979). One junior high school science teacher got so frustrated with her female students' lack of confidence that she organized a summer program to teach them to climb ropes, scale walls, and use power tools (Solomon, 1991). The greater freedom permitted to boys has its costs, in that boys are more likely to be injured and to die from accidents as the result of unsupervised play. In my quiet rural town in the last few years alone one boy lost his hands to an exploding illegal firecracker, two were buried alive in an industrial sand pit, and another drowned while exploring an abandoned copper mine. Such risks are seen as a regrettable but natural part of growing up for boys but something from which girls must be carefully protected.

■ Achievement

A recent television commercial for wall paint showed a proud father carrying his tiny infant son around an empty, freshly painted bedroom as he pointed out the locations for the boy's future trophies, his home computer, and his gym equipment. Although admiring hard work, self-reliance, persistence and initiative in both sexes, U.S. parents value these qualities more in sons than daughters and have higher hopes for their sons' career and academic accomplishments (J. H. Block, 1977; Brooks-Gunn & Matthews, 1979; L. Hoffman, 1975). Parents also often have a more narrowly defined idea of what a successful son should be. Newson and Newson (1986) found that mothers tended to discount many of their sons' "romantic" career goals, such as becoming an astronaut, in favor of more practical alternatives, suggesting that boys face a narrower set of career options acceptable to parents. One college student told me that his parents insisted that he go to a professional school although they didn't much care which one—law, medicine, and business were all fine—but becoming a teacher (his real interest) was not. In my experience, women students are more likely to say that their parents have left the choice of major and career up to them, which sometimes sounds like, "It really doesn't matter what she does as long as she's happy." Parents also react differently to failure in the sexes; when things do not go well, the girl may hear, "That's OK, honey, you tried your best and that's what counts," while the boy hears, "How could you do this to us?" Even women with demanding professional careers of their own report that they would be more disappointed by a son's lack of accomplishment than a daughter's (L. Hoffman, 1977).

The "Farmer's Daughter" Effect

Parents' expectations for their sons and daughters interact with social class and ethnicity: Poor and working-class parents have higher hopes for daughters than sons, while the opposite is true of wealthier families (Bock, 1969). This is because parents know that boys' and girls' actual chances for success vary with social class. In middle-class and wealthy families, parents expect more from their sons because a daughter faces more gender discrimination in the workplace and will realistically have a harder time becoming a chief executive officer (CEO) of a major corporation or the owner of a professional football franchise. But among poor and working-class families *girls* are seen as more likely to succeed for several reasons: First, as we will see in Chapter 8, girls tend to do better in school than boys, so education provides them an avenue for advancement. Second, some traditionally female jobs can represent a step up the social and economic ladder. Studies of working-class parents in Britain show that mothers assumed their sons would become manual laborers or tradesmen but hoped that their daughters would become professional secretaries, teachers, or nurses. Even though these careers are often not very well paid, they represent a move up into the professional class, a route that was much easier for girls than boys (Newson & Newson, 1986). Third, ethnic prejudice is often stronger against boys than girls. African-American mothers expect that their daughters will do better than sons, who face more hostility from teachers, administrators, and potential employers (Hare & Castenell, 1985; Swanson & Cunningham, 1991). At the same time, black parents tend to be more supportive and controlling of their children than white or Hispanic parents and push the child to do his or her best regardless of gender (Bartz & Levine, 1978).

Instruction

Parents not only expect great achievements from their sons, they help them get there, doing more actual teaching and giving boys more detailed explanations and specific guidance about solving a problem, even social problems such as having a fight with a friend (Dino, Barnett, & Howard, 1984; Frankel & Rollins, 1983; Radin, 1982). In a Baby X study in which adults taught a task to a toddler they believed to be a boy or girl, adults who thought the child was a boy were more focused on the task goal and expected the child to learn more than those who thought they were teaching a girl (J. H. Block, 1983). Mothers even do more teaching when reading bedtime stories with sons than daughters, for example, by supplying unfamiliar names ("Look, here's a giraffe; can you say 'giraffe'?") (N. Weitzman, Birns, & Friend, 1985). With girls, the emphasis is on being together and enjoying the event, not so much on actually arriving at the solution.

Parents promote independence in problem solving by not giving a boy as much help as a girl. While they are quick to respond to a girl's request for help, they ignore the same request in a boy about half the time (Fagot, 1978; Rothbart & Rothbart, 1976). Mothers are almost too quick to step in (called "anxious intrusion") when a daughter makes a mistake on a problem or if she asks for help, implying that they do not think she can cope or perhaps wanting to spare her the experience of failure. Again, however, this deprives girls of the chance to learn that they can overcome problems through their own efforts, and girls become more dependent on adults for help with problems that they could solve for themselves (Gold, Crombie, Brender, & Mate, 1984). Parents' reactions to shyness and withdrawal in their children also varies by gender: Fathers in particular are less tolerant of shy, uncertain behavior in sons than in daughters, and will use more intrusive teaching strategies to try to draw the boy out, for example, making more demands ("Put that piece right here") and showing less warmth ("No, you're not doing it right") while being more protective of daughters (Kemple, 1991). As we will see in Chapter 8, some of these differences can also be observed in teachers' behavior toward male and female students; in particular, teachers are less likely to push girls when they are not doing well.

"Smother Love"

The studies described above suggest that boys are expected to be more independent and achievement-oriented than girls, who learn to remain close to their parents and to rely on their help (J. A. Martin, Maccoby, & Jacklin, 1981). In some cases this can interfere with the daughter's autonomy, making it hard for her to develop the confidence to strike out on her own. One mother said of her 2-year-old, "If I go into another room, she has to keep coming to check. My shadow I call her, always bumping into her" (McGuire, 1991, p. 155). Among older children, having a very close, warm, emotional bond with mother has been found to be *negatively* related to achievement and autonomy in daughters (Baumrind, 1989; L. Hoffman, 1972). Often, girls who are typically smothered with parental concern can actually benefit from being challenged and provided with more opportunities to be self-reliant. One top Wall Street financial analyst who earned $1.5 million a year reported that her success was due to the fact that her mother deliberately treated her like her brothers. When she played sports after school, her mother told her, "Don't come home if you don't win" (Antilla, 1991, p. 51).

At the other extreme, boys tend to show more behavioral problems than girls when parents are less attentive than usual, for example, during a divorce when parents tend to be preoccupied with their own problems. Because boys get less support, affection, and supervision to begin with, a further reduction can hit them hard and leave them without the support they need (J. H. Block, Block, & Gjerde, 1986; Clarke-Stewart, 1980). The effects of having a poor emotional relationship with the mother or other caregiver in the first few years of life are also more apparent in boys than girls; while both sexes suffer when the mother is not sufficiently responsive and warm, boys are more likely to have behavior problems and poor relationships with peers as preschoolers (Carlson, Cicchetti, Barnett, & Braunwald, 1989; Cohn, 1990; M. Lewis, Feiring, McGuffog, & Jaskir, 1984). Thus, the types of problems associated with poor family relations are different for the sexes: Girls suffer more from excessive concern and protectiveness, while boys suffer more from parental neglect and inattention.

■ Other Cultures

The research described so far shows that in western cultures boys from the toddler period on are encouraged by parents to be more independent and achievement-oriented than girls. This pattern has also been found in many other cultures, according to anthropological records collected in the 1950s on 110 diverse societal groups around the world (M. Welch & Page, 1981; Zern, 1984). In most communities girls were more often encouraged to develop a sense of commitment to a social group, such as the family, village, or tribe. Girls were often, although not always, raised to be obedient to adults, nurturant, and responsible, for example, by taking on household chores at a young age. Boys were usually encouraged to take an individualistic orientation; they were more often pressured to achieve and to be independent, and they were more likely to be punished for failure to show self-reliance. The socialization of girls was less consistent across cultures than that of boys, which again illustrates that boys' behavior is usually more carefully socialized than girls'.

Boys' and Girls' Work

Most social learning research has focused on whether boys and girls learn to act differently by receiving different consequences for the *same behavior*; for example, a girl who picks up a Barbie finds that her mother smiles and sits down to join her, whereas a boy who does the same finds that his mother sits down near the Legos and begins to stack them up while ignoring the doll. Such subtle processes have been studied in part because we do not really make many overt distinctions between boys and girls in western cultures. Many parents feel that boys and girls should be treated similarly, and the sexes spend much of their time in joint activities; for example, most children now attend schools that are coeducational.

In contrast, in other cultures there are very clear distinctions between what boys and girls do on a daily basis, and the gender role training provided in childhood is directly related to the roles of adult men and women in the culture. Boys and girls are given different tasks as soon as they are capable of independent and productive work (Greenfield & Lave, 1982; Weisner, 1979; Whiting & Edwards, 1988). Girls usually take over domestic chores, such as watching younger siblings, cleaning, sweeping, and preparing food, so that their mothers can work outside the home, for example, by walking several miles for water, going to the family's garden plot, weaving cloth to sell, sewing for pay, or trading in a nearby village. Boys are more likely to do chores out of the home, to work with large animals, or to be sent to the next village on errands (Weisner, 1979; Whiting & Edwards, 1988). Similar distinctions are made in children's chores in the United States and Britain. Girls help with "indoor" housework, such as doing dishes, vacuuming, and making beds, while boys do "outside" chores, such as taking the garbage out, mowing the lawn, and washing the car. One of my high school girlfriends had to spend Saturday mornings cleaning while her brothers went out with their friends; her mother told her (only half in jest), "You're not a woman until you know how to clean a toilet."

The chores assigned to boys and girls reflect their future roles as adults, in which women will be responsible for the home and men work outside the home. But sometimes a small boy cannot realistically be given a "man's work" when men's work requires considerable strength, is dangerous, or involves travel away from the home; for example, a small boy on his own could not possibly plow a distant rice field with the family water buffalo. In such cases, adults create artificial gender distinctions in children's household chores, so that boys are not doing "girls' work." In one Native Indian tribe in rural Mexico, boys rather than girls feed chickens, although, among adults, caring for poultry is considered "women's work." When boys and girls must do the same work, the boys often have their own style; for example, they will carry water in a different type of container than that used by girls and women (Whiting & Edwards, 1988).

Thus far we have learned that consistent with the social learning perspective, the same behavior in boys and girls can receive a different reaction from parents and that parents structure the social environment differently for the sexes so that boys and girls do different things. In the next section we look at the second component of social learning theory, children's learning of gender roles by observing role models.

ROLE MODELS IN THE FAMILY

One of the up-and-coming race-car drivers on the international scene today is Michael Andretti, following in the footsteps of his famous father, Mario Andretti; the two can even be found on the same track in some races. Clearly, the father has served as a role model for his son. Even if children do not grow up to adopt the same career as their parents, they learn aspects of gender roles through observing their parents on a daily basis, for example, a girl who sees that her mother never leaves the house without putting on lipstick might find herself unconsciously doing the same thing as a teenager. Of course, children can some-times react by doing the exact opposite of what they see their parents do, in an effort to establish their own identity. For example, a woman who grew up resenting the fact that her mother traveled frequently on business might decide that when she has children, she will quit her job and be a full-time homemaker. Even this sort of reaction shows that children are aware of their parents as role models and make choices about what aspects of the parents' behavior to incorporate and what to avoid in their own lives.

If children learn by observing and imitating role models, as suggested by social learning theory, then we should find that children are influenced by parents who provide different illustrations of male and female behavior. In the following sections we look at some typical variations in family patterns, to see whether children's gender role develop-ment varies according to the employment status of the mother, the presence or absence of the father in the home, and the presence of male and female siblings.

■ Employed Mothers

We often think of the ideal mother as being at home after school, waiting with a bowl of hot soup or a plate of warm cookies, and ready to drive the child to soccer practice or music lessons. Yet this idealized image is terribly misleading; mothers in almost all areas of the world have always worked to help support their families, and in the United States, the mother-at-home ideal was always limited primarily to white middle-class women. The idealized image was also limited to times of relative prosperity. Women were strongly encouraged to work when it was beneficial to the national economy, as in World War II, and when men's real earning power began to decline in the 1970s, mothers again moved back into the work force (Brookins, 1985; Scarr, 1984). Women's wages have become essential for their families' survival and economic advancement, and most children now have mothers who will be employed at least some of the time.

What are the effects of having an employed mother on children's gender role development? Seeing Mom go to work, earning wages, and having responsibilities outside the home clearly expands a girl's own ideas about what the future holds and makes her less stereotyped. Across ethnic groups, daughters of employed mothers are more likely to consider work to be an important part of their future identities as adults and to be interested in more prestigious occupations, a beneficial effect given that most girls growing up today will be employed on average for about 30 years even if they marry and have children (Brookins, 1985; Gold & Andres, 1978; L. Hoffman, 1972; Katz, 1987; Marantz & Mansfield, 1977). Having an employed mother not only provides a role model for female achievement, it may also work to reduce the intensity of the emotional bond with the daughter. As we saw earlier, a very close affectionate relationship with mother tends to be associated with lower achievement in daughters (L. Hoffman, 1972). Thus, girls seem to be positively affected by having an employed mother.

Boys are less directly affected when their mother works outside the home, because she is a less salient role model for them. However, boys' perceptions of the father change when their mother works, in ways that interact with social class. In middle-class and wealthy families, sons of employed mothers show less traditional attitudes about the roles of men and women, view their fathers as good role models, and see fewer differences between men and women than sons of mothers who are primarily homemakers. In contrast, among working-class families the sons of employed mothers show *more* traditional attitudes about gender roles and view their fathers as less desirable role models. Boys tend to view their mother's employment as resulting from their father's failure to provide adequate support for the family, which in their eyes is one of a man's primary obligations; thus, they may see him as an inadequate role model (Flanagan, 1990; Katz, 1987). Some tend to compensate by adopting exaggerated stereotypes, for example, by insisting that women should remain at home with their children and that their future wives will not have to work.

■ Absent Fathers

Many children now live in homes with only one parent involved in their upbringing on a regular basis; in fact, about half of all children in the United States will live with only one parent at some point before they reach age 18 (Biller, 1981; M. Stevenson & Black, 1988). That parent is almost always the mother; despite the recent proliferation of television shows about single fathers struggling to raise their children, in reality about 90 percent of children in one-parent families live with their mother.

What are the effects of father absence on children's gender development? Social learning theory would predict that children from one-parent families should be less stereotyped, because the remaining parent probably provides a more androgynous role model; the single mother may be more likely to reglaze the storm windows and take the car in for its oil change than a mother who shares household chores with a spouse and divides tasks according to gender. In addition, the absent parent is typically the father, and, as we saw earlier, the father strongly influences children's sex-typed play. Therefore, the absence of the father should have a particularly clear effect on boys because he is a more salient role model for them, as well as a greater source of pressure to avoid feminine behaviors. Let us see if these predictions are supported.

Effects on Boys

Consider first the prediction that father absence affects the development of gender-typed play. Several studies indicate that the absence of a father before the boy is 4 to 5 years old does lead the boy to be less aggressive and less likely to engage in rough-and-tumble, stereotypically masculine play. In addition to the absence of messages from the father, mothers also tend to be less concerned with stereotypic play when they are single, or when the father is away often, and to be more protective of their children than mothers with a partner in the home. The father usually provides a balance to the mother's protectiveness, encouraging more independence and risk taking in the son (Biller, 1970, 1981; Biller &

Bahm, 1971; Kurdek & Siesky, 1980; Leaper, Smith, Sprague, & Schwartz, 1991; M. Stevenson & Black, 1988).

In addition to encouraging masculine play, the father provides a model of male self-control (Hetherington, 1991). The male gender role actually requires a delicate, difficult-to-learn blend of assertiveness and restraint. For example, a boy has to learn that he should stand up for himself in some situations but also must know how to work with others, for instance, as part of a team. A father can be a living illustration of the many facets of the male role, including the delay of gratification (going off to work every morning), long-term goal setting (next year we'll build the garage), and cooperating with others toward a common goal (let the quarterback call the plays). Boys who grow up without a father do seem to have more trouble mastering appropriate levels of self-control. Several studies have found that boys react to father absence with increased hostility and aggression, as well as acting-out behavior in the classroom and less ability to delay gratification than boys whose fathers are present in the home (Biller, 1981; Santrock, 1977). When children were given the choice of receiving a small candy bar immediately or a large candy bar several days later, the father-absent boys were more likely to opt for immediate gratification than other children (Mischel, 1961).

Biller (1981) suggests that early father absence can lead boys to feel uncertain about their masculine identity and, in some cases, to develop a kind of "compensatory masculinity," which includes difficulty in establishing close relationships, an excessive dependence on the male peer group, rebellion against the authority of adult males, and an avoidance of anything that is perceived to be feminine. This leads them to avoid being involved with their own children, so that the effects of father absence are then passed along to a new generation. Biller (1981) has found that the "compensatory masculinity" pattern is more prevalent among poor and working-class boys who hold traditional attitudes about gender roles and for whom appearing "tough" is essential to being accepted by male peers. These patterns can be found across ethnic groups, but researchers and community leaders have been increasingly concerned that the absence of adult male role models has hit the African-American community particularly hard because black children frequently live in mother-headed families due to the history of social and economic discrimination in this country. Many communities are now working to provide male role models for black children through mentor programs and by increasing the number of African-American male teachers in the public schools (Allen, 1985; P. Smith, 1991).

Although father absence does seem to affect boys' gender role development, it does not inevitably have a *detrimental* effect. Often, the effects reflect the mother's attitude: Single mothers who are more accepting of traditional masculine behavior and willing to tolerate some aggressiveness and rough play have sons who are more stereotypically masculine than mothers who are highly protective and uncomfortable with "boy" behavior. The availability of other potential male role models, such as media figures, older brothers, uncles, teachers or day-care workers, is another important factor. In one study, boys in one-parent homes were actually *more* knowledgeable about gender role stereotypes than those living with two parents, as if those who lacked a father were making a greater effort to learn by observation (Brenes, Eisenberg, & Helmstadter, 1985). Even in studies where early paternal deprivation was related to lower rates of masculine play, the boys were by no means effeminate. Four-year-old boys whose mother was divorced were less likely to play with male-typed toys than boys from two-parent families but more likely to play with such gender-neutral toys as puzzles. In other words, the father-absent boys were more flexible in their play, not more feminine (Brenes et al., 1985). We should also keep in mind that in many other cultures both boys and girls often reside exclusively with their mothers until puberty, at which time boys move to live with their father and other adult men. Thus father absence in itself is not necessarily an unusual arrangement for young children nor one that inevitably has detrimental effects on their learning of gender roles.

Effects on Girls

During childhood girls seem less directly influenced by father absence than boys, which is not surprising as fathers are less salient role models for girls. However, when the girl reaches adolescence, the absence of a father has been found to influence her interactions with male peers (Hetherington, 1972; M. Stevenson & Black, 1988). Without a father, the girl may not have learned to interact comfortably with males, although the reason for the father's absence—death or divorce—seems to be as important as the absence itself. In one study, girls whose father had died seemed anxious and inept around males, while girls whose parents were divorced were sexually assertive. For example, the daughters of widows were uncomfortable with a male interviewer, while daughters of divorcees often flirted with him; there were no differences when the girls were interviewed by a woman. When the girls were observed in a community recreation center, girls whose father had died had much less casual contact with boys than daughters of two-parent families, while daughters of divorcees often lingered near the carpentry shop and basketball courts where the boys hung out. At a school dance the daughters of divorcees were often seen near the boys' stag area, while the daughters of widows remained with groups of other girls, and two even hid in the ladies' restroom for the entire evening! Girls in both groups were asked to dance equally often (when they were actually in the dance hall, that is) suggesting that the shyness exhibited by daughters of widows was not due to unpopularity or lack of attractiveness (Hetherington, 1972).

The reason for the father's absence is important to girls' development because the mother provides a different role model in the two situations. The divorcees were much more likely than widows to date themselves, which conveyed "permission by example" to daughters, who were in turn more likely to date earlier and more frequently than other girls (Belsky, Steinberg, & Draper, 1991; Booth, Brinkerhoff, & White, 1984; Hetherington, 1972; Maccoby, 1991, p. 680). One divorcee said of her daughter, "Pow! At eleven she really turned on. She went boy crazy" (Hetherington, 1972, p. 322). A letter to the advice columnist Ann Landers described teenage girls as "sex-crazed, out-of-control estrogen bombs." According to one parent, "My teen-age son was propositioned by two girls who taped roses with sexy notes to the windshield of his car in the school parking lot," while another wrote, "I caught a 13-year-old girl throwing pebbles at my son's bedroom window at 1:30 in the morning" (*Boston Globe*, 1991b). Another concluded, "Those 'aggressive girls' are starved for affection . . . They are the first generation to grow up in broken homes . . . Show me a 15-year-old girl who is 'boy-crazy' and I will show you a young girl who is hungering for her father" (*Boston Globe*, 1991a). In contrast, one widow said about her daughter, "[She] is almost too good. She has lots of girl friends but doesn't date much . . . she clams up when a man comes in. Even around my brother she never says much . . . When boys do phone she often puts them off . . . She says she has lots of time for that later" (Hetherington, 1972, p. 322).

Clearly, father absence influences both sons and daughters but in different ways: Boys who lack a male role model in the home tend to be less strongly stereotyped in their play, although some develop an exaggerated masculine style to compensate. Girls do not seem as directly affected until adolescence, at which point his absence seems to affect their ability to interact in a comfortable, casual manner with male peers.

Mother Absence

Most research has focused on the effect of father absence rather than mother absence, because the latter is relatively rare. One exception is the work of Santrock and his colleagues, who conducted a study of children living with a parent of the same or other sex (Santrock & Warshak, 1979). The results showed that children who lived with the same-sex parent generally seemed better adjusted in terms of their social development. Boys living with their fathers had fewer behavior problems, while girls living with their mothers seemed a bit more mature. However, there were no apparent effects on the children's masculinity or femininity. Similar conclusions have been made in studies of families in which the mother was employed outside the home while the father took care of the children. Having a father as the primary caregiver did not affect children's gender role behavior despite the reversal of traditional gender roles in the home (Pruett, 1987; Radin, 1982). Father absence probably has a greater impact on gender role development because it is not really equivalent to mother absence in terms of the availability of role models. Children who live with their father have more frequent and regular contact with their mother than children who live with their mother do with their father (Santrock, Warshak, & Elliott, 1982). In addition, fathers often rely on mother-substitute figures, such as nannies, baby-sitters, and female relatives to share child care, while mothers are probably less likely to hire or borrow father substitutes to play with children, admire girls when they wear pretty dresses, and do "guy stuff" with boys.

■ Gay and Lesbian Parents

If parents are important role models, as social learning theory predicts, how does having a gay or lesbian parent influence a child's gender role learning? Reseachers have found that children of homosexual parents are remarkably similar to children of heterosexuals; they usually adopt role behaviors typical for their biological sex, have no confusion about their own sex, and have no interest in being the other sex (Golumbok, Spencer, & Rutter, 1983; Green, 1978; Kirkpatrick, Smith, & Roy, 1981; C. Patterson, 1992). In one study, the children of lesbian mothers were so similar to children of single heterosexual mothers that the interviewers could not tell them apart (Kirkpatrick et al., 1981). A similar conclusion was reached by Green (1978) who studied children who had grown up with a transsexual parent and who were old enough to observe and remember the parent begin to dress as the other sex, undergo hormone treatment and surgery, and establish relationships with new partners. Despite the sometimes dramatic changes in their parents' lives, the children themselves were remarkably similar to children growing up in more traditional households: They showed typical role behaviors, preferred playmates of their own sex, and were happy with their own sex. Those who were entering adolescence reported heterosexual interests and sexual fantasies, and those who had become sexually active were heterosexual.

If parents are important role models, why are the children of gay parents so un-affected? Green (1978) concluded that there were many role models available in the media, peer influences, and other family members and that children tended to follow the more conventional role models; as we saw at the start of the chapter, children tend to avoid copying role models who seem unrepresentative. In addition, the homosexual parents often made special efforts to provide role models of the other sex for their children. Lesbian mothers were significantly more likely than single heterosexual mothers to arrange for their children to spend time on a regular basis with uncles, grandfathers, male friends, and the children's biological father (Golumbok et al., 1983). The homosexual parents also discussed their life-styles in terms appropriate for their children's developmental level, which helped the children understand that there are various ways of being male or female. Most children were deeply attached to their gay or lesbian parents without feeling any need to imitate their parents' sexuality. One 12-year-old boy said of his lesbian mother, "She can be anything she wants as long as she's still my mother" (Green, 1978, p. 695).

Despite the evidence, there is strong societal prejudice against homosexual parents. Gay and lesbian parents can lose custody of their children after divorce, and applications and paperwork for adoption and foster-parenting programs often have spaces for "man's" and "woman's" names, clearly indicating that heterosexual parents are preferred. Negative community reaction is sometimes cited as one justification, and indeed, lesbian mothers worried that their children would be teased and ostracized. However, Green (1978) found that the children themselves reported little teasing. When a child shouted, "Your mom's a lezzie!" to one boy, he responded, "So what?" and the subject was not raised again. Objections are sometimes raised that gay parents will abuse children, although homosexuals are no more likely to abuse children than are heterosexuals. In one case, two preschool boys who had been cared for by a gay foster-parent couple were removed and placed in a new foster home after a public outcry. The men had met all the requirements for being foster parents, and by all accounts the boys were doing very well. One of the boys was subsequently sexually abused by the heterosexual son of the new foster mother, and the policy was later changed to permit placement of foster children with gay and lesbian couples (*Boston Globe*, 1985). Given the research evidence, there is no reason to believe that having a gay or lesbian parent interferes with children's social, emotional, or gender role development (C. Patterson, 1992).

■ Siblings

Parents are not the only role models in the home; there are often other children as well; about 80 percent of U.S. children have brothers or sisters. We know that younger children imitate and learn from their older brothers and sisters in play, and there is evidence that children are more likely to acquire sexist attitudes from their older siblings than from their parents (R. Abramovitch, Corter & Pepler, 1980; Barry, 1980; B. Bryant & Crockenberg,

1980; Cicirelli, 1973, 1975; DeHart & Smith, 1991; Falbo & Polit, 1986). But do they learn about being a boy or girl from their older siblings?

When there are two children of the same sex in the family, the older one does seem to serve as a role model for the younger child. Research on college students found that women with older sisters were often conventionally feminine and men with older brothers were conventionally masculine. However, when the two children were not the same sex, the picture was different for boys and girls. A girl with an older brother often tended to have been more of a tomboy, because she emulated him, tagged along with his friends, and learned athletic skills. But while a boy with an older sister is somewhat more likely to play with gender-neutral toys, he does not necessarily become feminine; as with father absence, he seems to become more flexible in his behavior (Graham-Bermann & Gest, 1991; Stoneman, Brody, & MacKinnon, 1986). On the other hand, a boy with several older sisters can border on the "macho" side, as if rebelling against the influence of all those girls in the home (J. Dunn, 1985; Katz & Boswell, 1984).

If there are several children in the family, the picture becomes considerably more complex because the pattern of sibling influence reflects not only the children's gender but also their birth order and their need to differentiate themselves. Siblings often unconsciously create distinct roles for themselves within the family, such as "the smart one," "the jock," "the social one," and even "the dumb one." With several siblings, this attempt to diversify may overwhelm any direct influence of older siblings as role models (L. Hoffman, 1991; Huston, 1983; Katz, 1987; Schachter, Gulutz, Shore, & Adler, 1978; Sutton-Smith & Rosenberg, 1970). Thus, a girl with several older sisters is often a tomboy; this suggests that she has tried to "go in the other direction" in terms of gender role behavior (Grotevant, 1978). Similarly, one study found that extremely effeminate boys (see Chapter 13) often had several older brothers; this implies that the younger boy might have moved toward the feminine role to try to distinguish himself from the other boys in the family (Harrington, 1970).

Only Children

Girls who are the only child in the family tend to be less traditionally feminine than girls who have siblings; they play with boys and identify more with their father than their mother. This is because parents whose first and possibly only child is a girl treat her in some ways as a firstborn son, encouraging her to be more of a tomboy than they would if they already had a boy. Boys who have no siblings are in a bind in terms of their parents' expectations: Their mother treats them a bit like the daughter that she does not have, encouraging more feminine and gender-flexible behavior than a mother who has several children. At the same time their father wants his only son to be even more conventionally masculine than does a father who has several children. Boys in this predicament apparently decide to go along with their father's expectations instead of their mother's: Boys without siblings report having even more masculine interests and preferences than other boys (Katz & Boswell, 1984).

To summarize, siblings serve as role models when they are the same gender, unless there are more than two or three in the same family, when the children try to carve out unique roles within the family by behaving in a way distinct from their older siblings. Among mixed-gender siblings brothers serve as role models for girls, but sisters do not serve as role models for their brothers, another example of the asymmetry of gender socialization. When parents have only one child, children of both sexes tend to move toward the masculine role, reflecting the importance to parents of having a son.

So far, the two components of social learning theory seem to have considerable empirical support: Boys and girls do receive different patterns of reinforcement in specific areas, most notably play, independence, and achievement orientation. They are also influenced by same-sex role models: Girls with working mothers and older brothers tend to move more toward the masculine role, whereas boys who grow up without a father tend to be less strongly stereotyped in their play. The influence of role models is asymmetric: Boys seem more affected by the absence of male models than the presence of females; that is, they do not become more feminine with an older sibling, but they do become more flexible with fewer male role models in the family. In the last section of this chapter we look more specifically at the strengths and weaknesses of the theory.

EVALUATION OF THE SOCIAL LEARNING APPROACH

■ Comparison with Psychoanalytic Theory

Social learning theory shares some themes with the psychoanalytic approach, primarily, the idea that gender roles are learned during childhood and the emphasis on the importance of same-sex role models. The two approaches differ, however, in a number of ways: First, the theories differ in their view of the child's role in the process of gender role learning. Freud's theory viewed the child as the primary instigator of learning, motivated to identify with the same-sex parent in order to resolve the emotional crisis of the oedipal stage. The parents themselves were seen as relatively uninvolved except for serving as adequate role models. In contrast, social learning theory places more emphasis on the power of the surrounding social environment to influence children's development, that is, the motivation for learning comes more from outside the child.

Second, the reasons why the child looks to role models and begins to try to be like them are different in the two approaches. As we saw in the last chapter, Freud proposed that the development of masculinity and femininity occurred through a very specific developmental process, the resolution of the oedipal crisis. Social learning theory, on the other hand, suggests that children become masculine or feminine because they are rewarded for gender-typed behavior and ignored or punished for cross-gender behavior. This is an advantage because gender role learning is viewed as resulting from a general principle of learning, that of reinforcement; we do not have to propose a special mechanism to account for one particular aspect of development as if it were isolated from other behaviors.

Third, the methodology associated with the two theories is quite different. As we saw in the last chapter, Freud developed his theory on the basis of his work with adults in therapy who recalled their early years and relations with their parents. In contrast, social learning theory focuses on the development of typical children, using observation of naturally occurring behavior in the home, as well as studies in the laboratory, to test its predictions.

■ Strengths and Weaknesses of the Social Learning Approach

Social learning theory offers several advantages in terms of explaining children's gender role learning. First, the theory can explain why boys and girls start to behave differently so early in life, before they even know they are boys or girls. The shaping of children's behavior through reinforcement can begin very early, before children or their parents realize it is happening, and can produce striking differences in the behavior of boys and girls relatively quickly. For example, boys' and girls' earliest aggressive behaviors elicit different reactions from adults, and this in turn alters the future frequency of aggression in the sexes. One-year-old boys and girls are equally likely to use physical assertion to get what they want, such as hitting or pushing an adult or another child or trying to grab a toy away. They are also equally likely to try to communicate by whining, gesturing, and gently touching the other person. However, adults' reactions to these efforts vary strikingly by gender. Adults responded positively to 90 percent of girls' attempts to communicate, while ignoring 90 percent of girls' efforts to use physical assertion. In contrast, adults responded to boys' efforts to communicate only 15 percent of the time; boys who whined or babbled at an adult were usually simply picked up and put down in front of some toys, but adults did respond to 41 percent of boys' attempts to use physical assertion. By the time the children were 2, the girls had given up on aggression because they had learned that they would only get a reaction through using words. The boys had learned the reverse lesson: Their rate of aggressive acts remained high (Fagot, Hagan, Leinbach, & Kronsberg, 1985). Overall, the sexes started out with similar behaviors but looked quite different a year later as the result of different reinforcement histories.

Another strength of the theory is the component of observational learning, which shows that children can learn by watching others and can store away knowledge about gender roles without having to try things out directly for themselves. Again, this suggests that learning can occur very quickly. Children do often know more than they will show in their own behavior, including things typically associated with the other sex. In a classic study young children first watched an adult hit and punch a large inflated plastic "Bobo" clown doll. When the children were later left alone in the playroom, the boys were more likely than girls to imitate the adult by hitting Bobo and by hitting and punching the doll in exactly the same way as the adult. However when children were given a prize for showing that they remembered what the adult had done, the girls imitated as accurately as the boys. The girls had watched, learned, and remembered as much as the boys, but they were careful not to act in an aggressive manner themselves until they were sure that it was socially acceptable to do so (Bandura, Ross, & Ross, 1961).

Social learning theory also accounts for the fact that boys show stronger avoidance of feminine things than girls do of masculine activities (Bussey & Perry, 1982). This is because reinforcements and models give stronger messages to boys about the costs of engaging in feminine behavior; for example, Langlois and Downs's (1980) study showed that there was greater pressure on boys than girls to avoid playing with the toys typically associated with the other sex.

Although social learning theory helps account for the process of gender role learning, it also has several weaknesses. First, it does not explain the wide individual variation within each gender. We do not know why some girls are much more feminine than others and why some boys are more masculine than others. This does not seem to be related to the parent's degree of gender typing; Maccoby (1980) concluded that there was no relation between children's degree of gender typing and the femininity or masculinity of their parents. Rather, children tended to be most like the more forceful, dominant parent regardless of that parent's sex. In fact, if the same-sex parent is a weak or unattractive role model, children sometimes show a "compensatory" pattern and become even more strongly gender-typed; this pattern is particularly strong for boys (J. Block, von der Lippe, & Block, 1973). Thus the theory fails to explain why some children are apparently not strongly influenced by parents, who are presumably the most salient and accessible role models or why reinforcements for gender role behavior have more impact on some children than others.

Another limitation is that social learning theory views the child as producing behaviors according to the reinforcement contingencies learned from past experiences. Yet as any parent knows, children do things for which they will be punished and they also fail to do things for which they would be rewarded. This is particularly true for boys, who are often reluctant to do things that they view as feminine even if they see another boy or an adult man perform the behavior and even if parents or teachers praise them for it (Bussey & Bandura, 1984; Fagot, 1985b; Fein, Johnson, Kosson, Stork, & Wasserman, 1975; Raskin & Israel, 1981). In one study, preschool children first selected a small toy as a prize; not surprisingly, all of them chose gender-typical toys. The child and experimenter then asked the child's favorite teacher over to see the toy, but to the child's surprise the teacher suggested that the child trade it for a cross-gender toy and gave four reasons why it would be a better toy. Both boys and girls resisted the teacher's suggestions, but while the girls simply said that they wouldn't like playing with a boy's toy (one said her brother might take it!), the boys appeared very uncomfortable. They actively argued with her and even tried to discredit her advice, for example, by saying that she must be ill or overworked or she would never have told them to swap the truck for a necklace. One boy nervously told the experimenter, "She has too much to do today. You shouldn't ask her to do more things. Let's pretend we never asked her" (Ross & Ross, 1972, p. 345). Clearly, children's own ideas about appropriate behavior for boys and girls influence their receptiveness to reinforcements and their attention to potential role models (Fagot, 1985a,b). The influence of children's own developing ideas about gender roles is explored in further detail in the next chapter.

6

THEORIES OF GENDER ROLE DEVELOPMENT: COGNITIVE-DEVELOPMENTAL APPROACHES

A father told me that his 3-year-old daughter always insisted on wearing her pink pajamas. One evening when he and his wife were getting ready to go out, he was in a hurry and quickly put the little girl to bed in a set of printed blue pajamas before the baby-sitter arrived. Later as they left the house, they looked up and saw the little girl waving from the upstairs window—and wearing pink. She had climbed out of bed, rummaged through the chest of drawers, and changed into the pink set.

Why would a little girl be so insistent on wearing pink? Such examples make us wonder whether little girls really are "naturally" feminine and boys "naturally" masculine, since it is the child who seems to be insisting on conforming to gender role expectations, not the parents. Children's at times fervent desire to adhere to traditional gender roles can be puzzling and even discouraging to parents who have tried hard to avoid making gender distinctions in the home. A mother who had struggled through medical school, in part so that she would be a strong role model for her daughter, was startled when the little girl told her that she must be a nurse because only men could be doctors. Another little girl said, "Mommy cleans the living room," even though she had only ever seen her father doing the vacuuming and dusting. When another girl was given a toy truck to play with, she said, "My mommy would want me to play with this, but I don't want to" (Bussey & Bandura, 1992). Clearly, there is more to the gender socialization story than differential reinforcements from parents!

As we saw at the end of Chapter 5, while the social learning perspective shows that boys and girls are treated differently in many ways, it is apparent that children have their own ideas about what it means to be a boy or girl and that adults have only limited influence. In contrast, the cognitive-developmental perspective focuses on the child's active role in the process of gender socialization. Specifically, children's own need to establish a clear self-concept leads them to form a *gender identity*, a sense of themselves as male or female. Once established, gender identity provides a powerful motivation to identify with role models and to learn by observation. In addition, gender provides a powerful tool with which children can make sense of their social world. In other words, gender becomes an "organizing principle" for children, helping them understand and interpret the behavior of those around them.

THEORISTS AND SCHEMAS

◼ Major Theorists

The cognitive-developmental perspective includes several theories focusing on related components of gender role learning. Kohlberg (1966) introduced the notion of gender identity as a critical component in the process of gender role learning. The social learning view had argued that children eventually inferred from the patterns of reinforcement that they were boys or girls: "If I'm doing things that boys do and receiving approval for it, I must be a boy." However, part of social learning theory is learning by observation of same-sex role models, which implied that children would need to know their own sex or at least perceive a match between themselves and certain role models before this kind of learning could take place. This led Kohlberg to place more emphasis on gender identity in the process; he suggested instead that the child might think, "If I'm a boy, I'd better figure out what kinds of things boys do." The cognitive-developmental perspective thus is not inconsistent with the social learning view but "adds on" to it by arguing that in addition to reinforcements behavior is guided by the child's own need to do things that fit his or her concept of the self (Serbin, Powlishta, & R. Gulko, 1993; Ullian, 1984).

In this early theory Kohlberg placed special emphasis on a particular component of gender identity: gender permanence. He argued that once children realized they were always going to be a boy or girl, they became highly motivated to adopt masculine or feminine behaviors. However, he felt that it was not until children were about 5 to 7 years old that they would really understand that they were boys or girls, in the sense of being able to understand that their gender assignment was *permanent*. He focused on the 5- to 7-year stage because according to Piagetian theory, children's general cognitive capacities were thought to become much more flexible during these years, while younger children's reasoning abilities were too limited for them to really understand gender permanence. However, recent studies indicate that understanding gender permanence is only one component of gender identity and that considerable learning takes place well before children understand that they will always be boys and girls (Hort, Leinbach, & Fagot, 1991; Martin & Little, 1990). This has led other researchers to extend Kohlberg's original theory to include other components of learning in addition to gender identity, in particular, the notion of gender schemas.

Gender Schemas

Several theorists have proposed that children build up knowledge structures termed *gender schemas*, which organize gender-related information in memory and which become the cognitive window through which the child interprets the world (Bem, 1981; Markus, Crane, Bernstein, & Siladi, 1982; Martin & Halverson, 1981). Gender schemas might include knowledge about what males and females look like; their typical interests, activities, and personality characteristics; and expectations about how the sexes will behave in various situations. Schemas are built up through repeated experience and observation of males and females, examples that are eventually abstracted or summarized to become stereotypes. For example, the child might notice that when the family goes out, the father usually drives; when the car is broken, he fixes it or takes it to be repaired; television ads often show men driving and caring for cars; and little boys enjoy playing with cars and trucks. Although the child will have seen many counterexamples of women driving, the correlation between being male and driving is high enough that the child could develop a rule stating, "Cars are for men."

Children are thought to build up schemas for both sexes to help guide their own behavior by determining if new information is appropriate for them. The child might encounter a new toy, notice that the picture on the box shows a girl, reason, "I am a girl, this toy is for girls, and therefore this toy is something I might like to play with," and open the box, explore the toy, and learn about it. A boy, on the other hand, would reason, "I am a boy, this toy is for girls, and therefore this toy is not for me," and lose interest in it (Martin & Halverson, 1981). The own-sex schema will thus be more detailed; in this case, because the boy has coded the toy as "for girls," he will not learn as much about it as the girl (Bryan & Luria, 1978; Masters & Wilkinson, 1976). Despite the relative lack of detail, having an other-sex schema is still useful because it allows the child to know what to avoid as well as what to approach, a guideline that, as we have seen, is particularly important for boys.

The two theories forming the cognitive-developmental perspective emphasize different aspects of it: Kohlberg's theory focuses on gender identity as a critical source of motivation for learning, while gender schema theory retains the idea that gender identity is an important component of learning but extends the notion of children as active processors of information by suggesting that they use schemas to interpret the world around them. In the following sections we explore these claims in detail by examining the development of gender identity and then turning to evidence that children use gender as an organizing principle for understanding their social world.

GENDER IDENTITY

What do we know about early awareness of one's sex, that is, the beginnings of gender identity? In the past, researchers have relied on studies in which children are asked whether they are a boy or girl, to point to pictures of boys and girls, and to indicate which they are most like. These techniques required that the child understand language and, as described below, generally led to the conclusion that children knew their own sex between the second and third birthday. However, more recent studies of preverbal infants suggest that gender identity may be forming at the end of the first year of life. This possibility is explored in the following section.

■ Infancy

The first step in constructing a gender identity would be to discriminate males and females. One needs to establish that there are two groups before identifying the self as a member of one. To test whether the infant can tell men and women apart, the infant is typically presented with examples from one category (e.g., slides of female faces) until the infant becomes bored and merely glances at each new example as if to say, "Oh, another one of those . . . I've seen enough already." An example from another category (e.g., a male face) is then presented to see whether the infant shows renewed interest, implying that the category shift has been detected. Studies using this method have shown that by about the middle of the first year infants can distinguish between male and female faces (Fagan, 1979; Leinbach, 1991; Walsh, Katz, & Downey, 1991). Babies seem to rely primarily on hair length to make the discrimination, as they cannot tell men and women apart if photographs of women with short haircuts are used.

Infants can also discriminate men and women by other sensory systems. Babies can tell the difference between male and female voices by 6 months, even if voice pitch is artificially equalized, suggesting that they notice sex differences in intonation and speech patterns (C. Miller, 1983). Two-month-olds who heard a single syllable spoken by a man noticed the gender change when the same syllable was spoken by a woman (Leinbach, 1991). Babies also match on the basis of gender across sensory modalities: 9- to 12-month-olds look longer at a female face when they hear a female voice and longer at a male face when they hear a male voice (Poulin-Dubois, Serbin, Kenyon, & Derbyshire, 1991). Although newborns are highly sensitive to odors, there is so far no evidence that they can make male-female discriminations on this basis, for example, telling Daddy and Mother apart by sense of smell alone. However, babies can tell their own mother from other women by smell when they are only a few days old, so it is not implausible they could make gender discriminations as well.

Babies' early ability to tell males and females apart might be taken to imply that gender is somehow a fundamental or distinctive characteristic of human beings, one so basic that it is perceived before babies have had much social experience or exposure to the surrounding culture. However, this implication is false; infants also easily make other types of distinctions, such as on the basis of facial expressions (e.g., smiling versus frowning faces) or race. For example, 9- to 12-month-old infants show renewed interest and attention to the face of a black person after seeing a series of white faces or to a white face after seeing a set of black faces. This seems to be based on opportunities to observe and learn about people from diverse backgrounds. Black infants recognize race category shifts more quickly than white infants, who are less likely to have seen other-race faces (Walsh et al., 1991). Thus, there does not appear to be anything particularly special about gender as a social dimension for infants.

Early Gender Identity

The beginnings of gender identity appear in the second year, based on evidence that infants start to show a preference for others of their own gender, as if at some level they are beginning to learn that the other person is "like me." M. Lewis and Brooks-Gunn (1979) found that infants 12 to 18 months old looked longer at photographs of babies of their own sex than those of the other sex. Another study also found that infants looked longer at a photograph of a same-sex child as long as the child was dressed in sex-typical clothing. Babies became confused when the other child was cross-dressed, suggesting that they relied on clothing cues to determine the other child's gender. Infants even preferred to watch the pattern of biological motion produced by a same-sex child. The patterns were produced by attaching lights to the joints of a boy and a girl and filming the children walking in the dark (T. Bower, 1982). Slightly different patterns were produced because girls' wider hips gives them a more rolling gait. There are also hints in some studies that 6-month-old boys show increased attention to male faces (Kagan, Henker, Hen-Tov, Levine, & Lewis, 1966; Langlois, Ritter, Roggman, & Vaughn, 1991; M. Lewis, 1969; Moss & Robson, 1968). While more research needs to be done to confirm the findings, these studies suggest that our earliest sense of self may be tinted with pink or blue (M. Lewis & Weinraub, 1979). However, it is not yet clear how this knowledge would be acquired. T. Bower (1982) suggests that girls may detect a correspondence between the girl-produced pattern of lights and proprioceptive feedback from their own bodies. Gender identity might also be related to early language comprehension. It is generally thought that many concepts are understood before the corresponding linguistic terms are attached and that the ability to understand language precedes the ability to speak. It is not implausible that being repeatedly called a boy or girl would become a component of early self-concept and that language is a mediator for gender identity in the second year of life when most children are beginning to speak.

The possibility that gender identity is forming in late infancy may also be relevant to the case discussed in Chapter 2—the boy baby who was reassigned as a girl after his penis was damaged in a circumcision accident and who was raised as a girl but then returned to the male role as an adult. Since the sex assignment was done when the baby was 17 months old, it is possible that a male identity had already started to become established, with the switch contributing to lingering ambivalence about gender identity. On the other hand, other sex reassignments have been apparently successful up to the time the child uses verbal labels to refer to the self as a boy or girl. More studies will need to be done to learn whether in fact the preverbal infant has a sense of the self as a boy or girl, and if so, whether early gender identity is still malleable enough for sex reassignments to be successful.

◼ The Toddler Period: Using Gender Labels

Once the child begins to use language to express himself or herself and to communicate with others, it becomes possible to test the child's knowledge about gender stereotypes much more directly than can be done with preverbal babies. Slaby and Frey (1975) showed toddlers a series of dolls and photographs of men and women and of boys and girls. The children were asked if the dolls and photographs were male or female and what sex they were themselves. About 80 percent of the 3- to 3 $^1/_2$-year-olds could accurately identify the sex of other people and knew their own sex. Converging results were obtained by Thompson (1975), who asked toddlers to sort photographs by sex and then to add their own picture to the appropriate pile. Some children as young as 2 $^1/_2$ years could do so accurately, and most children knew their own sex by the time they were about 3 years old.

Like infants, toddlers continue to make their judgments primarily on the basis of how people look and what they do, rather than on an understanding of the biological basis of gender. For example, young children initially believe that someone who has short hair, wears pants, and enjoys rough, outdoor games must be a boy. Relying on appearance and activity cues makes sense; the biological information is often not available, and appearance cues are quite reliable indicators of gender in our culture. For example, men rarely wear skirts or cosmetics or push baby carriages. Yet Thompson and Bentler (1971) found that young children continued to rely on appearance cues even when the biological information was also provided. The researchers used a doll that could be modified through the use of snap-on parts to have male or female genitals, large breasts or a flat chest, and long or short hair. Each child in the experiment was shown the doll with a particular combination of masculine and feminine features. For example, the doll might have a penis, a flat chest, and long hair. The child was asked to pick out clothes for the doll (dress or pants), to give it a name, and to say whether it would grow up to be a mommy or daddy. Adults who were shown the doll relied exclusively on its genitals to determine its sex, but the children relied primarily on hair length. Only 16 percent of the children mentioned the doll's genitals as the reason for their gender assignment. One of my graduate school friends had a very short haircut, and one day when she happened to wear overalls to her job at a local preschool, she looked up to see a little girl staring at her with a puzzled expression. The little girl tentatively whispered, "Are you a man?" When my friend said no, the little girl became quite distressed, convinced that my friend was lying to her because she was unable to believe that a woman could have short hair and wear pants.

In addition to establishing a gender identity, young children also quickly acquire an astonishingly extensive set of stereotypical beliefs about males and females (Cann & Haight, 1983; Fein, Johnson, Kosson, Stork, & Wasserman, 1975; J. E. Williams, Bennett, & Best, 1975). Kuhn, Nash, and Brucken (1978) asked 2- and 3-year-olds which sex was associated with particular activities, future roles, and personality traits. To avoid taxing the children's emerging verbal skills, the researchers trained children to point to one of two paper-doll drawings, "Lisa" and "Michael," to indicate their responses. For example, the adult would ask who would most like to play with dolls, and the child would point to either the Lisa or Michael doll. The researchers found that even 2-year-olds had clear beliefs about boys and girls. For example, children thought that Lisa liked to play with dolls, liked to clean house and cook dinner, talked a lot, and never hit, while Michael liked to play with cars and build things, liked to fight, and was loud, naughty, and made girls cry. They thought that Lisa would grow up to clean the house and be a nurse or teacher, while Michael would grow up to mow the grass and be "the boss." Children also hold stereotyped beliefs about more abstract qualities associated with gender, such as color: When shown a set of stuffed toy animals, children selected the pink and lavender animals as the "girls" and the brown, blue, and maroon ones as the "boys" (Picariello, Greenberg, & Pillemer, 1990). Similarly, children assign a fierce bear, fire, and a piece of rough sandpaper to males, while giving butterflies, flowers, and soft textures to females (Leinbach & Hort, 1989). They also associate natural objects such as trees, flowers, and lakes with females, while artifacts such as buildings, sunglasses, and cameras are associated with males (Mullen, 1990). Thus, many of the stereotypic associations about masculinity and femininity are learned early in the life span.

Gender identity seems to provide the impetus for conforming to gender role expectations and learning such stereotypes. In the studies described above, the most stereotyped 2- and 3-year-olds were those who already knew their own sex (Hort, Leinbach, & Fagot, 1991). In addition, once children use gender labels accurately, their actual behavior changes as they try to fit what they think is expected for their own sex. For example, girls and boys initially start out with similar levels of aggression, but girls' aggression rates then decline once they start to call themselves girls, as if they have figured out that such actions are not expected for females. Similarly, boys who call themselves boys begin to avoid girls' toys and activities that they had previously enjoyed, such as playing in the "housekeeping corner" (Fagot, 1985b; Fagot, Leinbach, & Hagan, 1986). Toddlers who know their sex also spend more of their time playing with other children of the same sex than those who have not yet acquired gender identity.

✓To summarize, toddlers can tell males and females apart, know which sex they are, have learned many cultural stereotypes about the sexes, and have altered their behavior accordingly—all by the time they are 3 years old. No wonder many parents, including the parents of the little girl who insisted on wearing pink pajamas, start to wonder whether sex stereotypes are programmed by nature! By the time most parents even begin to consider the issue of gender stereotyping, much of the learning has already taken place. The rate at which different children acquire stereotypes and gender labels does suggest that these concepts are learned (Reis & Wright, 1982). Brighter children acquire gender stereotypes more quickly than their less intelligent peers. The speed with which toddlers acquire gender labels and stereotypes is also related to how much gender is emphasized in the surrounding social environment; children in more traditional homes master these concepts sooner than their peers whose parents place less emphasis on gender (Fagot & Leinbach, 1989; Weinraub et al., 1984).

■ The Preschool Period

By the preschool period, children know they are boys or girls, but they still do not really understand why, that is, because they are biologically male or female, and, in particular, that their identity as male or female is permanent. The realization that they will always be the same sex is an important aspect of development because it appears to trigger a renewed and more serious search for appropriate role models and to increase children's conforming to traditional gender role expectations. This realization is marked by several milestones or components of gender permanence which are acquired gradually in an ordered sequence.

Gender Stability and Consistency

Many young children can accurately label themselves as a boy or girl while believing that they could become the other sex if they wanted to, by dressing and behaving like a child of the other sex. Slaby and Frey (1975) found that children first learned to label themselves reliably and accurately as male or female (identity), then learned that they stayed the same gender over time (stability), and finally learned that they stayed the same gender across situations (consistency), including changes in their appearance and activities. This ordered sequence has been observed across several cultures, including children in Belize, Kenya, Nepal, and Samoa, although children from working-class families and those living in nonindustrialized cultures tend to reach the identity, stability, and consistency milestones a year or so later than children from upper-middle-class U.S. samples (Frey & Ruble, 1992; Munroe, Shimmin, & Munroe, 1984).

Gender Permanence

Children can know that they are male or female and that they will not change sex, but their knowledge is still incomplete. Recall that Kohlberg (1966) emphasized the importance of gender permanence: understanding that being male or female is biologically determined and that while outward signs such as clothing and hairstyle are correlated with one's sex, these characteristics do not determine one's sex. This knowledge has traditionally been assessed by the *sex constancy* task (Emmerich, 1981; Wehren & De Lisi, 1983). The task begins with a drawing or photograph of a boy or a girl which is gradually altered by overlaying sheets or add-on paper-doll clothes so that the picture begins to resemble the other sex. For example, the experimenter might add a long hairstyle to a drawing of a boy and ask the child if "John" is now a boy or girl. Next, a frilly dress might be substituted for John's pants and t-shirt. Finally, a doll and toy baby carriage might be added to the picture. After each change, the child is asked if John is a boy or girl. In order to answer correctly, the child must discount the altered appearance and realize that the changes in hairstyle, clothing, and behavior cannot affect John's status as a male. Sex constancy is a more advanced concept than the previously acquired notions of gender stability and consistency in the following sense: While young children may realize that people do not typically change sex, they might believe that this is a matter of custom or preference, based on observation of those around them, without necessarily understanding that one *cannot* change sex because of one's biology.

When shown the sex constancy task, many preschool children agree that John has become a girl by adopting long hair, a dress, and girls' toys. One of my nephews had hair that had grown quite long one summer. Before he started kindergarten, he asked his mother to cut his hair short; he thought he was turning into a girl and wanted be a "real boy" again before going to school. As Kohlberg had hypothesized, most children master sex constancy between 5 and 7 years, first realizing that they themselves cannot change sex by changing how they look. This knowledge is then generalized to others (Gouze & Nadelman, 1980; Marcus & Overton, 1978). Among children who were quite sure that they themselves could not change sex, many were considerably less certain when asked about their classmates, particularly when they saw another child actually dressed up to look like the other sex!

Preschoolers' belief that they could change sex seems a little odd, particularly since they seem so knowledgeable about other aspects of gender roles. However, this reasoning is understandable given that they first learn to tell the sexes apart on the basis of appearance cues. This reasoning also may not be unique to gender; there are some indications that a similar phenomenon occurs with children's concepts of ethnicity. Until they are about 7 to 8 years old, children report that a black child could change into a white child by putting on light makeup and wearing a blond wig or that a white child could become a Native American by donning a leather shirt with beaded fringe and a feather headdress (Aboud, 1988; Wyche, 1991). Similarly, children often do not realize that they were born with their skin tone or that a person's skin color is permanent; many children reason that people become black by going out into the sun or white by staying in the shade all the time. Believing that ethnicity is a matter of wearing and doing certain things is analogous to believing that being a boy or girl is due to wearing and doing particular things.

The Role of Biological Knowledge

Children's reliance on outward appearance is quite reasonable given that most do not have the relevant knowledge about the biological basis of gender and ethnicity. Children who have the relevant biological knowledge are more likely to show sex constancy than their peers who lack this knowledge (Bem, 1989; McConaghy, 1979). In one study, children were first shown a photograph of a nude toddler, who was referred to with a sex-neutral name (e.g., "This is a picture of Gaw") (Bem, 1989). Children were asked, "Is Gaw a boy or a girl? Is there a part of Gaw's body that makes Gaw a boy or girl?" The child was then shown another photograph of Gaw dressed as the other sex and was asked if Gaw was a boy or girl. About 40 percent of Bem's sample of 3- to 5-year-olds could accurately tell Gaw's sex, and most of these children also said that Gaw was still the same sex even when dressed in cross-sex clothes. These children were also more likely than others to say that they could not really change their own sex and to refer to their own anatomy as a reason. For example, children said they could not change sex because "that's how I was made"; "Jesus made me a boy"; and "I was born a girl." Children who could not tell if a naked toddler was a boy or a girl relied on dress and hairstyle to determine sex and also reported that people could change their sex if they wanted to. In some cases, however, children who do know the difference between male and female genitals still believe that gender can change; for example, a girl might develop a penis and turn into a boy as she grew up (Frey & Ruble, 1992).

Once children understand that gender is related to biology and is unchangeable they asume that biology is the *reason* that the sexes behave differently and have different interests. In fact, preschoolers are little nativists, believing that sex differences are due to nature rather than to nurture! When told a story about a little girl who was raised on an island with only boys and men, preschoolers thought that despite growing up in an exclusively masculine environment, the girl would still play with dolls, wear dresses, cry a lot, want to be a nurse when she grew up, and be good at taking care of babies (M. Taylor & Gelman, 1991). When asked why the sexes behaved differently children often referred to physical characteristics, such as, "Boys have different things in their innards to girls. Only girls can get milk out of their bosoms, and they haven't got a penis" (J. Smith & Russell, 1984, p. 1114). These biological attributions decline in frequency beginning between 7 and 10 years, with most older children and adults saying that boys and girls act differently because their mothers and fathers treat them differently (J. Smith & Russell, 1984; Ullian, 1976). Girls shift from biological to socialization explanations for sex differences sooner than boys, perhaps realizing more quickly that they are physically capable of doing certain things, such as riding their bike home from the library in the evening, but are limited by social conventions or parental restrictions.

The Role of Cognitive Development

In addition to acquiring the relevant biological knowledge, children's greater understanding of sex constancy is also due to their increasing cognitive capacities. With age and experience, children become better able to consider multiple representations of events and discrepancies between appearance and reality, for example, recognizing that someone who appears to be a boy could really be a girl underneath the masculine clothes. Many preschoolers say that John has become a girl as the result of wearing a dress, having long hair, and playing with dolls because the appearance of the altered picture is more salient and compelling than their memory of the initial reality. Because the task involves a conflict between immediate appearance and remembered reality, children can be easily confused about what is being asked. C. Martin and Halverson (1983b) found that when some children claimed that a person had changed sex, they seemed to mean that the person was "dressing up" or "pretending" to be the other sex. When these children were asked if a person could change sex "for real," most said no. Similarly, if reminders of the starting point are available, children tend to perform better. For example, when the same proper name ("John") was used throughout the task, children were more likely to say John was still a boy than when only a neutral phrase ("this child") was used (Beal & Lockhart, 1989). The sex constancy task may therefore underestimate children's knowledge in the sense that some young children may know perfectly well that biology determines one's sex but become temporarily confused when they see the picture transformed to resemble the other sex. Of course, it could also be argued that the reason children become confused by the task in the first place is that they do not really understand what makes one male or female.

Children's reasoning on the sex constancy task is correlated with their general level of cognitive development, as measured by several Piagetian tasks that involve conflicts between appearance and reality (Marcus & Overton, 1978). For example, the child who understands that pouring liquid from a short, wide container into a tall, thin one does not change the amount, and who realizes that a sponge painted to look exactly like a piece of black and white granite is still really a sponge, is also likely to realize that a boy does not become a girl by changing into girls' clothing and wearing a ribbon in his hair (S. Brown & Pipp, 1991). A similar correlation has been found between children's understanding of conservation and ethnic constancy (Aboud, 1988). Knowing that external appearances do not necessarily correspond to an underlying reality seems to be the specific aspect of cognitive flexibility that is most important to understanding gender permanence. Another study found no relation between performance on the sex constancy task and another measure of general cognitive flexibility, a test of "divergent thinking" (Carter & Patterson, 1982). This task involves asking the child to think of possible novel uses for a common object, such as a bowl (e.g., use as a bucket or wear as a hat). Performance on the divergent thinking task is correlated with general intelligence, but not gender permanence.

■ Gender Identity: Effects on Behavior

One of my students was writing a paper on sex typing in children's play and posed the following hypothetical question to his 8-year-old brother: "Ben, if I gave you a Barbie doll to play with, would you make her play house or would you make her shoot guns and do karate kicks?" Ben's response was, "I wouldn't do it. I wouldn't do it. I wouldn't touch the Barbie doll." When asked to explain why not, he looked at his big brother and said condescendingly, "Because they're for girls, you dumbhead!"

One tenet of the cognitive-developmental perspective is that as children learn their own sex, they will be motivated to learn more about gender role expectations, to seek out appropriate role models, and to conform to what they think is expected of them as boys or girls. We have already seen an example of this in the earliest stages of gender identity:

Toddlers who know their own sex are more stereotyped in attitudes and behavior than their age-mates who have not yet learned to use gender labels accurately. Similarly, preschoolers who have reached subsequent milestones in gender identity become more strongly stereotyped and more selective in their patterns of attention to role models, their willingness to adopt new behaviors, and avoidance of cross-gender behaviors (Eaton, Von Bargen, & Keats, 1981; G. Levy, 1991; C. Martin & Little, 1990; Stangor & Ruble, 1987, 1989). For example, once children master gender consistency, that is, the notion that one stays the same sex across situations, they are more likely to watch same-sex role models. In one study, children were shown a movie of a male and a female actor (Slaby & Frey, 1975). The screen was divided so that the child could watch either the male or female actor but could not see both simultaneously. Children who had not yet acquired sex consistency spent equal amounts of time looking at the two sides of the screen, while children who had mastered consistency spent more time watching the actor whose sex matched their own. Similar patterns have been found in children's attention to male and female actors when they watch TV at home; gender-constant children are more likely to watch the program when same-sex actors are on the screen (Luecke & Anderson, 1993).

Knowing that they are boys or girls also helps children decide whether to adopt new behaviors, since they can match their own sex to the sex of a potential role model. For example, in a study by Ruble, Balaban, and Cooper (1981), children saw a film that included a short commercial for a plastic movie-viewer toy. The viewer had been previously established to be highly attractive to both sexes. Half the children saw the viewer demonstrated by a boy in the commercial, while the remaining children saw it demonstrated by a girl. Later, children were given the opportunity to play with the movie viewer themselves. Children who still thought that they could change sex played with the viewer regardless of the model's sex; for example, a boy would happily play with the viewer even if he had seen a girl use it in the commercial. In contrast, children who knew they would always be a boy or girl carefully avoided playing with the viewer when it had been demonstrated by a model of the other sex. In another study, gender-constant boys played more with an uninteresting toy that had been demonstrated by a male model than a very attractive toy demonstrated by a female model (Frey & Ruble, 1992). Gender constancy did not strongly affect girls' behavior in this study, possibly because girls are generally less strongly sex-typed even after acquiring gender constancy and probably felt less conflict about approaching a highly attractive boys' toy. In contrast, boys were careful to play it safe and leave the girls' toy alone even if they secretly thought it was pretty neat.

In general, gender identity predicts both children's attention to same-sex role models and their avoidance of new behaviors that are perceived to be for the other sex. However, gender identity does not always mean that a gender-stereotyped behavior will increase in frequency, because many behaviors have already been well established by this point. For example, achieving sex constancy does not increase children's preference for same-sex toys because most have already shown this preference for several years (Blakemore, LaRue, & Olejnik, 1979; Bussey & Bandura, 1992; Emmerich & Shepard, 1984; Marcus & Overton, 1978; Stangor & Ruble, 1987). Similarly, girls who had achieved sex constancy were more likely to seek out other girls as play partners than girls who had not yet acquired sex constancy, but no relation was found for boys, probably because, as we will see in the next chapter, the boys had already learned to avoid playing with girls (Fagot, 1985a; Smetana & Letourneau, 1984). In contrast, in the movie-viewer study described above, children had not seen the toy before and were therefore in the position of deciding whether it was appropriate to play with; in this situation, gender identity was clearly influential.

GENDER AS AN ORGANIZING PRINCIPLE

Besides gender identity, the other side to the cognitive-developmental coin is children's use of gender schemas to make sense of their social world. Children learn to organize information in memory according to whether it is associated with males or females. Because gender is thought to be an either-or category, children resist the notion that males and females might sometimes behave in similar ways, are critical of others who deviate from traditional gender roles, and exaggerate the differences between the sexes. Gender thus becomes a sort of mental filter through which children can interpret and evaluate others' behavior. In addition, children begin to guide their own behavior in terms of its perceived appropriateness for their own sex. Over time, children's need to be like others of the same sex and, by definition, different from the other sex leads them to act differently. Children's interests, skills, and even speech styles become increasingly gender-typed as a way of enhancing their sense of being male or female. In the following sections we look at children's use of gender as an organizing principle for interpreting others' behavior and guiding their own.

■ Reasoning about Others

Reasoning about other people is much easier when they can be classified as male or female, because schemas organize information in memory under the category labels "male" and "female." These categories or clusters of information allow us to make inferences about what a particular unknown male or female might be like, by looking up the typical characteristics of males or females and assuming that the new exemplar will be similar to those who have already been encountered. Categorical processing is a powerful cognitive mechanism that can be very useful; after all, if we had to treat each person we met as a completely unique individual without being able to make any assumptions about what they might be like, we would not have time to do very much else in life. The corresponding drawback is that our tendency to rely on stereotyped information in our schemas often leads us to ignore the unique characteristics of the individual.

Although adults are susceptible to stereotyping, children are more likely to rely heavily on gender labels to make predictions about others, even when more detailed information is available (Berndt & Heller, 1986; Eisenberg, Murray, & Hite, 1982; C. Martin, 1985). For example, when children were told a story about a little boy who liked to play with dolls, they still predicted that he would also like to play with a truck, despite the information that this particular boy had feminine play interests. In contrast, adults reasoned that if this boy happened to like dolls, he might also like to play with a kitchen set. Conversely, children find it very hard to reason about someone's interests when they do *not* know if the person is male or female (C. Martin & Wood, 1987). Even when children are told that the person likes dolls, they cannot imagine what other toys the person might like unless they know whether the person is a boy or girl.

Additional evidence of the inferential power of gender schemas comes from a study in which children were either told that someone was a boy or girl (gender category) or told about a particular characteristic the person had (gender property) (Gelman, Collman, & Maccoby, 1986). In the study, children were first taught that boys had "andro" in their blood, while girls had "estro." Children were then shown a picture of a child that was sex-ambiguous. Some children were told that the picture had andro and were asked if it was a boy or girl. That is, they were given a specific characteristic and had to figure out if it was typical of boys or girls. Most of the children found this very difficult to do. In contrast, children who were told that the picture was a boy and were asked if it had estro or andro easily inferred that it had andro. Gender schemas make it easy for children to make inferences about others, in this case, that if someone is a boy, he must also have various characteristics that are associated with being male.

■ Memory Effects

Gender schema theory argues that children will attend to, process, and store more information perceived to be sex-appropriate, while information that is inconsistent with the schema will be ignored or forgotten. Several studies have shown that children remember actions and characteristics that fit their stereotypes better than information that is schema-inconsistent (Meehan & Janik, 1990). In one case children were told stories about male and female characters who engaged in both traditional and atypical actions; for example, in one story about a circus, the girl was described as fixing a broken bicycle seat, while the boy sewed a clown costume (Koblinsky, Cruse, & Sugawara, 1978). Later, the children were asked which character had done the different things in the story; for example, did the girl or boy sew the clown costume? Children remembered the gender role–consistent information in the story much more accurately than the inconsistent actions. The same pattern was found in a study of children's memory for pictures. Liben and Signorella (1980) showed children a set of pictures, including some of boys engaged in feminine activities such as sewing and girls in masculine activities such as directing traffic. After a 5-minute delay the children had to pick out the original pictures from a larger set; again, they recognized pictures showing gender-consistent activities more than those showing gender-inconsistent activities. Picture recognition is generally extremely good, so the children's failure to recognize some images that they had seen only a few minutes before was striking. Children even remembered more information about a song if the lyrics were gender role–consistent (Britain & Coker, 1982). C. Martin and Halverson (1981) suggest that children's tendency to recall only stereotype-consistent examples creates an "illusory data base" which leads to gender distinctions being exaggerated in the child's image of the world.

How do we know that children's memory is actually being influenced by schemas, rather than that they simply have trouble remembering some stories and pictures? First, the memory errors are highly selective; children do not appear to have trouble remembering information as long as it fits their expectations. Also, information about male characters who had been shown engaged in feminine activities is particularly likely to be forgotten; if memory errors were random, children should remember these examples at least as well as those showing females engaged in masculine activities. Second, there is evidence that children with stronger gender stereotypes are more likely to forget the inconsistent information than their peers who hold more egalitarian beliefs (Liben & Signorella, 1980; List, Collins, & Westby, 1983; Signorella & Liben, 1984). That is, the stronger the schemas, the more children overlook schema-inconsistent information. This pattern has not been observed consistently, perhaps because most children are already strongly stereotyped at this age and so the relation is hard to demonstrate (Cann & Newbern, 1984; C. Martin & Halverson, 1983a).

In some cases, schema-inconsistent information may attract special attention and be remembered because of its novelty (C. Martin & Halverson, 1981; Trepanier-Street & Kropp (1986). For example, when children heard a story about a boy who wanted to be a ballet dancer, they recalled more details from the story than those who heard the same story about a girl (Jennings, 1975). Although they remembered it better, many children did not like the male version of the story, called it "stupid," and asked for a different story!

Whether schema-inconsistent information will be remembered or forgotten depends on how long it is before children are asked to remember and on whether they must recall the information or recognize it. Recognition is generally easier and more accurate. Trepanier-Street and Kropp (1986) showed kindergarten and second-grade children photographs of children playing with various toys, including some toys that were atypical for the models' sex (e.g., a boy playing with a Barbie doll). When the children were asked to pick out the original photographs from a larger set of distractor pictures a week later, even the kindergartners were quite good. The sight of a boy playing with Barbie apparently had made a strong impression! When children have to recall the information instead of recognize it, they are more likely to rely on schemas to fill in gaps and missing information, leading to distorted memories. C. Martin and Halverson (1983a) showed children pictures of boys and girls engaged in gender role–consistent and –inconsistent activities. For example, some children saw pictures of a boy fixing a stove and a girl cooking at a stove, while others saw a girl fixing a stove and a boy cooking. Recalling the inconsistent pictures accurately on an immediate memory test, children showed that they had noticed the gender role reversals. However, after a week's delay they often reversed the sex of actors to be consistent with the activity (e.g., the picture of the boy cooking was remembered as a picture of a girl cooking). Often seeming completely unaware that their memories had changed, the children were very confident that they had seen a girl cooking and explicitly denied that they had seen the picture of a boy at a stove. In general, children who have relatively strong gender stereotypes are more likely to show such memory distortions than are less stereotyped children (Liben & Signorella, 1980; C. Martin & Halverson, 1983a).

Such memory distortions can occur very quickly (Cordua, McGraw, & Drabman, 1979; Drabman et al., 1981). In one study, children saw one of four films depicting a doctor and nurse examining a patient (Cordua et al., 1979). Actually, there were four versions of the film: one showed a male doctor and female nurse, the second a male doctor and nurse, the third a female doctor and male nurse, and the fourth female doctor and nurse. The respective roles were clearly emphasized in the script: the nurse took the patient's temperature, and the doctor came in, examined the patient, and wrote a prescription. After watching the film, the children were asked to describe what they had seen a few moments before. All the children who had seen the film of the male doctor and female nurse recalled the film correctly, as did 91 percent of those who saw the film of the female doctor and female nurse. However, when the role of the nurse was played by a man, there were many memory errors. Only 22 percent of those who had seen the male nurse and female doctor identified them correctly, and most reversed the information in memory and said that they had seen a male doctor and a female nurse. Similarly, when children saw a male doctor and male nurse, half said that both men in the film were doctors. Note that the distortions centered around the male character; many children accepted that the woman could be a doctor but not that the man could be a nurse!

Not only can gender schemas induce memory distortions, they can interfere with learning new information. Carter and Levy (1991) taught children to play a game in which they had to pick the "right one" out of a pair of pictures of toys. The picture sets varied along two dimensions: size and gender typicality. For example, on one trial a child would be shown a picture of a small doll and a picture of a large truck and on the next trial a large kitchen set and a small baseball bat and ball. On each trial the child guessed which picture was "right" and received feedback. Although the children were not told explicitly what made one picture right and the other wrong, they quickly figured out that choosing the toy that was typical for their sex was the right strategy. After the game had been played for a while, the adult switched from rewarding one dimension (i.e., gender typicality) to the other (i.e., size). Thus, a child who had figured out to always choose the sex-typical picture suddenly found that this was no longer the "right one." Most children quickly picked up on the shift and began choosing on the basis of the other dimension, that is, size. However, individual children who were highly stereotyped took significantly longer to recognize a shift away from gender to size than other children who were less sex-typed. Strong gender schemas made the gender typing of the pictures highly salient, making it hard for children to ignore the gender information when it was no longer relevant to the game.

■ Exaggerated Stereotyping

Gender schema theory also helps explain why many children go through a period of rigid stereotyping. Many parents have heard their children say that only women can be teachers or only men can drive cars, remarks that are puzzling when parents know perfectly well that the children have encountered male teachers and female drivers. One mother reported that her little girl said one day, "Women don't fish," although they lived on a canal, had often seen women fishing, and the girl had asked for a fishing rod of her own only a few days before (Statham, 1986). While children's cognitive capacities are still fairly limited, it is easier to ignore the exceptions than to revise their emerging gender schemas to include them. Maccoby (1980) suggested that children may even temporarily exaggerate gender distinctions in an effort to get them clearly in mind. Confronted with an apparent exception to a gender stereotype, they often mark it as special. When children were asked to label pictures of people performing various jobs, such as nurse, carpenter, pilot, secretary, with each occupation being illustrated once with a man and once with a woman, they either mislabeled the picture (e.g., calling a female doctor a nurse) or used a linguistic marker (e.g., saying, "It's a *lady* spaceman"). The errors and linguistic markers occurred as often for males in gender-atypical occupations as for females (D. Rosenthal & Chapman, 1982).

In addition to trying to deny that exceptions exist, children at this stage can also be quite critical of others who deviate from traditional gender roles. Damon (1977) told children a story about a little boy named George who liked to play with dolls and who

Calvin and Hobbes

by Bill Watterson

wanted to wear a dress to school. Children were asked what they thought of George's behavior, if his parents should make him stop playing with dolls, and what they thought he should do instead. Four-year-olds generally thought that George should do whatever he wanted to. As one child eloquently put it, "It's his mind, not mine." Yet by the time children were 5 or 6 they had become quite critical of George. They thought that he was wrong to play with dolls or wear a dress to school and argued that his parents should punish him to make him to stop. Many preschoolers are made uneasy by deviations from expected roles because they do not yet really understand what makes someone male or female—that is, they have not yet mastered sex constancy concepts. Children often become more tolerant when they realize that being a boy or girl depends on biology, not on how one is dressed or what one does (Ullian, 1976; Urberg, 1982). Eight- and nine-year-olds thought that George was not really doing anything wrong and should be allowed to continue, although they pointed out that other children would probably tease him. One child said that George's parents might be disappointed if he kept playing with dolls but that they should be more understanding and try to remember what it was like to have a favorite toy!

Stereotyping eventually declines when children realize that many gender role behaviors are merely social conventions adopted out of convenience, habit, or custom (Carter & Patterson, 1982). At first, children view them as moral imperatives, and so violations are perceived to be very serious. Stoddart and Turiel (1985) told kindergartners and elementary school students several stories that included gender role transgressions (e.g., a boy who wore barrettes and nail polish) as well as other types of social transgressions (e.g., a boy who pushed another child off a swing or a girl who broke school rules by eating a cookie in class). The kindergartners thought the gender role violations were just as bad as hurting other children or breaking school rules, while the older children regarded them as comparatively harmless matters of personal choice.

■ In-Group, Out-Group

In children's minds, the same-sex and other-sex schemas are not equal; their own is better. One father was horrified to overhear his 5-year-old son tell his little sister, "Too bad you're a girl. Boys are better" (Meltz, 1991). C. Martin and Halverson (1981) term this the "in-group, out-group" phenomenon and suggest that it increases children's motivation to fit in with one group and to avoid the behaviors that characterize the other group. This begins almost as soon as children learn that they are boys or girls; for example, toddler girls think that girls are nice and boys are mean, while boys think that boys are nice and girls are mean (Kuhn et al., 1978). Older children often simply assert that their own sex is better, tossing out negative remarks about the other sex, such as, "boys are the best, girls have no brains"; "girls have brains, boys are just dirt" (J. Smith & Russell, 1984, p. 1114). Children also claim various socially desirable traits (e.g., sticks with a problem, is clever) are more typical of their own sex than the other sex (Albert & Porter, 1983; Koblinsky et al., 1978). Part of the motivation for learning to be a member of one group probably comes from constructing that group as superior.

Of course, the in-group, out-group phenomenon eventually creates a conflict for little girls, who start out believing that being a girl is better but later realize that feminine characteristics are less valued within the surrounding culture (Kohlberg, 1966). Girls do acquire certain stereotypes more slowly than boys, perhaps as a result of this conflict. For example, 3- and 4-year-old girls do not yet believe that certain careers, such as fire fighter, doctor, and pilot, and certain personality attributes, such as independence and bravery, are exclusively masculine, but 3- and 4-year-old boys do (Albert & Porter, 1983; Kuhn et al., 1978). Five- to nine-year-old girls claim that both sexes would like certain toys, while boys are more likely to say that particular toys are only for boys (Frey & Ruble, 1992). Older girls recognize the advantages of being male: Baumgartner (1983) asked elementary school children to describe how their lives would change if they became a member of the other sex and found that girls often thought they would be better off as boys; in particular, many girls mentioned that they thought they would have had closer relationships with their father if they had been a boy. One said, "If I were a boy, my Daddy might have loved me." In contrast, boys thought that girlhood would be a fate worse than death; one wrote, "If I woke up and I was a girl, I would go back to sleep and hope it was a bad dream" (Tavris & Wade, 1984, pp. 209–210). Girls generally are more flexible and more aware of the costs of rigid stereotyping than boys. Since boys' beliefs that they are superior to girls are reinforced by their observations of the surrounding culture, they have little motivation to change. A similar pattern has been observed in studies of children's developing sense of ethnic identity. Identification with one group often seems to involve a corresponding denigration of other groups. In contrast to children of minority groups, white children have been found to identify with their own group and to be biased against other groups relatively early, because these tendencies are reinforced by discriminatory attitudes in the surrounding culture (Aboud, 1988; Kleinke & Nicholson, 1979).

■ Self-Regulation of Behavior

We saw that children who are advanced in gender identity concepts are more careful to avoid other-sex activities than their peers. Generally, children's behavior depends on their perceptions of whether an action is sex-appropriate and enhances their sense of themselves as belonging to one gender role rather than the other. The either-or nature of gender roles is apparent in that if children think a new toy or activity or behavior is for the other sex, they will avoid it for themselves. Children also tend to exaggerate differences in how the sexes act, for example, in their ways of talking.

New Interests

Children's willingness to adopt a new activity is determined by its perceived gender-appropriateness. If they know that other children of the same sex have played with a toy, they tend to choose it also, and their interest and persistance in an activity is higher if they think it is something that others of the same sex have done (Bradbard & Endsley, 1983; Liebert, McCall, & Hanratty, 1971; Perry & Perry, 1975; A. Stein, Pohly, & Mueller, 1971). In one case children were asked to try out a new game which involved tossing marbles into the body cavity of a plastic clown as it spun around on a rod (Montemayor, 1974). Some of the children were told that the game was "a toy for boys, like basketball," others were told it was "a toy for girls, like jacks," and the remaining children were told only that it was a brand new toy, with no gender-related information provided. When children thought the clown game was appropriate for their sex, they rated it as much more fun than those who perceived it as gender-inappropriate, and they actually played the game better, in the sense that they tossed significantly more marbles into the clown. Perceived appropriateness thus predicts both interest and task performance, a finding that, as we will see in Chapter 11, has considerable implications for girls' difficulties with math and boys' problems with reading in school. In other words, if you believe that a task such as husking corn is something that the other sex typically does and does well, then you will be less interested in learning to husk corn yourself, you will not try quite as hard to learn how to do it, and you will accept lower performance as being about the best you can expect—even though you actually had the ability to be a star corn husker if you thought it was something your own sex usually did. One international track coach noticed that female athletes' times were now low enough to suggest that a woman could run a 4-minute mile and suggested that only the psychological barrier of being considered unfeminine was preventing a woman from doing so (Turnbull, 1988).

Speech: Talking like a Lady

Children regulate other aspects of their behavior to conform to their ideas about what is appropriate for their gender role and to distinguish themselves from the other gender. For example, boys and girls learn to speak differently, with girls generally using more correct and polished speech than boys (Andersen, 1984; J. Coates, 1986; Edelsky, 1977; Graddol & Swann, 1989). The differences reflect the assumption that gender roles should be opposites: Boys should talk "rough" and girls should talk "posh." Most of the research on boys' and girls' speech has been conducted in England where there are strong regional and social class accents, making it easier to see how sex differences in speech styles emerge over childhood and adolescence.

One way boys and girls learn to differentiate their speech is by adjusting the pitch of their voices. Among adults, the average pitch of male voices is lower than that of females, but there is so much overlap in range that the two sexes could speak at the same pitch if they chose to do so. With practice, women can adjust the pitch of their speaking voice to fall within the typical range for males. For example, the actress Lauren Bacall acquired her distinctive husky voice by sitting in her car and reading aloud. Margaret Thatcher had professional speech training to lower her voice into the male range for her political speeches, because lower voices were considered to be more authoritative (Graddol &

Swann, 1989). Conversely, there are cases of men whose voices had apparently never dropped at puberty. However, when they spoke through a masking device that prevented them from hearing their own voice, their pitch dropped, suggesting that they had unconsciously trained themselves to speak in the pitch range typical for women (Graddol & Swann, 1989). These findings suggest that the sexes tend to choose pitch ranges that will clearly distinguish women's and men's voices. In some cultures the differences are exaggerated, for example, Japanese women speak at a much higher pitch than men, while in other cultures the differences are not as extreme (Loveday, 1981).

In addition to learning to speak at different pitches, girls generally use more correct, standard speech, while boys adopt more "vernacular" speech, which involves slang, stronger accents, and more use of nonstandard grammatical constructions, such as "ain't": "How come that ain't working?" or "You ain't been around here." Vernacular forms of "what" and "be" are found in working-class British English and U.S. black English: "The new record what they've got out" and "Sometime she be fighting in school" (Romaine, 1984). Differences in boys' and girls' use of vernacular speech are apparent by middle childhood and early adolescence. Cheshire (1982) studied a group of adolescents in Reading, an English town where people spoke with a very strong regional accent and used many nonstandard grammatical constructions. Vernacular speech can be difficult to study because people usually shift into more formal, correct speech when talking to a stranger. To get around this problem, Cheshire hung around the local playground with a tape recorder for several weeks; she explained that she had a job to find out what people thought of the town, shared her candy and cigarettes with the boys and girls who played there, and recorded their speech. She found that while both boys and girls used nonstandard speech with their friends, boys did so more than girls, often to display their masculinity and "toughness." Similar patterns of girls using more polite and "correct" speech than boys of the same age have been observed among schoolchildren in Scotland, Sweden, and Japan and among Italian-American children in Boston. In some languages, such as Japanese, males and females must use different terms and grammatical forms for the same sentence, and parents and teachers correct Japanese schoolgirls who use boys' words by saying, "You're a girl, don't forget" (Rudolph, 1991).

Girls not only speak more grammatically, they tend to lose regional accents as they get older. Margaret Thatcher's accent became noticeably more "refined" over the years of her career in British politics. In contrast, boys tend to retain distinctive regional or working-class accents. In fact, linguists who study vanishing dialects try to find elderly men as informants because they are the only ones who are likely to still have their childhood accents (Romaine, 1984). Why do girls lose their accents while boys retain them? For males, a strong working-class accent and slang speech are associated in listeners' minds with physical labor and, thus, masculinity (Trudgill, 1972). In contrast, a woman's femininity is enhanced by sounding more wealthy and educated—more like a lady of leisure. Listeners do interpret stronger accents as more masculine. In one study, adults listened to tape recordings of young boys' and girls' speech and tried to guess whether the speaker was a male or female. Half the children were from working-class families, while the others were from British aristocratic families. Adults could usually tell if the speaker was a boy or girl, but when they made a mistake, working-class girls were usually mistaken for boys, while upper-class boys were thought to be girls (Edwards, 1979). So boys who keep their lower-class accents are in fact emphasizing their masculinity in a way that listeners recognize.

Two lines of evidence suggest that boys and girls actually learn to speak differently to enhance their identity as a boy or girl. First, most children can switch from standard to vernacular speech when the situation calls for it, showing that they choose to speak in a particular style in order to fit in with a particular group. Most of the Reading children recorded by Cheshire (1982) used standard English in school but switched to the vernacular style when with their friends. There are also some situations where boys speak more correctly than girls. One study of Swedish students found that when rehearsing for job interviews, boys were less likely than girls to use the local dialect. The researchers suggested that boys were more concerned with making a good impression on a prospective employer. Second, children themselves are conscious of the sex differences in pitch and grammar. Children raise their voices when pretending to be a female, and even babies babble at a higher pitch when near a woman instead of a man (Andersen, 1984; Graddol & Swann, 1989). Children associate grammatical, nonaccented speech with being ladylike. One child said, "The boys just talk any old way. The girls take more care in talking" (Romaine, 1984, p. 131). Some 12- to 14-year-old British girls denied they had a Birmingham accent (a broad, nonprestigious accent) even when hearing themselves on tape. Children also disapprove of girls using slang (de Klerk, 1990). Cheshire found that "good" girls used more standard speech than "bad" girls, that is, those who skipped classes, smoked, and engaged in petty crimes. Thus, girls who have rejected the traditional feminine role also avoid some of the speech patterns typically associated with girls.

At this point it should be clear that children are not passive recipients of gender role socialization messages from parents and other adults; rather, they actively observe the world around them, notice that males and females tend to do different things, figure out their own gender assignment, and then alter their behavior accordingly. Some of the otherwise-puzzling aspects of children's behavior, such as their attempts to deny that men can be nurses and their assumption that their own gender is superior, can by explained by the notion of gender schemas, cognitive structures that are organized around the assumption that the sexes are different and that influence children's view of the social world, increasing their convictions that males and females do different things and that they had better figure out what is appropriate for their gender and be careful to avoid behaviors associated with the other gender. This process begins early in children's lives, and gender becomes part of their sense of who they are, with being a boy or girl forming one of the building blocks of their developing self-concept.

THE POSSIBILITIES FOR CHANGE

It is something of an understatement to say that children are not passive recipients of gender role stereotyping; if anything, their internal motivation to conform to gender role expectations can lead parents to feel that the task of raising nonsexist children is hopeless. However, understanding that this occurs because of the child's need to organize information about the social world and his or her place within it can reassure parents and reveal possibilities for change. Two approaches have been suggested, first, programs that challenge children's gender stereotypes once they have been established and, second, strategies for preventing the formation of gender schemas in the first place.

■ Direct Intervention

Work has been done on effective ways to alter children's stereotypes (Katz, 1986). This is not always easy, because gender schemas lead to selective attention and memory and are self-sustaining once established. As we have seen, showing the child examples of male nurses will probably have little immediate effect if a child has already decided that only women can be nurses, because the inconsistent information will be distorted or misinterpreted to confirm the stereotype. Bigler and Liben (1990) found that a much more direct intervention was needed to help children widen their beliefs about appropriate occupations for men and women. In a 5-day program at a summer camp they taught children that interest and skill, rather than gender, were important in deciding who could get various jobs. For example, children learned that if Ann liked to build things (interest) and had learned how to drive big machines (skill), she could be a construction worker. At the end of the program, children thought a larger number of occupations were appropriate for both men and women. Such intervention programs should include both men and women instructors because other researchers have found that children, especially boys, are more willing to try nontraditional activities when asked by a male interviewer rather than a female (Katz & Walsh, 1991).

■ Raising Gender-Aschematic Children

While direct teaching about the irrelevance of gender challenges the underlying premises of children's gender schemas and can be effective, it is clearly a somewhat laborious task. Bem (1983) proposes an alternative, namely, that children should be prevented from latching onto gender as an organizing principle in the first place. Children form schemas based on gender because their observations of the world around them reveal that gender is predictive. If the child sees that most of the child-care workers, shoppers in the grocery store, and people at the laundry are women, the inference will be made that these are the tasks that females do, even if parents say that girls can do anything. Thus, the solution is to create a world in which, from the young child's point of view, these activities are *not* correlated with gender. Some support for this prediction is found in studies of European children which suggest that those growing up in cultures with relatively flexible gender roles (e.g., Holland) have fewer stereotypes than their age-mates who live in cultures with more traditional gender role divisions (e.g., Italy) (Best et al., 1977; Zammuner, 1982).

To reduce children's tendency to form schemas based on gender, parents can use several strategies. First, they can work to reduce the "cultural correlates" of gender. In the early years of the child's life, they could take turns sharing household tasks, driving, lawn mowing, repairs, and other activities, so that the child does not assume that some tasks are done by women and others by men. Parents can also seek out examples of adults in nontraditional occupations, for example, by enrolling the child in a nursery school which has male teachers or taking their pets to a clinic run by a female veterinarian. The child's exposure to television programs and books would need to be monitored so that sexist portrayals are avoided; Bem suggests rewriting stories and changing illustrations by drawing over them to change male characters into females and vice versa. In the classroom, when a new toy or activity is introduced, teachers can clearly signal that it is appropriate for both sexes. For example, if a teacher asks a boy and girl to demonstrate a fishing game, children of both sexes will play with it later.

A second strategy is to provide the child with a more narrowly defined schema for males and females, one based on biology. People are males if they have a penis and testicles, females if they have a vagina and clitoris, and it does not matter how they dress or wear their hair. As we saw earlier in the chapter, children who have the relevant biological knowledge early are less likely to rely on external cues to determine gender. Although this has not yet been tested directly, the implication is that young children with biological knowledge should also be less strongly stereotyped. Of course, explaining to children that the primary difference between males and females is biological rather than cultural can lead to some amusing episodes when children act on this knowledge. Bem (1983) described how her young son wore barrettes to school one day and was told by another little boy that he must be a girl because "only girls wear barrettes." Exasperated, her son pulled his pants down to show the other boy that he had a penis, but the other child found this evidence unconvincing and said, "Everyone has a penis. Only girls wear barrettes." One parent found that her children would greet visitors to the home with remarks such as, "Have you got a penis? Can I see it?" (Statham, 1986, p. 60). After explaining to her 2-year-old daughter that boys had penises and girls had vaginas, a mother found that while shopping, the little girl would shout exuberantly to clerks and passersby, "We're girls! We have 'ginas!"

Parents can also try other strategies to reduce gender schematic processing in children. When children make overgeneralized inferences, such as, "Men mow the lawn," parents can gently point out the wide range of individual variation, for example, by saying that while some men do, some women also mow their lawn, such as Mommy and Mrs. Allen down the street, and some men do not, such as Mr. Rankin next door. As children get a bit older, parents can also discuss sexism directly with them by pointing out that some beliefs about and restrictions on males and females are simply unfair and wrong.

While some of these suggestions would be time-consuming for parents to follow, they are not in themselves particularly extreme. Even parents who are not strongly committed to feminist ideology might want to limit the child's exposure to commercial television programming, make sure the child has a clear understanding of the biological differences between the sexes, and help the child avoid relying on stereotypes about other people.

SUMMARY

In this chapter we have examined the third theoretical perspective regarding children's learning of gender roles, one that emphasizes the role of the child in his or her own socialization. Beginning in the toddler period, possibly even toward the end of the first year of life, children come to know their own sex, and this provides considerable motivation for them to learn the corresponding gender role through observation of role models and to adhere quite rigidly at times to what they believe is appropriate behavior for their gender. In addition, children seize on gender as an organizing principle, classifying people and objects as male or female, memorizing information in schemas organized in terms of gender, and making inferences about others according to gender stereotypes. Once established, gender schemas are difficult to alter, making children quite ruthless in their tendency to view the world in terms of gender.

■ Comparisons with Other Theories

Both the cognitive-developmental and psychoanalytic perspectives emphasize the importance of biological knowledge as a key component of children's gender role learning. Cognitive-developmental theory shows that once children understand the permanence of gender, that is, its genital basis, they are increasingly motivated to conform to gender role expectations. The psychoanalytic perspective also emphasizes children's understanding of anatomical differences between the sexes and its role in the oedipal crisis. Both theories also assume that the effect of the biological information may depend on the child's state of receptiveness. Very young children might have seen that people are physically different but not yet be cognitively capable of relating these observations to people's behavior. Similarly, Freud thought that young children might have noticed that the sexes were anatomically different but that this knowledge did not have special impact until the child was in the oedipal crisis. The two theoretical perspectives differ, however, in that Freud thought that the discovery of the anatomical difference between the sexes served to exacerbate the psychological crisis and push development forward. The cognitive perspective does not claim that children's awareness of the physical differences between the sexes is necessarily accompanied by envy on the part of girls and fear of castration on the part of boys and, in fact, shows that much learning about gender roles occurs well before children understand much about reproductive biology.

While the social learning and cognitive-developmental theories emphasize different mechanisms—patterns of reinforcement and observational learning versus gender identity and gender schematic processing—both assume that children's own conception of the self as male or female is important and that children will rely on role models as sources of information to guide their behavior. In social learning theory, children must be able to match their own sex to the sex of a potential role model for observational learning to be possible, implying that gender identity is necessary. In cognitive-developmental theory children may know their own sex, but they must look to others around them to know what this means in terms of actual behavior. Thus, the theories are complementary; neither is sufficient alone. By "adding on" components of the cognitive-developmental perspective, we can account for some of the inconsistencies left unexplained by social learning theory; for example, some reinforcements are ineffective because they conflict with the child's emerging gender identity or are provided by someone perceived by the child to be an inappropriate role model.

■ Strengths and Weaknesses of the Cognitive-Developmental Perspective

A strength of the cognitive-developmental perspective is that gender role learning is thought to occur as a function of more general developmental processes. Young children need to establish a self-concept and need to construct schemas to organize information about the world; while gender is one basis on which to accomplish these developmental goals, it is by no means the only dimension that children consider. In addition, unlike the psychoanalytic perspective, no special developmental mechanisms are required to account for the learning that occurs.

The cognitive-developmental perspective assumes that gender, rather than other characteristics such as age, religious background, or ethnicity, becomes a central component of our identity and schemata because gender is emphasized so much in the surrounding world. This leads to the prediction that if gender were not given so much social emphasis, then children would probably not rely so heavily on it as an organizing principle. Of course, this claim has yet to be tested, and it is hard to see if it ever could be subjected to a strong test since although gender roles have changed dramatically over the last century or so, they have been revised rather than eliminated completely. It is possible that gender is so powerful an organizing principle that human society could not be structured without some sort of division between male and female roles; certainly no such society has ever existed that we know of. Yet the evidence that gender identity is learned during late infancy and early childhood, rather than being an inborn part of our sense of self, suggests that it is not necessarily an inevitable social distinction.

The primary weakness of cognitive-developmental theory is that it is incomplete; we have not yet accounted for the entire process of gender role socialization. We know that children are not passive recipients of messages about gender roles, but we still need to consider the sources of these messages, particularly since we know that while parents' influence is important, it is also limited: Children clearly look beyond their own homes to determine the cultural correlates of gender. The additional sources of information in the larger society, including peers, schools, and the media, will be the topics of the following chapters.

7

BEYOND THE FAMILY: THE POWER OF PEERS

"Boy, I hate girls. Don't you just hate girls, Michael?" At his friend's question, Michael, a 5-year-old, looked puzzled for a moment. He hesitated and then responded heartily, "Yeah, I really hate girls too!" His mother, who described this incident, doubts that Michael will hesitate at all the next time he is called to pledge allegiance to his gender. She also felt that 5 years of careful parental effort to avoid gender stereotyping in his upbringing had instantly been neutralized by his little friend's remark!

For the young child, other children are an important source of information about gender roles, clearly rivaling parents in their influence. Sex differences in behavior are often more apparent when children are observed with their peers than when they are alone or with adults (Carpenter, Huston, & Holt, 1986; Maccoby, 1990). The strong influence of peers is related to children's need to establish a gender identity, which as we saw in the last chapter becomes important in the toddler and preschool periods, because one way to feel that you are a real boy or girl is to act like others of the same sex. Both boys and girls are strongly influenced by their peers, but the asymmetry of gender socialization will be especially apparent in this chapter. We often think of girls as being the more sociable sex, but boys are actually more peer-oriented during development, imitating one another and influencing what they will and will not do. Far from being rugged John Wayne–type individualists, most little boys have a strong need to fit into the male peer group. Boys rely on one another as role models because they must avoid doing anything that might be perceived as feminine, while girls have relative freedom to act like boys and so do not need to copy their female peers quite as closely.

In this chapter we examine why children start to play primarily with other children of the same sex, the nature of boys' and girls' friendships, and the interactions of mixed-sex groups, specifically, how the skills of friendship developed with one sex put children at a disadvantage with the other sex. Finally, we consider how adults can influence children's peer relationships and whether they should attempt to do so.

SEPARATE WORLDS: GENDER SEGREGATION IN PLAY

▮ Toddlers and Preschoolers: Pulling Apart

One striking feature of children's play is that boys like to play with other boys, while girls generally prefer other girls. This preference begins in the toddler period, continues through the preschool years, and increases during middle childhood (Fagot, 1991; LaFreniere, Strayer, & Gauthier, 1984; Maccoby & Jacklin, 1987; Serbin, Moller, Powlishta, & Gulko, 1991). Observations of 1- to 6-year-old children attending a large daycare center showed that girls started the process: Girls made most of their social overtures to other girls by about 2 years, but boys did not show a clear preference for boys until about 3 years. By the time children were 5 to 6 years old, 70 percent of their social approaches were made to same-sex peers. Children also smile more at others of the same sex and rate others of their own sex as much more likable (Cheyne, 1976; Hayden-Thomson, Rubin, & Hymel, 1987; LaFreniere et al., 1984). This preference for others of the same sex has been observed in many other cultures and seems to follow roughly the same time course, emerging in the toddler period and increasing through middle childhood; for example, observations of the recess play of kindergartners in mainland China showed no instances of mixed-gender play (Shepard, 1991; Whiting & Edwards, 1988).

Dominating other characteristics such as ethnicity, gender is one of the most salient characteristics in children's decisions about a potential playmate (Hartup, 1983). For example, a white boy would rather play with a Hispanic boy than a white girl. Observational studies of the cafeteria of an integrated school revealed that white and African-American boys would sit together at one lunch table rather than join a group of girls at another table (Schofield, 1981, 1982). While these preferences are strong, they are not completely rigid; children will play with a child of the other sex when the supply of same-sex peers is limited—for example, in a neighborhood with only a few children—and they will also play with an other-sex child who is different in age. Deaf and hearing-impaired children are also less likely to show gender segregation in their play because they will overlook gender differences if they find another child who can sign (Lederberg, Chapin, Rosenblatt, & Vandell, 1986). In general, however, gender dominates children's decisions to play with or avoid another child.

Children's preference for their own sex does not seem to be due to adult influence; in fact, it is most obvious in situations that are not directly supervised by adults (Carpenter et al., 1986). If a parent or teacher is present, boys and girls are often quite willing to play or work with one another, although there may be some token complaining. An adult's presence apparently frees children from the social consequences of appearing to have chosen freely to interact with the other sex. A boy who with a girl is handing out milk cartons in the lunchroom does not have to defend himself to his friends, since the teacher made him do it. Maccoby (1986) gives an example from a private school in which teachers and parents were strongly committed to the avoidance of stereotypical gender roles. Boys and girls interacted easily, with one exception: The teachers had organized an early-morning baseball program for children who arrived at the school before classes began and made sure that the girls were fully integrated into the teams. There was only one aspect of the game that had not been structured by the adults: the two benches where players sat while waiting for their turn at bat. The children decided among themselves that the girls would sit on one bench and the boys would sit on the other. A similar pattern has been observed in other cultures. For example, Harkness and Super (1985) studied boys and girls in Kokwet, an agricultural village community in the highlands of Kenya in which even very young children have regular household tasks, such as watching chickens and weeding the garden. Children are supervised by adults until they are about 6 years old and show relatively little preference for their own sex during this period. However, as soon as parents give children greater autonomy, boys and girls choose to be with others of the same sex. For example, boys might meet together to supervise cattle, while girls share their tasks of watching babies and gardening. Some of the sex segregation is due to the different types of work that boys and girls are given, but their preference to be with same-sex others is most apparent when adults are not around.

If not the result of adult influence, what causes gender segregation in children's play? There are two reasons: First, children prefer playmates of the same sex because of compatible styles and, second, their need to establish a gender identity motivates them to want to be with others who are like them.

Behavioral Compatibility

One reason children prefer their own sex is that they simply get along better, with similar styles of interaction and similar interests. The key factor in compatibility seems to be the partner's social responsiveness, with girls being more responsive and cooperative, while boys are more often assertive and even domineering. Jacklin and Maccoby (1978) observed pairs of previously unacquainted 3-year-olds in a playroom stocked with several attractive toys. The children had not yet attended nursery school programs or day care and were thus having one of their very first meetings with another child of the same age. Their parents had been asked to dressed them in sex-neutral clothing, such as corduroy pants and a plain t-shirt, and adult observers could not always reliably tell whether the children were boys or girls. Despite the lack of obvious cues to the other child's gender, when two toddlers of the same sex were paired, there was quite a bit of social interaction; boys got along well with boys, and girls with girls. However, when a girl and boy were paired, the level of interaction dropped, and the girl was more likely to stand near the adult while quietly watching the boy play with a toy.

Why do girls decide that they do not want to play with boys? Girls do not seem particularly afraid of their male peers and can defend themselves and their property quite well if attacked. In particular, girls use their verbal skills to insult boys; one 3-year-old girl shouted, "You cucumber!" to a bewildered—and intimidated—boy (Pitcher & Schultz, 1983). Rather, girls begin to avoid boys because they discover that boys are often not very cooperative playmates. In the playroom, when one child tried to take a toy, the other would often say, "No!" or "Mine!" Girls tended to comply when told no by another child, but boys often did not. If little girls learn that their male peers are socially uncooperative, it would not be surprising if they preferred to play with other children who are more responsive, namely, other girls. In fact, the little girls who are the most tomboyish, confident, and assertive are the first to seek out other girls as playmates in preschool (Jacklin & Maccoby, 1978; Maccoby, 1986).

While girls are the first to seek same-sex play partners, boys subsequently show an even stronger preference for their own sex than do girls. The challenging style of play that girls dislike seems to attract other boys (Pitcher & Schultz, 1983). Thus, the sexes seem to move away from one another during early childhood because they enjoy the way that others of the same sex play and are less enthusiastic about the style of the other sex. A major component of this style difference is the presence or absence of mock aggression, termed *rough-and-tumble play*, which is more common in male-male pairs.

Rough-and-Tumble Play

Rough-and-tumble play typically includes wrestling, mock punching, shoving, tussling, and chasing, but it can be distinguished from true aggression because there is no intent to hurt, it occurs usually between boys who are already good friends, and it is accompanied by smiles and laughter rather than hostility. In addition, the roles of dominant and submissive partner (e.g., the one chasing and the one being chased) are frequently exchanged in rough-and-tumble play but not in real fighting. Boys show more rough-and-tumble play than girls when children are about 3 or 4 years old and continue to do so throughout childhood (DiPietro, 1981; Humphreys & Smith, 1987; Pitcher & Schultz, 1983). Boys do not initiate this type of play with girls, and girls do not seem to enjoy it very much, which again increases the division of the sexes into separate play groups. Boys' greater enjoyment of rough-and-tumble play may well have a biological component, as similar sex differences are found in the play of young primates (Maccoby, 1988; Maccoby & Jacklin, 1980). In addition, fathers encourage more active physical play with boys beginning in infancy. Boys can find girls' style of play relatively boring by comparison. In one study of children's conversational skills children interacted with an "E.T." puppet that could engage in an animated conversation with them but did not move. Girls clearly enjoyed talking with the puppet but boys found the session tedious because the puppet did not *do* anything—it just talked (Benenson, 1991).

Cognitive Motivation

Children also seek out friends of the same sex because of their need to establish a gender identity. As we saw in Chapter 6, toddlers know they are boys or girls and think that their own sex is better. Preference for others of their own sex also begins at about this time, and children who are more advanced on milestones of gender knowledge, such as stability and constancy, are more likely to play with same-sex peers than their peers who lack this knowledge (Fagot, 1985b; C. Martin, 1991). Thus, once children get the idea that they are members of one group they are motivated to stick to that group. They also seem to assume that group membership confers privileges. When they approach a group of unfamiliar children, they are more friendly and less cautious if the others are the same sex, as if shared gender ensures them a certain amount of acceptance. C. Martin (1989) found that children assumed they would like another child of the same sex more than one of the other sex, even if the child had gender-atypical interests. That is, shared gender membership was more important to them than mutual interests, and as a result, children increasingly spend time only with those of the same sex.

Within their respective play groups boys and girls socialize one another into traditional gender role behavior by punishing those who deviate from gender role–appropriate activities through making critical remarks, abandoning play with the friend who persists in doing something that seems inappropriate, or trying to get the friend to do something else. Expressions of approval and disapproval of peer play according to gender appropriateness begin by the age of 3, again, just as gender identity is being consolidated, and children quickly adjust their play accordingly (Lamb, Easterbrooks, & Holden, 1980; Lamb & Roopnarine, 1979; Roopnarine, 1984). Children are more careful to play with gender-appropriate toys when another child is present than when they are alone, even if the peer is doing something else and not actually interacting with them (Serbin, Connor, Burchardt, & Citron, 1979). Children who violate their peers' gender role expectations face social risks: Girls who try to join boys' rough-and-tumble games are usually unpopular with other girls, and they are not particularly well liked by boys, either (Humphreys & Smith, 1987; Serbin, Marchessault, Lyons, & Schwartzman, 1987). Similarly, cross-gender boys who do not like rough play tend to be strongly disliked by their peers, especially by other boys (see Chapter 13). One boy who had asthma and was not very strong was often targeted by other boys in soccer and football games; they would deliberately tackle him when he had the ball and then mock him for falling down and crying (P. Adler, Kless, & Adler, 1992). As the result of this mutual socialization into different types of play and interaction styles, the separation of the two sexes increases further.

■ Middle Childhood: "Border Work"

Avoidance of the other sex becomes quite pointed in the elementary school years. In one classroom children wrote letters to their classmates on a computer mail system as part of a new writing curriculum; over the course of the 6-month project boys wrote only to boys while girls wrote only to girls (Cazden & Michaels, 1985). Children become less sympathetic to the other sex and less willing to help them in the classroom, and they often invent rules that prohibit contact with the other sex during this stage (B. Bryant, 1982; Nelson-LeGall & DeCooke, 1987). Boys run from girls, because girls have "cooties," and create elaborate "disinfectant" rituals for cleaning themselves after contact with a girl. When contact between the two groups does occur, it is often tinged with romantic or sexual overtones. For example, a group of boys might dash through a jump rope game and deliberately entice the girls to chase them, or girls might run up and threaten to kiss a boy or call him after school and leave pseudo-sexy messages on the family answering machine (Adler et al., 1992). These brief contacts are often accompanied by shrieks of laughter and much excitement, considerably more so than occurs within the same-sex groups. Thorne (1986) calls this sporadic contact between boys' and girls' groups "border work." By acting as though contact with the other sex is forbidden and dangerous, children emphasize that there are clear boundaries between the two groups. The excitement connected with "raids" into the forbidden territory also suggests that children are highly aware of the other sex; Thorne suggests that border work serves as a sort of rehearsal for romantic activity while minimizing any extended contact or emotional involvement between the sexes that would be premature before adolescence. Supporting the idea that border work provides a rehearsal for adult romantic relationships, cross-cultural research shows that games where girls are chased by boys (rather than boys by girls) are typically found in societies where girls marry outside their own communities (Sutton-Smith & Roberts, 1973). Boys often pick on a girl whom they secretly admire, and send their friends to find out how she feels about them without ever talking directly to her themselves (Adler et al., 1992). Avoidance of the other sex is most commonly observed when children are around others of the same age; presumably the possibility of romantic interest does not come up when a boy and girl are significantly different in age (Ellis, Rogoff, & Cromer, 1981). One girl said that while she liked playing with boys she generally avoided doing so because, "...you can't say two words to a boy without them thinking you're immediately in love or something." (Statham, 1986, p. 37).

Elementary school children who violate these implicit rules will usually face considerable teasing from their peers, and few cross-sex friendships survive during this period. While studying friendship development, Gottman (1986) found that it was not unusual for preschool boys and girls to be best friends but that when he tried to study friendships among school-aged children, he could not locate any boy-girl friendship pairs among the children in his sample. He sent research assistants door to door in local neighborhoods to ask adults about children who might have a best friend of the other sex and was eventually able to locate several pairs of boys and girls who had been friends since they were preschoolers. These children still met after school to play and study together, but they now did so secretly. They did not play outdoors where they might have been observed by other children, and they ignored each other completely at school to avoid being teased about "going together."

BOYS' AND GIRLS' FRIENDSHIPS

As we have seen so far, young boys and girls create separate social worlds based on different styles, interests, and the need to be with others similar to themselves. Within boys' and girls' peer groups qualitative differences emerge in the nature of their friendships and their preferred activities. Boys become concerned with establishing status within a group of buddies, while girls are likely to create and maintain intimate relationships with one or two close friends. In the next sections we examine how these differences are expressed in the structure of boys' and girls' play groups, their preferred activities and games, and the language of friendship.

■ The Structure of Play Groups

Boys: "Top Dog"

Boys usually have larger friendship networks than girls and play in groups rather than pairs. These groups typically have an internal structure that reflects the relative social and physical power of the individual members. There will generally be an acknowledged leader, several of his close friends, and several peripheral members who are associated with the group through connections with one or two of the central group members. This type of organization is called a *dominance hierarchy*, because members higher in the hierarchy can safely challenge the ones below who have less social status and power. Dominance hierarchies among children are established by threats and challenges, the taking of toys to see if the other child will defend or retaliate, and sometimes through physical aggression (Pettit, Bakshi, Dodge, & Coie, 1990).

Boys are often concerned with maintaining or bolstering their status within the dominance hierarchy. Believing that they are more popular and powerful than they really are, boys tend to overestimate their own social status, and so they often react negatively when another child whom they perceive to be less prestigious or powerful tries to take something from them or to boss them around (Boulton & Smith, 1990). In one study children were brought into a playroom and had to try to join a board game that was already in progress with several children of the same sex—a situation somewhat analogous to joining an adult cocktail party. Asking bluntly for a turn and trying to draw attention to themselves, boy "guests" were more assertive than girls, but their assertive approach did not work very well because other boys did not want to yield a turn to a low-status stranger. Girl guests were less obtrusive; they waited quietly, watched, and made occasional comments until they were offered a turn and were actually more successful at getting into the game (Borja-Alvarez, Zarbatany, & Pepper, 1991).

Because boys need to establish and maintain status within their peer group, their style of interaction tends to be "restrictive," meaning that their behavior shortens or interrupts a play episode rather than prolongs it. For example, a boy might grab a toy away from another boy, making the other child leave to do something else; while this establishes the grabbing boy's dominance, it also effectively ends the social encounter! As a result, pairs of boys tend not to play together as long as pairs of girls who, as we will see below, avoid such direct challenges in their play (Benenson & Apostoleris, 1993). Boys' play themes also shift more quickly; for example, if two boys are pretending to fly a plane and cannot agree who will be the pilot, they might change to being race-car drivers and then to Ninja Turtles. Boys' concerns with being better, stronger, and more powerful than others also leads to the incessant themes of fighting, guns, and superheroes that are so prevalent in boys' play. Paley (1984) noted that the boys in her kindergarten class constantly pretended to be Batman, Superman, Darth Vader, He-Man, and other superhero characters so that they could feel powerful and invulnerable—like being at the top of a dominance hierarchy.

Girls: "Best Friends"

In contrast to boys, girls tend to play with one or two "best friends," and they try to maintain a relationship in which both parties have equal status (Eder & Hallinan, 1978). Because girls do not want status differences between friends, they try to avoid conflicts that create a clear winner and loser. Groups of three preschool boys or three girls were observed as they played on a small trampoline; boys argued with and challenged one another for turns on the trampoline, while girls set up turn-taking rules to avoid arguments about whose turn it was (DiPietro, 1981). When overt conflicts do come up—as they inevitably do—girls try to defuse the problem by suggesting a compromise, changing the topic, giving in, or trying to clarify what the other child wants, rather than by standing their ground and forcing the issue. For example, when two children were arguing over who found a toy first, one said, "We both . . . hey, we both found it, OK? OK?" (P. M. Miller, Danaher, & Forbes, 1986, p. 545). In another case two girls playing house each wanted a plastic pickle and began arguing. One proposed cutting it in half, but the other rejected this solution. The first girl evaded the problem by taking an orange and offering it as a conciliatory gesture, and they ended up agreeing that their quarrel had actually been part of their pretense, a face-saving solution that allowed them to continue the play (Sheldon, 1990). If girls are unhappy about something that another girl has done or said about them, they deal with the problem indirectly, by passing along criticisms from one girl to another without specifying the source (Goodwin, 1990). They also refer to abstract or adult standards of social behavior to make their point: "You have to put on your shoes. I'm going to tell the teacher." These strategies allow girls to express their feelings without appearing to be putting their own opinions or concerns above those of a friend. In contrast, boys exchange direct reprimands and insulting personal remarks with friends: "Hey, don't do that again ever. You put the blocks in my place," or, "Get off that board, you big stupid" (Pitcher & Schultz, 1983).

Girls' indirect approach to conflict resolution does not seem to be due to fear or a lack of self-confidence, because they can be very direct and confrontational with boys and with girls whom they do not consider to be friends. Rather, they avoid confrontations with friends because their priority is to maintain a relationship in which both partners are equally valued and of similar status, a goal that is inconsistent with a situation having a winner and loser. When one girl does take charge in a group, she will use much less direct strategies than a "top dog" boy would in the same situation. In one study, groups of four boys or four girls played with a movie projector that had been diabolically designed so that one child could watch the movie through a viewer only if another child held down a light button while a third child turned a crank. In both boys' and girls' groups there was usually one child who got more viewing time than the others by making the others do the work of running the projector, but the dominant boys and girls got their way by using different strategies: Boys tended to use physical strategies, such as pushing other boys away, while the dominant girls combined physical strategies with verbal persuasion, such as asking another girl to help, appealing to turn-taking rules, and saying she really *needed* to see the movie (Charlesworth & Dzur, 1987).

Although there are clear differences in the way that boys and girls relate to their friends, it is not merely that boys are dominant while girls are deferential. Boys do try to dominate others, but not everyone can be the leader in a dominance hierarchy, and everyone meets his match at some point. Thus, boys learn not only to assert themselves; they also learn how to defer, that is, to submit to and take commands from other boys who have higher status by merit of greater size, confidence, age, experience, or other factors. Just as boys are not always dominant in their peer groups, girls are not exclusively deferential either. Girls can be rather mean to others whom they do not consider to be their friends. One 4-year-old girl turned to her friend as another girl approached them and said, "Tell her we don't want to play with her. Tell her we don't like her" (Shapiro, 1990, p. 58). I recall forming with a friend in second grade a "horses" club whose primary activity seemed to be concocting devious membership tests to prevent other girls from joining. Girls resist forming new friendships, because establishing a new relationship takes away from existing friendships; by definition there can only be one "best friend." Girls talk explicitly about who their best friends are and negotiate where their ultimate loyalties lie. One sixth-grade girl wrote to a classmate, "Would you like to be my best friend, or are you O—'s best friend?" (Cazden & Michaels, 1985, p. 8). They spend much time in school passing notes in class and starting rumors and gossip about girls they do not like (Adler et al., 1992). One girl explained that while she wanted to spend less time with Laura, a popular girl, she was afraid of Laura's retribution:

> I don't know when I go in to school every day if she's been calling up other girls talking about me behind my back and getting everybody against me or not. She might decide at school that I've done something she doesn't like and turn everyone against me . . . she controls everybody, and I wouldn't have any friends. (Adler et al., 1992, p. 179)

While two girls may sometimes include another girl as a friend, these triadic structures tend to revert to dyads over time, when one girl insists on establishing which two of the three are really best friends (Eder & Hallinan, 1978). One of the saddest experiences of female childhood is for a girl to watch her best friend become best friends with somebody else and leave her out. In contrast, boys' friendship pairs tend to expand over time to include other boys, and boys do not make as sharp distinctions between who is a friend and who is not. Thus, while girls' social world is characterized by deference to friends, it also has a dark side of exclusivity and rejection of others.

■ Sex Differences in Favorite Games

Differences in the friendship patterns of boys and girls—dominance hierarchies versus dyads—influence the games and activities that boys and girls prefer. Lever (1978) asked fifth graders to record their play activities in diaries and then analyzed the children's games according to their relative complexity. Complexity was defined in terms of the number of different roles required in the activity, the relative interdependence of players, the total number of players, the number of rules, whether teams were involved, and whether the activity was competitive in nature. For example, according to this analysis basketball would be a more complex play activity than tennis, because tennis involves only two players, each of whom have similar roles, while basketball involves a team of five players who have different roles. Lever's analysis of the children's diary entries, supplemented by her playground observations, showed that boys were more likely to play competitive team games, that is, that boys' play was more complex, while girls were more likely to be involved in individual activities such as reading or listening to records. When girls did report playing competitive games, they tended to be individual sports, such as gymnastics and ice skating, which typically involve indirect competition, where the quality of each player's performance is evaluated against an absolute standard rather than through a direct challenge to another player or team.

Boys' and girls' game preferences reflect boys' greater enjoyment of rough play and competitive activities that will allow them to gain status, but adult influence is also involved. Sutton-Smith (1979) found that neither sex played many team sports a century ago, and it was only when adults began supervising children's play at school that boys' play became structured into team activities. Since the 1960s girls, too, have become increasingly involved in team games, such as soccer and basketball, and the proportion of time spent in such traditional girls' games as jacks, skipping, jump rope, and board games has steadily declined. However, boys still report liking skateboarding, wrestling, hockey, football, and war games more than girls (Bensoussan et al., 1992).

Boys' play, especially participation in team sports, is often thought to provide boys with important lessons—about cooperating with others, working toward a common goal, celebrating victory, and accepting defeat without taking it personally—to prepare them for handling competition as adults and working within hierarchically structured organizations such as the military or large corporations; by implication, girls are at a disadvantage for not having had these experiences (Borman & Frankel, 1984; Lever, 1978). This was one rationale for the effort to increase girls' participation in organized sports through the passage of the Educational Amendments Act (Title IX) in 1972. Before Title IX girls had few opportunities to participate in team sports. At one school in Michigan girls would practice for an entire season for *1 day* of competition with other teams, because the school buses were occupied with transporting boys' teams to their events. In another case a school rather desperately argued in court that it could not support a girls' swim team because the boys would no longer have been able to swim nude in the school pool. A similar situation still exists in Washington, D.C., today; female senators must arrange an appointment to use the Senate pool because some of the male senators still prefer to swim nude.

Girls' participation in team sports has increased significantly since the passage of Title IX, yet inequities in funding and opportunities still remain 20 years later. Girls' sports never attained the same level of support, and in tight financial times "the girls' programs were the first to be cut and the last to be reinstated," as one lawyer put it (Roche, 1992, p. 24). While most parents no longer object to girls' sports in principle, tempers can flare when giving girls more opportunities would mean cutting back on boys' programs. One father complained on behalf of his junior high school daughter that it was unfair for the school to support four boys' team sports but not one girls' team. He insisted on remaining anonymous because he was afraid that parents of boys would retaliate against his family.

Team activities probably do provide important developmental experiences for both sexes, but there are also advantages to girls' more collaborative style of play. For example, learning negotiation skills that will prevent the eruption of overt conflicts can lead to effective resolutions in which both parties are satisfied with the outcome. Increasingly, business leaders suggest that people who try to resolve disagreements by considering the needs of all parties are more effective managers than those who rely on a traditional zero-sum notion of competition, in which one party must lose if the other is to win. Those who cite Vince Lombardi's famous quote, "Winning isn't everything; it's the only thing," in defense of cut-throat competitive activities for children should keep in mind that he retracted this statement later in his life and said that he had not meant that winning was so important to be worth any cost.

■ The Language of Friendship

The qualitative differences in boys' and girls' friendships are also evident in their use of language. Boys enjoy games that allow them to achieve status and recognition through winning, and they also use talk to establish and defend their place within the group. Leaper (1991) arranged pairs of same- and mixed-sex children to play together and then analyzed their conversations in terms of whether talk was used to increase collaboration with the other child ("What do you want to do?" "Let's play superheroes," "I'll help you with that") or to dominate and control the play ("Don't do that," "You jerk," "That's not right"). Girl-girl pairs were more collaborative in their conversations; girls have also been found to make more self-effacing remarks ("I'm not very good at this; you try it") and to ask their partner questions, which gives the other person an opportunity to speak (McCloskey, 1987). In contrast, domineering remarks and insults are more common among the boy-boy pairs, for example, two African-American boys who were good friends had the following interchange:

CHILD 1: Why don't you get out of my yard.
CHILD 2: Why don't you *make* me get out the yard.
CHILD 1: I *know* you don't want that.
CHILD 2: You're not gonna make me get out the yard cuz you can't.
CHILD 1: Don't force me.
CHILD 2: You can't. Don't force me to hurt you. (*snickers*) (Goodwin, 1990, p. 37)

Other researchers have found that boys even lecture their friends and try to tell them what to do on the assumption that they know best: the "me better" approach (Cook, Fritz, McCornack, & Visperas, 1985)! Boys try to gain status and the attention of their peers by interrupting others and holding the floor by telling jokes and stories (Maltz & Borker, 1983). In a hierarchy, the only way to gain status is to displace someone else, so boys also learn to put others down through the use of verbal insults and tricks, termed "catches." For example, one boy began to explain to his friends that he had obtained a set of coathangers for making slingshots. He mentioned that his mother had some coathangers which led another boy to anticipate, "So she let you have 'em." The speaker triumphantly corrected him by saying that he had actually gotten the hangers elsewhere, a verbal score which was acknowledged by an appreciative whistle from the group leader (Goodwin, 1980).

In contrast to boys, girls' conversations with their friends are less directive and confrontational. In analyzing conversations between girls who were trying to make rings from bottlenecks, Goodwin (1980) found that girls typically used indirect verbal forms, such as "let's" and "we gonna," when discussing their plans. These forms suggest a possible plan of action and include the speaker as a potential actor, in contrast to direct commands for someone else to perform a task, such as boys' more explicit requests ("Gimme the pliers!"). The use of indirect forms can make girls' talk appear more tentative than that of boys, but it can be more effective because it avoids the social awkwardness that can result if no one thinks the suggestion is a good idea. In contrast, a boy whose request or suggestion is ignored by his peers is publicly embarrassed and loses status.

Linguists have proposed that, as adults, men and women sometimes have trouble communicating across sexes because they have learned to use language for different purposes while growing up in their separate worlds (Leaper, Bell, & Carson, 1991). Girls enjoy using conversations to establish and consolidate their friendships through sharing secrets and talking about their feelings. When asked to talk with their best friend about "something serious and intimate," 7- and 8-year-old girls quickly found things to talk about, while boys were uncomfortable in the situation with nothing to do but talk, and most of the boys' conversation focused on what they would do after the session (Tannen, 1990a)! As adults, men are often less likely to engage in general conversation with those close to them, since they have no reason to display or defend status to them, which can leave women disappointed with the lack of male conversational responsiveness (Tannen, 1990b). On the other hand, men are more likely than women to enjoy argument for its own sake, because it involves the use of language to establish and reinforce one's position.

When men and women were assigned to debate a topic, men liked their female partners more after the debate, but women liked their male partners less (Hogg & Turner, 1987).

Differences in conversational style are again not a simple matter of girls being deferential while boys are domineering. Boys often use deferential suggestions and indirect requests when addressing the group leader or boys of higher status ("Can I please have those pliers?" "Maybe we could go down to the river"). Girls' efforts to avoid verbal confrontations and to diffuse conflicts are apparent only in their interactions with their friends. With boys, and with girls whom they do not consider to be friends, they will often use heavy-handed strategies to get what they want, such as threatening to hit or issuing blunt commands: "You'd better get off there!" "Give me that!" In fact, girls can rank quite high in a classroom dominance hierarchy when their interactions with boys are evaluated (Strayer & Strayer, 1976). In the following conversation between a boy and girl who are playing checkers, the girl more than holds her own as she lectures him about moving his piece across the board:

> BOY: I'm moving here.
> GIRL: No, you can't.
> BOY: I don't care. (moves piece)
> GIRL: No! You gotta be right here and you go like that.
> BOY: No, you gotta be there and you go.
> GIRL: If you jump I'll jump you. (McCloskey, 1987, p. 149)

Boys and girls both have a dominant and deferential social style available; what develops is the recognition of when each approach is most appropriate and, in particular, which style works best with others of the same sex.

SEPARATE WORLDS: IMPLICATIONS FOR MIXED-SEX INTERACTION

One consequence of growing up in separate social worlds is that as children learn a style of interaction that works well with peers of their own sex, they become progressively less effective with the other sex (Bryant, 1982; Leaper, 1991; Serbin, Sprafkin, Elman, & Doyle, 1984). Girls learn to use polite suggestions rather than direct demands or requests, and other girls in turn are more likely comply with a polite suggestion than a direct request; that is, their emerging styles mesh well. In contrast, boys begin to use and respond only to direct commands. When the two sexes are later paired, boys end up dominating the interaction because they ignore girls' indirect suggestions and try to order girls about. When mixed-sex groups were observed in the movie-viewer studies described earlier, boys achieved the dominant viewing position *three times* as often as girls, who were willing to yield a place on the expectation of a reciprocal turn that never came (Charlesworth & LaFreniere, 1983; Powlishta, 1987).

Boys also end up dominating girls in conversation. Interruption rates are similar for boy-boy and girl-girl pairs, but in mixed-sex pairs boys interrupt girls twice as often as girls interrupt boys (Esposito, 1979)! Boys are also more likely to use direct requests and commands ("Gimme the red block") with girls than with other boys, as if secure in their superior social status (Hass, 1981). Adult speech has similar patterns, suggesting that children may learn by observation that male speech can be more forceful and direct (Bellinger & Berko-Gleason, 1982; Walters, 1981; Wanska & Bedrosian, 1991). Girls might also learn to expect softer speech from others, because parents use less direct language with girls and allow girls to have longer turns in a conversation (Cherry & Lewis, 1976; Golinkoff & Ames, 1979; Walters, 1981) . For example, parents say, "Put the wheel on there," and, "No, you can't have that," to boys and, "I think maybe it needs a wheel, don't you?" and "Not right now, sweetie, maybe another time," to girls. This might later leave girls unprepared to deal with boys' more dominating conversational style.

Not only do boys ignore girls' less direct style, girls' behavior also changes in mixed-sex groups; they become less assertive when paired with a boy than with a girl. In a mixed-sex play session girls make fewer direct requests to a boy than they do to another girl, they laugh more with boys, and they join in boys' topics of conversation, namely, sports (Hass, 1981). There is also evidence that girls hold back in competition with boys; they do not perform as well as they can when competing with other girls, even when the boys have less skill (Cronin, 1980)! For example, girls playing dodgeball with other girls showed as much skill as boys in avoiding the ball and hitting the target. But when they played against a male team, they did not play as well as they could, even when the boys had less skill and experience with the game. A similar pattern was found in an academic competition, a spelling contest. Boys volunteered to try spelling a word consistently more often than girls, even when they were worse spellers. While girls who were good spellers were willing to compete against girls, they would not do so against boys even when they could easily have won.

It seems unlikely that girls "back off" around boys because they are worried about being considered unattractive; some of these patterns are apparent in children as young as 4 years old who presumably are not yet aware that a girl who is too direct will not get many dates. As we saw in the last chapter, preschool girls have not yet accepted the idea that boys are better or are higher in social status, so it seems unlikely little girls' behavior is driven by feelings of relative inadequacy. A explanation based on social status also cannot explain why girls are highly deferential to other girls whom they view as their friends, that is, who are of equal status. It seems more likely that girls learn a way of relating to others that works well with female peers but later puts them at a disadvantage around boys; they do not like boys' domineering style of interaction or want to adopt it themselves, and this makes them cautious when they have to interact with boys. Regardless of the initial reason, continual practice from preschool in yielding to boys when the two are working or playing together is going to make it very difficult for a girl to challenge a boy to the best of her ability as an adult, particularly when the social costs of being considered less attractive are factored in when children move into adolescence.

While girls may not necessarily acknowledge boys as having higher social status, boys do seem to assume that they are superior to girls, as may be seen in their assumption that they can interrupt girls and tell them what to do. Boys can be hostile when they feel that girls are not sticking to their proper place. Ugly incidents of peer harassment on college campuses are an example, in which groups of young men surround and taunt a woman by exposing their genitals or insisting that she show her breasts before they will let her go. Women who are active in women's studies programs and feminist organizations and who most clearly threaten the assumption of masculine superiority are generally the targets of such peer harassment (Hughes & Sandler, 1988). On the other hand, boys are occasionally more willing to cooperate with a girl than with another boy, as if feeling that they can afford to be magnanimous and yield to a girl's suggestion or request without losing status as they would if they deferred to another boy.

Styles vary across cultures too; boys' focus on competition, status, and winning is most apparent among white children (Knight & Kagan, 1977). Conflicts can develop regardless of gender when the parties do not share similar values about dominance and the importance of winning. For example, in an informal basketball game between white and Navajo men, the whites were out to win while the Navajo seemed more to enjoy the activity for its own sake and did not always stick to the rules; the whites became frustrated and left early (Freedman, 1980). On President Bush's 1991 visit to Japan he viewed a ceremonial ritual in which several Japanese men tossed a ball back and forth. The U.S. President assumed it was a game and joined the activity; after a few turns he shouted, "We won!" to the consternation of his hosts.

ASYMMETRY IN PEER SOCIALIZATION

Peers are clearly important influences for both boys' and girls' gender role development, but in many ways little boys are more oriented than girls toward their peers. Boys still receive most of their care from mothers and from female teachers in school, and because male role models are relatively inaccessible, boys have to rely on their friends as guides for proper boy behavior. Boys are more likely than girls to imitate one another, for example, by shooting balls of clay across the art table, chanting, "Oh-oh-spaghettio," and bending over while ripping a newspaper for sound effects (A. Abramovitch & Grusec, 1978). Paley (1984) noticed that the boys in her kindergarten class often copied one another. For example, during one music lesson a high-status boy got up on one knee, tilted his head as if he was wearing a cowboy hat, and clapped to the rhythm of the song. Most of the other boys quickly copied him. Paley concluded that boys take all opportunities to distinguish themselves from girls: "If I am doing something only boys do, then I must be a boy" (Paley, 1984, p. 18). For boys, male peers can be even more influential than adults. Observations in a nursery school showed that the behavior of 2-year-old boys was more influenced by the reactions of other boys than by female teachers or girls. "[T]he male peer group starts defining what is *not male* very early, and . . . the behaviors that are defined as not male drop out of the boy's repertoire" (Fagot, 1985a, p. 1102; Lamb & Roopnarine, 1979).

Boys also do what their friends do because the social costs of deviating from expected roles are much greater for them than for girls. K. Zucker, Wilson, and Bradley (1983) presented elementary school children with versions of a story about a boy who engaged in varying ratios of feminine to masculine behavior. For example, one story described a boy who did typically masculine things during the day but also played with his favorite toy, a Barbie doll, after school. The mention of *one* feminine behavior led boys to say that they would not like the boy in the story, and their dislike increased steadily as more examples of feminine behavior were mentioned in the story. These findings are consistent with the results of observational studies showing that even as toddlers boys receive negative

ROBOTMAN® by Jim Meddick

Robotman reprinted by permission of NEA, Inc.

reactions from other boys for doll play, dress-up, dance, and art activities, including snatching away the offending toy, bumping or hitting the other child, walking away, or saying, "That's dumb, that's for girls" (Fagot, 1977; 1985a). A grade-school boy who has feminine mannerisms can become a social pariah, a target for teasing and rejection. One fifth-grade boy said of the class "sissy":

> When he sits in his chair, he crosses one leg over the other and curls the toe around under his calf, so it's double-crossed, like this [shows]. It looks so faggy with his "girly" shoes. And he always sits up erect with perfect posture, like this [shows].
> (Adler et al., 1992, p. 174)

In contrast to the strong rejection of boys who have even minor feminine characteristics, tomboys are generally accepted by their peers or at least do not meet with open hostility. As one mother said, "Little boys *have* to act like other boys if they are going to remain anywhere near the top of the food chain!"

THE POSSIBILITIES FOR CHANGE

We have seen in this chapter that peers are a strong influence on children's gender role behavior. Beginning in the toddler period boys and girls create separate social worlds in which they learn different lessons, with boys learning to assert themselves with a group of buddies, while girls establish intimate bonds with one or two close friends and learn to maintain those friendships through indirect conflict resolution. The learning that occurs within same-sex peer groups is valuable, but it is also one-sided and creates problems when boys and girls interact in the classroom or on the playground, because the social skills that work well with same-sex peers are less effective with the other sex. This asymmetry is particularly hard on girls, who often end up being interrupted and ignored by boys who have not yet learned the same skills of collaboration and conflict resolution.

Although gender segregation in childhood is not caused by adults, adults can influence the process by organizing activities to enhance interaction between boys and girls or to keep them apart. In many cultures cross-sex contact is strongly discouraged by adults; for example, in one Japanese school students are required to fill out an application form before talking with a schoolmate of the other sex (*Toronto Daily Telegraph*, 1991). Similarly, before the 1970s U.S. parents and teachers discouraged cross-sex play, particularly in organized sports activities. One reason was that adults were worried about the negative effects on boys of being beaten by a girl. No matter how athletically inept a boy was, he could reassure himself that at least he was better than the girls, without ever having to put this assumption to the test. Parents and teachers also worried that competing with boys would masculinize and would be too stressful for girls (Committee, 1974).

Support for girls' participation in mixed-sex sports has increased in the last 20 years, and parents and teachers have also become more interested in encouraging cross-sex interaction out of concern that boys and girls become strangers to one another as they grow up in their separate worlds. When children later become interested in romantic relationships, they often have very little knowledge about how the other sex thinks and feels, making them particularly vulnerable to stereotypic information in the media about love and sex. Encouraging children to interact would give them the chance to develop and maintain cross-sex friendships which might provide a better foundation for work and love relationships with the other sex later in life. Separation also means that boys and girls are excluded from the lessons and values learned within their respective play groups.

Interventions designed to increase cross-sex play can be quite effective, as long as adults are involved (Bianchi & Bakeman, 1978; Carpenter et al., 1986). Serbin, Tonick, and Sternglanz (1977) worked with nursery school teachers who wanted to encourage boys and girls to play together in their classrooms. After obtaining baseline rates of cross-sex play—which were low—the teachers were trained to recognize and reward instances of cross-sex play with attention, for example, by saying, "I like the way you're playing today." The teachers worked to provide such feedback every 5 minutes during the daily free-play periods, and over the 2-week experiment the frequency of cross-sex play increased steadily. The children were clearly sensitive to the adults' goals and willing to comply. However, when the teachers stopped commenting, the level of cross-sex play dropped again, suggesting that play with a child of the other sex was not sufficiently rewarding for children to keep doing it in the absence of adult rewards. The adults' attention during the intervention phase of the experiment may also have signaled to other children that the boy and girl had not necessarily chosen to play together on their own initiative. Without this "cover" children may have feared teasing from their peers.

Teachers and parents are sometimes discouraged at the difficulty of integrating boys' and girls' play, and some researchers are doubtful that it can be sustained without continued adult involvement. At times, there may even be unanticipated negative reactions. For example, in hopes of promoting positive cross-sex interactions, one study had boys and girls assigned to work in collaborative learning groups (Lockheed & Harris, 1984). While girls helped peers of both sexes, boys helped other boys in the group almost exclusively. By the end of the school year girls reported that they were even less interested in working with boys than they had been to start, as if their worst fears had been confirmed! Despite these drawbacks, providing children with opportunities to play and work with the other sex, even if under the continual direction of adults, probably still has long-term benefits. If adults emphasize that it is important to work and play with the other sex, children might be less likely to devalue the other sex, and it is probably especially beneficial for boys to learn that they will have to work with females as equals.

SUMMARY

As we have seen in this chapter, young children start to show a preference for play with others of their own sex during the toddler period, a preference that appears to be universal. While adults can influence the process, the development of sex-segregated play seems to result from children's finding the behavioral style of their own sex more compatible rather than from adult pressure. Once separate play worlds are established, boys and girls focus on different aspects of friendship, with girls being more concerned with mutual support and intimacy, while boys focus on issues of status and dominance. Playing with others of the same sex who have similar values helps children create a sense of group membership and reinforces their developing sense of gender identity. The peer group seems to be particularly important for boys, who are more likely than girls to imitate their peers and criticize those who violate gender role standards.

Although peers are strong influences, we have not yet shown where many of boys' and girls' ideas about friendships and appropriate interaction with peers originate. The family is one influence, but there is a wealth of information about expected gender role behavior available to children through schools and the media. Research on how this information influences children's developing concept of gender roles is discussed in the following chapters.

8

BEYOND THE FAMILY: SCHOOLS AND THE HIDDEN CURRICULUM

Within six months of starting school my child had abandoned the term "firefighter" for "fireman." He told me that I was not capable of rescuing him in play, as women had not got any muscles . . . I made special arrangements to leave work early to have a discussion with the teacher. But, at the end of the day, she was always surrounded by parents with specific concerns about their offspring. A quick glance at the queue, the photograph money to be collected, the pictures to be mounted, the part-finished wall display, the books awaiting marking, the equipment to be tidied and the work to be prepared for the next day and no wonder my tentative comments received a weary reply. (J. Rose, 1989, p. 15)

As this mother found, schools can have as much impact as parents on children's ideas about gender roles. Even if parents do not place much emphasis on being a boy or girl, gender is a highly salient dimension in the classroom. Informal distinctions are made between boys and girls about 20 times during a typical school day, including different lines for assembly, separate places for boys and girls to hang up their coats, separate listings on the class roster, different tasks such as collecting milk money versus carrying crates of milk cartons, spelling competitions between the boys and girls, and so on (Delamont, 1990). School is also a setting in which children have extended contact with their peers which, as we saw in the last chapter, tends to increase their adherence to traditional gender roles. In addition, schools are often the child's first point of contact with the expectations of the larger society beyond the family. One of the functions of school is to prepare children to fit into this larger world of adults by instilling the kinds of behavior that are considered appropriate within the society, such as "acting like a lady" or being "a leader among men." Along with learning academic subjects such as reading and math, an implicit educational goal is for children to learn the behaviors that are considered appropriate for boys and girls. These

135

implicit lessons have been termed the "hidden curriculum" (R. Best, 1983; Kessler, Ashenden, Connell, & Dowsett, 1985).

Several decades of research have documented that boys and girls have very different experiences within the same classroom. There is also clear evidence that gender socialization in the classroom is asymmetric: Boys absorb the bulk of the attention and instruction from teachers and the relative neglect of female students contributes to a loss of confidence by the end of high school. In addition, there is growing evidence that school serves as a setting in which boys learn to feel superior to their female classmates, increasing girls' sense of discouragement. As one researcher put it, "There is no other group, other than females, who come into school ahead and end up falling behind. . . . This suggests that there is something fundamentally wrong with their schooling" (Black, 1990). Yet as the mother quoted above found, few teachers have the resources and support to tackle the problem on their own even if they are sympathetic to parents' concerns about gender stereotyping in schools; thus, the problem has persisted.

In this chapter we explore how teachers interact with boys and girls, analyze why teachers treat boys and girls differently, and examine the consequences for the sexes in terms of their interest in challenging work and their self-confidence. Then we consider how school serves as a setting in which peer influence is exacerbated. Finally, we consider the possibilities for change.

INTERACTIONS WITH TEACHERS

In most classrooms teachers spend the majority of their time watching and interacting with boys, leaving girls to work and play quietly on their own. Teachers do not *deliberately* favor boys, yet somehow the classroom becomes organized around the needs and interests of boys. Boys demand attention, teachers provide it, and girls learn to politely wait their turn.

Compliant Girls, Rambunctious Boys

In a typical classroom girls can be seen waiting quietly in line to have a worksheet checked, waiting with their hands up to be called on during a lesson, and playing indoors at the art table or in the dress-up area, while boys yell out answers during lessons, race around the yard on big-wheel tricycles, topple over block towers, and push each other in line. Teachers' patterns of attention to boys and girls enhance boys' assertiveness while encouraging girls to be compliant and dependent. Teachers are most likely to pay attention to them when the girls play quietly indoors, which encourages girls to adopt quieter, more sedentary, and structured activities (Carpenter & Huston-Stein, 1980). Teachers generally notice when a girl does something wrong, such as poke the class gerbil with a stick through its cage bars or yell at a classmate, only when the misdeed occurs close by, and teachers reprimand a girl quietly, as if out of concern that the girl not be publicly embarrassed (Serbin, O'Leary, Kent, & Tonick, 1973).

Teachers' behavior with boys is quite different; teachers are always watching boys, even if they are across the room, in anticipation of some misbehavior that could result in someone getting hurt, and they respond quickly to any hints of impending mischief in boys. If a boy picks up a block and looks threateningly at another child, the teacher will often quickly call out ("Joey, stop that!") or come over to intervene (Serbin & O'Leary, 1975). Teachers' watchfulness inadvertently has the opposite effect than intended: Many boys enjoy the public attention they receive for behaving badly; even though the attention often consists of a scolding, reprimand, or lecture about why the behavior is unacceptable, the boy is still "in the limelight" for a moment, with everyone in the class staring at him. This, of course, tends to increase the probability that the boy will misbehave again in the future, while girls do not have the same incentive to act out in the classroom.

These patterns reinforce the lessons that boys and girls have already learned at home. Recall from Chapter 5 that parents responded warmly to daughters who stay close by and ask for help and often overlooked girls' early attempts to be assertive, while boys were encouraged to play independently and learned to misbehave to attract parental attention. Not surprisingly, when a boy or girl develops problem behaviors in the classroom, they tend to be on different ends of the behavioral spectrum: A child who is undercontrolled, unable to sit still and attend to lessons, and who is always pestering and distracting friends is more often a boy than a girl. In contrast, the student who is overly quiet and passive, afraid to try something new without being shown exactly what to do, is more likely to be a girl. These patterns are extreme forms of the everyday behaviors encouraged in typical boys and girls. One little girl had begun to irritate her preschool teachers because she clung to them so closely and refused to play with other children. The teachers were at their wits' end from nearly tripping over her every day and finally made the difficult decision to speak to her only when she was with another child. After a few days she ventured away and quickly became much more independent (Serbin & O'Leary, 1975). This suggests that it is not the children that are so different but that they are reacting to different patterns of adult attention.

■ Instruction

When we turn to actual instruction, we find that boys again garner the bulk of teacher attention. In preschool classes boys get twice as much informal learning contact with teachers than girls do. In one class experimenting with Piagetian concepts of volume that are important for cognitive development, children poured liquids from one container into another. After the teacher let several of the boys try pouring the liquids, she put the materials away without giving a little girl a turn, although the girl had asked several times for a chance (Serbin & O'Leary, 1975). At elementary school, boys also receive more formal instruction than girls even though the two groups are sitting in the same classroom. In one study researchers observed over 100 fourth-, fifth-, and sixth-grade classrooms from widely differing communities over a 3-year period. Teachers were consistently more likely to call on boys during lessons and engage them in class discussions. Boys were considerably more assertive—they were eight times more likely than girls to call out an answer in class—but this was encouraged by the fact that teachers accepted boys' spontaneous contributions but not girls'. If a girl shouted an answer, the teacher would often tell her to raise her hand, and wait her turn, but when a girl did raise her hand, she was much less likely to be called on than a boy (G. Jones, 1989; L. Morse & Handley, 1985; M. Sadker & Sadker, 1985; Windass, 1989). The *type* of instruction boys receive is also of higher quality; teachers ask boys more open-ended questions, whereas girls are more often asked for simple facts or

Doonesbury

BY GARRY TRUDEAU

questions that can be answered with a "yes" or "no" (Meece, 1987; Stitt, 1988). In a demonstration history lesson William Bennett, former secretary of education, frequently pushed male students for more critical analysis of the issue but responded to girls' contributions with brief comments of "Fine," "Good,"and "OK." Praise is rewarding, but it cuts off contact with the teacher and does not require the girl to defend her points and come up with a deeper analysis of the problem (Shuy, 1986).

Not only do boys receive more instruction, they receive more help than girls when they have trouble with a question. Teachers will give a boy more hints and second tries if he answers incorrectly, as if suspecting that he might really know the right answer, as in the following example from a fourth-grade class:

> TEACHER: What's the capital of Maryland, Joel?
> JOEL: Baltimore.
> TEACHER: What's the largest city in Maryland, Joel?
> JOEL: Baltimore.
> TEACHER: That's good. But Baltimore isn't the capital. The capital is also the location of the U.S. Naval Academy; Joel, do you want to try again?
> JOEL: Annapolis.
> TEACHER: Excellent. Anne, what's the capital of Maine?
> ANNE: Portland.
> TEACHER: Judy, do you want to try?
> JUDY: Augusta.
> TEACHER: OK. (M. Sadker & Sadker, 1985, p. 56)

Note that Joel received help from his teacher in figuring out the right answer, and then she praised him for his success! This kind of adult support in problem-solving is called "scaffolding." It is a very effective kind of instruction because the child's self-confidence is enhanced if he or she comes up with the right answer, and it promotes independent problem solving in the future. As the example shows, girls get less scaffolding help; when a girl gives the wrong answer, the teacher will often simply supply the right one or move on to another child, without giving her a hint or second try. One reason is that teachers, like parents, are more protective of girls; when they do push girls, it can be quite uncomfortable. At a recent colloquium I sat behind a female graduate student who rather timidly asked a question after the talk. Unfortunately, her question was not very well thought out, and she struggled a bit to explain her point. The speaker first listened calmly, letting her try to articulate her idea, and then responded with a strong criticism of the student's point and kept her on the hook by asking, "And if what you suggest is correct, how would you account for the following finding?" By this point most people in the room felt terribly uncomfortable; it was almost painful to watch the interchange. Yet the speaker—a distinguished woman professor from another university—was being perfectly polite and, more important, was taking the woman student seriously. Several of us realized later that if the student had been a young man, we would not have thought twice about the incident but viewed it as training in intellectual debate which is part of the graduate school experience and which male students have received since elementary school.

Gender and Ethnicity

Although girls receive less attention overall than boys, the extent of this differential treatment also depends on ethnicity and social class. Teachers pay more attention to children from middle- and upper-middle-class families than those from working-class families, and white children are expected to be higher achievers than minority children (Alvidrez & Weinstein, 1993; Dusek & Joseph, 1983; M. Sadker, Sadker, & Klein, 1991). White girls receive more teacher attention than black girls, who are equally likely to approach their white teachers but are sometimes unconsciously rebuffed and more often feel isolated and left-out in school as a result (American Association of University Women [AAUW], 1992; Damico & Scott, 1987; L. Grant, 1983). One teacher reluctantly admitted that her stereotyped expectations of her middle-class white female students as "nice girls" led her to favor them over the working-class black girls in her class; she said, "I think it does influence me . . . I do let them off the hook sometimes, and I shouldn't" (Askew & Ross, 1988, p 28). Correspondingly, although teachers give more attention to boys than girls, most is directed to white boys. African-American, Hispanic, or Native American boys receive less instruction and more criticism than white boys, and when they are disruptive, their behavior is viewed as much more serious than the same behavior in a white boy. For example, a black kindergarten boy was suspended for teasing a female classmate by lifting up her dress on the playground; it is unlikely that the same act by a white 5-year-old boy would have triggered such a strong reaction (Murrell, in press). Teachers do give positive feedback to minority students, but it tends to be more qualified than praise given to white students, for example, "Well, this section is pretty good, but you missed some of the long division problems," rather than "Excellent job on your arithmetic this week!" (AAUW, 1992; Askew & Ross, 1988; Freiberg, 1991).

■ What about Male Teachers?

Teaching *is* a strongly feminine-typed profession—about 86 percent of elementary school teachers are women, and many female teachers tend to hold relatively traditional views about gender roles themselves, believing that little girls should act like ladies and that "boys will be boys" (Delamont, 1990; Simpson & Erickson, 1983; Spender, 1984). Perhaps male teachers would be less stereotyped because their own career choice is nontraditional? Actually, researchers have found that male teachers also treat boys and girls differently. In fact, in some cases, by joining in boys' block play and outdoor games while praising girls who dressed up in princess costumes, male teachers made clearer distinctions than female teachers. In one study, male teachers were found to make comments on girls' appearance much more often than female teachers, for example, "You look pretty today," or saying to a girl in a science class, "She walks, she talks, she can even read" (S. Hill, 1991). Male teachers tend to have fewer years of teaching experience than females, and relatively inexperienced teachers tend to allow themselves to be influenced by gender stereotypes more than teachers who have been in the classroom for many years and put academic objectives first by rewarding quiet, task-oriented behavior in both sexes. There is also little evidence that merely having a male teacher improves boys' achievement in school (Etaugh, Collins, & Gerson, 1975; Fagot, 1981; Gold & Reis, 1982; S. Hill, 1991; Meece, 1987).

However, most of this research has focused on white students. In the 1990s there has been a renewed interest in increasing the number of male teachers, particularly among African-Americans. School districts in several states, including Michigan, New York, Maryland, and Florida, have begun to experiment with gender-segregated classrooms with African-American men teachers and special academic programs in hopes of encouraging more boys to stay in school. At present there is little research on how teacher gender and ethnicity interact; it is possible that boys who are academically at risk might respond especially well to a male teacher of the same ethnicity (Murrell, in press; Riley, Holmes, Cornwell, & Blume, 1985; Sciarra, 1972). Unfortunately, the supply of such teachers is limited; fewer men are becoming elementary school teachers today than 30 years ago, and the percentage of teachers who are white remains steady at about 85 to 90 percent (Freiberg, 1991; *Valley News*, 1992a). And, there has been little discussion of the academic needs of black *girls*. Currently, federal courts have ruled that girls must be admitted to special programs for minority boys. As one judge put it, "There is no evidence the school system is failing males because girls attend school with them. Girls fail too" (*Boston Globe*, 1991d; E. Ray, 1991).

So far we have seen that teachers pay more attention to boys, both in terms of management and actual instruction. Girls become almost invisible; they are noticed only when they are nearby, they are given fewer opportunities to speak, and their errors and misdeeds are minimized. When teachers talk about their classes, the child who is repeatedly overlooked or whose name is frequently forgotten is most often a girl (Spender, 1982). Researchers have shown that these patterns are pervasive but generally overlooked; just as parents often feel that they treat boys and girls similarly, teachers and observers underestimate the extent of differential treatment of the sexes in the classroom. In one case teachers watching a film of a classroom discussion were convinced that the girls had made more frequent comments than the boys, when in reality the boys had talked *three* times as often as the girls (D. Sadker & Sadker, 1985). Why does this happen? In the next section we review factors that lead teachers to give boys more attention, often without realizing it or intending to do so.

■ Why Are Boys and Girls Treated Differently?

Are teachers just sexist? Some certainly are, like the male science teacher who shouted, "One thing I hate and detest is ignorant females . . . and this school is lousy with them these days," at his class (Delamont, 1990, p. 58). But there is more to it than the personal prejudices of a few teachers. Even teachers who are personally opposed to sexism find it hard to treat boys and girls similarly, often complimenting girls when they wear dresses ("My, you look pretty today!") and admiring boys for standing up for themselves with other children or for challenging the teacher ("What a tough guy!") (Joffe, 1971). Teachers respond to the characteristics of male and female students and to stereotyped beliefs about their intellectual potential.

Characteristics of Male and Female Students

Teachers certainly treat boys and girls differently, but we need to keep in mind that boys and girls have also learned to behave differently by the time they enter school, and that children influence their teachers as well as the other way around (Irvine, 1986; Meece, 1987). One reason teachers give boys more attention and instruction is that boys tend not to be quite as successful in school as girls of the same age. Boys find it harder to adapt to the demands of the classroom and feel a conflict between the behaviors that lead to academic success—being quiet, attentive, and adult-oriented—and those encouraged by the male peer group, such as being loud, independent, and peer-oriented (Brophy & Good, 1973; L. Grant, 1983; Meece, 1987).

Classroom management. "The boys plunge into things, interrupt discussion, can't keep still, can't wait. Ten boys in a class of 29 and they demand 50 percent or more of my time" (Askew & Ross, 1988, p. 29). As this teacher pointed out, boys more frequently call out answers, talk with their friends during lessons, get into fights, or burst out of line on the way to the cafeteria. Teachers often feel that girls can be safely left on their own for a few moments but that boys must be monitored to make sure that they are not getting into trouble. Although teachers give boys up to five times as much attention as girls, most of this extra contact involves teachers telling boys to behave themselves (Cherry, 1975; Serbin & O'Leary, 1975). Little boys are especially likely to become disruptive if they feel they cannot do something, in an attempt to cover up their inadequacies. One teacher started an indoor "Skip to my Lou" game one day, with the children skipping around the room in a large circle. All the girls knew how to skip, but some of the boys were not quite coordinated enough, and they quickly started pushing and shoving each other before anyone noticed their awkwardness. The game dissolved into an unruly brawl (Paley, 1984).

One way that teachers try to manage boys is through competition with girls, as in the following example from a British school:

> A male teacher informed a games class in Dock Side, who were clambering over items of sports apparatus, that the girls were "beating" the boys in climbing up the rope. Almost immediately the boys went into a paroxysm of activity in order to prove that they were "better." (Delamont, 1990, p. 28)

Teachers also try to discipline boys by the threat of forced association with girls; for example, by telling a boy that if he does not quiet down, he will have to work on an assignment with a girl. One teacher told the girls to line up first for recess and said, "Oh, Billy thinks he's a girl" when a boy stood up and tried to head out the door; he promptly sat down again. The problem with using such gender-based competition and control strategies is that the distinctions between the sexes are emphasized rather than minimized, and, in effect, girls' presence in the classroom is reduced to providing the motivation for appropriate classroom behavior in male students. Note that most girls do not seem to need the same efforts at motivation and control.

Achievement differences. Teachers also appear to favor boys not because they are sexist but because of boys' lower average achievement. Girls get higher grades on average throughout school, are more likely to graduate and go on to college, and are less likely to be diagnosed with learning difficulties than boys (AAUW, 1992). In classes of 25 to 30 students, teachers cannot give everyone individual attention in every subject, so they let the better students work quietly and learn the material with minimal instruction, and they give the bulk of their attention to those who do not appear to be mastering the material and who need prodding to focus on the work; more of these students are boys. Teachers often organize lessons with boys in mind to encourage them and keep them interested in the topic, for example, by planning activities that involve hands-on work, such as using microscopes, or competitions, such as math show downs and "Bookworm" contests. These activities are much more time-consuming than straightforward lessons and desk work but tend to involve students who might otherwise become disruptive. The focus on boys in planning lessons means that activities that girls enjoy, such as collaborative projects, are rarely used (AAUW, 1992; Askew & Ross, 1988; M. Sadker et al., 1991).

Stereotypes about Boys and Girls

Although teachers are influenced by the behavior of their students, teachers' treatment of boys and girls also reflects stereotyped assumptions about boys' and girls' ability. A child who is thought to be bright will often receive extra attention and more detailed feedback about the quality of his or her work ("Excellent job on these multiplication problems, but you can do better on your division; I want you to remember to check your digit carrying next time"). Such feedback can be a powerful influence on children's academic performance, regardless of their actual ability. In the following sections we look at teachers' beliefs about boys and girls and how these beliefs influence the kinds of feedback given to children about the quality of their work.

"Good student" versus "smart." Teachers generally report that girls are better students, nicer, more likely to concentrate on their work, and better-behaved in the classroom. More positive evaluations of female students are found across different ethnic and social class groups: Studies in Britain showed that teachers rated West Indian, Asian, and Cypriot children as poorer students than white children, but within each ethnic group they considered girls to be better students than boys. Similarly, in the United States teachers consider working-class children to be less promising students than middle-class children, but girls are more favorably evaluated than boys in both groups (Delamont, 1990). Girls' gender role behavior more often matches the behavior teachers expect in the classroom: The image of the "good student"—attentive, listening carefully to instructions, following the rules, focusing on the work, and not disrupting the class—matches the image of the "good girl" (Levitan & Chananie, 1972). Unfortunately, this suggests that the reason that girls get good grades is because they are careful, attentive workers, not necessarily because they

are smart. Again, these expectations interact with ethnicity; teachers are most likely to assume that an African-American girl's academic success must be due to hard work and that a white boy's success must reflect high ability (Askew & Ross, 1988; Cornbleth & Korth, 1980; Damico & Scott, 1987; L. Grant, 1984).

Teachers do associate masculine characteristics with intelligence, and have higher expectations for male students even though girls get better grades (Benz, Pfeiffer, & Newman, 1981; Bernard, 1979; Meece, Parsons, Kaczala, Goff, & Futterman, 1982). In one study teachers were asked to read descriptions of hypothetical students and to make predictions about how well the students would do in various subjects in the future. In the descriptions masculine and feminine characteristics were crossed with sex of student; for example, "John" was a good listener who encouraged others in classroom discussions, while "Jane" used logical arguments and was a discussion leader, and vice versa. Teachers predicted that both male and female students with feminine characteristics would have trouble in future studies. Even so, they expected that John the good listener would do better than Jane the good listener; that is, feminine qualities in John were taken as a sign of independence, self-confidence, and initiative, but the same qualities in Jane were viewed as a sign of lower ability! Girls with feminine characteristics were expected to have the most trouble in future classes, particularly in subjects such as math and physics (Bernard, 1979). Boys who ask questions, challenge the teacher about solutions, and do not follow the rules in working on problems are interpreted as showing real mastery of the material, whereas girls' correct solutions are dismissed as resulting merely from conscientious work. In both British and Israeli schools, teachers have been found to nominate many more boys to take national mathematics tests even though girls received the top class grades. The boys' undisciplined work suggested potential brilliance to their teachers, while the girls were viewed as good but not really creative students (Askew & Ross, 1988; Safir, 1986).

"Bad girls." If a girl is *not* a "good student," meaning that she does not sit quietly, pay attention, and do careful work, teachers view her much less favorably than a boy in whom disruptive behavior is perceived as natural (Levitan & Chananie, 1972; Meece, 1987). In one study, child "confederates" worked on two tasks with an adult, building with Tinker Toys and copying designs with an Etch-A-Sketch. The child was trained either to be socially responsive, that is, to smile, talk enthusiastically, and ask the adult for feedback ("How does this look, Miss Twinkles?"), or to be unresponsive, not looking or smiling at the adult and speaking as little as possible. When a girl behaved sociably and asked for help, her adult partners rated her as brighter and gave her more praise, help, and attention than when the same girl behaved in an unresponsive and sullen manner. In contrast, boys received similar amounts of praise and help regardless of their level of responsiveness (Cantor & Gelfand, 1977; Cantor, Wood, & Gelfand, 1977). In another case, teachers read the file of a poor student which showed low marks in some subjects, comments about inattentiveness in class, and careless work on several assignments. Half the teachers received the file labeled "Jane Smith," while the others received an identical file labeled "John Smith." Their resulting recommendations were strikingly different; John was viewed as intellectually capable, "possibly very bright," with a good career in business or government service ahead. One teacher enthused, "This boy could do anything he wanted." His careless work was interpreted as showing that he needed more personal attention and more challenging work to help him perform up to his true potential. In

contrast, teachers gave up on Jane; they did not mention her intellectual potential, her carelessness was viewed as a sign that she was more interested in her friends and social activities than in her studies, and she was predicted to soon drop out of school (Spender, 1984).

As the result of stereotyped expectations girls face a double bind: The more they conform to the demands of the classroom in terms of concentrating on their work, listening attentively, and pleasing their teacher, the less likely they will be viewed as bright and creative. On the other hand, girls who do not fit the "good student" stereotype risk losing attention, support, and help from teachers, and, in fact, girls who are assertive and who do not conform to the expectations for quiet, passive behavior are particularly at risk for dropping out of high school (Fine, 1991). In contrast, boys are considered to have intellectual potential regardless of whether they are "good students," and a boy's poor performance is interpreted as a sign that he needs more attention. Given these different experiences, it is striking that girls continue to do as well as they do in the classroom. Yet as we will see in the next section, even though girls get better grades than boys on average, there are serious long-term costs to their self-confidence; this in turn undermines their interest in pursuing such subjects as math and science.

THE EFFECTS OF DIFFERENTIAL TREATMENT

■ Academic Self-Confidence

One afternoon an elementary school class held a spelling contest. After a few rounds it became clear that several girls were the best spellers, but as the words became more difficult, the girls started to hang back, reluctant to volunteer even though they had been doing very well. In contrast, several of the worst spellers were little boys. Despite their repeated failures, they kept putting up their hands and saying, "I can get this one!" Even the anticipatory groans from the other children did little to discourage them (Omark, Strayer, & Freedman, 1980). Clearly, children's perceptions of their ability do not necessarily match their actual performance. How do such discrepancies between perception and performance develop, and why is it that boys often leave school convinced that they can do whatever they set their minds to, while girls begin to doubt themselves despite a track record of academic successes?

Thinking about Success and Failure

Imagine that a test was just handed back in your math class and you see that you received one of the highest scores in the class! You might feel a glow of pride, a satisfying sense of accomplishment, and optimistic about the future, anticipating that you will do well on future tests and end up with an A in the class. Or you might be relieved that all your hard work paid off but mildly worried about whether you will be able to repeat your good performance on the next test when the material gets more difficult. Or you might be surprised that you had done so well and recall that you happened to study the right problems the night before; of course, there's no guarantee that you will be so lucky again, so you would not necessarily expect to be able to repeat your good performance.

Analyzing your own performance in this way involves making *attributions* about the reasons for your successes and failures, including factors such as intellectual ability, hard work, and luck. The implications of these factors are quite different; if you think that you did well because you are bright, then you can expect to do well again in the future, because intellectual ability is a relatively unchangeable factor. On the other hand, if you decide that you are doing well because you are working at it, then you might feel as though your effort is making up for a lack of ability. The problem is that effort is a changeable factor; if you stopped working so hard, your grades might plummet. Luck, of course, is entirely uncontrollable, so attributing your success to a teacher who likes you, to having studied the right problems by chance, or to an easier-than-expected test leaves you uncertain about the future. Simply doing well is not necessarily enough to ensure that you will feel competent; rather, your feelings of competence depend on the reasons why you think you succeeded.

Success built on a foundation of sand. For girls, the problem is that although on average they do well in school when compared to boys, they gradually learn to believe that they do well because they work hard rather than because they are bright. As a result, their successes do not necessarily enhance their confidence; it doesn't matter how many A's you get if you believe that your achievements would vanish if you stopped trying so hard or if the material became so difficult that effort alone would not be enough. In contrast, more boys learn to think about their successes in ways that enhance their self-confidence over the long term. These differences were illustrated in a study in which children worked on puzzles and math problems. Some of problems were very easy, while others were difficult or impossible to solve, and children were asked why they had succeeded or failed on each of the tasks. More girls thought that they had solved a particular problem because they had tried hard or gotten lucky, while more boys attributed their success to aptitude because they were good at puzzles or math (Dweck, 1981; Erkut, 1983; Stipek & Hoffman, 1980). Similar patterns have been found in children's reasoning about why they did well on a test in school: More girls than boys say they got a high score because they had studied hard (Bar-Tal & Darom, 1979; D. Phillips, 1984; Stipek & Gralinski, 1991). A good grade then seems like a castle built on sand, easily washed away in the future when circumstances change.

Failures written in stone. Imagine that instead of seeing that you received a high grade on your test, you saw that you had done very poorly; in fact, you had failed. You might be disappointed but brush it aside, reminding yourself that you really hadn't studied as much as you could and had missed a couple of classes, so what else could you expect? You know that you can hit the books and make up the points by doing better on the next test. Or you might think bitterly that your teacher Mr. Buchanan is a real ogre who gives unfair tests; you went to most of the classes and studied all the chapters, but he put in some different kinds of problems—how can you be expected to do well with such a mean teacher? Or you might feel very depressed, thinking that you had been to most of the classes and had done all the reading and homework and it wasn't enough, so maybe you just aren't very good at this stuff. It's probably not worth it to kill yourself studying; maybe you could transfer to an easier class, one for the dumb kids.

As with reasoning about success, how we think about our failures has implications for what we do in the future: whether we increase our effort or give up, assuming that failure is inevitable because we do not have what it takes to succeed. When children were asked why they had not solved some of the puzzles and math problems mentioned above, more girls than boys said they just weren't very good at those kinds of problems, which left them discouraged because internal factors such as aptitude and ability are not easily changed in the future. One can always work harder, but it is not so easy to figure out how to increase one's brainpower or talent for a particular subject. Blaming yourself for failure and not taking credit for your successes is a "self-derogating" pattern of reasoning that saps confidence. In contrast, more boys said that they had failed because the problems were too hard, or they hadn't tried as hard as they could. In the classroom, more boys assume that they did not do well because the teacher is mean and does not like them (Dweck, 1981; Lochel, 1983). That is, they made *external* attributions, blaming their failures on something other than themselves. Taking credit for success and blaming others for failure is a "self-enhancing" pattern of reasoning that preserves confidence.

The Role of Teachers

Children learn a self-derogating or self-enhancing style of attribution from teachers, who tend to appraise boys' and girls' performance differently as a result of the stereotyped expectations discussed earlier. Teachers analyze boys, failures in terms of controllable factors, such as not paying attention or not following instructions, and emphasize that if the boy tried harder, he would do better next time. By telling boys that "you could do this if you would just settle down and concentrate!" teachers help boys interpret their failures in a way that does not detract from their overall self-confidence. In addition, teachers' criticism of boys' schoolwork is often submerged in a wave of reprimands about poor conduct, diluting its impact (J. S. Eccles & Blumenfeld, 1985). In contrast, teachers rarely criticize girls, and their few negative comments are focused almost exclusively on girls' schoolwork, so criticism of girls seems more pointed and forceful. Teachers also do not provide the "excuses" for poor performance supplied to boys, because they assume that girls have already concentrated and done their best work, letting girls infer that their failures were due to lack of ability and that their performance probably could not be improved.

"Classroom chivalry." We saw earlier that teachers will prod a boy after a wrong answer on the assumption that he was not really trying, but if a girl does not know the answer to a problem, teachers move on, on the assumption that she must really not know the information—and implying that perhaps she is not quite up to the work. If teachers think a child is less capable, they may not always demand extra effort or top performance, out of an understandable desire to protect the child from embarrassment or discouragement about failure. One teacher mused, "Maybe we haven't wanted to embarrass girls or maybe we haven't had faith that they could actually do the work" (Manuel, 1991, p. A21). This protective reasoning is also apparent in teachers' greater willingness to solve problems for girls rather than make girls learn to do it for themselves. One woman asked a male teaching assistant a question about her computer account and found that, as she put it, "he started doing all this stuff with my account without telling me what he was doing. He started messing around, 'You need this. Let's see, I'll give you this file.' It's like, what are you doing? He wouldn't tell me!" His well-meaning behavior prevented her from learning

how to manage her computer files herself (Frenkel, 1990). Studies of Coast Guard and other military training facilities revealed that male instructors gave detailed instructions about how to use the equipment to their male students but often completed the assignments for their female students. While it was easy for the women to accept this well-intentioned assistance, they were subsequently less likely to pass the exams (M. Sadker & Sadker, 1985). This protective attitude parallels the "anxious intrusion" parents sometimes show with daughters at home by stepping in prematurely to solve the problem while letting boys struggle along on their own and allowing them to learn that they can overcome failure.

Why do teachers respond differently to boys and girls who are having difficulty? Giving help, praising successes, prodding, and suggesting more effort are strategies teachers use with low-achieving students, at least those whose failures are believed to be due at least in part to poor classroom behavior; these patterns have not been found among high school teachers whose students are generally more attentive in the classroom (Heller & Parsons, 1981; Parsons, Kaczala, & Meece, 1982). Elementary school teachers have also been found to praise and push their low-achieving *female* students, giving them the same sorts of feedback that boys typically receive, suggesting that the child's achievement level is as important as gender in determining teacher feedback (Dusek & Joseph, 1983). But when a high-achieving, well-behaved female student is discouraged or having trouble with some work, teachers assume that she has already done her best and often try to motivate her by praising her successes—"You did so well on your spelling last week!" or "You did get these words right" (ignoring the errors further down the page)—rather than by suggesting that she could try a bit harder ("I know you usually can get these pretty well, but these are harder words than you've seen before; you're going to have to spend more time reviewing them before the test"). Yet past successes do not necessarily build confidence about the future, and vague praise does not provide much guidance about what girls could do to improve—information that boys receive *eight* times as frequently as girls (Boggiano & Barrett, 1991).

As with the amount of instruction, feedback patterns provided by teachers depend on the child's ethnicity as well as gender. In one study both white and black girls were more likely than boys to show a self-derogating pattern of reasoning, but black girls had the strongest tendency to blame themselves for failure and to discount their successes (Brown, Fulkerson, Furr, & Voight, 1984). As we saw earlier, teachers are especially likely to assume that a high-achieving black girl has only done well because of effort, and so may be even more likely to use ineffective praise-oriented feedback to try to help her improve or, worse, to imply that she cannot really be expected to do better. Some studies have found that black girls have lower academic self-esteem than black boys even when the girls get better grades (AAUW, 1992).

Consequences for Schoolwork

The attributions you make about your performance are important because they shape your interest in pursuing difficult subjects and your persistence in encountering difficulties. If you believe that you are bright and that success will be yours if you put your mind to it, the sky is the limit—you will be willing to accept a challenge and work through the hard times to reach your goal. On the other hand, if you believe that you have done well through trying hard, you might be considerably more cautious about each new challenge you accept, fearing that perhaps the limits to what hard work and being a conscientious student can do have been reached. And you may eventually lose interest and give up, tired of feeling that you can never coast, worried that your lack of ability will be discovered, and never fully enjoying the self-satisfaction and pride that come with high achievement. A survey of highly successful women graduate students in demanding, male-dominated science and engineering programs at Stanford University showed that despite the fact that they were doing as well or better than the male students the women were more likely to doubt their ability and to assume that they were doing well because of their effort. Hard work is certainly important in academic success, but these women clearly also had extraordinary intellectual ability; they had simply learned to discount it as the result of their earlier classroom experiences. The researchers concluded, "The good news is that women don't have to learn to be more intelligent, they just have to learn to appreciate their talents" (Zappart & Stansbury, 1983).

The delibitating effects of low self-confidence are also apparent in the types of tasks that children choose to work on. Confident children choose more ambitious problems, and they persist longer through initial difficulties than children who are equally bright but who have learned to discount their abilities (Harter, 1975; D. Phillips, 1984). In the third grade, both boys and girls think that they are good at math, but girls' self-confidence has declined significantly by junior high school, along with their enrollment in optional math classes. If girls have learned to think that they only do well when they study hard, it is not suprising that they choose not to take math classes when they can avoid them, even though they get grades equal to or better than those of boys when the same classes are required (Entwisle & Baker, 1983; Heller & Parsons, 1981; Kimball, 1989; Lockheed, Thorpe, Brooks-Gunn, Casserly, & McAloon, 1985; Stockard & Wood, 1984; Wigfield et al., 1989). Low confidence also reduces students' persistence in the face of challenges. Female students are more likely than males to be turned away from a major or a career plan by a single negative encounter with a teacher, one failed test, or a single poor course grade. One woman chose a particular college because of its prestigious physical therapy program. Within weeks of her arrival on campus, she gave up her dream, because she did not do as well on her first college tests as she had done with ease in high school. Instead of deciding to devote more time to her classes or to seek help with her study skills, she assumed that she did not have the ability to do the work (Holland & Eisenhart, 1990).

The "illusion of incompetence" in boys. Although we have focused primarily on the undermining effects of teacher feedback on girls, high-achieving boys can also develop a cautious attitude about approaching difficult work and become easily discouraged when they receive the pattern of teacher feedback that is typically given to girls (D. Phillips, 1984). In one study boys were given difficult or impossible-to-solve anagram problems; when a boy failed to get a problem right, the adult reassuringly said that he had clearly done the best he could and that perhaps he should be given easier problems next time. Boys who received this apparently supportive feedback later said that they had not done well on the problems because they just weren't smart enough. They also had great difficulty solving new problems even when the new problems were quite easy and well within their ability. Conversely, girls who were told that they had failed because they hadn't concentrated hard enough expected to do well in the future, and they persisted longer on a new set of difficult problems; their reasoning resembled that of boys in the classroom (Dweck, 1981). This shows us that self-enhancing and self-derogating attributional styles are learned by children and that we can enhance girls' self-confidence by changing the messages that we give them about their schoolwork and their ability. There is no reason to think that girls are naturally somehow less able to cope with challenge than boys. In fact, in preschool, boys and girls start out equally confident, equally interested in challenging tasks, and equally likely to persist in the face of initial difficulty, but girls' initial persistence and interest in challenge are gradually whittled away during the early school years by undermining feedback about their performance from adults (Callard, 1968; Molnar & Weisz, 1981; Parsons & Ruble, 1977; Stipek & Hoffman, 1980).

The "illusion of competence." So far we have focused on the drawbacks of a lack of self-confidence and how it leads students to discount their achievements, to choose less challenging work, and to be overly discouraged by failure. There are also drawbacks to overconfidence, which is more often apparent in boys but can be seen in some girls too. Believing in yourself is a good thing, but not if it means you never actually get around to studying and mastering the material, and if you always brush aside your poor grades with external attributions and the comforting belief that one day, when it counts, you will buckle down to work. Research with adults suggests that men are more likely than women to discount others' evaluations of their ability and to take credit for their successes and blame others for their failures, but this creates problems in situations in which they need to pay careful attention to the implications of feedback from others. For example, if you repeatedly ignore poor performance appraisals on the job, you may retain your self-confidence but not your position, and never figure out what you are doing wrong or how you could improve (T. Roberts, 1991). There is evidence that at the college level males do not as quickly recognize the implications of feedback on their performance, for example, how they scored on a psychology exam relative to others in the class (Bender & Standage, 1992). When the illusions of competence are eventually shattered, the pain and frustration can be devastating. The young man who dreamed of being a doctor but who failed his first-year organic chemistry class, because he never really learned to study properly, and blamed his weak grades on unfair tests, mean teachers, and a busy schedule is just as sad a case as the young woman who did not even sign up for organic chemistry because she had heard how difficult and competitive the class was and didn't think she had what it took to become a doctor. For most of us, there is an ideal balance between an unrealistically optimistic view of our ability that ignores the role of effort and an overly pessimistic view that ignores all our past achievements.

Cultural views of ability versus effort. In U.S. classrooms, the feedback patterns given to boys and girls both derive from the underlying western assumption that ability is a relatively fixed quantity. If one believes, as U.S. students and their parents do, that one is born either smart or not so smart, then poor schoolwork implies that one is not really very bright and there is little to be done about it. Teachers and parents reason that it would be cruel or unfair to push the child to do better, particularly when the child already seems to be making some effort. In contrast, Asian parents, teachers, and students emphasize effort much more than ability, believing that whatever ability one has must be developed and enhanced by work, that one's intellect can be expanded through studying hard, and that one can always work a bit harder and do better. The Japanese educational system's hours of homework, special tutors, and rigorous examinations are probably more demanding and stressful than U.S. parents and students would ever be willing to accept. Yet more emphasis on the importance of effort would benefit *both* male and female students in U.S. classrooms, encouraging boys to put their minds to their work and girls to learn to push themselves and not give up so easily when they encounter difficult work. The overall level of academic achievement in the United States is so low relative to that of students in other industrialized countries that there is considerable room for increased effort on the part of both male and female students.

Earlier we saw that children's beliefs about their ability do not necessarily match reality; some children do well in school but feel unnecessarily gloomy about the future, while others seem oblivious to past failures and remain confident. We have seen that such discrepancies between beliefs and performance develop as the result of the attributions children make about their successes and failures and that boys and girls learn to analyze their performance differently as the result of different patterns of feedback from their teachers. Yet there is more to the school experience than taking tests; the hidden curriculum also includes other sources of information about how boys and girls are expected to behave, including messages from peers.

PEER RELATIONS IN SCHOOL

Teachers are a powerful influence but, as we saw in the last chapter, so are children. Typically organized by age, U.S. schools surround children with same-age peers for much of the day; about 30 percent of the contacts students have during the classroom day are with peers (Lockheed & Klein, 1985). Classrooms therefore provide an ideal setting for peer influences to proliferate, along with the informal contacts that occur in the hallways, lunchrooms, buses, and playgrounds. Peers have a particularly strong impact on the types of classes that students will venture to take, and they also foster a culture of male superiority in the classroom.

■ Why Are You Taking *That?*

Students at a small college had to enroll in a writing seminar during their first term, and one young man signed up for a women's studies seminar because it was the only one open at a convenient time in his schedule. He found, somewhat to his surprise, that he really enjoyed the material, but when the instructor asked if he would be interested in a more advanced class, he said that he was sick of having to justify himself to his friends and that he would "catch hell" if he took any more classes in the program. Negative reactions from classmates do make it hard for students to try subjects or classes that are a little different from what would typically be expected for their sex. Students report being more worried about what their friends will think than about whether they can handle the classwork. When such vocational classes as home economics, graphic arts, metal shop, and woodworking were first opened to both sexes at one junior high school, the students were initially enthusiastic, but by the end of the school year many were unhappy with their choices, and within the classrooms boys and girls chose to work in separate groups. Although teased or chided by their friends, some boys who took home economics effectively defended themselves by saying that they only signed up to meet girls or bragged that they got to sit around and eat the cookies the girls baked in class!

Peer culture also contributes to boys' tendency to devalue schoolwork and academic achievement. While girls can do well in school, and still be popular, starting in mid-elementary school, boys begin to suggest to one another that sliding off on homework, ignoring assignments, and challenging the teacher are ways to gain social status and to be "cool." We have seen that boys tend not to concentrate in school or give their best effort; this is in part because boys learn that they should not do as well as they can for fear of being labeled a "nerd," "brain," "goody-goody," or "teacher's pet" by their male peers. One fifth-grade boy explained why he did not do put more effort into his assignments:

> I can't do more than this. If I do, then they'll make fun of me and call me a nerd. Jack is always late with his homework, and Chuck usually doesn't even do it at all [two popular boys]. I can't be the only one. (P. Adler et al., 1992, p. 177)

■ "Just Ignore It"

Schools also become a medium through which boys freely express their feelings of being better than girls. Reports of boys harassing girls in school have significantly increased in recent years (AAUW, 1992). Researchers have found that even 4-year-old boys act "as if they own the classroom," claiming access to toys and play areas, as well as to the teacher's attention. In one first-grade classroom the boys hoarded the Lego building blocks set; one girl said rather sadly, "I like playing but all the boys keep it and don't let us have it. They think girls can't use it" (Burn, 1989, p. 146; Windass, 1989). At the elementary school level groups of boys have been observed to engage in an ongoing campaign of petty tyranny toward girls by making rude remarks about their work, kicking them with their feet during a lesson, taking over equipment or materials that girls were using, pushing them away from play areas—and teachers generally did not interfere, either not noticing or not considering it serious (AAUW, 1992; Askew & Ross, 1988; C. Jones, 1985). At the junior high and high school level, harassment takes on increasingly sexual and abusive overtones. Boys snap girls' bras, pinch them in the hallways, and even burn them with cigarettes (C. Jones, 1985; S. Kessler, Ashenden, Connell, & Dowsett, 1985). One girl had to use crutches because she had lost a leg in an accident; taking advantage of the fact that she could not use her arms to defend herself, boys in the hallway between classes would lift up her skirt and try to pull down her underpants (*Boston Globe*, 1992b). A girl's letter to an advice columnist illustrates how painful such peer harassment can be, particularly for young adolescents who are often at the stage of being quite self-conscious:

> Last week I was on the school bus and some boys in my class stole my bag . . . [they] found my tampons. I just burst into tears and got off the next stop. Now they all laugh and tease me, calling me Little Miss Tampon. Please help me. I hate school and sometimes I want to kill myself. (Delamont, 1990, p. 65)

Gender inequality is thus perpetuated, with girls becoming deferential and trying to blend in to avoid being picked on. One girl was careful not to get higher scores than one of the boys in her class, not because she wanted to date him but because she did not want to be punched and kicked in the hallway. By dominating girls, boys continue to feel superior, especially when teachers and adminstrators do not interfere. When one parent complained to the school superintendent about boys' harassment of girls, he replied, "Oh, that isn't anything. Kids do that all the time. Just ignore it" (*Boston Globe*, 1992c). Yet it is discouraging for girls to be in an environment in which they are demeaned on a daily basis and treated with a lack of respect by their male classmates. It is no longer a matter of "boys will be boys"; state and federal courts have ruled that schools can be held liable if they allow an atmosphere that interferes with students' ability to work and learn (J. Adler & Rosenberg, 1992; Strauss, 1988). In one case a girl's parents sued her school district and won after obscene graffiti about her was repeatedly written in the boys' restroom at the school and the school did nothing to stop the merciless teasing and sexual threats from her male classmates.

THE POSSIBILITIES FOR CHANGE

"Don't misunderstand me. I'm against sexism like the next person. But I think discussion about sexism in school takes time away from the really important thing, and that's getting kids through the exams, isn't it?" (Askew & Ross, 1988, p. 99)

Well, no, passing exams is not the only important goal for students. As we saw at the start of this chapter, schools have a hidden as well as a formal curriculum. In addition to passing along knowledge to children and preparing them for the world of work, we expect our schools to teach students how to get along with others and to know how to behave, including the behavior expected of boys and girls. Therefore, it is reasonable to suggest that schools should be a positive force for change, rather than a mechanism for the perpetuation of stereotypes that limit the possibilities for both sexes.

■ Teachers as Agents of Change

Several studies have shown that when teachers change their behavior, boys and girls respond accordingly. For example, when girls were assigned to "boys'" activities and boys to "girls'" activities, each group began to behave more like the other sex. Girls who were told to play with blocks and trucks became more peer-oriented and more assertive, while boys who were told to read books or play house spent more time interacting with their teacher. This suggests that some of the compliance shown by girls and the assertiveness exhibited by boys result from the types of activities that they typically engage in. Adults can alter these patterns by providing more teacher-supervised activities and making sure that children actually try different things, rather than scheduling unlimited "free-play" or unstructured "discovery" activities which tend to encourage children to stick to familiar, stereotyped behaviors (Carpenter & Huston-Stein, 1980; Carpenter, Huston, & Holt, 1986; J. Johnson & Ershler, 1981). In another case teachers realized that they often unconsciously signaled that a new toy or activity was either for boys or girls, for example, by asking, "Bobby, would you show us how to use the fishing game?" or, "Perhaps Peggy would like to show us the new kit for making pot holders." They began to choose children of both sexes as models and to explicitly mention both sexes when introducing activities, for example, "We can all pretend to be policemen and policewomen driving the new police cars," and found that children were much more likely to try new activities as a result (Serbin, Connor, & Iler, 1979).

Reorganizing the Classroom

Teachers have also begun to analyze the dynamics of the classroom and to experiment with management techniques and lesson plans that are not always based on the needs of boys. One group of teachers worked on ensuring equal access to materials for both sexes. Boys typically hogged the computers, clustering around the keyboard, and making it hard for girls to get near the equipment. At first, the teachers had assumed that the girls were simply not as interested in the computers and preferred to read instead, but the teachers developed "fair use" rules to allocate time at the equipment and found that the girls used the computers as much as boys when they did not have to battle constantly to get and keep a place (Kiesler, Sproull, & Eccles, 1985). Another group of teachers decided to encourage their female students and supported one another as they learned not to respond immediately to boys' excessive demands for their attention, a task that they found quite difficult at first ("Mrs. Schnurr! Mrs. Schnurr! *Mrs. Schnurr!!*). One novice teacher prepared a lesson on space travel for his fourth-grade class and recalled that "when I was in school I used to think it was great when we did anything about space." When he found that the lesson did not go very well, one of his colleagues helped him pinpoint the problem: The girls had been bored and restless. The next year he added some books and materials on women astronauts and found that the girls were much more interested and involved (Skelton, 1989, p. 54). In addition to developing new materials and sharing strategies for organizing activities in the classroom, teachers have also tackled the problem of gender equity more directly, through workshops and discussions with students. Several teachers have reported that talking with students about why boys and girls avoid one another and behave in stereotyped ways helped them become more aware of the problem and led to more casual mixed-sex interaction and less teasing in the classroom (R. Best, 1983; Lockheed & Klein, 1985).

Spender (1984) claims that preferential treatment of boys in the educational system is so pervasive that its true extent is unrecognized by teachers and children alike; as a result, even modest changes seem as though they are giving girls much more than their "fair share" of attention. One mathematics professor noticed that her women students usually sat in the back of the classroom and rarely asked questions or made comments. She decided to try to get the women more involved and started to talk directly to them and refer back to their ideas when they did make a comment. Within a few weeks the women were sitting in the front rows, enthusiastic, making regular contributions, and scoring higher on the tests. She thought that perhaps she had neglected the men but reasoned, "This experiment was not fair to everyone. But one has to bear in mind that ordinarily the social climate is the reverse—it favors the men" (Harrison, 1991, p. 731). Boys do become accustomed to preferential treatment and can feel that even tiny changes in the classroom are unfair. When a teacher prepared a single 2-week unit on outstanding women in U.S. history, the boys protested, claiming they were being "left out" and "brainwashed" (Stitt, 1988). Teachers need the support of their colleagues, administrators, and parents to cope with resistance and to effect lasting changes in the classroom, as well as more preparation and training to promote gender equity.

■ Teacher Training

Unfortunately, most teacher education programs do not really provide training in issues of gender role stereotyping and do not yet emphasize the need to encourage, challenge, and attend to girls as well as boys. Nor is there much focus on issues of gender equity in national discussions of educational reform. One review of more than 22,000 articles on education showed that less than 1 percent discussed gender and racial equity, and another survey of 138 articles focusing specifically on how U.S. schools could be improved again found that only 1 percent mentioned the need for more gender fairness (AAUW, 1992; C. Grant & Sleeter, 1986; D. Sadker & Sadker, 1985; M. Sadker et al., 1991). New teachers are not alerted to the risks of having their attention inadvertently captured by boys or provided with strategies to deal with the problem, and few teacher education textbooks and lesson planning materials mention the issue of sexism. A survey of 125 "master teachers" (experienced teachers who supervise and train student teachers) found that while they agreed it was important for boys and girls to receive equal treatment, overcoming gender biases in instruction was only sixth on their list of objectives and addressing ethnic biases was *twenty-sixth*, suggesting that many teachers still do not recognize the extent of differential treatment of students (Bautz, 1993). Thus, teachers who are concerned about overcoming gender stereotyping can find themselves pretty much on their own. School principals and administrators, the majority of whom are male, can facilitate teachers' efforts to create change, or impede them. One researcher who had been hired by a local school district to give workshops on overcoming gender inequities in the classroom found that most of the teachers, both male and female, were very interested in attending. However, the principals at several schools were resistant, saying, "I think the money could be better spent," or, "I don't want women to become too masculine," and even, "Does this mean you would allow boys to come to school in dresses?" (Gibbs, 1989, pp. 111–112; M. Sadker et al., 1991).

Some of the differences in how boys and girls are treated, although unfair to girls, probably result as much from the conditions under which teachers often work than from teachers' lack of training to deal with gender issues or stereotyped beliefs. Teachers' focus on boys might be considered a reasonable compromise given overcrowded classrooms, lack of help and support, and the greater number of boys who are low achievers. One student teacher, who wrote a term paper on the dangers of gender stereotyping in the classroom, insisted that when he got his first class, things would be different; 2 years later he admitted that it had not been quite as easy as he had thought to keep from overlooking the girls. Individual teachers cannot be expected to solve the problem on their own without providing the support to facilitate change.

SUMMARY

School represents the first major step away from home for most children, giving them an initial glimpse at what will be expected of them as adult men and women, expectations that are conveyed through the hidden curriculum. As we have seen in this chapter, although boys and girls sit in the same classroom, they have quite different experiences. Boys receive more attention and instruction from teachers in response to the belief that girls get by through being conscientious students, while boys are bright but need extra encouragement and attention to do their best. As a result, girls become increasingly discouraged about their ability the longer they are in school, and their discouragement is exacerbated by the growing problem of harassment by their male peers. In response to the problem, teachers are beginning to try new ways of working with students that do not favor boys at the expense of girls. One step is to consider the books and materials that children are exposed to in school, along with other media influences such as television. We consider these sources of gender role messages in the next chapter.

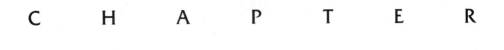

9

BEYOND THE FAMILY: MEDIA MESSAGES

BOY: *Do you want to be a clown when you grow up?*
GIRL: *No, I'm going to be a farmer.*
BOY: *You can't be a farmer. Farmers are men.*
GIRL: *Oh, yes I can. Here's a book about a farmer who raises sheep and she's a woman.*
BOY: *Hmm . . .* (looking through the book). *Maybe I could shave the wool off the sheep on your farm. I could still be a clown on weekends. (Pogrebin, 1980, p. 518).*

This conversation between two 6-year-olds illustrates the power of words and images to influence children's beliefs about the sexes, in this case, to challenge the boy's assumption that only men can be farmers. Like schools, messages in the media are influences that originate beyond the family and transmit values and expectations about gender roles that are part of the larger culture. Textbooks used in schools have the weight of community authority behind them, as do children's storybooks that win national awards and programs shown on public and commercial television stations. Gender role messages in the media are pervasive. Most parents find it very difficult to control their children's exposure to particular books and television shows. Even parents who refuse to have a TV in their homes have children who report watching 1 to 2 hours of TV a day—they watch at their friends' houses (J. Condry, 1989). To examine the impact of the media on children's gender role learning, we focus on the influence of television and then consider children's books, including storybooks, classic fairy tales, and textbooks, as well as the effects of sexist language.

TELEVISION: THE UNIVERSAL CURRICULUM

Several years ago nursery school teachers reported an increase in fighting and war play among children who were imitating the Teenage Mutant Ninja Turtles they had seen in

157

the movies and on television. One teacher said, "They all started calling each other Butt Head and Party Dude and making all their Legos into swords and weapons" (*Amherst Record*, 1990). A similar phenomenon occurred a few years earlier when children re-created in their play the epic battles they had seen in *Star Wars* films and *Masters of the Universe* cartoons. These examples suggest that children imitate what they see in movies and television and that these sources can help to shape children's gender role behavior, turning boys into macho warriors and girls into beautiful princesses waiting to be rescued. Conversations with parents about the difficulties of raising less stereotyped children often end with the parent sighing helplessly, "We try, but then they see it all the time on TV."

Is television really such a strong influence on children's development? On the one hand we know that TV cannot be an *essential* component of the process of gender role learning—it has only been around for about 40 years, after all. On the other hand, there are several reasons why TV might be an especially strong influence: First, it reaches almost all U.S. children. There is at least one television set in nearly all (98 to 99 percent) households in the United States; a U.S. home is more likely to have a television set than running water. Second, the level of exposure is extraordinarily high. Children begin watching TV in infancy, when their parents put them in front of the set to soothe or distract them, and are watching their own specific favorite programs by about 2½ to 3 years. By preschool, children watch 3 to 4 hours a day on a regular basis (J. Condry, 1989; Singer & Singer, 1981). Third, children's cognitive limitations make them particularly receptive to television's messages (J. Bryant & Anderson, 1983; P. M. Greenfield, 1984). Young children often assume that they are watching real people and events because the images *look* real. Children also tend to take characters' actions at face value, so exaggerated depictions of males and females probably have a greater influence on them than older viewers. Finally, as we will see below, television provides a highly repetitive, uniform message about the sexes. Children in very different communities across the country all see the same programs with the same portrayal of the sexes. As a result, television has been called the "universal curriculum," leading viewers from diverse backgrounds to have homogenized expectations about gender role behavior.

Clearly, television is a potentially powerful socializing force; children's overall level of exposure is high; and they are receptive to its messages. But what are those messages? In the following sections we analyze the male and female role models available on TV and then consider whether television actually teaches children anything new or merely reinforces what they have already learned about being male or female.

■ What Do Children See on TV?

The first step in investigating the potential impact of television is to examine the portrayal of the sexes. This kind of appraisal requires a *content analysis*: examining the number of characters shown and evaluating how they are presented to the viewer. In early research on the stereotyping of blacks and other minorities in the media, Clark (1972) suggested that inaccuracies and biases in how characters are depicted could occur in two forms. First, a group might received diminished *recognition*, with members of a particular group shown in relatively few numbers. Second, members of the group could be shown with a lack of *respect*, portrayed in degrading, stereotyped, or unattractive roles. When this analysis was extended to the representation of males and females, it became clear that females do not receive a realistic level of recognition, while males are overrrepresented on television relative to their actual numbers in the real world. About two-thirds of the characters in both commercial programming and in public broadcasting programming are males (M. Cantor, 1977; J. Condry, 1989; Huston et al., 1992; Liebert & Sprafkin, 1988). This figure has remained stable from the 1950s into the 1990s, possibly because between 75 and 90 percent of television writers, directors, and producers are male (D. Davis, 1990; Liebert & Sprafkin, 1988). Not only are females underrecognized, but the sexes are depicted in ways that are unrealistic and stereotyped, that is, with a lack of respect. This is apparent in the personal attributes, relationships, and activities that are emphasized for the two sexes in prime-time programming, commercials, and programming targeted to children and adolescents.

Appearance

By far the most powerful TV message about females is that they should be young, thin, and beautiful. Most female characters are either under 35 or over 50. Middle-aged women are systematically underrepresented, although most male TV characters are middle-aged. Female TV characters are decorative as well as young: They are twice as likely to have blonde or red hair as are women in the real world and are four times more likely than male characters to be provocatively dressed (Atkin, Moorman, & Lin, 1991). One girl said, "Girls think they have to be pretty all the time," and explained that this idea came "[f]rom TV where women wear frilly dresses and have lots of makeup" (Short & Carrington, 1989, p. 31). Fat female characters are particularly unusual; when such a part does occur, it is often played by an African-American actress, which implies that the cultural ideal is a thin white woman (Huston et al., 1992). In contrast, male characters usually appear fully clothed, and they can be fat, old, bald, sloppy or homely and still be the star of their own program (Tavris & Wade, 1984).

Relationships

Female characters are consistently defined in terms of their relationships with males. Females usually appear on the screen in the company of males, and while there are many examples of male-male interaction, female-female encounters are relatively rare (Mackey & Hess, 1982). The marital status of TV female characters is usually clearly indicated, while it is not always apparent whether male characters are single, divorced, widowed, or married. Television also implies that relationships should come first for female characters. Marriages and romantic relationships are shown as full of conflicts if both partners are achievement-oriented but harmonious if the couple follows a traditional assignment of roles (J. Condry, 1989). If a female TV character is single, she is shown as the victim of accidents, murders, and assaults far more often than occurs in reality. Television thus implies that it is dangerous for women not to have a male partner—although women are actually most at risk from assault by males in their own families (Gerbner, 1972; Signorielli, 1987).

Employment

Whether or not a female TV character has a paid job depends on the current social norms. In the 1950s and 1960s television programs rarely showed women working outside the home, except as a nurse or secretary or, in a surprising number of programs, as a witch. Sternglanz and Serbin (1974) found that four of the five female characters with their own programs used magic to accomplish their goals, including the housework (e.g., *Bewitched*). When many women began to work outside the home in the 1970s, several popular programs had women with responsible jobs, including *Mary Tyler Moore* (a single woman with a full-time job as a TV producer) and *Star Trek* (men and women working together on a spaceship, although admittedly the women wore painfully short miniskirts). By the 1980s, there had been a significant increase in the number of women in such professional fields as medicine, law, and business (e.g., *LA Law*), which has increased adolescent girls' interest in professional careers (Wroblewski & Huston, 1987). But the television world is misleading on this point. Little information about how one obtains such jobs is presented, and television suggests that far more women have such jobs than is true in the real world in which less than 10 percent of U.S. women make more than $50,000 a year.

Although more women are shown working on TV today than in the past, it is not clear that this has had a significant impact on young children. Many of the programs showing professional women are typically on late at night (e.g., the 10 to 11 P.M. slot) when relatively few children are watching, and older programs are still shown as reruns on afternoon time slots. Children watching after school today can see *Gilligan's Island, Lassie, Leave It to Beaver, My Three Sons, Mister Ed, The Brady Bunch,* and *I Dream of Jeannie,* just as children did 20 or more years ago. In addition, the changes have been limited to prime-time programming. In daytime TV and soap operas men are four times more likely to work than women, and the employment status of half the female characters is never even mentioned. In addition, female characters with professional careers tend to become more traditional over time. During the run of the popular detective program *Miami Vice* the female police officers became progressively less involved in the plots and were more often shown standing around the office in skimpy costumes. In several programs, such as *LA Law* and *Murphy Brown*, the concerns of the female characters shifted from professional issues in the early seasons to conflicts about motherhood, marriage, and family after several years on the air.

Images of Men

While most content analyses have focused on the portrayal of women, TV images of males are often inaccurate and unattractive as well. Men in prime-time programs have an unrealistically limited range of jobs, generally in law enforcement. They rarely reveal their emotions, but when they do, they are more likely than women to be shown as unhappy or deranged (M. Harris & Voorhees, 1981). Not only are males portrayed as relying on violence to accomplish their goals, but they are also frequently the victims of violence, being shot, blown up, or run over by unscrupulous business associates and wives who are interested only in their life insurance. Television fathers in situation comedies are not always very appealing, often serving as the target of jokes and constantly being outwitted by their cute children, their clever wives, and cleverer pets (*Dick Van Dyke, Family Ties, Mister Ed*) (Ruhl, 1987). However, again following societal changes in the late 1980s, several programs appeared with men in nurturing, nontraditional roles, including the *Cosby Show, Growing Pains,* and *Who's the Boss.* In fact, in the world of television half of the children who live with one parent live with their father, while in real life 90 percent of children in single-parent homes live with their mother (Press, 1991).

Advertisements

It is easy to forget that the primary purpose of television is not to entertain us but to make us buy things. Commercials take up about 12 to 14 minutes of each program hour, and while the male-female ratio is more realistic than in the accompanying programs (about 1:1), the roles are even more highly stereotyped. Females are shown primarily in ads for household and beauty products, while men are shown in ads for cars, alcohol, and such financial products as insurance. Women in commercials are concerned with their appearance, cleanliness, and health. Although both sexes may be shown in need of the various products being advertised, the announcer—the voice of authority that explains the advantages of the product—is almost always male. When women are portrayed as experts, it is primarily in the home arena; they know just how to treat a spouse's cold, remove a pesky chocolate stain on a little girl's party dress, and wrap leftovers to maintain freshness. In the 1980s more employed women were shown in commercials, but the number of men shown involved in household and child-care tasks did not change.

Children's Programming

Gender images in children's programs and commercials are often even more stereotyped than in programs targeted to adults (Feldstein & Feldstein, 1982). Male cartoon characters are active problem solvers, while females follow the lead of the males. On the *Smurfs,* a program about elflike cartoon characters, the male Smurfs have actual names, while the one female is named "Smurfette." She wears pink, tags along on their adventures, often gets into trouble, and requires rescue, as does April, the one female character in the Ninja Turtles series. Female cartoon characters are designed to be childlike and sweet, such as "Strawberry Shortcake," "Holly Hobbie," and "Rainbow Brite." Minority characters have also been consistently underrepresented in children's programming. One analysis of Saturday morning cartoons found a total of six minority characters in all programs, and five were clustered in one program, a show about a black rap group with a white manager (Swan, 1992).

Educational programming for children is also male-dominated, with a 2:1 male-female ratio of characters and a preponderance of such male hosts as Captain Kangeroo and Mister Rogers (M. Cantor, 1977). Even *Sesame Street,* generally lauded as an example of good programming for children, succumbed to gender role stereotyping in its early seasons (Gardner, 1974). *Sesame Street* was originally intended to reach poor children from inner-city communities, and the program was designed to include positive male characters as role models for children who might not have an adult male in the home. The result was that many of the original characters were and still are male. Only one of the Muppets—Miss Piggy—has a female voice, and she is not a particularly appealing character, with her obsessive concern with her appearance and her troubled romance with Kermit the Frog. One mother who called recently to complain about the all-male Muppets was told that the producers were still "working on it," although the show has now been on the air for a quarter of a century (Pollitt, 1991).

Why is children's television so dominated by males? Programmers and advertisers believe that using male characters is the safest strategy to ensure an audience. Boys' favorite TV characters are almost always male, while girls are about equally likely to have a favorite character of either sex (Cullingford, 1984; Hodge & Tripp, 1986). When networks were challenged about the male-dominated lineup of Saturday cartoons, one network executive explained, "It is well known that boys will watch a male lead and not a female lead . . . but girls are willing to watch a male lead" (*New York Times*, 1991, p. 1). Similarly, advertisers explain, "Most general products can be sold to both sexes by the use of boy models, and even with girl viewers, boys tend to attract greater interest than girl models" (Brooks-Gunn & Matthews, 1979, p. 198; Feldstein & Feldstein, 1982; C. Schneider, 1987). While it is true that boys will often lose interest in a toy if they see it demonstrated by a girl (as we saw in Chapter 6), TV is designed to reinforce children's assumptions that certain toys and activities are only for one sex. In U.S. television, children's commercials are typically designed to signal clearly the gender associated with the product. Commercials for boys use loud music and rapid cuts from one scene to the next, while those targeted to girls use camera fades and dissolves between scenes along with soft background music. Children are familiar with these signals and adjust their viewing behavior accordingly (Huston, Greer, Wright, Welch, & Ross, 1984). This strong gender typing of commercials was not found in a sample of commercials for children's toys and products on South Korean television (Bu & Condry, 1991).

Girls will sometimes watch male-dominated programs often because they have no other option. However, girls can be extremely loyal viewers of programs designed with their interests in mind. Over the years the consistently popular series of female heroines includes *Wonder Woman*, Farrah Fawcett-Majors in *Charlie's Angels*, (described as "Barbie in the flesh"), the *Bionic Woman*, and *She-Ra, Princess of Power* (C. Schneider, 1987).

Programming for Adolescents

Television targeted toward adolescents is perhaps the most extreme in its depiction of the sexes, particularly of teenage girls. One study found that teenaged girls on television were shown as primarily concerned with dating, shopping, and their appearance while rarely discussing their school or career plans. Attractive girls were often portrayed as "airheads" (e.g., Mallory, the sister on the popular program *Family Ties*) and intelligent girls as unattractive. One episode of the program *Mr. Belvedere* showed a smart girl as homely, awkward, and so desperate for a date that she was willing to go out with a boy who only asked her as part of a fraternity initiation joke (C. Campbell, 1988).

Television programming directed to teens also conveys highly stereotyped images of how the sexes relate to each other (Hansen & Hansen, 1988). Commercials for beer often show young men surrounded by smiling, subservient women in bathing suits or short skirts, with a ratio of several women per man. One infamous example showed a group of men on a backpacking trip greeted on the trail first by "the Swedish Women's Bikini Team" (whatever that is) and then by a case of beer—the intended implication being that the beer was even better than the women. Such images are of special concern when directed to adolescents who are forming their notions of romantic relationships and may imagine that this is how the sexes should interact. Arguing that it contributes to excessive drinking and demeaning attitudes toward women on the part of young men, Antonia Novello, the U.S. surgeon general, recommended that beer companies voluntarily reduce their reliance on this sort of advertising, and even an advertising trade journal recently admonished advertising agencies and brewers to reduce their reliance on sexist ads to sell beer to teens (Hohler, 1992; *Valley News*, 1992b).

Another highly stereotyped form of programming specifically targeted toward teenage

ROBOTMAN® by Jim Meddick

Robotman reprinted by permission of NEA, Inc.

viewers is rock music videos. MTV and similar all-video channels were introduced in the early 1980s in an attempt to reach an untapped market: teenagers, who typically watched less TV than other age groups and were relatively affluent, with money to spend on clothes, cosmetics, and cars. MTV was remarkably successful, becoming profitable within 3 years by attracting a strong audience. Teenagers now report watching MTV about an hour a day during the week and more on the weekends. Unfortunately, what they see is highly stereotyped and is often specifically slanted to a male audience. The focus on male viewers was apparent from the beginning when the sets were designed to look like a 15-year-old boy's ideal bedroom, with rock posters, video games, and albums, and female video announcers were chosen based on their ability to "make the young boys . . . go nuts" (L. Lewis, 1990, p. 41). The strong slant toward male viewers is also apparent in the content of videos. As with beer commercials, there are frequent scenes of parties at which women significantly outnumber men. Women are twice as likely to be dressed provocatively in videos as in prime-time programming, and, in direct contrast to prime-time programming, aggressive acts are often perpetrated by females; for example, there may be a scene of a woman pushing a recalcitrant man to the ground, lying on him, holding him down, and kissing him (Sherman & Dominick, 1986). MTV has been described as a teenage boy's "dreamworld" populated by beautiful, aroused women who outnumber men, who seek out and even assault men to obtain sex, and who always mean yes even when they say no (Jhally, 1990). As with children's programming, the assumption seems to be that adolescent females would watch anything, while male viewers would only watch programming that was specifically oriented to them; thus, it is difficult for videos that are not male-oriented to receive exposure. One singer said of his new video, "[T]here are no tarts or supermodels in the video, so you know they won't play it!" (Morse, 1992, p. 42). Yet female performers in the late 1980s, such as Cyndi Lauper and Madonna, attracted tremendous numbers of loyal female viewers, suggesting that much of the potential female audience had been missed by the reliance on traditional male-oriented programming (L. Lewis, 1990).

■ The Impact of TV on Children's Gender Stereotypes

Does It Matter?

Although it is clear from the content analyses reviewed above that the sexes are depicted unrealistically on television, we cannot automatically conclude that children's and adolescents' ideas about men and women are actually shaped by what they see on the screen. After all, children had no trouble acquiring gender stereotypes in the centuries before television became widely available, suggesting that its overall influence may be limited. Television may merely reinforce what children have already learned about gender roles rather than teach them anything new. Or it is entirely possible that children may not be influenced at all by what they see. Tavris and Wade (1984) point out that people who saw the film *Bonnie and Clyde* did not go out and rob banks the next day. Similarly, a little girl may watch *I Dream of Jeannie* every day after school but still know perfectly well that she will not grow up to wear chiffon trousers and live in a bottle. The actual impact of TV also depends on the viewer's characteristics. For example, while the bigoted Archie Bunker in *All in the Family* was very popular, some viewers liked him because they felt he was expressing attitudes similar to their own, while other viewers enjoyed the program because they recognized that the character was a parody (Vidmar & Rokeach, 1974). Similarly, young children may not have the cognitive capacity to understand and be directly influenced by much of what they see on television, even if the portrayals are highly stereotyped (Durkin, 1985).

On the other hand, television is organized and funded on the premise that viewers will be influenced to buy the advertised products or, in the case of children, to get their parents to buy them. There is considerable evidence that children do influence adult purchasing decisions in this way as the result of viewing TV commercials; this is no surprise to parents who have heard pleas for Cocoa Puffs cereal or Flintstones vitamins (Huston et al., 1992). One of the first demonstrations of the power of children's TV advertising came in 1963 when the Mattel toy company introduced a new model of the popular Barbie doll through a TV commercial that encouraged girls to "trade in" their old Barbie. The commercials were shown in several midwestern cities during February, normally not a month in which many toys are sold. Although severe blizzards made shopping even more difficult than usual, within 3 weeks of the commercials the new Barbies were sold out in the test cities as "girls and their mothers went out into the snow to purchase the new dolls" (C. Schneider, 1987, p. 36). A similar effect was observed when MTV was first introduced in several test cities in 1981; performers whose videos were shown repeatedly had a significant increase in sales in those cities within 6 weeks. Today, nearly half of all tape and CD purchases can be traced to a teenager's viewing of the accompanying video on television. If television can influence purchasing behavior so dramatically, it seems reasonable to argue that it may also influence children's and adolescents' ideas about gender roles.

Research Approaches

Believing that television is influential is one thing, but proving it is another. It has been difficult to demonstrate convincingly that exposure to television actually causes increased gender stereotyping in children (Durkin, 1985). One serious methodological problem is that there are few children left who do not watch television and who could provide a representative control group. The few remaining children who are nonviewers are by definition highly unusual, making comparisons difficult. For example, it would be misleading to compare the gender concepts of Amish children, who do not watch television, with those of mainstream children with more typical viewing habits, as any differences in their gender concepts would probably be due to the profound differences in cultural values than to the effects of television. This problem has forced researchers to rely on several different research strategies to assess the possible influence of television viewing on children's gender stereotyping.

The correlational approach. One strategy is to compare the gender concepts of children who are heavy or light television viewers. Studies relying on this method have consistently shown that children who are heavy television viewers are more likely to have traditional gender role expectations and attitudes (Beuf, 1974; Frueh & McGhee, 1975; McGhee & Frueh, 1980; Morgan & Rothschild, 1983; Zuckerman, Singer, & Singer, 1980). However, it is not clear that watching a lot of traditional TV programming causes children to become more stereotyped. It is equally possible that stereotyped children enjoy watching TV because what they see on the screen is consistent with their interests and the way they imagine the world to be. A girl who daydreams about being a fashion designer might become an avid fan of *Dynasty* and similar programs because she likes the costumes and characters of the shows. Her heavy viewing would be the result of her preexisting interests rather than the cause. This relation is especially strong for boys; that is, boys who are initially more conservative in their attitudes about gender roles tend to watch increasing amounts of TV, showing that their preexisting attitudes influence their viewing behavior (Morgan, 1982).

The longitudinal approach. Other researchers have tried to find out if watching television causes children to become more stereotyped over time. Morgan (1982) followed sixth graders over a 3-year period and found that television viewing had the greatest effect on the attitudes of children who were least stereotyped to begin with. Specifically, the amount of television watched by girls in sixth grade predicted their "sexism" scores 3 years later, with heavier viewing leading to greater stereotyping. Watching a lot of TV had the strongest effect on those who had started out with the most flexible gender concepts to begin with, that is, on girls. Viewing rates had relatively little observable effect on boys because they were already fairly strongly stereotyped at the start of the study. Morgan concluded that television gradually merges everyone to a "mainstream" view of gender roles because it confirms the preexisting beliefs of traditional viewers and leads to increased stereotyping among less traditional viewers. Similar results were obtained by Eron, Husemann, Brice, Fischer, and Mermelstein (1983), who followed overlapping samples of children from first through fifth grade, and by Morgan (1987) with a sample of eighth graders who were followed for 6 months. In each case the amount of TV viewing at one point in time was a small but significant predictor of children's subsequent gender role attitudes.

Although research based on the longitudinal approach does suggest that TV might cause children to become more stereotyped, it has two limitations: First, the studies have focused on children's attitudes about gender roles rather than their actual behavior, and second, the attitude measures themselves have been relatively weak. In one case children were asked only five questions, such as whether they thought women were happiest at home raising children (Morgan, 1982). Durkin (1985) suggested that children's responses to such questions might be based on their increasing awareness about what the world is typically like, rather than reflecting their ideas about what it should or could be like. As a result children might appear to become more sexist with age, but this might not be due entirely to the influence of television.

Before and after television. Another approach to testing the impact of TV is to compare children's attitudes before and after they have been exposed to it. Access to television had become nearly universal by the late 1970s, but there was a small town in western Canada that had never received television because its location within a deep valley interfered with reception. The families in the town were comparable to other families in that they were interested in viewing TV; in fact, they lobbied the provincial government for the installation of a more powerful transmitter and even bought television sets in advance so that they would be ready when the transmissions began. A team of researchers studied the town during the year before and 2 years after the introduction of television to see if attitudes and behavior had changed as a result. Two other towns were selected as comparison groups; one had received one Canadian Broadcasting Corporation channel (similar to PBS in the United States) for several years, while the other town had several commercial channels with programming comparable to what children might see in the United States (Kimball, 1986).

The first step was to assess children's level of gender stereotyping in the three communities. These initial assessments suggested that gender stereotyping and TV viewing were correlated. Children in the no-TV town were significantly less stereotyped than those living in the town with access to several commercial programming channels. In the town with only one channel girls were less stereotyped than those living in the town with several commercial channels, although there was no difference for boys. Although these patterns were suggestive, they did not indicate that TV was necessarily the cause of the variations in stereotyping. The next step was therefore to evaluate children's stereotyping 2 years after TV had been introduced into the town that had been without it. The follow-up assessments in the "no-TV" town showed clearly that there had been a significant increase in gender stereotyping after exposure to TV, with the effect being particularly large for boys (Kimball, 1986). The pattern of results strongly suggested that watching TV actually caused children to become more traditional in their ideas about how men and women should behave.

Changing the message. Another research strategy has been to study the effectiveness of "counterprogramming," that is, to look at how children's ideas are affected by viewing programs designed to challenge their gender role stereotypes. The logic is as follows: If the message of television is changed and children's ideas about males and females change as a result of watching the new programs, we can infer that their original beliefs might also been derived in part from their earlier viewing of more traditional programs. (In Chapter 8 we saw a similar research strategy used by Dweck, 1981, who reversed the typical teacher feedback given to boys and girls and observed the effects on children's attributions for academic success and failure.)

The largest experiment in counterprogramming involved a 13-part series of half-hour programs called *Freestyle* (J. Johnston, Ettema, & Davidson, 1980; F. Williams, LaRose, & Frost, 1981). The project was sponsored by the National Institute of Education, with the goal of altering 9- to 12-year-old children's stereotyped beliefs about appropriate careers for the sexes, particularly females. The programs were professionally produced and included themes about female leadership and achievement, lessons about reasonable risk taking and working to overcome failure, and the importance of following one's own interests even if they are not traditional. For example, in one program a girl ran for class president against a popular boy, while another show portrayed a girl who overcame her fear of mountain climbing and coped with being temporarily lost while on a hike. In another program a boy and a girl resisted peer pressure to stick to sports and cheerleading in order to collaborate on a prize-winning entry at the school science fair. Several additional programs showed males engaged in nurturing behavior. For example, two boys helped a bilingual classmate with her English so that she would be able to keep up with her math homework. More than 7000 children watched the programs in seven test-site cities around the country in 1978 and 1979. Some children viewed the programs during school, and some of these children also participated in classroom discussions and accompanying activities conducted by their teachers. Other children watched at home, with teachers and community project leaders reminding them and their parents to watch the shows each week.

Freestyle was clearly successful in the sense that it was highly attractive to children. One teacher commented, "The shows certainly held the interest of the children. . . . During viewing time . . . you could hear a pin drop. The children loved the programs and were very attentive" (Johnston et al., 1980, p. 58). Teachers also felt that the programs increased children's awareness of stereotyping, and two-thirds enthusiastically recommended the series to other teachers. However, simply showing that children would watch and enjoy TV shows about nontraditional gender role behavior was not enough; it was also important to learn whether viewing the programs actually had an effect on the children's preexisting attitudes and beliefs. Thus, preprogram and postprogram assessments were conducted of the children's beliefs about males and females, and their beliefs were compared with those of similar children who did not view the programs. These analyses showed that *Freestyle* did have a substantial impact on children's attitudes: Both sexes were significantly more open to nontraditional career possibilities after watching the series. Boys even became more receptive to the idea that men could be secretaries or nurses! The magnitude of the effect varied by geographic region and ethnicity, but overall *Freestyle* led to less traditional attitudes among all the groups regardless of their initial level of stereotyping. This is similar to Morgan's (1982) finding, discussed above, that TV viewing tends to reduce differences among viewers and move everyone toward a similar view of the world, although in this case it was a more egalitarian view.

While *Freestyle* was generally effective for most viewers, its benefits were greatest for students who viewed the programs in the classroom and who participated in the discussion groups led by their teachers. Classroom discussion was especially helpful in altering boys' beliefs, as they were more stereotyped than girls' to begin with. As we saw in Chapter 6, children tend to distort information that is inconsistent with their preexisting beliefs; adults can correct this tendency and reinforce the message of the programs. Adult involvement is not a bad thing in practical terms—most researchers would encourage parents to monitor and discuss TV programs with their children—but it does limit our conclusions about the power of TV as a unique influence, in that some of the effects attributed to the TV show might have been due to adult involvement. In addition, the effects of *Freestyle* were demonstrated with an audience that was already highly committed to the goal of decreasing stereotyping, enough to sign on for the 13-week project. In contrast, other communities would not even host the project because parents felt that a girl's primary adult role should be that of wife and mother and so were not happy about programs designed to encourage girls to think about possible paid employment and independence. Children in these communities probably would have been much less influenced by the programs even if they had been shown.

Despite these limitations, the *Freestyle* project showed that TV can influence children's attitudes and beliefs, as have other smaller-scale projects using the counterprogramming approach (Corder-Bolz, 1980; Davidson, Yasuna, & Tower, 1979; Flerx, Fidler, & Rogers, 1976; M. Miller & Reeves, 1976; O'Bryant & Corder-Bolz, 1978; Rosenwasser, Lingenfelter, & Harrington, 1989). However, this strategy can backfire with young adolescents who are likely to resist the nontraditional messages (Eisenstock, 1984; Pingree, 1978). In one study conducted in Britain, 12- to 13-year-olds saw TV sketches about people who held nontraditional jobs, including a male secretary, a male nurse, and a female plumber (Durkin & Hutchins, 1984). The male secretary described his training and explained that he had chosen secretarial work because it had good long-term prospects. He mentioned that he had been kidded a bit at first, but that his friends and colleagues soon accepted his unusual job, and that he would definitely recommend it to others. After viewing the series, the teenagers still held traditional views about appropriate careers for males and females, and in some cases they were even more disapproving of the alternative careers than they had been before viewing the interviews. (The researchers ruefully concluded that "at least they got a clear answer" about the power of television to expand teenagers' notions of career possibilities [Durkin, 1985, p. 96]!) This is similar to the point we made about correlational research; children's preexisting attitudes about the sexes can determine whether they like and will watch a particular TV program. In addition, TV alone probably cannot overcome strong stereotypes once they are in place, and while it might reinforce such stereotypes, it probably does not create them in isolation.

The drench effect. The steady diet of stereotyped images on TV seems as though it might shape children's attitudes gradually, much as dripping water slowly shapes a rock. For some children the effects of TV might be more like a bucket of water being poured over one's head, with a single compelling TV character or program having a substantial impact. That is, TV influences might be more like a sudden drench than a slow drip (Greenberg, 1988). Producers of children's programming and commercials are careful to avoid risky scenes of "imitable behavior" because they recognize that some children might try to copy what they see on the screen. For example, a cartoon skit of a cat hiding from a monster in a bowl of pasta was changed out of concern that children might actually try to push the family kitty into their spaghetti (C. Schneider, 1987). So far there is little research directly on this possibility with children, but there certainly are sporadic cases of children imitating a particular act that they had seen on television. In one case a 9-year-old girl was sexually assaulted with a bottle by a group of older girls and one boy 4 days after a similar attack was shown in a network television movie (J. Condry, 1989; Liebert & Sprafkin, 1988). In another case near my hometown a mentally handicapped young man murdered a 20-year-old woman; he had been obsessed with the character Jason in the *Friday the 13th* movie series and had collected a hockey mask and other apparel just like Jason's in the films (Miedzian, 1991).

Of course, it is hard to know what to make of the role of television in such tragic cases. It is entirely possible that these adolescents would have assaulted or murdered someone without the impetus of a television show or movie or that the drench effect only works on viewers who are already vulnerable due to psychological disturbances or limited intelligence. Because it is difficult to predict why a particular program would have a strong influence on a particular child but not on others, the drench model will be hard to evaluate systematically. From the parents' and teachers' perspective, however, it is important to recognize that children can learn very quickly from a few salient images on television. One mother said, "I slipped *once* and let Timmy watch *The Dukes of Hazzard*. Five months later he's still acting it out—racing and smashing cars and calling himself Bo and Luke" (Lickona, 1983, p. 351). Clearly, then, it is quite possible that in a few hours of television viewing, children could acquire a great deal of information about gender roles.

TV as a Positive Force

Let us now look on the bright side. Expanding a child's world beyond the immediate environment and providing illustrations of gender role behavior that the child might never see in daily life, along with access to inspirational role models, TV can be a positive force in gender socialization. For example, the child who has never been on a plane trip might see an airline commercial and notice that one of the pilots is a woman. A young girl whose family thinks that sports are unfeminine can watch the Olympics and see many inspiring examples of successful female athletes. For minority children, those living in isolated rural areas and those from low-income families, television can provide a window to the dominant culture and provide guidelines and role models for assimilation if that is their goal. Television can also challenge and expand white and affluent children's assumptions about gender and ethnicity (Gorn, Goldberg, & Kanungo, 1976; Greenberg, 1972; P. M. Greenfield, 1984; Powell, 1982; Zuckerman et al., 1980). For example, the *Cosby Show*, a popular comedy program about a black upper-middle-class family, had a significant impact on many white viewers' attitudes about African-Americans. Thus, TV in itself is not necessarily a negative influence; its effects depend on the content that is depicted.

Our original questions were, What do children see on TV? and Does it matter? At this point we can conclude that for the most part males and females are not accurately represented either in terms of numbers or roles and that media portrayals of the sexes do influence children's beliefs and attitudes. These lessons are reinforced through other important influences: books and language.

THE POWER OF WORDS

> When my then nine-year-old daughter announced . . . that she wanted to raise horses when she grew up and would marry a rich man to finance the project, I realized that all those stories she had been reading about a girl and her horse were getting to her. She was modeling herself on fictional and cultural projections of a woman's role, and the fact that I was a career-oriented Ph.D. candidate was not sufficient by itself to overcome the seduction of those images. (Schumacher, 1974, p. 113)

As this mother recognized, even simple children's stories are not gender-neutral. The words we use and the books that children read convey messages about gender, and children are quite sensitive to these messages. We now consider how books and sexist language influence children's gender role stereotypes.

■ Children's Books

When something is written down, it gains authority, and when books are given awards, designated to be "classics," or are used in a school classroom, their hidden messages seem to be given an official stamp of approval. Unfortunately, females have long been under-represented in written materials for children, just as they are in television programming. Although there has been progress in recent years, traditional stereotypes still linger in many of the storybooks and textbooks for children.

Children's Literature

Many parents enjoy reading stories to their children, and older children are often encouraged to visit the library and to read for pleasure. Studies conducted in the 1970s found that males dominated the stories, titles, and illustrations in children's literature, even award-winning books. There were three times as many books about boys as girls, and minority characters rarely appeared at all (Feminists on Children's Literature, 1971; P. Roberts & Chambers, 1977; M. Sadker, Sadker, & Klein, 1991). One survey of award-winning picture books for young children found that males were shown in the illustrations 11 times as often as females, and male animal characters outnumbered females by 95:1 (M. Sadker et al., 1991; L. Weitzman, Eifler, Hodaka, & Ross, 1972)! Male characters dominated because authors, editors, publishers, and teachers assumed that boys would not be interested in a book about a girl but that girls would be willing to read a story about a boy. This assumption is questionable, but the safest strategy seemed to be to produce books with male main characters. Scott O'Dell, the author of *Island of the Blue Dolphin*, a best-selling book about a girl's survival alone on an isolated island, was asked by several publishers to change the main character from a girl to a boy. He refused, and in 1961 his book won the Newbery Award from the American Library Association as the year's best book for elementary school children (M. Sadker et al., 1991).

A second reason for the prevalence of male characters in children's books was that females were usually limited to the roles of mother or teacher, with books including such comments as, "It's girls' work to do dishes," and "A woman's place is in the kitchen among the pots and pans" (McDonald, 1989, p. 392). Such narrow ideas about females' typical activities restricted the number of stories in which they appeared; it is not very easy to write an exciting children's story about washing the dishes. In contrast, male characters were shown as ranchers, space explorers, and big game hunters, roles that allowed authors to create stories about conflicts and challenges through which characters could exercise their resourcefulness and learn important lessons about life. As with TV programs and videos there is evidence that the female market was underserved by the focus on attracting male readers. One survey of high-achieving women found that despite large differences in their backgrounds and family environments, one aspect they had in common was an enjoyment of Nancy Drew stories while growing up. Although the stories were not great literature, they at least were about a female main character who drove her own car, had adventures, and solved mysteries (Unger & Crawford, 1992).

When it became clear in the 1970s that children's books were overwhelmingly dominated by males, publishers and authors responded to the need for a more equitable depiction of the sexes and for more representation of minority characters. In children's books published in the 1980s, there were almost as many female main characters as males (Kinman & Henderson, 1985; Purcell & Stewart, 1990; White, 1986). Boys and girls are now more likely to be shown as friends, and when girls get into trouble, they are more likely to appear brave and resourceful rather than terrified and helpless. However, there are still more male supporting characters, and other more traditional differences remain as well: Female characters are still more likely to need help than male characters, males are more likely to give it, and males' help is more likely to be required in situations calling for bravery and adventurous action (Barnett, 1986; McDonald, 1989; White, 1986). The reasons why storybook boys and girls need help are also still different. Boys often help girls with personal difficulties such as being fat or shy, while girls help boys with larger missions such as escaping from politically repressive regimes. One exception was a girl who helped a male character by trying to clear his reputation: He was *dead* and so presumably his masculinity could not be threatened by her assistance (White, 1986). One of my students recently examined Newbery Award winners from 1985 through 1991 and found that of the five fiction books during this period (two were biographies), three were still quite strongly stereotyped: In one, a princess killed a dragon to win a crown but then was rescued by a prince, to whom she gave her kingdom. Another was about an unruly prince and his adventures, with a ratio of nine males to one female (and the one female main character needed to be rescued). A third focused on a boy confronting the problem of racism in his town, but few girls appeared in the story. Thus, parents still need to monitor contemporary children's literature for lingering gender stereotypes.

Classics. While contemporary children's literature has become more egalitarian, parents still buy and read classic children's stories and fairy tales, which are more highly stereotyped than contemporary books. Male characters appear four times as often as females, and are shown as strong and active, while the female characters are typically beautiful and in need of rescue. The theme "someday my prince will come" is repeated in the stories of Snow White, Cinderella, Sleeping Beauty, Rapunzel, and many other less well known fairy tales (Lieberman, 1972). If females are not beautiful princesses, they are mean stepmothers, nasty sisters, and wicked witches. When we turn to stories about animal characters, we find that most of them are male. Winnie-the-Pooh and his friends are all male except for Kanga the mother, and most of the fantasy characters in the popular Dr. Suess stories are male. Even when the gender of fantasy or animal characters is not marked in the text or illustrations, when mothers read to their toddlers, they refer to such characters as male 95 percent of the time (DeLoache, Cassidy, & Carpenter, 1987). Fantasy stories for preadolescents are dominated by male characters, including the *Narnia Chronicles* and the *Lord of the Rings*. Bias can even be found in nursery rhymes: A student analyzed a book of 301 Mother Goose rhymes for a class project and found that about 30 percent were about males, 22 percent about females, 9 percent about both, and 35 percent were about gender-neutral characters (e.g., animals). While this seemed reasonably equitable, she then examined the illustrations for the neutral rhymes and found that males were twice as likely to be pictured as females!

The stereotyping in fairy tales, rhymes, and classic children's books creates a dilemma for parents, who might object to the hidden messages but who recall their own enjoyment of the stories and want to share them in turn with their own children. Bem's (1983) suggestion is that parents can enjoy reading the stories with their children but also point out that the ideas are old-fashioned; for example, "Isn't it funny that people back then thought that girls needed to be rescued all the time?" One girl reinterpreted a fairy tale herself, saying, "I know the princess is asleep, but her mind is not. She's figuring out her next move" (McCabe, 1992, p. 37). Parents can also provide contemporary books as an alternative in which female characters are more independent and competent than Cinderella and Sleeping Beauty (A. Davis, 1984; St. Peter, 1979). In some cases older books have actually been updated. For example, the popular "Noddy" books in Britain, a 40-year-old series about doll characters in "Toytown," were recently rewritten to eliminate derogatory terms for black dolls and to increase the self-reliance of females who formerly had always waited for Noddy, the main character, to rescue them when they got into trouble. As the publishers commented, "Certain changes were long overdue" (*Valley News*, 1990).

Children's textbooks. The situation has not been much better with books used in the classroom. One analysis of 134 textbooks used for reading instruction revealed that boys were four times more likely to be main characters than girls (Women on Words and Images [WOWI], 1974). Not only did boys appear more frequently in the stories, their activities made for much more interesting and appealing reading. Boys traveled to China, panned for gold in Yellowstone, sledded to the North Pole, drove submarines, and captured grizzly bears, while girls sewed outfits for a brother competing in a rodeo and baked cookies for the state fair. Boys faced challenges that taught them bravery, initiative, and persistence, while girls waited to be assisted by their fathers or older brothers. In one story a female main character's big problem was a dirty tennis dress—it is hard to imagine what valuable personal qualities a girl would acquire as the result of dealing with such a challenge (WOWI, 1974).

Have things changed in the last two decades? One study found that recent textbooks for reading instruction had been significantly updated (Purcell & Stewart, 1990). There were almost as many female characters as males, and girls had more active roles in the stories. The number of biographies of women had also increased significantly, thus providing more role models for girls. Other analyses of recently published children's schoolbooks have not been quite so positive. Boy characters had been changed to girls to increase the number of female characters, but the stories that were revised in this way were judged to be weaker in plot and less interesting to children (Purcell & Stewart, 1990; Stitt, 1988). For example, there were more stories about women doctors but not many women explorers or big game wardens. The names of white male characters were sometimes changed to minority names ("Mark" to "Manual") without updating the cultural content of the story. In addition, the decrease in the number of stories about boys was matched by an increase in the number of stories about male animals and animated-object characters (e.g., a talking clock). Thus, although there have been significant changes in instructional materials, traces of male dominance and stereotyping remain.

The Impact of Nonsexist Materials

If children's literature and textbooks tend to be stereotyped, perhaps the solution is to look for materials that show the sexes in more flexible roles. This counterprogramming approach would also help confirm that children are actually influenced by what they read, as we saw in our evaluation of television discussed earlier. Several studies have demonstrated that sex-equitable materials can significantly alter children's behavior and beliefs about the sexes (Ashby & Wittmaier, 1978; Scott & Feldman-Summers, 1979; Stitt, 1988; Zimet, 1976). In one case, 3- to 5-year-olds chose a nonstereotyped toy after hearing a story about another child of the same sex who had played with the toy (Ashton, 1983). Flerx, Fidler, & Rodgers, (1976) used the classroom story time in several kindergartens to compare children's responses to two sets of stories presented over a 5-day period. One set included traditional books, while the second set included books that showed both males and females working outside the home and sharing household tasks. Children who heard the egalitarian stories were significantly less stereotyped in their responses to questions like, "Who rakes the leaves, sets the table, works in an office, is afraid of a bug, helps a hurt child, is the smartest," and so on, when compared with children who had heard the traditional stories. The effect was striking given that the total intervention time was only about 2½ hours. Children's ethnic prejudices can also be reduced by exposure to nonstereotyped materials (Berg-Cross & Berg-Cross, 1978; Litcher & Johnson, 1969). In a review of instructional materials for elementary school children Schau and Scott (1984) recommended that schools use sex-equitable materials whenever possible. Ensuring that much of the written material that children see in school is nonsexist could help counteract children's formation of gender schemas and counter their tendency to assume that only boys can be doctors, explorers, and pilots while only girls can be nurses and teachers.

These recommendations run counter to those made in many teacher education textbooks, which argue that while girls will read stories about boys, boys will not read stories about girls, and so the school library collection should have twice as many books about boys and teachers should select instructional materials that are specially designed to appeal to boys' interests (Segel, 1986). One survey of several hundred elementary teachers found that eight of the ten favorite stories for reading aloud in the classroom were about males (N. Smith, Greenlaw, & Scott, 1987). When children are asked what they would prefer to read, boys and girls at times do express a preference for stories with same-sex characters, but sex-typed preferences are small in elementary school relative to the junior high and high school periods (Bleakley, Westerberg, & Hopkins, 1988; Connor & Serbin, 1978; Kropp & Halverson, 1983; Schau & Scott, 1984). In addition, this can become a self-fulfilling prophecy, leading to a preponderance of "boys' books," limiting boys' chance to experience different points of view through literature, and making female experiences invisible (Segel, 1986). A preference does not mean that boys will not read or listen to stories about girls, especially now that there are more interesting books with female main characters. One teacher found that both her male and female second-grade students enjoyed *Little House on the Prairie* when she read it aloud to her class, even though it focused on the girls in the pioneer family. One boy nominated *A Wrinkle in Time* by Madeleine L'Engle as his favorite book, although when the teacher mentioned that the story was about a girl, he quickly dismissed her as not really a main character (Segel, 1986)!

When teachers are interested in using sex-equitable materials in their classrooms, they often find it difficult to do so. It is very expensive for school districts to replace books, so teachers may have to use books that are decades old, and new texts, workbooks, and films are often selected by a central school district office rather than by individual teachers. Teachers may also encounter resistance from some parents to the use of updated textbooks and storybooks in the classroom (Britton & Lumpkin, 1977; Cohen, 1985; Hemp, 1991). In a recent case the state court of Tennessee ruled in support of a group of parents who had objected to a second-grade textbook that did not depict women exclusively in their traditional role as homemakers.

◼ The Effects of Sexist Language

Media influences are not limited to obviously stereotyped images on TV and in children's books. Even the language we use acts as a subtle influence on children's gender stereotypes.

Some linguists have suggested that language has the power to shape how we think about concepts. While there is considerable disagreement about this claim, it is certainly the case that what things are called can have important social and emotional significance. For example, the term *sissy* has such strong negative connotations that it can overwhelm common sense: In 1992, a man dove off a Maine bridge to his death when a relative called him a sissy for hesitating, and in 1979 a boy fatally stabbed another child for calling him a sissy (Pogrebin, 1980).

Language often provides cues to children about the relative status of males and females. In the English language, many terms of reference are male in their basic form, and special "marked" forms have been developed to refer to females, such as actress, mistress, duchess, waitress, majorette, and Smurfette (Graddol & Swann, 1989). Many female proper names are marked forms of male names, including Joanne, Roberta, Patricia, Christine, Andrea, and Paula. The terms used to refer to people also have a basic masculine form ("mankind," "he") that is sometimes claimed to be generic, that is, to refer to both sexes, as in the original *Star Trek* television series mission, "to boldly go where no *man* has gone before" (italics added). However, researchers have found that adults typically assume that the supposedly generic terms "he" and "man" refer specifically to males; in other words, people assume that females are not included unless they are specifically mentioned, which is why the new series lead-in speaks of going "where no *one* has gone before" (italics added; Hamilton, 1988, 1991; MacKay, 1980; Martyna, 1978; Moulton, Robinson, & Elias, 1978; J. Schneider & Hacker, 1973).

Like adults, children also assume that "he" and "man" mean males, not females (Fisk, 1985; Hyde, 1984a; Switzer, 1990). One girl read the instructions for a new board game and said, "This game isn't for girls, Mommy, look how it says a player should move *his* piece when *he* draws a card" (Pogrebin, 1980, p. 375). When schoolchildren were asked to draw pictures of "early cavemen," they drew men, but when they were asked to draw "early cave people," they drew families with men, women, boys, and girls (Stitt, 1988). In one experiment children heard the first sentence of a story: "When a kid goes to school, —— often feels excited on the first day." The blank was filled in with "he," "he or she," or "they." Children were then asked to complete the story. When children heard the "he" or "they" version, most of their stories were about boys. In contrast, when "he or she" was used in the opening sentence, almost half the children told stories about girls (Hyde, 1984a).

Children's assumption that "he" usually means only males could contribute to girls' increasing lack of confidence in school, since many texts and materials use sexist language (Hyde, 1984a). To investigate this possibility, Hyde had children read a description of the fictitious job of "making wudges." Some children read the description referring to wudgemakers as "he," while others read "she," "he or she," or "they" versions. Children were then asked to rate how well they thought men and women would make wudges. Those who read descriptions which referred to wudgemakers as "he" thought that men would do a better job. Those who read the "they" and "he or she" versions gave similar ratings to men and women, and the "she" version produced high ratings for women, along with high ratings for men. In other words, children assumed that men would always be good wudgemakers, but the children needed a specific linguistic marker to infer that the job could also be done well by women.

Since children are sensitive to the gender cues in language, it is important to use both "he" and "she" in speech and writing, or at least to alternate between them on different occasions. Admittedly, efforts to alter language to include females can sometimes irritate readers who insist that "he" is truly generic. I once tried to solve the sexist language problem in my own writing by alternating "he" in one paragraph and "she" in another. One of the reviewers of the article unconsciously overlooked all the instances of "he" and angrily questioned why I had included only female children in my study. An elementary school teacher encountered male resistance when she changed all the "he" pronouns in the materials for a lesson about space travel to "she." Her female students wrote essays about space*women* for the first time, but the boys in the class loudly resisted the idea of spacewomen and defiantly wrote only about space*men* (Sarah, 1980). Despite occasional problems it is better in the long run for boys to realize that certain careers are not the exclusive domain of males, even if the notion makes them a bit uncomfortable at first, and for girls to hear language that specifically includes them.

SUMMARY

As we have seen, television and books provide an additional curriculum about gender roles. Content analyses of television and books reveal a preponderance of male characters, as well as stereotypical depictions of both sexes. Although the effects of such materials are not always easy to tease apart, several research strategies have confirmed that exposure to such materials contributes to children's gender stereotyping and that sex-equitable materials can help to change children's beliefs. In general, gender stereotypes in the media are so prevalent and exaggerated that it seems it would be hard for children to escape getting the picture. Even if children learn nothing new from these sources, what they see and hear is consistent with what they have learned at home, in school, and with their peers. All these factors acting together create a powerful lesson about what it means to be male or female.

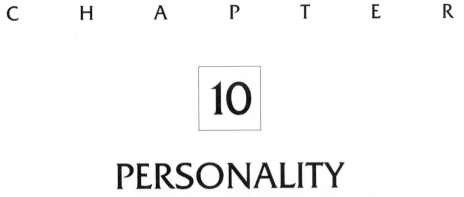

PERSONALITY CHARACTERISTICS OF BOYS AND GIRLS

Sugar and spice and everything nice,
that's what little girls are made of;
snakes and snails and puppy dog tails,
that's what little boys are made of.

Up to this point, concentrating primarily on the processes through which children learn to be male and female, we looked at several theories of how this learning takes place in the family and examined the influence of peers, schools, and the media. In this chapter and the next we turn to look at some of the *consequences* of growing up male or female in terms of personality and intellectual characteristics. As the traditional rhyme above illustrates, we tend to believe that girls are sweet-natured, kind, and caring, while boys are feisty, rambunctious, and ready to stand up for themselves—or, if not, that they should be. As we have seen, children themselves believe these stereotypes: One girl said, "Boys are smelly, horrid and wild," while her male classmate retorted, "Girls are silly and soft and they are not strong; they all want to be nurses and they all want to be flowers" (Statham, 1986, p. 6).

In this chapter our first goal is to consider whether boys and girls do in fact differ in certain personality areas, including aggressive behavior, prosocial behavior such as helping and nurturing others, and moral reasoning. In these areas we must often balance our own needs with those of others; for example, if we stand up for ourselves and go after what we want without concern for others, we are considered aggressive, whereas if we put our own desires to one side in order to help someone else, we are considered altruistic and nurturing. As you can probably anticipate by this point, these alternatives are linked with gender, so that aggression is more often considered appropriate for males—a girl who stands up for herself may find others call her a "bitch"—while prosocial behavior is more

177

often expected of females—a boy who is too quick to help others may earn the label "wimp." Yet are these behaviors really linked to gender, or are they merely stereotypes?

In addition to examining the evidence regarding possible gender differences, we consider potential explanations for the patterns of aggression, prosocial behavior, and moral reasoning. Although both biology and differential socialization are no doubt involved in the development of personality characteristics, it is especially important not to underestimate the role of socialization. It is often relatively easy, for example, to assume that boys are just naturally more aggressive because of "hormones" while overlooking the social factors that contribute to aggression. Most people are not in a position to verify or challenge biological arguments, and so such claims tend to have an aura of authority that sometimes overstates the case. In addition, the power of socialization is easy to overlook because we are so accustomed to tailoring behavior along gender lines that we do not always recognize the extent of differential treatment. Therefore, a second goal of the chapter is to discuss both the contribution of biology and differential socialization where appropriate.

We begin with a discussion of gender differences by reviewing what constitutes a difference in terms of group averages and relative variability. Then we consider the area of aggression, followed by prosocial behavior and, finally, moral reasoning. Within each section we look at whether boys and girls really differ and consider possible explanations for the patterns.

WHAT IS A GENDER DIFFERENCE?

Claims about differences in boys' and girls' behaviors in areas such as aggression and altruism often sound plausible and authoritative. "Men and women: our differences are here to stay," reported *Cosmopolitan* magazine, adding, "does biology give boys the edge?" (1989). Without some inside knowledge about what constitutes a "difference," there is no way to verify or question the conclusions. Because knowledge is power, in this section we work through a short example of a straightforward gender difference (in height) to give you the tools to understand and assess claims about gender differences. If you can add, subtract, multiply, and divide, you already have the basic skills; one does not need an advanced degree in statistics to be a reasonably informed reader of the gender differences literature.

■ Example: Gender Differences in Height

Suppose we wanted to investigate differences in height between high school boys and girls. To obtain initial information, we stood outside the local high school school gym and measured the height of 10 boys and 10 girls who passed by on their way to gym class. The heights we collected are shown in Table 10.1. The group of 10 boys includes a very tall young man who led his basketball team to the state championship and who is currently being recruited by the local university as a potential center. The boys' group also includes a very short male who is clinging to the hope that he is just a late bloomer. The remaining eight boys are more typical students, hovering between $5^{1}/_{2}$ and 6 feet.

TABLE 10.1 Heights of 10 Boys and 10 Girls, in Inches	
Boys	Girls
88	60
68	66
68	63
72	60
75	63
60	63
76	72
70	68
64	66
56	61

Group Averages

The heights in the table are listed in inches; if you add the inches and divide by 10 (the number in the group), you can see that the average (or *mean*) height for the boys' group is about 69.7 inches, or 5 feet, 8 inches. The average height for U.S. adult men is about 5 feet, 10 inches; some of our male high schoolers are still growing and have not yet reached their full adult height.

We also measured 10 girls. Again, as you can see from their heights listed in Table 10.1, there is a considerable range, including girls who are taller than some of their male classmates, and thus feel self-conscious on dates, and girls who are quite short. Adding up the girls' heights and dividing by 10 (the number in the group), you find that the group average for females is about 5 feet, 3 inches. The average for U.S. women is 5 feet, 4 inches, so our high school girls are closer to their final height, which is consistent with the fact that girls mature physically earlier than boys.

Now that we have collected the initial data, we can begin to examine it for patterns. Figure 10.1 shows both the girls (the X's) and boys (the O's) marked against a height chart; for example, you can see the basketball center up near the top at the 88-inch mark. The group averages are marked by bars on the height chart. The difference between the average heights for the boys and girls passes what my first statistics professor used to call the "interoccular trauma" test—it jumps out and hits you between the eyes! In other words, the 5-inch difference between the two averages is noticeable, both on the chart and in real life. Most group differences in psychology are not *nearly* this large.

Overlap between Groups

There are several points to notice about the data in our height chart. First, there is an overlap between the groups. Several of the boys are shorter than many of the girls (leading to the high heels problem). Our 72-inch girl feels especially awkward because there are only a few boys in her class who are as tall as she is, and she does not want a boyfriend who

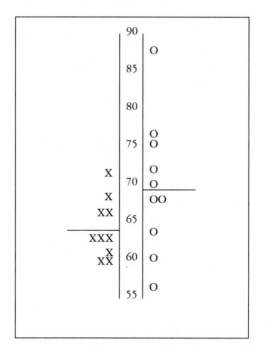

FIGURE 10.1 Height Chart of 10 Boys (Os) and 10 Girls (Xs).

is shorter than she is. (In fact, the world's tallest woman wants to marry someone even taller than she is, arguing that she is an "old-fashioned gal.") There is enough overlap of boys' and girls' heights that if we knew a child was 65 inches tall, we couldn't tell whether the child was male or female; both would be reasonable guesses.

Groups versus Individuals

A more subtle point about our collection of height measurements is that characteristics of the groups do not necessarily apply to any individual person who belongs to a group. For example, an upper-middle-class suburb may have mostly large homes with manicured lawns and expensive shrubbery, but there may still be several run-down homes on the block with rusting old cars parked in the front yard. A group of couples may go on skiing weekends and rent a condo and equipment together to reduce costs; while most of the individuals enjoy skiing, it is perfectly possible than one or two might not actually ski, preferring to relax by the fire with a hot drink. Similarly, a group average does not necessarily match the score of any one person. The boys' average is 69 inches, but in our example no particular boy happens to be 69 inches tall. The group average also does not tell you very much about how tall any particular person is. In the case of the boys, knowing that the group average for boys is 69 inches does not help us guess how tall other boys are because there are just as many who are shorter or taller. This illustrates that a group may possess certain characteristics or tendencies but those properties may not be found in any one person, and there may be several members who don't fit the general pattern at all.

In our discussion of personality characteristics we will be comparing large groups of boys and girls, and our conclusions will be limited to the groups, not to any one individual within a group. We might, for example, conclude that a group of boys is taller than a group of girls, without assuming that all the boys are taller than all the girls. Or drawing on an example that we have previously encountered, we might find that parents of boys as a group tend to leave their sons alone to play more often than parents of girls as a group, but there may well be some parents who never let their little boys out of their sight and some parents who push their daughters out the backdoor in the morning to play and tell them not to come home until dark. In most cases we cannot make conclusions about particular individuals on the basis of group characteristics.

Variation within a Group

Another point to notice on the height chart is that the boys' range is wider than the girls'. Some boys are close to the average height but others are quite far away, while most of the girls are clustered pretty close to the group average. Notice that each individual is a different distance from the group average; for example, our basketball star is about 18 inches taller than the group average ($88 - 69.7 = 18.3$). The tendency for a group's scores to be clustered or spread out is measured by the *standard deviation*, meaning how much the scores tend to deviate away from the group average in both directions. The standard deviation is calculated by subtracting the group average from each person's score (this gives you the "deviation" of each person from the average). Then we *standardize* these deviation scores by squaring each one, adding them up, dividing by the total group size, and taking the square root. Now we examine our calculations in detail.

To illustrate, in the case of the boys, we first find the deviations by subtracting each score from the average, and then square each deviation, as shown in Table 10.2. We add the squared deviations and get 727.97 inches; we divide by the number of boys in the group ($727.97/10 = 72.79$); and we take the square root of 72.79 inches, which is 8.53 inches. Therefore, the boys' group has a standard deviation of about $8\frac{1}{2}$ inches. If you follow the same steps for the girls, the standard deviation is about 3.8 inches. Reflecting

TABLE 10.2 Finding and Squaring Deviations		
Score − average	Square	Result
$88 - 69.7 = 18.3$	18.3×18.3	334.8
$68 - 69.7 = -1.7$	-1.7×-1.7	2.9
$68 - 69.7 = -1.7$	-1.7×-1.7	2.9
$72 - 69.7 = 2.3$	2.3×2.3	5.3
$75 - 69.7 = 5.3$	5.3×5.3	28.0
$60 - 69.7 = 9.7$	9.7×9.7	94.1
$76 - 69.7 = 6.3$	6.3×6.3	39.7
$70 - 69.7 = 0.3$	0.3×0.3	0.0
$64 - 69.7 = -5.7$	-5.7×-5.7	32.5
$56 - 69.7 = -13.7$	-13.7×-13.7	187.7

the fact that the boys are a more variable group, the standard deviation is larger for boys than girls. Computing a standard deviation is admittedly tedious to do by hand, but most calculators can produce it instantly if you type in a set of scores. (Differences in conventions for rounding off the decimal places and variations in the particular formula being used can lead to minor differences in the results, but this is not a major concern for our purposes.) Squaring the standard deviation gives you the *variance*, another value occasionally used to represent the variability of a set of scores around the average.

You are probably wondering why we even need to worry about how spread out the scores are; why can't we just say the boys are 5 inches taller than the girls, and leave it at that? One reason is that if the group is highly variable, as our boys' group is, knowing only the average can give you a misleadingly, limited idea of typical height. Although the average boy is about 5 feet, 8 inches, a boy could quite easily fall into a range of almost 9 inches (the standard deviation) in height while still being perfectly typical. In contrast, the standard deviation for girls tells us that a typical girl is likely to be within a 4-inch range. A second reason for being concerned about the standard deviation is that it can alert you that there may be unusual individuals in the group you happened to measure. For example, in our boys' sample the one very tall boy raises the average for the entire group by about 2 inches! The large standard deviation alerts us to this possibility.

A third reason to be concerned about the standard deviation is that it becomes important when we want to compare two groups and decide if they are really different. To consider this issue, we need to talk about distributions.

Samples and Distributions

If we turn our height chart on its side, we see a *histogram* representation of our boys and girls. The heights of the bars show the number of people who are a particular height: In this example, there is only one person at most of the heights, but there are two boys who are 68 inches tall, so that bar is twice as tall as the others, and three girls who are 63 inches tall. In Figure 10.2*a*, the very short boy is shown as the bar on the far left (at 56 inches), while the basketball center is represented as the bar on the far right (at 88 inches).

Of course, our set of 10 boys and 10 girls is only a "sample," or a subset of the students at the high school. We might want to look at a larger group, to make sure that the students we happened to encounter on their way to gym class are a good representation of the entire set of students. After all, we did include a very tall person in our first group; maybe he is so unusual that his inclusion has distorted the boys' average too much. Clearly, we would want to look at larger groups to get a sense of whether our preliminary information is reliable and reasonably accurate.

Figure 10.3 shows the histograms with 25 more boys and girls added in. You can see the original students are still represented; the basketball star is still there at 88 inches, for example. The average heights for the groups of 35 boys and 35 girls are still at about 70 and 64 inches, respectively. Notice that the gaps in the bars are starting to "fill in," as we run into more people of different heights.

Figure 10.4 shows histograms with even larger samples: 100 boys and 100 girls. The averages are still about the same, and the diagrams are beginning to look more rounded. With these larger groups we see two things: First, the gaps are filled in even more; now we have encountered at least one person of almost every height. Second, most of the people are

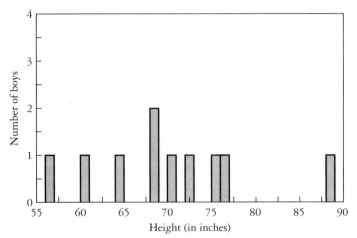

FIGURE 10.2a Distribution of 10 Boys' Heights.

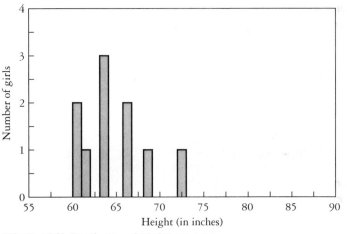

FIGURE 10.2b Distribution of 10 Girls' Heights.

clustered around the average. There are more people who are about 71 inches tall, than 61 or 81 inches.

If we drew a line connecting the tops of the bars, we would see a curved outline, or what is called a *distribution*. While our example shows a distribution of heights, we could also construct similar distributions representing the annual salaries, IQ scores, or bowling scores of a group of people. A distribution is simply a list of possible scores or values, showing the number of people in a sample who have each of the various scores or values. The distribution has a group mean and a standard deviation that represent the variability of the scores.

Distributions can have different shapes: If we made a distribution of annual salaries, it might have a long "tail" that represents a small number of extremely wealthy people, with the bulk of the scores in the middle-class range, and a sizable group of people living below the poverty line (about $14,000 annually for a family of four). This distribution would have an *enormous* standard deviation; the average income might be about $16,000 but the

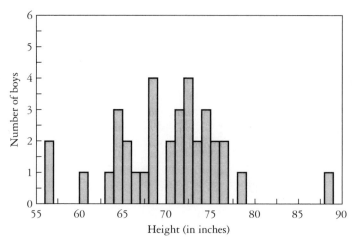

FIGURE 10.3a Distribution of 35 Boys' Heights.

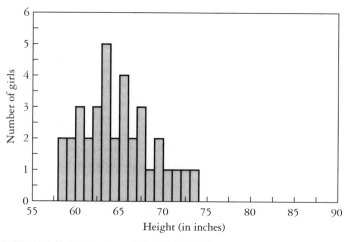

FIGURE 10.3b Distribution of 35 Girls' Heights.

range of zero to several million dollars is so large that the average is not very meaningful. In contrast, if we made a distribution of the number of hours of TV watched per week, it might be considerably tighter: Hardly anyone watches less than 10 hours per week, most people watch about 40, and there is an upper limit of about 60, set by the fact that people also have to work and sleep!

Comparing Distributions

Recall that with our initial group of 10 boys and 10 girls we compared the averages using our height chart, and it was fairly easy to see that the boys were taller on average. If we superimpose the distributions for the larger groups, it is not quite so easy to tell just by looking. This is where statistical tests come in; various tests can be used to compare the group averages while taking into account the "spread," or variance, of the groups. For example, the boys' group still has a very tall boy (the 88-incher), so we want to be sure to

WHAT IS A GENDER DIFFERENCE?

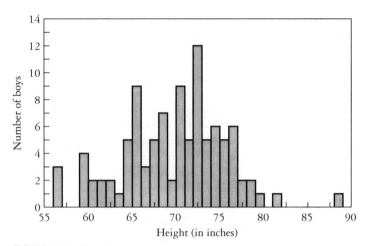

FIGURE 10.4a Distribution of 100 Boys' Heights.

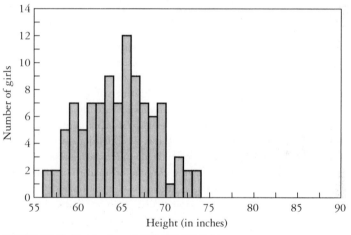

FIGURE 10.4b Distribution of 100 Girls' Heights.

take that into account. In addition, statistical tests take the overall scale of the scores into account. A difference of 5 inches seems like a lot, but only because the scores fall into a range of about 2 feet, from about $4^{1}/_{2}$ to $6^{1}/_{2}$ feet tall. If we were 30 feet tall, a difference of 5 inches would be meaningless!

We will not go into particular tests here, but you should not be overly intimidated by them; a statistical difference merely means that two averages are reliably different in the sense that they are probably not due to the chance inclusion of some unusual scores. For example, after we have measured the heights of 25 boys and 25 girls, we would be fairly sure that the average differences were not due only to the one boy who happens to be 88 inches tall. Detecting that a consistent, reliable difference exists often depends on the number of cases we have examined, because it is numerically easier to detect small consistent patterns with large groups. Most gender differences in behavior that are reported by psychologists are much smaller in scale than our height example, and the psychological or behavioral differences are only noticeable when data from very large samples are analyzed.

This again means that the properties of a large group are even less likely to apply to any one person than is the case with small groups.

Interpreting Group Differences

In psychological research, when someone claims that "males are better at X than females," they are usually comparing two distributions of scores, one for males and one for females, just as we have done with our height example. Again, the claim is not that all males are better than all females, only that there is a higher group average for males than females. In addition to knowing the group averages, it is also reasonable to ask how large the difference is, how much overlap there is between the groups, and how wide a range of performance there is within each group. It is also reasonable to ask if the group differences are consistent in direction. Perhaps if we took our measurements at many schools, we would find cases in which a particular group of girls happened to be taller than a group of boys. We would also want to know if the difference varies across the life span. In the case of height, girls are taller on average than boys during the transition to puberty, because they enter their adolescent growth spurt sooner. The conclusion, "boys are taller on average than girls," would depend on the age of the children.

It's also important, after establishing that two groups are reliably different, to ask whether it is a meaningful difference. In our example of height, the difference is statistically significant, meaning that the 5-inch difference is reliable and not due to the accidental inclusion of a few people who are extremely tall or short, but it is hardly an important or meaningful difference. For most people, height variations do not make any practical difference in life. Most men and women can pass through doorways without ducking, and most people see over the theater seats in front of them without sitting on a telephone book. There is no particular advantage to being very tall or very short, other than to play professional basketball or to ride thoroughbred racehorses. Most women are not tall enough to play for the Boston Celtics but neither are most men, and very few people of either sex are short enough to be champion jockeys. In fact, height requirements for many jobs have been eliminated because there is no evidence that being a certain height is necessary for good job performance (at most, it may make it easier to order standard-sized uniforms).

All this information is necessary to put a discussion about differences between males and females in perspective, which is especially important because of a strong tendency in the media to exaggerate the size and importance of sex differences—at least those differences that relate to the overall structure of a society and to power relations between males and females. There are many differences between groups of men and women, but most are so trivial that we pay little attention to them. We do not see headlines about the fact that most (but not all) U.S. women wear makeup while most U.S. men do not (although some do).

Now that we are armed with some basic terminology, we can turn to look at the personality characteristics of boys and girls. We focus on aggression, prosocial behavior, and moral reasoning because there are stereotypes about the sexes in these areas which influence how children are treated by parents, teachers, and peers; namely, boys are more aggressive, and girls are more empathetic, nurturant, and concerned for other people. Some of these stereotypes reflect real differences in the behavior of boys and girls, as in the case of aggression. However, other stereotypes are much less accurate; for example, as we will see, girls have a reputation for being helpful and empathetic but the reputation is not particularly well deserved.

AGGRESSION

If asked how men and women are most different, people would probably mention aggression. Greater male aggression is apparent in warfare and combat, as well as in terms of antisocial behavior; at all points in the life span, men are more likely than women to be imprisoned and to die as the result of violence (Tavris & Wade, 1984). Among adolescents, five times as many boys are arrested for violent crimes as girls (Parke & Slaby, 1983). Even 2-year-olds think that boys are more likely to hit than girls (Kuhn, Nash, & Brucken, 1978). We accept high levels of male violence as "normal," while feminine aggression attracts attention because it is relatively unusual. For example, men kill members of their family with dismaying frequency, but Lizzie Borden, who was suspected of murdering her parents with an axe, is still famous after a century even though she was exonerated of the crime! In my former home state of New Hampshire a young school administrator was convicted of enticing several teenagers to murder her husband. The news media coverage and public interest in her case reached obscene levels, including telephone polls conducted during the trial by newspapers in which callers could register their "guilty" or "innocent" verdicts. In contrast, local cases of husbands who killed their wives were considered to be almost routine, including a husband who murdered his wife and then put her dismembered body through a tree chipper and another man who allegedly hired two teenagers to take his pregnant wife to an empty construction site and stab her while he watched and laughed (*Boston Globe*, 1991e).

■ Patterns of Aggression in Boys and Girls

Differences in the amount of aggressive behavior displayed by the sexes are found early in the life span, beginning in the toddler period when children first become capable of hostile intentions. For most children the first target for aggressive impulses is the parent. In the second and third year, boys are more likely than girls to have tantrums and to lash out at their parents. After the third year, the overall rate of tantrums and aggression toward parents drops steadily, but it drops faster for girls than boys. One reason for greater male aggression during this period is that, as we saw in Chapter 5, boys are encouraged to be more independent than girls and thus are more often frustrated when parents eventually step in to control them, while girls are more likely to be compliant because they have been encouraged to mesh their activities with those of the parent (Maccoby, 1980). I found these data particularly compelling after a party in which a parent brought his 3-year-old son to our apartment. The little boy became overtired and responded to all parental efforts to restrain him by lying on his back, howling, and kicking the walls that I had just laboriously repainted pale sage green.

Although aggression toward parents declines by the preschool period for both boys and girls, aggression toward other children increases. The reason is clear: Aggressive acts toward peers are very often rewarded by positive consequences, such as getting food or an attractive toy away from another child (P. K. Smith & Green, 1975). Both boys and girls clearly learn from other children how to be aggressive. In one study children were observed with their playmates during their first year in preschool; those who did not hit or attack others at the start of the school year had learned to do so by the spring (G. Patterson, Littman, & Bricker, 1967). Children also learn aggression from their siblings. Sibling conflicts are the most frequent form of family aggression; almost half the interactions between 2- to 5-year-old siblings were found to be hostile, with the highest rates of aggression episodes occurring between brother-brother pairs (R. Abramovitch, Corter, & Lando, 1979; Parke & Slaby, 1983).

The gender difference in aggressive behavior is found consistently in cross-cultural data. Whiting and Edwards (1973) studied preschool children in several cultures, including Kenya, Japan, India, the Philippines, Mexico, and the United States, and recorded incidents of verbal (e.g., insults) and physical aggression. Across the cultures, boys outscored girls on both forms of aggression. In the United States, higher rates of male aggression have been found across social class. Children from working-class and poor families show more aggression overall than those from wealthy families, but within each group boys have higher rates of aggression than girls (Parke & Slaby, 1983; Shaffer, 1988).

Several factors contribute to greater aggression in boys. First, boys' play tends to involve more gross motor activity and rough-and-tumble play which can create the antecedent conditions for aggression (DiPietro, 1981). If one boy playfully punches or shoves another, the other child can easily misperceive hostility or even be accidently hurt and thus counterattack in earnest. Second, as we saw in Chapter 7, boys are more concerned with dominance relations, and implied or explicit aggression is often the means by which dominance is established and acknowledged. Dave Barry gives the following example: "Guys at sporting events getting into shoving matches and occasionally sustaining fatal heart attacks over such issues as who was next in line for pretzels." As a result of boys' focus on establishing dominance, rates of aggression are higher for male-male pairs than for mixed or female-female pairs (P. K. Smith & Green, 1975). Men who are, or who feel that they are, low in the dominance hierarchy relative to other men may direct aggression toward women, as if to reassure themselves that they are at least "better" than females. Perhaps this is why several members of the New England Patriots football team harassed a female reporter in the locker room in the 1990–1991 season; the team had won only one game that year.

How Substantive Is the Sex Difference?

As we discussed earlier, the fact that a gender difference is consistent does not necessarily mean that it is large or meaningful. In a review of 143 studies of children's aggressive behavior, Hyde (1984b) discovered that only about 5 percent of the variance between individual children could be attributed to the child's sex and that the average aggression scores for boys and girls were about half of a standard deviation apart. This is not a trivial difference, but there is a vast overlap in the distributions and for most children, for whom aggression rates are in the average range, gender therefore yields little predictive power. In addition, the male average is inflated by the fact that most extremely aggressive children are boys (Dodge, 1980; Eme, 1979; Olweus, 1979, 1980; G. Patterson, 1980). Take the perspective of a school counselor who finds several new case files on your desk. You open one file and see that "Leslie" has been reported by several teachers as a bully who has been making the younger children's recess periods and bus rides a living hell by starting fights and threatening them. You can make a reasonable inference that Leslie is male; in fact, you would be surprised if Leslie was female because there are relatively few female bullies. In the next file you read that "Chris," who is generally well behaved, was referred for pushing another child off a chair in the school cafeteria when the other child allegedly stole a piece of pizza (a prized asset in cafeteria lunchrooms). This incident does not really give you much clue about whether Chris is a boy or a girl because either sex would be likely to respond with hostility in this situation.

Not all studies note sex differences in aggressive behavior. Girls are perfectly capable of aggression when they think the situation calls for it. For example, a 14-year-old Massachusetts girl was pushed to the ground, beaten, and kicked by several girls who thought she had snitched to the school authorities that a friend was drunk in the school restroom, while in another case a girl ordered her male friends to beat and orally rape another girl who had flirted with her boyfriend (Lipsitt, 1988). There has also been a decrease in the number of studies reporting a gender difference in aggression in the last decade. This could reflect a change in socialization practices such that girls are actually becoming more aggressive than in the past. It is also possible that more examples of girls' aggressive behavior are now being reported, or that studies reporting no differences between boys' and girls' aggression are now more likely to be published than in previous decades (Hyde, 1984b).

The "Boys Will Be Boys" Effect

Observers' stereotyped expectations might have led to a systematic *underreporting* of male aggression. J. C. Condry and Ross (1985) found that observers tend to overlook aggression in boys while immediately noticing it in girls and mixed-sex pairs. In their study, subjects were shown a videotape of two children roughhousing, including punches and tussles, in the snow. The children were dressed in bulky snowsuits so that their gender was not apparent. Subjects were told that the videotape showed two boys, two girls, or a mixed pair. Their job was to rate how aggressive and affectionate one of the children was toward the other, with all subjects rating the same target child in the pair. Although all subjects observed the same behavior, their judgments of the target child's aggressiveness varied with gender label. Observers' ratings of aggression were highest when they thought both children were girls and lowest when they thought both children were boys. The researchers called this the "boys will be boys" effect, meaning that observers unconsciously expect boys to play roughly so a boy's action must be *highly* aggressive before it will be registered and reported. In contrast, relatively modest signs of aggression in girls will be immediately noted and recorded because they are unexpected. Because children are clearly recognizable as male or female after the toddler stage, this bias may be difficult to overcome, and the sex difference might actually be more substantial than the data suggest.

◼ Theories of Aggressive Behavior

The 2-year-old son of one of my colleagues saw a large cannon monument in a public park. He immediately insisted on climbing up onto it, pounded on the barrel, and shouted, "Shoot, shoot!" His mother was puzzled that a child so young would even know that the object was a gun and wondered if this early interest was biologically based. At the same time, she recognized that it is highly unlikely that boys are genetically programmed to recognize antique cannons as weapons. As she put it, the only plausible explanation was that her son had been a European military officer in a previous life.

Past lives aside, what accounts for aggressive behavior? Why are some kids ready to pummel everyone in their path, while others are easygoing and slow to anger? In this section we look at biological and socialization factors and examine how each contributes to a sex difference in aggressive behavior.

Biological Factors

Differences in the aggressive behavior of boys and girls appear very early in the life span and seem to be universal, raising the possibility that greater male aggression has a biological foundation (Maccoby & Jacklin, 1974, 1980). Many people do assume that male aggression is biologically based, as does the author of the following letter:

> Dear Ann Landers:
> What is wrong with men? Every day you read about men who beat up their wives and children, murder girlfriends, torture animals, and commit atrocious crimes. Driving with a man is enough to make you a nervous wreck . . . Last week I saw a man get out of his car at a stoplight and punch a stranger in the face because he slowed down at a yellow light and stopped at a red one. The guy screamed, "I could have made that light if you weren't such a dumb "!&x!" and then he socked him. Women don't do things like that. It's standing room only in the prisons for men . . . Why don't our scientists do some serious studies and find out what is in the genetic makeup of males that makes them so vicious?

In fact, considerable scientific research *has* been conducted on aggression in both humans and animals. Few serious researchers would claim that biology alone makes people aggressive; we clearly learn when and how to be aggressive, as we will see below. But it is quite possible that male children are in some sense more "prepared" to learn these lessons than females. For example, males might have stronger reactions to challenges and threats than females, which could lead them into situations where aggression becomes inevitable.

Violent genes? One possibility considered by researchers is that, as the letter writer suggested above, there is something in the genetic makeup of males that predisposes them toward aggression. When Richard Speck was arrested in Chicago for the infamous murder of several nursing students in the 1960s, he was believed to have had an extra Y chromosome, that is, to be an XYY male (Fausto-Sterling, 1985). The report was not accurate, but it created considerable public excitement about the possibility that we had at last figured out what led some men to be so violent: If one Y chromosome made a male appropriately bold and assertive, two might tip him into antisocial behavior. Initial studies showed that some prison inmates did have the XYY pattern, but it subsequently turned out that many men who were *not* in prison also had an extra Y chromosome and that having an extra chromosome was correlated with reduced intelligence, which in itself is related to higher rates of antisocial behavior (Fausto-Sterling, 1985). In addition, as we saw in Chapter 2, prisoners with the double-Y characteristic had less violent criminal records than genetically normal prisoners (Doyle & Paludi, 1991). The double-Y pattern is clearly not the cause of male aggression.

Hormones. Another possibility is that higher levels of androgen hormones in males predisposes them to behave aggressively. Comparing hormone levels between the sexes does not get us very far; we already know that males have higher levels of androgens than females and that adult males are more overtly aggressive, but we cannot conclude on that basis alone that there is a causal relation between the two factors. The research strategy has been to try to explain *within-gender* variations in terms of variations in androgen levels, in other words, to demonstrate that some males are more aggressive than others because they have more testosterone (one of the androgen hormones) and that altering their hormone levels also alters their behavior (Maccoby & Jacklin, 1980).

Not all studies have shown a relation, but some have found higher levels of testosterone among men who were incarcerated for delinquent, criminal, or violent behavior (Dabbs, Frady, Carr, & Besch, 1987). Similar patterns were also found in a study of men who were not prison inmates. As part of a large study on the aftereffects of the Vietnam war, over 4600 military veterans provided extensive personal histories, and testosterone levels were measured for each subject. Men who had higher levels of testosterone reported more episodes of delinquent behavior while growing up and while in military service, as well as higher levels of substance abuse (Dabbs & Morris, 1990). The effects were not very large; in fact, the patterns were probably only apparent because of the enormous sample size. However, converging evidence for the potential role of hormones is found in studies of bullies, children who show a consistent predisposition to be highly aggressive. Bullies were found to have higher levels of testosterone than other boys (Olweus, Mattsson, Schalling, & Low, 1980). Individual levels of aggression are also fairly stable in childhood and adolescence, again suggesting that physiological factors might be involved (Cummings, Iannotti, & Zahn-Waxler, 1989; Olweus, 1979).

But let us not conclude that hormones act as an ON–OFF switch in producing aggressive behavior. After all, sex hormone levels are relatively low in childhood, when sex differences in aggressive behavior first appear. In addition, although higher levels of testosterone were found to be correlated with antisocial behavior in the study of veterans, the effect was limited to those men who had little education and low incomes. Showing that hormones do not directly affect their behavior, men with more education and money are not especially likely to be antisocial even if they have high levels of testosterone. One way to reconcile these results is to suggest that testosterone encourages a general "sensation-seeking" tendency. A desire for excitement and stimulation could certainly lead to antisocial behavior among males having few social and economic opportunities, but it could also lead to increased drive and motivation among those who are in a position to, as the author of one study put it, "do things that are both exciting and socially acceptable— driving fast cars instead of stealing them, arguing instead of fighting, playing college football instead of assaulting" (Dabbs & Morris, 1990, p. 209). The memory of a duel in the adjacent racquetball court engaging two middle-aged doctors—red-faced, sweaty, intense, and screaming at each other—comes to my mind. If they could not take potshots at each other on the court, would they have beaten each other up in the hospital parking lot? Aggressive tendencies depend as much on a person's social situation and the opportunities for socially acceptable aggression as on hormones.

Not only is androgen related indirectly to behavior, but the direction of causality is not always clear. The levels of androgen hormones within an individual are known to vary according to an individual's social situation. Male rhesus monkeys show increased testosterone levels when they are given the chance to dominate females or when they successfully challenge a high-ranking male but lower hormone levels when they are caged with males who dominate them (R. M. Rose, Gordon, & Bernstein, 1972; R. M. Rose, Holaday, & Bernstein, 1971; Tieger, 1980). A similar pattern has been observed in humans: Among men confined to a boat on a sailing holiday, those who established social dominance over the others, for example, by bossing others around or insisting on deciding where to turn the boat or when to drop anchor, showed an increase in testosterone while the others showed a decrease, although there were no differences at the start of the holiday (Cacioppo & Bernston, 1992). Stress and fear can also depress the production of androgen; men who were about to engage in combat during the Vietnam war showed reduced levels of androgen (R. Rose, 1969). Prison inmates might have higher testosterone levels because they are housed in an environment characterized by extreme dominance relations; they are not necessarily in prison because high hormone levels got them into trouble to begin with. We are left with the conclusion that male sex hormones seem to be linked to aggressive behavior but that levels of male sex hormones are set by the opportunity and the need to be dominant and aggressive—in other words, androgen and behavior are probably related, but we cannot be sure of the direction of causality.

Let's look at the possible role of sex hormones from another perspective, what Tieger (1980) terms the "organizing function." During prenatal growth, androgens produced by the developing testes of the male fetus could influence the developing central nervous system, with the effects on behavior appearing only later in the life span. In other species, such effects are clearly evident. For example, if infant male mice, who are not normally very aggressive, are injected with testosterone they will become as aggressive as adult males. If females are exposed to extra testosterone prenatally, they show higher levels of aggression as adults than nontreated females.

Such experiments would not be done deliberately with humans, but in some cases the fetus is exposed to unusual levels of sex hormones as the result of medical treatment provided to the mother. Recall that in Chapter 2 we described the case of girls who were exposed to excess androgen during prenatal development. These girls were reported to be more physically active than their sisters and to have a greater tendency to start fights with their siblings. Conversely, boys whose mothers were treated with estrogen or progesterone during pregnancy were reported to be less active than other boys. Although these results are consistent with the animal studies, the conclusions are limited, for several reasons. First, the evidence of greater activity in androgenized girls and estrogen-exposed boys was not obtained by direct observations but through maternal reports of the children's behavior. The interviewers were also aware of the children's medical history, so the reported differences may have been unconsciously exaggerated by parental and interviewers' expectations that the children would be more active as the result of their prenatal androgen exposure. Second, even if there were real and substantial differences in the level and intensity of physical activity between the prenatally treated children and the controls, other factors besides prenatal hormones could have been responsible (Fausto-Sterling, 1985). Boys whose mothers had been treated with estrogen or progesterone to maintain the pregnancy might well have been less active than other boys because they had grown up in a household with a parent who was chronically ill. Conversely, girls exposed to prenatal androgen might have developed more of their tomboy interests because they had had considerable medical treatment, including surgery on their reproductive organs and ongoing hormone therapy. The androgenized girls might have worried that they would have some trouble conceiving, reasoned that it would not make sense to make the traditional feminine goals of an early marriage and children a priority, and thus allowed themselves to develop their tomboyish side. Finally, the behaviors reported to be affected by prenatal exposure to unusual levels of sex hormones primarily involved the children's activity level and interest in sports, not aggressive behavior. Although it remains a possibility, there is little direct and compelling evidence that sex hormones have an organizing function for aggression in humans.

Recent studies suggest that androgen hormones might be influential at puberty, when hormone levels rise. One study of normal teenagers going through puberty found that for adolescent boys, higher levels of two types of androgens produced by the adrenal glands (androstenedione and dehydroepiandrosterone) were correlated with increased acting out, rebellious, and generally nasty behavior reported by their parents (Susman et al., 1987). There was no direct relationship between negative behavior and boys' testosterone levels in the study by Susman and colleagues. However, Olweus and his colleagues studied older boys in later stages of puberty and did find that higher testosterone levels were related to aggressive behaviors (Olweus et al., 1980). So far, the patterns seem to explain only the variations among individual males; no such links between sex hormones and aggressive behavior were found for teenage girls. In fact, Susman and colleagues (1987) found no overall difference in the amount of problem behavior reported for boys and girls, and the problem behaviors consisted of irritability, talking back, and rebelliousness, not physical aggression.

Attacks versus retaliation. The picture regarding the effects of hormones on human behavior is still incomplete, but it seems reasonable to allow for the possibility that androgen hormones are somehow related to temperament characteristics and aggressive behavior, either directly or indirectly. Perhaps higher levels of androgen make the person more likely to seek out higher levels of excitement and stimulation, as well as to be more excitable, impatient, and irritable than others. Someone with a "short fuse" may not be more likely to instigate hostile actions but could respond more quickly and strongly to provocation and perceived threats. In fact, among preschool children, boys are only about 25 percent more likely than girls to initiate an attack but are four times more likely to retaliate with aggression to an attack (Barrett, 1979; Parke & Slaby, 1983).

Learning

Whatever the importance of sex hormones, the social environment clearly has a powerful influence on the expression of aggression (Tieger, 1980). For example, while boys do retaliate to an attack more than girls, they typically do so only when their attacker is another boy and inhibit their response if their attacker is a girl (Parke & Slaby, 1983). There is considerable evidence that children learn both specific aggressive behaviors and when to display them and that the rewards for aggression are greater for boys than for girls.

Many parents react with frustation when they see their child bop another over the head with a plastic gun because they feel they have not encouraged this behavior. In fact, several

Calvin and Hobbes   by Bill Watterson

reviews confirm that parents do not encourage or reward boys for being aggressive, at least not directly (Maccoby & Jacklin, 1974, 1980). Parents rate incidents of aggressive behavior as equally serious regardless of the sex of the child (Wenger & Berg-Cross, 1980). In fact, parents sometimes come down harder on boys who fight or challenge the parents than on girls, who escape some harsher forms of punishment because they are thought to be more fragile. Girls probably also seem less in need of strong controls because they tend to be more compliant in the first place, while parents may feel that they need to be very firm with boys right from the start in order to retain control.

Role models and reinforcements. Although not directly rewarding aggression in sons, parents sometimes facilitate it indirectly. The way boys are punished has the unintended effect of teaching them that the way to solve problems is to hit or to lash out (Tavris & Wade, 1984). Parents are more likely to use physical punishment with boys, thus providing a model of aggression ("Don't hit your sister" [swat!]), while using inductive reasoning and verbal methods of discipline with girls ("It hurts your sister when you kick her like that; how would you like it if someone did that to you?"). Boys not only experience more punishment themselves, they probably see more examples of aggression within their own families. There is some evidence that parents are more likely to fight in front of sons than daughters and that troubled marriages drag on longer in families with sons; thus boys see more examples of family hostility (Hetherington & Camara, 1984). Parents are also implicated in the development of hyperaggressive, out-of-control children. While no one would deliberately set out to create a bully, Olweus found that parents of such children used harsh, arbitrary discipline themselves and allowed the children to be aggressive within the home without setting clear limits on their behavior (Olweus, 1980). Given that parents encourage boys to be independent and treat them more harshly than girls to begin with, boys are probably more likely to experience these extreme home conditions (G. Patterson, 1980).

Boys not only see more examples of physical aggression within the home, they have more available role models in the media. Television is both extremely violent and dominated by male role models who use aggression to meet their goals. By about 3 years, children imitate male aggressive models more than female ones, as if they have already inferred that aggression is more appropriate for males. Feminine aggression is more likely to be punished, and even when it is rewarded, it is usually performed in the service of someone else, not for personal gain. For example, *Aliens* and *Terminator 2* were popular films with strong, militant female characters, but in both cases the women were aggressive in order to defend a child. In the cult film *La femme Nikita*, the woman's aggression is initially motivated by her emotional attachments. The story has a superficially hard edge; it is about a young French woman who works as a government assassin. But it is established early in the plot that she has taken the job only because she has been sentenced to death for shooting a police officer (who had just killed her companions), and if she quits, she will be killed herself. Thus, the story provides considerable justifications for her aggression, and in the end, she escapes her employers and goes into hiding, risking her own death rather than to continue to take others' lives. Somehow, it is hard to imagine Arnold Schwarzenegger in the same role.

In addition to having more role models, boys receive more rewards for aggression than do girls, for whom aggression has social and personal costs. Among adults, what is viewed as legitimate assertiveness in a male is seen as excessive aggressiveness in a female. In one recent case heard by the Supreme Court, a woman at a prominent accounting firm was denied a partnership because her colleagues felt she was unfeminine, even though she had brought in business worth $25 million and her clients valued her for being "a determined go-getter" (Fiske, Bersoff, Borgida, Deaux, & Heilman, 1991, p. 1051). The negative responses to feminine aggression come not only from men; other women can be made uneasy by another woman who stands up for herself. In one study, business professionals, including supervisors and midlevel managers, watched a staged videotaped argument between a male and female manager, both strongly assertive characters. Both men and women described the male manager as competent and professional, but the assertive female manager was considered pushy and overly aggressive, especially by other women!

Little boys find that aggression "works," while girls find that other methods of problem solving are more effective. As we saw in Chapter 5, Fagot and her colleagues demonstrated that differential reinforcements led to greater aggressiveness in boys by the time they were 2 years old (Fagot & Hagan, 1985; Fagot, Hagan, Leinbach, & Kronsberg, 1985). Adults responded to 13-month-old boys when they hit or kicked the adult to get attention but ignored girls who did the same thing. A year later, the little boys were still physically assertive, but the girls had abandoned aggressive overtures. Children themselves report that boys should resolve conflicts through fighting but girls should not and that boys are more likely to get away with aggressive actions (D. Best et al., 1977; Gates, 1982; Kuhn et al., 1978; Perry, Perry, & Weiss, 1989). Perry and his colleagues have found that when children are asked about the consequences for aggressive acts, boys expect less disapproval from their parents as well as more concrete benefits, for example, that the way to successfully retrieve a soccer ball is by hitting the child who has grabbed it away (Perry et al., 1989). Among 11- to 15-year-olds, boys were more likely than girls to say that they used hitting and yelling as strategies to cope with anger, while girls said that they would talk with the person with whom they were angry, or get away from the situation, or try to distract themselves from the problem (Whitesell, Robinson, & Harter, 1991).

In contrast, girls experience negative social reactions and personal costs for aggression. Compared with boys, girls expect to feel more guilt and anxiety over aggressive acts and they think the victim will suffer more than do boys, who tend to minimize the suffering of their victim and to believe that aggression will make them feel better about themselves (Boldizar, Perry, & Perry, 1989; Perry, Perry, & Rasmussen, 1986; Perry et al., 1989; Sears, 1961). Similar patterns are found in studies of adults. For example, when men and women are induced to administer shocks to a confederate in the guise of a teaching task, women report more guilt and anxiety over the suffering they believe they are causing the victim (Eagley & Steffen, 1986). Girls' empathetic focus on the victim may lead them to learn to inhibit their aggressive impulses sooner than boys. Brodzinsky, Messer, and Tew (1979) asked children to make up stories about two characters in a picture and found that while both boys and girls introduced aggressive elements in the story, girls were more likely to mention events that controlled or eliminated the aggression early in the story. For example, girls said that a hostile action would be prevented by an adult or that the intended victim would get help from another person. Adult women report becoming angry when someone cuts in front of them in line or blocks them in traffic, just as men do, but women also report that they "hold back" their anger and their desire to retaliate (A. Frodi, Maccaulay, & Thome, 1977). Thus, the gender difference in aggression could be due in part to the fact that little girls learn faster than boys to keep their anger under control.

"Hit him right back." Far from being an uncontrolled outburst of anger, aggression is often highly regulated; few boys will dare challenge a boy much higher in the dominance hierarchy even if they are furious with him. Boys and girls alike learn that aggression in self-defense is acceptable and often expected. In one survey of British parents more than half of the mothers had told their children to hit back if they were attacked by another child, and both mothers and fathers feel it is more important for a boy to respond aggressively than a girl (Gates, 1982; Newson & Newson, 1968). Both sexes also learn that unprovoked attacks are frowned upon; as we saw earlier, boys are not much more likely to initiate an attack than are girls. Bob Greene, a journalist who wrote a book based on his high school diary, recalled walking up to another boy with whom he was angry and hitting him in the face without warning. He realized immediately that he had lost prestige and that he would have to do something quickly to save his social reputation, so he made a dramatic apology and invited the other boy to hit him back. Although he was knocked to the ground and had bruises for a week, it was worth it to regain the respect he had lost by being aggressive out of turn (Greene, 1987). Bullies are disliked by other children precisely because their aggression seems to be so unprovoked and unpredictable (Coie, Dodge, Terry, & Wright, 1991). Bullies assume that others have hostile intentions; for example, when told a story about a boy who spills a carton of milk all over another child in the cafeteria, bullies think the damage was intentional and that hitting the unfortunate milk spiller is a reasonable retaliatory response. Other boys assume it was an accident and perceive the bully's aggression as unwarranted (Dodge, 1980).

"Don't hit girls." In addition to learning that unprovoked aggression is prohibited, boys learn that they should not hit girls or younger children, even in response to an attack (Maccoby, 1980). I conducted an informal survey of male colleagues and students for several weeks and found that few recalled ever actually hitting a girl during childhood, even when one was attacked by what he described, with a reminiscent shudder of horror, as "a vicious neighborhood tomboy." The exception to the rule "don't hit girls" was their own sisters, for whom all bets were off. Even then, one man described an incident in which his little sister had bitten him and was "hanging on with her teeth embedded in his arm."

His parents finally told him, "Just hit her, Scott," but he begged her to let go so that he would not have to. Another man recalled that the only time he had hit a girl involved a situation of extreme provocation: She had taunted and then socked his physically and mentally handicapped twin brother, behavior that was so abhorrent that he felt completely justified in, as he put it, "punching her lights out." In fact, experimental studies of aggressive behavior in game-playing tasks show that men are less competitive with women opponents than with other men, as long as the woman appears cooperative. Once she violates feminine stereotypes by making strong competitive moves herself, she is targeted for even more aggressive competition in the game than men. Some of girls' immunity from aggression rests on their not being overtly aggressive themselves (Frodi et al., 1977).

■ Aggression: The Bottom Line

What can we conclude about the causes of male and female aggression? There may well be a biological foundation to the sex difference in aggression, based on an organizing or an activating function for androgen hormones. At the same time there is considerable evidence that, far from being a natural, uncontrollable impulse, aggression is highly socialized; we learn when and in what ways to express our hostile intentions toward others. As we have seen, boys have more accessible role models for aggression, and boys expect to receive more benefits through aggression than do girls. The specificity of aggressive behavior in childhood also suggests that it is highly regulated through socialization. As noted above, parents strongly discourage children, especially boys, from directing aggression toward them. In addition, most children do not go around attacking others indiscriminately; rather, aggression appears in certain specific situations, such as self-defense (Maccoby, 1980). The more complex contingencies for male aggression, as well as the greater rewards it brings boys, probably make it harder for boys to learn to inhibit their aggressive impulses. It is not so easy to figure out when to hit and when to hold back. For girls, the lesson is relatively simple: There are few situations in which aggression is really expected, and the social costs are high.

Girls might be considerably more aggressive if they expected higher payoffs or if the social costs were reduced. In fact, cross-cultural comparisons show that girls in some cultures can be even more aggressive than U.S. boys. For example, preschool girls in Israel have been found to be involved in fights about 20 percent more often than U.S. boys, although the Israeli boys are even more aggressive than the girls. Similarly, studies of *cholo* teenage groups, or cliques, in several Mexican cities show that teenage girls engage in fistfights with the leader in order to be admitted into a girls' *cholo*, and are ready to back up their male companions in fights with rival groups by using rocks and other weapons. One of the researchers commented, "Girls and boys follow cultural dictates that can overwhelm any genetic influences on aggressive behavior" (B. Bower, 1991, p. 359). Not only can girls be considerably more aggressive when the social context permits, but boys are much less aggressive when parents and community members frown on physical aggression in children. Observations of children growing up in two villages in southern Mexico, one in which there was little violence and parents did not allow children to fight with one another ("La Paz") and one in which parents condoned a certain amount of roughhousing and fighting ("San Andres"), showed no gender differences in either village. Girls rarely fought in La Paz but neither did boys, while in San Andres both sexes tended to be more often involved in bouts of play fighting and threats as well as in serious fighting. The differences could be traced to parents' attitudes; when one father in La Paz was asked what he would do if he saw his children fighting, he replied, "Tell them not to do it, that it is bad for brothers and sisters to fight. This is not good." In contrast, parents in San Andres had a more resigned attitude; when one mother saw her two sons attacking each other with rocks, she simply remarked that they always fought and did not intervene. Another parent encouraged his daughter to hit her brother in retaliation for something he had done. These findings point to the strong influence of culture on the expression of aggression in both boys and girls (Fry, 1988).

It is admittedly a little frustrating when there is no simple answer to a question like, Why are males so vicious? But human aggression is not a straightforward matter of either hormones or learning. Unlike other species, we have many ways to express aggression. A sweet smile and the comment, "You look just wonderful—how on earth do you do it, at your age?" can be as nasty as hitting someone over the head with an iron frying pan (although the comment will not land you in jail). Human behavior is also multidetermined. Let me give you a personal example. Anyone who has flown recently knows that air travel is stressful. Flights are inevitably delayed, seating arrangements are confused, luggage goes astray, and the planes are hot, grubby, and crowded. Over the years, I have realized that my spouse reacts more to such stresses, leading him to act in what might be termed an aggressive manner—snapping at people, thumping the luggage, muttering at the computer displays of departure times, angrily flapping the flight coupons, and so on. His stronger reaction is not a simple matter of hormones or socialization; rather, it reflects the interaction of several factors. First, he seems genuinely more uncomfortable and restless, which then makes him even more vulnerable to additional irritations. Second, he has fewer reasons to inhibit his behavior. People would have a much stronger negative reaction to me screaming at a travel clerk than to him ("Of course he's angry, they screwed up the seating.") Third, we interpret the situation differently; I don't really care if others are ahead in line or first at the boarding gate, whereas he becomes annoyed at having to yield to large numbers of other people. The point of this example is not to display the superior nature of women (except possibly as traveling companions) but to emphasize again the interactive nature of biology and socialization in the expression of aggression.

PROSOCIAL BEHAVIOR

If the stereotypical view of boys is that they are rough, tough, and ready to fight at a moment's notice, the corresponding view of girls is that they are sweet, caring, empathetic, and willing to help others, even at their own expense (Eagly & Crowley, 1986). We examine this view in two areas: *altruism*, the willingness to help others without direct benefit to the self, and *nurturance*, the willingness and ability to care for babies and younger children.

Altruism

One day an 11-year-old girl who lives on the street came by with two of her girlfriends to show me their "save the animals" campaign. They carried clipboards, a petition letter to the President about endangered species, and copies of a newsletter they had written that included a checklist of "things to do," such as clipping through the plastic soda-can rings that can strangle seabirds. After a lively 10-minute discussion about what we could all do to reduce the world trade in ivory, the girls moved off to the next neighbor. Discreet questioning had established that the girls were not working on a school project, and they refused a donation for their newsletter; rather, they seemed quite happy to spend their afternoon working on this cause for its own sake.

Are girls really more helpful and concerned about others? Studies of children's helping behavior have established that when gender differences are observed, the pattern is most often for girls to help others more than boys do (Radke-Yarrow, Zahn-Waxler, & Chapman, 1983). But the differences are often minimal, and, in fact, girls' reputation for helpfulness is much greater than their behavior warrants. Fifty years ago, teachers rated the girls in their classes as more helpful, but when actual helping behavior was observed directly, it was found that the girls helped others only slightly more than the boys did (Hartshorne, May, & Maller, 1929). The same pattern of results was observed again when teachers rated the helpfulness of nearly three hundred fifth and sixth graders, and the children themselves were also asked to nominate classmates who were helpful and those who were selfish (Shigetomi, Hartmann, & Gelfand, 1981). These measures of reputation were compared to children's actual altruistic behavior on six tasks, including making a donation of game prizes to a charity, helping collect pictures for hospitalized children, and volunteering to put the pictures in booklets. Girls exceeded boys in both reputed and actual altruism, but the discrepancy between reputation and behavior was much greater for girls. In other words, people thought that girls were much more helpful and concerned for others than they actually were.

Where does this glowing reputation for helpfulness come from? One contributing factor is that girls sometimes do verbally express more concern than boys do for others in distress. For example, girls more often said that they felt sorry for a crying baby than boys did, although girls did not actually do anything more to help, such as fetching an adult or helping the mother look for the baby's bottle (Zahn-Waxler, Friedman, & Cummings, 1983). Boys might also want to help but be more reluctant to admit empathic concern for others. Evidence for this possibility comes from a study by M. Hoffman and Levine (1976), who told children stories in which a character experienced a problem or difficulty, such as losing a pet dog. Girls reported feeling more sad and unhappy for the story characters, but more boys spontaneously made concrete suggestions about solving the problem ("I'd follow his tracks") which could also be considered an expression of concern. Suppose you are miserable in your job; is the man who brusquely drops the phone number of a prospective new employer on your desk any less helpful than the woman who commiserates endlessly with you over lunch?

A second factor contributing to girls' altruistic reputation is that girls inflate their helping behavior more than boys do when others are present. In one study, kindergartners and fifth graders were paired and asked to clip tickets into sets of five, in order to earn tokens that could be exchanged for a prize. The younger child in each pair was given twice as many tickets as the older child. With an adult present, older girls were more likely than boys to help the younger child, but girls were no more likely than boys to make *private* charitable donations of the tokens they had earned (O'Bryant & Brophy, 1976; Rosenhan & White, 1967).

A third factor is that girls are more likely than boys to help their own friends, which again may make them appear more caring and concerned for others. In a zero-sum game, that is, a game in which one person wins only when the other loses, boys are more likely than girls to maximize their own gain (Shaffer, 1988). But this pattern depends on who the partner is; while girls help their friends more than strangers, boys do not necessarily favor their friends and, in fact, are more likely to compete with them. In one study children were asked to complete a drawing in return for a small amount of money, but the experimenter deliberately provided only a few crayons of the necessary colors so the children had to share. Sharing therefore meant that the child was less likely to finish the drawing and earn the reward. In this situation, girls shared more with their friends than with acquaintances, while boys showed the reverse pattern (Berndt, 1981). As we saw in Chapter 7, competition is an important component of male-male friendship. The boy who hogs the crayons is ensuring that he will do at least as well as his friend, rather than expressing dislike or a wish that the other child not do well. In fact, boys who had at least one close friendship were found to be more helpful toward an unfamiliar partner in a game than boys who did not have a good friend, suggesting that male-male competition enhances altruism toward those with whom the boy is not interested in competing (Mannarino, 1976).

Rewards, Risks, and Reinforcements

Several studies have examined parents' training of prosocial behavior in the home and found that in general girls are more likely than boys to receive encouragement for helping behavior and to be given more "empathy training," although parents actually do surprisingly little to encourage children of either sex to think about the feelings of others (Grusec, 1991). In the preschool classroom, teachers also react more warmly when girls help and share with others. One study found that teachers *never* reacted positively to any of the boys' prosocial behaviors, such as sharing a toy, helping another child with a task, or trying to help another child in distress (Eisenberg, Cameron, Tryon, & Dodez, 1981). In addition, children who complied very often when asked to help or share by other children were not particularly popular with their peers; they were viewed as "easy targets" by others. While more research is needed to fill out the picture, it seems likely that boys receive fewer rewards from adults for being helpful and that they would lose status with their peers if they appeared overly concerned about others; gender typing and willingness to help and share are negatively related for boys (Doescher & Sugawara, 1990). When children are asked to nominate their classmates who are "generous, always willing to share, considerate of others," girls typically receive many nominations because boys are reluctant to nominate their male friends as illustrations of such stereotypically feminine behavior. When asked who would "help another kid out of a tough spot" and "help get another child's cat out of a tree," boys are more likely to nominate their male friends (Zarbatany, Hartmann, Gelfand, & Vinciguerra, 1985).

■ Nurturance

"The baby is here! The baby is here!" Several preschool girls shouted excitedly as the researcher brought in the baby who had been a regular visitor to the classroom. In contrast, the boys ignored the baby even though she smiled, gurgled, and babbled at them when they happened to come near her playpen (Blakemore, 1991, 1993). Why do many girls seem to find infants appealing and spend much of their time playing with dolls?

When we look at nurturant behavior, we find a strong gender difference among adults, in that females are much more likely than males to spend time caring for children. This difference begins in childhood; in most cultures girls from about 7 to 11 years receive "nurturance training" and are given child-care tasks, while boys are assigned such chores as animal care, errands, and selling. Older sisters are more likely than big brothers to offer help and comfort to a younger sibling in distress (R. Abramovitch, Corter, & Pepler, 1980; R. Abramovitch et al., 1979; B. Bryant, 1982; Cicirelli, 1973, 1975; Stewart, 1983; Stewart & Marvin, 1984). Mothers do most of the child care; in one study of English families 40 percent of the fathers had never changed the baby's diapers (C. Lewis, 1986). Even among couples with strongly egalitarian views the birth of an infant tends to push them toward more traditional roles, especially if the mother is breast-feeding. One woman recalled that after the birth of their new baby, they had gone to visit some friends, and when they arrived, her spouse took the baby ahead into the house. When she came in from the car a few minutes later, she found he had put the infant carrier down on the floor inside the door, walked off into the living room to greet their hosts, and left the baby sitting there alone still strapped in the carrier in its snowsuit. She realized at that moment that things were not going to work out quite as equally as they had agreed before the baby was born! Moving outside the home, careers that involve caring for young children are dominated by females: day care and elementary school teaching are "pink-collar" careers, and even pediatrics is seen as a feminine medical speciality.

A Maternal Instinct?

One factor that often limits males' involvement with children is the belief that females are somehow naturally better-suited for nurturant behavior. There is clear evidence that in some species hormones in pregnancy elicit maternal behavior. Virgin rat females will exhibit maternal behavior toward pups if they are injected with blood plasma from a new mother rat, which presumably contains hormones that elicit the behavior. In other species, early separation of the mother and infant can interfere with nurturant behavior when the two are reunited, suggesting that there is a period immediately after birth when the mother is hormonally primed for caregiving behavior (Rosenblatt, 1969). Injections of hormones can even make male rats show such maternal behaviors as building nests and fetching pups who stray too far away (Fisher, 1956).

In humans, the evidence for a maternal instinct is much less clear. Girls in early adolescence are more interested in infants than younger girls, and those who have begun to menstruate have a greater preference for pictures of infants than their peers who have not yet reached menarche, but it is not known if this is due to the biological changes associated with puberty or to the fact that the ability to bear children is one of the few benefits of menstruation emphasized by the surrounding culture (S. Feldman & Nash, 1977; Goldberg, Blumberg, & Kriger, 1982). Among women who have just given birth, immediate contact with the infant can help establish an emotional bond, particularly for women who were somewhat ambivalent about becoming a mother in the first place. This might suggest that the mother is in an especially receptive state immediately after the infant's birth (Klaus & Kennell, 1983). On the other hand, hormones are obviously not necessary for an emotional bond to be established because fathers seem to be as excited and aroused as new mothers at the birth of their baby, as are adoptive parents at their child's arrival. In addition, after a long pregnancy, labor, and delivery, many women are not immediately overwhelmed with love for their infants in the minutes or hours after the birth. In fact, in one study 40 percent of new mothers reported that they were so exhausted from the birth process that their initial reaction to their baby was one of utter indifference (Robson & Kumar, 1980)! Parental love emerges within the first week after birth through exposure to the infant, and the onset of this parental affection can be delayed by medication or a difficult labor (Klaus & Kennell, 1983). In addition, if a human maternal instinct exists, it has not kept women throughout history from abandoning, killing, or abusing their infants when under stress, when they cannot provide for their offspring, or when infanticide is required by custom (Tavris & Wade, 1984).

Berman (1980) surveyed many studies of women's interest in infants and found that although the patterns change over the life span, women's changing interest does not correspond to changes in their hormone levels. For example, mothers and grandmothers are more responsive to babies than pregnant women, single women, and married women who do not have children. Women do not become less interested in babies after they enter menopause, when estrogen levels drop. Conversely, they do not become more interested in or attracted to babies while taking certain types of oral contraceptives that mimic the hormonal state of pregnancy. Girls who had been exposed to excess androgen before birth described themselves as not very interested in dolls, playing house, babysitting, or becoming mothers, but most of them did marry and have children when they grew up. So if there is a hormonal contribution to women's interest in babies, it is hardly a direct effect.

The Importance of Experience

Regardless of the role of hormones, learning is clearly an important element of nurturant behavior in new parents. In other species, new mothers are not automatically skilled at taking care of infants; they need a role model or some previous experience to do it successfully. For example, female monkeys who had been raised in isolation or with age-mates were not very successful mothers once they had matured and been mated with a male. Human mothers are often inexpert with a first baby. The behaviorist John Watson reported, "We have observed the nursing, handling, and bathing, etc. of the first baby of a good many mothers. Certainly there are no new ready-made activities appearing except nursing. The mother is usually as awkward about that as she can be. The instinctive factors are practically nil" (cited in Tavris & Wade, 1984, p. 160). The skill that we attribute to maternal instinct may more often be due to the fact that in most cultures women give birth with the support of more experienced women who share the baby's care and are always available with advice and guidance. The mother herself has often already learned a great deal about infants by taking care of her younger siblings and relatives. It is not typical of our species for young, inexperienced parents to take their first baby home from the hospital with only a free sample of baby powder and a couple of pamphlets for guidance!

Is there any evidence for a *paternal* instinct? In some species, male aggression interferes with nurturant behavior, but if the adult is prevented from attacking, exposure to infants will eventually elicit parenting behavior in the male. For example, after a few days a male rat will groom and retrieve infant pups when they fall out of the nest. Male rhesus monkeys will also play and care for infants in the lab, although, again, this caretaking behavior is elicited only after a delay. In other species, such as penguins, kiwis, wolves, and some subspecies of baboons, males routinely help care for their infants (Tavris & Wade, 1984). In humans, males tend to be less interactive with unfamiliar infants (Blakemore, 1981). But human fathers have a level of interest and capacity for nurturance equal to that of human mothers. When fathers must care for their babies, as when the mother is bedridden for several weeks after a cesarean delivery or the baby is premature and requires extra feedings, they quickly master the skills and do as well as mothers; for example, they can get the infant to take as much milk and can soothe it as well as mothers (Parke, 1981). Thus, there is little evidence that human females have a special advantage in nurturing skills.

The Influence of Gender Stereotypes

If human fathers have this capacity for nurturance, why is it not expressed more often in their behavior? One reason is that males learn early that baby and child care is "girls' stuff" (Blakemore, 1990; D. Dunn, Gustafson & Budzik, 1992; Melson & Fogel, 1988; Nash & Feldman, 1981). Berman, Monda, and Myerscough (1977) studied preschoolers' interest in babies by placing a real, live infant in a playpen in the schoolroom. Both boys and girls were quite intrigued by the baby, and approached it equally often. But once the boys got to be about 5 years old, their interest declined, as if they were starting to realize that babies, like dolls, were the business of females. Berman and her colleages found that parents subtly encouraged this process; when parents of daughters saw their little girl playing with a doll, they often referred to the doll as "your baby" and the girl as "the mommy," but they rarely talked to boys about being a daddy (Gordon, 1991). White boys are especially likely to distance themselves from an infant, while black boys and both white and black girls appeared more willing to interact with the baby (Reid, Trotter, & Tate, 1991).

Further evidence for the role of stereotypes in shaping nurturant behavior is a little sad: Males are often quite interested in young children but learn to suppress their responses, perhaps for fear of being thought effeminate. When males and females are shown pictures or videotapes of young children and infants and their physiological reactions are compared, both sexes respond with heart rate acceleration, increased blood pressure, and pupil dilation, all indications of attention and interest. Yet females report more interest and attraction than males do to the pictures (Berman, 1980; A. M. Frodi & Lamb, 1978). Among parents, fathers and mothers showed equally strong physical reactions to the sound of a crying infant, although mothers reported more concern (A. M. Frodi et al., 1978). Berman (1975) asked college students to rate the attractiveness and appeal of pictures of infant monkeys. When students indicated their ratings by a public vote in a group situation, women's scores were higher and men's scores were lower than when their ratings were made privately. These patterns suggest that men may well be more interested in babies than they feel comfortable admitting. One man recalled:

> When I was a teenager, my mother cared for many foster children. I loved it when the toddlers fell down and came to me for comfort. It made me feel great inside . . . but I would never tell anyone how good I felt. Men weren't supposed to enjoy taking care of babies and young children. (Wessel, 1990)

I will never forget the sight of my department chairman at a dinner party; his eyes lit up at the sight of a colleague's new baby, and he began cuddling and playing with it. He suddenly realized that everyone was watching him (the contrast with his office demeanor was somewhat startling) and responded defensively, "I *like* little babies."

■ Prosocial Behavior: The Bottom Line

The research discussed above strongly suggests that boys and girls have similar capacities for caring for others, including infants and younger children, but that males avoid appearing too interested in babies or too willing to help others because such behaviors are inconsistent with the masculine gender role. However much males like babies, they do not spend much time with them for several reasons. Parke (1981) found that many fathers thought that mothers had a special maternal instinct and that the fathers assumed they would become more involved when the children were older. Mothers also sometimes act as "gatekeepers," wanting an exclusive, special relationship with the baby, and subtly restrict the father's involvement (Scarr, 1984). One woman reported that she was devastated when her husband was able to quiet their crying baby after she could not, because she thought that she should naturally know more about the baby's needs. A third factor is that time and money are limited in most families. Without an adequate national child-care system, parental leave, and flexible employment schedules, someone must usually trade off work responsibilities for child care. Most families decide, consciously or unconsciously, that the mother will make this compromise, and as long as men still earn significantly more on average, it would be economic suicide for most families to do otherwise.

MORAL REASONING

Like altruism and nurturance, moral reasoning draws on such capacities as empathy and requires you to think about the needs of other people. However, moral decisions often involve your own needs as well. For example, you may discover that your friend Mildred is about to hand in a term paper that she copied from her sister's master's thesis completed at another university. You may empathize with Mildred's desire to do well on the assignment, and if you say something, you will pay certain costs yourself: She will be angry, others will think you are a snitch, and you will cause problems for her, such as guilt, fear of discovery by others, and potential disciplinary action. Yet if you don't speak up you will violate your own standards of what is right and a promise to abide by the school's honor principles; Mildred will have missed learning the rewards of doing her own work; and others in the class could be hurt if their papers are perceived to be substantially inferior to her plagiarized version. There are abstract principles to be considered, such as the value of being honest, but there are also immediate considerations based on the particular people involved; for example, it would probably be an easier decision if Mildred were not a close friend or if you were not in the class yourself.

We now look at two major theories of moral development, first, the cognitive approaches of Piaget and Kohlberg, and, second, the more recent work of Gilligan and her colleagues. The theories emphasize different values, namely, justice as the basis for moral decisions versus the need to be responsive to others. It has been argued that these values are systematically linked with gender during development, but this is an example of a stereotype that is not strongly supported by the data: Although there is evidence that both values are important in people's moral reasoning, these values are not necessarily linked to gender in childhood.

Cognitive Theories of Morality: Fairness and Justice

Piaget (1965) argued that conflicts with peers are vital in helping children recognize differing points of view and learning that rules can help resolve conflicts in a fair way. Kohlberg continued Piaget's work by focusing on the hypothesis that as cognitive capacities developed, children's ability to reason about moral problems would become more objective and less influenced by immediate, personal concerns and the opinions of other people. Kohlberg's original study included 72 boys, aged 10, 13, and 16, from middle- and working-class families living in Chicago. Because Piaget had pointed to peer interaction as an important factor in moral development, Kohlberg included boys who were either popular or rejected by their peers. While the addition of the "popularity" factor to the design of the study was theoretically reasonable at the time, it led Kohlberg to exclude girls, to keep the design and the sample size of his initial study manageable. Thus, his theory of moral development was constructed solely on the basis of responses provided by males.

Hypothetical Dilemmas

To test children's developing ability to think about moral problems, Kohlberg presented them with stories that were constructed to put the rights of individuals in conflict. For example, in one story a druggist develops a new drug for treating cancer and sells it for far more than it cost him to prepare. A man desperately needs the drug for his dying wife, but he does not have enough money to buy it. Should he steal the drug? The dilemmas are designed so that no claim is obviously better than another. For example, to steal the drug would violate the druggist's right to benefit from his labor and to control his property, but the husband also has an obligation to help his wife, and the druggist is being unfair by overcharging for the drug. Kohlberg was more interested in the reasoning used by the child than in the particular solution (Colby & Kohlberg, 1986; Colby, Kohlberg, Gibbs, & Lieberman, 1983).

Kohlberg found that, with increasing age and cognitive development, children's answers reflected more and more abstract reasoning about fairness and justice and less focus on the particular people involved in the dilemma. For example, a young child would often talk about the problem in terms of the immediate costs and benefits of stealing. The child might argue that the husband should not steal the drug because he would go to jail and if his wife died, he could just get married again. Or a child might say that the husband should steal the drug because he would have no one to cook for him if his wife died. This type of reasoning is termed *preconventional* because the child shows little awareness of anything other than personal needs. At the next level, *conventional* reasoning, which is shown by most adolescents and adults, the person shows a focus on society and what people will think. The person might argue that the husband should steal the drug because other people will think he is not a good, loving person if he lets his wife die. Or the husband should not steal the drug because laws are meant to be obeyed; if everyone did illegal acts for their own convenience, society would fall apart. Finally, some adults show a more advanced type of reasoning in which certain principles, such as the sanctity of human life, are described as more important than particular laws. Such reasoning is termed *post-conventional*.

Gender Differences in Objective Reasoning?

There has been considerable debate about whether there are gender differences in responses to Kohlberg's dilemmas, particularly at the conventional level of reasoning (Holstein, 1976). Conventional reasoning includes both arguments about personal considerations, such as the argument that the husband should steal the drug out of love or because of what people will think of him, and arguments that stress the needs of the larger society and the importance of laws. While both kinds of arguments focus on the needs of others, those involving a discussion of society and laws are considered more advanced than those that are more immediate and personal, because the former involve more detached, abstract reasoning. Kohlberg found that his male subjects did progress from the personal to the societal kinds of arguments as they grew older, but he had no female subjects for comparison.

Several researchers have argued that there are gender differences at the conventional level; specifically, that females are less willing to accept the hypothetical nature of the problem and that they try to reason about the dilemma as if real people were involved. For example, a girl might insist that the druggist is only being so recalcitrant because he just does not understand how sick the wife really is and propose that if the husband talks to the druggist again, he will surely lower the price of the drug or accept a delayed payment; after all, no one would really be quite so obstinate. This approach, of thinking about the problem as if real people were involved, leads to responses that appear to be based on immediate personal concerns and, consequently, to be judged less mature. In contrast, those who take it to be, as one boy put it, "like a math problem with humans," end up sounding more crisp and objective and to be judged as more sophisticated in their reasoning (Bussey & Maugham, 1982; Gilligan, 1982, p. 26).

Although it is now clear that people show both types of reasoning, an orientation toward the more abstract, detached approach does not seem to be gender-related. L. Walker (1984) surveyed 79 studies of moral reasoning from childhood through adulthood and found no evidence that males' reasoning was more detached and impersonal than females' of the same age. In addition, Rest (1983), L. Walker (1984), and Baumrind (1986) concluded from their reviews that educational level is a more important influence on moral reasoning than is gender; often, taking a hypothetical, detached approach to problem solving is a skill acquired in college and graduate school.

■ The Voice of Care

Clearly, there are other moral concerns and values to be considered besides those of abstract, detached justice. One important alternative has been proposed by Gilligan (1982): the "voice" in which expressions of care, compassion, and concern for others are articulated. From this perspective, moral problems are not limited to those that develop when the rights of individuals are in conflict but also include those that arise when one's actions threaten to disrupt the network of ongoing relationships and the bonds of attachment between individuals. Such hypothetical dilemmas as the druggist problem are best solved by stepping back from the individuals involved to examine the situation from an objective perspective and to find a solution that will be fair to everyone. But in many moral problems we *are* deeply involved in the situation, and it can even be counterproductive to try to view the situation objectively. Rather, the solution comes from exhibiting compassion for others' needs, by engaging in a dialogue in which feelings are integrated with reasoning and trying to construct an understanding of the problem in terms of how it is experienced by each participant.

Real-Life Moral Problems

Hypothetical dilemmas, such as the story of the druggist and the husband, cannot effectively tap into a person's concerns about maintaining and restoring the ties of trust, attachment, and care between people and promoting others' well-being. An alternative task developed by Gilligan and her colleagues is to ask the person to describe a real moral problem from his or her own life, a time when he or she was not sure of the right path to take. This allows the person to select and frame a problem in terms of genuine attachment relationships and concerns about the self and others, if those issues are important to him or her. Gilligan and her colleagues found that when children were asked about their real-life problems, girls seemed to talk more than boys about issues of trust, friendship, and concern for others (Gilligan, 1982). For example, "Amy" could not decide whether to tell one friend that another friend had stolen a book; the dilemma resulted from the fact that Amy had commitments to both friends and not telling would be as hurtful to one as telling would be to the other. In contrast, "Jake's" moral problem involved a conflict between his own personal standards, specifically, not to break his word once given, and the need to be fair to others. Jake had told the school principal that a friend was being beaten up unfairly, and, as a result, the principal was ready to punish strongly any fighting that took place in the school in the next few weeks. Jake had promised the principal not to say anything about their talk, and his dilemma was whether to warn another friend not to fight because he, too, would probably be punished (Gilligan, 1982).

The real-life dilemma reveals the issues that are of most concern to each person, which might be the need to keep to one's standards of behavior, to be loyal to others, or to be compassionate. Gilligan and her colleagues found that women tended to describe dilemmas that emphasized the voice of care, while men talked about issues of fairness and justice (Gilligan & Attanucci, 1988). However, although there was an link between gender and moral concerns, both sexes often showed both types of concerns in their descriptions (Donenberg & Hoffman, 1988; Gilligan & Attanucci, 1988; L. Walker, 1987). Subsequent studies have shown that the differences more often reflect the kinds of problems that are realistically experienced by men and women in their daily lives than differences in their personal system of values. For example, a woman whose elderly mother wants to come live with her might well talk more about emotional ties and obligations than a man who must decide whether to fire an employee who works hard and needs the job but who really is not qualified. The man and woman might sound very similar if they discussed the same problems, but the nature of life is such that this tends not to happen.

The "Fables" Task

When young children are asked to describe real-life dilemmas, there is little evidence that girls are more concerned than boys about the needs of other people (Donenberg & Hoffman; 1988; L. Walker, 1987). One problem in accurately assessing children's moral orientation is that it is hard for young children to reason about abstract hypothetical dilemmas and real-life problems. (One little boy looked baffled when asked to talk about a time when he wasn't sure what to do and said, "I ain't had no problems yet!") A compromise that works well with children is D. K. Johnston's (1988) "fables" task: The child is told a fable involving animal characters who have a problem and is asked how the animals could solve their problem. For example, a porcupine looks for a home for the winter and asks if he can share a cave occupied by a family of moles. The generous moles agree to let him stay, but he is so large and prickly that they are very uncomfortable. They eventually ask him to move out, but he refuses, saying that the cave suits him nicely! The fables are constructed so that a solution can be based either upon issues of rights and fairness—it is the moles' cave, they were there first, and they have the right to ask him to leave—or upon issues of compassion—it is winter, the porcupine has nowhere to go, and they could work together to enlarge the cave so that everyone could be housed comfortably.

Several studies using the fables task have shown that younger boys and girls both usually approach the problem from the perspective of compassion and care for others (Garrod & Beal, 1993; Garrod, Beal, & Shin, 1990). For example, one 8-year-old child suggested that the moles could put marshmallows on the porcupine's quills; then the moles would be comfortable, the porcupine could remain in the cave, his big body would help keep the cave warm, and everyone would have "tasty tidbits!" As children get older, they start to talk more about issues of rights and fairness, but this change is common to both boys and girls (Donenberg & Hoffman, 1988). One 13-year-old said that the moles should not hesitate to kick the porcupine out: "It's not their fault he has quills. They have a right to be comfortable in their own home . . . It's like if a homeless man moved into my home while my family was vacationing in Florida. We'd definitely call the police. Call it harsh, but it's reality" (Garrod & Beal, 1993). D. K. Johnston (1988) found that among 15-year-olds, boys were more likely than girls to talk about competing rights, so it is possible that consistent links between moral values and gender are forged during adolescence.

■ Moral Reasoning: The Bottom Line

It seems clear that there is more to morality than justice; other values, such as compassion, loyalty, and concern for relationships, are important in determining the kinds of conflicts that people face, as well as the types of solutions that they try to generate. Gilligan's work on alternative systems of morality has become very popular; in particular, many women students find that the values reflect issues that are important to them, and it is reassuring to have those values recognized as legitimate. However, at this point it does not appear that these values depend on gender; rather, moral reasoning reflects the level of education, life experiences, and the nature of problems faced by the individual person in everyday life.

Despite the lack of empirical support, the notion that moral values are gender-linked has been remarkably persistent. Gilligan's own writing and research shows that she did not assume that the voice of care was exclusively feminine, but this point is often overlooked. When it comes to moral decisions, there seems to be an inherent conflict between justice in the abstract and justice for individuals. We want a system that is fair to everyone while wanting to consider the particular circumstances and unique characteristics of each individual case. Stereotypes about rational males and nurturing females allow us to preserve both values but at the cost of perpetuating traditional views of the sexes. One of my colleagues became exasperated by a conversation with several students who held Gilligan's (1982) book like a bible and talked about their special feminine sensitivity. She mused, "Don't they see where this kind of reasoning is taking them? Right back to the kinds of low-paying, stressful, under-appreciated jobs taking care of children and sick people that were all they would have been able to get forty years ago."

Gilligan's examples of the themes of care and justice in real-life dilemmas share some resemblance to Freud's psychoanalytic theory, in that both suggest that females are focused more on interpersonal relationships than abstract ideas about justice. As we saw in Chapter 4, Freud concluded that boys would identify more strongly with their fathers than girls would with their mothers and that males would have a stronger superego as a result. (Recall that the superego is the psychological structure that maintains the ideals, the values, and the behavioral standards to live up to.) He concluded, "For women, the level of what is ethically normal is different from what it is in men. Women show less sense of justice than men . . . they are more often influenced in their judgments by feelings of affection or hostility." In other words, Freud concluded that females would not solve moral problems by using a rational, impersonal set of rules based on the values of the society but would base their reasoning on their feelings about the people involved and the particular situation. If a system of justice must be "blind" to be administered fairly, then by his logic, females would clearly have less sense of justice than men. Although there are similarities in their approaches, Gilligan differs from Freud in arguing that both types of reasoning are valuable and that there is no principled reason why blind justice should be considered superior to justice that is tempered with compassion and that takes the specifics of each case into account.

STEREOTYPES: A KERNEL OF TRUTH?

In this chapter we have seen one gender difference in behavior that appears early in the life span, is consistent in direction, and appears to be consistent across cultures: aggression. This difference fits with our stereotypes about the sexes, namely, that males are bolder, more assertive, and more concerned with protecting and advancing their own interests, even at the expense of others. In contrast, stereotypes about females' greater propensity for altruism and nurturance are not strongly supported by the behavioral data. Similarly, in the case of moral reasoning, both boys and girls express concerns about the needs of the self and those of others, despite popular assumptions that females are more self-sacrificing and sensitive to others' needs.

Although stereotypes often present a biased or inaccurate view of reality, they sometimes have a kernel of truth (D. Campbell, 1967). This may well be the case for aggression and nurturant behavior. As we have seen, there is evidence for males' greater tendency to be aggressive, and it is quite possible that there is a biological foundation to male aggression, although much more research is necessary to clarify this relation in humans. In the case of nurturant behavior, females are consistently more likely, across the life span and across cultures, to be responsible for infant and child care. Perhaps the physical fact that only women carry, give birth to, and nurse infants makes it seem natural for females also to be given the care of young children, and from that point, it is a small step to train girls for the role and to assume that females are inherently better suited to such tasks (Maccoby & Jacklin, 1980). The drawback to the kernel-of-truth position is the implication that differences based in biology are inevitable and unchangeable. This conclusion is unwarranted. The behaviors examined in this chapter are clearly highly regulated through strong socialization, including aggression, the area of behavior for which biological factors probably play the most influential role.

At best, stereotypes are caricatures or exaggerations of small-scale differences between groups, which raises the question of what purpose these stereotypes serve within a society and why they have endured in the cases where there is relatively little empirical support. For example, why do we continue to believe that only a baby's biological mother can properly care for it, rather than its father, despite evidence to the contrary (Scarr, 1984)? In the case of aggression, popular beliefs about males are consistent with a real behavioral difference, but the stereotypes are somewhat more positive in tone than is perhaps warranted. While it is admirable to be assertive and to defend oneself, the higher rates of incarceration, homicide, and violent behavior among males are hardly a source of pride. We will come back to these questions about the cultural function of stereotypes at the end of the next chapter, after examining evidence for sex differences in intellectual and cognitive abilities.

SUMMARY

We have seen that boys and girls differ in several personality characteristics, again, meaning only that groups of boys and girls tend to be different; we cannot make any strong predictions about individual children's aggressiveness, altruism, or moral reasoning based solely on their gender. Two of the characteristics we have considered, aggression and nurturant behavior, are associated with fairly strong gender differences: Boys are more likely than girls to express aggression, and females are much more likely than males to take care of babies and children. In contrast, two other areas, altruisim and moral reasoning, show few consistent gender differences, despite stereotypes that girls are more caring and concerned for others.

As we have argued throughout this book, gender differences in behavior can have different causes. Higher levels of aggression in boys represent a good candidate for a behavior that reflects the interaction of biology and socialization. Although we do not yet have definitive evidence for the role of sex hormones in aggression, it seems possible that more boys than girls are primed to learn to use aggression, particularly in response to an attack. Even if this is true, it is also clear that boys grow up in a social environment that offers many more role models, rewards, and reinforcements that permit their aggression, whereas girls find that it is relatively ineffective for them and has high social costs. With regard to nurturance, the fact that females are so often responsible for child care does not necessarily mean that they are biologically better suited to the task, aside from the early months of breast-feeding. Fathers have been found to be as interested in their infants and as skillful in caring for them as mothers; however, males are socialized away from nurturance beginning in the preschool period when little boys learn that babies are "girls' stuff," and most families find that a traditional division of responsibilities makes sense after the arrival of an infant. Turning to the areas of altruism and moral reasoning, there is little need to propose explanations for gender differences that do not appear to be either consistent or strong, at least during the childhood stage.

Most of the topics that we have considered in this chapter involve what psychologists call the "warm" areas of behavior, involving empathy, emotional reactions, and interactions with others. As we have seen, stereotypes about the sexes have been constructed so that boys are viewed as more on the "hot" end of the behavioral scale—more quick-tempered and aggressive than girls—and more self- than other-oriented. There are also stereotyped beliefs about boys and girls in the "colder" behavioral areas, including language skills, cognitive abilities, and math achievement. Here again we find that the sexes tend to be viewed in opposition to one another, with boys being considered to be good at math and spatial reasoning while girls are viewed as better in the language areas. We consider the accuracy of these beliefs in the next chapter.

11

INTELLECTUAL CHARACTERISTICS OF BOYS AND GIRLS

While I was in junior high school, an issue of *Seventeen* came out that showed teenage models with the recommended "looks" for various school activities. The head cheerleader had her hair in a perky flip, bright lipstick to emphasize her ready smile, and white powder under her eyebrows to highlight her eyes on the field. The editor of the school paper wore her hair pulled back in a ponytail (functional, but with a ribbon to break the severity) and used concealer cream to hide the dark circles brought on by late nights of copy editing. The images were stereotypes, to be sure, but the recommendations actually made a certain amount of sense. In contrast, the science fair prize winner was delicate and flowerlike, and the recommendations did not relate to the activity: The model had waist-length hair, gently curled to hang about her face (not very practical for working in the lab); the approved makeup was delicately pink; and she wore a dress with a lace collar. The message seemed to be that a girl could certainly be interested in science but she would have to make a special effort to be feminine in compensation.

As with personality characteristics, the kinds of cognitive abilities, reasoning skills, and intellectual interests that emerge in a child are likely to be influenced by his or her gender. In this chapter, we focus specifically on the development of language skill, spatial ability, and mathematical reasoning in boys and girls. There are stereotypes about the sexes in these areas; namely, girls are better at verbal tasks and boys at math. In some cases these stereotypes have a kernel of truth, while in others they are inaccurate. Next, we look at possible explanations for these patterns. There are several theories about gender differences in cognitive abilities; one approach suggests that sex differences in the hemispheric organization of the brain might be a factor, while other theories place more emphasis on the influence of social expectations and differential treatment in leading the sexes to develop certain skills at the expense of others. Finally, we consider why it is especially

213

important to look for differential socialization as an explanation for gender differences in these areas, before turning to theories that emphasize the role of biology.

COGNITIVE ABILITIES OF BOYS AND GIRLS

Let's first see what the differences are, if any, in verbal, spatial, and mathematical skills in boys and girls before turning to theoretical explanations. Some researchers have suggested that these skills might be related: Specifically, there might be a trade-off between being good with linguistic information and being good at spatial (i.e., nonlinguistic) tasks; if one is good at one kind of nonverbal task, such as mental imagery, it might help with another nonverbal task, such as solving algebra problems; and there might be different average balances between these skills for the sexes.

■ Verbal Skills

Females have been reported to perform better on average on various verbal tasks, including correct use of grammatical forms, spelling accuracy, relative ease of acquiring reading skills, solving verbal analogies, and speed of pronouncing speech sounds. Obviously, this does not mean that all girls are better at language skills than all boys but that the group averages are different. The female advantage in verbal skills is apparent when children first begin to talk in the toddler period; girls talk a bit earlier than boys, have larger vocabularies, and produce utterances that are slightly longer on average than do boys of the same age (Huttenlocher, Haight, Bryk, Seltzer, & Lyons, 1991; Schachter, Shore, Hodapp, Chalfin, & Bundy, 1978). Males' language functioning also appears to be less resilient than females'. Boys are more likely to stutter than girls and to have problems in learning to read (Skinner & Shelton, 1985). Males have more trouble than females in recovering their full-language capabilities after brain damage caused by tumors, strokes, surgery, or accidents, although this is confounded by the fact that males are more likely to suffer severe head injuries, as the result of their higher rate of involvement in auto accidents (Inglis & Lawson, 1981; Marchand, 1991; McGlone, 1980). The only language problem more common in girls than boys is elective mutism, a syndrome in which the child is capable of speech but refuses to talk; it is usually caused by an emotional reaction to great trauma and is often related to the effects of child sexual abuse.

The differences in average male and female language abilities are not substantive, especially when we limit our analysis to studies of typical children, that is, those who do not have serious linguistic disabilities. Hyde and Linn (1988) reviewed data from 165 studies and found that although there was a consistent female advantage in verbal skills across the life span, it was trivially small. Macaulay (1978) also questioned the claim of feminine superiority in early language acquisition by pointing out that the original data show only weak differences between boys and girls and that some of the studies are so dated that it is difficult to be sure of the actual findings. Plomin and Foch (1981) examined the data from 86 studies of verbal ability originally reviewed by Maccoby and Jacklin (1974), which included about 67,000 children. With such a large sample size even very minor differences between two groups will be statistically significant but of little practical interest, because the two groups overlap almost completely. Only about 1 percent of the variance in verbal performance between children was explained by gender; in other words, knowing a particular child's sex gives little indication of the quality of that child's verbal skills. The gender difference is also minimal for written language. In the past, girls had received higher scores on the verbal section of standardized achievement tests, such as the SAT, but average scores for females have declined since the 1970s and males now have a slightly higher average score (Feingold, 1988; Hyde & Linn, 1988). For example, in 1992 the national verbal average score for males was 428, compared to 419 for females (scores run from 200 to 800) (Henry, 1992).

■ Spatial Ability

Phil Donahue (1985), the television talk show host, argues that the males in the family should pack the car trunk because they have better spatial skills than women. Quite a few men must listen to Donahue; on an airplane I had my carrier bag lifted right out of my hands and stowed in the overhead compartment by a stranger who seemed convinced that his superior spatial skills allowed the jamming of more stuff into the bin. I commented that, as far as I knew, most baggage handlers were still men, and their spatial skills weren't preventing an awful lot of luggage from going astray. "Not the same thing at all!" was the terse response.

What *do* we mean by spatial ability? Linn and Petersen (1985, p. 1482) describe it as "skill in representing, transforming, generating and recalling symbolic, *nonlinguistic* information" (italics added). In other words, many tasks that do not involve the use of verbal labels could be considered to utilize spatial skills. Such tasks include imagining how objects will look if they are folded or rotated, detecting patterns, and seeing how objects are related to one another in space. One review of many studies, including a wide variety of spatial-reasoning tasks, found that there was an average male advantage of about half a standard deviation and that gender accounted for about 4 percent of the variation between individuals (Hyde, 1981). While not an enormous difference, it is not trivial either. More recent reviews have found fewer differences in the average performance of males and females than in previous decades. In addition, when specific types of spatial reasoning are considered separately, gender differences are found to be more prevalent on certain types of tasks (Linn & Hyde, 1989; Richmond, 1980).

Types of Spatial Reasoning

Linn and Petersen (1985) classified various tests of spatial reasoning into three categories. First, there are tests of the ability to locate a simple pattern or shape within a group of other shapes, as quickly as possible. Different strategies can be used to solve these *embedded figure tasks:* You can take an analytic approach of looking at one part of the shape, trying to find a corresponding part in the field, and, once a match is found, testing whether the adjacent part also fits and so on. Or you can work with a mental image of the shape, superimposing it on the field and rotating it to see where it fits. Simple versions of this kind of problem can be given to children, and in a summary analysis of the data from 81 studies, no gender differences in accuracy were found for any age. Males and females do seem to use different strategies; males tend to use the mental rotation method, while females use the analytic step-by-step method, but both approaches work well on this task.

A second type of spatial task assesses your ability to judge spatial relationships in the presence of distracting information. For example, hanging a picture in a sagging old New England farmhouse might require you to judge the true horizontal in the presence of a sloping floor line. A commonly used test is the *rod and frame task*, in which you must adjust a rod that is hanging within a tilted picture frame to the true vertical position. A similar task that can be used with children is Piaget's *water-level task*, in which the child is shown the outline of a tilted bottle and is asked to draw a line indicating where the water level would be. In middle childhood, that is, after about 8 years, males show a small average advantage (about a third of a standard deviation) on these tasks. Surprisingly, adolescents and college students sometimes make errors on the bottle task by drawing the water line perpendicular to the walls of the bottle rather than along the true horizontal, and women do less well than men. In adults, this failure can be erased by clarified instructions or brief training, but it is still not clear why women tend to make more errors than men (Liben, 1991; Liben & Golbeck, 1984; McGillicuddy–De Lisi, De Lisi, & Youniss, 1978; Meehan & Overton, 1986).

The third type of spatial task is mental rotation. The subject is shown one object and must find the same object in a different position (e.g., upside down and rotated to the left) in a set of alternatives as quickly as possible. The optimal strategy is to rotate a mental image of the entire figure, rather than calculate the view from another angle or check it against the alternatives piece by piece, since those strategies take more time. Linn and Petersen (1985) found that mental rotation problems revealed the strongest gender difference in adolescents and adults, in favor of males (about a standard deviation). Similarly, E. Johnson and Meade (1987) investigated the performance of about 1800 children in one school system and found that starting at about age 10, there was a consistent male advantage on tasks involving mental rotation. However, other studies have not found gender differences on mental rotation tasks before adolescence (Kail, Pellegrino, & Carter, 1980; Waber, Carlson, & Mann, 1982). It is not yet clear what accounts for these inconsistencies across studies with children; they may reflect variations in stimulus materials—whether the child is asked to imagine rotating a nonsense figure or to recognize a familiar letter in a rotated orientation—and whether the test is timed or not. We do know that while females are as accurate as males on mental rotation tasks, they tend to take longer to arrive at the answer. This might suggest that girls are more cautious about getting the right match and use a piece-by-piece strategy, which works to their disadvantage when speed is important. There is other evidence that girls are more cautious in their test-taking behavior; for example, they are more likely to check their work and are reluctant to guess when they are not sure of an answer. Linn and Petersen warn that in the future we are likely to see an increasing use of mental rotation tasks to assess spatial ability, with the result that gender differences in the literature will become exaggerated because these tasks are more likely than others to yield a clear difference between males and females.

In most studies, a male advantage only appears after about 8 to 10 years. It is not definitively known if a gender difference exists earlier in the life span due to the lack of appropriate tests that can be used with young children. In particular, mental rotation problems require too much concentration to be administered reliably to children under about 10 years. However, studies of when infants and young children learn to use landmarks, search for objects, and move through space show no gender differences. There are also no differences on perspective-taking tasks, in which the preschooler must imagine how a three-dimensional model looks to someone sitting on the other side; presumably, this should involve mental rotation of either the self or the model. The fact that boys and girls in preschool and elementary school perform similarly on such tests of spatial cognition suggests that differences in spatial reasoning do not emerge until late childhood or early adolescence.

Does It Matter?

Before becoming overly concerned about the patterns for boys and girls, we should step back and ask if the differences are significant in practical terms. In particular, while verbal abilities are central to most aspects of human life, including interpersonal relationships and academic endeavors, it is not clear that individual variations in spatial abilities are great enough to be particularly important in practical terms (Hyde & Linn, 1988). I remember reading a letter to Ann Landers from a woman complaining that she constantly got lost and could not find her way out of large shopping malls because she had no sense of direction, but this was an extreme case. In jobs that specifically require spatial reasoning, such as architecture, there is no evidence that those with higher spatial skills are better architects (Salthouse, Babcock, Skovronek, Mitchell, & Palmon, 1990). As E. Johnson and Meade put it, "There is as yet no overwhelming evidence that, other things being equal, it is desirable to be a high scorer on spatial tests or undesirable to be a low scorer" (1987, p. 738).

■ Mathematical Reasoning

What about mathematics performance? Doesn't a child need good spatial abilities to do well in math? Not exactly. Spatial ability and mathematics performance do tend to be correlated, meaning that if you are good at one, you tend to be good at the other, and there seems to be a single underlying cognitive factor predicting performance on both (Halpern, 1986). In other words, a proficiency at working with symbolic, nonlinguistic information would be equally helpful for spatial problems, such as packing a car trunk, and for mathematics, such as balancing a checkbook. But that does not mean that good spatial skills are directly implicated in mathematical reasoning, any more than balancing the checkbook accurately means good packing skills, for several reasons. First, girls and boys acquire arithmetic skills at the same age, and as we will see below, girls perform as well or better than boys in math classes. Clearly, then, even if girls have poorer spatial skills, it does not hinder their performance in math. Second, training and practice in spatial-reasoning skills, such as solving mental rotation problems, has not been shown to help mathematical reasoning, or vice versa, and in fact, there is no systematic relation between spatial skill and mathematics achievement, even on math problems that would seem to involve spatial reasoning such as geometry (Pattison & Grieve, 1984). In any case, spatial reasoning is not really essential for the introductory levels of mathematics taught in U.S. elementary and high schools; even geometry problems can for the most part be solved with an analytic, verbal approach. One could imagine that good spatial skills might be an advantage for some esoteric branches of higher mathematics involving topological relations, but in fact, many of these problems would be extremely difficult to visualize. Mathematics researchers report that they just rely on their equations or use computer programs to generate the images for them!

"Math Class Is Tough" — Or Is It?

In 1992 the Mattel toy company released a Teen Talk Barbie doll; one of her recorded phrases was, "Math class is tough." Barbie's message was quickly reprogrammed in the face of public protests that such messages would discourage preteen girls who, it was assumed, already had enough trouble with math class without Barbie telling them they were dumb (*Boston Globe*, 1992d; *Denver Post*, 1992). Yet Barbie was wrong: Girls outperform boys in their math classes, although boys do better on standardized tests of math achievement (Hyde, Fennema, & Lamon, 1990; Kimball, 1989). The female advantage in classes begins in early elementary school and continues through college and graduate school, as long as the girls and boys being compared within the same class have had equal levels of prior preparation.

Although girls get better math grades than boys, they tend not to do as well on math achievement tests as their class grades would suggest that they should. In one study of several thousand high school students taking advanced algebra and calculus courses, girls received significantly higher grades than the boys in the classes but did less well on the SAT (Rosser, 1989). College-bound men score an average of about 40 points higher on the math portion of the SAT than women; in 1992, for example, the national average for males was 499, compared to 456 for females (Henry, 1992).

The male advantage on the SAT math exam is inflated by the fact that the boys who take the exam tend to have taken more math classes than the girls; about two-thirds of the gender gap can be explained by differential preparation. However, when boys and girls with the same number of classes are compared, there is still a gender difference in favor of boys. This difference has remained constant since the 1960s, putting girls at a disadvantage in competing for college admission and for scholarships and awards programs that use SAT scores to select winners. For example, two-thirds of all National Merit Scholarships have gone to men. A federal court ruled in 1989 that the use of the SAT for awarding scholarships discriminated against girls, because it systematically underestimated how well they would do in college (Mensh & Mensh, 1991).

Math Prodigies

Among extremely gifted students, there is a clear male advantage on standardized tests of math skill. Benbow and Stanley (1980, 1983) have conducted math "talent searches" since 1972 and have administered the SAT exam, which is usually taken by high school seniors, to about 100,000 junior high school students. Those who score in the top 2 to 5 percent are considered to have an unusually strong aptitude for mathematics because they have not yet taken classes in the material covered by the test. On average, the talented boys scored 30 points higher than the talented girls, and among children who scored above 700 on the exam, there were 13 boys for every girl! Benbow and Stanley made special efforts to encourage more high-achieving girls to take the exam, but the gender difference remained.

What is often overlooked is the fact that the gifted girls continued to do well or better than the boys in the math classroom even at the high school level (Benbow & Stanley, 1982). In addition, some researchers have pointed out that describing the gender differences in terms of ratios gives a misleading impression; only about 5 percent of the already talented children who volunteered to take the exam scored above 600 points, and the gender differences were trivial for the remainder (Halpern, 1986; Rossi, 1983). Thus, although there seem to be more male math prodigies than girl prodigies, we are clearly talking about a *very* select sample of children.

THEORIES OF COGNITIVE ABILITIES

In the last section we saw there are slightly different patterns of cognitive performance for males and females, although often one has to be really searching for the differences to notice them. Overall, there is some evidence that males have a higher rate of vulnerability to language problems during acquisition and in recovery after language loss. In spatial reasoning, females have a recognizably lower group average than males, particularly on tasks involving mental rotation. In mathematics, girls do not perform as well as expected on standardized tests, and among extremely gifted children, boys significantly outnumber girls on tests of math ability. We now look at possible *explanations* for the findings, including theories suggesting that differences in how male and female brains might be organized could lead to varying patterns of cognitive performance and explanations that emphasize the role of social factors encouraging verbal development in girls and non-linguistic skills in boys.

■ Hemispheric Organization: Sex Differences in the Brain?

Several theories argue that the way the hemispheres of the brain are organized might be different for the sexes, leading to different patterns of strengths and weaknesses in cognition (Buffery & Gray, 1972; Kimura, 1985; J. Levy, 1969). The brain looks a bit like a walnut, with two halves that control mental functioning and that are connected by a band of fibers called the *corpus callosum*. There are no obvious physical differences between male and female brains. If one was plopped down on a table in front of you, you would not be able to tell whether it came from a man or woman, at least not without examining the individual cells for their chromosomal patterns. Deep within the brain itself are certain areas, particularly in the hypothalamus, known to be involved in reproductive functioning and correspondingly differ for the sexes, for example, to regulate menstruation in women (Springer & Deutsch, 1981). But there is considerable debate over whether the hemispheres, the upper layers that control higher-mental functions, are organized differently for the two sexes.

Specialization of Function

The hemispheres of the brain seem to be specialized, in that each appears to process certain types of information a bit more efficiently than the other. In most people, the left hemisphere processes verbal information more efficiently than the right hemisphere. As a result, many people have a "right-ear advantage" for hearing speech sounds. Because nerves from the right ear connect directly to the left hemisphere of the brain, the person will respond more quickly to spoken words presented to the right ear, than to the same stimuli presented to the left ear, which connects to the right hemisphere. Using other techniques, researchers have found that certain *nonverbal* responses (e.g., depth judgments, detecting the orientation of a line, locating a point in space) are made more quickly and efficiently by the right hemisphere, again suggesting that the hemispheres specialize in function. This is not a strict dichotomy; rather, it is a matter "of degree rather than kind" (Bradshaw & Nettleton, 1981, p. 51).

Relation to Hand Preference

In addition to relative ear advantage and nonverbal judgments, hemispheric organization is often indicated by a person's hand preference. About 90 percent of the population is right-handed, and 95 percent of right-handed people process language in their left hemisphere (Halpern, 1986). Left-handers, the majority of whom are male, are a more variable group. About two-thirds process language primarily in the left hemisphere, just like right-handers. The remaining third is split between lefties who process language more efficiently in the right hemisphere (15 percent) and those who seem to distribute processing across both hemispheres (15 percent). One study found that the corpus callosum, the area that connects the two hemispheres, was often slightly larger in left-handers than right-handers. Whether such differences are related to cognitive processes is not yet known, but it does seem likely that left-handers are a bit different in hemispheric organization. As an extremely left-handed person myself, I was in high demand as a research subject during college because many people conducting cognitive experiments wanted to include both left- and right-handed individuals for comparison.

■ Tradeoffs: Specialization versus Collaboration?

While there are several theories of sex differences in hemispheric organization, J. Levy's (1969) theory is most closely related to the areas of cognitive performance that differ for the sexes. The theory argues that males and females might show different patterns of verbal and spatial performance if their brains tend to be organized with different degrees of specialization. In particular, we know that males are a more variable group: They have a greater risk of more serious linguistic deficits (e.g., stuttering, dyslexia, loss of speech after strokes), but they also have a greater chance of outstanding performance on certain nonverbal tasks (e.g., scoring 700 on the SAT at age 12). A possible explanation for this variability is that male brains might have a higher probability of being relatively specialized, or "lateralized," in terms of how their hemispheres are organized (J. Levy, 1969; J. Levy & Reid, 1968).

This explanation does not claim that one type of brain is better than another. Rather, there are trade-offs. A distributed processing style and a more specialized type of processing could both offer advantages. Greater specialization might lead to more efficient processing of that specific type of information, while greater shared processing could offer more resilience; if one area of the brain is damaged, another area could also handle the information. Let's use the analogy of a hiring decision for a faculty position. Our final two candidates are both excellent, but they have different strengths. Candidate A is an outstanding, well-rounded individual; he can teach the fundamentals of the field, such as introductory psychology and basic statistics, as well as courses in his area, social psychology, and he has a solid, interesting research program underway. Candidate B is known to be absolutely brilliant in his particular topic, structural causal equation modeling. However, this special skill in one relatively obscure area might have come at the cost of his not being as knowledgeable about other areas, and no one would be able to work with him on shared projects or cover his courses if he became ill or took a sabbatical. Following this analogy, the argument is that more male brains could be highly specialized; more like Candidate B. Depending on the exact balance of specialization, males might have a higher chance of being extremely good at spatial reasoning, which is thought to require more specialization. But males as a group might also have a higher risk of being not very good at language, because extra specialization could start to detract from other, more basic kinds of processing.

There is some suggestive evidence to support the hypothesis that male brains have a greater likelihood of being specialized. In the listening tasks mentioned above, males have a stronger right-ear advantage than females and a greater discrepancy between hemispheres for spatial tasks. Boys can identify a hidden shape better if they hold the object in their left hand, presumably because the right hemisphere is processing the tactile information, while girls do as well as boys with either hand, suggesting that neither hemisphere has an advantage in processing nonlinguistic information (Witelson, 1976). Males are more likely to suffer language problems than females with similar levels of damage to the left hemisphere and to recover less completely (McGlone, 1980). Levy's theory also predicts that a group of left-handed people should show lower average performance than right-handers on spatial tasks, because a group of left-handers would include more people with reversed or shared processing across hemispheres. Preliminary support for this prediction was obtained in one study, in which a group of left-handed men did worse than right-handed men on a battery of spatial reasoning tasks. However, the participants in this study were extremely bright graduate students at a technical university; it is not yet known whether a similar pattern holds for a more typical group (Halpern, 1986).

Developmental Theories of Lateralization

If sex differences in hemispheric organization exist, how would they come about in development? One possibility is that exposure to excess androgen in the prenatal stage might have an "organizing function" (Geschwind & Galaburda, 1987). As we saw in the last chapter, research on animals suggests that exposure to hormones during prenatal development can alter the developing nervous system, with the effects on behavior not appearing until much later in the life span. If exposure to androgen during the prenatal stage enhanced the development of the right hemisphere, this could improve spatial skills for some people but could also hinder verbal processing in others, depending on the exact balance of hormones and the stage of development of the brain when the excess hormone exposure occurred. The argument is that this pattern of strong right-hemisphere dominance would be more likely to occur with male fetuses, who are exposed to androgen anyway, than with female fetuses.

Support for the prenatal hemispheric organization theory is suggestive, although weak. As we have seen, more males do well at spatial processing, suffer language problems, and are left-handed. Could this be related to prenatal hormone levels? Boys who are insensitive to androgen score more like girls than other boys, as do males who have been feminized by severe malnutrition (Dawson, 1967). Mathematically gifted students tend to be left-handed and to suffer from minor immune system disorders, such as allergies and asthma, which can be an indication of androgen sensitivity. The idea is that a male fetus whose developing cells happened to be especially sensitive to the effects of testosterone might be more affected by the hormone than are other males (Kolata, 1983). However, a subsequent study found that other very good students were just as likely to be left-handed.and to have allergies as the mathematically gifted children. Thus, if the hypothesized androgen effect exists at all, it may enhance general intellectual functioning, without necessarily being related to one particular kind of cognitive processing, such as mathematics reasoning (*Science News*, 1990a).

In the case of girls, fetally androgenized girls score higher on spatial-reasoning tests than other girls (Lambert, 1978; Resnick, Berenbaum, Gottesman, & Bouchard, 1986). Girls who were exposed to diethylstilbestrol (DES) before birth showed stronger lateralization of their brains than their unexposed sisters, although the DES girls did *not* show different patterns of spatial and verbal performance (Hines & Shipley, 1984). A synthetic estrogen, DES has a masculinizing effect on the brain when administered to laboratory animals. Another study found that right-hemisphere dominance correlated with performance on the Piagetian water-level task for females, although the measure of dominance was fairly crude and did not relate to spatial performance in males (W. Ray, Georgiou & Ravizza, 1979).

Other evidence is inconsistent with the organizing function hypothesis. First, male sex hormone levels at birth, as measured from samples of umbilical cord blood collected at the delivery, did not predict boys' spatial reasoning at age 6 years; that is, boys with higher testosterone levels before birth did not score better on spatial-reasoning tests than boys with lower levels of male hormones. In the case of girls, higher levels of male hormones at birth predicted *lower* spatial reasoning at 6 years, a pattern opposite to what we would expect if testosterone levels enhance right-hemisphere development (Jacklin, Wilcox, & Maccoby, 1988). Second, a review of data from several hundred fetal brains found no observable sex differences in structure, casting additional doubt on the idea of hormone influence (Bleier, 1988). Overall, while the idea that fetal hormone levels might shape the developing brain is an intriguing possibility, it has little direct empirical support at this point.

Timing of Maturation

An alternative theory is also based on the idea that hemispheric specialization patterns differ for the sexes but argues that specialization develops gradually during childhood and then "freezes" at puberty, rather than being established during prenatal development. If timing of puberty is important in stabilizing hemispheric organization, females might be less specialized because more of them reach puberty earlier than boys, who have an extra year or two to gain additional specialization. If maturation is the critical factor, then early maturers of both sexes should have less lateralized brains, better verbal skills, and worse spatial skills. Several studies of young adolescents have shown a relation between early maturation and poorer spatial reasoning in both sexes (L. Harris, 1979; Newcombe & Bandura, 1983; Waber, 1976, 1977). In addition, there is evidence that spatial-reasoning performance levels off in adolescence and then declines steadily over the life span, even among men who have decades of experience using spatial visualization abilities on a daily basis, such as practicing and recently retired architects (Salthouse et al., 1990). This suggests again that physical maturation might be an important factor in determining an individual's spatial-reasoning capacity.

One problem with the timing of maturation theory is that there is quite a bit of evidence that specialized processing of linguistic information is already present early in life. For example, most infants show left-hemisphere dominance when listening to speech sounds, and hand preference is established by about age 4 in both sexes and possibly even before birth (*Science News*, 1990a; Tan, 1985). There is also evidence that by the preschool period certain types of nonverbal processing are performed by the right hemisphere and linguistic processing by the left hemisphere (Hisock & Kinsbourne, 1978; Kee, Gottfried, Bathurst, & Brown, 1987; Saxby & Bryden, 1984; Witelson, 1987). It is certainly possible that specialization for various types of processing is established early and that the different types of processing then continue to develop on different timetables for the sexes during childhood (Rueckert, Sorensen, & Levy, 1991). However, it is then less clear how or why one process could affect the other, specifically, why being better at verbal tasks should be paralleled by poorer average performance on spatial tasks.

The advantage of these theories is that they suggest reasons for the greater variability of performance among males, specifically, why more males have language deficits after brain injuries and why boys predominate among the most mathematically gifted students. However, as we have seen, the evidence for sex differences in hemispheric organization is extremely weak, and the details of the theories are not clear (Hahn, 1987; McManus & Bryden, 1991). In addition, alternate explanations can be found for much of the evidence used to support the theories, as we will see below. In any case, these theories only offer an explanation for the children at the extremes of performance, that is, prodigious talent in mathematics, on the one hand, and speech aphasia and dyslexia, on the other hand. Thus, we are still left with questions about the performance of more typical children. For example, many children have some trouble learning to read; it seems very unlikely that all boys who struggle with first-grade reading have some sort of deficit in their brains. Girls often seem to do less well on spatial and mathematics problems because they adopt the wrong approach, rather than because they are incapable of a particular kind of reasoning. Thus, the differences in cognitive performance might not result because males and females have differently organized brains but because they have been encouraged and expected to develop some cognitive abilities over others. We look at this possibility in the next section.

THE SOCIALIZATION OF COGNITIVE ABILITIES

Verbal Abilities

Children first learn to talk in a social context that varies by gender: Parents talk more to baby girls and they respond more to girls' early attempts to use language to communicate.

For example, when talking with toddlers about past events, such as a trip to the zoo, parents engage daughters in longer, more elaborative discussions than they do with sons, and they encourage more responses from daughters (Reese & Fivush, 1993). Parents also use more verbal methods of discipline with girls than boys.

During the school years, it looks as though social factors also contribute to boys' relative difficulty with reading. Teachers spend more time instructing girls in reading while boys receive more instructional attention in math which leads to gender differences in achievement (Leinhardt, Seewald, & Engel, 1979). Not surprisingly, American children believe that reading is a feminine activity, a belief that is probably enhanced by the fact that most children are taught to read by female teachers. Boys do not have the same difficulty in other cultures in which there are more male teachers. For example, studies of German children show that boys learn to read ahead of girls, and that more girls are diagnosed with reading problems; there are more male primary teachers in Germany than in the United States. Other countries for which boys have been found to read at least as well as girls include England, Nigeria, Japan, and Israel (Bank, Biddle, & Good, 1980; Preston, 1962). In one study, boys did worse than girls on a reading task when taught by a teacher, but they did as well as girls on a computer-presented reading lesson (McNeil, 1964). The gender difference in reading achievement in the United States is also inflated by the fact that teachers are quicker to notice boys' reading problems than girls' (Scott, Dwyer, & Lieb-Brilhart, 1985; Shaywitz, Shaywitz, Fletcher, & Escobar, 1990).

Not only do patterns of verbal achievement vary across cultures, they vary within culture as a function of the relative status of boys and girls. Studies of Israeli schoolchildren found that among urban children boys outscored girls on most tests of verbal skills, but that among kibbutz children there was no gender difference. Girls who lived in kibbutzim in which gender equity was strongly stressed had particularly high scores, while boys outscored girls in more orthodox, patriarchal communities (Safir, 1986). Similarly, boys from orthodox Jewish families in New York outscored girls on tests of verbal skill, reflecting their families' strong traditional emphasis on scholarly achievement in males (Levinson, 1959). Such variations in the patterns of gender differences cannot easily be explained in terms of biology; rather, they support the notion that cultural expectations have a strong role in determining boys' and girls' achievement in language areas.

Social factors have also contributed to the decline over the last 20 years in female scores on the verbal SAT (a decline that cannot be explained by hemispheric organization theories; brains do not evolve that quickly). For one thing, the groups of males and females who volunteer to take the SAT exam are not equivalent. Males who are poor students are more likely than females to drop out of high school and thus are not likely to sign up for the SAT. Female students who are less well prepared have been increasingly likely to take the exam over the last few decades, and the females come from less advantaged family backgrounds than the male volunteers (Halpern, 1989). The decline in scores could therefore be due to the fact that an increasingly broad sample of females is compared to a group of males that was, and still is, largely made up of good students. But the sex difference holds within each socioeconomic group, so population differences cannot be the entire explanation. An additional factor is that according to Educational Testing Service researchers, adjustments to the verbal section of the exam were made beginning in the early 1970s when the female advantage began to disappear. Questions on which girls outscored boys were dropped, and questions with science-oriented content were added to reduce the gender difference on the verbal section, in order to create "a better balance for the scores between the sexes" (American Association of University Women [AAUW], 1992; Donlon & Angoff, 1971, pp. 25–26, cited in Rosser, 1989; Mensh & Mensh, 1991). No such adjustments have been made to reduce the differences that favor boys on the mathematics section.

■ Spatial Abilities

There is considerable evidence that an individual's spatial abilities can be developed through practice, experience, and use of relevant strategies. I am famous in my family for being able to generate shortcuts, detect that we are heading in the wrong direction, and remember routes to locations that we have not visited for years. This is not because I have some special mental capacity for spatial reasoning; rather, while growing up in San Diego, I learned to quickly work out the appropriate direction by locating my destination on a mental grid with the Pacific Ocean as an anchor point on the left. My navigational performance plummeted dramatically when we went to India, because the Pacific was now on the right!

Do Games and Toys Enhance Boys' Spatial Abilities?

Perhaps more boys do well on such tasks as mental rotation because they have had access to relevant experiences; for example, playing football might help them discover how objects move through three-dimensional space. Several studies suggest that children's spatial skills are related to practice, training, and experience with toys that might provide opportunities to notice spatial principles. Traditionally masculine toys, such as trucks, blocks, and action figures (e.g., GI Joe), have been found to promote more physically active play, and boys who frequently engage in masculine play, including ball games, blocks and transportation toys, and cube puzzles, showed better performance on an embedded figures task than other boys (Connor & Serbin, 1977; Liss, 1983; M. O'Brien & Huston, 1985; Serbin & Connor, 1979). The connection between experience and spatial skill has also been found for girls: Females with higher involvement in traditionally masculine activities and with more masculine-typed personality traits have superior spatial reasoning (Baenninger & Newcombe, 1989; Nash, 1975). This link is particularly strong among adolescent girls (Signorella & Jamison, 1986). Differential interests and experience also seemed to be related to the early maturation hypothesis discussed above, in which children who reach puberty relatively late tend to have better spatial skills. Newcombe and Bandura (1983) found that early-maturing girls tended to have more conventionally feminine interests, while later-maturing girls were more likely to have masculine interests, which were in turn correlated with high spatial ability. In fact, by age 16, masculine interests were a stronger predictor of spatial ability than timing of puberty (Newcombe & Dubas, 1987). These findings predict that a teenage girl who spends her weekends rock climbing or bike riding probably will have better spatial ability than either the girl who looks at fashion magazines and tries out new combinations of accessories with her outfits or the boy who rehearses rock songs with his band in the garage.

Females' performance on tests of spatial reasoning has improved over the last two generations, and girls' greater involvement in sports might account for this change

(Caplan, MacPherson, & Tobin, 1985; Feingold, 1988). Even so, activities that might enhance spatial reasoning are probably still more accessible to boys. Most schools run organized sports programs, such as football and baseball, which are legally open to both sexes but are in practice limited to boys. As one researcher pointed out, "[We] really don't know what the majority of girls are doing while adolescent boys are engaged in sports" (Halpern, 1986, p. 128). Watching afternoon soap operas and trying on makeup are not activities that will enhance spatial skills in anyone.

Cultural Variations

Another factor that could contribute to differences in spatial ability is that girls are usually restricted to their homes, while boys can roam freely about their neighborhood or city. When I lived at the edge of a large nature preserve, I often saw groups of boys running and riding bikes on the trails, but girls were never there without an adult along. Cross-cultural research shows that such experiences help develop or retard spatial skills (Monroe & Monroe, 1971). In societies where children, particularly girls, are kept close to home, both sexes score relatively low on spatial tests, and girls score worse than boys. In cultures where children are encouraged to roam and learn their way around, for example, in certain Inuit tribes, children do very well on spatial-reasoning problems, and gender differences are reduced (Berry, 1966; MacArthur, 1967). Males' average scores also vary enormously between different cultures, depending on the patterns of travel and the local environment. For example, males from some Bushmen tribes in Australia performed much better on a maze problem than males from other tribes, and the difference between males across tribes was much greater than the sex difference within each tribe (L. Harris, 1979). A study of Native American children in Peru found cognitive gender differences in favor of boys among those who lived in the urban shantytowns outside of Lima and in villages in the Andean highlands. However, there were few gender differences among children who lived in an isolated community deep in the rain forest; these patterns were attributed to the greater status and parental attention given to boys in the more urban settings (H. Stevenson, Chen, & Booth, 1990). Biological theories cannot easily account for such wide variations in performance within and across cultures.

Although there is strong evidence that children learn to develop their spatial skills and that boys have more opportunities to engage in activities that could enhance spatial reasoning, it is not altogether clear that such factors can account entirely for the male advantage. First, several studies have found that both sexes benefit from training and practice on spatial problems, so that although girls do improve considerably, boys still outperform girls after the training (Baenninger & Newcombe, 1989; Ben-Chaim, Lappan, & Houang, 1988; Connor, Schackman, & Serbin, 1978). Second, it is not always obvious that stereotypically masculine toys and activities are really more relevant to spatial development than are feminine toys (Tracy, 1987). Why should block building teach more about spatial relations than nesting a set of toy pots and pans or working with clay? Does making a treasure map involve more spatial representation than working with a dress pattern? Does setting up a play in football provide more opportunities to observe spatial trajectories than learning a gymnastics or ballet routine? There is no systematic and independent way to determine how much spatial reasoning is involved in many children's activities, other than by intuition, or by inferring that it is a masculine-stereotyped task and boys have a spatial advantage, so the task must involve spatial reasoning—a rather circular argument. Third, even when boys and girls are given the same toys, they tend to play with them differently, so spatial learning may reflect boys' style of play more than their greater experience with a particular type of toy (Liss, 1981). Thus, it would be premature to conclude that differential experience accounts entirely for the male advantage in spatial reasoning.

In some cases, boys' socialization can actually interfere with their spatial performance, as occurs in studies of children's ability to maintain a sense of direction while in a "swivel chair" (Young, 1989). In these experiments the children are blindfolded and then placed in a chair that turn, tilts, and twists wildly for several minutes, rather like a carnival ride. When the chair stops, they have to report the direction they think they are facing. Before early adolescence, children are not very good at this task, but after about 11 years, girls start to do very well, while boys continue to fail dismally. The reason is that boys try to keep track of the chair's movements and actively calculate their position. In contrast, girls realize quickly that they cannot follow the chair's trajectory and instead rely on their unconscious sense of direction, which turns out to be quite accurate. Girls showed a sharp decline in accuracy when they wore a magnet on their head, suggesting that their sense of direction was based on a subtle awareness of the earth's magnetic field—information that the boys overlooked because they viewed the task as a challenge and relied on active problem-solving methods that did not work in the situation.

Mathematics

In one school district the first prize for the junior high school mathematics competition was a tie pin; a fairly clear indication that a boy was expected to win (Tobias, 1978). There is considerable evidence that boys and girls, as well as their parents and teachers, do have different attitudes and expectations about math and that these expectations affect children's interest in math and their feelings of competence in the subject (J. Jacobs, 1991). Beginning in first grade, children and their parents consider reading to be a girl's subject, while math is for boys; these stereotyped expectations have been found in Asian classrooms, as well as in the United States (Lummis & Stevenson, 1990; Wigfield et al., 1989). Entwisle and Baker (1983) found that first-, second- and third-grade girls were pessimistic about math—expecting to do worse than they actually did—while boys were optimistic— expecting to do better than they actually did. The discrepancies between children's expectations and their performance were matched by their parents': Parents did not expect girls to do as well in math as boys, and girls apparently internalized their parents' expectations, doubting their competence even in first grade. Parents who have seen such headlines as, "Hormones Add Up to Boys' Math Superiority," in media accounts of sex differences in prodigious math achievement expect even less of daughters and more of sons than in the past (J. S. Eccles & Jacobs, 1986). Parents' lower expectations have the most debilitating influence on white, middle-class girls. For students at a racially mixed, working-class school, parents expected girls to do fairly well, perhaps reflecting the belief that daughters have a better chance of doing well in school.

Effects on Confidence

Despite their lower expectations, girls continue to get good grades throughout elementary school, but by the time children reach junior high school, girls have lost considerable confidence in their math ability, while boys continue to be confident (J. E. Eccles et al., 1983; Wigfield et al., 1989). Not surprisingly, girls begin to prefer their English and language classes at this point, while boys like their math and language classes about the same. Decreasing enjoyment of math is problematic because when math courses become optional in high school, girls "bail out" faster than boys and thus graduate on average with less mathematics preparation for college.

The Role of Attributions

In addition to low expectations and stereotypes about math as unfeminine, the type of performance feedback provided in math classes may be part of what eventually puts girls off the subject and leads them to prefer language classes. Grades on a book report or an essay in an English class seem more subjective. There can be genuine differences of opinion in the interpretation or analysis of a novel, and one is assessed as much on one's expressive abilities as on producing a particular answer. In contrast, math involves a clear answer, and errors are highly visible. Because girls are indirectly encouraged to make internal attributions for failure, the frequent minor failures that are inevitable in learning math might eventually be more discouraging to girls, who tend to overestimate the importance of ability for doing well in math relative to other subjects and who believe that they only succeed in math class through high levels of effort (Newman, 1989; Wigfield et al., 1989). Stipek and Gralinski (1991) found that elementary and junior high school girls expected to do less well than boys on an upcoming classroom math test. After the test was over, the girls who had done well attributed their high score to effort, and were less proud of their success than were boys. Among those who had failed the test, girls were more likely than boys to assume they had low math aptitude and that hard work would not help them do better and to report that they would like to avoid math in the future if they could. I realize now that in some ways I was lucky to study statistics back in the dark ages before computer programs were widely available. We had to do all the calculations by hand, which was admittedly extremely tedious but provided an easy external attribution for failure: If the answer to a problem was wrong, I assumed that a simple calculation error was probably responsible, which kept me from being overwhelmed with the feeling "I'll never get this" that can be so discouraging.

Another factor that may contribute to girls' avoidance of math in junior high is their fear of being considered unfeminine; early adolescence is a time when children cling to stereotypical notions of gender, and a 13-year-old girl can say she is not good at math to signal her femininity. In a study of West German teenagers, girls who were more traditionally feminine and more interested in dating than other girls did less well in math than would have been predicted on the basis of their general intelligence and their grades in other subjects, suggesting a trade-off between attractiveness and good performance in masculine-stereotyped subjects (Tobias, 1978). J. C. Condry and Dyer (1977) found that many junior high school girls said explicitly that they would rather have a boyfriend than outperform a boy! A survey of women mathematicians found that most recalled being told that boys did not like smart girls, although clearly this message did not keep them from pursuing math (Becker, 1990). Yet we have to keep in mind that even if girls feel that math is unfeminine, it does not inhibit them from getting better grades than boys do. One study of wealthy, mostly white, high school students found that the girls scored as high as the boys on a mathematics achievement test and reported liking math more than did the boys; the researchers attributed this pattern of results to the high degree of career orientation in these relatively advantaged students and the high expectations of their parents, which may have helped them discount messages about math being unfeminine (Paulsen & Johnson, 1983).

What about Tests?

It makes intuitive sense to suggest that adolescent girls turn away from math because they lack confidence, they think it is unfeminine, and their parents and peers do not expect them to do well. But this explanation cannot entirely account for several aspects of the data, including why girls get better grades in math but lower scores on standardized tests. Are teachers unconsciously giving girls better grades than they deserve, perhaps because girls are better behaved or more conscientious about their work? Grade inflation might conceivably be a possibility at the elementary school level, but it seems less plausible that high school math teachers are rewarding girls with good grades for good behavior in calculus, particularly given that performance evaluations in math are often more objective than in other subjects (Kimball, 1989). It also seems equally likely that stereotypes could work against girls when teachers assign grades, if teachers unconsciously assume that girls are not as interested and capable in math as are boys. In fact, about two-thirds of teachers think that boys are better at math, and the rest think there is no sex difference; no one thinks that girls are better. In other words, girls are actually getting higher grades in a classroom atmosphere that is less hospitable in terms of teacher expectations, support, and instruction (see Chapter 8).

The Issue of Test Bias

There is also more evidence that standardized tests underestimate girls' real skill than that their classroom grades are artificially inflated. The formal, tightly timed test-taking situation works against girls, who are reluctant to guess or to use quick estimation strategies when they are not sure of an answer, and who tend to spend more time on each problem and then to have to rush through the more difficult problems at the end of the section (Becker, 1990; Linn, De Benedictis, Delucchi, Harris, & Stage, 1987). A discrepancy between grades and test scores might also be due to the inclusion of more questions that involve male-oriented content (Hyde, Fennema, & Lamon, 1990). One SAT question that produced a large sex difference involved the calculation of a basketball team's win-loss ratio for the season; more boys reported that they could simply guess the answer based on their general familiarity with team averages, while more girls carefully set up the appropriate equation and calculated the correct answer. Gender differences in performance on particular items are related to students' judgments of whether the items are "for boys" or "for girls" (Chipman, 1988). On the other hand, it seems less than plausible—almost insulting—to suggest that girls somehow become incapable of solving problems merely because the content involves sports. In addition, while girls do report being more nervous about taking the SAT on average than do boys, test anxiety does not correlate with individual performance; a finding that should reassure those readers who tend to worry about such exams. Overall, it seems unlikely that item content and the test format can entirely account for the gender difference in test performance. Although more research is needed to find out why there is a gender gap in performance on standardized tests, it is known that the discrepancy between males and females is greater on the SAT math test than on other standardized tests (AAUW, 1992; Feingold, 1988; Linn & Hyde, 1989; Rosser, 1989). To address this concern, the math section of the SAT exam is currently being revised to include more items and a wider range of problems in hopes of more accurately reflecting girls' real skills and yielding more accurate predictions of how boys and girls will do in their college classes.

Math Prodigies

Just as stereotypes about math being unfeminine do not inhibit girls from getting good grades, such beliefs also do not seem to explain completely the male advantage among the most mathematically talented students. Mathematically gifted boys and girls report no differences in their view of math as either a masculine or feminine subject. They like math equally well and report equal levels of parental encouragment for studying math, although girls take one less semester of math, usually high school calculus (Benbow & Stanley, 1982, 1984; C. L. Raymond & Benbow, 1986). If gifted girls do well in math and do not view it as masculine, why are they less likely to pursue it in high school and college? One possibility is that the gifted girls also enjoy other classes, particularly their English and language classes, more than do the boys. Several of my advisees have been women who have always done well in math but who in their second year of college report that they are not going to take any more math because it is just not as rewarding and interesting as other subjects. They do not seem to think that math is unfeminine or appear to lack confidence. Rather, they feel free to pursue their other interests, while their male counterparts stick it out in math classes because they consider math to be important for their future careers. Another possibility is that gifted girls find a mathematics career less appealing than their male counterparts because of its relative isolation and they have realistic concerns about the difficulties of combining a science career with their anticipated family responsibilities. Gifted girls tend to scale down their ambitions accordingly, for example, by seeking masters degrees rather than doctorates, and only about half planned to work full time throughout their careers (C. Raymond, 1992).

■ Does It Matter?

We have seen that although girls do well in math class relative to boys, they tend not to take more math than they absolutely have to and they like math less than other subjects. Although the precise reasons for the different patterns of math achievement among males and females are not yet known in detail, the long-term consequences are clear: In the United States, only about 13 to 15 percent of math- and science-related jobs that require mathematics training are held by women, and the proportion of women "in the pipeline," that is, those gaining enough training to qualify for such jobs, is not increasing (Benbow & Stanley, 1984; Hyde, Fennema, & Lamon, 1990; Linn & Hyde, 1989; Maple & Stage, 1991; Oakes, 1990). Math proficiency has been calculated to add more than 35 percent to a girl's future income (Pogrebin, 1980). There are two general approaches to solving the problem of girls' underachievement in math: one difficult, the other comparatively straightfoward.

The Hard Way

One approach is to try to build girls' self-confidence in math and to encourage them to continue taking classes. A number of colleges, including traditionally black institutions and women's colleges, offer summer programs for girls to build their self-confidence in math; for example, Mount Holyoke offers a 6-week program for high school girls that includes a review of math skills and confidence-building activities, at a cost of about $3000 per student (*Hampshire Life*, 1992; Stage, 1985). Spelman College, a historically black college in Atlanta, offers half-day science-and-math academies for elementary and secondary students (Raloff, 1991). These workshops seem to be most successful when they are all female. In one case, researchers found that in mixed-gender summer school classes for gifted students, the girls would drop out because they were teased by their peers, and they thought that their gifted male classmates were "nerds" (L. Fox & Cohn, 1980). In addition, intervention programs need to take into account the specific reasons why girls abandon math. There is some evidence that the reasons vary with ethnicity; parental education and expectations appear to be more influential for black and Hispanic girls, while gender stereotypes seem to have more of a debilitating influence on white girls (Maple & Stage, 1991).

A related approach is to increase girls' understanding of the importance of math for their future, as beliefs about math utility are correlated with achievement for both sexes (MacDonald, 1980; Midgley, Feldlaufer, & Eccles, 1989). At Dartmouth College, a group of women science and engineering faculty created a "Women in Science" program in which first-year women students worked as research assistants with faculty members so that they could see for themselves how mathematics is used in various fields. The program was so successful that men students started to ask if they, too, could participate. The image of math as a career also needs a cosmetic overhaul. Students' image of a female mathematician is of an elderly lady wearing spectacles and oxford shoes, not a particularly attractive option compared to the elegant female lawyers and doctors often seen on television (Halpern, 1986). A woman in one of my classes cited the gorgeous blonde physicist in the popular film *Top Gun* as an example that encouraged her to sign up for a math class, although having the character wear black seamed stockings with sky-high heels while lecturing to her male Air Force students was perhaps not the most believable costume choice!

The Easy Way

Although special programs and workshops can encourage girls to continue studying math and to be more confident of their skills, this is an expensive approach that reaches relatively few students. An alternative strategy is to recognize the gender gap in confidence but simply navigate around it, at least temporarily, by requiring more mathematics of all students, boys and girls. We know that girls on average will do well in math classes; the problem is not a lack of ability. With more required math in the curriculum, girls might still feel doubtful of their abilities, but they would at least graduate with the math training necessary to continue at the college level or to take jobs in science industries. Girls might also encounter less resistance from male classmates protective of "their" domain if math classes were compulsory for all students, rather than being presented as an optional choice, one that is gender-atypical for girls (Kimball, 1989).

A second reason to require more mathematics training in the curriculum is that boys also need more encouragement to continue. It is not as if there are large numbers of male students who are taking every math class they can find, having "calculator wars" in their dorm rooms and, after graduation, filling all the available scientific and technical jobs in the country that require mathematics training. In fact, there is growing concern in the United States, as well as other countries, that too few students of either sex have sufficient math training to meet the demands of science and industry in future decades (Raloff, 1991). The difference in mathematics achievement between U.S. male and female students is *trivial* compared to the vast gap between U.S. students and those in other countries. One comparison of fifth graders in U.S., Taiwanese, and Japanese schools found that on a 70-question exam covering material taken directly from the students' math textbooks, the average difference between U.S. boys and girls was about one-quarter of a point, while the Asian students scored between 9 and 10 points higher than the U.S. students (H. Stevenson & Lee, 1990). Efforts to encourage girls need to be part of a larger effort to raise the overall level of mathematics achievement in U.S. children.

INTERPRETING GENDER DIFFERENCES

By this point, it should be apparent that many factors interact in determining an individual's personality and cognitive characteristics and that biology and socialization are probably both involved in aggression, prosocial behavior, and cognitive performance. Differences based in biology are only the starting point for behavioral differences, but it is possible to highlight one influence or the other, depending on one's particular theoretical or political bias. My own bias is that before we conclude that one sex is somehow fundamentally less capable in a particular cognitive area—for example, because of differences in the organization and function of their brains—we must establish that alternative explanations cannot account for their poorer performance. For example, if we discover that more girls have trouble with a particular type of spatial reasoning, rather than immediately assuming it is because their right hemispheres are somehow deficient, we should first look at other factors: Perhaps girls have had less relevant experience while growing up, or they tend to select inappropriate strategies on tests, or they have experienced more overt discouragement for good performance and more tolerance for poor performance. If none of these other possibilities receives much support then it makes sense to turn to theories that include a more explicit biological component. The socialization-first approach is warranted because, to date, socialization explanations for different patterns of cognitive performance between the sexes have considerable support and offer more detailed explanations than biologically oriented theories are currently able to provide (Boles, 1980; Lambert, 1978; McManus & Bryden, 1991).

There are several additional reasons to look toward socialization explanations for differential performance by the sexes. First, chalking up poor performance on a task to biology can often leave us with the helpless feeling that there is nothing to be done other than to learn to live with the situation. We do tend to assume that our personality and cognitive traits are stable attributes: "That's just the way I am," "I was never any good at math," "You can't teach an old dog new tricks." Yet this conclusion is inaccurate; in fact, our behavior is highly determined by the situation and our previous experiences. A bias to assume that our traits and abilities are fixed by some mysterious biological process makes attempts to modify our behavior seem superfluous when such efforts usually yield considerable rewards. A young man might consider himself to be hopelessly shy, meaning that he tends to hang back at large parties having lots of new people, even though he is actually quite comfortable at parties at his own fraternity and even though he could fairly easily overcome his shyness in new situations with a bit of effort and tolerance of a few initial awkward moments. Similarly, a girl who is struggling with algebra can almost certainly master it with some encouragement and persistence, but may give up prematurely if she assumes she just isn't smart enough and if no one pushes her. Even in cases where a specific cognitive ability seems relatively fixed, such as laboratory tests of mental rotation, our performance is rarely the best it could be, and minor interventions, training, and practice usually lead to a significant improvement. World-class runners do not consider their last race time to be an indication of a biologically based upper limit on their speed or endurance; rather, they assume that their past performance is an indication of a possible range within which improvement is always possible and devote their training time to achieving even better performance. The same approach toward social and cognitive abilities can have significant payoffs for the individual.

Second, attributing lower performance to biological causes is often not limiting merely for a particular individual but to groups as well. Intentionally or otherwise, biological explanations for group differences tend to be emphasized only when this view will justify the traditional societal advantages of one group while limiting the opportunities of other groups. For example, parents, teachers, the media, and children themselves seem quite willing to accept that girls "just aren't as good at math," and thus there is little point in trying to help and encourage them. Such headlines as, "Hormones Add Up to Boys' Math Superiority," have attracted wide attention, while the discrepancy between girls' lower SAT math scores and their better college grades was overlooked for many years, with the result that more boys received college scholarships. The male advantage in spatial reasoning is often emphasized, although there is little evidence that variations in spatial skills make much practical difference in life. Most people can manage to wedge a few suitcases into a car trunk and find their way out of a shopping mall, even if they are terrible at mental rotation. While the supposed limitations of females are highlighted, those of males are almost delicately avoided. Little attention is given to the fact that excessive male violence is a serious and extremely expensive societal problem. When boys have trouble learning to read, it is not assumed to be due to biological constraints, and considerable economic resources are quietly devoted to helping them by providing special reading teachers, remedial classes, and reading resource rooms. No comparable institutional efforts are made at the junior high and high school levels to encourage girls to continue with mathematics.

While there are reasons to look first for socialization explanations for sex differences in behavior, this does not mean that we should never consider the role of biology or adopt a head-in-the-sand attitude to the possibility that biological factors influence what children can do. Biology probably does set some limits on performance. Gender may indeed be an important factor in the prognosis and treatment of a little boy who has sustained severe brain damage in a car accident. A girl may have her heart set on playing quarterback but simply not be able to throw the football far enough to make the team. Children who get perfect scores on the math SAT at age 9 might well have brains that were shaped by a prenatal hormonal fluke. We can recognize the possibility that biological influences and constraints might exist while not using this possibility as an excuse for setting limits on the opportunities open to particular individuals. For example, we would not want to reduce our efforts to provide speech therapy for the little boy, on the belief that a male's chances of recovery are more limited. We would not want to say that only junior high school boys can try the SAT exam. Similarly, the federal judge who ruled in 1978 that girls could not be excluded from school sports solely on the basis of gender wrote:

> Where is it written that girls may not, if suitably qualified, play football? . . . It may well be that there is a student today in an Ohio high school who lacks only the proper coaching and training to become the greatest quarterback in professional football history. Of course, the odds are astronomical against her, but isn't she entitled to a fair chance to try? (Brooks-Gunn & Matthews, 1979, pp. 276–277)

The odds of becoming the next Joe Montana or Randall Cunningham are astronomical against most boys too, but we allow them their chance. When it comes to intellectual pursuits, we can encourage children to find their areas of special aptitude and come to terms with their individual limitations, without allowing gender to restrict their opportunities.

SUMMARY

In the last two chapters we have reviewed evidence about the personality characteristics and intellectual talents of boys and girls and found that, for the most part, the sexes are similar. In fact, in almost every case, knowing a child's gender does not allow one to make any reliable predictions about that child's capacity for nurturance, friendship, or performance in school. It is clear that our popular stereotypes about the characteristics of the sexes— that boys are ready to beat up other kids, while girls are timid and fearful; that boys are selfish and mean, while girls are sweet and caring; that boys are good at math, while girls are good at language—are exaggerated well beyond the reality, another example of how we tend to treat gender characteristics as polar opposites.

Although in most cases the sexes are more similar than different, we have seen some instances in which the proportion of males and females is recognizably different, namely, boys' greater tendency to respond to aggressive attacks, girls' greater resilience in language areas, and the greater number of male math prodigies. In both chapters we have considered the potential contribution of biological factors, including the role of hormones in aggressive behavior and in shaping patterns of cognitive performance, as well as the contribution of differential expectations and socialization. It is impossible to rule out entirely the contribution of biology to these differences, particularly at the extremes of performance, such as bullies, math prodigies, and children with serious linguistic disabilities, who are mostly boys. However, as we have argued throughout the book, biological tendencies are always shaped by the social environment: The bully finds that he can get what he wants through aggression, while the girl learns it does not work for her; the 14-year-old girl math prodigy decides not to take calculus because she does not want to be the only girl in the class; the 8-year-old girl who still cannot read goes without help for another year because her teachers have overlooked her reading disability. Clearly, biology interacts with the experience of growing up male or female.

12

GROWING UP: THE TRANSITION TO ADULT ROLES

I provoke my first fight between boys when I am in third grade, looking from one to the other with the old up-from-under-the-lashes whammy, smiling a small secret smile. The boys would find another reason to fight if I am not there, but I am and I make the most of it. They give each other a pretty solid pounding, but nobody really gets hurt . . . I have three boyfriends during grade school . . . I keep them all on a string and never make a choice, but that is because sex isn't part of our lives yet. (J. Phillips, 1991, pp. 39–40).

Although third graders do not worry too much about sex, they will soon begin to do so as they enter puberty and move into adolescence. In the last 10 chapters we have traced the development of the gender-neutral infant into a boy or girl and have discovered that much of the learning of an appropriate gender role is accomplished within a few short years. Yet as this quote illustrates, children do not stay little boys or girls forever. In fact, gender role learning in childhood is only the foundation for the task of becoming an adult man or woman, and many aspects begin to change in late elementary school and early adolescence. Not only do children's bodies change at puberty, but their cognitive capabilities expand, and they notice that members of their own families react to them differently. Their peers are also changing. The best friend who used to read Batman comic books and who thought that girls were dumb now talks a lot about "getting it" and wants to hang out at the mall in hopes of running into some girls, while the girl who loved playing with her collection of plastic horses now wants to practice kissing on pillows in her room while listening to love songs on the radio.

The focus of this chapter is on adolescence, the years of transition between childhood and adulthood. One goal of the chapter is to provide an overview of the changes during adolescence in several of the areas that we have examined in earlier chapters, including physical, cognitive, and social development. Another goal is to consider why growing up often seems harder for girls than boys. Much of the earlier asymmetry of gender role socialization disappears in adolescence as a result of the new pressure on girls to be attractive to the other sex, along with parents' and teachers' increasing insistence that the girl act like a lady. As we will see, the constraints of the mature feminine role are received with some ambivalence by girls, and adolescent girls are more likely than boys to suffer from low self-esteem, eating disorders, and depression.

PUBERTY: PHYSICAL CHANGES

The physical process of becoming a man or woman takes several years during which time the child's body grows dramatically and takes on its sexually mature form. Puberty is still largely a mystery; we know that it is triggered by the hypothalamus, an area of the brain that signals the pituitary gland to allow the ovaries or testes to produce larger amounts of sex hormones. The processes of puberty are naturally different for the sexes given that their reproductive functions as adults are biologically different: Females menstruate and have the potential to become pregnant and nurse the infant, while males have the capacity to impregnate. Thus puberty, like the prenatal stage, is a point where the path of development diverges sharply for boys and girls.

■ Female Development

A famous painting by Norman Rockwell shows a girl in front of a mirror; she wistfully compares her childish figure and braids to the photograph in a magazine resting on her lap and is clearly anxious to grow up but doubtful that she will ever look like the glamorous model in the picture. Growing up is not only an exciting time for girls but also one that for many girls creates a sense of uncertainty and ambivalence. The discovery that a female grade school classmate has started to wear a bra can trigger excited discussion among other girls and requests for "training bras" to skeptical mothers at home, yet at the same time the girl whose breasts *have* developed often hunches her shoulders, tries to hide her chest, and bursts into tears if her parents give her a bit of gentle teasing about it. I once overheard a group of third-grade girls talk for an entire recess period about another girl who had started to shave her legs. One announced, with a mixture of awe, envy, and disapproval, that the girl in question even rubbed baby oil on her legs so that the boys would notice them!

Puberty in girls begins when, in response to signals from the pituitary, the girl's ovaries begin to produce more sex hormones. Estrogen levels rise up to eight times their levels in childhood, and rising progesterone levels also help the breasts to develop, the uterus to mature, and the hips and thighs to accumulate layers of fat, producing the typical "eggplant" shape of the mature female body. The ovaries also produce some androgen which leads to the growth of pubic and underarm hair. The process of physical maturation usually takes several years. One of the early signs that puberty has started is the girl's growth spurt, which generally occurs about 2 years earlier than in boys, meaning that for a few years at least girls are generally taller than their male classmates (Marshall & Tanner, 1986; Weirman & Crowley, 1986). Breast development usually begins during or just after the girl's growth spurt and then continues for several years. The appearance of pubic hair is then followed by *menarche*, the girl's first menstruation, as the ovaries begin to produce sex hormones in a regular cycle. In some cultures parents would schedule a girl's betrothal or marriage as soon as they noticed the early signs of puberty, confident that her first menstrual period would follow within the year. Note that menarche, the most obvious indication of maturation, actually occurs relatively late in the process of puberty, meaning that girls can be affected by the physical and hormonal changes of puberty well before parents and siblings really recognize that she is growing up. The average age of puberty in the United States is now about $12\frac{1}{2}$ years; thus some girls within the normal range can be starting the early stages of puberty at 8 to 9 years.

Menarche

Some years ago while at the movies I went into the ladies' restroom during the film and noticed a girl standing outside the stalls alone. She was still there when I came out and started washing my hands, and I realized she was looking at the sanitary napkin dispenser. Feeling sympathetic—most females have occasionally been caught unprepared by an unexpected menstrual period—I asked if she needed a quarter, dug in my bag for some change, and operated the machine. As I handed her the cardboard box, something in her embarrassed face struck me and I said doubtfully, "Have you had your period before?" Stifling an internal groan when she looked down and said no, I explained how she should use the pad and waited while she went into a stall and put it in her underpants. When she came out, I said something cheerful about growing up and asked if she wanted to call her parents. No, she was with her friends, and if she left the movies, everyone would want to know what had happened, and she most definitely didn't want *anyone* to know. She then bolted out the door and back into the dark theater.

Menarche is a major milestone in female development; it is a clear sign to the girl and others that she is no longer a child (Golub, 1983; Ruble & Brooks-Gunn, 1982). Most girls look forward to their first period as a sign of growing up, and there is often quite a bit of competition over who will "get it" first and worried anticipation among those who have not yet "gotten it." Researchers have found that girls who have reached menarche show many signs of being more conscious of what it means to be an adult female. When compared with girls of the same age who have not yet begun to menstruate, post-menarcheal girls report thinking more about dating, marriage, and having children, and they draw themselves with makeup, jewelry, and breasts, in contrast to the simple stick figures of premenarcheal girls (Brooks-Gunn & Warren, 1988; Henton, 1961; Koff, Rierdan, & Jacobson, 1981; Koff, Rierdan, & Silverstone, 1978; Rierdan & Koff, 1980). However, the excitement girls feel about growing up is often mixed with ambivalence, as in the case of the girl I encountered in the restroom. One source of ambivalence is that girls feel they must give up some of the freedom of childhood. Girls report that they feel as though they can no longer ride bikes or go swimming even though there is no reason not to continue athletic activities during menstruation. Some girls even deny that they have started to menstruate; one mother found her daughter's stained underpants in the laundry for several months although the girl would not admit she was having periods and refused to use the supplies her mother purchased for her and left in her room (Petersen, 1983).

There are other indications of resistance to the idea of maturation in girls. Girls report that their strongest reaction to their first period is surprise, as if they did not really believe it would actually happen to them, and even though menstruation is often a hot topic of discussion at sleepovers and play sessions, girls often do not tell their friends for several months after they have begun to menstruate. Adult women have been found to recall surprisingly little about their menarche relative to other events at that time, a phenomenon that has been termed *pubertal amnesia* (Brooks-Gunn & Ruble, 1983, p. 157; Greif & Ulman, 1982). Another indication of ambivalence is that although most girls nowadays have learned about menstruation from their parents, school health education classes, and books, they do not always completely take in the information. One mother had carefully talked with her daughter several years in advance, provided her with books about menstruation, pointed out the napkins and tampons in the supermarket, and made her a celebration supper when her first period arrived. Everything seemed fine until the mother mentioned, "Now you'll know exactly what to do when your period comes next month." The girl gasped in horror, "Next month? You mean this happens *again?*" (Weltner, 1991). Many girls apparently do not wholeheartedly embrace the idea of "becoming a woman."

The "Fat Spurt"

Another source of ambivalence about growing up is the normal weight gain that is associated with puberty. The average girl gains about 24 pounds during puberty, with most of the fat going to her breasts, hips, and thighs. Thus, just as she is becoming aware of the need to be attractive, her body begins to evolve in the direction exactly opposite to the cultural ideal of a thin, leggy, boyish female figure. The fat spurt is exacerbated in many girls because the basal metabolic rate typically drops about 15 percent in adolescence, and girls often give up their participation in sports activities, making it even harder to avoid gaining weight. Currently, about 25 percent of American teenagers are overweight, and the typical adolescent diet of fast food and high-fat snack foods such as tortilla chips and chocolate chip cookies does not help the problem (Santrock, 1990). Although at the time I was mortified, I now look back and applaud my mother for refusing to help sell doughnuts as a PTA fund-raising event at my junior high school; she said that the last thing young teenagers who were worried about their weight and their complexions needed was to be encouraged by adults to eat doughnuts between classes!

Unfortunately, the problem for U.S. girls is not merely achieving a normal, healthy weight; it is that their idea of a desirable weight is highly unrealistic. Girls' worries about being too fat are reinforced by media images that show models who are on average about 5 feet, 11 inches, tall and weigh 110 pounds—a good 6 inches taller and 20 to 30 pounds lighter than the average U.S. woman. Girls' worries about their weight has led to chronic dieting even in grade school and a risk of eating disorders, such as anorexia and bulimia. It has also contributed to the continued high level of smoking among women, most of whom start smoking in adolescence, often in an effort to keep their weight down. It is no coincidence that cigarettes marketed to women are longer and thinner than those marketed to men, and have names such as "Virginia Slims." For teenage girls, body image and self-esteem are strongly correlated, meaning that if a girl feels unhappy with her body, other potential sources of pride and self-esteem—such as doing well in school, enjoying a rewarding hobby, or having good friends—do not make up for the feeling that she is too fat (Attie & Brooks-Gunn, 1989).

Variation in the Timing of Menarche

Although researchers still need to learn what triggers the hypothalamus to begin the process of puberty, we do know that its timing in females is affected by physical and social stress. Damage to the hypothalamus, for example, from a lesion or tumor, can trigger puberty in a young child. One Peruvian girl was reported to begin menstruating at age 3 and gave birth to a baby when she was 5½ years old (J. Williams, 1987). On the other hand, poor health, physical stress, and inadequate diet can delay puberty for several years. In western societies the average age of menarche has declined considerably; a century ago girls reached menarche at about age 16, whereas today the average age of menarche is about 12½ years. Conversely, girls growing up today in areas of Africa that are suffering from severe drought and famine now reach menarche between 13 and 14 years (Marshall & Tanner, 1986). Social stress can also affect the timing of puberty. Girls whose parents divorce or whose family life is very stressful tend to reach puberty earlier than other girls. Again, the precise reason for earlier puberty in this situation is not known, but it seems possible that the neuroendocrine system would respond to stress by accelerating the process of physical maturation. Some researchers have suggested that the variability in the timing of puberty might reflect evolutionary adaptation. When the natal family setting is full of conflict, it would be optimal for the girl to mature, find a partner, and leave the family early. On the other hand, under conditions of extreme stess, such as starvation, it would be advantageous for menarche to be delayed; this would reduce the likelihood that the girl would become pregnant when she could not provide for her offspring (Belsky, Steinberg, & Draper, 1991).

We have seen that many girls feel that they should give up sports at puberty. Is there any evidence that the physical stress of being involved in serious athletics is harmful or delays a girl's menarche? An initial hypothesis was that the girl would have to attain a certain percentage of body fat before puberty would begin and that strenuous activity might therefore interfere with pubertal development. This idea was based on the observation that girls who are involved in intense physical training for competitive athletics or professional dance and who maintain lean bodies through dieting reach menarche later than less active girls (Bailey, Malina, & Mirwald, 1986). However, it now appears that weight alone is not the critical factor. Girls who mature relatively late tend to have somewhat better athletic skills to begin with and to be thinner after puberty as well as before (Bailey et al., 1986). Thus, later-maturing girls might be more interested in and more proficient at athletics and dance than their earlier-maturing peers and will probably receive more encouragement to continue their participation. The petite girls who reach the stellar level of international gymnastics competitions are an example. A 12-year-old girl who gains 25 pounds, grows 5 inches, and develops breasts and hips is unlikely to be a world-class gymnast no matter how hard she trains, whereas the girl whose puberty begins at age 14 or 15 will have an ongoing competitive advantage. In all, there is no evidence that being active in sports or even competitive athletics is harmful to adolescent girls; in fact, continuing to be physically active can reduce the risk of obesity.

■ Male Development

On average, about 2 years later than girls, boys begin puberty when the pituitary signals the testes to produce sex hormones. Boys' androgen levels rise as much as 18 times what they were a few years earlier, leading to the development of muscle bulk and body hair. Boys' estrogen levels increase as well, which can in some cases lead to breast enlargement. Although this condition is usually temporary it can be quite embarrassing to be a 12-year-old-boy who appears to need a bra. One of the first indications of puberty in boys is the enlargement of the testes, penis, and scrotum. This is followed by the growth spurt, the appearance of pubic hair, the growth of facial hair, and the lowering of the voice. As with girls, the more obvious signs of puberty tend to occur relatively late in the process, which can now begin anywhere between 9 and 14 years. Parents and teachers need to keep in mind that it is not uncommon for boys in third or fourth grade to be going through puberty and to be interested in girls. One mother had not yet thought about her son's impending puberty until she collected laundry from his room one day: "It hit me one day, going into his room, a smell of underarm sweat. I suddenly thought, he's grown up!" (Statham, 1986, p. 51).

Another sign of puberty is the boy's increasing interest in sex and its expression in frequent erections and thoughts about sex, reflecting the surge in testosterone levels. One girl wrote, "It seems like the guys I know want sex twenty-four hours a day . . . Why can't they ever think about anything else?" (Kent, 1992, p. 50). Although females have a similar capacity for sexual arousal, there does seem to be a gender gap in adolescence, with boys being faster to become aroused, feeling greater urgency about sex, and being more likely to explore their sexuality through masturbation. Many doctors and researchers consider *spermarche*, the boy's first ejaculation, to be the marker of sexual maturity that is analogous to menarche in girls. Spermarche can occur as the result of masturbation, intercourse, or as a nocturnal emission (a "wet dream"). In contrast to research on menarche, there have been very few studies of spermarche, probably because its more explicit connection with masturbation and sexuality makes it difficult to discuss. One parallel with girls' menarche experience is that boys tend not to talk about it with others. Even with male peers, boys referred to ejaculation only indirectly, by way of jokes and "locker room talk" rather than explicit discussion of their own personal experiences. About two-thirds said they would not even tell a younger brother about spermarche unless he specifically asked for information. One said, "I would tell him something if he asked, but I just don't see how I would work it into a conversation" (Gaddis & Brooks-Gunn, 1985, p. 61). Most had learned about ejaculation from adult magazines, such as *Playboy*, rather than from fathers, other adult males, or male peers. In some cases boys knew more about girls' physical development at puberty than about their own (Brooks-Gunn & Matthews, 1979).

In some ways, the physical changes of puberty are analogous to those we saw in Chapter 2 during the prenatal period, in that sex hormones signal the process of differentiation into the male or female form in both stages. Of course, the major difference is that while as far as we know the fetus is not aware of its own development, the teenager is definitely conscious of his or her sprouting hair, spreading pimples, enlarging genitals, increasing underarm odor, and broadening hips, an awareness that is heightened even more by media advertisements for acne treatments, deodorants, and diet drinks. Teenagers are especially aware of their own development and of others' reactions to them because of the new cognitive capacities that emerge during early adolescence; some of these changes are reviewed in the next section.

COGNITIVE DEVELOPMENT

We saw in Chapter 6 that preschoolers organize their knowledge about gender into schemas and become better able to reason about such issues as appearance and reality, recognizing, for example, that a boy is still a boy even if he puts on a dress and plays with a doll. At adolescence teenagers become able to reason at an even more abstract and flexible level. Their new cognitive capacities, termed *formal operations*, allow teenagers to consider others' points of view in addition to their own and to engage in self-reflection and self-evaluation. At first, these changes are a bit scary. Teens spend much time imagining what others are thinking of them and feeling self-conscious, especially about the changes in their bodies. Girls often wear loose sweatshirts and walk around with their notebooks hugged to their chest to hide their developing breasts, and if they have begun to menstruate, they worry about whether others can tell or will notice that they have to stop in the restroom between classes. Boys in turn worry about erections that develop at inconvenient times. One boy went through torments of embarrassment on the bus ride home from school each day because the vibrations of the bus would trigger an erection, and he was never sure if it would subside before he had to walk down the bus aisle in front of his classmates.

One way to cope with extreme self-consciousness is to try to blend in by doing what everyone else is doing. This explains why teenagers so often dress the way their friends do; at the mall you can often see groups of young adolescents wearing a near uniform of jeans and t-shirts, or tights with big sweatshirts, or one pair of baggy boxer shorts over another, or particular brand-name sneakers or jackets. One girl cried with despair because her father bought her the wrong brand of bike lock; she said, "It's not the kind the other kids have!" (Zimbardo, 1982, p. 161). When we feel unsure of ourselves, we often fall back on the security of familiar things, and teenagers often adopt traditional ideas about gender roles during early adolescence (Alfieri, Thompson, Ruble, Harlow, & Higgins, 1991; B. Brown, Clasen, & Eicher, 1986; Carter & Patterson, 1982; Huston & Alvarez, 1990; Sigelman, Carr, & Begley, 1986; Stoddart & Turiel, 1985; Thompson, 1988; Ullian, 1976). For example, when asked about gender role deviations, such as a boy wearing nail polish or a girl with a crew cut, 12- to 13-year-olds were less tolerant than younger children and more likely to say that they would not want to go to a school that allowed students to do such things, even though the teenagers actually understood more clearly than the younger children that such behaviors were a matter of personal choice. Expectations of the other gender are also highly stereotyped in early adolescence. When asked to describe the ideal man, teenage girls said he would be kind, honest, fun-loving and smiling, and would bring flowers, a picture that the researchers termed the "chivalrous football player." Teenage boys described the ideal woman as the "smiling sunbather," meaning a female who was good looking, sexy, and spent her time in leisure activities such as tanning rather than working or studying (Stiles, Gibbons, & Schnellmann, 1987). The strong need to conform also contributes to the intolerance many teenagers show toward their peers who do not "fit in," for example, those who are overweight, wear the wrong clothes, or are gay or lesbian. One boy walked up to a gay classmate in the school cafeteria, asked, "Are you a faggot?" and then sat at a nearby table and bombarded him with hostile remarks throughout lunch (Savin-Williams, 1990). Such intolerance usually stems from the person's own internal doubts and uncertainty; when you are not too sure yet about your own sexuality, lashing out at a classmate who seems different is a way to reassure yourself.

■ The "Flight into Femininity"

While both boys and girls become more self-conscious during early adolescence, the increase is highest for girls, especially where issues of appearance are concerned. In one study children and teenagers were asked what they would do in various hypothetical situations, such as getting an awful haircut the day of the big school basketball game, being called on to solve a problem at the blackboard when you have an obvious split in your pants seam, or wearing a costume to a party only to discover that it wasn't a costume party after all. In general, 12- to 13-year-olds showed more self-consciousness than younger children or older adolescents, but the girls were the most self-conscious group of all. This is because the strongest predictor of girls' popularity is being thin, pretty, and wearing the "right" clothes; the old saying, "Her face is her fortune," is almost literally true for adolescent girls (P. Adler et al., 1992). The girl who is outgoing and friendly, has lots of energy and enthusiasm, and is a great tennis player, skiier, and dancer cannot hope to be popular if she has bad skin, is a bit chubby, or wears beige cardigan sweaters and lime-green cotton skirts to school. Conversely, no girl is so attractive that she is unaffected by others' evaluations. The television announcer Diane Sawyer won a national beauty pageant as a teenager, but when she overheard a boy at a dance say, "Is that her? She's not so great," she ran back to her room and avoided dating for several years afterward (Bosworth, 1985). Teenage girls respond to the pressure to be attractive by spending considerable time, money, and energy on their appearance, a change from childhood that researchers have termed the *flight into femininity* (Douvan & Adelson, 1966). *money, energy, time.*

■ Media Messages

Female beauty has always been a valuable commodity, bringing admiration, marriage proposals, and movie contracts, but in the past not everyone was expected to achieve it. Today, through the pervasive messages of the media, the overall standards of feminine beauty have been raised so that everyone now knows what the cultural ideal is and assumes that it is within reach (N. Wolf, 1991). Magazines and advertisements directed to teenage girls send out the message that the right "in" look can be attained if the girl diets, uses the right cosmetics, styles her hair every morning, or even opts for cosmetic surgery (Evans, Rutberg, Sather, & Turner, 1991). We have seen how girls learn in school to view their academic accomplishments as resulting from hard work, and how exhausting this can be; similarly, media messages convey that girls could always do more to look better. One article described the daily regimen of a contestant "in training" for the Miss America beauty pageant: She rose at dawn to bone up on current events by watching the early morning news shows and then spent the entire day experimenting with her makeup and hair, exercising, tanning, trying on outfits, taking speech lessons, and practicing her walk in a swimsuit and high heels. Such examples imply that a girl who is chubby, has blotchy skin, or flat hair simply has not tried hard enough. Often, however, the cultural ideal is not in fact attainable, for example, some girls simply cannot achieve a slim, leggy body no matter how much they diet and exercise. Similarly, girls who are not white are given the message that they cannot succeed in the area emphasized as most important for girls: their appearance. Although more black and Hispanic women are shown in magazines now, they are still underrepresented; only about 3 to 5 percent of models in advertisements are nonwhite, and the most popular African-American models often have straightened hair, relatively light skin, and white or Asian features (F. Taylor, 1991).

Of course, it is not as if boys today can obtain peer acceptance if they are fat, pimply, greasy-haired, or dress like a nerd. Wearing "cool" clothes, sporting a tan and the right hairstyle, and the right brand of sunglasses, skateboard, or bike equipment are essential for fitting in. Increasingly, advertisements for products such as dandruff shampoos and deodorant are targeted to teenage boys as well as girls. One print ad shows a pretty blonde woman looking at a man while thinking, "It's such a turn-off when a guy smells," while a television commercial shows a handsome young man extolling the power of his antiperspirant and concluding that his gorgeous girlfriend is proof that the product really works. Some of the expectations placed on girls at adolescence are being extended to boys too.

■ Timing of Puberty: The Interaction of Biology and Cognition

Biological and cognitive changes tend to hit at the same time, meaning that not only does the teenager grow taller, heavier, hairier, and smellier, he or she also realizes that everyone else is watching. This can be especially hard if you are the only one in your group to whom these events are happening or if it has happened to everyone else except you; it is no fun to be the only one with a pancake-flat chest when your girlfriends hit the Victoria's Secret lingerie shop at the mall on Saturday. The onset of puberty can vary over several years for both boys and girls; thus some will inevitably be ahead, while others will be left behind. Researchers have found that being out of sync with peers adds to the stress of adolescence, especially for girls who mature early.

Girls

We have already considered the double bind for teenage girls who find that their appearance is increasingly important to their social success at the same time that they become less and less happy with how they look, especially with their bodies. For two reasons, this conflict is greatest for girls who mature relatively early. First, early-maturing girls tend to be heavier children to begin with, and they remain heavier after puberty. Thus they are more likely than later-maturing girls to worry about their weight and to have a negative view of their bodies, which as we have seen is a strong predictor of low self-esteem. Second, early-maturing girls are especially likely to get the message that their physical appearance is their major asset because they are often asked out by older boys; as one girl said, "A pair of D-cups in a sweater tends to get their attention." Placing a high value on something—your appearance—that you feel you are not good at is a prescription for depression, and early-maturing girls have lower self-esteem, less self-confidence, and a higher rate of emotional problems and depression than girls who reach puberty at the same time as most of their friends (Belsky, Steinberg, & Draper, 1991; Conger, 1991). Later-maturing girls actually have a better chance of experiencing what Unger and Crawford (1992) term *positive social deviance*: By not fleeing into femininity, they benefit from a few extra years of close friendships with their girlfriends, less worry about their appearance and weight, and less risk of becoming prematurely involved in potentially exploitive relationships with older boys.

The "princess effect." While early-maturing girls are especially vulnerable to a loss of self-confidence and an excessive concern with their appearance, these problems also relate to social class and ethnicity. The girl who worries most about her weight and shows the strongest decline in self-confidence and self-esteem is likely to be a white girl from an upper-middle-class family. At first glance this seems paradoxical: Why should the girl who seems on the surface to have the most advantages in life have the least confidence? The answer seems to be that she is also most affected by cultural expectations of being thin, beautiful, and marrying well because, to put it bluntly, in purely economic terms she has the greatest need to attract a partner to maintain the standard of living she enjoyed while being supported by her father. In contrast, working-class girls have been found to retain a higher sense of self-worth during high school. They do not necessarily expect to have to rely on a spouse for support; they are less affected by media portrayals of wealthy, ultrathin white women as the ideal of beauty and femininity; and black parents in particular place strong emphasis on the importance of educational advancement for girls and tell daughters that they do not have to accept negative evaluations from others (E. Smith, 1982; Ward, 1989). Unfortunately, recent studies have found that minority girls are also now increasingly likely to worry about being too fat, suggesting that they are also becoming vulnerable to media images and the cultural ideal of extreme thinness (Unger & Crawford, 1992).

Boys

In contrast to girls, maturing early offers social advantages to boys, at least in the short term. A boy who reaches puberty early is likely to have a size advantage over his peers and to be successful in sports, which is the major key to social status for boys; the 14-year-old boy who is 6 feet tall is likely to be the big wheel on campus. As with girls, however, these early benefits come with a cost. First, the physical advantage is only temporary; within a few years the other boys catch up in size, height, and athletic ability, so the boy who was star quarterback in junior high school can find himself carrying the Gatorade keg in college. Second, like their female counterparts, early-maturing boys are more likely to get involved with older friends and, as a result, to have a higher rate of school problems, substance abuse, and delinquency. Third, boys who have a few extra years of childhood have more time to grow up emotionally and to develop more coping skills. It is cold comfort to tell a boy who in seventh grade still does not have a beard and who feels lonely and left out that he is going through a valuable learning experience, but there appears to be some truth to it. Recent studies have found that later-maturing boys are just as successful in adulthood as their early-maturing peers, and they also seem to be more creative and to enjoy life more than those whose "glory days" were in junior high school (Steinberg, 1993).

So far we have described some of the physical and cognitive changes that occur in early adolescence and seen that these changes tend to affect girls more than boys, particularly girls who go through puberty earlier than their classmates and who become caught by traditional expectations of femininity, including being thin, pretty, and popular. In the following sections we look at changes in the young adolescent's social life, including relationships with parents and peers, before turning to examine how institutions, such as schools and the larger culture, can support the boy's or girl's transition to adulthood.

FAMILY INFLUENCES

Early adolescence resembles the toddler phase: The child is moving out on his or her own, with the parent watching anxiously and trying to keep the child safe, and the two squabble whenever the child wants to do something that the parent forbids. The difference of course is that while parents can make the toddler comply, they cannot really force a teenager to do anything! Many parents dread the teenage years, anticipating an increase in moodiness and conflicts. "She seems OK so far; we're holding our breath, hoping it lasts," said one parent. Another called one day and said, "It's starting," as if announcing the arrival of bubonic plague; her son had yelled at her in frustration when she told him she could not afford to buy him the $150 sneakers that "all the other kids have." Squabbling does increase in early adolescence; one study found that parents and their teenager argued about once every other day, with most of the arguments being about relatively minor issues such as chores, schedules, the way the teenager dresses, and the state of his or her room (Santrock, 1990). Researchers have found that changing sex hormone levels have little to do with such squabbles; rather, teenagers argue because they want more autonomy than parents are willing to grant, just as a 2-year-old often wants to try something that parents think is inconvenient, dirty, or dangerous (Brooks-Gunn & Warren, 1989; Paikoff & Brooks-Gunn, 1990). In general, however, in spite of parents' worries that their child will suddenly become a sulky airhead or a hostile "metalhead," the transition is actually quite smooth in most families. Serious problems rarely appear unless there were also signs of difficulties in childhood, and researchers have found that most teens continue to rely heavily on their parents for emotional support and guidance (Steinberg, 1993).

As we saw in Chapter 5 parents give more autonomy and independence to boys than girls of the same age, and this pattern continues in adolescence because parents worry about the possibility that their daughter will become pregnant; they are notably less concerned that their teenage son will impregnate someone else's daughter (V. Meyer, 1991). The boy's increasing independence in adolescence does lead to changes in his relationships with his parents. With sons, fathers have been found to become more controlling and competitive as the boy enters puberty, and in most cases sons yield. Fathers seem to be trying to make sure that their authority is still recognized, perhaps because of their growing awareness of their own limitations. Most parents of young teenagers are moving into middle age themselves, meaning that just when the father begins to realize that he cannot cover the tennis court the way he used to, he finds that his son can now give him a real run for his money. At the same time fathers also yield to sons; perhaps fathers feel that they need to promote independence, rather like a coach who wants to make sure that his players follow his overall game plan but is willing to let them go out on the field and run a few plays as a learning experience. In contrast, when mothers and sons argue, usually over household chores which teenage boys often deeply resent being asked to help with, mothers usually end up giving in. In a family discussion about where to go on vacation, fathers and sons might bicker a bit but eventually agree on a solution, whereas sons are more likely to keep pushing their own agenda with mothers (Grotevant & Cooper, 1985; Welsh & Powers, 1991).

Some of these changes are especially difficult for single mothers who do not have the backup authority of a spouse to enforce household rules. One single mother found that her 13-year-old son had become remarkably uninformative about his plans:

> JEANNE: Where are you going?
> JOSH: Out.
> JEANNE: Around here, or far?
> JOSH: I'd tell you if I was going far. Bye. (Statham, 1986, p. 51)

The same mother added that it was hard to shout at someone who was now taller than she was! Another boy said that he had previously fought a lot with his mother but once she gave up trying to enforce household rules, they got along fine. Another described his mother as "superintelligent and mature": She let him do whatever he wanted (Arnett, 1991, p. 88). However, complete freedom in adolescence is not necessarily good, being correlated with school truancy, substance abuse, and other problems. Teenage sons of divorced mothers tend to do better in school when the mother remarries because the addition of a father-figure means that the boy benefits from increased monitoring, supervision, and support (Hetherington, 1989; Zimiles & Lee, 1991).

Adolescence also brings some changes in the relationships between daughters and parents. In contrast to their continued involvement with sons, fathers have been found to become more distant with their daughters in adolescence. This has been interpreted as a reflection of the incest taboo, with the father perhaps becoming uncomfortable at his daughter's sexual maturation. A father who had been his little girl's hero might also be put off by her increasing desire for privacy at puberty and her growing interest in being with her friends rather than with her family. The increasing distance between fathers and teenage daughters could also simply reflect the fact that, as we saw in Chapter 3, some fathers are less emotionally invested in their daughters to begin with and may therefore be more willing to let go as the child moves into adolescence. In contrast, daughters often remain close to mothers, especially after a divorce, and daughters typically adjust less well to the mother's remarriage because their close relationship with the mother is disrupted. They are also accustomed to having more independence and resent a stepfather's imposition of authority, and unfortunately, there is a genuine risk to daughters of sexual abuse by their stepfathers (Doherty & Needle, 1991; Hetherington, 1989). Some of these patterns resemble those we saw in Chapter 5, in that adolescent boys suffer when parents give them too little discipline, attention, and support, rationalizing that boys need to learn to stand on their own feet, while girls are more likely to be excessively restricted (Dubow, Huesmann, & Eron, 1987; Leaper et al., 1989; Lempers, Clark-Lempers, & Simons, 1989; Vaughn, Block, & Block, 1988).

In general there appears to be continuity in family relationships as the child moves into adolescence: Mothers and daughters remain close despite superficial bickering and boys continue to have more independence and autonomy than girls. However, although parents remain important to the adolescent, the balance does shift more toward peers, for both boys and girls.

PEERS

There is a story about a mother who one summer enjoyed spending time at the family pool with her preteen son and his best friend, bringing out iced tea, listening to their conversations, and feeling her own youth being renewed by their boyish exuberance and acceptance of her presence. One evening she steps out into the yard and sees a third figure in the pool, a girl of her son's age, and realizes with a chill that she is no longer the center of his universe; his attention and interest have shifted to another world of friends, hormones, and dates as abruptly as a spotlight moves from one scene to another. Of course, teens do not abandon their families overnight, but it is true that peer relationships become increasingly important in the early adolescent years, both same-gender friendships and the new and exciting prospect of relationships with peers of the other gender who have been studiously avoided throughout childhood.

■ Same-Gender Friendships

We saw earlier that teenagers become more self-conscious as the result of their new cognitive capacities; one benefit of teenagers' new ability to consider others' perspectives is that their friendships move to a new level of intimacy. They are able to really think about the other friend's concerns and share the friend's worries, for example, about whether he will be cut from the basketball team this week or whether her rear end looks too big in her new jeans to wear them to the party. Teenagers' friendships are characterized by much more emotional support, sharing, and commitment than is typically found in younger children's friendships. However, the way that this support is expressed and accepted between friends differs for girls and boys.

Girls' Friendships

We saw in Chapter 7 that during childhood girls typically have one or two close friends, while boys tend to belong to larger groups that are organized by dominance relations. Similarly, intimate friendships are formed earlier for teenage girls than boys, and girls work hard to cultivate their friendships by sharing secrets, asking for the friend's advice, complimenting the friend's popularity, and avoiding doing anything that would indicate they feel superior to their friends (Buhrmester & Furman, 1987; Savin-Williams 1979). In fact, a popular girl can easily become disliked because she obviously cannot be best friends with everyone who approaches her, and if she turns some girls away, she can gain the reputation of being "stuck up," that is, implying that she thinks she is better than the other girls (Eder, 1985). Similarly, when one girl begins to date, her friendships with other girls are often disrupted because they feel that her primary allegiance has shifted to a boyfriend, as illustrated in the following letter to the "Ask Beth" advice column:

> Dear Beth,
> My best friend and I used to be so-o-o close. Then Shana got involved with this guy. We're 14, he's 17. She barely sees me now because they're always together. All we do is fight about her not having time for me anymore. I said we shouldn't hang around each other any more. Was I right?
> SAD ABOUT EX-FRIEND. (*Boston Globe*, 1992a)

Close, intimate friendships help the teenager cope with the self-consciousness of early adolescence by sharing and receiving emotional support in return; it is easier if one can see that someone else feels equally awkward. They also provide the teen with the opportunity to learn that others have similar feelings and to care about someone else's welfare as much as his or her own. Early-maturing girls who start dating ahead of their peers are especially likely to miss out on the benefits of friendships with other girls (Miller, 1993; Steinberg, 1993).

Although teenage girls benefit from the emotional support they find in their intimate friendships, there are some costs to their autonomy. When compared with boys, 12- to 14-year-old girls worry more about what others will think of them, are more concerned about being popular with friends of both sexes, worry more that their friends do not really like them, and try to figure out what their friends want from them, termed the *chameleon syndrome* (J. Hill & Lynch, 1985). One girl recalled her junior high school days:

> Now, well, in friendships before, I felt like I was just part of the group and I would mold myself to a group, and what that group needed I would be. I would change or act a certain way. If they needed an airhead, I would be an airhead. If they needed a jock, I would act like a jock, or whatever. (Lyons, 1989, p. 60)

When combined with the self-consciousness and self-doubt that is characteristic of early adolescence, girls can end up wanting so desperately to fit in and to be popular that they create exclusive cliques, defending their membership through rejection of those who do not rank high enough to eat lunch with or who do not have the money to dress in the latest styles and would therefore, if included, "drag down" the rest of the group. What one writer called "careful and cruel distinctions" are made on the basis of such characteristics as a girl's appearance and clothes, her parents' wealth and professional background, her social adeptness with boys, and ethnicity (Elkind, 1984, p. 73). One sixth grader explained bluntly why certain girls were not popular: "They're not rich and not pretty enough" (P. Adler et al., 1992, p. 180). Girls are also much less likely than boys to have friends who are of a different ethnic background, and social contact between white and African-American girls is especially limited (Berndt, 1981, 1982; Hallinan & Teixeira, 1987; Sagar, Schofield, & Snyder, 1983; Steinberg, 1993). Cliques operate on a principle of exclusion, and because places are limited within a clique, its members must constantly worry about whether they are really accepted. At times, the social jockeying at a junior high school can rival that of an eighteenth-century European royal court in terms of who is stuck up, who said something nasty about someone else, who doesn't like someone anymore, and who is starting rumors about someone who thinks she is the most popular girl at the school even though everyone knows it is really someone else.

Some of these patterns resemble those we saw in Chapter 7 in that female friendships have positive aspects—mutual support—but also a dark side of rejection of others who are not friends. As in childhood, adolescent girls seem to dislike competition with friends. A study at one private all-girls school found that the students did well when they worked in collaborative learning groups but poorly when they had to compete with one another (Gilligan, Lyons, & Hanmer, 1989). Similarly, the college coach of a women's athletic team once told me that her biggest coaching problem was that the team members were often close friends and would not really compete with one another in practice. Adolescent girls' declining interest in math and science has often been attributed to their worries about appearing unfeminine to boys but may also reflect their reluctance to stand out as high achievers in a subject that their girlfriends do not like.

Boys' Friendships: A Gender Gap?

Although teenage girls say that their friends mean more to them than do boys, there is some reason to believe that this gender gap reflects stereotypes rather than reality and that boys may just be more cautious than girls about admitting that their friends are important to them (Berndt, 1992; D. Coates, 1987; Furman & Buhrmester, 1985; F. Hunter & Youniss, 1982; Sharabany, Gershoni, & Hofman, 1981). Boys probably *are* somewhat careful about disclosing personal concerns and appearing too intimate with other boys out of fear that close friendships might be mistaken for homosexual interest. Also, intimacy in boys' friendships develops a year or two later than in girls', which can make a sex difference appear to exist if children of the same age are compared. Yet when teens were asked to list people they felt close to and who were sources of advice and support, girls listed their mother, female friends, and male friends, while boys listed mostly their male friends. Teenage boys had as much intimate knowledge about their best friends as girls did about theirs, such as how the friend would feel if teased and what the friend worried most about, and boys' friendships actually lasted longer than girls' (Blyth, Hill, & Thiel, 1982; D. Coates, 1987; Diaz & Berndt, 1982; Montemayer & Van Komen, 1985; Reis, Senchak, & Solomon, 1985; Sharabany et al., 1981; Wintre, Hicks, McVey, & Fox, 1988). Intimacy and mutual support are not necessarily expressed through hours of conversation about one's deepest feelings; one boy said that he and his best friend just listened to heavy metal music together when "girls stomp on our egos" (Arnett, 1991, p. 83). Being rejected by peers is also a strong predictor of mental health problems for boys. In one case in New Hampshire an adolescent boy became depressed because he had no friends; he did not want to go to the cafeteria alone and so he ate lunch every day with a sympathetic teacher. One day he brought a shotgun to school, threatening his classmates, and when the police arrived, he turned the gun on himself. These findings imply that just as during the childhood years boys have a strong capacity and need for same-gender friendships but that socialization pressures make adolescent boys cautious about expressing overt affection for their friends (Blyth & Foster-Clark, 1987).

Status and Dominance Revisited

Recall from Chapter 7 that a major theme of boys' peer groups in childhood was competition and efforts to establish and maintain status. Junior high school is often a time when these concerns resurface because whenever things change, such as going to a new school, meeting new people, being in a new environment, or trying out for new teams, the boy's status has to be reestablished all over again. This is often expressed through the blustering talk about fighting, who is going to "kick someone's ass" after school and who is just a wimp or a "wuss" (A. Wolf, 1991). One man recalled how in fifth grade he had to tackle the biggest kid in the school in a football game: "I was afraid of him, but my greater fear was to show my fear" (Miedzian, 1991, p. 201). The incredible popularity of televised professional wrestling among older elementary school boys also illustrates their renewed interest in issues of dominance. They will talk for hours about the hierarchy of the flamboyant, boastful characters and compare notes on who "kicked butt" in the latest matches. Status for boys is also established through being "cool," meaning that you wear the right things, are seen in the right places, and have perfected an attitude of casual confidence with an undertone of surly defiance toward adults (P. Adler et al., 1992).

The drive for status is also evident in the competitive element of boys' early experiments with sexual activity, beginning with masturbation contests after school—who can achieve an erection most quickly, ejaculate most often or over the longest distance, or maintain the largest number of fishing weights tied to his erect penis—and continuing on to weekly score sessions and newsletters at college fraternities in which boys share their sexual exploits and heap scorn on those who have not kept up. Often they do not recognize the effects on girls of their efforts to impress their friends. One girl recalled:

> When I was 16, I went with three of my friends to this concert. These really cute guys sat behind us and flirted with us. Soon, one of them sat next to me. Then he started putting the moves on me really fast. Before I knew it, he was fully kissing me. I opened my eyes and saw him giving his friend a thumb's up signal, meaning, he'd won the game. He'd made the move on someone first . . . I just sat in my chair, not talking to anyone. I was devastated and humiliated. (Karlsberg, 1992, p. 98)

On the other hand, boys can be surprisingly kind if they feel secure among their peers. Many a young girl has blossomed under the occasional compliment of an older brother's best friend who knows perfectly well that she has a crush on him. We once attended a large party hosted by a neighbor whose high school–age daughter and her friends had their own band and dance area in the backyard. Several fifth- and sixth-grade girls hovered hopefully near the older teens who pretty much ignored them all evening. As people began to leave the party, I noticed a couple of the older boys look over at the girls, who were wilting a bit by this point. The young men exchanged glances, and then each one walked over and asked an obviously thrilled girl to dance.

Dating and Sexual Relationships

One of the biggest changes in adolescence is in mixed-sex relationships. The peers of the other sex who previously seemed like creepy aliens from another planet now become highly attractive, although we should keep in mind that not all teenagers experience feelings of attraction to the other gender. The boundaries between boys' and girls' worlds that had been established and vigorously defended during childhood start to crumble in mid- to late-elementary school. Currently, most girls date by about 12 to 13 years—that is, by about the sixth grade—and boys start dating at about 13 to 14 years. Clearly, the days of the "sweet sixteen" birthday party as the son or daughter's first boy-girl event are long over.

"Going Together"

Usually, girls are the first to become interested in the other gender, and boys initially react to their overtures with a certain amount of bemusement. One 10-year-old boy who was besieged by girls asking him to go steady said yes to everyone, not really caring one way or the other, which led to many frantic phone calls to his home after school until his mother finally put her foot down. "Going with" someone is desirable because it enhances a child's social status with same-gender peers, but often the relationship is more form than content; the two may not even talk to one another directly at school but pass along messages through intermediaries or rely on the phone. One sixth-grade boy described how he and his buddy spent a Saturday afternoon:

> We started calling girls we liked on the phone, one at a time. We'd each call the girl the other one liked and ask if she wanted to go with the other one . . . Usually they wouldn't say too much. So sometimes we'd call her best friend to see if she could tell us anything. Then they would call each other and call us back. If we got the feeling after a few calls that she really was serious about no, then we might go on to our next choice, if we had one. (P. Adler et al., 1992, p. 176)

Most of us can recall the self-consciousness about actually being around the other gender, making events such as school dances indescribably awkward for all but the most confident children. While it is painful for girls to wait, hoping to be noticed, it is equally difficult for boys. One boy recalled:

> When I was twelve years old, I went to my first junior high school dance. I was really scared that none of the girls would dance with me. I didn't ask any of them, for fear that they would say no to me. Looking back . . . I realize that very few of them actually would have rejected me if I had just taken the risk. But I didn't take the risk and spent the night sitting in a corner with some friends. I was so depressed by that dance that I didn't go to another dance for two years. (Zimbardo, 1982, p. 167)

Dating?

In many communities young adolescents no longer date in the old-style boy-girl couple fashion; rather, groups of boys and girls will meet at the mall, go to the movies or parties together, or meet and hang out on the street. One mother, confused by the changes since she was a teenager, wrote:

> What are the rules of dating these days? When we were dating, which was in the stone age, of course, my husband had to call me by Tuesday if he wanted to go out on Saturday, come to get me even though my campus was a long bus ride away, pay for the movies and food, and take me back to the door. (J. Martin, 1985, p. 228)

Although she went on to say that she did not like the sound of the new, more casual mixed-gender interactions, such group activities actually appear to be quite beneficial to girls. They have the chance to interact with boys on a casual basis and to build their confidence about being with the other gender in low-key situations with others around. Conversely, early couple dating is risky for young adolescent girls because they often date older boys and are pressured to become sexually active before they are ready. In addition, becoming overly involved with a single boyfriend in early adolescence has been found to inhibit personal growth and autonomy which, as we have seen in earlier chapters, tends to be more difficult for girls to begin with. One psychiatrist explained, "A girl who enters into a serious relationship with a boy very early in life may find out later that her individuality was thwarted. She became part of him and failed to develop her own interests, her sense of independent identity" (Lickona, 1983, p. 379). One 14-year-old girl found that after 5 months of dating, her boyfriend was telling her what to wear every morning, when to cut her hair, and when she could see her girlfriends; her parents finally stepped in and ended the near-abusive relationship.

■ Sexual Activity

Rates of sexual activity vary considerably across gender, social class, and ethnicity, but we know that teenagers are more likely to have had sexual intercourse during adolescence than in previous decades and that the increase has been much greater for girls (Steinberg, 1993). Attitudes have also changed: A young teenage girl known to have had sex is no longer automatically viewed as a whore who had disgraced her parents and ruined her chance for a decent marriage, as she would have been 40 years ago. In fact there is now strong peer pressure in some communities on both boys and girls to be sexually active. One girl said, "At this school you have to be a slut to be popular," and another explained:

> I was part of a group in junior high school that was into partying, hanging out and drinking. I started to have sex with my boyfriend and it was a real downer. It was totally against what I was, but it was important to be part of a group. Everybody was having sex. I couldn't handle the pressure. (Lickona, 1983, p. 366; Zimbardo, 1982, p. 165)

Similarly, a boy who is not yet sexually active can find himself embarrassed around other boys and even be quizzed by girls about whether he is gay. Long before his days as a mainstream television star the comedian Bill Cosby performed a monologue in which he described how in the fifth grade an "older woman," a sixth-grade girl with a hot reputation, asked him to come over to her house after school. Later, his envious friends ask how they "did it," and having no idea what they are talking about, he tries to bluff by saying casually, "Oh, the regular way . . . yeah, for maybe three, four hours."

"Scoring" versus "Swept Away"

In spite of more accepting attitudes and the increase in rates of teenage girls' sexual activity, researchers have found that the nature of early sexual experiences is often very different for boys and girls. Traces linger in teenagers' reasoning of the old double standard in which a boy is expected to sow a few wild oats with "bad girls" before finding a "good girl" to settle down with, while a girl should have sex only if she is "in love" (Kallen & Stephenson, 1982; Komarovsky, 1976). By implication, "too much" sexual experience makes her a "slut," not a girl with whom to have a serious relationship.

Media messages. Many of these ideas about romance seemed derived directly from soap operas, romance novels, videos, and movies, with boys being encouraged to "go for the score," while girls dream of being "swept away" into a passionate affair by true love. One mother said of her 14-year-old daughter, "All of my daughter's friends watch the soap operas religiously the first thing when they get home from school, and I mean *religiously*. Then they get on the phone and talk about it for an hour. I told Karen I didn't like her watching that stuff, but she didn't want to be cut out of the action" (Lickona, 1983, p. 353). Romance novel series, such as *Sweet Valley High, Young Love, Wildfire,* and *First Love,* are very popular with 9- to 16-year-old girls and have massive sales to school libraries and school-based book clubs (Christian-Smith, 1990). Many parents, teachers, and librarians have objected to the books for emphasizing the importance of appearance for girls, sending the message that a girl's real role in life is to compete with other girls to find love with the right boy, and involving only wealthy, white, suburban teenagers. In romance novels, heroines often have relationships that begin with abuse, rape, or abduction by hostile and mysterious men with whom they fall in love and eventually marry, thus presenting teenage girls with a highly unrealistic and damaging portrait of love between men and women (Radway, 1991). (On the other hand, romances are so popular that they have been used to motivate adolescent girls who are poor readers, for example, by allowing a student to read a romance for every "good" book read. And in contrast to many of the children's books we saw in Chapter 9, they at least have female main characters.)

The confusion of sex and love. The media messages and the lingering double standard lead girls to rationalize that they are in love before becoming sexually active, and in fact they are more likely to have their first intercourse with a boyfriend, someone to whom they feel an emotional commitment or with whom they hope to establish an ongoing relationship (Kallen & Stephenson, 1982). The confusion of sex and love leads 12- to 13-year-old girls to try maneuvers they have read in *Cosmopolitan*, such as leaving explicit messages on the family answering machine at a boy's house or sexy notes with lipstick kisses on his locker; the girls end up puzzled and hurt when early sexual experiences do not lead to true romance and grand passion or when they are emotionally exploited by boys. One young man explained that the way to obtain sex was, "Tell her you love her; women fall for it all the time" (Collison, 1991, p. 1). One 14-year-old girl said sadly, "I never expected the guy to marry me, but I never expected he would avoid me in school" (Lickona, 1983, p. 377).

Other indications of a lingering double standard are found in teenagers' reactions to losing their virginity. Teenage boys report feeling happy, proud, and grown-up after their first sexual experience, and many immediately tell their friends; one said, "It was like I had become a man and I wanted to tell everyone about it" (Elkind, 1984, p. 87; Kallen & Stephenson, 1982). In contrast, girls more often report feeling disappointed, guilty, worried, and afraid and are slower to tell a friend. They are also less likely to find the experience physically gratifying (Lewin, 1985; Tavris & Wade, 1984). If a girl's initial partner is a highly aroused but inexperienced teenage boy and if she does not feel comfortable telling him what she wants or does not even know from her own experience with masturbation what she would enjoy—as we saw earlier, girls are less likely than boys to masturbate—the whole episode may well be somewhat disappointing at first (J. H. Williams, 1987). One girl said, "It was over so fast; I just thought, 'was that it?'" Teenage girls more often report that they have sex to maintain the relationship or to please their boyfriend than for their own pleasure (Lewin, 1985; Tavris & Wade, 1984).

Adolescent Sexual Aggression

Differing expectations also contribute to the risk of rape for girls. Teenage boys consider many behaviors to be signals of sexual interest, including wearing tight jeans, looking into a date's eyes, paying him compliments, or going to his house or dorm room, although girls do not think that these signs means that they want to have sex (Abbey, 1987; Goodchilds & Zellman, 1984). If a girl later refuses, he may feel that she "led him on," which teens consider legitimate motivation for rape. Many teenagers also think that a boy is entitled to force intercourse on an unwilling girl—that is, to rape her—if he has spent a lot of money on her—defined as about $10 to $15—or if they have been dating longer than 6 months, or if she has had sex with other boys, that is, if she can be labeled a "bad girl" (Goodchilds & Zellman, 1984; B. Levy, 1991; Miedzian, 1991).

Blaming the victim. Not only do traditional dating scripts contribute to tolerant attitudes among teens toward rape, but they encourage teens to blame the victim. Girls are expected both to attract a boy's interest and to set limits, and if this delicate balancing act goes wrong, teenagers consider it to be her responsibility. Girls often agree with boys that a girl who was raped should not have had a beer at a boy's house, worn a short skirt, or left the party with a boy (Goodchilds & Zellman, 1984). One college woman who had been raped at a party cried in my office when she told me that her best friend had said, "You must have asked for it." This blame-the-victim reasoning allows other girls to avoid facing the reality that they could be raped regardless of how they dress or act.

Date-rape prevention programs have sometimes inadvertently contributed to this reasoning by focusing primarily on alerting girls to the problem and telling them not to drink at parties and to say no clearly. It has to be recognized that there are limits to what girls can do to control male partners, particularly given that teenage boys appear to be subject to wishful thinking and will read sexual interest into almost anything the girl does or says. In addition, many date-rape education programs have involved women counselors and speakers, and, as we have seen throughout the book, boys are socialized not to be influenced by females. As a result, many programs have now shifted to using male coaches, teachers, and peers to get across the message that boys have to be sure that their partner is willing (Collison, 1991). Unfortunately adults have not always supported this message, as in the following report from a New England university:

> Students performing a skit on sexual assault and harassment prevention entitled, "But I said no," before 700 student-athletes were ridiculed and harassed by athletes who hurled obscene jeers and catcalls, such as "bitch" and "fag," at the cast *in the presence of their coaches.* (Kittredge, 1992, p. 28, italics added)

Clearly, more work is needed to change some of the lingering double standards in reasoning about boys' and girls' rights both to engage in sex and to say no.

Media messages. Some of the problem may be traceable to the media. As a student in one of my classes put it, "Teenage boys do not need the movies to tell them that they are horny; they kind of figure that out for themselves." What videos, films, and music may do is imply to adolescent boys that they are entitled to sex by any means necessary. In general, male characters in films accept any opportunity for sexual contact even if it involves peeping (*Porky's, Animal House, Stakeout*), pimping (*Risky Business*), rape (*Fast Times at Ridgemont High*), sleeping with a best friend's mother or nanny (*Class, Rambling Rose*), or driving across the country in hopes of obtaining sex (*The Sure Thing*). Media messages may also suggest to adolescent boys that a disrespectful attitude toward the other gender and even violence and rape are "cool," as in the following song lyrics: "I used to love her . . . but I had to kill her," (Guns'n'Roses), "Killing you helped me keep you home" (Motley Crue), "Black and blue" (Rolling Stones), and "I creeped on my bitch with my Uzi machine" (Niggas With Attitude) (Miedzian, 1991, p. 255). On the other hand, we saw in Chapter 9 that exposure to sexist television and videos does not necessarily mean that children are affected by the media messages. Several researchers have found that teenagers do not really pay much attention to song lyrics and often may not even understand them; for example, young adolescents thought that Bruce Springsteen's "Born in the USA" was a song about patriotism and completely missed its harsh critical message about the Vietnam war (P. M. Greenfield et al., 1987). Similarly, adolescent boys who enjoy rock and heavy metal music say that it helps them to relax and forget their problems, and they scoff at the idea that it might have a negative effect on their attitudes (Arnett, 1991).

Endless Love

The above discussion sounds a bit as though the risks of mixed-gender dating and sexual activity are all on the female side, but this is not necessarily true. As we saw above, friendships with others of the same sex often serve as a model for intimacy, allowing the young adolescent to learn to care deeply about another person and consider his or her needs without the additional complexities of sexual attraction. If homophobia keeps a boy from establishing this sort of friendship with another boy, his first experience of emotional dependence and true intimacy may well come in a relationship with a girl, whereas most girls have already had such relationships with other girls (Buhrmester & Furman, 1987). This can make the boy more vulnerable when the relationship ends (and almost all teenage relationships *do* end). One psychologist found that his teenage clients who were truly brokenhearted after a breakup, sometimes in despair to the point of attempting suicide, were mostly boys (A. Wolf, 1991). Scott Spencer's novel *Endless Love* portrays a teenage boy so caught up in an obsessive relationship with his girlfriend that when her parents finally prohibited her from seeing him, he set fire to their house in an irrational hope that they would somehow then come to understand how much she meant to him. Boys often do not have the luxury of sharing their feelings with friends—after all, mooning around over a girl who has rejected him is not exactly cool!—and even if his friends sympathize, they may not really know what to say or how to help him, while teenage girlfriends will often commiserate for hours and endlessly discuss the breakup, analyze what went wrong, and share ideas about what the girl should do about it. This gender difference foreshadows the patterns in adulthood in which men suffer more loneliness, depression, and physical health problems than do women after the breakup of a serious relationship or a divorce because they are less likely to have other sources of emotional support.

As we have seen so far, adolescence is a time of transition in many areas, including physical development, increased self-awareness, changing family dynamics, and new peer relationships. No wonder teens have the reputation for being a bit on the moody side! We now look at how larger social institutions support or inhibit these changes for boys and girls, first, by looking at the role of school and, second, examining how different cultures have helped teenagers move into adulthood by providing rituals and rites of passage to ease the transition.

SCHOOL

Imagine that you have gained 20 pounds over the last year, started to wear a bra, found that your best friend has started to date and doesn't have time to hang out with you anymore, and learned that your mother is getting married to someone who will be bringing along several small children when he moves in. In addition, you have just started a new school, you don't know any of the teachers, you don't have many of your old friends in your classes, you have to move around to different classes all day instead of staying in one room, and you are surrounded by much older kids who all seem to be extremely cool and intimidating. Changes in the school environment clearly add to the stress of early adolescence, and these changes have been shown to affect girls more than boys (Simmons & Blyth, 1987).

■ School Structure

One of the major difficulties for young adolescents, especially girls, is that often they move to a new school where they may not have classes with their childhood friends and are at the bottom of the school social hierarchy. School districts vary in their approach to middle school education, but in most cases children shift from an elementary school to a separate junior high at about age 12. However, in some communities even children as young as fifth grade—about 11 years old—are sent to a large school with high school students. In general, researchers have found that children adjust best when they remain in an extended elementary school that includes sixth, seventh, or even eighth grade (Simmons & Blyth, 1987). Remaining in one class with a familiar teacher, a neighborhood location, and the same friends provides security at a time when the child is already experiencing many changes. Being the "top dogs" of the school also enhances children's self-esteem. They have the admiration of the younger children and the chance to fill leadership positions, such as the editor of the school paper, the sports team captain, and the first chair in the violin section of the school orchestra. In a school with older students young adolescents are usually crowded out of such positions by 16- and 17-year-olds. One girl said that when she went to junior high, "I thought it was going to be so great, like I'd feel so grown-up, and then I saw all of these new, older kids who really had it together and I didn't. So I felt terrible" (Steinberg, 1993, p. 263).

The effects of school structure are especially critical for early-maturing girls who, as we have seen, are most at risk for emotional problems and depression. When transferred to a high school, they are around older boys, date earlier, become more concerned about their appearance, and show a greater loss of self-esteem than do girls who remain in an extended elementary school. Unfortunately, maintaining neighborhood extended elementary schools is financially difficult for most communities; it is usually more economical to send children to a large central school as soon as possible. However, costs can be measured in many ways, and the likely emotional adjustment and academic success of the students also need to be considered when making up the school district budget.

■ Class Participation

We saw in Chapter 8 that girls are less visible in the classroom; they receive relatively little attention, instruction, and support from teachers. Although we also found that girls do well in terms of their average grades, by the time they reach adolescence, much of their confidence has drained away and they tend to avoid new subjects and challenging classes when they can. This decline in confidence is accelerated in adolescence for several reasons: Junior high school teachers are more likely than those who teach elementary school to believe that children's ability is relatively fixed and that instruction cannot really do much to help a student who is having difficulties. Second, "tracking," the practice of grouping students for instruction on the basis of past achievement and perceived ability is often more explicit in secondary school than at the elementary level; everyone knows who made the college-prep track and who is stuck in remedial classes. Third, the average grades for both sexes generally start to decline in junior high school because teachers set higher grading standards (Steinberg, 1993). We saw in Chapter 8 that girls are more likely than boys to interpret criticism as an indication of low ability, and thus these changes in the academic environment have a greater impact on girls than on boys. Adding to the problem is that beginning in secondary school, the type of academic work for which girls have been rewarded, that is, careful, quiet, conscientious work, becomes less valued (Huston & Alvarez, 1990). Classes gradually shift from lectures and tests, where detailed notes and a good memory ensure success, to seminars, with discussion and debate, and independent projects. In such classes, confidence, assertiveness, and a willingness to take risks, for example, by debating with the teacher or trying a novel approach on a project, are rewarded, and the person who merely sits and takes notes does not create the impression of intellectual competence that can lead to good recommendations from teachers and nominations for scholarships. It can be especially hard for girls to join in class discussions because they have been systematically overlooked throughout elementary school; too often, the quiet, conscientious, attentive "A" student who never says a word in class is a girl.

Some of the imbalance in classroom participation is due to instructor bias of the sort we saw in Chapter 8, but beyond the elementary level it also reflects the dynamics between male and female students; girls worry about what boys will think of them, and boys often indicate that they resent girls' contributions. One teacher looked forward to teaching a particular group of students whom she remembered from an earlier grade, but that fall she found that they had changed; now when she posed a question the girls looked at the boys to see if it was all right to answer (*Hampshire Life*, 1992). Even in college classrooms boys dominate discussions; one researcher said that if you asked, "What is the meaning of life?" five male hands would instantly shoot up while girls would hold back (Krupnick, 1985). One girl who transferred to a private all-girls high school found herself feeling much more free in the classroom and explained:

> I think a lot of it is that I am not around boys anymore, and that used to intimidate me a lot. I was scared to death that if I said something wrong, so-and-so wouldn't like me any more . . . and when you are here they are not even part of your life, which in some ways is good, because you don't have that pressure. (Mendelsohn, 1989, p. 237)

Although instructors often do not want to put quiet women students on the spot, calling on them directly ("And, Mary, what do *you* think is the meaning of life?") gives them the chance to speak without appearing "too" assertive and relieves them of the potential social backlash outside the classroom (Krupnick, 1985).

THE ROLE OF CULTURE: RITES OF PASSAGE

Aside from the move to junior high school, we have few markers in our culture to indicate the child's move into adolescence. There are some religious ceremonies, such as confirmation and the bar and bat mitzvah, along with the acquisition of a driver's license, but in general there is no formal social custom through which the teenager is recognized within the community as having left childhood. In contrast, in many other cultures there are clear rites of passage that mark this important transition in the boy's or girl's development.

Male Rites

In many nonindustrialized cultures boys grow up with their mothers and rarely see their fathers or spend much time with adult men. Then, at puberty, ceremonial rites of passage shift the boys' focus to the world of males. These rites have common elements around the world; they usually involve a period of seclusion in which the boys live with adult men and learn the knowledge and customs of the community. Hazing and tests of endurance are another common component. For example, in one South African tribe boys of 10 to 16 years are hazed over a 3-month period during which time they are regularly beaten, given tainted food, and forced to sleep exposed to the elements. A third common component is circumcision or other genital mutilations such as subincision, in which the underside of the penis is slit, as well as ritual scarring of the chest and other areas of the body so that the boy can be quickly recognized as an adult man (Tavris & Wade, 1984). Rites of passage are usually held apart from the women, and the boys are threatened with death if the secret activities are revealed to females. In communities where children of both sexes are very close to their mother, puberty rites tend to be more severe and hazardous to break the close bond between the boy and his mother and establish the authority of the adult males (Gilmore, 1990; Raphael, 1988).

Female Rites

Whereas male rites of passage tend to be held for groups of boys of a particular age, ceremonies for females are typically held when an individual girl begins to menstruate, and the nature of the rite reflects the community's attitude toward menstruation. Some Native American tribes viewed a girl's first menstruation as a holy blessing to be celebrated with elaborate dances, special clothing, and long ceremonies, while in other groups around the world the girl is isolated for the duration of her menstrual flow or for longer periods; in some communities the girl was kept inside a closed hut for 40 days before being "reborn" as an adult woman. Menarche ceremonies are most common when the girl will remain within her own community after her marriage, to emphasize her new status to those who have known her since she was an infant (Paige, 1983).

Female Circumcision

Paralleling ritual circumcision for boys is the custom of female circumcision, currently practiced in a number of African countries, among Muslim groups in Asia, in several South American countries, and among immigrant communities in Europe (Ebomoyi, 1987; Koso-Thomas, 1987). Female circumcision involves the removal of the clitoris and inner labia; in some cases the outer labia are stitched together, with a small opening left for urine and menstrual flow. The operation is performed by an older woman when the girl reaches puberty or is betrothed. The operation has a high risk of infection and shock because an unsterilized razor blade, broken bottle, or pair of scissors is typically used, although some wealthy families now fly their daughters to European hospitals for the operation. After the operation there are often celebrations, periods of religious instruction, and the awarding of a new name to recognize the girl's new status. The practice of female circumcision reflects traditional beliefs about the role of women, for example, that sex should be for procreation rather than female pleasure, that the clitoris will grow and dangle on the thighs if it is not cut off, or that contact with the clitoris will kill an infant when the woman gives birth. Undergoing circumcision also signals a girl's loyalty to her community, as it does for the boy who is ritually circumcised and hazed. In one recent case a young Mali woman refused to be circumcised after seeing her best friend die of the operation; when she fled to France, her mother was ostracized by the community for raising a disobedient daughter. The practice of female circumcision has been targeted for elimination by a United Nations task force and the governments of several dozen countries because in addition to limiting a woman's sexual responsiveness, the operation carries a high risk of infection, serious ongoing health problems, and death.

■ Benefits?

It is probably safe to assume that most U.S. teenagers would not eagerly await the genital mutilations, tests of endurance, and the prospect of an immediate marriage that form the basis of most rites of passage. Yet in spite of the unpleasant and dangerous components, such rituals do provide a certain security to the adolescent who knows that once the test is over, he or she will no longer be a child. Without such adult-controlled rituals, adolescents are often left with a lingering sense of uncertainty, particularly boys who do not have such a clear physical sign of maturity as menarche in girls (Gilmore, 1990; Raphael, 1988). This uncertainty can lead to self-constructed tests of maturity and masculinity: drinking contests, car races, substance abuse, and peer-hazing rituals. These peer-oriented tests are considerably riskier than events that are arranged and monitored by adults, in which each adolescent's success is nearly always ensured because underneath the atmosphere of mystery and fear adults adjust the tests so that no one fails (Raphael, 1988)! Teens therefore move into adulthood knowing that they are now accepted as a grown-up and with the confidence that comes from a successful initiation, even though this confidence is often hard won in terms of stress and physical suffering.

SUMMARY

We have seen in this chapter that adolescence is both a time of change and of continuity for gender roles. On the one hand, several themes that were introduced in childhood continue into adolescence. These include the continued importance of peers for both boys and girls, although same-gender friendships shift to a new level of intimacy, and the ongoing central role of parents, who still allow boys more freedom while wanting to know where girls are going, who they will be with, and what time they will be home. On the other hand, there are some rather major differences in the gender role issues that face adolescents as compared to children. First, teenagers have to cope with the enormous physical changes of puberty, changes that are exacerbated by the teen's expanding cognitive abilities and increased awareness of how he or she appears to others. Second, relations with the other gender change markedly as dating relationships begin and the teenager confronts the possibility of sexual activity. Teens often cope with the stress of these changes by becoming more conservative and traditional in their ideas about gender roles, a tendency that is enhanced by media messages about the importance of being attractive and about the double standard for sex and love.

We have also seen that on average adolescence seems to be more difficult for girls than boys. This is not to deny that boys can also find the teenage years to be perfectly miserable! However, a significant gender difference in self-confidence and self-esteem, rates of depression, and the incidence of eating disorders appears at the point when girls begin to grow up, that is, when they enter puberty and adopt the mature female role. There is some reason to believe that these problems have worsened in recent decades as girls' childhoods have become compressed. This reflects the fact that with menarche occurring 4 or 5 years earlier than a century ago, most girls now become interested in boys and dating by the end of elementary school rather than in high school. In addition, researchers suggest that in our culture the general concept of childhood is disappearing and that many of the traditional demarcations between children and adults have disappeared; for example, girls now wear makeup and clothes like those of adult women (Elkind, 1984). (I have even seen a sixth-grade girl wearing a garter belt to school, presumably for the benefit of her boyfriend; it was definitely a back-to-the-future sight for someone who attended junior high school before pantyhose were even invented.) In all, girls have lost several important years of development in the childhood female role when compared to girls growing up 50 or 100 years ago. Not surprisingly, girls who mature relatively early today are especially at risk for developmental problems.

■ Pay Now, Pay Later?

Perhaps the difficulties that girls have in adolescence merely represent a righting of the gender role asymmetry that pervaded the childhood years: Although boys have to learn early to avoid everything feminine, girls eventually run into equally tight and costly constraints in the form of the adult female role. While boys are also subject to peer pressure and media influences in early adolescence, the pressure on girls to be attractive and popular does appear to be higher. Many adolescent boys seem reasonably content to have a couple of friends with whom to hang out after school and a steady girlfriend or two later on, while girls are more likely to get themselves into paroxysms of despair over not being part of the "in crowd" in junior high school (A. Wolf, 1991). One girl wrote:

> I go to the local hangout and sit there for hours talking about clothes and hairdos and the twist and I'm not that interested, so it's an effort. But I found out that I could make them like me—just do what they do, dress like them, talk like them, not do things that are different. I guess I even started to make myself not different inside . . . I used to write poetry. The guidance office says I have this creative ability and I should be at the top of the class and have a great future. But things like that aren't what you need to be popular. The important thing for a girl is to be popular. (Friedan, 1983, p. 73)

Thus, we might say that boys pay early in terms of having to fit into the masculine role by preschool, while girls pay later in adolescence, but that no one gets completely away from the constraints of gender roles without suffering the social consequences. We consider this issue in more detail in the next chapter when we discuss the case of children who actively resist adopting the gender role that would normally be considered appropriate for their sex.

13

GENDER IDENTITY
DISTURBANCE IN
CHILDHOOD

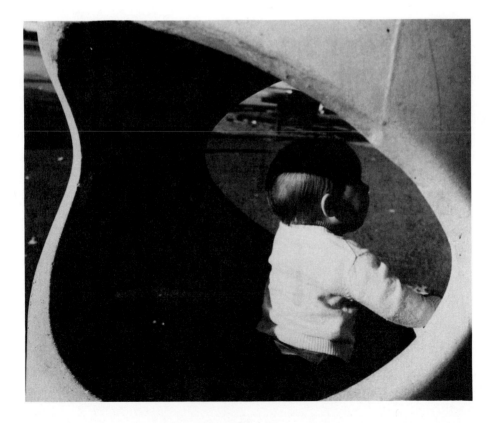

My problem to begin with is of very long standing, in fact, all my conscious life, I have been aware that I was the wrong sex. There was a place way up in the branches of a tree where I grew up that branched out close enough I could lie in it like a hammock. I would lie there and look up through the leaves to the sky and pray. I would promise, and I would offer anything if God would do a miracle for me and make me a girl some day. Any day. (Green, 1987, pp. 9–10)

We have seen throughout the book that most children quickly and eagerly adopt the gender role behaviors that are expected for their sex. In contrast, some children seem to decide that they are the other gender; that is, they develop a gender identity that is inconsistent with their biological sex and the gender in which they have been raised. Such "gender-disturbed" children are very rare, perhaps 1 in 25,000, and within this very small group it is more common among boys than girls (Rekers, 1979; Rekers, Crandall, Rosen, & Bentler, 1979). Despite its rarity, gender disturbance is of interest to us for two reasons: First, the existence of children who believe that they are the other sex raises questions about the power of gender role socialization. After all, if gender socialization is as consistent and pervasive as the previous chapters have claimed, we should not find children without "the message." Second, gender identity disturbance raises questions about the importance of consistency between one's biological sex and the social roles that one learns while growing up.

In this chapter we discuss how gender disturbance is diagnosed in children and review possible contributing causes in the child's family situation. We then consider whether a child who is considered to be gender-disturbed should receive therapy and look at examples from other cultures that have provided blended gender roles for such children as a social alternative.

DIAGNOSING GENDER IDENTITY DISTURBANCE

Suppose you are observing in a preschool classroom and notice that a little boy has spent the entire morning playing in the dress-up area with the girls, enjoying trailing scarves behind him, and piling on glittery play jewelry. Or a little girl comes up as you observe the boys run around the playground and says despondently, "I wish I was a boy." Are such children gender-disturbed? Probably not; in fact, such behaviors and comments are not particularly rare in young children, and mild deviations from the expected gender role behaviors do not seem to be anything to worry about. A boy who enjoys wearing bracelets might live in a home in which no particular fuss is made about the issue and may simply be more flexible in his behavior than most children. On the other hand, suppose the child only wants to do things that are typical for the other sex; for example, the little girl flatly refuses to wear a dress—ever. Or the little boy says that he wishes his penis would disappear, or, as in the case of the man quoted above, he hopes every night that he will turn into a girl by the next morning. At this point we might become concerned that the child's gender identity development has gone awry. Children who are gender-disturbed are distinguished by an early, strong rejection of the expected gender role and a strong preference for the other role. In the next section we review the characteristics that therapists would consider when gender disturbance is suspected in a young child.

◼ Diagnostic Criteria

Therapists first consider whether the child is developing a *gender identity*—a fundamental sense of the self as male or female—that is inconsistent with his or her physical self. We saw in Chapter 6 that for most children gender identity is established in the toddler period and provides the motivation for learning the associated gender role. Clinicians also consider whether the child's *role behaviors*—including preferred activities, toys, friends, clothes, speech patterns, and mannerisms—generally fit what would be expected for his or her physical sex. These considerations are necessarily different for boys and girls because of the asymmetry in gender roles. There is much greater social acceptance of tomboy girls than so-called sissy boys, and clinicians must take this difference into account when evaluating a particular child.

Gender Disturbance in Boys

A boy who insists repeatedly that he is a girl or that he wants desperately to be a girl may be indicating that his gender identity is female rather than male. A boy might indicate his sense of being a girl by lining up with the girls at school or insisting on using the girls' restroom (Kantrowitz, 1991). One 5-year-old boy ran home from playing in a wooded area so that he could urinate while sitting down on the toilet and told his mother, "Girls can't go to the bathroom in the woods" (K. Zucker, 1985, p. 157). Other indications of a female identity involve the boy's rejection or dislike of his male anatomy. He might hide his penis between his legs, say that he wants to have it taken off, or try to pull it off. One teenager recalled that as a little boy he would go to sleep at night with his penis tucked between his thighs and hope that when he woke up the next morning, it would be gone

(Green, 1987). Another little boy was actually happy when he developed a skin rash around his groin because he hoped that if the rash did not improve, the doctors might finally be willing to remove his penis. This feeling of being the other sex is often apparent very early in life. One boy started trying to dress as a girl when he was 2 years old. Another 3-year-old said he wanted to be a girl, and when his mother asked him what was wrong with being a boy he replied, "Just don't want to be a boy, want to be a girl" (Green, 1987, p. 116). The fact that these children report being the other sex almost as soon as they are able to talk suggests that their *initial* gender identity may be "wrong," that is, inconsistent with their physical self. It does not appear that they first form a sex-matching identity and then for some reason change their mind later.

In addition to evidence of a female identity, a therapist would also look for feminine role behaviors, that is, whether a boy acted like a girl as well as thought of himself as a girl. Gender-disturbed boys prefer feminine clothes and games, and may try to fashion girls' clothes, for example, by wearing a towel like a skirt, or tie on ribbons to resemble long hair. Many gender-disturbed boys also seem to dislike boys' games and to be frightened by the rough-and-tumble play of other boys. One boy told his mother, "I don't want to go to school today because I'll have to play baseball," and complained that the ball hurt his legs when it hit him (Bates & Bentler, 1973; Green, 1987, p. 3). Their mannerisms can also appear feminine, including limp-wristed or fluttering hand gestures, standing with one hip or elbow cocked to the side or with the hands on the hips, and a hip-swinging walk. Green, Neuberg, and Finch (1983) compared the nonverbal behavior of a group of gender-disturbed boys (aged 4 to 10 years) with that of a group of typical boys. Each child was dressed in a plain jumpsuit, sneakers, and a bathing cap to hide his hair and was videotaped while running, throwing a ball, and telling a story (with the sound turned off to focus attention on the child's nonverbal behavior). Adults watched the videotapes and decided whether the child was a boy or girl. They could easily recognize the comparison children as boys, but they could not reliably decide whether the gender-disturbed boys were boys or girls because their behavior appeared quite feminine. Another common characteristic, although not a diagnostic criterion in itself, is that the gender-disturbed boy may show signs of general immaturity when compared to other children of the same age. For example, as a young grade school child the boy might still have temper tantrums, problems with bed-wetting and pants soiling, and be unable to wait his turn and whine if he does not get his own way in the classroom (Bates, Bentler, & Thompson, 1973; 1979).

Gender Disturbance in Girls

There are also girls who feel that they are boys or who would like very much to be boys. Although gender-disturbed boys outnumber girls by about 3:1, this ratio seems to have been equalizing in recent years for unknown reasons (Steiner, 1985). It is more difficult to diagnose gender disturbance in a girl because it is so common for girls to enjoy boys' games, clothes, and activities that this alone can hardly be indications of a problem with gender identity. The key distinction is that most tomboys usually enjoy feminine activities as well and will play with girls as well as boys. A gender-disturbed girl would show a more extreme avoidance of the feminine role by refusing to wear a skirt or dress for any occasion, trying to walk like a boy, lowering the pitch of her speaking voice, playing only with boys, and insisting on being called by a boy's name or nickname (Blanchard & Freund, 1983; Rekers & Jurich, 1983).

In addition to trying to behave as much like a boy as possible, a gender-disturbed girl would insist repeatedly that she *is* a boy, which is quite different from merely saying she would like to be a boy because she thinks that boys have it better in life. One child said she would rather be dead than remain a girl. She repeatedly failed her gym classes because she would not play sports with the girls, and the school could not legally allow her to take gym with the boys (Rekers & Jurich, 1983). As with boys, the indications of a gender identity problem in girls is usually apparent from early childhood. One survey of parents found that they felt something was "different" or "not right" with their daughter from the toddler stage (Benjamin, 1964). Some clinicians argue that a girl cannot really be considered to have a gender identity disturbance unless she also seems to be rejecting her feminine anatomy, for example, by saying that she does not have a vagina; that she will not have breasts, menstruate, or be able to bear children when she grows up; or by binding down her breasts at puberty and denying that she has started to menstruate (Ehrhardt, Grisanti, & McCauley, 1979). Others do not necessarily agree with this criterion by pointing out that a boy must only say that he dislikes his genitals or wishes that he did not have them to be considered gender-disturbed and arguing that a girl might well have a problem with her gender identity without necessarily denying physical reality (K. Zucker, 1985).

■ Gender Identity versus Gender Role

In some cases, an inconsistency can develop in a child's core identity or role behaviors independently. For example, a child may behave more like the other gender while still knowing and accepting his or her true sex. One preschool boy acted much like a girl; he had girlish gestures and a high-pitched voice, he hated playing sports with other boys, his favorite television shows had female stars such as Mary Tyler Moore, and he wanted to be an interior designer when he grew up. Yet he never claimed to be a girl or said that he wanted to be a girl, thus suggesting that his identity was male (K. Zucker, 1985). Other children may secretly wish to be or believe they are the other sex but not reveal this in their role behavior. Kidnapped by his father at the age of 3 the boy was dressed as a girl for a year as a disguise while they were in hiding from the police. When the boy was 8 years old, he appeared on the surface to be a typical boy, but he had secret thoughts about really being a girl which he believed came from a devil in his brain: "He always bugs me, he tells me in my mind to think about being a girl" (K. Zucker, 1985, p. 161). Most clinicians consider signs of problems with the child's core identity to be much more serious than deviations in role behaviors. While a boy who does "sissy stuff" is probably not going to be terribly popular with his classmates, a boy who believes he is really a girl faces the risk of considerably more serious adjustment problems later in life.

As the cases described above illustrate, some children believe they are or would like to be the other sex. These children are not merely tomboy girls or boys who happen to enjoy quiet indoor play; they strongly reject the expected role as well as prefer the other role. In the next section we examine factors that are known to contribute to gender disturbance and then turn to the question of intervention—should parents try to help a child who shows signs of wanting to be the other sex?

CHILDHOOD GENDER DISTURBANCE: "FAILED" SOCIALIZATION?

As we have seen in previous chapters, the process of gender role learning begins very early in the child's life, and parents and other family members are an important part of the process, although they are by no means the only source of influence. Some clinicians have suggested that the family environment might also contribute to gender disturbance, at least in some cases. This does *not* mean that parents can easily or accidentally cause gender disturbance in a child or that they should be excessively concerned about the possibility. For the vast majority of children the process of learning to be a boy or girl seems to be remarkably smooth and resilient; almost all children quickly and easily master the role of boy or girl despite wide variations in home, school, and cultural settings. Studies of gender-disturbed children suggest that their situations are often quite unusual or that they had characteristics, such as developmental immaturity, causing them to be particularly vulnerable to inconsistent socialization or unusually resistant to traditional socialization. Keeping these qualifications in mind, researchers have found several characteristics that have been associated with families of gender-disturbed children. Most of these studies have focused on gender disturbance in boys; very little is known about the corresponding case of girls.

■ Gender Lessons: Mixed Messages?

Most parents, particularly fathers, react negatively to signs of feminine behavior in young boys, for example, frowning or making a sarcastic remark if the boy puts on lipstick and plays with a doll. This suggests that if the boy does not receive such clear signals, he might not learn to avoid feminine behavior as quickly as do other boys. A mother may have thought that her son's early experiments with feminine clothes or her makeup were "cute" and encouraged it, or she allowed it to continue past the point when most other parents would have said, "That's enough of that." In one study, parents of gender-disturbed boys often had photographs of the boy dressed up as a girl displayed on their mantel or in family albums. In contrast, although some typical boys had occasionally dressed up as girls, for example, at Halloween, none of their parents had taken photographs and displayed them in the home, suggesting a much lower tolerance for feminine behavior in their sons (Green, 1987). In some cases parents may genuinely not realize that their son's behavior is relatively unusual. When one mother was asked about her son's repeated episodes of dressing up as a girl, she said, "I thought, well, maybe it's just a stage he's going through . . . it's just one of those normal things kids do, and I probably didn't think too much of it" (Green, 1987, pp. 136–137). Although it is true that many boys do try out feminine activities, most quickly learn to avoid doing so when others react negatively. In other cases the parents may be preoccupied with their own depression and marital problems, and the little boy may discover that if he dresses and acts as a girl, he will elicit his parents' attention and concern. One boy reasoned that "daddies came home from work to be with mommies," and thought that if he dressed up as a girl, his daddy might want to spend more time at home (Bradley, 1985; Holden, 1988).

Occasionally, parents deliberately encourage feminine behavior in a son, for example, a parent who had wanted a daughter might let the little boy's hair grow long and dress him in frilly outfits, as illustrated by the following letter:

> Dear Ann Landers,
> This letter will sound bizarre and I'm sure most of your readers will think it was made up by a student at Yale. Every word is true, so help me. I am praying that you will print it because my wife refuses to listen to me and I need some help with this problem. She respects you, Ann. "Susan" and I have been married for seven years. We have a 6-year-old son and cannot have any more children. She was hoping for a girl and was deeply disappointed when "Jack" was born. Susan has treated our son like a girl from the day he came home from the hospital. She dresses him in frilly pinafores and puts ribbons in his hair. My family thought Susan was nutty at first and told her so. She threatened to keep them from seeing "Jackie" if they continued to be critical, so they caved in and now they even buy him tea sets and dolls. When Jackie started kindergarten last year, he was registered as a girl. No one at school knows he's a boy. He wears dresses with fancy underwear and plays with dolls. He seems quite comfortable as a girl and loves to go shopping with his mom . . . I get a sick feeling when I see her teaching him to sit like a lady and apply lipstick. This child should be playing with boys and learning how to be a boy. Do you believe what my wife is doing will cause a problem to our son later in life?

(Landers' response is basically yes.) This particular letter may or may not be truthful, but similar situations do occur; for example, Ernest Hemingway's mother dressed him as a girl for most of his childhood, and it has been suggested that the repeated exploration of strong masculine themes in his work stemmed from his effort to compensate for this early experience. In another case, a girl was born with an enlarged clitoris, as the result of exposure to masculinizing hormones during prenatal development. Although the baby was recognized to be a girl, the father decided to raise her as a boy, against medical advice and over the mother's protests, because he desperately wanted a son. This led to disagreement and inconsistency in the gender of rearing within the family. Not surprisingly, the child was extremely confused, feeling that although he was a boy he was also, or should have been, a girl (Dearsley, 1990). As we saw in Chapter 2, a child will often try to resolve such ambivalence by identifying with the other gender; in this case, the child decided to live in the female role when she left home. Occasionally, other family members besides the parents may be the source of the problem. One older sister who was deeply resentful of her younger brother secretly taught him to dress up as a girl and to think of himself as a girl (Bradley, 1985). In several other cases a grandmother was eventually discovered to have encouraged cross-dressing and doll play by the little boy as a regular play activity without the knowledge of other family members (Halle, Schmidt, & Meyer, 1980).

The Role of Fathers

As we saw in Chapter 5, fathers are an important influence in shaping children's gender-typed play. In some families, if the father's influence is absent, the young boy may not learn to avoid feminine behavior, particularly if he does not receive such messages from other sources, such as male peers, older brothers, relatives, or teachers. Some studies have suggested that gender-disturbed boys had had much less frequent contact with their fathers before the age of 3 than typical boys (Green, 1987; Roberts, Green, Williams, & Goodman, 1987). Some support for this relation is found in studies of typical children whose fathers were absent during their first 5 years of life because of death, divorce, military service, or employment that required regular, extended travel. Father-absent boys were less stereotypically masculine than boys whose fathers had been present continuously during this period, although all these boys were well within the typical range and none was gender-disturbed (M. Stevenson & Black, 1988). If there is no father in the family, the boy probably has more intense or exclusive contact with his mother than would be the case for a boy in a two-parent family. Mothers tend to encourage feminine behavior in children of both sexes, so a boy who lacks counterbalancing attention from an adult male might not learn to avoid feminine behavior as quickly as other boys. Other times fathers may be physically present but not providing the usual signals to avoid feminine behavior because they themselves enjoy the child's feminine behavior. For example, a father might enjoy taking the little boy to events and activities that his wife does not enjoy and unconsciously begin treating the child as an "understudy" for his wife. This could explain why mothers rather than fathers are usually the first to become concerned about their child's feminine behavior (Holden, 1988).

Although some parents do seem to have conveyed mixed messages to the gender-disturbed child, in other cases the preference for other-sex clothes and activities seems to originate in the child and to persist despite the parents' protests. For example, one 3-year-old boy put on his mother's pink-and-white blouse and danced excitedly around the room; his mother made him take it off and put the blouse away; but he asked for it over and over despite her anger. Another mother offered to get her little boy a much-wanted puppy if he would stop putting on dresses in the play corner at preschool; she found him wearing a skirt in school the next day (Green, 1987). Thus, cross-gender behavior can persist in the face of clear signals from the child's parents that they do not like it; this suggests that other factors, such as peer influence, may also be important.

The Role of Peers

We saw in Chapter 7 that peers are a significant influence for young children, especially for little boys who use one another as role models of masculine behavior. This suggests that a boy who does not have much contact with other boys might miss some of the feedback that would teach him to avoid dolls and other stereotypically feminine behavior. Consistent with this possibility, some gender-disturbed boys have been found to have had much less peer contact than was the case for most children. For example, one boy had missed an entire year of school due to a serious illness. Another was restricted to playing at home alone because his parent was very ill; he could not go to other boys' homes and was not allowed to invite friends over to his house to play.

Later, the boy who missed early peer influences and who did not learn to avoid feminine behavior will probably discover that the boys at school or in the neighborhood do not like him. Seventy percent of elementary school children say that they would not want to be friends with a child who displayed even moderate examples of cross-gender behavior, for example, a boy who plays with a doll or a girl who talks in a loud voice (Hemmer & Kleiber, 1981; Stoddart & Turiel, 1985; K. Zucker, Wilson, & Stern, 1985). Preschool boys who show even moderate amounts of feminine behavior are strongly rejected by their male classmates and play alone three times as often as other boys (Fagot, 1977). Whereas typical boys quickly abandon feminine behavior in the face of peer reprisals, the gender-disturbed boy tends not to change his behavior for two reasons. First, he often has trouble figuring out exactly what it is that makes the other boys dislike him; for example, he does not realize that when he stands with his hands on his hips, the other boys think, "girl." Second, although the boys ignore or reject him, the girls will occasionally play with him, providing just enough social acceptance to keep the feminine behavior going. He then misses additional information about masculine gender role behavior as he becomes increasingly isolated from the other boys.

In contrast to boys, cross-gender girls do not elicit such strong negative reactions from peers, and some are even admired and popular (Oltmanns, Neale, & Davison, 1991; Rekers & Jurich, 1983). In one study, third and sixth graders were asked to nominate and rate the popularity of one "sissy boy" and one tomboy from their class. The cross-gender boys were much less popular than other boys, while the tomboys received similar or in some cases higher ratings than their more feminine classmates. Once again we see the asymmetry of gender roles, with girls having more freedom to cross gender role boundaries than boys have.

■ Does Failed Socialization Explain Gender Disturbance?

The idea that instances of gender identity disturbance could be due to mixed messages or the absence of contact with peers and fathers is consistent with the general pattern of gender role learning. Some cases of gender identity disturbance seem to develop because parents or other family members do not provide the usual messages about avoiding certain gender role behaviors while sticking to others, or different family members give inconsistent messages, so that the child has trouble figuring out what he should and should not do. It also can help explain why more boys than girls are affected. As we have seen throughout this book, the male gender role is more narrowly defined and harder to learn, compared to the relative freedom allotted girls. Boys would be particularly vulnerable when socialization messages are unclear, making it difficult to figure out exactly what they should and should not do. For example, a boy might put on lipstick and find that on one occasion his father yells at him, "Get that stuff off your face," while the next time his mother and sister laugh, say he is cute, and take his picture. Behaviors that are occasionally but unpredictably rewarded tend to persist long after the rewards have stopped coming.

Inconsistent or unclear socialization can account for some aspects of gender disturbance, but it has two limitations. First, it does not explain why some children show such an early, strong preference for being the other sex and why gender disturbance appears in families in which the parents do not seem to have encouraged it, are quite upset at their son's feminine behavior, and provide very clear signals that they would like him to stop. Second, the failed socialization model does not really account for gender disturbance in girls; socialization influences on girls are fairly weak to begin with, and it is relatively uncommon for a girl to grow up without being exposed to adult female role models. In fact, we know very little about why a girl decides that she is or would like to be a boy. Thus, although it seems that inconsistent socialization can contribute to the development of gender identity disturbance, as yet it does not completely explain the phenomenon.

THE QUESTION OF INTERVENTION

Should we try to help a gender-identity disturbed child? At first, the answer seems obvious; it is hard to see a child become rejected by his peers and who seems to be deeply confused about an aspect of his self-concept as basic as whether he is a boy or girl. Yet a certain amount of loneliness and self-questioning is a natural component of normative development, not always a reason to jump in with therapy. We might also hesitate to try to tamper with a fundamental part of the child's personality unless we are very sure that it will be beneficial to the child in the long run, that is, once he or she has become an adult. We next consider the developmental outcomes associated with gender identity disturbance, review the therapy programs that have been developed, and consider whether therapy is warranted.

■ Adult Outcomes

One reason that gender identity disturbance is of concern to therapists is that there is some risk that the child will have emotional difficulties in adulthood. Estimates are that about 60 percent of gender-disturbed children will become homosexual, 30 percent heterosexual, and 7 to 10 percent transsexual (Green, 1987; B. Zucker, 1984; K. Zucker, 1985). Homosexuality is not considered by psychologists to be a deviant or problematic outcome, aside from lingering societal prejudice, and it is not particularly unusual—about 5 percent of women and about 10 percent of men are exclusively homosexual, and a much higher proportion of adults has engaged in occasional or periodic episodes of homosexual behavior (Feldman, 1984; Kinsey, Pomeroy, & Martin, 1948). In contrast, gender-disturbance in childhood is extremely rare. Most gay and lesbian adults were not gender disturbed children, and it would not be justified to intervene with a child's development out of fear that the child will grow up to be gay, that is, out of homophobia. Only the possibility of transsexualism is of concern when gender identity disturbance is diagnosed in a child.

■ Transsexualism

Transsexualism is a rare disorder in which an adult man or woman believes that he or she is the other sex "trapped" in the wrong body. One estimate has 1 male transsexual per 18,000 males and 1 female transsexual per 54,000 females, although accurate estimates are difficult to establish because some individuals may never seek treatment (Eklund, Gooren, & Bezemer, 1988). The deep sense of gender disturbance and extreme discomfort with their physical sex is emotionally debilitating, and transsexuals have high rates of serious psychological problems, including depression, repeated suicide attempts, violent behavior, social isolation, and even attempts at self-mutilation or self-castration when it seems unbearable to remain in the "wrong" body any longer.

Transsexualism is difficult to treat effectively. Although the person can adopt the role behaviors of the desired sex, for example, a man can live convincingly as a woman for many years without discovery, the fact that the person's body does not match his or her gender identity creates ongoing tension and unhappiness for many. Sex reassignment surgery is a possibility, in which a penis or vagina is constructed following steps similar to those used for sex correction or reassignment of pseudo-hermaphroditic children, as we saw in Chapter 2 (Kaplan, 1983; Latham & Grenadier, 1982; Roberto, 1983; Steiner, 1985). Transsexuals who have had sex reassignment surgery almost universally say they are happier, that they feel better, and that it was the right decision (Fleming, MacGowan, Robinson, Spitz, & Salt, 1982; Pauly, 1968, 1969). Other measures are somewhat less optimistic. Follow-up studies have found that clients who have had surgery have the same rates of drug abuse, criminal activity, and psychiatric treatment as those who did not (Langevin, 1985; McCauley & Ehrhardt, 1984; J. Meyer & Peter, 1979). As a result, some medical centers have stopped performing sex reassignment surgery, and most insurers no longer pay for it. Its high cost (about $15,000) puts it out of reach of most patients, although cheaper, unregulated surgery can apparently still be obtained outside the United States.

Because the treatment for transsexualism in an adult is fairly difficult and not always successful, some therapists have suggested that it would be better to intervene when signs of gender identity disturbance first appear in a child, even though most gender-disturbed children will not become transsexual adults (Rekers, 1979; Rekers, Bentler, Rosen, & Lovaas, 1977). In most cases the decision to provide treatment for a cross-gender child must be made by the parents. A young child cannot anticipate the long-term benefits and risks of the therapy, particularly the consequences for his or her adult sexuality and, therefore, cannot give informed consent for the treatment.

■ Treatment Programs

Most therapy programs for childhood gender disturbance are designed to replace one set of gender role behaviors with those that are considered more appropriate for the child's sex, rather than to add new behaviors to those the child has already adopted. For example, the goal for Paul, an 8-year-old boy, was to teach him stereotypically masculine behaviors and to eliminate his feminine behaviors which included putting towels around his waist like a skirt, asking to wear a girl's dress, tying ribbons on his head to make long hair, playing with dolls, and fluttering his hands with limp-wristed gestures. Paul also told his foster mother, "I want to be a girl so I can have a baby" (Rekers, Willis, Yates, Rosen, & Low, 1977).

The first step in treatment is to determine if the child wants to change. Paul admitted that he was unhappy, complained that the boys at school called him a sissy, and said he did not know why they did not like him. Once convinced that he wanted to change, the therapists worked on eliminating his feminine behaviors. They used videotapes to point out his feminine mannerisms and then used behavior modification techniques to help him avoid the mannerisms; for example, they would play a game with Paul and take away some of his winnings whenever he fluttered his hands. Then, masculine role behaviors were gradually added. A male college student taught Paul some basic athletic skills, such as throwing a baseball and football. As his behavior changed, Paul was less often teased and avoided by his peers, and greater social acceptance provided additional motivation for him to abandon his feminine behaviors. Although he was not completely accepted by the other boys, he did make several friends and was even elected captain of his class kickball team.

He told his foster mother that he felt more like the other boys, and he seemed to be much happier after the 8 months of treatment.

In addition to behavior modification programs, other types of intervention can be effective. K. Zucker, Bradley, Doering, and Lozinski (1985) found that play therapy, analyzing the underlying motivation for the child's behavior, and working directly with the family reduced cross-gender behavior in about 80 percent of their sample of gender-disturbed children, although the children still showed more cross-sex play than did their siblings. Other successful programs help children see some of the positive aspects of their physical sex, reduce their stereotyped beliefs about what boys and girls can do, and, in the case of boys, provide a male therapist as a positive role model (Roberto, 1983). Thus, gender disturbance in children can be effectively treated through a variety of approaches.

■ Do Gender-Disturbed Children *Need* Therapy?

Treatment programs can be effective, but they also raise several ethical questions. One concern is that the success of such programs may be more apparent than real. Although some children, such as Paul in the case described above, seem to appreciate the chance to change, other children may quickly learn to adopt the trained behaviors while being observed but revert to cross-gender behavior or thoughts when they are alone. One gender-disturbed boy admitted to his mother after a therapy play session, "I played with the boys' toys because that's what I knew I was supposed to do" (K. Zucker, 1985). What the child may really be learning from therapy is that his true interests and preferences are unaccept-able to others, even his own parents, and must be kept deeply hidden. The long-term psychological and emotional costs of attempting to deny or hide one's feelings in this way are not known but are probably considerable.

A second concern is the motivation behind the parents' desire to change the child's behavior, particularly in the case of boys. Adults are often overly sensitive about what constitutes feminine behavior in a boy: they become worried if their son would rather stay indoors and read a book than play baseball or ride dirt bikes and afraid that their child will be homosexual. Homophobia is still strong in many areas, and there remains societal, religious, and legal prejudice against those who are not hetereosexual. Parents might well want to spare their child from those consequences, much as parents of a chubby child might wish to help their child lose weight to avoid being teased and rejected by other children. Yet the vast majority of homosexual adults were not gender-disturbed children, so parental concern is misplaced. Although the causes of sexual orientation, either homosexuality or heterosexuality, are not known at this time, there is no evidence that it can be altered once established, and little evidence that it is beneficial to try (Gladue, 1987; Hoenig, 1985).

Parents might legitimately worry about the consequences of potential transsexualism, but it is important to keep in mind that this disorder is very rare. In one study of about 60 extremely feminine boys, only one could have been classified as transsexual as an adult (Green, 1987). Thus, the risks may not be great enough to justify intensive intervention for each child. Huston (1983) argues that in most cases of gender disturbance the child is not really at risk for anything beyond the negative reactions of other people and that adults should therefore not try to tamper with the child's developing gender identity. Others have suggested that the goal of intervention should be to expand the child's behavioral repertoire, rather than to replace one stereotypical gender role with another. For example, rather than training an effeminate boy not to use particular mannerisms, he might be given some help in learning how to throw a ball or ride a bike and to handle teasing from other boys with a show of confidence or by tossing off a joke of his own. Such approaches might give the child a greater choice about how to behave to reach different social goals, without conveying that he is fundamentally unacceptable to other people, including his own parents.

Blended Gender Roles

Another way to view the issue of childhood gender disturbance is to reexamine the assumption that gender must be an either-or category. As we have seen throughout this book, we tend to exaggerate the differences between the male and female role and are uncomfortable when someone does not seem to fit neatly into one or the other. Other cultures have allowed people more freedom to cross gender role boundaries and to blend aspects of both the male and female role. For example, women in several communities in Africa have traditionally been able to adopt the male social role through economic success. Women who had acquired considerable wealth through trading did not have to marry a man to survive; they could behave as men in everyday life and hold positions of authority in the community that were usually limited to men. These women were called "female husbands" because they could maintain their own households and support other women to perform the traditional tasks of a wife, including cooking and child care (O'Brien, 1977; Whitam, 1977). There is also evidence from anthropological studies that blended roles were created in some societies to accommodate children who would be considered gender-disturbed in our contemporary society. One such role was the Native American *berdache*.

The Berdache

The berdache role was part of the social fabric of many Native American tribes until the middle of this century, particularly in the plains areas of North America. The male berdache was a man who lived as a woman, dressing in women's clothes, wearing a female hairstyle, using the language of women, living with the women of the tribe, and doing women's work (Blackwood, 1984; Callender & Kochems, 1983; Whitehead, 1981). Berdaches were highly respected for their hard work and their skill in women's work, such as weaving, and in fact, they were often quite wealthy because their work was never limited by pregnancy and child care. In addition, they often had prestigious ceremonial or spiritual functions within the community —naming children, performing burials, or serving as matchmakers—because they could move freely between the worlds of men and women. Some berdaches became men's wives, which was accepted as an essentially heterosexual arrangement; the husbands were not considered to be homosexual. The berdache role was not exclusively feminine; rather, the berdache combined elements of both male and female roles. He could engage in such male activities as hunting, and although he lived as a woman in everyday life, he could dress as a man and carry weapons for the men of the tribe when they went to war, while the women could not.

At least some berdaches may have been what today we would call gender-disturbed children (Callender & Kochems, 1983). Some were reported to have shown a great interest and unusual proficiency in women's work and to have had a strong preference for feminine clothing as children. When the parents suspected that the child might be a future berdache, they could arrange a test to determine the child's true identity, for example, by placing the child with a man's hunting bow and a woman's basket, inside a circle of brush. The brush would then be set on fire, and the adults would observe which object the child took while escaping from the enclosure. If a boy chose the basket, he would be officially recognized as a future berdache. It is clear that the cross-gender behavior was the child's preference rather than the parents, as at times appears to be the case with children who today are diagnosed as gender-disturbed. One Mohave informant explained:

> When there is a desire in a child's heart to become a [transvestite] that child will act different. It will let people become aware of that desire. They may insist on giving the child the toys and garments of its true sex, but the child will throw them away. (Whitehead, 1981, p. 95)

Note that the quote is a translation, and "transvestite" refers to gender role behavior rather than sexual activity. An older boy or young man might realize that he was a berdache through a dream or vision in which female spirits or forces transformed him. One boy dreamed that the spirit of the full moon gave him the choice of a bow and arrow (a male symbol) or a burden-strap (a female symbol). When he tried to take the bow, the moon pulled it away and forced the burden-strap on him. After living in the male role, an adult man could also become a berdache as the result of a sign or vision; attributing his decision to supernatural forces helped make it acceptable in the eyes of the community. Similarly, there were rituals in many tribes in which a child would be recognized as a berdache, which formally relieved parents of any sense of guilt or responsibility for raising a "different" child. While the role was socially accepted, many parents were still not particularly pleased if their son showed signs of preferring the woman's role.

Women could also become berdaches, dressing and living as men and marrying women. Again, the role was more of a blending of the male and female roles than a complete gender transformation; for example, female berdaches were not allowed to participate in male warfare activities no matter how strong and skillful they were. In addition, prohibitions against contact with menstruating women made it difficult for a woman to become a berdache; several are reported to have denied that they menstruated to preserve their berdache status. There is little recorded information about the process by which a woman became a berdache, although there are indications that a girl who was an exceptionally good hunter might adopt the role. One Crow woman was such a skilled hunter that she was able to support four wives! Female berdaches were apparently much rarer than the male version, possibly because women were already able to gain some of the advantages of the male role without making a formal gender change; for example, they could hunt if no man in the family was available for the task or if it was economically necessary. They could also gain considerable honor and prestige within the female role by being productive workers and helping with battle preparations; such women were called "manly hearted." But if such role flexibility was not sufficient for a particular woman, the berdache role provided an additional option.

SUMMARY

Gender identity disturbance is a rare disorder in which the child believes that he or she is the other sex; most cases involve a boy who thinks he is a girl, although there are cases of girls who believe that they are boys. Sometimes the disturbance can be traced to inconsistent or ambivalent socialization within the home, including the absence of clear messages to a boy from parents and peers to avoid feminine behavior. These cases are similar to several of this examples of pseudo-hermaphroditic children discussed at the start of this book, in that when there is some uncertainty within the family about the child's sex the child may decide to adopt the other gender role. However, in other cases, the very early onset of the child's belief that he or she is the other sex and the strength of this belief suggest that more than "failed socialization" may be involved in the development of gender identity disturbance. Although gender disturbance in childhood is extremely rare, anthropological research suggests that it has occurred in other cultures as well as our own. Gender-disturbed children can be treated through behavior modification and other programs; an alternative solution adopted in some cultures is to allow them to blend aspects of male and female roles, as in the Native American berdache role.

14

CONCLUSIONS

I occasionally think of Cory, the child mentioned at the start of the book and who could have been either a boy or a girl, and wonder what he or she is doing now. If I had to guess, I would bet that Cory is a girl because of the greater flexibility in gender role behavior permitted girls and the greater need for boys to clearly establish their masculinity around other boys. In either case, Cory would be well into high school by now and has no doubt clearly become a young man or woman in terms of physical, social, and personality development. One can delay adopting a gender role only so long; some aspects of development are inevitable.

We began this book by asking how most children learn so quickly and easily to be boys and girls, Cory being the rare exception, and suggested that many of the differences we see in their behavior result from the fact that they are born into a world that emphasizes gender distinctions, which range from the trivial to the momentous, and that does so even before they are born. It would be an insult to children's intelligence and powers of observation to suggest that they would not notice that men and women look different and do different types of things or that they would not be affected by these observations. Of course, common sense would tell you that children learn some aspects of gender roles by observation; you did not need to read this book to know that. In the next section we review some of the more detailed conclusions we can now make about how children learn to be boys and girls and about the potential interaction of biology and socialization.

GENDER ROLE LEARNING

■ Beyond Parents

Parents are clearly part of the socialization process; we have seen that parents who are expecting a child do in most cases have a preference for its gender and that they treat boys and girls differently in particular areas, most notably in how much independence and autonomy they allow the child. But one point that we have learned is that parents are not everything, and for gender role development they may even be rather peripheral to the process. There are many other sources of information about gender roles and other formal and informal pressures on children to become boys or girls, including children's own need to establish a gender identity and the power of peers, schools, and the media (Serbin et al., 1993). It seems unlikely that any one of these influences would be sufficient alone, but together they seem to do the job most effectively. I once posed the following exam question to my students: "Imagine that we discovered that parents actually treat boys and girls identically; do you think that boys and girls would still develop different behavior?" Almost every student agreed that they would, as the result of these other influences. This should be somewhat reassuring to parents who have actively tried to avoid raising gender-stereotyped children and found themselves living with Barbie and Rambo.

■ Punctuated Socialization

We have seen that gender role learning is more punctuated than continuous, meaning that at transitional points in development children appear to be particularly sensitive to gender lessons, for example, during the toddler stage and early adolescence. Also, some sources of influence may have much more impact than others. Increasingly, researchers point to the role of peers as important socializing agents in early childhood, possibly outweighing parents in their power to influence children's behavior in particular areas. As one of my students explained, "Your parents *have* to love you; their approval is unconditional. But your friends, well, you have to act right or they won't like you anymore. So you care more about what they think." "Acting right," of course, means acting like a regular boy or girl. One possibility for future research is to investigate whether the type of learning associated with sources of influence outside the family might conform more to the "drench" model of learning suggested for television (Chapter 9), in that one rude remark by a playmate about your selection of toys could have an immediate and long-lasting effect on your play behavior or a carelessly critical comment by an overtired or distracted teacher could lead you to believe for years that you aren't a very good writer. In contrast, learning from parental feedback might fit a "drip" model of slow, gradual learning, with the true effects only becoming apparent in late adolescence or the college years or beyond (Sedney, 1987).

We have also seen that gender role socialization is asymmetric and that lessons provided to one gender are not necessarily matched for the other in terms of the degree of emphasis and the social costs. As we saw in Chapter 12, the asymmetry depends on when you look in development; boys are constrained to avoid the feminine role beginning at about 2 years, while many girls in early adolescence feel compelled to be feminine by internal and peer pressures that are as forceful as anything a parent could say. So if we want to know which gender is most restricted in development, the answer depends on when we look—early childhood or later development. Overall, however, the male role appears to be more restrictive, to the point of being so oppressive that some children refuse it. We saw in Chapter 13 that many more boys than girls actively resist conforming to the expected gender role.

■ The Role of Biology

Some of the behaviors we have examined may also reflect biological predispositions that are expressed more frequently in one sex, for example, aggression and rough-and-tumble play in boys, the development of genius-level math talent, and differential vulnerability to certain language problems and brain injury. We can accept this possibility without concluding that biology means behavioral destiny (J. E. Mitchell, Baker, & Jacklin, 1989). As we described at the start of this book, biological influences do not work in isolation; children always develop within a social context, and thus nature and nuture inevitably interact. Something as apparently "biological" as the onset of puberty and menarche in girls depends on the social context, as does the probability that a child will be diagnosed and labeled as dyslexic or that a boy will become a horrible bully. Biological correlates also do not mean that all boys or all girls are equally affected; as we saw in Chapters 10 and 11, the overlap between male and female groups is so great that we cannot really anticipate much about a particular child's abilities and characteristics based only on gender. I am especially cautious about this issue because the contributions of biology are so often raised as a justification for keeping things the way they are, implying that there is nothing to be done about girls' lower achievement on the SAT math exam or boys' reluctance to be involved in nurturing activities. Yet as we have seen throughout this book, such arguments are unwarranted and often terribly misleading, denying individuals the chance to what they might very much enjoy and are quite successful at when given the opportunity, such as signing up for a session at a summer computer camp or working part-time at the college child-care center.

We may find in the future that biology plays a more important role than we have been able to establish thus far; even so, it does seem that there is much socialization going on as well, from infancy through adolescence. Before turning to consider the possibilities for change, let us ask about some of the relative costs and benefits of adopting gender roles.

ARE GENDER ROLES GOOD OR BAD?

■ Benefits

One benefit of having a gender role is that growing up male or female provides support for identity development. Knowing their gender provides toddlers who are first beginning to recognize themselves and to develop a self-concept, a clear guideline that structures future learning across many situations and gives a reassuring sense of security. A similar process is at work whenever we become part of a group, whether it is part of a group at work, a sports team, a sorority, or a college class; our membership becomes part of who we are, and, as the advertisement says, it has its privileges in that we know there are others who will always accept us and with whom we share certain common experiences. I do not think we can underestimate the benefits this provides young children, especially when they first begin to establish social relationships with others besides their parents.

Another benefit of gender role stereotypes is that they crystallize facets of human behavior that we think are important, including sheer physical power, caring and sensitivity to friends, physical beauty, a quick, logical mind, the willingness to put another first, and to care for those in need. By associating these various qualities with one or the other gender, we help preserve them and keep them clear in our minds. Finally, like all stereotypes, gender roles facilitate decisions; for example, if a young woman is not sure which major to select, signing up for early childhood education is familiar, safe, and no one will question her excessively or imply that she is not suited for the field. At times, we do need this sort of support, and sometimes we cannot consider all the options that are open to us, or we would be paralyzed, unable to make a choice at all. Thus, we do gain some advantages from gender role stereotypes, but naturally these benefits do not come for free.

■ Costs

First, gender role stereotypes bring some disadvantages in terms of how we perceive others. When we classify someone as a male or female, we make assumptions, assumptions that may or may not hold for them as individuals. Sometimes these costs are relatively trivial. When looking for a house several years ago, I was constantly dragged into kitchens by beaming realtors and forced to inspect lazy Susan corner cupboards, appliance garages, and the latest countertop grills, while my spouse was shown the heating arrangements in dozens of dank basements, although he does all the cooking and I make the elaborate arrangements necessary for the care and nurturance of a New England furnace. Not surprisingly, we ended up working with the one realtor who actually related to us as unique individuals rather than stereotypes. At other times the costs can be quite high; we saw at the start of the book that women whose parents had originally wanted a boy tended to have more difficult family relationships while growing up. Such problems can also impact boys' development as well; for example, at one school the football coach found that some of his players were deliberately playing poorly so that they would be thrown off the team. They could not cope with trying to live up to their fathers' image of them as star players, but at the same time they did not feel able to simply quit the team. One can only imagine the anguish these boys felt about not being the "men" their fathers expected them to be (Miedzian, 1991).

■ What If?

Other costs come in terms of lost or limited opportunities. Imagine how your life path might have evolved if you had been born the other gender: What options would have opened up easily and automatically for you, what benefits were you able to assume apparently by rights, without question, and what opportunities were set just a few critical steps farther away for you than for others, so that in the end you turned back to the more familiar path? I think back to my friend who in high school wanted to be a fabric designer and whose parents let him set up a loom in the garage, along with buckets of dye and pots of wax for making batiks. Today he is a salesperson working in a large textbook publishing house. As a sixth grader I wanted to be an astronomer; I read every book in the science fiction section of our small-town library and spent warm summer evenings lying on my back looking at the stars and wondering if any had planets and if we would ever know. Of course, it is part of childhood to dream, and we do not expect that all children will follow their early career fantasies—the world would be awfully full of astronauts, fire fighters, princesses, and horse trainers if they did—and both of us are perfectly happy with the choices we did make. Yet biology did not make him a corporate salesperson or me a psychologist, and so we both occasionally wonder what would have happened if we had been the other gender.

Poignant musings of childhood aside, gender stereotypes do offer some benefits, but clearly we can pay a high price for those benefits, both as individuals and as a larger society when we lose the talents and contributions of those whose developmental options were prematurely constrained by gender role expectations.

THE POSSIBILITIES FOR CHANGE

Ursula Le Guin's (1976) science fiction novel *The Left Hand of Darkness* portrays a world, the planet Winter, in which gender is pretty much irrelevant to daily life and social organization. People live in a neuter form except for the sexually active part of a monthly cycle in which they change physically into a male or female. Each individual has the potential to become either sex, so that a person who was male the last time might be female the next, and the father of a child might be the mother of several others. This idea is actually not quite as implausible as it sounds at first; recall that as we saw in Chapter 2, there is great similarity in the male and female form early in development, with each embryo having the potential to develop as a male or female. Much of the novel deals with other characters' difficulties in dealing with people whose gender cannot be classified along traditional social boundaries and with a society that is not organized around gender-linked careers, interests, and family responsibilities. It is a stunning vision of a world in which most ordinary gender distinctions are absent and which by contrast reveals the prevalence of those distinctions in our world.

We may not want to create a society like that out of a science fiction novel—in fact, I have never met anyone who actually found the vision of Winter appealing—but more and more, parents, teachers, students, and children and adolescents themselves have the goal of reducing some of the more arbitrary and unnecessary gender distinctions within our society. Having examined the process of gender role socialization in some detail, does it seem possible to achieve this goal?

■ Changing the Message

In the short term, the answer is a clear yes, based on the examples of "reversal" experiments in which the usual gender messages were altered and children's attitudes and behavior changed accordingly, for example, in Chapter 8 when the teacher feedback typically given to boys was delivered to girls and in Chapter 9 in which children read books and viewed TV programs that presented gender-atypical characters. Gender stereotypes are clearly not inevitable; change the message and you change what is learned, although children's receptiveness to the new messages does vary with their developmental stage. Of course, so far we have only been able to demonstrate this on a local level; no one has yet shown that children's gender role ideas can be entirely revised by altering parental feedback and other influences, and most researchers would probably agree that it would not be possible without a complete overhaul of society as we know it.

■ Nonsexist Child Rearing?

A somewhat less optimistic view is presented by parents and teachers who have tried to bring up children who are less strongly stereotyped and who have begun to conclude that, no matter what they do, little girls will inevitably want pink satin ballet slippers and Barbie dolls dressed in wedding white, while little boys will run over to the toy chest and dig through the proper "educational" toys to find the one rusty, old toy pistol left buried at the bottom by an earlier generation of small cowboys (S. Stein, 1983). As one parent ruefully admitted after her kindergarten daughter begged piteously to have her ears pierced, "This was not supposed to happen" (Span, 1987, p. 15). What can we say to parents whose children still seem to persist in creating a pink-and-blue world?

First, as we saw in Chapter 6, we can interpret children's apparent focus on gender in terms of their developmental needs, including their efforts to make sense of the social world and to feel that they belong somewhere within that world (Serbin et al., 1993). We can recognize that some of the more exaggerated remarks, such as "women can't be doctors," reflect children's attempt to organize their burgeoning knowledge about the world around them, and we can anticipate that these phases will pass. Second, we can be reassured by the fact that the strength and ferocity of early gender typing does not appear to predict a particular child's interests and capabilities as an adult. The frilly 6-year-old girl who is devoted to her "my little pony" figurines is not doomed to become an empty-headed clothes horse in high school or a professional cheerleader at 22. Individual development simply does not appear to be so continuous from early childhood to adult-hood. Parents might therefore want to grit their teeth and bide their time through some of the more exaggerated stereotyping phases and to choose their battles, for example, to let the 6-year-old girl have her Barbies but draw the line at allowing her to grow Rapunzel hair or to let the boy create guns out of sticks and cardboard if he wishes but decline to purchase the latest toy sidewinder missile with rocket launcher attachment advertised on television. With older children, we can also step in and insist that gender not be a justification for a choice that will limit the child's future options unnecessarily, for example, not letting a boy persist in football if his grades are poor or not letting a girl drop a math class at the first sign of difficulty.

Finally, we can shift our attention from wondering why we cannot eliminate gender differences to achieving the goal of gender equity. Most of us would agree that the denial of opportunities to children on the basis of their gender is as unfair as discrimination based on disability or ethnicity or age or sexual orientation or any personal characteristic that the person cannot alter. For example, we can make sure that girls have the opportunity to participate in organized sports. This does not mean that boys and girls should necessarily play on the same teams but that the chance to participate should not be limited by district policies that fund only "big-team sports," (meaning that there is no part-time coach for girls who want to play field hockey) or policies that keep girls from using the school field because it is "reserved to protect the turf for the varsity football team home games," as once happened at the high school in my former hometown before parents' cries of outrage got the policy changed. The goal of gender equity applies to boys as well as girls; why should boys feel left out if they do not like contact sports but there are no other activities available, such as cross-country track, the school band, or a computer club?

■ Just a Matter of Time

Finally, we can also step back, look at this issue from a broader angle, and recognize how much change has already occurred. Legal barriers have fallen, along with restrictive policies, and we now have extraordinary flexibility in the options open to both males and females. Many of the social roles that previously were gender-linked have changed to the point where women astronauts now go into orbit so routinely that we hardly do more than yawn at the latest example and the President is married to a woman who earns more money than he does. Of course, informal barriers remain in many fields, and there are certainly high personal costs to those who do not follow the job and family roles that would have been typical for their gender a generation ago: The woman who flies military jets encounters derogatory graffiti in the pilots' lounge; the man who leaves faculty meetings promptly at 4 P.M. to meet his children's school bus overhears his colleagues' snide comments of "boy, his wife's sure got him whipped." But many have already overcome these barriers and are joined by more every day. There are still changes ahead and more work to be done to make options more easily available for both boys and girls, but there is no going back now. Even football, long considered the ultimate bastion of masculinity, is now including girls in many small communities not out of principle but because there are not enough boys who want to play, and the interested girls are as good or better than many of their male teammates and competitors. So far, there has been occasional grumbling from a few parents, a couple of patronizing comments from insecure boys, and some awkward moments trying to find ladies' rooms at strange schools for the girls to change in, but the sky has not fallen. One high school football coach who signed up a girl as a tight end on the team said, "I don't think it's a big deal. It's the 90s; stranger things have happened . . . She's willing to do what all the others do. We have fat people, thin people, fast people, slow people. All we ask is that you do the best you can" (Burris, 1992, p. 19). Surely this is the lesson we want all children to learn, regardless of their gender.

REFERENCES

Abbey, A. (1987). Misperceptions of friendly behavior as sexual interest: A survey of naturally occurring incidents. *Psychology of Women Quarterly, 11*, 173–194.

Aboud, F. (1988). *Children and prejudice.* New York: Basil Blackwell.

Abramovitch, A., & Grusec, J. E. (1978). Peer imitation in a natural setting. *Child Development, 49*, 60–65.

Abramovitch, R., Corter, C., & Lando, B. (1979). Sibling interaction in the home. *Child Development, 4*, 997–1003.

Abramovitch, R., Corter, C., & Pepler, D. J. (1980). Observations of mixed sex sibling dyads. *Child Development, 51*, 1268–1271.

Adler, J., & Rosenberg, D. (1992, October 19). Must boys always be boys? *Newsweek*, p. 77.

Adler, P. A., Kless, S. J., & Adler, P. (1992). Socialization to gender roles: Popularity among elementary school boys and girls. *Sociology of Education, 65*, 169–187.

Albert, A. A., & Porter, J. R. (1983). Age patterns in the development of children's gender role stereotypes. *Sex Roles, 9*, 59–67.

Aleksandrowicz, M. K., & Aleksandrowicz, D. R. (1974). Obstetrical pain-relieving drugs as predictors of infant variability. *Child Development, 45*, 935–945.

Alfieri, T. J., Thompson, E. P., Ruble, D. N., Harlow, R., & Higgins, E. T. (1991, April). *Developmental changes in gender stereotyping: A closer look.* Paper presented at the biennial meeting of the Society for Research in Child Development, Seattle, WA.

Allen, W. R. (1985). Race, income and family dynamics: A study of adolescent male socialization processes and outcomes. In M. B. Spencer, G. K. Brookins, & W. R. Allen (Eds.), *Beginnings: The social and affective development of black children* (pp. 273–295). Hillsdale, NJ: Erlbaum.

Alvidrez, J., & Weinstein, R. S. (1993, March). Early teacher expectations and later academic achievement. Paper presented at the biennial meeting of the Society for Research in Child Development, New Orleans.

American Association of University Women. (1992). *How schools shortchange girls.* Washington, DC: AAUW Educational Foundation.

Amherst Record. (1990, April 8). Ninja turtles banned, p. 3.

Andersen, E. S. (1984). The acquisition of sociolinguistic knowledge: Some evidence of children's verbal role-play. *Western Journal of Speech Communication, 48*, 125–144.

Antilla, S. (1991, August). The hottest woman on Wall Street. *Working Woman*, pp. 49–51.

Arnett, J. (1991). Adolescents and heavy metal music: From the mouths of metalheads. *Youth and Society, 23*, 76–98.

Ashby, M. S., & Wittmaier, B. C. (1978). Attitude changes in children after exposure to stories about women in traditional or nontraditional occupations. *Journal of Educational Psychology, 70,* 945–949.

Ashton, E. (1983). Measures of play behavior: The influence of sex role stereotyped books. *Sex Roles, 9,* 43–47.

Ashton, R. (1971). Behavioral sleep cycles in the human newborn. *Child Development, 42,* 2098–2100.

Askew, S., & Ross, C. (1988). *Boys don't cry: Sexism in education.* Milton Keynes, England: Open University Press.

Atkin, D. J., Moorman, J., & Lin, C. A. (1991). Ready for prime time: Network series devoted to working women in the 1980s. *Sex Roles, 25,* 677–685.

Attie, I., & Brooks-Gunn, J. (1989). Development of eating problems in adolescent girls: A longitudinal study. *Developmental Psychology, 25,* 70–79.

Baenninger, M., & Newcombe, N. (1989). The role of experience in spatial test performance: A meta-analysis. *Sex Roles, 20,* 327–344.

Bakeman, R., & Brown, J. V. (1977). Behavioral dialogues: An approach to the assessment of mother-infant interaction. *Child Development, 48,* 195–203.

Baker, S. W. (1980). Biological influences on human sex and gender. *Signs, 6,* 80–96.

Bandura, A., Ross, D., & Ross, S. A. (1961). Transmission of aggressive models. *Journal of Abnormal Social Psychology, 63,* 572–582.

Bank, B. J., Biddle, B. J., & Good, T. L. (1980). Sex roles, classroom instruction, and reading achievement. *Journal of Educational Psychology, 72,* 119–132.

Barkley, R. A., Ullman, D. G., Otto, L., & Brecht, J. M. (1977). The effects of sex typing and sex appropriateness of model behavior on children's imitation. *Child Development, 48,* 721–725.

Barnett, M. A. (1986). Sex bias in the helping behavior presented in children's picture books. *Journal of Genetic Psychology, 147,* 343–351.

Barrett, D. E. (1979). A naturalistic study of sex differences in children's aggression. *Merrill-Palmer Quarterly, 25,* 193–203.

Barry, R. J. (1980). Stereotyping of sex role in preschoolers in relation to age, family structure, and parental sexism. *Sex Roles, 6,* 795–806.

Bar-Tal, D., & Darom, E. (1979). Pupils' attributions of success and failure. *Child Development, 50,* 264–267.

Bartz, K. W., & Levine, E. S. (1978). Childrearing by black parents: A description and comparison to Anglo and Chicano parents. *Journal of Marriage and the Family, 40,* 709–719.

Bates, J. E., & Bentler, P. M. (1973). Play activities of normal and effeminate boys. *Developmental Psychology, 9,* 20–27.

Bates, J. E., Bentler, P. M., & Thompson, S. K. (1973). Measurement of deviant gender development in boys. *Child Development, 44,* 591–598.

Bates, J. E., Bentler, P. M., & Thompson, S. K. (1979). Gender-deviant boys compared with normal and clinical control boys. *Journal of Abnormal Child Psychology, 7,* 243–259.

REFERENCES

Baumgartner, A. (1983). *"My daddy might have loved me": Student perceptions of differences between being male and being female.* Unpublished paper, Institute for Equality in Education, Denver, CO.

Baumrind, D. (1986). Sex differences in moral reasoning: Response to Walker's (1984) conclusion that there are none. *Child Development, 57,* 511–521.

Baumrind, D. (1989, April). *Sex differentiated socialization effects in childhood and adolescence in divorced and intact families.* Paper presented at the biennial meeting of the Society for Research in Child Development, Kansas City, MO.

Bautz, B. J. (1993, March). Elementary school teachers' priorities for instruction. Paper presented at the biennial meeting of the Society for Research in Child Development, New Orleans.

Bayley, N. (1965). Comparisons on mental and motor test scores for ages 1–15 months by sex, birth order, race, geographical location, and education of parents. *Child Development, 36,* 379–411.

Beal, C. R., & Lockhart, M. E. (1989). The effect of proper name and appearance changes on children's reasoning about gender constancy. *International Journal of Behavioral Development, 12,* 195–205.

Becker, B. J. (1990). Item characteristics and gender differences on the SAT-M for mathematically able youth. *American Educational Research Journal, 27,* 65–87.

Bee, H. L., Mitchell, S. K., Barnard, K. E., Eyres, S. J., & Hammond, M. A. (1984). Predicting intellectual outcomes: Sex differences in response to early environmental stimulation. *Sex Roles, 10,* 783–803.

Belenky, M. F., Clinchy, B. M., Goldberger, N. R., & Tarule, J. M. (1986). *Women's ways of knowing.* New York: Basic Books.

Bell, M. A. (1991, April). *Crying at maternal separation is related to sex differences in hemispheric maturation.* Paper presented at the biennial meeting of the Society for Research in Child Development, Seattle, WA.

Bell, N. J., & Carver, W. (1980). A reevaluation of gender label effects: Expectant mothers' responses to infants. *Child Development, 51,* 925–927.

Bell, R. Q. (1960). Relations between behavior manifestations in the human neonate. *Child Development, 31,* 463–477.

Bell, R. Q., & Costello, N. S. (1964). Three tests for sex differences in tactile sensitivity in the newborn. *Biologia Neonatorum, 7,* 335–347.

Bellinger, D., & Berko-Gleason, J. (1982). Sex differences in directives to young children. *Sex Roles, 8,* 1123–1139.

Belsky, J. (1980). A family analysis of parental influence on infant exploratory competence. In F. A. Pedersen (Ed.), *The father-infant relationship* (pp. 87–110). New York: Praeger.

Belsky, J., Gilstrap, B., & Rovine, M. (1984). The Pennsylvania infant and family development project: I. Stability and change in mother-infant and father-infant interaction in a family setting at one, three, and nine months. *Child Development, 55,* 692–705.

Belsky, J., Steinberg, L., & Draper, P. (1991). Childhood experience, interpersonal development, and reproductive strategy: An evolutionary theory of socialization. *Child Development, 62,* 647–670.

Bem, S. L. (1981). Gender schema theory: A cognitive account of sex typing. *Psychological Review, 88,* 354–364.

Bem, S. L. (1983). Gender schema theory and its implications for child development: Raising gender aschematic children in a gender schematic society. *Signs, 8,* 598–616.

Bem, S. L. (1989). Genital knowledge and gender constancy in preschool children. *Child Development, 60,* 649–662.

Benbow, C. P., & Stanley, J. C. (1980). Sex differences in mathematical ability: Fact or artifact? *Science, 210,* 1262–1264.

Benbow, C. P., & Stanley, J. C. (1982). Consequences in high school and college of sex differences in mathematical reasoning ability: A longitudinal perspective. *American Educational Research Association Journal, 19,* 598–622.

Benbow, C. P., & Stanley, J. C. (1983). Sex differences in mathematical reasoning ability: More facts. *Science, 222,* 1029–1031.

Benbow, C. P., & Stanley, J. C. (1984). Gender and the science major. In M. W. Steinkamp & M. L. Maeher (Eds.), *Advances in motivation and achievement* (pp. 165–195). Greenwich, CT: JAI Press.

Ben-Chaim, D., Lappan, G., & Houang, R. T. (1988). The effect of instruction on spatial visualization skills of middle school boys and girls. *American Educational Research Association Journal, 25,* 51–71.

Bender, T. A., & Standage, T. H. (1992, April). *Influences on students' uses of classroom examination feedback.* Paper presented at the annual meeting of the American Educational Research Association, San Francisco, CA.

Benenson, J. F. (1991, April). *Sex differences in dyadic and group interaction in early childhood.* Paper presented at the biennial meeting of the Society for Research in Child Development, Seattle, WA.

Benenson, J. F., & Apostoleris, N. H. (1993, March). Gender differences in group interaction in early childhood. Paper presented at the biennial meeting of the Society for Research in Child Development, New Orleans.

Benjamin, H. (1964). Clinical aspects of transsexualism in male and female. *American Journal of Psychotherapy, 18,* 458–469.

Bensoussan, S., Batchie, M., Catania, P., Del Vasto, R., Marchese, S., & Derevensky, J. (1992, June). *Game preferences in children: A contemporary analysis.* Paper presented at the annual meeting of the Canadian Psychological Association, Quebec City.

Benton, C. J., Hernandez, A. C. R., Schmidt, A., Schmitz, M. D., Stone, A. J., & Weiner, B. (1983). Is hostility linked with affiliation among males and with achievement among females? A critique of Pollak and Gilligan. *Journal of Personality and Social Psychology, 45,* 1167–1171.

Benz, C., Pfeiffer, I., & Newman, I. (1981). Sex role expectancies of classroom teachers, grades 1–12. *American Education Research Journal, 18,* 289–302.

Berch, D. B., & Bender, B. G. (1987, December). Margins of sexuality. *Psychology Today,* pp. 54–57.

Berg-Cross, L., & Berg-Cross-G. (1978). Listening to stories may change children's social attitudes. *Reading Teacher, 31,* 659–663.

Berko-Gleason, J. (1989). *The development of language* (2nd ed.). Columbus, OH: Merrill.

Berman, P. W. (1975). *Attraction to infants: Are sex differences innate and invariant?* Paper presented at the annual meeting of the American Psychological Association, Chicago, IL.

Berman, P. W. (1980). Are women predisposed to parenting? Developmental and situational determinants of sex differences in responses to the young. *Psychological Bulletin, 88,* 668–695.

Berman, P. W., Monda, L. C., & Myerscough, R. P. (1977). Sex differences in young children's responses to an infant: An observation within a day-care setting. *Child Development, 48,* 711–715.

Bernard, M. E. (1979). Does sex role behavior influence the way teachers evaluate students? *Journal of Educational Psychology, 71,* 553–562.

Berndt, T. J. (1981). The effects of friendship on prosocial intentions and behavior. *Child Development, 52,* 636–643.

Berndt, T. J. (1982). The features and effects of friendship in early adolescence. *Child Development, 53, 1447–1460.*

Berndt, T. J. (1992). Friendship and friends' influence in adolescence. *Current Directions in Psychological Science, 1,* 156–159.

Berndt, T. J., & Heller, K. A. (1986). Gender stereotypes and social inferences: A developmental study. *Journal of Personality and Social Psychology, 50,* 889–898.

Berry, J. W. (1966). Temne and Eskimo perceptual skills. *International Journal of Psychology, 1,* 207–229.

Best, D. L., Williams, W. E., Cloud, J. M., Davis, S. W., Robertson, L. S., Edwards, J. R., Giles, H., & Fowles, J. (1977). Development of sex trait stereotypes among young children in the United States, England, and Ireland. *Child Development, 48,* 1375–1384.

Best, R. (1983). *We've all got scars: What boys and girls learn in elementary school.* Bloomington: Indiana University Press.

Beuf, A. (1974). Doctor, lawyer, household drudge. *Journal of Communication, 24,* 142–145.

Bianchi, B. D., & Bakeman, R. (1978). Sex-typed affiliation preferences observed in preschoolers: Traditional and open school differences. *Child Development, 49,* 910–912.

Bigler, R. S., & Liben, L. S. (1990). The role of attitudes and interventions in gender-schematic processing. *Child Development, 61,* 1440–1452.

Biller, H. B. (1970). Father absence and the personality development of the male child. *Developmental Psychology, 2,* 181–201.

Biller, H. B. (1981). Father absence, divorce, and personality development. In M. E. Lamb (Ed.), *The role of the father in child development* (2nd ed. pp. 489–552). New York: Wiley.

Biller, H. B., & Bahm, R. M. (1971). Father absence, perceived maternal behavior, and masculinity of self-concept among junior high school boys. *Developmental Psychology, 4,* 178–181.

Black, C. (1990, May 20). The case for single-sex colleges. *Boston Globe,* pp. A19, 22.

Blackwood, E. (1984). Sexuality and gender in certain Native American tribes: The case of cross-gender females. *Signs, 10,* 27–42.

Blakemore, J. E. O. (1981). Age and sex differences in interaction with a human infant. *Child Development, 52,* 386–388.

Blakemore, J. E. O. (1990). Children's nurturant interactions with their infant siblings: An exploration of gender differences and maternal socialization. *Sex Roles, 22,* 43–57.

Blakemore, J. E. O. (1991). The influence of gender and temperament on children's interaction with a baby. *Sex Roles, 24,* 531–537.

Blakemore, J. E. O. (1993, March). Preschool children's interest in babies: Observation in naturally-occurring settings. Paper presented at the biennial meeting of the Society for Research in Child Development, New Orleans.

Blakemore, J. E. O., LaRue, A. A., & Olejnik, A. B. (1979). Sex-appropriate toy preference and the ability to conceptualize toys as sex-role-related. *Developmental Psychology, 15,* 339–340.

Blanchard, R., & Freund, K. (1983). Measuring masculine gender identity in females. *Journal of Consulting and Clinical Psychology, 51,* 205–214.

Bleakley, M. E., Westerberg, V., & Hopkins, K. D. (1988). The effect of character sex on story interest and comprehension in children. *American Educational Research Association, 25,* 145–155.

Bleier, R. (1988). Sex differences research: Science or belief? In R. Bleier (Ed.), *Feminist approaches to science.* New York: Pergamon Press.

Block, J., von der Lippe, A., & Block, J. H. (1973). Sex role and socialization patterns: Some personality concomitants and environmental antecedents. *Journal of Consulting and Clinical Psychology, 41,* 321–341.

Block, J. H. (1973). Conceptions of sex role: Some cross-cultural and longitudinal perspectives. *American Psychologist, 28,* 512–526.

Block, J. H. (1977). Another look at sex differentiation in the socialization behaviors of mothers and fathers. In J. Sherman & F. Denmark (Eds.), *Psychology of women: Future directions of research* (pp. 29–87). New York: Psychological Dimensions.

Block, J. H. (1983). Differential premises arising from differential socialization of the sexes: Some conjectures. *Child Development, 54,* 1335–1354.

Block, J. H., Block, J., & Gjerde, P. F. (1986). The personality of children prior to divorce: A prospective study. *Child Development, 57,* 827–840.

Blyth, D. A., & Foster-Clark, F. S. (1987). Gender differences in perceived intimacy with different members of adolescents' social networks. *Sex Roles, 17,* 595–609.

Blyth, D. A., Hill, J. P., & Thiel, K. S. (1982). Early adolescents' significant others: Grade and gender differences in perceived relationships with familial and nonfamilial adults and young people. *Journal of Youth and Adolescence, 11,* 425–450.

Bock, W. E. (1969). Farmer's daughter effect: The case of the Negro female professionals. *Phylon, 30,* 17–26.

Boggiano, A. K., & Barrett, M. (1991). Strategies to motivate helpless and mastery-oriented children: The effect of gender-based expectancies. *Sex Roles, 25,* 487–510.

Boldizar, J. P., Perry, D. C., & Perry, L. C. (1989). Outcome values and aggression. *Child Development, 60,* 571–579.

Boles, D. B. (1980). X-linkage of spatial ability: A critical review. *Child Development, 51,* 625–635.

Booth, A., Brinkerhoff, D., & White, C. (1984). The impact of parental divorce on courtship. *Journal of Marriage and the Family, 46,* 85–94.

Borja-Alvarez, T., Zarbatany, L., & Pepper, S. (1991). Contributions of male and female guests and hosts to peer group entry. *Child Development, 62,* 1079–1090.

Borman, K. M., & Frankel, J. (1984). Gender inequalities in childhood social life and the adult work life. In S. Gideonse (Ed.), *Women in the workplace: Effects on families* (pp. 55–83). Norwood, NJ: Ablex.

REFERENCES

Boston Globe. (1985, January 19). Foster care controversy resurfaces, pp. 33, 35.

Boston Globe. (1991a, July 8). Ann Landers: The good news about teenagers, p. 34.

Boston Globe. (1991b, April 22). Ann Landers: Super-aggressive girls won't give up, p. 38.

Boston Globe. (1991c, July 10). China jails pair in child case, p. 68.

Boston Globe. (1991d, August 16). Detroit plan for all-male schools halted, p. 70.

Boston Globe. (1991e, October 4). Husband suspected of hiring pair to kill wife is freed.

Boston Globe. (1991f, August 12). Saudi sheik held in India for marrying a 10-year-old, p. 9.

Boston Globe. (1992a, November 10). Ask Beth: Her friend doesn't make time for her anymore, p. 73.

Boston Globe. (1992b, February 20). Ask Beth: Sexual harassment at school, p. 64.

Boston Globe. (1992c, October 1). Ask Beth: Teen's fed up with immature boys, p. 54.

Boston Globe. (1992d, October 1). Dim doll, p. 50.

Boston Globe. (1992e, October 19). Schooled in life, p. 35.

Bosworth, P. (1985, February). Diane Sawyer. *Ladies' Home Journal,* pp. 28–34.

Boulton, M. J., & Smith, P. K. (1990). Affective bias in children's perceptions of dominance relationships. *Child Development, 61,* 221–229.

Bower, B. (1991). Females show strong capacity for aggression. *Science News, 140,* 359.

Bower, T. G. R. (1982). *Development in infancy* (2nd ed.). San Francisco: Freeman.

Bower, T. G. R. (1989). *The rational infant.* New York: Freeman.

Brackbill, Y. (1975). Continuous stimulation and arousal level in infancy: Effects of stimulus intensity and stress. *Child Development, 46,* 364–369.

Bradbard, M. R. (1985). Sex differences in adults' gifts and children's toy requests at Christmas. *Psychological Reports, 56,* 569–570.

Bradbard, M. R., & Endsley, R. C. (1983). The effects of sex-typed labeling on preschool children's information-seeking and retention. *Sex Roles, 9,* 247–260.

Bradley, S. J. (1985). Gender disorders in childhood: A formulation. In B. Steiner (Ed.), *Gender dysphoria: Development, research, management* (pp. 175–188). New York: Plenum Press.

Bradshaw, J. L., & Nettleton, N. C. (1981). The nature of hemispheric specialization in man. *Behavioral and Brain Sciences, 4,* 51-91.

Brenes, M. E., Eisenberg, N., & Helmstadter, G. C. (1985). Sex role development of pre-schoolers from two-parent and one-parent families. *Merrill-Palmer Quarterly, 31,* 33–46.

Britain, S. D., & Coker, M. (1982). Recall of sex-role appropriate and inappropriate models in children's songs. *Sex Roles, 8,* 931–934.

Britton, G., & Lumpkin, M. (1977). *A consumer's guide to sex, race, and career bias in public school textbooks.* Corvallis, OR: Britton and Associates.

Brodzinsky, D. M., Messer, S. B., & Tew, J. D. (1979). Sex differences in children's expression and control of fantasy and overt aggression. *Child Development, 50,* 372–379.

Brookins, G. K. (1985). Black children's sex role ideologies and occupational choices in families with employed mothers. In M. B. Spencer, G. K. Brookins, & W. R. Allen (Eds.), *Beginnings: The social and affective development of black children* (pp. 257–271). Hillsdale NJ: Erlbaum.

Brooks, J., & Lewis, M. (1974). Attachment behavior in thirteen-month-old opposite-sex twins. *Child Development, 45,* 243–247.

Brooks-Gunn, J., & Matthews, W. S. (1979). *He and she: How children develop their sex role identity.* Englewood Cliffs, NJ: Prentice-Hall.

Brooks-Gunn, J., & Ruble, D. N. (1983). The experience of menarche from a developmental perspective. In J. Brooks-Gunn & A. C. Petersen (Eds.), *Girls at puberty: Biological and psychological perspectives* (pp. 155–177). New York: Plenum Press.

Brooks-Gunn, J., & Warren, M. P. (1988). The psychological significance of secondary sexual characteristics in nine- to eleven-year-old girls. *Child Development, 59,* 1061–1069.

Brooks-Gunn, J., & Warren, M. P. (1989). Biological and social contributions to negative affect in young adolescent girls. *Child Development, 60,* 40–55.

Brophy, J., & Good, T. (1973). Feminization of American elementary schools. *Phi Delta Kappan, 54,* 564–566.

Brown, B. B., Clasen, D. R., & Eicher, S. A. (1986). Perceptions of peer pressure, peer conformity dispositions, and self-reported behavior among adolescents. *Developmental Psychology, 22,* 521–530.

Brown, D., Fulkerson, K. F., Furr, S., & Voight, N. L. (1984). Locus of control, sex role orientation, and self concept in black and white third- and sixth-grade male and female leaders in a rural community. *Developmental Psychology, 20,* 717–721.

Brown, J. V., Bakeman, R., Snyder, P. A., Fredrickson, W. T., Morgan, S. T., & Hepler, R. (1975). Interactions of black inner-city mothers with their newborn infants. *Child Development, 46,* 677–686.

Brown, S. R., & Pipp, S. (1991, April). *The role of the appearance-reality distinction and the genital basis of gender in the development of gender constancy.* Paper presented at the biennial meeting of the Society for Research in Child Development, Seattle, WA.

Bryan, J. W., & Luria, A. (1978). Sex role learning: A test of the selective attention hypothesis. *Child Development, 49,* 13–23.

Bryant, B. K. (1982). An index of empathy for children and adolescents. *Child Development, 53,* 413–425.

Bryant, B. K., & Crockenberg, S. B. (1980). Correlates and dimensions of prosocial behavior: A study of female siblings with their mothers. *Child Development, 51,* 529–544.

Bryant, J., & Anderson, D. R. (1983). *Children's understanding of television.* New York: Academic Press.

Bu, K. H. P., & Condry, J. C. (1991, April). *Children's commercials in the U. S. and Korea.* Paper presented at the biennial meeting of the Society for Research in Child Development, Seattle, WA.

Buffery, A. W. H., & Gray, J. A. (1972). Sex differences in the development of spatial and linguistic skills. In C. Ounsted & D. C. Taylor (Eds.), *Gender differences: Their ontogeny and significance* (pp. 123–157). Edinburgh: Churchill Livingstone.

Burhmester, D., & Furman, W. (1987). The development of companionship and intimacy. *Child Development, 58,* 1101–1113.

Burn, E. (1989). Inside the Lego house. In C. Skelton (Ed.), *Whatever happens to little women? Gender and primary schooling* (pp. 139–148). Milton Keynes, England: Open University Press.

Burris, J. (1992, October 15). A new field of dreams: Mass. girls making mark in boys' sports. *Boston Globe*, pp. 1, 19.

Busby, L. J. (1975). Sex role research on the mass media. *Journal of Communication, 25*, 107–131.

Bussey, K., & Bandura, A. (1984). Influence of gender constancy and social power on sex-linked modeling. *Journal of Personality and Social Psychology, 47*, 1292–1302.

Bussey, K., & Bandura, A. (1992). Self-regulatory mechanisms governing gender development. *Child Development, 63*, 1236–1250.

Bussey, K., & Maugham, B. (1982). Gender differences in moral reasoning. *Journal of Personality and Social Psychology, 42*, 701–706.

Bussey, K., & Perry, D. G. (1982). Same-sex imitation? *Sex Roles, 8*, 773–784.

Cacioppo, J. T., & Bernston, G. G. (1992). Social psychological contributions to the decade of the brain. *American Psychologist, 47*, 1019–1028.

Caldera, Y. M., Huston, A. C., & O'Brien, M. (1989). Social interactions and play patterns of parents and toddlers with feminine, masculine, and neutral toys. *Child Development, 60*, 70–76.

Callard, E. D. (1968). Achievement motive of four-year-olds and maternal achievement expectancies. *Journal of Experimental Education, 36*, 14–23.

Callender, C., & Kochems, L. M. (1983). The North American berdache. *Current Anthropology, 24*, 443–470.

Campbell, C. Y. (1988, August 24). Group raps depiction of teenagers. *Boston Globe*, p. 44.

Campbell, D. T. (1967). Stereotypes and the perception of group differences. *American Psychologist, 22*, 817–829.

Cann, A., & Haight, J. M. (1983). Children's perceptions of relative competence in sex-typed occupations. *Sex Roles, 9*, 767–773.

Cann, A., & Newbern, S. R. (1984). Sex stereotype effects in children's picture recognition. *Child Development, 55*, 1085–1090.

Cantor, M. G. (1977). Women and public broadcasting. *Journal of Communication, 27*, 14–19.

Cantor, N. L., & Gelfand, D. M. (1977). Effects of responsiveness and sex of children on adults' behavior. *Child Development, 48*, 232–238.

Cantor, N. L., Wood, D. D., & Gelfand, D. M. (1977). Effects of responsiveness and sex of children on adult males' behavior. *Child Development, 48*, 1426–1430.

Caplan, P. J., MacPherson, G. M., & Tobin, P. (1985). Do sex differences in spatial abilities exist? A multilevel critique with new data. *American Psychologist, 40*, 786–799.

Carlson, V., Cicchetti, D., Barnett, D., & Braunwald, K. (1989). Disorganized/disoriented attachment relationships in maltreated infants. *Developmental Psychology, 25*, 525–531.

Carpenter, C. J., Huston, A. C., & Holt, W. (1986). Modification of preschool sex typed behaviors by participation in adult structured activities. *Sex Roles, 14*, 603–615.

Carpenter, C. J., & Huston-Stein, A. (1980). Activity structure and sex-typed behavior in preschool children. *Child Development, 51*, 862–872.

Carter, D. B., & Levy, G. D. (1991). Gender schemas and the salience of gender: Individual differences in nonreversal discrimination learning. *Sex Roles, 25*, 555–567.

Carter, D. B., & Patterson, C. J. (1982). Sex roles as social conventions: The development of children's conceptions of sex role stereotypes. *Developmental Psychology, 18*, 812–824.

Cazden, C. B., & Michaels, S. (1985, October). *Gender differences in sixth grade children's letters in an electronic mail system.* Paper presented at the Boston University Child Language Conference, Boston, MA.

Charlesworth, W. R., & Dzur, C. (1987). Gender comparisons of preschoolers' behavior and resource utilization in group problem solving. *Child Development, 58*, 191–200.

Charlesworth, W. R., & LaFreniere, P. (1983). Dominance, friendship utilization and resource utilization in preschool children's groups. *Ethology and Sociobiology, 4*, 175–186.

Cherry, L. (1975). The preschool teacher-child dyad: Sex differences in verbal interaction. *Child Development, 46*, 532–535.

Cherry, L. J., & Lewis, M. (1976). Mothers and two-year-olds: A study of sex-differentiated aspects of verbal interaction. *Developmental Psychology, 12*, 278–282.

Cheshire, J. (1982). *Variation in an English dialect.* Cambridge, England: Cambridge University Press.

Cheyne, J. A. (1976). Development of forms and functions of smiling in preschoolers. *Child Development, 47*, 820–823.

Chodorow, N. (1978). The reproduction of mothering: Psychoanalysis and the sociology of gender. Berkeley: University of California Press.

Christian-Smith, L. K. (1990). *Becoming a woman through romance.* New York: Routledge.

Cicirelli, V. G. (1973). Effects of sibling structure and interaction on children's categorization style. *Developmental Psychology, 9*, 132–139.

Cicirelli, V. G. (1975). Effects of mother and older sibling on the problem solving behavior of the younger child. *Developmental Psychology, 11*, 749–756.

Clark, C. (1972). Race, identification, and television violence. In G. A. Comstock, E. A. Rubinstein, & J. P. Murray (Eds.), *Television and social behavior: Vol. 5. Television's effects: Further explorations* (pp. 120–184). Washington, DC: U.S. Government Printing Office.

Clarke-Stewart, K. A. (1973). Interactions between mothers and their young children: Characteristics and consequences. *Monographs of the Society for Research in Child Development, 38*(6–7, Serial No. 153).

Clarke-Stewart, K. A. (1980). The father's contribution to children's cognitive and social development during early childhood. In F. A. Pederson (Ed.), *The father-infant relationship.* New York: Praeger.

Coates, D. L. (1987). Gender differences in the structure and support characteristics of black adolescents' social networks. *Sex Roles, 17*, 667–687.

Coates, J. (1986). *Men, women, and language.* London: Longman.

Cohen, M. (1985, December 1). Critics say textbooks dull, call for higher standards. *Boston Globe,* pp. 1, 28.

Cohn, D. A. (1990). Child-mother attachment of six-year-olds and social competence at school. *Child Development, 61*, 152–162.

REFERENCES

Coie, J. D., Dodge, K. A., Terry, R., & Wright, V. (1991). The role of aggression in peer relations: An analysis of aggression episodes in boys' play groups. *Child Development, 62,* 812–826.

Colby, A., & Kohlberg, L. (Eds.).(1986). *The measurement of moral judgment.* New York: Cambridge University Press.

Colby, A., Kohlberg, L., Gibbs, J., & Lieberman, M. (1983). A longitudinal study of moral judgment. *Monographs of the Society for Research in Child Development, 48*(1–2, Serial No. 200).

Collison, M. N. K. (1991, November 13). Men talk frankly with counselor to assess harassment and acquaintance rape. *Chronicle of Higher Education,* pp. 1, 39–40.

Committee to Eliminate Sexual Discrimination in the Public Schools. (1974). Let them aspire: A plea and proposal for equal opportunity for males and females in the Ann Arbor public schools. In D. Gersoni-Stavn, (Ed.), *Sexism and youth* (pp. 127–160). New York: Bowker.

Condry, J. (1989). *The psychology of television.* Hillsdale, NJ: Erlbaum.

Condry, J., & Condry, S. (1976). Sex differences: A study of the eye of the beholder. *Child Development, 47,* 812–819.

Condry, J. C., & Dyer, S. L. (1977). Behavioral and fantasy measures of fear of success in children. *Child Development, 48,* 1417–1425.

Condry, J. C., & Ross, D. F. (1985). Sex and aggression: The influence of gender label on the perception of aggression in children. *Child Development, 56,* 225–233.

Conger, J. J. (1991). Adolescence and youth: Psychological development in a changing world (4th ed.). New York: Harper & Row.

Connor, J. M., Schackman, M., & Serbin, L. A. (1978). Sex-related differences in response to practice on a visual-spatial test and generalization to a related test. *Child Development, 49,* 24–29.

Connor, J. M., & Serbin, L. A. (1977). Behaviorally based masculine and feminine activity preference scales for preschoolers: Correlates with other classroom behaviors and cognitive tests. *Child Development, 48,* 1411–1416.

Connor, J. M., & Serbin, L. A. (1978). Children's responses to stories with male and female characters. *Sex Roles, 4,* 637–645.

Cook, A. S., Fritz, J. J., McCornack, B. L., & Visperas, C. (1985). Early gender differences in the functional usage of language. *Sex Roles, 12,* 909–915.

Corder-Bolz, C. R. (1980). Mediation: The role of significant others. *Journal of Communication, 30,* 106–118.

Cordua, G. D., McGraw, K. O., & Drabman, R. S. (1979). Doctor or nurse: Children's perceptions of sex typed occupations. *Child Development, 50,* 590–593.

Cornbleth, C., & Korth, W. (1980). Teacher perceptions and teacher student interaction in integrated classrooms. *Journal of Experimental Education, 48,* 259–263.

Corter, C. M. (1973). A comparison of the mother's and a stranger's control over the behavior of infants. *Child Development, 44,* 705–713.

Corter, C. M., & Bow, J. (1976). The mother's response to separation as a function of her infant's sex and vocal distress. *Child Development, 47,* 872–876.

Corter, C. M., Rheingold, H. L., & Eckerman, C. O. (1972). Toys delay the infant's following of his mother. *Developmental Psychology, 6,* 138–145.

Cosmopolitan. (1989, July). Men and women: Our differences are here to stay, pp. 198–201.

Cronin, C. L. (1980). Dominance relations and females. In D. R. Omark, F. F. Strayer, & D. G. Freedman (Eds.), *Dominance relations: An ethological view of human conflict and social interaction* (pp. 299–318). New York: Garland Press.

Cullingford, C. (1984). *Children and television.* New York: St. Martin's Press.

Culp, R. E., Cook, A. S., & Housley, P. C. (1983). A comparison of observed and reported adult-infant interactions: Effects of perceived sex. *Sex Roles, 9,* 1983.

Cummings, E. M., Iannotti, R. J., & Zahn-Waxler, C. (1989). Aggression between peers in early childhood: Individual continuity and developmental change. *Child Development, 60,* 887–895.

Dabbs, J. M., Frady, R. L., Carr, T. S., & Besch, N. F. (1987). Saliva testosterone and criminal violence in young adult prison inmates. *Psychosomatic Medicine, 49,* 174–182.

Dabbs, J. M., & Morris, R. (1990). Testosterone, social class, and antisocial behavior in a sample of 4,462 men. *Psychological Science, 1,* 209–211.

Damico, S., & Scott, E. (1987). Behavior differences between black and white females in desegregated schools. *Equity and Excellence, 23,* 63–66.

Damon, W. (1977). *The social world of the child.* San Francisco: Jossey-Bass.

Davidson, E. S., Yasuna, A., & Tower, A. (1979). The effects of television cartoons on sex-role stereotyping in young girls. *Child Development, 50,* 597–600.

Davis, A. J. (1984). Sex-differentiated behaviors in nonsexist picture books. *Sex Roles, 11,* 1–16.

Davis, D. M. (1990). Portrayals of women in prime-time network television: Some demographic characteristics. *Sex Roles, 23,* 325–332.

Davis, M. (1991, April). *Perinatal sex differences in physiological and behavioral stress reactivity.* Paper presented at the biennial meeting of the Society for Research in Child Development, Seattle, WA.

Dawson, J. L. M. (1967). Cultural and physiological influences on spatial perceptual processes in West Africa. *International Journal of Psychology, 1,* 115–128, 171–185.

DeAngelis, T. (1992, October). The "who am I" question wears a cloak of culture. *APA Monitor,* pp. 22–23.

Dearsley, G. (1990, November 27). He longed to be a girl. *Woman's Own,* p. 7.

DeHart, G., & Smith, B. (1991, April). *The role of age and gender composition in sibling pretend play.* Paper presented at the biennial meeting of the Society for Research in Child Development, Seattle, WA.

de Klerk, V. (1990). Slang: A male domain? *Sex Roles, 22,* 589–606.

Delamont, S. (1990). *Sex roles and the school* (2nd ed.). London: Routledge.

DeLoache, J. S., Cassidy, D. J., & Carpenter, J. C. (1987). The three bears are all boys: Mothers' gender labeling of neutral picture book characters. *Sex Roles, 19,* 785–799.

Denver Post. (1992, October 18). Barbie's negative vibes get the ax, p. 1.

Desor, J. A., Maller, O., & Turner, R. A. (1973). Taste in acceptance of sugars in human infants. *Journal of Comparative Physiological Psychology, 84,* 496–501.

Diamond, A. (1985). Development of the ability to use recall to guide action, as indicated by infants' performance on the AB̄. *Child Development, 56,* 868–883.

Diamond, M. (1982). Sexual identity, monozygotic twins reared in discordant sex roles and a BBC follow-up. *Archives of Sexual Behavior, 11,* 181–185.

Diaz, R. M., & Berndt, T. J. (1982). Children's knowledge of a best friend: Fact or fancy? *Developmental Psychology, 18,* 787–794.

Dino, G. A., Barnett, M. A., & Howard, J. A. (1984). Children's expectations of sex differences in parents' responses to sons and daughters encountering interpersonal problems. *Sex Roles, 11,* 709–717.

DiPietro, J. A. (1981). Rough and tumble play: A function of gender. *Developmental Psychology, 17,* 50–58.

Dodge, K. A. (1980). Social cognition and children's aggressive behavior. *Child Development, 51,* 162–170.

Doescher, S. M., & Sugawara, A. I. (1990). Sex role flexibility and prosocial behavior among preschool children. *Sex Roles, 22,* 111–123.

Doherty, W. J., & Needle, R. H. (1991). Psychological adjustment and substance abuse among adolescents before and after a divorce. *Child Development, 62,* 328–337.

Donahue, P. (1985). *The human animal.* New York: Simon & Schuster.

Donenberg, G. R., & Hoffman, L. W. (1988). Gender differences in moral development. *Sex Roles, 18,* 701–717.

Douvan, E., & Adelson, J. (1966). *The adolescent experience.* New York: Wiley.

Doyle, J. A., & Paludi, M. A. (1991). *Sex and gender: The human experience* (2nd ed.). Dubuque IA: William C. Brown.

Drabman, R. S., Robertson, S. J., Patterson, J. N., Jarvie, G. J., Hammer, D., & Cordua, C. (1981). Children's perceptions of media-portrayed sex roles. *Sex Roles, 7,* 379–389.

Dubignon, J., Campbell, D., Curtis, M., & Parrington, M. (1969). The relation between laboratory measures of sucking, food intake, and perinatal factors during the newborn period. *Child Development, 40,* 1107–1120.

Dubow, E. F., Huesmann, L. R., & Eron, L. D. (1987). Childhood correlates of adult ego development. *Child Development, 58,* 859–869.

Dunn, D. A., Gustafson, G. E., & Budzik, K. (1992, November). *The acquisition of caregiving behaviors in boys 5 to 9 years of age.* Paper presented at the New England Psychological Association meeting, Fairfield, CT.

Dunn, J. (1985). *Sisters and brothers.* Cambridge, MA: Harvard University Press.

Durkin, K. (1985). *Television, sex roles and children.* Milton Keynes, England: Open University Press.

Durkin, K., & Hutchins, G. (1984). Challenging traditional sex role stereotypes via careers education broadcasts: The reactions of young secondary school pupils. *Journal of Educational Television, 10,* 25–33.

Dusek, J. B., & Joseph, G. (1983). The bases of teacher expectancies: A meta-analysis. *Journal of Educational Psychology, 75,* 327–346.

Dweck, C. S. (1981). Learned helplessness and negative evaluation. In E. M. Hetherington & R. D. Parke (Eds.), *Contemporary readings in child psychology* (2nd ed. pp. 360–366). New York: McGraw-Hill.

Eagly, A. H., & Crowley, M. (1986). Gender and helping behavior: A meta-analytic review of the social psychological literature. *Psychological Bulletin, 100,* 283–308.

Eagly, A. H., & Steffen, V. J. (1986). Gender and aggressive behavior: A meta-analytic review of the social psychological literature. *Psychological Bulletin, 100,* 309–330.

Eaton, W. O., & Enns, L. R. (1986). Sex differences in human motor activity level. *Psychological Bulletin, 100,* 19–28.

Eaton, W. O., & VonBargen, D. (1981). Asynchronous development of gender understanding in preschool children. *Child Development, 52,* 1020–1027.

Eaton, W. O., VonBargen, D., & Keats, J. G. (1981). Gender understanding and dimensions of preschooler activity choice: Sex stereotypes versus activity level. *Canadian Journal of Behavioral Science, 13,* 203–209.

Ebomoyi, E. (1987). Prevalence of female circumcision in two Nigerian communities. *Sex Roles, 17,* 139–151.

Eccles, J. E., Adler, T. F., Futterman, R., Goff, S. B., Kaczala, C. M., Meece, J. L., & Midgely, C. (1983). Expectancies, values, and academic behaviors. In J. T. Spence (Ed.), *Achievement and achievement motives* (pp. 75–146). San Francisco: Freeman.

Eccles, J. S., & Blumenfeld, P. C. (1985). Classroom experiences and student gender: Are there differences and do they matter? In L. C. Wilkinson & C. B. Marrett (Eds.), *Gender influences in classroom interactions* (pp. 79–114). New York: Academic Press.

Eccles, J. S., & Jacobs, J. E. (1986). Social forces shape math attitudes and performance. *Signs, 11,* 367–380.

Edelsky, C. (1977). Acquisition of an aspect of communicative competence: Learning what it means to talk like a lady. In S. Ervin-Tripp & C. Mitchell-Kernan (Eds.), *Child discourse* (pp. 225–243). New York: Academic Press.

Eder, D. (1985). The cycle of popularity: Interpersonal relations among female adolescents. *Sociology of Education, 58,* 154–165.

Eder, D., & Hallinan, M. T. (1978). Sex differences in children's friendships. *American Sociological Review, 43,* 237–250.

Edwards, J. R. (1979). Social class differences and the identification of sex in children's speech. *Journal of Child Language, 6,* 121–127.

Ehrhardt, A. A., & Baker, S. W. (1974). Fetal androgens, human central nervous system differentiation, and behavior sex differences. In Richard C. Friedman, R. M. Richart, & R. L. Vande Wiele (Eds.), *Sex differences in behavior* (pp. 33–51). New York: Wiley.

Ehrhardt, A. A., Grisanti, G., & McCauley, E. A. (1979). Female-to-male transsexuals compared to lesbians: Behavioral patterns of childhood and adolescent development. *Archives of Sexual Behavior, 8,* 481–490.

Ehrhardt, A. A., & Meyer-Bahlburg, H. F. L. (1981). Effects of prenatal sex hormones on gender related behavior. *Science, 211,* 1312–1318.

Eisenberg, N., Cameron, E., Tryon, K., & Dodez, R. (1981). Socialization of prosocial behavior in the preschool classroom. *Developmental Psychology, 17,* 773–782.

Eisenberg, N., Murray, E., & Hite, T. (1982). Children's reasoning regarding sex typed toy choices. *Child Development, 53,* 81–86.

Eisenberg, N., Wolchik, S. A., Hernandez, R., & Pasternack, J. F. (1985). Parental socialization of young children's play: A short-term longitudinal study. *Child Development, 56,* 1506–1513.

Eisenstock, B. (1984). Sex role differences in children's identification with counter-stereotypical televised portrayals. *Sex Roles, 10,* 417–430.

Eklund, P. L. E., Gooren, L. J. G., & Bezemer, P. D. (1988). Prevalence of transsexualism in the Netherlands. *British Journal of Psychiatry, 152,* 638–640.

Elkind, D. (1984). All grown up and no place to go. Reading, MA: Addison Wesley.

Ellis, S., Rogoff, B., & Cromer, C. C. (1981). Age segregation in children's social interaction. *Developmental Psychology, 17,* 399–407.

Eme, R. F. (1979). Sex differences in childhood psychopathology: A review. *Psychological Bulletin, 86,* 574–595.

Emmerich, W. (1981). Non-monotonic developmental trends in social cognition: The case of gender constancy. In S. Strauss (Ed.), *U-shaped behavioral growth* (pp. 249–269). New York: Academic Press.

Emmerich, W., & Shepard, K. (1984). Cognitive factors in the development of sex-typed preferences. *Sex Roles, 11,* 997–1007.

Entwisle, D. R., & Baker, D. P. (1983). Gender and young children's expectations for performance in arithmetic. *Developmental Psychology, 19,* 200–209.

Erikson, E. H. (1963). *Childhood and society* (2nd ed.). New York: Norton.

Erikson, E. H. (1968). *Identity, youth, and crisis.* New York: Norton.

Erkut, S. (1983). Exploring sex differences in expectancy, attribution, and academic achievement. *Sex Roles, 9,* 217–231.

Eron, L. D., Husemann, L. R., Brice, P., Fischer, P., & Mermelstein, R. (1983). Age trends in the development of aggression, sex typing, and related television habits. *Developmental Psychology, 19,* 71–77.

Esposito, A. (1979). Sex differences in children's conversation. *Language and Speech, 22,* 213–220.

Etaugh, C., Collins, G., & Gerson, A. (1975). Reinforcement of sex-typed behaviors of two-year-old children in a nursery school setting. *Developmental Psychology, 11,* 255.

Evans, E. D., Rutberg, J., Sather, C., & Turner, C. (1991). Content analysis of contemporary teen magazines for adolescent females. *Youth and Society, 23,* 99–120.

Fagan, J. F. (1979). The origins of facial pattern perception. In M. H. Bornstein & W. Kessen (Eds.), *Psychology development from infancy: Image to intention* (pp. 83–113). Hillsdale, NJ: Erlbaum.

Fagot, B. I. (1974). Sex differences in toddlers' behavior and parental reaction. *Developmental Psychology, 10,* 554–558.

Fagot, B. I. (1977). Consequences of moderate cross-gender behavior in children. *Child Development, 48,* 902–907.

Fagot, B. I. (1978). The influence of sex of child on parental reactions to toddler children. *Child Development, 49,* 459–465.

Fagot, B. I. (1981). Male and female teachers: Do they treat boys and girls differently? *Sex Roles, 7,* 263–271.

Fagot, B. I. (1985a). Beyond the reinforcement principle: Another step toward understanding sex role development. *Developmental Psychology, 21,* 1097–1104.

Fagot, B. I. (1985b). Changes in thinking about early sex role development. *Developmental Review, 5,* 83–98.

Fagot, B. I. (1991, April). *Peer relations in boys and girls from two to seven.* Paper presented at the biennial meeting of the Society for Research in Child Development, Seattle, WA.

Fagot, B. I., & Hagan, R. (1985). Aggression in toddlers: Responses to the assertive acts of boys and girls. *Sex Roles, 12,* 341–351.

Fagot, B. I., & Hagan, R. (1991). Observation of parent reactions to sex-stereotyped behaviors: Age and sex effects. *Child Development, 62,* 617–628.

Fagot, B. I., Hagan, R., Leinbach, M. D., & Kronsberg, S. (1985). Differential reactions to assertive and communicative acts of toddler boys and girls. *Child Development, 56,* 1499–1505.

Fagot, B. I., & Kavanagh, K. (1990). Sex differences in response to the stranger in the Strange Situation. *Sex Roles, 23,* 123–132.

Fagot, B. I., & Leinbach, M. D. (1989). The young child's gender schema: Environmental input, internal organization. *Child Development, 60,* 663–672.

Faison, S. (1991, September 15). Teen-age girl found chained in Bronx residence. *New York Times,* p. L35.

Falbo, T., & Polit, D. F. (1986). Quantitative review of the only child literature: Research evidence and theory development. *Psychological Bulletin, 100,* 176–189.

Farylo, B., & Paludi, M. A. (1985). Research with the Draw-A-Person test: Conceptual and methodological issues. *Journal of Psychology, 119,* 575–580.

Fausto-Sterling, A. (1985). *Myths of gender: Biological theories about women and men.* New York: Basic Books.

Fein, G., Johnson, D., Kosson, N., Stork, L., & Wasserman, L. (1975). Sex stereotypes and preferences in the toy choices of 20-month-old boys and girls. *Developmental Psychology, 11,* 527–528.

Feingold, A. (1988). Cognitive gender differences are disappearing. *American Psychologist, 43,* 95–103.

Feinman, S. (1981). Why is cross-sex-role behavior more approved for girls than for boys? A status characteristic approach. *Sex Roles, 7,* 289–299.

Feldman, P. (1984). The homosexual preference. In K. Howells (Ed.), *The psychology of sexual diversity* (pp. 5–41). Oxford, England: Basil Blackwell.

Feldman, S. S., & Nash, S. C. (1977). The influence of age and sex on responsiveness to babies. *Developmental Psychology, 16,* 675–676.

Feldstein, J. H., & Feldstein, S. (1982). Sex differences on televised toy commercials. *Sex Roles, 8,* 581–587.

Feminists on Children's Literature. (1971). A feminist look at children's books. *School Library Journal, 17,* 19–24.

Field, T. M. (1978). Interaction patterns of primary versus secondary caretaker fathers. *Developmental Psychology, 14*, 183–185.

Field, T. M. (1979). Visual and cardiac responses to animate and inanimate faces by young term and preterm infants. *Child Development, 50*, 188–194.

Fine, G. A. (1986). The dirty play of little boys. *Society, 24*, 63–67.

Fine, M. (1991). *Framing dropouts: Notes on the politics of an urban public high school.* Albany: State University of New York Press.

Fisher, A. E. (1956). Maternal and sexual behavior induced by intracranial chemical stimulation. *Science, 124*, 228–229.

Fisk, W. R. (1985). Responses to "neutral" pronoun presentations and the development of sex-biased responding. *Developmental Psychology, 21*, 481–485.

Fiske, S. T., Bersoff, D. N., Borgida, E., Deaux, K., & Heilman, M. E. (1991). Social science research on trial: Use of sex stereotyping research in *Price Waterhouse v. Hopkins. American Psychologist, 46*, 1049–1060.

Flanagan, C. A. (1990). Change in family work status: Effects on parent-adolescent decision-making. *Child Development, 61*, 163–177.

Fleming, M. Z., MacGowan, B. R., Robinson, L., Spitz, J., & Salt, P. (1982). The body image of the post-operative female-to-male transsexual. *Journal of Consulting and Clinical Psychology, 50*, 461–462.

Flerx, V. C., Fidler, D. S., & Rodgers, R. W. (1976). Sex role stereotypes: Developmental aspects and early intervention. *Child Development, 47*, 998–1007.

Fox, L. H., & Cohn, S. J. (1980). Sex differences in the development of precocious mathematical talent. In L. H. Fox, L. Brody, & D. Tobin (Eds.), *Women and the mathematical mystique* (pp. 94–112). Baltimore, MD: Johns Hopkins University Press.

Fox, N. A., Kimmerly, N. L., & Schafer, W. D. (1991). Attachment to mother/attachment to father: A meta-analysis. *Child Development, 62*, 210–225.

Frankel, M. T., & Rollins, H. A., Jr. (1983). Does mother know best? Mothers and fathers interacting with preschool sons and daughters. *Developmental Psychology, 19*, 694–702.

Freedman, D. G. (1980). Cross-cultural notes on status hierarchies. In D. R. Omark, F. F. Strayer, & D. G. Freedman (Eds.), *Dominance relations: An ethological view of human conflict and social interaction* (pp. 335–340). New York: Garland Press.

Freeman, M. G., Graves, W. L., & Thompson, R. L. (1970). Indigent Negro and Caucasian birth weight–gestational age tables. *Pediatrics, 46*, 9–15.

Freiberg, P. (1991, May). Separate classes for black males? *APA Monitor*, pp. 1, 47.

Frenkel, K. A. (1990, November). Women and computing. *Communications of the ACM*, pp. 34–46.

Freudigman, K. A., & Thoman, E. B. (1991, April). *Newborn sleep: Effects of age, sex and mode of delivery.* Paper presented at the biennial meeting of the Society for Research in Child Development, Seattle, WA.

Frey, K. S., & Ruble, D. N. (1992). Gender constancy and the "cost" of sex-typed behavior: A test of the conflict hypothesis. *Developmental Psychology, 28*, 714–721.

Friedan, B. (1983). *The feminine mystique.* New York: Dell. (Originally published 1963)

Friedman, E. A., & Neff, R. K. (1987). *Labor and delivery: Impact on the offspring.* Littleton, MA: PSG Publishing.

Frisch, H. L. (1977). Sex stereotypes in adult-infant play. *Child Development, 48,* 1671–1675.

Frodi, A., Macaulay, J., & Thome, P. R. (1977). Are women always less aggressive than men? A review of the experimental literature. *Psychological Bulletin, 84,* 634–660.

Frodi, A. M., & Lamb, M. E. (1978). Sex differences in responsiveness to infants: A developmental study of psychophysiological and behavioral responses. *Child Development, 49,* 1182–1188.

Frodi, A. M., Lamb, M. E., Leavitt, L. A., Donovan, W. L., Neff, C., & Sherry, D. (1978). Fathers' and mothers' responses to the faces and cries of normal and premature infants. *Developmental Psychology, 14,* 490–498.

Frueh, T., & McGhee, P. E. (1975). Traditional sex role development and amount of time spent watching television. *Developmental Psychology, 11,* 109.

Fry, D. P. (1988). Intercommunity differences in aggression among Zapotec children. *Child Development, 59,* 1008–1019.

Furman, W., & Buhrmester, D. (1985). Children's perceptions of the personal relationships in their social networks. *Developmental Psychology, 21,* 1016–1024.

Gaddis, A., & Brooks-Gunn, J. (1985). The male experience of pubertal change. *Journal of Youth and Adolescence, 14,* 61–69.

Gardner, J. E. (1974). Sesame Street and sex role stereotypes. In D. Gersoni-Stavn (Ed.), *Sexism and youth* (pp. 395–397). New York: Bowker/Xerox.

Garrod, A., & Beal, C. R. (1993). Voices of care and justice in children's responses to fable dilemmas. In A. Garrod (Ed.), *Approaches to moral development: New research and emerging themes* (pp. 59–71). New York: Teachers College Press.

Garrod, A. C., Beal, C., & Shin, P. (1990). The development of moral orientation in elementary school children. *Sex Roles, 22,* 13–27.

Gates, F. L. (1982). Socialization of sex differences in aggression: Peer and parental influences. *Dissertation Abstracts International, 43.* (University Microfilms No. 8213493)

Gaultieri, T., & Hicks, R. E. (1985). An immunoreactive theory of selective male affliction. *Behavioral and Brain Sciences, 8,* 427–441.

Gelman, S. A., Collman, P., & Maccoby, E. E. (1986). Inferring properties from categories versus inferring categories from properties: The case of gender. *Child Development, 57,* 396–404.

Gerbner, G. (1972). Violence in television drama: Trends and symbolic functions. In G. A. Comstock & E. A. Rubinstein (Eds.), *Television and social behavior: Vol. 1. Media content and control* (pp. 28–187). Washington, DC: U.S. Government Printing Office.

Gerwitz, H. B., & Gerwitz, J. L. (1968). Visiting and caretaking patterns for kibbutz infants: Age and sex trends. *American Journal of Orthopsychiatry, 38,* 427–443.

Geschwind, N., & Galaburda, A. M. (1987). *Cerebral lateralization.* Cambridge, MA: MIT Press.

Gibbs, J. (1989). Equal opportunities in Leicestershire. In C. Skelton (Ed.), *Whatever happens to little women? Gender and primary schooling* (pp. 109–121). Milton Keynes, England: Open University Press.

Gilligan, C. (1982). *In a different voice: Psychological theory and women's development.* Cambridge, MA: Harvard University Press.

Gilligan, C., & Attanucci, J. (1988). Two moral orientations: Gender differences and similarities. *Merrill-Palmer Quarterly, 34,* 223–237.

Gilligan, C., Lyons, N. P., & Hanmer, T. J. (Eds.).(1989). *Making connections: The relational worlds of adolescent girls at Emma Willard School.* Cambridge, MA: Harvard University Press.

Gilmore, D. D. (1990). *Manhood in the making: Cultural concepts of masculinity.* New Haven, CT: Yale University Press.

Gladue, B. A. (1987). Psychobiological contributions. In L. Diamont (Ed.), *Male and female homosexuality* (pp. 129–153). Washington, DC: Hemisphere.

Goff, D. M. (1991, April). *Gender differences in expectations for secure attachment behaviors.* Paper presented at the biennial meeting of the Society for Research in Child Development, Seattle, WA.

Gold, D., & Andres, D. (1978). Developmental comparisons between ten-year-old children with employed and unemployed mothers. *Child Development, 49,* 75–84.

Gold, D., Crombie, G., Brender, W., & Mate, P. (1984). Sex differences in children's performance in problem-solving situations involving an adult model. *Child Development, 55,* 543–549.

Gold, D., & Reis, M. (1982). Male teacher effects on young children: A theoretical and empirical consideration. *Sex Roles, 8,* 493–513.

Goldberg, S., Blumberg, S. L., & Kriger, A. (1982). Menarche and interest in infants: Biological and social influences. *Child Development, 53,* 1544–1550.

Goldberg, S., & Lewis, M. (1969). Play behavior in the year old infant: Early sex differences. *Child Development, 40,* 21–31.

Goleman, D. (1990, March 6). As a therapist, Freud fell short. *New York Times,* pp. C1, C12.

Golinkoff, R. M., & Ames, G. J. (1979). A comparison of fathers' and mothers' speech with their young children. *Child Development, 50,* 28–32.

Golub, S. (Ed.).(1983). *Menarche.* Lexington, MA: Heath.

Golumbok, S., Spencer, A., & Rutter, M. (1983). Children in lesbian and single parent households: Psychosexual and psychiatric appraisal. *Journal of Child Psychology and Psychiatry, 24,* 551–572.

Goodchilds, J. D., & Zellman, G. L. (1984). Sexual signaling and sexual aggression in adolescent relationships. In N. M. Malamuth & E. Donnerstein (Eds.), *Pornography and sexual aggression* (pp. 233–243). Orlando, FL: Academic Press.

Goodwin, M. H. (1980). Directive-response speech sequences in girls' and boys' task activities. In S. McConnell-Ginet, R. Borker, & N. Furman (Eds.), *Women and language in literature and society* (pp. 157–173). New York: Praeger.

Goodwin, M. H. (1990). Tactical uses of stories: Participation frameworks within girls' and boys' disputes. *Discourse Processes, 13,* 33–71.

Gordon, S. (1991, July 21). Snakes and snails are behavioral tales. *Boston Globe,* p. A27.

Gorman, C. (1992, January 20). Sizing up the sexes. *Time,* pp. 42–51.

Gorn, G. J., Goldberg, M. E., & Kanungo, R. N. (1976). The role of educational television in changing the intergroup attitudes of children. *Child Development, 47,* 277–280.

Goshen-Gottstein, E. R. (1981). Differential maternal socialization of opposite-sexed twins, triplets and quadruplets. *Child Development, 52,* 1255–1264.

Gottman, J. M. (1986). The world of coordinated play: Same- and cross-sex friendship in young children. In J. M. Gottman & J. G. Parker (Eds.), *Conversations of friends: Speculations on affective development* (pp. 139–191). Cambridge, England: Cambridge University Press.

Gouze, K. R., & Nadelman, L. (1980). Constancy of gender identity for self and others in children between the ages of three and seven. *Child Development, 51,* 275–278.

Graddol, D., & Swann, J. (1989). Gender voices. Oxford, England: Basil Blackwell.

Graham-Bermann, S., & Gest, S. (1991, April). *Sibling and peer relations in socially rejected, average, and popular children.* Paper presented at the biennial meeting of the Society for Research in Child Development, Seattle, WA.

Grant, C. A., & Sleeter, C. E. (1986). Race, class, and gender in education research: An argument for integrative analysis. *Review of Educational Research, 56,* 195–211.

Grant, L. (1983). Gender roles and statuses in school children's peer interactions. *Western Sociological Review, 14,* 58–76.

Grant, L. (1984). Black females' "place" in integrated classrooms. *Sociology of Education, 57,* 98–111.

Gray, J., Cutler, C., Dean, J., & Kempe, C. H. (1976). Perinatal assessment of mother-baby interaction. In R. Helfer & C. H. Kempe (Eds.), *Child abuse and neglect: The family and the community* (pp. 377–392). Cambridge, MA: Ballinger.

Green, R. (1978). Sexual identity of 37 children raised by homosexual or transsexual parents. *American Journal of Psychiatry, 135,* 692–697.

Green, R. (1987). *The "sissy boy syndrome" and the development of homosexuality.* New Haven, CT: Yale University Press.

Green, R., Neuberg, D., & Finch, S. (1983). Sex typed motor behaviors of "feminine" boys, conventionally masculine boys, and conventionally feminine girls. *Sex Roles, 9,* 571–579.

Greenberg, B. (1972). Children's reactions to TV blacks. *Journalism Quarterly, 49,* 5–14.

Greenberg, B. S. (1988). Some uncommon television images and the drench hypothesis. In S. Oskamp (Ed.), *Television as a social issue* (pp. 88–102). Newbury Park, CA: Sage.

Greene, B. (1987). *Be true to your school.* New York: Atheneum.

Greenfield, P., & Lave, J. (1982). Cognitive aspects of informal education. In D. A. Wagner & H. W. Stevenson (Eds.), *Cultural perspectives on child development* (pp. 181–207). San Francisco: Freeman.

Greenfield, P. M. (1984). *Mind and media: The effects of television, video games, and computers.* Cambridge, MA: Harvard University Press.

Greenfield, P. M., Bruzzone, L., Koyamatsu, K., Satuloff, W., Nixon, K., Brodie, M., & Kingsdale, D. (1987). What is rock music doing to the minds of our youth? A first experimental look at the effects of rock music lyrics and music videos. *Journal of Early Adolescence, 7,* 315–329.

Greif, E. B., & Ulman, K. J. (1982). The psychological impact of menarche on early adolescent females: A review of the literature. *Child Development, 53,* 1413–1430.

Grotevant, H. D. (1978). Sibling constellations and sex typing of interests in adolescence. *Child Development, 49*, 540–542.

Grotevant, H. D., & Cooper, C. R. (1985). Patterns of interaction in family relationships and the development of identity exploration in adolescence. *Child Development, 56*, 415–428.

Grusec, J. E. (1991). Socializing concern for others in the home. *Developmental Psychology, 27*, 338–342.

Gunnar, M. R. (1980). Control, warning signals, and distress in infancy. *Developmental Psychology, 16*, 281–289.

Gunnar, M. R., & Donahue, M. (1980). Sex differences in social responsiveness between six months and twelve months. *Child Development, 51*, 262–265.

Gunnar, M. R., Leighton, K., & Peleaux, R. (1984). Effects of temporal predictability on the reactions of 1-year-olds to potentially frightening toys. *Developmental Psychology, 20*, 449–458.

Gunnar-VonGnechten, M. R. (1978). Changing a frightening toy into a pleasant toy by allowing the infant to control its action. *Developmental Psychology, 14*, 157–162.

Hahn, W. K. (1987). Cerebral lateralization of function: From infancy through childhood. *Psychological Bulletin, 101*, 376–392.

Halle, E., Schmidt, C. W., & Meyer, J. K. (1980). The role of grandmothers in transsexualism. *American Journal of Psychiatry, 137*, 496–498.

Hallinan, M. T., & Teixeira, R. A. (1987). Opportunities and constraints: Black-white differences in the formation of interracial friendships. *Child Development, 58*, 1358–1371.

Halpern, D. F. (1986). Sex differences in cognitive abilities. Hillsdale, NJ: Erlbaum.

Halpern, D. F. (1989). The disappearance of cognitive gender differences: What you see depends on where you look. *American Psychologist, 44*, 1157–1158.

Hamilton, M. C. (1988). Masculine generic terms and misperception of AIDS risk. *Journal of Applied Social Psychology, 18*, 1222–1240.

Hamilton, M. C. (1991a). Masculine bias in the attribution of personhood. *Psychology of Women Quarterly, 15*, 393–402.

Hamilton, M. C. (1991b). *Preference for sons or daughters and the sex role characteristics of the potential parent.* Paper presented at the meeting of the Association for Women in Psychology, Hartford, CT.

Hammer, J. (1970). Preference for a male child: Cultural factors. *Journal of Individual Psychology, 26*, 54–56.

Hampshire Life. (1992, August 28). Math myth, pp. 10–14, 25.

Hansen, C. H., & Hansen, R. D. (1988). How rock music videos can change what is seen when boy meets girl: Priming stereotypic appraisal of social interaction. *Sex Roles, 19*, 287–316.

Hare, B. R., & Castenell, L. A. (1985). No place to run, no place to hide: Comparative status and future prospects of black boys. In M. B. Spencer, G. K. Brookins, & W. R. Allen (Eds.), *Beginnings: The social and affective development of black children* (pp. 201–214). Hillsdale, NJ: Erlbaum.

Hare-Mustin, R. T., & Maracek, J. (1990). *Making a difference: Psychology and the construction of gender.* New Haven, CT: Yale University Press.

Harkness, S., & Super, C. M. (1985). The cultural context of gender segregation in children's peer groups. *Child Development, 56,* 219–224.

Harrington, C. C. (1970). *Errors in sex role behavior in teenage boys.* New York: Teachers College Press.

Harris, L. J. (1979). Sex related differences in spatial ability: A developmental psychological view. In C. B. Kopp (Ed.), *Becoming female: Perspectives on development* (pp. 133–181). New York: Plenum Press.

Harris, M. B., & Voorhees, S. D. (1981). Sex role stereotypes and televised models of emotions. *Psychological Reports, 48,* 826.

Harrison, J. (1991). The Escher staircase. *Notices of the American Mathematical Society, 38,* 730–734.

Harter, S. (1975). Mastery motivation and need for approval in older children and their relationship to social desirability response tendencies. *Developmental Psychology, 11,* 186–196.

Hartley, R. E., Hardesty, F. P., & Gorfein, D. S. (1962). Children's perceptions and expressions of sex preference. *Child Development, 33,* 221–227.

Hartshorne, H., May, M. A., & Maller, J. B. (1929). *Studies in the nature of character: II. Studies in service and self-control.* New York: Macmillan.

Hartup, W. W. (1983). Peer relations. In E. M. Hetherington (Ed.), P. H. Mussen (Series Ed.), *Handbook of child psychology: Vol. 4. Socialization, personality, and social development* (pp. 103–196). New York: Wiley.

Hass, A. (1981). Partner influences on sex associated spoken language of children. *Sex Roles, 7,* 925–935.

Haugh, S. S., Hoffman, C. D., & Cowan, G. (1980). The eye of the very young beholder: Sex typing of infants by young children. *Child Development, 51,* 598–600.

Haviland, J. J., & Malatesta, C. Z. (1981). The development of sex differences in nonverbal signals: Fallacies, facts, and fantasies. In C. Mayo & N. M. Henley (Eds.), *Gender and nonverbal behavior* (pp. 183–208). New York: Springer-Verlag.

Haviland, J. M. (1977). Sex-related pragmatics in infants. *Journal of Communication, 27,* 80–84.

Hayden-Thomson, L., Rubin, K. H., & Hymel, S. (1987). Sex preferences in sociometric choices. *Developmental Psychology, 23,* 558–562.

Heller, K. A., & Parsons, J. E. (1981). Sex differences in teachers' evaluative feedback and students' expectancies for success in mathematics. *Child Development, 52,* 1015–1019.

Hemmer, J. D., & Kleiber, D. A. (1981). Tomboys and sissies: Androgynous children? *Sex Roles, 7,* 1205–1217.

Hemp, P. (1991, June 25). Houghton Mifflin's textbook troubles. *Boston Globe,* pp. 37–41.

Henry, T. (1992, August 2). SAT scores see first increase since 1987. *Boston Globe,* p. 3.

Henton, C. L. (1961). The effect of socio-economic and emotional factors on the onset of menarche among Negro and white girls. *Journal of Genetic Psychology, 98,* 255–264.

Herdt, G. H., & Davidson, J. (1988). The Sambia "Turnim-Man": Socialcultural and clinical aspects of gender formation in male pseudohermaphrodites with 5-alpha-reductase deficiency in Papua New Guinea. *Archives of Sexual Behavior, 17,* 33–56.

Hetherington, E. M. (1972). Effects of father absence on personality development in adolescent daughers. *Developmental Psychology, 7,* 313–326.

Hetherington, E. M. (1989). Coping with family transitions: Winners, losers, and survivors. *Child Development, 60,* 1–14.

Hetherington, E. M. (1991). The role of individual differences and family relationships in children's coping with divorce and remarriage. In P. Cowan & E. M. Hetherington (Eds.), *Advances in family research: Vol 2. Family transitions* (pp. 165–194). Hillsdale, NJ: Erlbaum.

Hetherington, E. M., & Camara, K. A. (1984). Families in transition. In R. D. Parke (Ed.), *Review of child development research* (Vol. 7, pp. 398–439). Chicago: University of Chicago Press.

Hill, J. P., & Lynch, M. E. (1985). The intensification of gender related role expectations during early adolescence. In J. Brooks-Gunn & A. C. Petersen (Eds.), *Girls at puberty: Biological, psychological and social perspectives* (pp. 201–228). New York: Plenum Press.

Hill, S. (1991, July 21). Researchers find subtle biases favor boys in science classes. *Boston Sunday Globe,* p. 81

Hines, M., & Shipley, C. (1984). Prenatal exposure to diethylstilbestrol (DES) and the development of sexually dimorphic cognitive abilities and cerebral lateralization. *Developmental Psychology, 20,* 81–94.

Hisock, M., & Kinsbourne, M. (1978). Ontogeny of cerebral dominance: Evidence from time-sharing asymmetry in children. *Developmental Psychology, 14,* 321–329.

Hittleman, J. H., & Dickes, R. (1979). Sex differences in neonatal eye contact time. *Merrill-Palmer Quarterly, 25,* 171–184.

Hodge, R., & Tripp, D. (1986). *Children and television: A semiotic approach.* Stanford, CA: Stanford University Press.

Hoenig, J. (1985). Etiology of transsexualism. In B. Steiner (Ed.), *Gender dysphoria: Development, research, management* (pp. 33–73). New York: Plenum Press.

Hoffman, L. W. (1972). Early childhood expectancies and women's achievement motives. *Journal of Social Issues, 28,* 129–155.

Hoffman, L. W. (1975). The value of children to parents and the decrease in family size. *Proceedings of the American Philosophical Society, 119,* 430–438.

Hoffman, L. W. (1977). Changes in family roles, socialization, and sex differences. *American Psychologist, 32,* 644–658.

Hoffman, L. W. (1991). The influence of the family environment on personality: Accounting for sibling differences. *Psychological Bulletin, 110,* 187–203.

Hoffman, M. L., & Levine, L. E. (1976). Early sex differences in empathy. *Developmental Psychology, 12,* 557–558.

Hogg, M. A., & Turner, J. C. (1987). Intergroup behavior, self stereotyping and the salience of social categories. *British Journal of Social Psychology, 26,* 325–340.

Hohler, B. (1992, October 13). Some see seeds of abuse in culture. *Boston Globe,* pp. 21, 24.

Holden, C. (1988, May). Doctor of sexology. *Psychology Today,* pp. 45–48.

Holland, D. C., & Eisenhart, M. A. (1990). *Educated in romance: Women, achievement and college culture.* Chicago: University of Chicago Press.

Holstein, C. B. (1976). Irreversible, stepwise sequence in the development of moral judgment: A longitudinal study of males and females. *Child Development, 47,* 51–61.

Hort, B. E., Leinbach, M. D., & Fagot, B. I. (1991). Is there coherence among the cognitive components of gender acquisition? *Sex Roles, 24,* 195–207.

Hughes, J. O., & Sandler, B. R. (1988). *Peer harassment: Hassles for women on campus.* Washington, DC: Project on the Status and Education of Women, Association of American Colleges.

Humphreys, A. P., & Smith, P. K. (1987). Rough and tumble, friendship, and dominance in schoolchildren: Evidence for continuity and change with age. *Child Development, 58,* 201–212.

Hunter, F. T., & Youniss, J. (1982). Changes in functions of three relations during adolescence. *Developmental Psychology, 18,* 806–811.

Hunter, M. (1990). *The sexually abused male: Prevalence, impact, and treatment* (Vol. 1). Lexington, MA: Lexington Books.

Hurtig, A. L., & Rosenthal, I. M. (1987). Psychological findings in early treated cases of female pseudohermaphroditism caused by virilizing congenital adrenal hyperplasia. *Archives of Sexual Behavior, 16,* 209–223.

Huston, A. C. (1983). Sex typing. In E. M. Hetherington (Ed.), P. H. Mussen (Series Ed.), *Handbook of child psychology: Vol. 4. Socialization, personality, and social development* (pp. 387–467). New York: Wiley.

Huston, A. C., & Alvarez, M. (1990). The socialization context of gender role development in early adolescence. In R. Montemayor, G. R. Adams, & T. P. Gullotta (Eds.), *From childhood to adolescence: A transitional period?* (pp. 156–179). Newbury Park, CA: Sage.

Huston, A. C., Donnerstein, E., Fairchild, H., Feshbach, N. D., Katz, P. A., Murray, J. P., Rubinstein, E. A., Wilcox, B. L., & Zuckerman, D. (1992). *Big world, small screen: The role of television in American society.* Lincoln: University of Nebraska Press.

Huston, A. C., Greer, D., Wright, J. C., Welch, R., & Ross, R. (1984). Children's comprehension of televised formal features with masculine and feminine connotations. *Developmental Psychology, 20,* 707–716.

Huttenlocher, J., Haight, W., Bryk, A., Seltzer, M., & Lyons, M. (1991). Early vocabulary growth: Relation to language input and gender. *Developmental Psychology, 27,* 236–248.

Hyde, J. S. (1981). How large are cognitive gender differences? *American Psychologist, 36,* 892–901.

Hyde, J. S. (1984a). Children's understanding of sexist language. *Developmental Psychology, 20,* 697–706.

Hyde, J. S. (1984b). How large are gender differences in aggression? A developmental meta-analysis. *Developmental Psychology, 20,* 722–736.

Hyde, J. S., Fennema, E., & Lamon, S. J. (1990). Gender differences in mathematics performance: A meta-analysis. *Psychological Bulletin, 107,* 139–155.

Hyde, J. S., & Linn, M. C. (1988). Gender differences in verbal ability: A meta-analysis. *Psychological Bulletin, 104,* 53–69.

Imperato-McGinley, J., Guerro, L., Gautier, T., & Peterson, R. E. (1974). Steroid 5a-reductase deficiency in man: An inherited form of male pseudohermaphroditism. *Science, 186,* 1213–1215.

Imperato-McGinley, J., Peterson, R. E., Gautier, T., & Sturla, E. (1979). Androgens and the evolution of male-gender identity among male pseudohermaphrodites with 5a-reductase deficiency. *New England Journal of Medicine, 300,* 1233–1237.

Inglis, J., & Lawson, J. S. (1981). Sex differences in the effects of unilateral brain damage on intelligence. *Science, 212,* 693–695.

Intons-Peterson, M. J., & Reddel, M. (1984). What do people ask about a neonate? *Developmental Psychology, 20,* 358–359.

Irvine, J. J. (1986). Teacher-student interactions: Effects of student race, sex, and grade level. *Journal of Educational Psychology, 78,* 14–21.

Jacklin, C. N., DiPietro, J. A., & Maccoby, E. E. (1984). Sex typing behavior and sex typing pressure in child/parent interaction. *Archives of Sexual Behavior, 13,* 413–425.

Jacklin, C. N., & Maccoby, E. E. (1978). Social behavior at thirty-three months in same-sex and mixed-sex dyads. *Child Development, 49,* 557–569.

Jacklin, C. N., & Maccoby, E. E. (1982). Length of labor and sex of offspring. *Journal of Pediatric Psychology, 7,* 355–360.

Jacklin, C. N., Maccoby, E. E., & Dick, A. E. (1973). Barrier behavior and toy preference: Sex differences (and their absence) in the year-old child. *Child Development, 44,* 196–200.

Jacklin, C. N., Wilcox, K. T., & Maccoby, E. E. (1988). Neonatal sex-steroid hormones and cognitive abilities at six years. *Developmental Psychobiology, 21,* 567–574.

Jacobs, B. S., & Moss, H. A. (1976). Birth order and sex of sibling as determinants of mother-infant interaction. *Child Development, 47,* 315–322.

Jacobs, J. E. (1991). Influence of gender stereotypes on parent and child mathematics ability. *Journal of Educational Psychology, 83,* 518–527.

Jacobvitz, D., & Sroufe, L. A. (1987). The early caregiver-child relationship and attention-deficit disorder with hyperactivity in kindergarten: A prospective study. *Child Development, 58,* 1488–1495.

Jennings, S. A. (1975). Effects of sex typing in children's stories on preference and recall. *Child Development, 46,* 220–223.

Jhally, S. (Producer) (1990). *Dreamworlds: Desire/sex/power in rock video* [Videotape]. Amherst, MA: Dept. of Communications, University of Massachusetts at Amherst.

Joffe, C. (1971). Sex role socialization and the nursery school: As the twig is bent. *Journal of Marriage and the Family, 33,* 467–475.

Johnson, E. S., & Meade, A. C. (1987). Developmental patterns of spatial ability: An early sex difference. *Child Development, 58,* 725–740.

Johnson, J. E., & Ershler, J. (1981). Developmental trends in preschool play as a function of classroom program and child gender. *Child Development, 52,* 995–1004.

Johnston, D. K. (1988). Adolescents' solutions to fables in dilemmas: Two moral orientations, two problem solving strategies. In C. Gilligan, J. Ward, J. Taylor, & B. Bardige (Eds.), *Mapping the moral domain* (pp. 49–71). Cambridge, MA: Harvard University Press.

Johnston, J., Ettema, J., & Davidson, T. (1980). *An evaluation of Freestyle: A television series to reduce sex-role stereotypes.* Ann Arbor, MI: Institute for Social Research, University of Michigan.

Jones, C. (1985). Sexual tyranny: Male violence in a mixed secondary school. In G. Weiner (Ed.), *Just a bunch of girls* (pp. 26–39). Milton Keynes, England: Open University Press.

Jones, G. (1989). Gender bias in classroom interactions. *Contemporary Education, 60,* 216–222.

Jurich, A. P., Bollman, S. R., & Moxley, V. M. (1976). Families of hospitalized adolescents: Sex differences. *Psychological Reports, 38,* 883–886.

Kadushin, A., & Seidl, F. W. (1971). Adoption failure: A social work post-mortem. *Social Work, 16,* 32–38.

Kagan, J., Henker, B. A., Hen-Tov, A., Levine, J., & Lewis, M. (1966). Infants' differential reactions to familiar and distorted faces. *Child Development, 37,* 519–532.

Kail, R., Pellegrino, J., & Carter, P. (1980). Developmental changes in mental rotation. *Journal of Experimental Child Psychology, 29,* 102–116.

Kakar, S. (1978). *The inner world: A psychoanalytic study of childhood and society in India.* Delhi: Oxford University Press.

Kakar, S. (1991, April). *Observations on male identity development in Hindu India.* Paper presented at the biennial meeting of the Society for Research in Child Development, Seattle, WA.

Kallen, D. J., & Stephenson, J. J. (1982). Talking about sex revisited. *Journal of Youth and Adolescence, 11,* 11–24.

Kantrowitz, J. (1991, June 25). When Jeffrey became Sarah, the journey had just begun. *Boston Globe,* pp. 53, 57.

Kaplan, H. S. (1983). *The evaluation of sexual disorders.* New York: Brunner/Mazel.

Karlsberg, E. (1992, December). I have an eating disorder. *'Teen,* pp. 96–98.

Katz, P. A. (1986). Modification of children's gender stereotyped behavior: General issues and research considerations. *Sex Roles, 14,* 591–602.

Katz, P. A. (1987). Variations in family constellation: Effects on gender schemata. In L. S. Liben & M. L. Signorella (Eds.), *Children's gender schemata* (pp. 39–56). San Francisco: Jossey-Bass.

Katz, P. A., & Boswell, S. L. (1984). Sex role development and the one-child family. In T. Falbo (Ed.), *The single-child family* (pp. 63–116). New York: Guilford Press.

Katz, P. A., & Walsh, P. V. (1991). Modification of children's gender-stereotyped behavior. *Child Development, 62,* 338–351.

Kee, D. W., Gottfried, A. W., Bathurst, K., & Brown, K. (1987). Left-hemisphere language specialization: Consistency in hand preference and sex differences. *Child Development, 58,* 718–724.

Kemple, K. M. (1991, April). *Toddlers' shyness as related to parental attitudes and behavior: A function of child and parent gender.* Paper presented at the biennial meeting of the Society for Research in Child Development, Seattle, WA.

Kent, D. (1992, December). Sexual response: Guys. *Seventeen,* pp. 50–52.

Kessler, S., Ashenden, D. J., Connell, R. W., & Dowsett, G. W. (1985). Gender relations in secondary schooling. *Sociology of Education, 58,* 34–48.

Kessler, S. J. (1990). The medical construction of gender: Case management of intersexed infants. *Signs, 16,* 3–26.

Kiesler, S., Sproull, L., & Eccles, J. S. (1985). Pool halls, chips, and war games: Women in the culture of computing. *Psychology of Women Quarterly, 9,* 451–462.

Kimball, M. M. (1986). Television and sex role attitudes. In T. M. Williams (Ed.), *The impact of television: A natural experiment in three communities* (pp. 265–301). Orlando, FL: Academic Press.

Kimball, M. M. (1989). A new perspective on women's math achievement. *Psychological Bulletin, 105,* 198–214.

Kimura, D. (1985, November). Male brain, female brain: The hidden difference. *Psychology Today,* pp. 50–52, 54, 55–58.

King, F. (1990, November 11). Born to win—and to lose [Review of *Hustle: The myth, life, and lies of Pete Rose*]. *New York Times Review of Books,* p. 9.

Kinman, J. R., & Henderson, D. L. (1985). An analysis of sexism in Newbery Medal Award books from 1977 to 1984. *Reading Teacher, 38,* 885–889.

Kinsey, A. C., Pomeroy, W. B., & Martin, C. E. (1948). *Sexual behavior in the human male.* Philadelphia, PA: Saunders.

Kirkpatrick, M., Smith, C., & Roy, R. (1981). Lesbian mothers and their children: A comparative survey. *American Journal of Orthopsychiatry, 51,* 545–551.

Kishwar, M. (1987). The continuing deficit of women in India and the impact of amniocentesis. In G. Corea (Ed.), *Man-made women* (pp. 30–37). Bloomington: Indiana University Press.

Kittredge, C. (1992, November 10). Student group says UNH fosters a "rape culture." *Boston Globe,* pp. 25, 28.

Klaus, M. H., & Kennell, J. H. (1983). *Bonding: The beginnings of parent-infant attachment.* New York: Mosby Press.

Klein, P. (1984). Behavior of Israeli mothers towards infants in relation to infants' perceived temperament. *Child Development, 55,* 1212–1218.

Klein, R. P., & Durfee, J. T. (1978). Effects of sex and birth order on infant social behavior. *Infant Behavior and Development, 1,* 106–117.

Kleinke, C. L., & Nicholson, T. A. (1979). Black and white children's awareness of de facto race and sex differences. *Developmental Psychology, 15,* 84–86.

Knight, G. P., & Kagan, S. (1977). Development of prosocial and competitive behaviors in Anglo-American and Mexican-American children. *Child Development, 48,* 1385–1394.

Koblinsky, S. G., Cruse, D. F., & Sugawara, A. I. (1978). Sex role stereotypes and children's memory for story content. *Child Development, 49,* 452–458.

Koff, E., Rierdan, J., & Jacobson, S. (1981). The personal and interpersonal significance of menarche. *Journal of the American Academy of Child Psychiatry, 20,* 148–158.

Koff, E., Rierdan, J., & Silverstone, E. (1978). Changes in representation of body image as a function of menarcheal status. *Developmental Psychology, 14,* 635–642.

Kofman, S. (1985). *The enigma of woman: Woman in Freud's writings.* Ithaca NY: Cornell University Press.

Kohlberg, L. (1966). A cognitive-developmental analysis of children's sex role concepts and attitudes. In E. E. Maccoby (Ed.), *The development of sex differences* (pp. 82–173). Stanford, CA: Stanford University Press.

Kolata, G. (1983). Math genius may have prenatal hormonal basis. *Science, 222,* 1312.

Komarovsky, M. (1976). *Dilemma of masculinity: A study of college youth.* New York: Norton.

Korner, A. F. (1969). Neonatal startles, smiles, erection and reflex sucks as related to state, sex, and individuality. *Child Development, 40,* 1039–1053.

Koso-Thomas, O. (1987). *The circumcision of women: A strategy for eradication.* London: Zed Books.

Kotelchuck, M. (1976). The infant's relationship to the father: Experimental evidence. In M. E. Lamb (Ed.), *The role of the father in child development* (pp. 329–344). New York: Wiley.

Kraemer, H. C., Korner, A. F., & Thoman, E. B. (1972). Methodological considerations in evaluating the influence of drugs used during labor and delivery on the behavior of the newborn. *Developmental Psychology, 6,* 128–143.

Kronsberg, S., Schmaling, K., & Fagot, B. I. (1985). Risk in a parent's eyes: Effects of gender and parenting experience. *Sex Roles, 13,* 329–341.

Kropp, J. J., & Halverson, C. F. (1983). Preschool children's preferences and recall for stereotyped versus nonstereotyped stories. *Sex Roles, 9,* 261–272.

Krull, M. (1986). *Freud and his father.* New York: Norton.

Krupnick, C. G. (1985). Women and men in the classroom: Inequality and its remedies. *Teaching and Learning, 1,* 18–25.

Kuczynski, L., & Kochanska, G. (1990). Development of children's noncompliance strategies from toddlerhood to age 5. *Developmental Psychology, 26,* 398–408.

Kuebli, J., & Krieger, E. (1991, April). *Emotion and gender in parent-child conversations about the past.* Paper presented at the biennial meeting of the Society for Research in Child Development, Seattle, WA.

Kuhn, D., Nash, S. C., & Brucken, L. (1978). Sex role concepts of two and three year olds. *Child Development, 49,* 445–451.

Kurdek, L. A., & Siesky, A. E. (1980). Sex role self concepts of single divorced parents and their children. *Journal of Divorce, 3,* 249–261.

LaFreniere, P., Strayer, F. F., & Gauthier, R. (1984). The emergence of same-sex preferences among preschool peers: A developmental ethological perspective. *Child Development, 55,* 1958–1965.

Lamb, M. E. (1977). Father-infant and mother-infant interaction in the first year of life. *Child Development, 48,* 167–181.

Lamb, M. E., Easterbrooks, M. A., & Holden, G. W. (1980). Reinforcement and punishment among preschoolers: Characteristics, effects, and correlates. *Child Development, 51,* 1230–1236.

Lamb, M. E., Frodi, A. M., Hwang, C., Frodi, M., & Steinberg, J. (1982). Mother- and father-infant interaction involving play and holding in traditional and nontraditional Swedish families. *Developmental Psychology, 18,* 215–221.

Lamb, M. E., & Roopnarine, J. L. (1979). Peer influences on sex role development in preschoolers. *Child Development, 50,* 1219–1222.

Lambert, H. H. (1978). Biology and equality: A perspective on sex differences. *Signs, 4,* 97–117.

Landerholm, E. J., & Scriven, G. (1981). A comparison of mother and father interaction with their six-month-old male and female infants. *Early Child Development and Care, 7,* 317–328.

Langer, P. (1989, July 20). Wife testifies Sudbury man cool to daughter. *Boston Globe*, pp. 25, 31.

Langevin, R. (1985). The meanings of cross-dressing. In B. W. Steiner (Ed.), *Gender dysphoria* (pp. 207–225). New York: Plenum Press.

Langlois, J. H., & Downs, C. (1980). Mothers, fathers and peers as socialization agents of sex-typed play behavior in young children. *Child Development, 51,* 1217–1247.

Langlois, J. H., Ritter, J. M., Roggman, L. A., & Vaughn, L. S. (1991). Facial diversity and infant preferences for attractive faces. *Developmental Psychology, 27,* 79–84.

Latham, A., & Grenadier, A. (1982, October). The ordeal of Walter/Susan Cannon. *Psychology Today*, pp. 64–72.

Leaper, C. (1991). Influence and involvement in children's discourse: Age, gender, and partner effects. *Child Development, 62,* 797–811.

Leaper, C., Bell, S., & Carson, M. (1991, April). *Gender relations in early adulthood: Interactions between same- and cross-gender friends.* Paper presented at the biennial meeting of the Society for Research in Child Development, Seattle, WA.

Leaper, C., Hauser, S. T., Kremen, A., Powers, S., Jacobson, A. M., Noam, G. G., Weiss-Perry, B., & Follansbee, D. (1989). Adolescent-parent interactions in relation to adolescents' gender and ego developmental pathway: A longitudinal study. *Journal of Early Adolescence, 9,* 335–361.

Leaper, C., Smith, L., Sprague, R., & Schwartz, R. (1991, April). *Single-parent mothers, married mothers, married fathers, and the socialization of gender in preschool children.* Paper presented at the biennial meeting of the Society for Research in Child Development, Seattle, WA.

Lederberg, A. R., Chapin, S. L., Rosenblatt, V., & Vandell, D. L. (1986). Ethnic, gender, and age preferences among deaf and hearing preschool peers. *Child Development, 57,* 375–386.

Le Guin, U. K. (1976). The left hand of darkness. New York: Ace.

Leinbach, M. D. (1991, April). *The beginnings of gender: What's happening before age 2?* Paper presented at the biennial meeting of the Society for Research in Child Development, Seattle, WA.

Leinbach, M. D., & Hort, B. E. (1989). *Bears are for boys: "Metaphorical" associations in the young child's gender schemata.* Paper presented at the biennial meeting of the Society for Research in Child Development, Kansas City, MO.

Leinhardt, G., Seewald, A. M., & Engel, M. (1979). Learning what's taught: Sex differences in instruction. *Journal of Educational Psychology, 71,* 432–439.

Lempers, J. D., Clark-Lempers, D., & Simons, R. L. (1989). Economic hardship, parenting, and distress in adolescence. *Child Development, 60,* 25–39.

Lever, J. (1978). Sex differences in the complexity of children's play and games. *American Sociological Review, 43,* 471–483.

Levinson, B. M. (1959). Traditional Jewish cultural values and performance on the Wechsler tests. *Journal of Educational Psychology, 50,* 179–181.

Levitan, T. E., & Chananie, J. D. (1972). Responses of female primary school teachers to sex-typed behaviors in male and female children. *Child Development, 43,* 1309–1316.

Levy, B. (1991). *Dating violence: Young women in danger.* Seattle, WA: Seal Press.

Levy, G. D. (1991, April). *Effects of gender constancy understanding, perception of figure's sex and size, and gender schematization on preschoolers' gender typing.* Paper presented at the biennial meeting of the Society for Research in Child Development, Seattle, WA.

Levy, J. (1969). Possible basis for the evolution of lateral specialization of the human brain. *Nature, 224,* 614–615.

Levy, J., & Reid, M. (1978). Variations in cerebral organization as a function of handedness, hand posture in writing, and sex. *Journal of Experimental Psychology: General, 107,* 119–144.

Lewin, M. (1985). Unwanted intercourse: The difficulty of saying no. *Psychology of Women Quarterly, 9,* 184–266.

Lewis, C. (1986). Early sex role socialization. In D. J. Hargreaves & A. M. Colley (Eds.), *The psychology of sex roles* (pp. 95–117). London: Harper & Row.

Lewis, L. A. (1990). *Gender politics and MTV: Voicing the difference.* Philadelphia PA: Temple University Press.

Lewis, M. (1969). Infants' responses to facial stimuli during the first year of life. *Developmental Psychology, 1,* 75–86.

Lewis, M., & Brooks-Gunn, J. (1979). *Social cognition and the acquisition of self.* New York: Plenum Press.

Lewis, M., Feiring, C., McGuffog, C., & Jaskir, J. (1984). Predicting psychopathology in six-year-olds from early social relations. *Child Development, 55,* 123–136.

Lewis, M., & Weinraub, M. (1979). Origins of early sex role development. *Sex Roles, 5,* 135–153.

Liben, L. S. (1991). Adults' performance on horizontality tasks: Conflicting frames of reference. *Developmental Psychology, 27,* 285–294.

Liben, L. S., & Golbeck, S. L. (1984). Performance on Piagetian horizontality and verticality tasks: Sex related differences in knowledge of relevant physical phenomena. *Developmental Psychology, 20,* 595–606.

Liben, L. S., & Signorella, M. L. (1980). Gender related schemata and constructive memory in children. *Child Development, 51,* 11–18.

Lickona, T. (1983). *Raising good children.* New York: Bantam Books.

Lieberman, M. R. (1972). "Someday my prince will come": Female acculturation through the fairy tale. In D. Gersoni-Stavn (Ed.), *Sexism and youth* (pp. 228–243). New York: Bowker/Xerox.

Liebert, R. M., McCall, R. B., & Hanratty, M. S. (1971). Effects of sex typed information on children's toy preferences. *Journal of Genetic Psychology, 119,* 133–136.

Liebert, R. M., & Sprafkin, J. (1988). *The early window: Effects of television on children and youth* (3rd ed.). New York: Pergamon Press.

Linn, M. C., De Benedictis, T., Delucchi, K., Harris, A., & Stage, E. (1987). Gender differences in National Assessment of Educational Progress items: What does "I don't know" really mean? *Journal of Research in Science Teaching, 24,* 267–278.

Linn, M. C., & Hyde, J. S. (1989). Gender, mathematics, and science. *Educational Researcher, 18,* 17–27.

Linn, M. C., & Petersen, A. C. (1985). Emergence and characterization of sex differences in spatial ability: A meta-analysis. *Child Development, 56,* 1479–1498.

Lipsitt, L. P. (1988). The changing population of bullies. *Brown University Child Behavior and Development Newsletter, 4,* 8.

Lipsitt, L. P., & Levy, N. (1959). Electrotactual threshold in the neonate. *Child Development, 30,* 547–552.

Liss, M. B. (1981). Patterns of toy play: An analysis of sex differences. *Sex Roles, 7,* 1143–1150.

Liss, M. B. (1983). Learning gender-related skills through play. In M. B. Liss (Ed.), *Social and cognitive skills: Sex roles and children's play* (pp. 147–166). New York: Academic Press.

List, J. A., Collins, W. A., & Westby, S. D. (1983). Comprehension and inferences from traditional and nontraditional sex role portrayals on television. *Child Development, 54,* 1579–1587.

Litcher, J. H., & Johnson, D. W. (1969). Changes in attitudes towards Negroes of white elementary school students after use of multiethnic readers. *Journal of Educational Psychology, 60,* 148–152.

Lochel, E. (1983). Sex differences in achievement motivation. In J. Jaspars, F. D. Fineham, & M. Hewstone (Eds.), *Attribution theory and research: Conceptual, developmental, and social dimensions* (pp. 193–220). London: Academic Press.

Lockheed, M. E., & Harris, A. M. (1984). Cross-sex collaborative learning in elementary classrooms. *American Educational Research Association Journal, 21,* 275–294.

Lockheed, M. E., & Klein, S. S. (1985). Sex equity in classroom organization and climate. In S. S. Klein (Ed.), *Handbook for achieving sex equity in education* (pp. 189–217). Baltimore MD: Johns Hopkins University Press.

Lockheed, M. E., Thorpe, M., Brooks-Gunn, J., Casserly, P., & McAloon, A. (1985). *Sex and ethnic differences in middle school mathematics, science and computer science.* Princeton NJ: Educational Testing Service.

Loveday, L. (1981). Pitch, politeness and sexual role: An exploratory investigation. *Language and Speech, 24,* 71–88.

Luecke, D., & Anderson, D. (1993, March). Gender constancy and attention to television. Paper presented at the biennial meeting of the Society for Research in Child Development, New Orleans.

Lummis, M., & Stevenson, H. W. (1990). Gender differences in beliefs and achievement: A cross-cultural study. *Developmental Psychology, 26,* 254–263.

Lyons, N. P. (1989). Listening to voices we have not heard. In C. Gilligan, N. P. Lyons, & T. J. Hanmer (Eds.), *Making connections: The relational worlds of adolescent girls at Emma Willard School* (pp. 30–72). Cambridge MA: Harvard University Press.

Lytton, H., & Romney, D. M. (1991). Parents' differential socialization of boys and girls: A meta-analysis. *Psychological Bulletin, 109,* 267–296.

MacArthur, R. (1967). Sex differences in field dependence for the Eskimo: Replication of Berry's findings. *International Journal of Psychology, 2,* 139–140.

Macaulay, R. K. S. (1978). The myth of feminine superiority in language. *Journal of Child Language, 5,* 353–363.

Maccoby, E. E. (1980). *Social development: Psychological growth and the parent-child relationship.* New York: Harcourt, Brace, Jovanovich.

Maccoby, E. E. (1986). Changing roles of the sexes. In P. Huston & D. M. McNulty (Eds.), *Being male and female: Traditions, changes and dilemmas.* Iowa City, IA: University of Iowa.

Maccoby, E. E. (1988). Gender as a social category. *Developmental Psychology, 24,* 755–765.

Maccoby, E. E. (1990). Gender and relationships. *American Psychologist, 45,* 513–520.

Maccoby, E. E. (1991). Different reproductive strategies in males and females. *Child Development, 62,* 676–681.

Maccoby, E. E., & Jacklin, C. N. (1974). *The psychology of sex differences.* Stanford CA: Stanford University Press.

Maccoby, E. E., & Jacklin, C. N. (1980). Sex differences in aggression: A rejoinder and reprise. *Child Development, 51,* 964–980.

Maccoby, E. E., & Jacklin, C. N. (1987). Gender segregation in childhood. In H. W. Reese (Ed.), *Advances in child development and behavior* (Vol. 20, pp. 239–288). New York: Academic Press.

Maccoby, E. E., Snow, M. E., & Jacklin, C. N. (1984). Children's dispositions and mother-child interaction at 12 and 18 months: A short-term longitudinal study. *Developmental Psychology, 20,* 459–472.

MacDonald, C. T. (1980). Facilitating women's achievement in mathematics. In L. H. Fox, L. Brody, & D. Tobin (Eds.), *Women and the mathematical mystique* (pp. 115–137). Baltimore, MD: Johns Hopkins University Press.

Macfarlane, A. (1977). *The psychology of childbirth.* Cambridge, MA: Harvard University Press.

MacKay, D. G. (1980). Psychology, prescriptive grammer, and the pronoun problem. *American Psychologist, 35,* 444–449.

Mackey, W. E., & Hess, D. J. (1982). Attention structure and stereotypy of gender on television: An empirical analysis. *Genetic Psychology Monographs, 106,* 199–215.

Malatesta, C. Z., Culver, C., Tesman, J. R., & Shepard, B. (1989). The development of emotion expression during the first two years of life. *Monographs of the Society for Research in Child Development, 54*(1–2, Serial No. 219).

Maltz, D. N., & Borker, R. A. (1983). A cultural approach to male-female miscommunication. In J. A. Gumperz (Ed.), *Language and social identity* (pp. 195–215). New York: Cambridge University Press.

Mannarino, A. P. (1976). Friendship patterns and altruistic behavior in preadolescent males. *Developmental Psychology, 12,* 555–556.

Manuel, D. (1991, January 20). Self-esteem in girls: How can it be kept high? *Boston Globe,* pp. A21–22.

Maple, S. A., & Stage, F. K. (1991). Influences on the choice of math/science major by gender and ethnicity. *American Educational Research Association Journal, 28,* 37–60.

Marantz, S. A., & Mansfield, A. F. (1977). Maternal employment and the development of sex role stereotyping in five- to eleven-year-old girls. *Child Development, 48,* 668–673.

Marchand, R. H. (1991, October). Psychological services for persons with traumatic head injury. *Network: Newsletter of the New Hampshire Psychological Organization,* pp. 4–5.

Marcus, D. E., & Overton, W. F. (1978). The development of cognitive gender constancy and sex role preferences. *Child Development, 49,* 434–444.

Margolin, G., & Patterson, G. R. (1975). Differential consequences provided by mothers and fathers for their sons and daughters. *Developmental Psychology, 11,* 537–538.

Markus, H., Crane, M., Bernstein, S., & Siladi, M. (1982). Self-schemas and gender. *Journal of Personality and Social Psychology, 42,* 38–50.

Marshall, W. A., & Tanner, J. M. (1986). Puberty. In F. Falkner & J. M. Tanner (Eds.), *Human growth* (2nd ed., pp. 171–209). New York: Plenum Press.

Martin, C. L. (1985, April). *The influence of sex stereotypes on children's impression formation.* Paper presented at the biennial meeting of the Society for Research in Child Development, Toronto.

Martin, C. L. (1989). Children's use of gender-related information in making social judgments. *Developmental Psychology, 25,* 80–88.

Martin, C. L. (1990). Attitudes and expectations about children with nontraditional and traditional gender roles. *Sex Roles, 22,* 151–165.

Martin, C. L. (1991, April). *Cognitive influences on the development of gender segregation.* Paper presented at the biennial meeting of the Society for Research in Child Development, Seattle, WA.

Martin, C. L, & Halverson, C. F. (1981). A schematic processing model of sex typing and stereotyping in children. *Child Development, 52,* 1119–1134.

Martin, C. L., & Halverson, C. F. (1983a). The effects of sex-typing schemas on young children's memory. *Child Development, 54,* 563–574.

Martin, C. L., & Halverson, C. F. (1983b). Gender constancy: A methodological and theoretical analysis. *Sex Roles, 9,* 775–790.

Martin, C. L., & Little, J. K. (1990). The relation of gender understanding to children's sex-typed preferences and gender stereotypes. *Child Development, 61,* 1427–1439.

Martin, C. L., & Wood, C. H. (1987, April). *Children's sex-typed interest attributions.* Paper presented at the biennial meeting of the Society for Research in Child Development, Baltimore, MD.

Martin, E. (1991). The egg and the sperm: How science has constructed a romance based on stereotypical male-female roles. *Signs, 16,* 485–501.

Martin, J. (1985). *Miss Manners' guide to rearing perfect children.* New York: Penguin Books.

Martin, J. A., Maccoby, E. E., & Jacklin, C. N. (1981). Mothers' responsiveness to interactive bidding and nonbidding in boys and girls. *Child Development, 52,* 1064–1067.

Martyna, W. (1978). What does "he" mean? Use of the generic masculine. *Journal of Communication, 28,* 131–138.

Masson, J. M. (1984). *The assault on truth: Freud's suppression of the seduction theory.* New York: Farrar, Straus & Giroux.

Masters, J. C., & Wilkinson, A. (1976). Consensual and discriminative stereotypy of sex type judgments by parents and children. *Child Development, 47,* 208–217.

McCabe, B. (1992, October 19). Making the world safe for Mario. *Boston Globe,* pp. 34, 37.

McCauley, E., & Ehrhardt, A. A. (1984). Follow-up of females with gender identity disorders. *Journal of Nervous and Mental Disease, 172,* 353–358.

McCauley, E., Kay, T., Ito, J., & Treder, J. (1987). The Turner syndrome: Cognitive deficits, affective discrimination, and behavior problems. *Child Development, 58,* 464–493.

McCloskey, L. A. (1987). Gender and conversation: Mixing and matching styles. In D. B. Carter (Ed.), *Current conceptions of sex roles and sex typing: Theory and research* (pp. 139–153). New York: Praeger.

McConaghy, M. J. (1979). Gender permanence and the genital basis of gender: Stages in the development of constancy of gender identity. *Child Development, 50,* 1223–1226.

McDonald, S. M. (1989). Sex bias in the representation of male and female characters in children's picture books. *Journal of Genetic Psychology, 150,* 389–401.

McGhee, P. E., & Frueh, T. (1980). Television viewing and the learning of sex role stereotypes. *Sex Roles, 6,* 179–188.

McGillicuddy–De Lisi, A. V., De Lisi, R., & Youniss, J. (1978). Representation of the horizontal coordinate with and without liquid. *Merrill-Palmer Quarterly, 24,* 199–208.

McGlone, J. (1980). Sex differences in human brain asymmetry: A critical survey. *Behavioral and Brain Sciences, 3,* 215–263.

McGuire, J. (1991). Sons and daughters. In A. Phoenix, A. Woollett, & E. Lloyd (Eds.), *Motherhood: Meanings, practices and ideologies* (pp. 143–161). London: Sage.

McManus, I. C., & Bryden, M. P. (1991). Geschwind's theory of cerebral lateralization: Developing a formal, causal model. *Psychological Bulletin, 110,* 237–253.

McNeil, J. D. (1964). Programmed instruction versus usual classroom procedures in teaching boys to read. *American Educational Research Journal, 1,* 113–119.

Mednick, B. R., Hocevar, D., Baker, R. L., & Teasdale, T. (1983). Effects of social, familial, and maternal state variables on neonatal and infant health. *Developmental Psychology, 19,* 752–765.

Meece, J. L. (1987). The influence of school experiences on the development of gender schemata. In L. S. Liben & M. L. Signorella (Eds.), *Children's gender schemata* (pp. 57–73). San Francisco: Jossey-Bass.

Meece, J. L., Parsons, J. E., Kaczala, C., Goff, S., & Futterman, R. (1982). Sex differences in math achievement: Toward a model of academic choice. *Psychological Bulletin, 91,* 324–348.

Meehan, A. M., & Janik, L. M. (1990). Illusory correlation and the maintenance of sex role stereotypes in children. *Sex Roles, 22,* 83–95.

Meehan, A. M., & Overton, W. F. (1986). Gender differences in expectancies for success and performance on Piagetian spatial tasks. *Merrill-Palmer Quarterly, 32,* 427–441.

Melson, G. F., & Fogel, A. (1988). The development of nurturance in young children. *Young Children, 43,* 57–65.

Meltz, B. F. (1991, May 25). Round 1 in the battle of the sexes. *Boston Globe,* p. 64.

Mendelsohn, J. (1989). The view from step number 16: Girls from Emma Willard School talk about themselves and their futures. In C. Gilligan, N. P. Lyons, & T. J. Hanmer (Eds.), *Making connections: The relational worlds of adolescent girls at Emma Willard School* (pp. 233–257). Cambridge MA: Harvard University Press.

Mensh, E., & Mensh, H. (1991). The IQ mythology: Class, race, gender and inequality. Carbondale: Southern Illinois University Press.

Meyer, J., & Peter, D. (1979). Sex reassignment: Followup. *Archives of General Psychiatry, 36,* 1010–1015.

Meyer, J. W., & Sobieszek, B. (1972). Effect of a child's sex on adult interpretations of its behavior. *Developmental Psychology, 6,* 42–48.

Meyer, V. F. (1991). A critique of adolescent pregnancy prevention research: The invisible white male. *Adolescence, 26,* 217–222.

Midgley, C., Feldlaufer, H., & Eccles, J. S. (1989). Student/teacher relations and attitudes towards mathematics before and after the transition to junior high school. *Child Development, 60,* 981–992.

Miedzian, M. (1991). *Boys will be boys: Breaking the link between masculinity and violence.* New York: Anchor Books.

Miller, C. L. (1983). Developmental changes in male/female voice classification by infants. *Infant Behavior and Development, 6,* 313–330.

Miller, K. E. (1993, March). *Same-sex and opposite-sex friendship quality and perceived social competence: Developmental overlap.* Paper presented at the biennial meeting of the Society for Research in Child Development, New Orleans.

Miller, M. M., & Reeves, B. B. (1976). Children's occupational sex role stereotypes: The linkage between television content and perception. *Journal of Broadcasting, 20,* 35–50.

Miller, P. H. (1989). *Theories of developmental psychology* (2nd ed.). New York: Freeman.

Miller, P. M., Danaher, D. L., & Forbes, D. (1986). Sex-related strategies for coping with interpersonal conflict in children ages five and seven. *Developmental Psychology, 22,* 543–548.

Minton, C., Kagan, J., & Levine, J. A. (1971). Maternal control and obedience in the two-year-old child. *Child Development, 42,* 1873–1894.

Mischel, W. (1961). Father absence and delay of gratification. *Journal of Abnormal and Social Psychology, 62,* 116–124.

Mischel, W. (1966). A social learning view of sex differences in behavior. In E. E. Maccoby (Ed.), *The development of sex differences* (pp. 56–81). Stanford, CA: Stanford University Press.

Mitchell, J. (1974). *Psychoanalysis and feminism.* New York: Pantheon.

Mitchell, J. E., Baker, L. A., & Jacklin, C. N. (1989). Masculinity and femininity in twin children: Genetic and environmental factors. *Child Development, 60,* 1475–1485.

Mittwoch, U. (1988). The race to be male. *New Scientist, 120,* 38-42.

Molnar, J. M., & Weisz, J. R. (1981). The pursuit of mastery by preschool boys and girls: An observational study. *Child Development, 52,* 724–727.

Money, J., & Ehrhardt, A. (1972). *Man and woman, boy and girl.* Baltimore, MD: Johns Hopkins University Press.

Money, J., & Matthews, D. (1982). Prenatal exposure to virilizing progestins: An adult follow-up study of twelve women. *Archives of Sexual Behavior, 11,* 73–83.

Money, J., & Tucker, P. (1975). *Sexual signatures: On being a man or a woman.* Boston: Little, Brown.

Monroe, R. L., & Monroe, R. H. (1971). Effect of environmental experience on spatial ability in an East African society. *Journal of Social Psychology, 83,* 3–10.

Montemayor, R. (1974). Children's performance in a game and their attraction to it as a function of sex-typed labels. *Child Development, 45,* 152–156.

Montemayor, R., & Van Komen, R. (1985). The development of sex differences in friendship patterns and peer group structure during adolescence. *Journal of Early Adolescence, 5,* 285–294.

Morgan, M. (1982). Television and adolescents' sex role stereotypes: A longitudinal study. *Journal of Personality and Social Psychology, 43,* 947–955.

Morgan, M. (1987). Television, sex-role attitudes, and sex-role behavior. *Journal of Early Adolescence, 7,* 269–282.

Morgan, M., & Rothschild, N. (1983). Impact of the new television technology: Cable TV, peers, and sex-role cultivation in the electronic environment. *Youth and Society, 15,* 33–50.

Morse, L. W., & Handley, H. M. (1985). Listening to adolescents: Gender differences in science classroom interaction. In L. C. Wilkerson & C. B. Marrett (Eds.), *Gender influences in classroom interaction* (pp. 37–56). Orlando, FL: Academic Press.

Morse, S. (1992, September 25). Parker fights to be heard. [Interview with Graham Parker]. *Boston Globe,* p. 42.

Moss, H. A. (1967). Sex, age, and state as determinants of mother-infant interaction. *Merrill-Palmer Quarterly, 13,* 19–36.

Moss, H. A., & Robson, K. S. (1968). Maternal influences in early social visual behavior. *Child Development, 39,* 401–408.

Moulton, J., Robinson, G., & Elias, C. (1978). Sex bias in language use: "Neutral" pronouns that aren't. *American Psychologist, 33,* 1032–1036.

Mullen, M. K. (1990). Children's classifications of nature and artifact pictures into female and male categories. *Sex Roles, 23,* 577–587.

Munroe, R. H., Shimmin, H. S., & Munroe, R. L. (1984). Gender understanding and sex role preference in four cultures. *Developmental Psychology, 20,* 673–682.

Murrell, P. (1993). Afrocentric immersion: Academic and personal development of African American males in public schools. In T. Perry & J. Fraser (Eds.), *Freedom's plow: Teaching for a multicultural democracy* (pp. 231–250). New York: Routledge.

Nash, S. C. (1975). The relationship among sex role stereotyping, sex role preference and the sex difference in spatial visualization. *Sex Roles, 1,* 15–32.

Nash, S. C., & Feldman, S. S. (1981). Sex-related differences in the relationship between sibling status and responsivity to babies. *Sex Roles, 7,* 1035–1042.

Nelson-LeGall, S., & DeCooke, P. A. (1987). Same-sex and cross-sex help exchanges in the classroom. *Journal of Educational Psychology, 79,* 67–71.

New York Times. (1989, February 13). Computing in America: A masculine mystique, pp. A1, B10.

New York Times. (1991, May 1). Children's TV, where boys are king, p. 1.

Newcombe, N., & Bandura, M. M. (1983). Age at puberty and spatial ability. *Developmental Psychology, 19,* 215–222.

Newcombe, N., & Dubas, J. S. (1987, April). *A longitudinal study of predictors of spatial ability in adolescent females.* Paper presented at the biennial meeting of the Society for Research in Child Development, Baltimore, MD.

Newman, R. S. (1989, April). *Developmental differences in children's motivation for academic help-seeking.*

Paper presented at the biennial meeting of the Society for Research in Child Development, Kansas City, MO.

Newson, J., & Newson, E. (1968). *Four years old in an urban community*. Chicago: Aldine.

Newson, J., & Newson, E. (1986). Family and sex roles in middle childhood. In D. J. Hargreaves & A. M. Colley (Eds.), *The psychology of sex roles* (pp. 142–158). London: Harper & Row.

Nisbett, R., & Gurwitz, S. (1970). Weight, sex and the eating behavior of human newborns. *Journal of Comparative Physiological Psychology, 73*, 245–253.

Oakes, J. (1990). Opportunities, achievement, and choice: Women and minority students in science and mathematics. In C. B. Cazden (Ed.), *Review of research in education* (Vol. 16, pp. 153–222). Washington, DC: American Educational Research Association.

Oakley, A. (1980). *Becoming a mother*. New York: Schocken Books.

O'Brien, D. (1977). Female husbands in Southern Bantu societies. In A. Schlegel (Ed.), *Sexual stratification: A cross-cultural view* (pp. 109–126). New York: Columbia University Press.

O'Brien, M., & Huston, A. C. (1985). Activity level and sex stereotyped toy choice in toddler boys and girls. *Journal of Genetic Psychology, 146*, 527–534.

O'Bryant, S. L., & Brophy, J. E. (1976). Sex differences in altruistic behavior. *Developmental Psychology, 12*, 554.

O'Bryant, S. L., & Cortder-Bolz, C. R. (1978). The effects of television on children's stereotyping of women's work roles. *Journal of Vocational Behavior, 12*, 233–244.

Oltmanns, T. F., Neale, J. M., & Davison, G. C. (1991). *Case studies in abnormal psychology*. New York: Wiley.

Olweus, D. (1979). Stability of aggressive reaction patterns in males: A review. *Psychological Bulletin, 86*, 852–875.

Olweus, D. (1980). Familial and temperamental determinants of aggressive behavior in adolescent boys: A causal analysis. *Developmental Psychology, 16*, 644–660.

Olweus, D., Mattsson, A., Schalling, D., & Low, H. (1980). Testosterone, aggression, physical, and personality dimensions in normal adolescent males. *Psychosomatic Medicine, 42*, 253–269.

Omark, D. R., Strayer, F. F., & Freedman, D. G. (Eds.).(1980). *Dominance relations: An ethological view of human conflict and social interaction*. New York: Garland Press.

Osofsky, J. D., & Danzger, B. (1974). Relationships between neonatal characteristics and mother-infant characteristics. *Developmental Psychology, 10*, 124–130.

Osofsky, J. D., & O'Connell, E. J. (1977). Patterning of newborn behavior in an urban population. *Child Development, 48*, 532–536.

Paige, K. (1983). A bargaining theory of menarcheal responses in preindustrialized countries. In J. Brooks-Gunn & A. Petersen (Eds.), *Girls at puberty* (pp. 301–322). New York: Plenum Press.

Paikoff, R. L., & Brooks-Gunn, J. (1990). Physiological process: What role do they play during the transition to adolescence? In R. Montemayor, G. R. Adams, & T. P. Gullotta (Eds.), *From childhood to adolescence: A transitional period?* (pp. 63–81). Newbury Park, CA: Sage.

Paley, V. G. (1984). *Boys and girls: Superheroes in the doll corner*. Chicago: University of Chicago Press.

Palkovitz, R. (1984). Parental attitudes and fathers' interactions with their 5-month-old infants. *Developmental Psychology, 20*, 1054–1060.

Parke, R. D. (1981). *Fathers.* Cambridge, MA: Harvard University Press.

Parke, R. D., Grossmann, K., & Tinsley, B. R. (1981). Father-mother-infant interaction in the newborn period: A German-American comparison. In T. M. Field, A. M. Sostek, P. Vietze, & P. H. Liederman (Eds.), *Culture and early interactions* (pp. 95–113). Hillsdale, NJ: Erlbaum.

Parke, R. D., & Sawin, D. B. (1980). The family in early infancy: Social interactional and attitudinal analyses. In F. A. Pedersen (Ed.), *The father-infant relationship* (pp. 44–70). New York: Praeger.

Parke, R. D., & Slaby, R. G. (1983). The development of aggression. In E. M. Hetherington (Ed.), P. H. Mussen (Series Ed.), *Handbook of child psychology: Vol. 4. Socialization, personality, and social development* (pp. 547–641). New York: Wiley.

Parsons, J. E., Kaczala, C. M., & Meece, J. L. (1982). Socialization of achievement attitudes and beliefs: Classroom influences. *Child Development, 53,* 322–339.

Parsons, J. E., & Ruble, D. N. (1977). The development of achievement-related expectancies. *Child Development, 48,* 1075–1079.

Patterson, C. J. (1992). Children of lesbian and gay parents. *Child Development, 63,* 1025–1042.

Patterson, G. R. (1980). Mothers: The unacknowledged victims. *Monographs of the Society for Research in Child Development, 45*(5, Serial No. 186).

Patterson, G. R., Littman, R. A., & Bricker, W. (1967). Assertive behavior in children: A step toward a theory of aggression. *Monographs of the Society for Research in Child Development, 32* (5, Serial No. 113).

Pattison, P., & Grieve, N. (1984). Do spatial skills contribute to sex differences in different types of mathematical problems? *Journal of Educational Psychology, 76,* 678–689.

Paulsen, K., & Johnson, M. (1983). Sex role attitudes and mathematical ability in 4th-, 8th-, and 11th-grade students from a high socioeconomic area. *Developmental Psychology, 19,* 210–214.

Pauly, I. B. (1968). The current status of the change of sex operation. *Journal of Nervous and Mental Diseases, 147,* 460–471.

Pauly, I. B. (1969). Adult manifestations of male transsexualism. In R. Green and J. Money (Eds.), *Transsexualism and sex reassignment* (pp. 37-87). Baltimore, MD: Johns Hopkins University Press.

Pederson, F. A. (1980). Overview: Answers and reformulated questions. In F. A. Pedersen (Ed.), *The father-infant relationship* (pp. 147-163). New York: Praeger.

Perkins, M. (1983). *Modal expressions in English.* London: Frances Pinter.

Perry, D. G., & Bussey, K. (1979). The social learning theory of sex differences: Imitation is alive and well. *Journal of Personality and Social Psychology, 37,* 1699–1712.

Perry, D. G., & Perry, L. C. (1975). Observational learning in children: Effects of sex of model and subject's sex role behavior. *Journal of Personality and Social Psychology, 31,* 1084–1088.

Perry, D. G., Perry, L. C., & Rasmussen, P. (1986). Cognitive social learning mediators of aggression. *Child Development, 57,* 700–711.

Perry, D. G., Perry, L. C., & Weiss, R. J. (1989). Sex differences in the consequences that children anticipate for aggression. *Developmental Psychology, 25,* 312–319.

Petersen, A. C. (1983). Menarche: Meaning of measures and measuring meaning. In S. Golub (Ed.), *Menarche: The transition from girl to woman* (pp. 63–76). Lexington, MA: Lexington Books.

REFERENCES

Peterson, R. E., Imperato-McGinley, J., Gautier, T., & Sturla, E. (1977). Male pseudoher-maphroditism due to steroid 5a-reductase deficiency. *American Journal of Medicine, 62*, 170–191.

Pettit, G. S., Bakshi, A., Dodge, K. A., & Coie, J. D. (1990). The emergence of social dominance in young boys' play groups: Developmental differences and behavioral correlates. *Developmental Psychology, 26*, 1017–1025.

Phillips, D. (1984). The illusion of incompetence among academically competent children. *Child Development, 55*, 2000–2016.

Phillips, J. (1991). *You'll never eat lunch in this town again.* New York: Signet.

Phillips, S., King, S., & DuBois, L. (1978). Spontaneous activities of females versus male newborns. *Child Development, 49*, 590–597.

Piaget, J. (1965). *The moral judgment of the child.* New York: Free Press. (Originally published 1932)

Picariello, M. L., Greenberg, D. N., & Pillemer, D. B. (1990). Children's sex stereotyping of colors. *Child Development, 61*, 1453–1460.

Pingree, S. (1978). The effects of nonsexist television commercials and perceptions of reality on children's attitudes about women. *Psychology of Women Quarterly, 2*, 262–277.

Pitcher, E. G., & Schultz, L. H. (1983). *Boys and girls at play: The development of sex roles.* New York: Praeger.

Plomin, R., & Foch, T. T. (1983). Sex differences and individual differences. *Child Development, 52*, 383–385.

Pogrebin, L. C. (1980). *Growing up free.* New York: Bantam Books.

Pollak, S., & Gilligan, C. (1982). Images of violence in Thematic Apperception Test stories. *Journal of Personality and Social Psychology, 42*, 159–167.

Pollak, S., & Gilligan, C. (1983). Differing about differences: The incidence and interpretation of violent fantasies in women and men. *Journal of Personality and Social Psychology, 45*, 1172–1175.

Pollak, S., & Gilligan, C. (1985). Killing the messenger. *Journal of Personality and Social Psychology, 48*, 374–375.

Pollitt, K. (1991, April 7). The Smurfette principle. *New York Times Magazine*, pp. 22, 24.

Pomerleau, A., Bolduc, D., Malcuit, G., & Cossette, L. (1990). Pink or blue: Environmental gender stereotypes in the first two years of life. *Sex Roles, 22*, 359–367.

Pooler, W. S. (1991). Sex of child preferences among college students. *Sex Roles, 25*, 569–576.

Poulin-Dubois, D., Serbin, L. A., Kenyon, B., & Derbyshire, A. (1991, April). *Intermodal gender concepts in 12-month-old infants.* Paper presented at the biennial meeting of the Society for Research in Child Development, Seattle, WA.

Powell, G. J. (1982). The impact of television on the self-concept development of minority group children. In G. L. Berry and C. Mitchell-Kernan (Eds.), *Television and the socialization of the minority child* (pp. 105–131). New York: Academic Press.

Power, T. G. (1981). Sex-typing in infancy: The role of the father. *Infant Mental Health Journal, 2*, 226–240.

Powlishta, K. K. (1987, April). *The social context of cross-sex interactions.* Paper presented at the biennial meeting of the Society for Research in Child Development, Baltimore, MD.

Press, A. L. (1991). *Women watching television: Gender, class and generation in the American experience.* Philadelphia: University of Pennsylvania Press.

Preston, R. C. (1962). Reading achievement of German and American children. *School and Society, 90,* 350–354.

Price, W. H., & Whatmore, P. B. (1967). Criminal behavior and the XYY male. *Nature, 213,* 815.

Price-Bonham, S., & Skeen, P. (1982). Black and white fathers' attitudes towards children's sex roles. *Psychological Reports, 50,* 1187–1190.

Pruett, K. D. (1987). *The nurturing father.* New York: Warner.

Purcell, P., & Stewart, L. (1990). Dick and Jane in 1989. *Sex Roles, 22,* 177–185.

Quinn, S. (1987). *A mind of her own: The life of Karen Horney.* New York: Summit Books.

Radin, N. (1982). Primary caregiving and role-sharing fathers. In M. E. Lamb (Ed.), *Nontraditional families: Parenting and child development* (pp. 173–204). Hillsdale, NJ: Erlbaum.

Radke-Yarrow, M., Zahn-Waxler, C., & Chapman, M. (1983). Children's prosocial dispositions and behavior. In E. M. Hetherington (Ed.), P. H. Mussen (Series Ed.), *Handbook of child psychology: Vol. 4. Socialization, personality, and social development* (pp. 469–545). New York: Wiley.

Radway, J. A. (1991). *Reading the romance: Women, patriarchy and popular literature.* Chapel Hill: University of North Carolina Press.

Raloff, J. (1991). Science: Recruiting nontraditional players. *Science News, 140,* 396–397.

Raphael, R. (1988). *The men from the boys: Rites of passage in male America.* Lincoln: University of Nebraska Press.

Raskin, P. A., & Israel, A. C. (1981). Sex role imitation in children: Effects of sex of child, sex of model, and sex role appropriateness of modeled behavior. *Sex Roles, 7,* 1067–1077.

Ray, E. (1991, August 1). All-male black schools put on hold in Detroit. *Boston Globe,* p. 3.

Ray, W. J., Georgiou, S., & Ravizza, R. (1979). Spatial abilities, sex differences, and lateral eye movements. *Developmental Psychology, 15,* 455–457.

Raymond, C. (1992, July). Sex differences in gifted math students' achievement. *APS Observer,* p. 5.

Raymond, C. L., & Benbow, C. P. (1986). Gender differences in mathematics: A function of parent support and student sex typing? *Developmental Psychology, 22,* 808–819.

Rebelsky, F., & Hanks, C. (1971). Fathers' verbal interaction with infants in the first three months of life. *Child Development, 42,* 63–68.

Reese, E., & Fivush, R. (1993, March). Remember when? Gender differences in parent-child conversations about the past. Paper presented at the biennial meeting of the Society for Research in Child Development, New Orleans.

Reid, P. T., Trotter, K. H., & Tate, C. S. (1991, April). *Children's self-presentations with infants: Age, gender, and race comparisons.* Paper presented at the biennial meeting of the Society for Research in Child Development, Seattle, WA.

Reis, H. T., Senchak, M., & Solomon, B. (1985). Sex differences in intimacy of social interaction: Further examination of potential explanations. *Journal of Personality and Social Psychology, 48,* 1204–1217.

Reis, H. T., & Wright, S. (1982). Knowledge of sex role stereotypes in children aged 3 to 5. *Sex Roles, 8,* 1049–1056.

Rekers, G. A. (1979). Psychosexual and gender problems. In E. J. Marsh & L. G. Terdal (Eds.), *Behavioral assessment of childhood disorders.* New York: Guilford Press.

Rekers, G. A., Bentler, P. M., Rosen, A. C., & Lovaas, O. I. (1977). Child gender disturbances: A clinical rationale for intervention. *Psychotherapy: Theory, Research and Practice, 14,* 2–11.

Rekers, G. A., Crandall, B. F., Rosen, A. C., & Bentler, P. M. (1979). Genetic and physical studies of male children with psychological gender disturbances. *Psychological Medicine, 9,* 373–375.

Rekers, G. A., & Jurich, A. P. (1983). Development of problems of puberty and sex roles in adolescence. In C. E. Walker & M. C. Roberts (Eds.), *Handbook of clinical child psychology* (pp. 785–812). New York: Wiley.

Rekers, G. A., Willis, T. J., Yates, C. E., Rosen, A. C., & Low, B. P. (1977). Assessment of childhood gender behavior change. *Journal of Child Psychology and Psychiatry, 18,* 53–65.

Resnick, S. M., Berenbaum, S. A., Gottesman, I. I., & Bouchard, T. J. (1986). Early hormonal influences on cognitive functioning in congenital adrenal hyperplasia. *Developmental Psychology, 22,* 191–198.

Rest, J. (1983). Morality. In J. H. Flavell & E. M. Markman (Eds.), P. H. Mussen (Series Ed.), *Handbook of child psychology: Vol. 3. Cognitive development* (pp. 556–629). New York: Wiley.

Reynolds, P. (1989). *Childhood at crossroads.* Grand Rapids, MI: Eerdmans.

Rheingold, H. L., & Cook, K. V. (1975). The contents of boys' and girls' rooms as an index of parents' behavior. *Child Development, 46,* 445–463.

Richards, M. P., Bernal, J. F., & Brackbill, Y. (1976). Early behavioral differences: Gender or circumcision? *Developmental Psychobiology, 9,* 89–95.

Richmond, P. G. (1980). A limited sex difference in spatial test scores with a preadolescent sample. *Child Development, 51,* 601–602.

Rierdan, J., & Koff, E. (1980). Representation of the female body by early and late adolescent girls. *Journal of Youth and Adolescence, 9,* 339–346.

Riger, S. (1992). Epistemological debates, feminist voices. *American Psychologist, 47,* 730–740.

Riley, M. T., Holmes, D. L., Cornwell, D., & Blume, L. (1985). *The male's role in early childhood education.* Lubbock: Texas Tech University, Dept. of Human Development and Family Studies. (ERIC Document Reproduction Service No. ED 266 863)

Roberto, L. (1983). Issues in diagnosis and treatment of transsexualism. *Archives of Sexual Behavior, 12,* 445–473.

Roberts, C. W., Green, R., Williams, K., & Goodman, M. (1987). Boyhood gender identity development: A statistical contrast of two family groups. *Developmental Psychology, 23,* 544–557.

Roberts, P., & Chambers, D. (1977, January). Sugar and spice and almost always nice: A content analysis of the Caldecotts. *Resources in Education,* p. 587.

Roberts, T. (1991). Gender and the influence of evaluations on self-assessments in achievement settings. *Psychological Bulletin, 109,* 297–308.

Robin, M. (1982). Neonate-mother interaction: Tactile contacts in the days following birth. *Early Child Development and Care, 9,* 221–236.

Robson, K., & Kumar, R. (1980). Delayed onset of maternal affection after childbirth. *British Journal of Psychiatry, 136,* 347–353.

Roche, B. J. (1992, July 13). Playing field still tilts in boys' favor. *Boston Globe,* pp. 17, 24.

Romaine, S. (1984). *The language of children and adolescents.* Oxford, England: Basil Blackwell.

Roopnarine, J. L. (1984). Sex-typed socialization in mixed-age preschool classrooms. *Child Development, 55,* 1078–1084.

Roopnarine, J. L., Talukder, E., Jain, D., Joshi, P., & Srivastav, P. (1990). Characteristics of holding, patterns of play, and social behaviors between parents and infants in New Delhi, India. *Developmental Psychology, 26,* 667–673.

Rose, J. (1989). A parent's voice. In C. Skelton (Ed.), *Whatever happens to little women? Gender and primary schooling* (pp. 11–21). Milton Keynes, England: Open University Press.

Rose, R. M., Gordon, T. P., & Bernstein, I. S. (1972). Plasma testosterone levels in male rhesus: Influence of sexual and social stimuli. *Science, 178,* 643–645.

Rose, R. M., Holaday, J. W., & Bernstein, I. S. (1971). Plasma testosterone, dominance rank and aggressive behavior in male rhesus monkeys. *Nature, 231,* 366–368.

Rosenblatt, J. S. (1969). The development of maternal responsiveness in the rat. *American Journal of Orthopsychiatry, 39,* 36–56.

Rosenblith, J. F., & DeLucia, L. A. (1963). Tactile sensitivity and muscular strength in the neonate. *Biologia Neonatorum, 5,* 266–282.

Rosenhan, D. L., & White, G. M. (1967). Observation and rehearsal as determinants of prosocial behavior. *Journal of Personality and Social Psychology, 5,* 424–431.

Rosenthal, D. A., & Chapman, D. C. (1982). The lady spaceman: Children's perceptions of sex-typed occupations. *Sex Roles, 8,* 959–965.

Rosenthal, M. K. (1983). State variations in the newborn and mother-infant interaction during breast-feeding: Some sex differences. *Developmental Psychology, 19,* 740–745.

Rosenwasser, S. M., Lingenfelter, M., & Harrington, A. F. (1989). Nontraditional gender role portrayals on television and children's gender role perceptions. *Journal of Applied Developmental Psychology, 10,* 97–105.

Ross, D. M., & Ross, S. A. (1972). Resistance by preschool boys to sex-inappropriate behavior. *Journal of Educational Psychology, 63,* 342–346.

Rosser, P. (1989). *The SAT gender gap: Identifying the causes.* Washington, DC: Center for Women Policy Studies.

Rossi, J. S. (1983). Ratios exaggerate gender differences in mathematical ability. *American Psychologist, 38,* 348.

Rothbart, M. K., & Rothbart, M. (1976). Birth order, sex of child, and maternal help-giving. *Sex Roles, 2,* 39–46.

Rothman, B. K. (1986). *The tentative pregnancy.* New York: Viking.

Rubin, J. Z., Provenzano, F. J., & Luria, Z. (1974). The eye of the beholder: Parents' views on sex of newborns. *American Journal of Orthopsychiatry, 44,* 47–55.

Ruble, D. N., Balaban, T., & Cooper, J. (1981). Gender constancy and the effects of sex typed televised toy commercials. *Child Development, 52,* 667–673.

Ruble, D. N., & Brooks-Gunn, J. (1982). The experience of menarche. *Child Development, 53,* 1557–1566.

Rudolph, E. (1991, September). Women's talk. *New York Times Sunday Magazine,* p. 8.

Rueckert, L., Sorensen, L., & Levy, J. (1991, April). *Sex differences in the development of inter-hemispheric communication.* Paper presented at the biennial meeting of the Society for Research in Child Development, Seattle, WA.

Ruhl, S. (1987, June 17). TV dads tend to be either omniscient or incompetent. *Amherst Bulletin,* p. 28.

Sadker, D., & Sadker, M. (1985). The treatment of sex equity in teacher education. In S. S. Klein (Ed.), *Handbook for achieving sex equity in education* (pp. 145–161). Baltimore, MD: Johns Hopkins University Press.

Sadker, M., & Sadker, D. (1985, March). Sexism in the schoolroom of the '80s. *Psychology Today,* pp. 56–57.

Sadker, M., Sadker, D., & Klein, S. (1991). The issue of gender in elementary and secondary education. In G. Grant (Ed.), *Review of research in education* (Vol. 17, pp. 269–334). Washington, DC: American Educational Research Association.

Safir, M. P. (1986). The effects of nature or of nurture on sex differences in intellectual functioning: Israeli findings. *Sex Roles, 14,* 581–590.

Sagar, H. A., Schofield, J. W., & Snyder, H. N. (1983). Race and gender barriers: Preadolescent peer behavior in academic classrooms. *Child Development, 54,* 1032–1040.

St. Peter, S. (1979). Jack went up the hill . . . but where was Jill? *Psychology of Women Quarterly, 4,* 256–260.

Salthouse, T. A., Babcock, R. L., Skovronek, E., Mitchell, D. R. D., & Palmon, R. (1990). Age and experience effects in spatial visualization. *Developmental Psychology, 26,* 128–136.

Santrock, J. W. (1977). Effects of father absence on sex typed behaviors in male children: Reason for absence and age of onset of the absence. *Journal of Genetic Psychology, 130,* 3–10.

Santrock, J. W. (1990). *Adolescence* (4th ed.). Dubuque, IA: William C. Brown.

Santrock, J. W., & Warshak, R. A. (1979). Father custody and social development in boys and girls. *Journal of Social Issues, 35,* 112–125.

Santrock, J. W., Warshak, R. A., & Elliott, G. L. (1982). Social development and parent-child interaction in father-custody and stepmother families. In M. E. Lamb (Ed.), *Nontraditional families: Parenting and child development* (pp. 289–314). Hillsdale, NJ: Erlbaum.

Sarah, E. (1980). Teachers and students in the classroom: An examination of classroom interaction. In D. Spender and E. Sarah (Eds.), *Learning to lose* (pp. 155–164). London: Women's Press.

Savin-Williams, R. C. (1979). Dominance hierarchies in groups of early adolescents. *Child Development, 50,* 923–935.

Savin-Williams, R. C. (1990). *Gay and lesbian youth: Expressions of identity.* New York: Hemisphere.

Saxby, L., & Bryden, M. P. (1984). Left-ear superiority in children for processing auditory emotional material. *Developmental Psychology, 20,* 72–80.

Scarr, S. (1984). *Mother care, other care.* New York: Basic Books.

Schachter, F. F., Gulutz, G., Shore, E., & Adler, M. (1978). Sibling deidentification judged by mothers: Cross-validation and developmental studies. *Child Development, 49,* 543–546.

Schachter, F. F., Shore, E., Hodapp, R., Chalfin, S., & Bundy, C. (1978). Do girls talk earlier? Mean length of utterance in toddlers. *Developmental Psychology, 14,* 388–392.

Schau, C. G., Kahn, L., Diepold, J. H., & Cherry, F. (1980). The relationship to parental expectations and preschool children's verbal sex-typing to their sex-typed toy play behavior. *Child Development, 51,* 607–609.

Schau, C. G., & Scott, K. P. (1984). The impact of gender characteristics on instructional materials: An integration of the research literature. *Journal of Educational Psychology, 76,* 173–183.

Schneider, C. (1987). *Children's television: The art, the business, and how it works.* Lincolnwood, IL: NTC Business Books.

Schneider, J. W., & Hacker, S. L. (1973). Sex role imagery and the use of the generic "man" in introductory texts: A case in the sociology of sociology. *American Sociologist, 8,* 12–18.

Schofield, J. W. (1981). Complementary and conflicting identities: Images of interaction in an interracial school. In S. A. Asher & J. M. Gottman (Eds.), *The development of children's friendships* (pp. 53–90). New York: Cambridge University Press.

Schofield, J. W. (1982). *Black and white in school.* New York: Praeger.

Schumacher, D. (1974). Changing the school environment. In G. Gersoni-Stavn (Ed.), *Sexism and youth* (pp. 113–119). New York: Bowker/Xerox.

Schwartz, L. A., & Markham, W. T. (1985). Sex stereotyping in children's toy advertisements. *Sex Roles, 12,* 157–170.

Sciarra, D. J. (1972). Men in young children's lives make a difference. *Child Care Quarterly, 1,* 111–118.

Science News. (1990a, August 25). Doubt cast on biology of giftedness, p. 124.

Science News. (1990b, July 28). Master gene makes maleness mandatory, p. 61.

Scott, K. P., Dwyer, C. A., & Lieb-Brilhart, B. (1985). Sex equity in reading and communication skills. In S. S. Klein (Ed.), *Handbook for achieving sex equity in education* (pp. 269–279). Baltimore, MD: Johns Hopkins University Press.

Sears, R. R. (1961). Relation of early socialization experiences to aggression in middle childhood. *Journal of Abnormal and Social Psychology, 63,* 466–492.

Seavey, C. A., Katz, P. A., & Zalk, S. R. (1975). Baby X: The effect of gender labels on adult responses to infants. *Sex Roles, 1,* 103–109.

Sedney, M. A. (1987). Development of androgeny. *Psychology of Women Quarterly, 11,* 311–326.

Segel, E. (1986). "As the twig is bent . . . ": Gender and childhood reading. In E. A. Flynn & P. P. Schweickart (Eds.), *Gender and reading* (pp. 165–186). Baltimore, MD: Johns Hopkins University Press.

Serbin, L. A., & Connor, J. M. (1979). Sex-typing of children's play preferences and patterns of cognitive performance. *Journal of Genetic Psychology, 134,* 315–316.

Serbin, L. A., Connor, J. M., Burchardt, C. J., & Citron, C. C. (1979). Effects of peer presence on sex-typing of children's play behavior. *Journal of Experimental Child Psychology, 27,* 303–309.

REFERENCES

Serbin, L. A., Connor, J. M., & Iler, I. (1979). Sex stereotyped and nonstereotyped introductions of new toys in the preschool classroom: An observational study of teacher behavior and its effects. *Psychology of Women Quarterly, 4,* 261–265.

Serbin, L. A., Marchessault, K., Lyons, J. A., & Schwartzman, A. E. (1987, April). *Social behavior on the elementary school playground: An observational study of normal and atypical boys and girls.* Paper presented at the biennial meeting of the Society for Research in Child Development, Baltimore, MD.

Serbin, L. A., Moller, L., Powlishta, K., & Gulko, J. (1991, April). *The emergence of gender segregation and behavioral compatibility in toddlers' peer preferences.* Paper presented at the biennial meeting of the Society for Research in Child Development, Seattle, WA.

Serbin, L. A., & O'Leary, K. D. (1975, December). How nursery schools teach girls to shut up. *Psychology Today, 9,* 56–58, 102–103.

Serbin, L. A., O'Leary, K. D., Kent, R., & Tonick, I. (1973). A comparison of teacher response to the preacademic and problem behavior of boys and girls. *Child Development, 44,* 796–804.

Serbin, L. A., Powlishta, K. K., & Gulko, J. (1993). The development of sex typing in middle childhood. *Monographs of the Society for Research in Child Development, 58*(2, Serial No. 232).

Serbin, L. A., Sprafkin, C., Elman, M., & Doyle, A. (1984). The early development of sex differentiated patterns of social influence. *Canadian Journal of Social Science, 14,* 350–363.

Serbin, L. A., Tonick, I. V., & Sternglanz, S. (1977). Shaping cooperative cross-sex play. *Child Development, 48,* 924–929.

Serr, D. M., & Ismajovich, B. (1963). Determination of the primary sex ratio from human abortions. *American Journal of Obstetrics and Gynecology, 87,* 63–65.

Shaffer, D. R. (1988). *Social and personality development.* Pacific Grove, CA: Brooks-Cole.

Shakin, M., Shakin, D., & Sternglanz, S. H. (1985). Infant clothing: Sex labeling for strangers. *Sex Roles, 12,* 955–963.

Shapiro, L. (1990, May 28). Guns and dolls. *Newsweek,* pp. 54–65.

Sharabany, R., Gershoni, R., & Hofman, J. E. (1981). Girlfriend, boyfriend: Age and sex differences in intimate friendship. *Developmental Psychology, 17,* 800–808.

Shaywitz, S. E., Shaywitz, B. A., Fletcher, J. M., & Escobar, M. D. (1990). Prevalence of reading disability in boys and girls. *Journal of the American Medical Association, 264,* 998–1002.

Sheldon, A. (1990). Pickle fights: Gendered talk in preschool disputes. *Discourse Processes, 13,* 5–31.

Shepard, G. B. (1991). A glimpse of kindergarten—Chinese style. *Young Children, 47,* 11–15.

Sherman, B. L., & Dominick, J. R. (1986). Violence and sex in music videos: TV and rock'n'roll. *Journal of Communication, 36,* 79–93.

Shettles, L. B., & Rorvik, D. M. (1984). *How to choose the sex of your baby.* Garden City, NY: Doubleday.

Shigetomi, C. C., Hartmann, D. P., & Gelfand, D. M. (1981). Sex differences in children's altruistic behavior and reputations for helpfulness. *Developmental Psychology, 17,* 434–437.

Short, G., & Carrington, B. (1989). Discourse on gender: The perceptions of children aged between six and eleven. In C. Skelton (Ed.), *Whatever happens to little women? Gender and primary schooling* (pp. 22–37). Milton Keynes, England: Open University Press.

Shuy, R. (1986). Secretary Bennett's teaching. *Teaching and Teacher Education, 2,* 315–324.

Sidorowicz, L. S., & Lunney, G. S. (1980). Baby X revisited. *Sex Roles, 6,* 67–73.

Siegal, M. (1987). Are sons and daughters treated more differently by fathers than by mothers? *Developmental Review, 7,* 183–209.

Sigelman, C. K., Carr, M. B., & Begley, N. L. (1986). Developmental changes in the influence of sex role stereotypes on person perception. *Child Study Journal, 16,* 191–205.

Signorella, M. L., & Jamison, W. (1986). Masculinity, femininity, androgeny, and cognitive performance: A meta-analysis. *Psychological Bulletin, 100,* 207–228.

Signorella, M. L., & Liben, L. S. (1984). Recall and reconstruction of gender-related pictures: Effects of attitude, task difficulty, and age. *Child Development, 55,* 393–405.

Signorielli, N. (1987). Children and adolescents on television: A consistent pattern of devaluation. *Journal of Early Adolescence, 7,* 255–268.

Simmons, R. G., & Blyth, D. A. (1987). *Moving into adolescence: The impact of pubertal change and school context.* New York: Aldine De Gruyter.

Simpson, W., & Erickson, M. T. (1983). Teachers' verbal and nonverbal communication patterns as a function of teacher race, student gender, and student race. *American Educational Research Journal, 20,* 183–198.

Singer, J. L., & Singer, D. G. (1981). *Television, imagination, and aggression: A study of preschoolers.* Hillsdale, NJ: Erlbaum.

Skelton, C. (1989). And so the wheel turns . . . Gender and initial teacher education. In C. Skelton (Ed.), *Whatever happens to little women? Gender and primary schooling* (pp. 53–67). Milton Keynes, England: Open University Press.

Skinner, P. H., & Shelton, R. L. (1985). *Speech, language and hearing: Normal processes and disorders* (2nd ed.). New York: Wiley.

Slaby, R. C., & Frey, K. S. (1975). Development of gender constancy and selective attention to same sex models. *Child Development, 46,* 849–856.

Sloman, S. S. (1948). Emotional problems in "planned for" children. *American Journal of Orthopsychiatry, 18,* 523–528.

Smetana, J. G., & Letourneau, K. J. (1984). Development of gender constancy and children's sex-typed free play behavior. *Developmental Psychology, 20,* 691–696.

Smith, C., & Lloyd, B. (1978). Maternal behavior and perceived sex of infant: Revisited. *Child Development, 49,* 1263–1265.

Smith, E. J. (1982). The black female adolescent: A review of the educational, career and psychological literature. *Psychology of Women Quarterly, 6,* 261–288.

Smith, J., & Russell, G. (1984). Why do males and females differ? Children's beliefs about sex differences. *Sex Roles, 11,* 1111–1120.

Smith, N., Greenlaw, M., & Scott, C. (1987, January). Making the literate environment equitable. *Reading Teacher,* 400–407.

Smith, P. (1991, September 4). Role models for troubled youth. *Boston Globe,* p. 53.

Smith, P. K., & Daglish, L. (1977). Sex differences in parent and infant behavior in the home. *Child Development, 48,* 1250–1254.

Smith, P. K., & Green, M. (1975). Aggressive behavior in English nurseries and play groups: Sex differences and responses of adults. *Child Development, 46,* 211–214.

Snow, M. E., Jacklin, C. N., & Maccoby, E. E. (1983). Sex-of-child differences in father-child interaction at one year of age. *Child Development, 54,* 227–232.

Sobieszek, B. I. (1978). Adult interpretations of child behavior. *Sex Roles, 4,* 579–588.

Solomon, W. E. (1991, August 4). Training tougher women. *New York Times,* Education Life, p. 11.

Span, P. (1987, July 19). Bringing up Barbie and raising Rambo. *Boston Globe Sunday Magazine,* pp. 15, 42–47.

Spender, D. (1982). *Invisible women.* London: Writers and Readers Publishing Cooperative.

Spender, D. (1984). Sexism in teacher education. In S. Acker & D. W. Piper (Eds.), *Is higher education unfair to women?* (pp. 132–143). Surrey, England: University of Guilford.

Springer, S. P., & Deutsch, G. (1981). *Left brain, right brain.* New York: Freeman.

Sroufe, L. A., Jacobvitz, D., Mangelsdorf, S., DeAngelo, E., & Ward, M. J. (1985). Generational boundary dissolution between mothers and their preschool children: A relationship systems approach. *Child Development, 56,* 317–325.

Sroufe, L. A., & Ward, M. J. (1980). Seductive behavior of mothers of toddlers: Occurrence, correlates and family origins. *Child Development, 51,* 1222–1229.

Stage, E. K. (1985). Increasing the participation and achievement of girls and women in mathematics, science, and engineering. In S. S. Klein (Ed.), *Handbook for achieving sex equity in education* (pp. 237–268). Baltimore, MD: Johns Hopkins University Press.

Stangor, C., & Ruble, D. N. (1987). Development of gender role knowledge and gender constancy. In L. S. Liben & M. L. Signorella (Eds.), *Children's gender schemata* (pp. 5–22). San Francisco: Jossey-Bass.

Stangor, C., & Ruble, D. N. (1989). Stereotype development and memory: What we remember depends on how much we know. *Journal of Experimental Social Psychology, 25,* 18–35.

Statham, J. (1986). *Daughters and sons: Experiences of nonsexist childraising.* Oxford, England: Basil Blackwell.

Stattin, H., & Klackenberg-Larsson, K. (1991). The short- and long-term implications for parent-child relations of parents' prenatal preferences for their child's gender. *Developmental Psychology, 27,* 141–147.

Stechler, G. (1964). Newborn attention as affected by medication in labor. *Science, 144,* 315–317.

Stein, A., Pohly, S., & Mueller, E. (1971). The influence of masculine, feminine, and neutral tasks on children's achievement behavior, expectancies of success, and attainment values. *Child Development, 42,* 195–207.

Stein, S. B. (1983). *Girls and boys: The limits of nonsexist childrearing.* New York: Scribner.

Steinberg, L. (1993). *Adolescence* (3rd ed.). New York: McGraw-Hill.

Steiner, B. W. (1985). The management of patients with gender disorders. In B. Steiner (Ed.), *Gender dysphoria: Development, research, management* (pp. 325–350). New York: Plenum Press.

Stern, M., & Karraker, K. H. (1989). Sex stereotyping of infants: A review of gender labeling studies. *Sex Roles, 20,* 501–522.

Sternglanz, S. H., & Serbin, L. A. (1974). Sex role stereotyping in children's television programs. *Developmental Psychology, 10,* 710–715.

Stevenson, H. W., Chen, C., & Booth, J. (1990). Influences of schooling and urban-rural residence on gender differences in cognitive abilities and academic achievement. *Sex Roles, 23,* 535–551.

Stevenson, H. W., & Lee, S. (1990). Contexts of achievement: A study of American, Chinese, and Japanese children. *Monographs of the Society for Research in Child Development, 55*(1–2, Serial No. 221).

Stevenson, M. R., & Black, K. N. (1988). Paternal absence and sex role development: A meta-analysis. *Child Development, 59,* 793–814.

Stevenson-Hinde, J., & Simpson, M. J. A. (1981). Mothers' characteristics, interactions, and infants' characteristics. *Child Development, 52,* 1246–1254.

Stewart, R. B. (1983). Sibling attachment relationships: Child-infant interactions in the Strange Situation. *Developmental Psychology, 19,* 192–199.

Stewart, R. B., & Marvin, R. S. (1984). Sibling relations: The role of conceptual perspective-taking in the ontogeny of sibling caregiving. *Child Development, 55,* 1322–1332.

Stiles, D. A., Gibbons, J. L., & Schnellmann, J. (1987). The smiling sunbather and the chivalrous football player: Young adolescents' images of the ideal woman and man. *Journal of Early Adolescence, 7,* 411–427.

Stipek, D. J., & Gralinski, J. H. (1991). Gender differences in children's achievement-related beliefs and emotional responses to success and failure in mathematics. *Journal of Educational Psychology, 83,* 361–371.

Stipek, D. J., & Hoffman, J. M. (1980). Development of children's performance related judgments. *Child Development, 51,* 912–914.

Stitt, B. A. (1988). *Building gender fairness in schools.* Carbondale: Southern Illinois University Press.

Stockard, J., & Wood, J. (1984). The myth of female underachievement: A reexamination of sex differences in academic underachievement. *American Educational Research Association Journal, 21,* 825–838.

Stoddart, T., & Turiel, E. (1985). Children's concepts of cross-gender activities. *Child Development, 56,* 1241–1252.

Stoneman, Z., Brody, G. H., & MacKinnon, C. E. (1986). Same-sex and cross-sex siblings: Activity choices, roles, behavior, and gender stereotypes. *Sex Roles, 15,* 495–511.

Strauss, S. (1988). Sexual harassment in the school: Legal implications for principals. *National Association of Secondary School Principals Bulletin,* pp. 93–97.

Strayer, F. F., & Strayer, J. (1976). An ethological analysis of social agonism and dominance relations among preschool children. *Child Development, 47,* 980–989.

Susman, E. J., Inoff-Germain, G., Nottlemann, E. D., Loriaux, D. L., Cutler, G. B., & Chrousos, G. P. (1987). Hormones, emotional dispositions, and aggressive attributes in young adolescents. *Child Development, 58,* 1114–1134.

Sutton-Smith, B. (1979). The play of girls. In C. B. Kopp (Ed.), *Becoming female: Perspectives on development* (pp. 229–257). New York: Plenum Press.

REFERENCES

Sutton-Smith, B., & Roberts, J. M. (1973). The cross-cultural and psychological study of games. In B. Sutton-Smith (Ed.), *The folkgames of children.* Austin: University of Texas Press.

Sutton-Smith, B., & Rosenberg, B. G. (1970). *The sibling.* New York: Holt, Rinehart and Winston.

Swan, K. (Ed.).(1992). *Saturday morning: Critical analyses of television cartoons* (Tech. Rep. No. 92-1). Albany: State University of New York at Albany, Learning Technologies Laboratory, School of Education.

Swanson, D. P., & Cunningham, M. (1991, April). *Issues in the gender and racial socialization of African-American children.* Paper presented at the biennial meeting of the Society for Research in Child Development, Seattle, WA.

Switzer, J. Y. (1990). The impact of generic word choices: An empirical investigation of age- and sex-related differences. *Sex Roles, 22,* 69–82.

Tan, L. E. (1985). Laterality and motor skills in four-year-olds. *Child Development, 56,* 119–124.

Tannen, D. (1990b). *You just don't understand: Women and men in conversation.* New York: Morrow.

Tanner, J. M. (1962). *Growth at adolescence.* Oxford, England: Basil Blackwell.

Tauber, M. A. (1979). Sex differences in parent-child interaction styles during a free-play session. *Child Development, 50,* 981–988.

Tavris, C., & Wade, C. (1984). *The longest war: Sex differences in perspective* (2nd ed.). San Diego: Harcourt, Brace, Jovanovich.

Taylor, F. G. (1991, August 16). Study: Minority models missing from magazines. *Valley News,* p. 20.

Taylor, M. G., & Gelman, S. A. (1991, April). *Children's beliefs about sex differences: The role of nature vs. nurture.* Paper presented at the biennial meeting of the Society for Research in Child Development, Seattle, WA.

Thoman, E. B., Leiderman, P. H., & Olson, J. P. (1972). Neonate-mother interaction during breast-feeding. *Developmental Psychology, 6,* 110–118.

Thompson, S. K. (1975). Gender labels and early sex role development. *Child Development, 46,* 339–347.

Thompson, S. K. (1988, March). *Adolescents' attitudes about sex role egalitarianism: 1976–1987.* Paper presented at the meeting of the Southwestern Society for Research in Human Development, New Orleans, LA.

Thompson, S. K., & Bentler, P. M. (1971). The priority of cues in sex discrimination by children and adults. *Developmental Psychology, 5,* 181–185.

Thorne, B. (1986). Girls and boys together, but mostly apart. In W. W. Hartup & Z. Rubin (Eds.), *Relationships and development* (pp. 167–184). Hillsdale, NJ: Erlbaum.

Tieger, T. (1980). On the biological basis of sex differences in aggression. *Child Development, 51,* 943–963.

Tobias, S. (1978). *Overcoming math anxiety.* New York: Norton.

Toronto Daily Telegraph. (1991, May 25). Cost of the rising son, p. 1.

Tracy, D. M. (1987). Toys, spatial ability, and science and mathematics achievement: Are they related? *Sex Roles, 17,* 115–138.

Trepanier-Street, M. L., & Kropp, J. J. (1986). Children's recall and recognition of sex role stereotyped and discrepant information. *Sex Roles, 16,* 237–249.

Tronick, E. Z., & Cohn, J. F. (1989). Infant-mother face-to-face interaction: Age and gender differences in coordination and the occurrence of miscoordination. *Child Development, 60,* 85–92.

Trudgill, P. (1972). Sex, covert prestige, and linguistic change in the urban British English of Norwich. *Language in Society, 1,* 179–195.

Turnbull, A. (1988). Woman enough for the Games? *New Scientist, 131,* 61–64.

Ullian, D. Z. (1976). The development of conceptions of masculinity and femininity. In B. Lloyd & J. Ascher (Eds.), *Exploring sex differences* (pp. 25–47). London: Academic Press.

Ullian, D. Z. (1984). "Why girls are good": A constructivist view. *Sex Roles, 11,* 241–265.

Unger, R. & Crawford, M. (1992). *Women and gender: A feminist psychology.* New York: McGraw-Hill.

Urberg, K. A. (1982). The development of the concepts of masculinity and femininity in young children. *Sex Roles, 8,* 659–668.

Valley News. (1990, August 22). Britain cleans up children's "Noddy" books, p. 30.

Valley News. (1992a, July 6). Fewer men teaching in elementary schools, p. 12.

Valley News. (1992b, January 8). Women used to persuade patrons to buy their brand, pp. 19, 32.

Vaughn, B. E., Block, J. H., & Block, J. (1988). Parental agreement on child rearing during early childhood and the psychological characteristics of adolescents. *Child Development, 59,* 1020–1033.

Vidmar, N., & Rokeach, M. (1974). Archie Bunker's bigotry: A study in selective perception and exposure. *Journal of Communication, 24,* 36–47.

Vines, G. (1992). Last Olympics for the sex test? *New Scientist, 135,* 39–42.

Vogel, S., Broverman, J., & Gardner, J. A. (1970). Sesame Street and sex role stereotypes. New York: Children's Television Workshop.

Waber, D. P. (1976). Sex differences in cognition: A function of maturation rate? *Science, 192,* 572–574.

Waber, D. P. (1977). Sex differences in mental abilities, hemispheric lateralization, and rate of physical growth at adolescence. *Developmental Psychology, 13,* 29–38.

Waber, D. P., Carlson, D., & Mann, M. (1982). Developmental and differential aspects of mental rotation in early adolescence. *Child Development, 53,* 1614–1621.

Walker, L. J. (1984). Sex differences in the development of moral reasoning: A critical review. *Child Development, 55,* 677–691.

Walker, L. J. (1987, April). *Moral orientations: A comparison of two models.* Paper presented at the biennial meeting of the Society for Research in Child Development, Baltimore, MD.

Walker, S. J. H. (1982). The relationship of parental educational levels, race, and sex to sex role stereotyping in young children. *Dissertation Abstracts International, 43,* 662A. (University Microfilms No. DA8219486)

Walsh, P. V., Katz, P. A., & Downey, E. P. (1991, April). *A longitudinal perspective on race and gender socialization in infants and toddlers.* Paper presented at the biennial meeting of the Society for Research in Child Development, Seattle, WA.

Walters, J. (1981). Variation in the requesting behavior of bilingual children. *International Journal of the Sociology of Language, 27,* 77–92.

Wanska, S. K., & Bedrosian, J. L. (1991, April). *Mothers' conversational style with sons and daughters.* Paper presented at the biennial meeting of the Society for Research in Child Development, Seattle, WA.

Ward, J. V. (1989). Racial identity formation and transformation. In C. Gilligan, N. P. Lyons, & T. J. Hanmer (Eds.), *Making connections: The relational worlds of adolescent girls at Emma Willard School* (pp. 215–232). Cambridge, MA: Harvard University Press.

Wasserman, G. A., & Lewis, M. (1985). Infant sex differences: Ecological effects. *Sex Roles, 12,* 665–675.

Wehren, A., & De Lisi, R. (1983). The development of gender understanding: Judgments and explanations. *Child Development, 54,* 1568–1578.

Weiner, B., Stone, A. J., Schmitz, M. D., Schmidt, A., Hernandez, A. C. R., & Benton, C. J. (1983). Compounding the errors: A reply to Pollak and Gilligan. *Journal of Personality and Social Psychology, 45,* 1176–1178.

Weinraub, M., Clemens, L. P., Sockloff, A., Ethridge, T., Gracely, E., & Myers, B. (1984). The development of sex role stereotypes in the third year: Relationships to gender labeling, gender identity, sex-typed toy preference, and family characteristics. *Child Development, 55,* 1493–1503.

Weinraub, M., & Frankel, J. (1977). Sex differences in parent-infant interaction during free play, departure, and separation. *Child Development, 48,* 1240–1249.

Weirman, M. E., & Crowley, W. F. (1986). Neuroendocrine control of the onset of puberty. In F. Falkner & J. M. Tanner (Eds.), *Human growth* (2nd ed., pp. 225–241). New York: Plenum Press.

Weisner, T. S. (1979). Some cross-cultural perspectives on becoming female. In C. B. Kopp (Ed.), *Becoming female: Perspectives on development* (pp. 313–332). New York: Plenum Press.

Weitzman, L., Eifler, D., Hodaka, K., & Ross, C. (1972). Sex role socialization in picture books for preschool children. *American Journal of Sociology, 77,* 1125–1150.

Weitzman, N., Birns, B., & Friend, R. (1985). Traditional and nontraditional mothers' communication with their daughters and sons. *Child Development, 56,* 894–898.

Welch, M. R., & Page, B. M. (1981). Sex differences in childhood socialization patterns in African societies. *Sex Roles, 7,* 1163–1173.

Welsh, D. P., & Powers, S. I. (1991). Gender differences in family interaction. In R. M. Lerner, A. C. Petersen, & J. Brooks-Gunn (Eds.), *Encyclopedia of adolescence* (pp. 334–339). New York: Garland Press.

Weltner, L. (1991, October 18). A parenting job well done . . . almost. *Boston Globe,* p. 46.

Wenger, S., & Berg-Cross, L. (1980). Parents' judgments of children's aggressive behavior. *Merrill-Palmer Quarterly, 26,* 161–168.

Wessel, M. A. (1990, June 15). Fathers past and present. *Boston Globe,* p. 80.

West, M. M., & Konner, M. J. (1981). The role of the father: An anthropological perspective. In M. E. Lamb (Ed.), *The role of the father in child development* (2nd ed., pp. 155–186). New York: Wiley.

Whitam, F. L. (1977). The homosexual role: A reconsideration. *Journal of Sex Research, 13,* 1–11.

White, H. (1986). Damsels in distress: Dependency themes in fiction for children and adolescents. *Adolescence, 21,* 251–256.

Whitehead, H. (1981). The bow and the burden strap: A new look at institutionalized homosexuality in native North America. In S. B. Ortner & H. Whitehead (Eds.), *Sexual meanings: The cultural construction of gender and sexuality* (pp. 80–115). Cambridge, England: Cambridge University Press.

Whitesell, N. R., Robinson, N. S., & Harter, S. (1991, April). *Types and effectiveness of coping strategies employed by young adolescent males and females in anger-provoking situations.* Paper presented at the biennial meeting of the Society for Research in Child Development, Seattle, WA.

Whiting, B. B., & Edwards, C. P. (1973). A cross-cultural analysis of the behavior of children aged 3–11. *Journal of Social Psychology, 91,* 171–188.

Whiting, B. B., & Edwards, C. P. (1988). *Children of different worlds: The formation of social behavior.* Cambridge, MA: Harvard University Press.

Wigfield, A., Eccles, J., Harold-Goldsmith, R., Blumenfeld, P., Yoon, K. S., & Feedman-Doan, C. (1989, April). *Gender and age differences in children's achievement self-perceptions during elementary school.* Paper presented at the biennial meeting of the Society for Research in Child Development, Kansas City, MO.

Williams, F., LaRose, R., & Frost, F. (1981). *Children, television and sex role stereotyping.* New York: Praeger.

Williams, J. E., Bennett, S. M., & Best, D. L. (1975). Awareness and expression of sex stereotypes in young children. *Developmental Psychology, 11,* 635–642.

Williams, J. H. (1987). *Psychology of women: Behavior in a biosocial context* (3rd ed). New York: Norton.

Williamson, N. E. (1976). *Sons or daughters.* Beverly Hills, CA: Sage.

Windass, A. (1989). Classroom practices and organization. In C. Skelton (Ed.), *Whatever happens to little women? Gender and primary schooling* (pp. 38–49). Milton Keynes, England: Open University Press.

Wintre, M. G., Hicks, R., McVey, G., & Fox, J. (1988). Age and sex differences in choice of consultant for various types of problems. *Child Development, 59,* 1046–1055.

Wiser, W. H., Wiser, C. V., & Wadley, S. S. (1989). *Behind mud walls: 1930–1960.* Berkeley: University of California Press.

Witelson, S. F. (1976). Sex and the single hemisphere: Specialization of the right hemisphere for spatial processing. *Science, 193,* 425–427.

Witelson, S. F. (1987). Neurobiological aspects of language in children. *Child Development, 58,* 653–688.

Wolf, A. E. (1991). *Get out of my life, but first, could you drive me and Cheryl to the mall?* New York: Noonday Press.

Wolf, N. (1991). *The beauty myth: How images of beauty are used against women.* New York: Morrow.

Wolpe, J., & Rachman, S. (1960). Psychoanalytic "evidence": A critique based on Freud's case of Little Hans. *Journal of Nervous and Mental Disease, 130,* 135–148.

Women on Words and Images. (1974). *Dick and Jane as victims: Sex stereotyping in children's readers.* Washington, DC: Resource Center on Sex Roles in Education.

REFERENCES

Wroblewski, R., & Huston, A. C. (1987). Televised occupational stereotypes and their effects on early adolescents: Are they changing? *Journal of Early Adolescence, 7,* 283–297.

Wyche, K. F. (1991). *The development of concepts of race, ethnicity and gender in children from diverse racial ethnic groups.* Paper presented at the biennial meeting of the Society for Research in Child Development, Seattle, WA.

Yang, R. K., & Moss, H. A. (1978). Neonatal precursors of infant behavior. *Developmental Psychology, 14,* 607–613.

Young, S. (1989, September 30). The mini-explorers of Middle Earth. *New Scientist,* pp. 38–41.

Zachau-Christiansen, B., & Ross, E. M. (1975). *Babies: Human development during the first year.* London: Wiley.

Zack, E. (1991, March 31). What's love got to do with it? *Boston Globe Sunday Magazine,* pp. 14–16.

Zahn-Waxler, C., Friedman, S. L., & Cummings, E. M. (1983). Children's emotions and behaviors in response to infants' cries. *Child Development, 54,* 1522–1528.

Zammuner, V. L. (1982). Children's sex-role stereotypes: A cross-cultural analysis. In P. Shaver & C. Hendrick (Eds.), *Sex and gender* (pp. 272-293). Newbury Park, CA: Sage.

Zappart, L. T., & Stansbury, K. (1983). *In the pipeline: A comparative analysis of women in graduate programs in science, engineering and medicine at Stanford University.* Unpublished monograph, Stanford University, Dept. of Psychiatry and Behavioral Sciences, School of Medicine, Stanford, CA.

Zarbatany, L., Hartmann, D. P., Gelfand, D. M., & Vinciguerra, P. (1985). Gender differences in altruistic reputation: Are they artifactual? *Developmental Psychology, 21,* 97–101.

Zern, D. S. (1984). Relationship among selected child-rearing variables in a cross-cultural sample of 110 societies. *Developmental Psychology, 20,* 683–690.

Zimbardo, P. G. (1982). *The shy child.* New York: Doubleday.

Zimeles, H., & Lee, V. E. (1991). Adolescent family structure and educational progress. *Developmental Psychology, 27,* 314–320.

Zimet, S. (1976). *Print and prejudice.* London: Hodder & Stoughton.

Zucker, B. (1984). Early effeminate behavior in boys: Outcome and significance for homosexuality. *Journal of Nervous and Mental Disease, 172,* 90–97.

Zucker, K. J. (1985). Cross-gender-identified children. In B. Steiner (Ed.), *Gender dysphoria: Development, research, management* (pp. 75–174). New York: Plenum Press.

Zucker, K. J., Bradley, S. J., Doering, R. W., & Lozinski, J. A. (1985). Sex-typed behavior in cross-gender-identified children: Stability and change at a one-year follow-up. *Journal of the American Academy of Child Psychiatry, 24,* 710–719.

Zucker, K. J., Wilson, D. N., & Bradley, S. J. (1983). *Peer appraisals of cross-gender boys: A pilot study.* Paper presented at Child Psychiatry Day, Hospital for Sick Children, Toronto.

Zucker, K. J., Wilson, D. N., & Stern, A. (1985, April). *Children's appraisals of sex typed behavior in their peers.* Paper presented at the biennial meeting of the Society for Research in Child Development, Toronto.

Zuckerman, D. M., Singer, D. G., & Singer, J. L. (1980). Children's television viewing, racial and sex role attitudes. *Journal of Applied Social Psychology, 10,* 281-294.

NAME INDEX

AAUW (American Association of University Women) 139, 142, 147, 151, 154, 225, 230
Abbey, A., 255
Aboud, F., 98, 100, 107
Abramovitch, A., 130
Abramovitch, R., 85, 188, 201
Adelson, J., 244
Adler, J., 152
Adler, M., 86
Adler, P., 121
Adler, P. A., 121, 122, 124–125, 131, 151, 244, 250, 252, 253
Albert, A. A., 107
Aleksandrowicz, D. R., 41
Aleksandrowicz, M. K., 41
Alfieri, T. J., 243
Allen, W. R., 82
Alvarez, M., 243, 259
Alvidrez, J., 139
American Association of University Women (AAUW), 139, 142, 147, 151, 154, 225, 230
Ames, G. J., 129
Amherst Record, 158
Andersen, E. S., 108, 110
Anderson, D., 101
Aderson, D. R., 158
Andres, D., 80
Andretti, Mario, 80
Angoff, 225
Antilla, S., 78
Apostoleris, N. H., 123
Arnett, J., 248, 251, 257
Ashby, M. S., 172
Ashenden, D. J., 136, 151
Ashton, E., 172
Ashton, R., 41
Askew, S., 139, 141–143, 151, 152
Atkin, D. J., 159
Attanucci, J., 207
Attie, I., 241

Babcock, R. L., 217
Bacall, Lauren, 108
Baenninger, M., 225, 226
Bahm, R. M., 82

Bailey, 241
Bakeman, R., 46, 132
Baker, D. P., 148, 227
Baker, L. A., 283
Baker, R. L., 40
Baker, S. W., 15, 23
Bakshi, A., 123
Balaban, T., 101
Bandura, A., 71, 88, 89, 91, 101
Bandura, M. M., 223, 225
Bank, R. J., 224
Barkley, R. A., 71
Barnard, K. E., 48
Barnett, D., 78
Barnett, M. A., 77, 171
Barrett, D. E., 193
Barrett, M., 147
Barry, Dave, 75, 188
Barry, R. J., 85
Bar-Tal, D., 145
Bartz, K. W., 77
Bates, J. E., 267
Bathurst, K., 223
Baumgartner, A., 107
Baumrind, D., 78, 206
Bautz, B. J., 154
Bayley, N., 40
Beal, Carole R., 100, 208
Becker, B. J., 228, 229
Bedrosian, J. L., 129
Bee, H. L., 48
Begley, N. L., 243
Belenky, M. F., 62
Bell, M. A., 47
Bell, N. J., 44
Bell, R. Q., 40, 41
Bell, S., 127
Bellinger, D., 74, 129
Belsky, J., 45, 46, 83, 241, 245
Bem, S. L., 65, 93, 99, 111, 112, 171
Benbow, C. P., 218–219, 230
Ben-Chaim, D., 226
Bender, B. G., 17
Bender, T. A., 149
Benenson, J. F., 120, 123
Benjamin, H., 268
Bennett, S. M., 96
Bennett, William, 138
Bensoussan, H., 125

Bentler, P. M., 96, 265, 267, 274
Benton, C. J., 62
Benz, C., 143
Berch, D. B., 17
Berenbaum, S. A., 222
Berg-Cross, G., 173
Berg-Cross, L., 173, 194
Berko-Gleason, J., 46, 74, 129
Berman, P. W., 202, 203
Bernal, J. F., 41
Bernard, M. E., 143
Berndt, T. J., 102, 200, 250, 251
Bernstein, I. S., 192
Bernstein, S., 93
Bernston, G. G., 192
Berry, J. W., 226
Bersoff, D. N., 195
Besch, N. F., 191
Best, D. L., 96, 111, 195
Best, R., 136, 153
Beuf, A., 165
Bezemer, P. D., 273
Bianchi, B. D., 132
Biddle, B. J., 224
Bigler, R. S., 111
Biller, H. B., 81, 82
Birns, B., 77
Bittle, Jerry, 38
Black, C., 136
Black, K. N., 81–83, 271
Blackwood, E., 276
Blakemore, J. E. O., 101, 201, 203
Blanchard, R., 267
Bleakley, M. E., 173
Bleier, R., 222
Block J., 78, 89, 248
Block, J. H., 8, 71, 76–78, 89, 248
Blumberg, S. L., 201
Blume, L., 140
Blumenfeld, P. C., 146
Blyth, D. A., 251, 258
Bock, W. E., 77
Boggiano, A. K., 147
Boldizar, J. P., 196
Bolduc, D., 42
Boles, D. B., 232
Boleyn, Anne, 16

Bollman, S. R., 75
Booth, A., 83
Booth, J., 226
Borden, Lizzie, 187
Borgida, E., 195
Borja-Alvarez, T., 123
Borker, R. A., 127
Borman, K. M., 126
Boston Globe, 34, 38, 75, 83, 85,
  140, 151, 152, 187, 218,
  249
Boswell, S. L., 86
Bosworth, P., 244
Bouchard, T. J., 222
Boulton, M. J., 123
Bow, J., 47
Bower, B., 197
Bower, T. G. R., 41, 95
Brackbill, Y., 41
Bradbard, M. R., 43, 108
Bradley, S. J., 130, 270, 275
Bradshaw, J. L., 220
Braunwald, K., 78
Brecht, J. M., 71
Brender, W., 77
Brenes, M. E., 82, 83
Brice, P., 165
Bricker, W., 188
Brinkerhoff, D., 83
Britain, S. D., 103
Britton, G., 173
Brody, G. H., 86
Brodzinsky, D. M., 196
Brokaw, Tom, 33
Brookins, G. K., 80
Brooks, J., 74
Brooks-Gunn, J., 36, 37, 74–76,
  94, 148, 162, 234,
  239–242, 247
Brophy, J., 141
Brophy, J. E., 199
Brown, B. B., 243
Brown, D., 147
Brown, J. V., 46
Brown, K., 223
Brown, S. R., 100
Brucken, L., 96, 187
Bryan, J. W., 93
Bryant, B. K., 85, 121, 128,
  201
Bryant, J., 158
Bryden, M. P., 223, 232
Bryk, A., 214
Bu, K. H. P., 162
Budzik, K., 203
Buffery, A. W. H., 219
Buhrmester, D., 249, 251, 257
Bundy, C., 214
Burchardt, C. J., 121
Burn, E., 151
Burris, J., 287
Bush, George, 130

Bussey, K., 71, 88, 89, 91, 101,
  206

Cacioppo, J. T., 192
Caldera, Y. M., 73
Callard, E. D., 75, 149
Callender, C., 276, 277
Camara, K. A., 194
Cameron, E., 200
Campbell, C. Y., 162
Campbell, D., 41
Campbell, D. T., 209
Cann, A., 96, 104
Cantor, M. G., 159, 161
Cantor, N. L., 143
Caplan, P. J., 226
Carlson, D., 216
Carlson, V., 78
Carpenter, C. J., 117, 118, 132,
  136, 152
Carpenter, J. C., 171
Carr, M. B., 243
Carr, T. S., 191
Carrington, B., 159
Carson, M., 127
Carter, D. B., 100, 105, 106,
  243
Carter, P., 216
Carver, W., 44
Casserly, P., 148
Cassidy, D. J., 171
Castenell, L. A., 77
Cazden C. B., 121, 124
Chalfin, S., 214
Chambers, D., 170
Chananie, J. D., 142, 143
Chapin, S. L., 118
Chapman, D. C., 105
Chapman, M., 199
Charles, Price of Wales, 37
Charlesworth, W. R., 124, 128
Chen, C., 226
Cherry, F., 73
Cherry, L., 141
Cherry, L. J., 46, 74, 129
Cheshire, J., 109, 110
Cheyne, J. A., 118
Chipman, 229
Chodorow, N., 62
Christian-Smith, L. K., 255
Cicchetti, D., 78
Cicirelli, V. G., 86, 201
Citron, C. C., 121
Clark, C., 158
Clarke-Stewart, K. A., 46–48,
  78
Clark-Lempers, D., 248
Classen, D. R., 243
Clinchy, B. M., 62
Coates, D. L., 251
Coates, J., 108
Cohen, M., 173

Cohn, D. A., 78
Cohn, J. F., 46
Cohn, S. J., 231
Coie, J. D., 123, 196
Coker, M., 103
Colby, A., 205
Collins, G., 140
Collins, W. A., 104
Collison, M. N. K., 255, 256
Collman, P., 103
Committee to Eliminate Sexual
  Discrimination in the Public
  Schools, 132
Condry, J., 44, 157–159, 168
Condry, J. C., 162, 189, 228
Condry, S., 44
Conger, J. J., 245
Connell, R. W., 136, 151
Connor, J. M., 121, 153, 173,
  225, 226
Cook, A. S., 44, 127
Cook, K. V., 43
Cooper, C. R., 248
Cooper, J., 101
Corder-Bolz, C. R., 168
Cordua, G. D., 104
Cornbleth, C., 143
Cornwell, D., 140
Corter, C., 85, 188, 201
Corter, C. M., 47
Cosby, Bill, 254
Cosmopolitan, 178
Cossette, L., 42
Costello, N. S., 40
Cowan, G., 45
Crandall, B. F., 265
Crane, M., 93
Crawford, M., 4, 18, 20, 24,
  28, 170, 246
Crockenberg, S. B., 85
Crombie, G., 77
Cromer, C. C., 122
Cronin, C. L., 129
Crowley, M., 198
Crowley, W. F., 238
Cruse, D. F., 103
Cullingford, C., 161
Culp, R. E., 44, 49
Culver, C., 46
Cummings, E. M., 191, 199
Cunningham, M., 77
Curtis, M., 41
Cutler, C., 39

Dabbs, J. M., 191
Daglish, L., 45, 73
Damico, S., 139, 143
Damon, W., 105–106
Danaher, D. L., 123
Danzger, B., 45
Darom, E., 145
Davidson, E. S., 168

Davidson, J., 28
Davidson, T., 166–167
Davis, A. J., 172
Davis, D. M., 159
Davis, M., 41
Davison, G. C., 272
Dawson, J. L. M., 222
Dean, J., 39
DeAngelis, T., 62
DeAngelo, E., 60
Dearsley, G., 270
Deaux, K., 195
De Benedictis, T., 229
DeCooke, P. A., 121
DeHart, G., 86
de Klerk, V., 110
Delamont, S., 135, 139, 141, 142, 151
De Lisi, R., 98, 216
DeLoache, J. S., 171
Delucchi, K., 229
DeLucia, L. A., 40
Denver Post, 218
Derbyshire, A., 94
Desor, J. A., 41
Deutsch, G., 219
Deutsch, Helene, 58
Diamond, A., 40
Diamond, M., 28
Diana, Princess of Wales, 37
Diaz, R. M., 251
Dick, A. E., 47, 72
Dickes, R., 46
Diepold, J. H., 73
Dino, G. A., 77
DiPietro, J. A., 73, 120, 123, 188
Dodez, R., 200
Dodge, K. A., 123, 188, 196
Doering, R. W., 275
Doescher, S. M., 200
Doherty, W. J., 248
Dominick, J. R., 163
Donahue, M., 47
Donahue, Phil, 215
Donenberg, G. R., 207, 208
Donlon, 225
Douvan, E., 244
Downey, E. P., 94
Downs, C., 72, 73, 88
Dowsett, G. W., 136, 151
Doyle, A., 128
Doyle, J. A., 40, 191
Drabman, R. S., 104
Draper, P., 83, 241, 245
Dubas, J. S., 225
Dubignon, J., 41
DuBois, L., 41
Dubow, E. R., 248
Dunn, D. A., 203
Dunn, J., 86
Durfee, J. T., 47

Durkin, K., 164, 165, 168
Dusek, J. B., 139, 147
Dweck, C. S., 145, 146, 149, 166
Dwyer, C. A., 224
Dyer, S. L., 228
Dzur, C., 124

Eagly, A. H., 196, 198
Easterbrooks, M. A., 121
Eaton, W. O., 41, 44, 101
Ebomoyi, E., 260
Eccles, J. E., 228
Eccles, J. S., 146, 153, 227, 231
Eckerman, C. O., 47
Edelsky, C., 108
Eder, D., 123, 125, 249
Educational Testing Service, 224
Edwards, C. P., 61, 79, 118, 188
Edwards, J. R., 109
Ehrhardt, A., 22, 23, 26, 28
Ehrhardt, A. A., 23, 268, 274
Eicher, S. A., 243
Eifler, D., 170
Eisenberg, N., 72, 73, 82, 102, 200
Eisenhardt, M. A., 148
Eisenstock, B., 168
Eklund, P. L. E., 273
Elias, C., 174
Elkind, D., 250, 255, 262
Elliott, G. L., 84
Ellis, S., 122
Elman, M., 128
Eme, R. F., 188
Emmerich, W., 98, 101
Endsley, R. C., 108
Engel, M., 224
Enns, L. R., 41, 44
Entwisle, D. R., 148, 227
Erikson, E. H., 58
Erikson, M. T., 139
Erkut, S., 145
Eron, L. D., 165, 248
Ershler, J., 152
Escobar, M. D., 224
Esposito, A., 128
Etaugh, C., 140
Ettema, J., 166–167
Evans, E. D., 244
Eyres, S. J., 48

Fagan, J. F., 40, 94
Fagot, B. I., 47, 49, 71, 72, 74, 77, 88, 89, 92, 96, 97, 101, 118, 120, 130, 131, 140, 195, 272
Faison, S., 75
Falbo, T., 86
Farylo, B., 28

Fausto-Sterling, A., 21, 190, 192
Fein, G., 89, 96
Feingold, A., 215, 226, 230
Feinman, S., 10
Feiring, C., 78
Feldlaufer, H., 231
Feldman, P., 273
Feldman, S. S., 201, 203
Feldman-Summers, 172
Feldstein, J. H., 161, 162
Feldstein, S., 161, 162
Feminists on Children's Literature, 170
Fennema, E., 218, 229, 230
Fidler, D. S., 168, 172–173
Field, T. M., 46, 48
Finch, S., 267
Fine, G. A., 9
Fine, M., 144
Fischer, P., 165
Fisher, A. E., 201
Fisk, W. R., 174
Fiske, S. T., 195
Fivush, R., 224
Flanagan, C. A., 81
Fleming, M. Z., 274
Flerx, V. C., 168, 172–173
Fletcher, J. M., 224
Foch, T. T., 214
Fogel, A., 203
Forbes, D., 123
Foster-Clark, F. S., 251
Fox, J., 251
Fox, L. H., 231
Fox, N. A., 45
Frady, R. L., 191
Frankel, J., 48, 126
Frankel, M. T., 77
Freedman, D. G., 130, 144
Freeman, M. G., 40
Freiberg, P., 139, 140
Frenkel, K. A., 147
Freud, Sigmund, 11–12, 49, 51–67, 87, 209
Freudigman, K. A., 41
Freund, K., 267
Frey, K. S., 95, 97, 99, 101, 107
Friedan, Betty, 262
Friedman, E. A., 41
Friedman, S. L., 199
Friend, R., 77
Frisch, H. L., 46
Fritz, J. J., 127
Frodi, A., 196, 197
Frodi, A. M., 48, 203
Frodi, M., 48
Frost, F., 166
Frueh, T., 165
Fry, D. P., 198
Fulkerson, K. F., 147

Furman, W., 249, 251, 257
Furr, S., 147
Futterman, R., 143

Gaddis, A., 242
Galaburda, A. M., 221
Gardner, J. E., 161
Garrod, A., 208
Gates, F. L., 195, 196
Gauthier, R., 118
Gautier, T., 27, 28
Gelfand, D. M., 143, 199, 200
Gelman, S. A., 99, 103
Georgiou, S., 222
Gerbner, G., 159
Gershoni, R., 251
Gerson, A., 140
Gerwitz, H. B., 36
Gertwitz, J. L., 36
Geschwind, N., 221
Gest, S., 86
Gibbons, J. L., 243
Gibbs, J., 154, 205
Gilligan, C., 62, 206–209, 250
Gilmore, D. D., 260, 261
Gilstrap, B., 45
Gjerde, P. F., 78
Gladue, B. A., 275
Goff, D. M., 74
Goff, S., 143
Golbeck, S. L., 216
Gold, D., 77, 80, 140
Goldberg, M. E., 169
Goldberg, S., 46, 47, 201
Goldberger N. R., 62
Goleman, D., 64
Golinkoff, R. M., 129
Golub, S., 239
Golumbok, S., 84, 85
Good, T., 141
Good, T. L., 224
Goodchilds, J. D., 255, 256
Goodman, M., 271
Goodwin, M. H., 124, 127
Gooren, L. J. G., 273
Gordon, S., 203
Gordon, T. P., 192
Gorfein, D. S., 39
Gorman, C., 7
Gorn, G. J., 169
Goshen-Gottstein, E. R., 42
Gottesman, I. I., 222
Gottfried, A. W., 223
Gottman, J. M., 122
Gouze, K. R., 98
Graddol, D., 108–110, 174
Grahan-Bermann, S., 86
Gralinski, J. H., 145, 228
Grant, C. A., 154
Grant, L., 139, 141, 143
Graves, W. L., 40

Gray, J., 39
Gray, J. A., 219
Green, M., 187, 188
Green, R., 84, 85, 265, 267, 269, 271, 273, 275
Greenberg, B., 169
Greenberg, B. S., 168
Greenberg, D. N., 96
Greene, B., 196
Greenfield, P., 79
Greenfield, P. M., 158, 169, 257
Greenlaw, M., 173
Greer, D., 162
Greif, E. B., 240
Grenadier, A., 274
Grieve, N., 217
Grisanti, G., 268
Grossmann, K., 48
Grotevant, H. D., 86, 248
Grusec, J. E., 130, 200
Gualtieri, 19
Guerro, L., 27
Guisewhite, Cathy, 73
Gulko, J., 92, 118
Gulutz, G., 86
Gunnar, M. R., 47, 48
Gunnar-VonGnechten, M. R., 48
Guns'n'Roses, 256
Gurwitz, S., 41
Gustafson, G. E., 203

Hacker, S. L., 174
Hagan, R., 71, 72, 88, 97, 195
Hahn, W. K., 223
Haight, J. M., 96
Haight, W., 214
Halle, E., 270
Hallinan, M. T., 123, 125, 250
Halpern, D. F., 217, 219–221, 224, 226, 231
Halverson, C. F., 93, 100, 103, 104, 106–107, 173
Hamilton, M. C., 32, 174
Hammer, J., 34
Hammond, M. A., 48
Hampshire Life, 231, 259
Handley, H. M., 137
Hanks, C., 48
Hanmer, T. J., 250
Hanratty, M. S., 108
Hansen, C. H., 162
Hansen, R. D., 162
Hardesty, F. P., 39
Hare, B. R., 77
Hare-Mustin, R. T., 4
Harkness, S., 119
Harlow, R., 243
Harrington, A. F., 168
Harrington, C. C., 86
Harris, A., 229
Harris, A. M., 132

Harris, L. J., 223, 226
Harris, M. B., 160
Harrison, J., 153
Harter, S., 148, 195
Hartley, R. E., 39
Hartmann, D. P., 199, 200
Hartshorne, H., 199
Hartup, W. W., 118
Hass, A., 129
Haugh, S. S., 45
Haviland, J. J., 46
Haviland, J. M., 45
Hayden-Thomson, L., 118
Heilman, M. E., 195
Heller, K. A., 102, 147, 148
Helmstadter, G. C., 82
Hemingway, Ernest, 270
Hemmer, J. D., 272
Hemp, P., 173
Henderson, D. L., 170
Henker, B. A., 95
Henry, T., 215, 218
Henry VIII (king of England), 16
Henton, C. L., 239
Hen-Tov, A., 95
Herdt, G. H., 28
Hernandez, R., 72
Hess, D. J., 159
Hetherington, E. M., 82–84, 194, 248
Hicks, 19
Hicks, R., 251
Higgins, E. T., 243
Hill, J. P., 250, 251
Hill, S., 140
Hines, M., 222
Hisock, M., 223
Hite, T., 102
Hittleman, J. H., 46
Hocevar, D., 40
Hodaka, K., 170
Hodapp, R., 214
Hodge, R., 161
Hoenig, J., 275
Hoffman, C. D., 45
Hoffman, J. M., 145, 149
Hoffman, L. W., 36, 75, 76, 78, 80, 81, 86, 207, 208
Hoffman, M. L., 199
Hofman, J. E., 251
Hogg, M. A., 128
Hohler, B., 162
Holaday, J. W., 192
Holden, C., 270, 271
Holden, G. W., 121
Holland, D. C., 148
Holmes, D. L., 140
Holstein, C. B., 206
Holt, W., 117, 152
Hopkins, K. D., 173
Horney, Karen, 51, 58–59
Hort, B. E., 92, 96

Houang, R. T., 226
Housley, P. C., 44
Howard, J. A., 77
Huesmann, L. R., 248
Hughes, J. O., 130
Humphreys, A. P., 120, 121
Hunter, F. T., 251
Hunter, M., 75
Hurtig, A. L., 23
Husemann, L. R., 165
Huston, A. C., 8, 45, 71, 73,
    75, 86, 117, 152, 159,
    160, 162, 164, 225, 243,
    259, 275
Huston-Stein, A., 136, 152
Hutchins, G., 168
Huttenlocher, J., 214
Hwang, C., 48
Hyde, J. S., 174, 188, 189,
    214, 215, 217, 218, 229,
    230
Hymel, S., 118

Iannotti, R. J., 191
Iler, I., 153
Imperato-McGinley, J., 27, 28
Inglis, J., 214
Intons-Peterson, M. J., 33
Irvine, J. J., 141
Ismajovich, B., 19
Israel, A. C., 89
Ito, J., 18

Jacklin, C. N., 8, 40, 41,
    45–48, 71–73, 75, 78,
    118–120, 190, 191, 194,
    210, 214, 222, 283
Jacobs, B. S., 46
Jacobs, J. E., 227
Jacobson, S., 239
Jacobvitz, D., 60
Jain, D., 48
Jamison, W., 225
Janik, L. M., 103
Jaskir, J., 78
Jennings, S. A., 104
Jhally, S., 163
Joffe, C., 141
Johnson, D., 89, 96
Johnson, D. W., 173
Johnson, E. S., 216, 217
Johnson, J. E., 152
Johnson, M., 229
Johnston, D. K., 208
Johnston, J., 166–167
Jones, C., 151
Jones, G., 137
Joseph, G., 139, 147
Joshi, P., 48
Jurich, A. P., 75, 267, 268, 272

Kaczala, C., 143
Kaczala, C. M., 147
Kadushin, A., 36
Kagan, J., 74, 95
Kagan, S., 130
Kahn, L., 73
Kail, R., 216
Kakar, Sudhir, 34, 61
Kallen, D. J., 254, 255
Kantrowitz, J., 266
Kanungo, R. N., 169
Kaplan, H. S., 274
Karlsberg, E., 252
Karraker, K. H., 44
Katz, P. A., 44, 80, 81, 86, 94,
    111
Kavanagh, K., 47
Kay, T., 18
Keats, J. G., 101
Kee, D. W., 223
Kempe, C. H., 39
Kemple, K. M., 78
Kennell, J. H., 201, 202
Kent, D., 242
Kent, R., 136
Kenyon, B., 94
Kessler, S., 136, 151
Kessler, S. J., 25
Kiesler, S., 153
Kimball, M. M., 148, 166, 218,
    229, 231
Kimmerly, N. L., 45
Kimura, D., 219
King, F., 32
King, S., 41
Kinman, J. R., 170
Kinsbourne, M., 223
Kinsey, A. C., 273
Kirkpatrick, M., 84
Kishwar, M., 38
Kittredge, C., 256
Klackenberg-Larsson, K., 39
Klaus, M. H., 201, 202
Kleiber, D. A., 272
Klein, P., 41, 46
Klein, R. P., 47
Klein, S., 139, 170
Klein, S. S., 150, 153
Kleinke, C. L., 107
Kless, S. J., 121
Knight, G. P., 130
Koblinsky, S. G., 103, 107
Kochanska, G., 74
Kochems, L. M., 276, 277
Koff, E., 239
Kofman, S., 63
Kohlberg, L., 92, 93, 98, 107,
    205–206
Kolata, G., 222
Komarovsky, M., 254
Konner, M. J., 48
Korner, A. F., 41

Korner, A. F., 41
Korth, W., 143
Koso-Thomas, O., 260
Kosson, N., 89, 96
Kotelchuck, M., 36
Kraemer, H. C., 41
Krieger, E., 75
Kriger, A., 201
Kronsberg, S., 74, 88, 195
Kropp, J. J., 104, 173
Krull, M., 52
Krupnick, C. G., 259
Kuczynski, L., 74
Kuebli, J., 75
Kuhn, D., 96, 107, 187, 195
Kumar, R., 202
Kurdek, L. A., 82

LaFreniere, P., 118, 128
Lamb, M. E., 45, 48, 121, 130,
    203
Lambert, H. H., 222, 232
Lamon, S. J., 218, 229, 230
Landerholm, E. J., 46
Landers, Ann, 35, 83, 190, 217,
    270
Lando, B., 188
Langer, P., 39
Langevin, R., 274
Langlois, J. H., 41, 72, 73, 88,
    95
Lappan, G., 226
LaRose, R., 166
LaRue, A. A., 101
Latham, A., 274
Lave, J., 79
Lawson, J. S., 214
Leaper, C., 82, 126–128, 248
Lederberg, A. R., 118
Lee, S., 232
Lee, V. E., 248
Le Guin, Ursula, 285
Leiderman, P. H., 41, 46
Leighton, K., 48
Leinbach, M. D., 72, 88, 92,
    94, 96, 97, 195
Leinhardt, G., 224
Lempers, J. D., 248
L'Engle, Madeleine, 173
Letourneau, K. J., 101
Lever, J., 125, 126
Levine, E. S., 77
Levine, J., 95
Levine, J. A., 74
Levine, L. E., 199
Levinson, B. M., 224
Levitan, T. E., 142, 143
Levy, B., 256
Levy, G. D., 101, 105
Levy, J., 219, 220, 223
Levy, N., 40

Lewin, M., 255
Lewis, C., 36, 201
Lewis, L. A., 163
Lewis, M., 46, 47, 74, 78, 94, 95, 129
Liben, L. S., 103, 104, 111, 216
Lickona, T., 169, 254, 255
Lieb-Brilhart, B., 224
Lieberman, M., 205
Lieberman, M. R., 171
Liebert, R. M., 108, 159, 168
Lin, C. A., 159
Lingenfelter, M., 168
Linn, M. C., 214–217, 229, 230
Lipsitt, L. P., 40, 189
Liss, M. B., 225, 227
List, J. A., 104
Litcher, J. H., 173
Little, J. K., 92, 101
Littman, R. A., 188
Lloyd, B., 44
Lochel, E., 146
Lockhart, M. E., 100
Lockheed, M. E., 132, 148, 150, 153
Lombardi, Vince, 126
Lovaas, O. I., 274
Loveday, L., 109
Low, B. P., 274
Low, H., 191
Lozinski, J. A., 275
Luecke, D., 101
Lummis, M., 227
Lumpkin, M., 173
Lunney, G. S., 44
Luria, A., 93
Luria, Z., 44
Lynch, M. E., 250
Lyons, J. A., 121
Lyons, M., 214
Lyons, N. P., 250
Lytton, H., 8, 71

McAloon, A., 148
MacArthur, R., 226
Macaulay, J., 196
Macaulay, R. K. S., 214
McCabe, B., 171
McCall, R. B., 108
McCauley, E., 18, 274
McCauley, E. A., 268
McCloskey, L. A., 127
Maccoby, E. E., 8, 40, 41, 45–48, 66, 71–73, 75, 78, 83, 89, 103, 105, 117–120, 187, 190, 191, 194, 196, 197, 210, 214, 222
McConaghy, M. J., 99
McCornack, B. L., 127
MacDonald, C. T., 231

McDonald, S. M., 170, 171
Macfarlane, A., 31, 33
McGhee, P. E., 165
McGillicuddy-De Lisi, A. V., 216
McGlone, J., 214, 221
MacGowan, B. R., 274
McGraw, K. O., 104
McGuffog, C., 78
McGuire, J., 69, 78
MacKay, D. G., 174
Mackey, W. E., 159
MacKinnon, C. E., 86
McManus, I. C., 223, 232
McNeil, J. D., 224
McPherson, G. M., 226
McVey, G., 251
Malatesta, C. Z., 46
Malcuit, G., 42
Malina, 241
Maller, J. B., 199
Maller, O., 41
Maltz, D. N., 127
Mangelsdorf, S., 60
Mann, M., 216
Mannarino, A. P., 200
Mansfield, A. F., 80
Manuel, D., 146
Maple, S. A., 230, 231
Maracek, J., 4
Marantz, S. A., 80
Marchand, R. H., 214
Marchessault, K., 121
Marcus, D. E., 98, 100, 101
Margolin, G., 73
Markham, W. T., 43
Markus, H., 93
Marshall, W. A., 238, 241
Martin, C. E., 273
Martin, C. L., 10,92, 93, 100–104, 106–107, 120
Martin, E., 21
Martin, H., 39
Martin, J., 253
Martin, J. A., 78
Martyna, W., 174
Marvin, R. S., 201
Masson, J. M., 65
Masters, J. C., 93
Mate, P., 77
Matthews, D., 23
Matthews, W. S., 36, 37, 74–76, 162, 234, 242
Mattsson, A., 191
Maugham, B., 206
May, M. A., 199
Meade, A. C., 216, 217
Meddick, Jim, 131, 163
Mednick, B. R., 40
Meece, J. L., 138, 140, 141, 143, 147
Meehan, A. M., 103, 216

Melson, G. F., 203
Meltz, B. F., 106
Mendelsohn, J., 259
Mensh, E., 218, 225
Mensh, H., 218, 225
Mermelstein, R., 165
Messer, S. B., 196
Meyer, J., 274
Meyer, J. K., 270
Meyer, J. W., 44
Meyer, V. F., 247
Meyer-Bahlburg, H. F. L., 23
Michaels, S., 121, 124
Midgley, C., 231
Miedzian, M., 168, 251, 256, 284
Miller, C. L., 94
Miller, K. E., 250
Miller, M. M., 168
Miller, P. H., 51, 52, 59
Miller, P. M., 123
Minton, C., 74, 75
Mirwald, 241
Mischel, W., 70, 82
Mitchell, D. R. D., 217
Mitchell, J., 63
Mitchell, J. E., 283
Mitchell, S. K., 48
Mittwoch, U., 17
Moller, L., 118
Molnar, J. M., 149
Monda, L. C., 203
Money, J., 22, 23, 26, 28
Monroe, R. H., 226
Monroe, R. L., 226
Montemayor, R., 108, 251
Moorman, J., 159
Morgan, M., 165, 167
Morris, R., 191
Morse, L. W., 137
Morse, S., 163
Moss, H. A., 41, 46, 47, 95
Mother Goose, 171
Motley Crue, 256
Moulton, J., 174
Moxley, V. M., 75
Meuller, E., 108
Mullen, M. K., 96
Munroe, R. H., 97
Munroe, R. L., 97
Murray, E., 102
Murrell, P., 139, 140
Myerscough, OR. P., 203

Nadelman, L., 98
Nash, S. C., 96, 187, 201, 203, 225
National Institute of Education, 166
Meale, J. M., 272
Needle, R. H., 248
Neff, R. K., 41

Nelson-LeGall, S., 121
Nettleton, N. C., 220
Neuberg, D., 267
New York Times, 35, 162
Newbern, S. R., 104
Newcombe, N., 223, 225, 226
Newman, I., 143
Newman, R. S., 228
Newson, E., 75–77, 196
Newson, J., 75–77, 196
Nicholson, T. A., 107
Niggas With Attitude, 256
Nisbett, R., 41
Novello, Antonia, 162

Oakes, J., 230
Oakley, A., 32
O'Brien, D., 276
O'Brien, M., 73, 225
O'Bryant, S. L., 168, 199
O'Connell, E. J., 41
O'Dell, Scott, 170
O'Leary, D., 136
O'Leary, K. D., 137, 141
Olejnik, A. B., 101
Olson, J. P., 41, 46
Oltmanns, T. F., 272
Olweus, D., 188, 191, 193, 194
Omark, D. R., 144
Osofsky, J. D., 41, 45
Otto, L., 71
Overton, W. F., 98, 100, 101, 216

Page, B. M., 78
Paige, K., 260
Paikoff, R. L., 247
Paley, V. G., 123, 130, 141
Palkovitz, R., 48
Palmon R., 217
Paludi, M. A., 28, 40, 191
Parke, R. D., 46–48, 187, 188, 193, 203, 204
Parrington, M., 41
Parsons, J. E., 143, 147–149
Pasternack, J. F., 72
Patterson, C. J., 84, 85, 100, 106, 243
Patterson, G. R., 73, 188, 194
Pattison, P., 217
Paulsen, K., 229
Pauly, I. B., 274
Pederson, F. A., 45, 49
Peleaux, R., 48
Pellegrino, J., 216
Pepler, D. J., 85, 201
Pepper, S., 123
Perry, D. C., 196
Perry, D. G., 71, 88, 108, 195, 196
Perry, L. C., 108, 195, 196
Peter, D., 274

Petersen, A. C., 215, 216, 239
Peterson, R. E., 27, 28
Pettit, G. S., 123
Pfeiffer, I., 143
Phillips, D., 145, 148
Phillips, J., 237
Phillips, S., 41
Piaget, Jean, 59, 205, 216, 222
Picariello, M. L., 96
Pillemer, D. B., 96
Pingree, S., 168
Pipp, S., 100
Pitcher, E. G., 119, 120, 124
Plomin, R., 214
Pogrebin, L. C., 157, 174, 230
Pohly, S., 108
Polit, D. F., 86
Pollak, S., 62
Pollitt, K., 161
Pomerleau, A., 42, 43
Pomeroy, W. B., 273
Pooler, W. S., 32
Porter, J. R., 107
Poulin-Dubois, D., 94
Powell, G. J., 169
Power, T. G., 48
Powers, S. I., 248
Powlishta, K., 118
Powlishta, K. K., 92, 128
Press, A. L., 160
Preston, R. C., 224
Price, W. H., 18
Price-Bonham, S., 73
Provenzano, F. J., 44
Pruett, K. D., 48, 84
Purcell, P., 170, 172

Quinn, S., 51

Rachman, S., 64
Radin, N., 77, 84
Radke-Yarrow, C., 199
Radway, J. A., 255
Raloff, J., 231, 232
Raphael, R., 61, 260, 261
Raskin, P. A., 89
Rasmussen P., 196
Ravizza, R., 222
Ray, E., 140
Ray, W. J., 222
Raymond, C., 230
Raymond, C. L., 230
Rebelsky, F., 48
Reddel, M., 33
Reese, E., 224
Reeves, B. B., 168
Reid, M., 220
Reid, P. T., 203
Reis, H. T., 97, 251
Reis, M., 140
Rekers, G. A., 265, 267, 268, 272, 274

Resnick, S. M., 222
Rest, J., 206
Reynolds, P., 58
Rheingold, H. L., 43, 47
Richards, M. P., 41
Richmond, P. G., 215
Rierdan, J., 239
Riger, S., 4
Riley, M. T., 140
Ritter, J. M., 41, 95
Roberto, L., 274, 275
Roberts, C. W., 271
Roberts, J. M., 121
Roberts, P., 170
Roberts, T., 149
Robin, M., 46
Robinson, G., 174
Robinson, L., 274
Robinson, N. S., 195
Robson, K., 202
Robson, K. S., 95
Roche, B. J., 126
Rodgers, R. W., 168, 172–173
Roggman, L. A., 41, 95
Rogoff, B., 122
Rokeach, M., 164
Rolling Stones, 256
Rollins, H. A., Jr., 77
Romaine, S., 109, 110
Romney, D. M., 8, 71
Roopnarine, J. L., 48, 121, 130
Rorvik, D. M., 36, 37
Rose, J., 135
Rose, Pete, 32
Rose, R., 192
Rose, R. M., 192
Rosen, A. C., 265, 274
Rosenberg, B. G., 86
Rosenberg, D., 152
Rosenblatt, J. S., 201
Rosenblatt, V., 118
Rosenblith, J. F., 40
Rosenhan, D. L., 199
Rosenthal, D. A., 105
Rosenthal, I. M., 23
Rosenthal M. K., 41, 46
Rosenwasser, S. M., 168
Ross, C., 139, 141–143, 151, 152, 170
Ross, D., 88
Ross, D. F., 189
Ross, D. M., 89
Ross, E. M., 19, 41
Ross, R., 162
Ross, S. A., 88, 89
Rosser, P., 218, 225, 230
Rossi, J. S., 219
Rothbart, M., 77
Rothbart, M. K., 77
Rothman, B. K., 31, 38, 43, 44
Rothchild, N., 165
Rovine, M., 45

Roy, R., 84
Rubin, J. Z., 44, 45
Rubin, K. H., 118
Ruble, D. N., 97, 99, 101, 107, 149, 239, 240, 243
Rudolph, E., 109
Ruechert, L., 223
Ruhl, S., 160
Russell, G., 99, 107
Rutberg, J., 244
Rutter, M., 84

Sadker, D., 137–140, 147, 154, 170
Sadker, M., 137–140, 142, 147, 154, 170
Safir, M. P., 143, 224
Sagar, H. A., 250
St. Peter, S., 172
Salt, P., 274
Salthouse, T. A., 223
Sandler, B. R., 130
Santrock, J. W., 82, 84, 240, 247
Sarah, E., 175
Sather, C., 244
Savin-Williams, R. C., 244, 249
Sawin, D. B., 46, 47
Sawyer, Diane, 244
Saxby, L., 223
Scarr, S., 80, 204, 210
Schachter, F. F., 86, 214
Schackman, M., 226
Schafer, W. D., 45
Schalling, D., 191
Schau, C. G., 73, 173
Schmaling, K., 74
Schmidt, C. W., 270
Schneider, C., 162, 164, 168
Schneider, J. W., 174
Schnellmann, J., 243
Schofield, J. W., 118, 250
Schultz, L. G., 119, 120, 124
Schumacher, D., 169
Schwartz, L. A., 43
Schwartz, R., 82
Schwartzman, A. E., 121
Sciarra, D. J., 140
Science News, 20, 222, 223
Scott, 172
Scott, C., 173
Scott, E., 139, 143
Scott, K. P., 173, 224
Scriven, G., 46
Sears, R. R., 196
Seavey, C. A., 44
Sedney, M. A., 282
Seewald, A. M., 224
Segel, E., 173
Seidl, F. W., 36
Seltzer, M., 214
Senchak, M., 251

Serbin, L. A., 92, 94, 118, 121, 128, 132, 136, 137, 141, 153, 160, 173, 225, 226, 282, 286
Serr, D. M., 19
Seuss, Dr., 171
Seventeen, 213
Shaffer, D. R., 188, 200
Shakin, D., 41
Shakin, M., 41–43
Shapiro, L., 6, 124
Sharabany, R., 251
Shaywitz, B. A., 224
Shaywitz, S. E., 224
Sheldon, A., 124
Shelton, R. L., 214
Shepard, B., 46
Shepard, G. B., 118
Shepard, K., 101
Sherman, B. L., 163
Shettles, L. B., 36, 37
Shigetomi, C. C., 199
Shimmin, H., 97
Shinn, P., 208
Shipley, C., 222
Shore, E., 86, 214
Short, G., 159
Shuy, R., 138
Sidorowicz, L. S., 44
Siegal, M., 73
Siesky, A. E., 82
Sigelman, C. K., 243
Signorella, M. L., 103, 104, 225
Signorielli, N., 159
Siladi, M., 93
Silverstone, E., 239
Simmons, R. G., 258
Simons, R. L., 248
Simpson, M. J. A., 74
Simpson, W., 139
Singer, D. G., 158, 165
Singer, J. L., 158, 165
Skeen, P., 73
Skelton, C., 153
Skinner, P. H., 214
Skovronek, E., 217
Slaby, R. C., 95, 97, 101
Slaby, R. G., 187, 188, 193
Sleeter, C. E., 154
Sloman, S. S., 39
Smetana, J. G., 101
Smith, B., 86
Smith, C., 44, 84
Smith, E. J., 246
Smith, J., 99, 107
Smith L., 82
Smith, N., 173
Smith, P., 82
Smith P. K., 45, 73, 120, 121, 123, 187, 188
Snow, M. E., 46, 48, 75
Snyder, H. N., 250

Sobieszek, B., 44
Sobieszek, B. I., 44
Solomon, B., 251
Solomon, W. E., 76
Sorensen, L., 223
Span, P., 286
Speck, Richard, 190
Spencer, A., 84
Spencer, Scott, 257
Spender, D., 139, 140, 144, 153
Spitz, J., 274
Sprafkin, C., 128
Sprafkin, J., 159, 168
Sprague, R., 82
Springer, S. P., 219
Springsteen, Bruce, 257
Sproull, L., 153
Srivastav, P., 48
Sroufe, L. A., 60
Stage, E., 229
Stage, E. K., 231
Stage, F. K., 230–231
Standage, T. H., 149
Stangor, C., 101
Stanley, J. C., 218–219, 230
Stansbury, K., 148
Statham, J., 105, 112, 122, 177, 242, 248
Stattin, H., 39
Stechler, G., 41
Steffen, V. J., 196
Stein, A., 108
Stein, S. B., 56, 57, 286
Steinberg, J., 48
Steinberg, L., 83, 241, 245–247, 250, 254, 258, 259
Steiner, B. W., 267, 274
Stephenson, J. J., 254, 255
Stern, A., 272
Stern, M., 44
Sternglanz, S., 132
Sternglanz, S. H., 41, 160
Stevenson, H. W., 226, 227, 232
Stevenson, M. R., 81–83, 271
Stevenson-Hinde, J., 74
Stewart, L., 170, 172
Stewart, R. B., 201
Stiles, D. A., 243
Stipek, D. J., 145, 149, 228
Stitt, B. A., 138, 153, 172, 174
Stockard, J., 148
Stoddart, T., 106, 243, 272
Stoneman, Z., 86
Stork, L., 89, 96
Strauss, S., 152
Strayer, F. F., 118, 128, 144
Strayer, J., 128
Sturla, E., 27, 28
Sugawara, A. I., 103, 200
Super, C. M., 119

Susman, E. J., 193
Sutton-Smith, B., 86, 121, 125
Swan, K., 161
Swann, J., 108–110, 174
Swanson, D. P., 77
Switzer, J. Y., 174

Talukder, E., 48
Tannen, D., 127
Tanner, J. M., 40, 238, 241
Tarule, J. M., 62
Tate, C. S., 203
Tauber, M. A., 73
Tavris, C., 6, 22, 65, 107, 159, 164, 187, 194, 202, 203, 255, 260
Taylor, F. G., 245
Taylor, M. G., 99
Teasdale, T., 40
Teixeira, R. A., 250
Terry, R., 196
Tesman, J. R., 46
Tew, J. D., 196
Thatcher, Margaret, 108, 109
Thiel, K. S., 251
Thoman, E. B., 41, 46
Thome, P. R., 196
Thompson, Clara, 59
Thompson, E. P., 243
Thompson, R. L., 40
Thompson, S. K., 95, 96, 243, 267
Thorne, B., 121
Thorpe, M., 148
Tieger, T., 192, 193
Tinsley, B. R., 48
Tobias, S., 227, 228
Tobin, P., 226
Tonick, I., 136
Tonick, I. V., 132
Toronto Daily Telegraph, 132
Tower, A., 168
Tracy, D. M., 226
Treder, J., 18
Trepanier-Street, M. L., 104
Tripp, D., 161
Tronick, E. Z., 46
Trotter, K. H., 203
Trudeau, Garry, 33, 138
Trudgill, P., 109
Tryon, K., 200
Tucker, P., 22, 23, 26
Turiel, E., 106, 243, 272
Turnbull, A., 16, 17, 198
Turner, C., 244
Turner, J. C., 128
Turner, R. A., 41

Ullian, D., 92
Ullian, D. Z., 99, 106, 243
Ullman, D. G., 71

Ulman, K. J., 240
Unger, R., 4, 18, 20, 24, 28, 170, 246
Urberg, K. A., 106

Valley News, 140, 162, 172
Van Komen R., 251
Vandell, D. L., 118
Vaughn, B. E., 248
Vaughn, L. S., 41, 95
Vidmar, N., 164
Vinciguerra, P., 200
Vines, G., 16, 24
Visperas, C., 127
Voight, N. L., 147
Von Bargen, D., 101
von der Lippe, A., 89
Voorhees, S. D., 160

Weber, D. P., 216, 223
Wade, C., 6, 22, 65, 107, 159, 164, 187, 194, 202, 203, 255, 260
Wadley, S. S., 4
Walker, L. J., 206–208
Walker, S. J. H., 46
Walsh, P. V., 94, 111
Walters, J., 129
Wanska, S. K., 129
Ward, J. V., 246
Ward, M. J., 60
Warren, M. P., 239, 247
Warshak, R. A., 84
Wasserman, G. A., 47
Wasserman, L., 89, 96
Watson, John, 202
Watterson, Bill, 106, 194
Wehren, A., 98
Weiner, B., 62
Weinraub, M., 48, 95, 97
Weinstein, R. S., 139
Weirman, M. E., 238
Weisner, T. S., 79
Weiss, R. J., 195, 196
Weisz, J. R., 149
Weitzman, L., 170
Weitzman, N., 77
Welch, M. R., 78
Welch, R., 162
Welsh, D. P., 248
Weltner, L., 240
Wenger, S., 194
Wessel, M. A., 203
West, M. M., 48
Westby, S. D., 104
Westerberg, V., 173
Whatmore, P. B., 18
Whitam, F. L., 276
White, C., 83
White, G. M., 199
White, H., 170, 171

Whitehead, H., 276, 277
Whitesell, N. R., 195
Whiting, B. B., 61, 79, 118, 188
Wigfield, A., 148, 227, 228
Wilcox, K. T., 222
Wilkinson, A., 93
Williams, F., 166
Williams, J. E., 96
Williams, J. H., 52, 59, 241, 255
Williams, K., 271
Williamson, N. E., 32, 34, 36
Willis, T. J., 274
Wilson, D. N., 130, 272
Windass, A., 137, 151
Wintre, M. G., 251
Wiser, C. V., 4
Wiser, W. H., 4, 10
Witelson, S. F., 221, 223
Wittmaier, B. C., 172
Wolchik, S. A., 72
Wolf, A. E., 251, 257, 262
Wolf, N., 244
Wolpe, J., 64
Women on Words and Images (WOWI), 172
Wood, C. H., 102
Wood, D. D., 143
Wood, J., 148
WOWI (Women on Words and Images), 172
Wright, J. C., 162
Wright, S., 97
Wright, V., 196
Wroblewski, R., 160
Wyche, K. F., 98

Yang, R. K., 47
Yasuna, A., 168
Yates, C. E., 274
Young, S., 227
Youniss, J., 216, 251

Zachau-Christiansen, B., 19, 41
Zack, E., 32
Zahn-Waxler, C., 191, 199
Zalk, S. R., 44
Zammuner, V. L., 111
Zappart, L. T., 148
Zarbatany, L., 123, 200
Zellman, G. L., 255, 256
Zern, D. S., 78
Zimbardo, P. G., 243, 253, 254
Zimeles, H., 248
Zimet, S., 172
Zucker, B., 273
Zucker, K. J., 130, 266, 268, 272, 273, 275
Zuckerman, D. M., 165, 169

SUBJECT INDEX

Ability vs. effort, 145–150
Abortion, for sex selection, 37, 38
Achievement:
  academic:
    effect of differential feedback on,
      147–150, 259
    gender differences in, 142, 258–259
      (*See also* Intellectual abilities)
  employed mothers as role models for, 80–81
  social learning of, 76–78
Achievement tests:
  gender bias in, 224–225, 229–230
  mathematics scores on, 218, 229, 230
  verbal scores on, 215, 224–225
Activity levels of infants, 41
Adolescents:
  cognitive development in, 243–247
  friendships of, 249–252
  media influence on, 162–163, 244–245,
    254–257
  overview of, 237–238
  parents' differential treatment of, 247–248
  rites of passage for, 259–261
  sexuality of, 242, 247, 254–257, 262
  spatial abilities in, 216, 225, 227
    (*See also* Peer influence, on adolescents; Puberty)
Adoption, gender preferences in, 35–36
Adrenal glands, 22, 193
Advertisements, 161, 162, 164, 245
Aggression:
  attacks vs. retaliation in, 193
  biological factors in, 190–193, 197, 283
  against females, prohibition of, 196–197
  gender stereotypes of, 188–189, 209, 210
  in other cultures, 197–198
  social learning of, 7–8, 88, 193–198
  in toddlers and preschoolers, 187–188
    (*See also* Sexual abuse/assault; Violent behavior)
Aliens (motion picture), 195
All in the Family (television program), 164
Altruism, 198–200
Ambiguous sexual differentiation (Pseudo-
    hermaphroditism):
  description of, 15, 22–25
  and socialization, 15–16, 23–29
Amnesia, pubertal, 240
Amniocentesis for sex testing, 17, 38
Anal stage, 54
Androgens:
  in aggressive behavior, 191–193
  in feminized males, 23–25, 27

Androgens (*Cont.*):
  and intellectual abilities, 221–22
  in masculinized females, 22, 23, 192, 193
  in normal prenatal development, 20, 221–222
  in normal pubertal changes, 238, 242
  and nurturant behavior, 202
    (*See also* Testosterone)
Animal House (motion picture), 256
Argument (debate), 127–128
Attacks vs. retaliation, 193
Attributions for success and failure, 145–150,
    228–29
Averages (statistics), 179

Barr body, 17
Beer commercials, 162
Berdaches, 276–277
Bewitched (television program), 160
Biological influence:
  in aggression, 190–193, 197, 283
  in intellectual abilities, 219–223,
    232–234, 283
  overview of, 7, 283
    (*See also* Hormones; Prenatal development)
Bionic Woman (television program), 162
Birth, parents' reactions to sex at, 15, 33–34
Blended gender roles, 276–277
Body image, 240–241
Books (*see* Children's literature)
Border work, 121–122
Boys:
  adolescent friendships of, 251–252
  childhood play groups of, 122–123
  gender identity disturbance diagnosis in,
    266–267
    (*See also* Males; Sons)
Brain development and function, 219–223
Bullying, 196

CAH (cogenital adrenal hyperplasia), 22–23
Captain Kangaroo (television program), 161
Castration fear, Freud on, 56–57, 65
Chameleon syndrome, 250
Change, intervention for (*see* Intervention for
    change)
Charlie's Angels (television program), 162
Childhood, loss of, 262
Children's literature:
  gender stereotypes in, 169–172
  impact of nonsexist, 172–173
  influence on adolescent sexuality, 254–255

Chores, children's, 79
Chromosomes
    abnormalities in, 17–19, 190
    and prenatal sex development, 16–20, 22
    and sex testing, 16–17
Circumcision:
    female, 260–261
    male, 41
Class (motion picture), 256
Class, social (*see* Social class)
Clitoris, 21, 22, 24
Clothing, gender-specific:
    and gender-disturbed children, 267, 268, 270
    for infants and toddlers, 42–43, 69
Cognitive development:
    in adolescents, 243–247
    theory of:
        compared to other theories, 92, 113
        evaluation of, 113–114
        overview of, 91–93, 112–113
        (*See also* Gender identity, in cognitive-developmental theory; Gender schemas; Intellectual abilities)
Commercials, television, 161, 162, 164, 245
Compassion, in moral reasoning, 206–208
Compatibility and gender segregation, 119–120
Competition:
    and adolescent girls' friendships, 250
    effect on altruism, 200
    in game preferences, 125–126
    by girls, with boys, 129
    in sexual behavior, 252
Competitive sports:
    level of participation in, 125–126, 226, 286–287
    and menarche, 241
    (*See also* Sports)
Compliance, 74–76, 136–137
Conception:
    artifical sex selection at, 36–37
    biology of sex determination during, 16
    gender stereotypes in descriptions of, 21–22
Conflict resolution strategies, 123–124
    (*See also* Aggression)
Congenital adrenal hyperplasia (CAH), 22–23
Consistency, gender (concept), 97, 101
Conventional reasoning, 205–206
Conversation, language used in, 108–110, 126–129
Corpus callosm, 219
Cosby Show (television program), 160, 179
Criminality and chromosome abnormalities, 18, 190
Cross-dressing, 267, 268, 270

Dartmouth College, 231
Date rape, 255–256
Dating, 249, 252–256
Daughters:
    as adolescents, 248
    effect of father absence on, 83–84
    as infants, 45–48

Daughters (*Cont.*):
    parents differential treatment of, 45–48, 248
    parents' preference for, 34
    psychoanalytic theory on, 57–58, 61–64
    (*See also* Females; Girls)
Debate (argument), 127–128
Dependence vs. independence:
    in adolescents, 247–248
    in infants, 47–48
    social learning theory on, 74–76, 77–78
    teachers' influence on, 136–137
DES (diethylstilbestrol), 222
Dick Van Dyke (television program), 160
Differential treatment (*see* Parents, differential treatment by; Teachers, differential treatment by)
Distributions (statistics), 182–186
Dominance hierarchy, 122–123, 124, 188, 251–242
    (*See also* Male dominance)
Drench effect, 168–169

Eating disorders, 240, 262
Educational Amendments Act (Title IX), 126
Effort vs. ability, 145–150
Ego, in psychoanalytic theory, 53–55
Elective mutism, 214
Elementary school children (*see* School-aged children [elementary level])
Employment:
    television portrayal of women's, 159–169
    working mothers as role models, 80–81
Endless Love (Spencer), 257
Estrogen:
    and nurturant behavior, 202
    prenatal effects on boys, 192
    and pseudo-hermaphrodites, 23, 24
    in pubertal changes, 23, 238
Ethnicity:
    effect on achievement expectations, 76–77, 231
    effect on gender segregation, 118
    effect on teachers' influence, 139, 140, 143, 147
    and emotional effects of puberty, 246
    media portrayal of, 158–159, 161, 172, 173

Fables task, 208
Failure and success, attributions for, 144–150, 228–229
Fairness, in moral reasoning, 205–206, 209
Fairy tales, 171
Fallopian tubes, 20–22
Family influence (*see* Fathers; Mothers; Parents; Siblings)
Family Ties (television program), 160
Fast Times at Ridgemont High (motion picture), 256
Fathers:
    absence of, 81–84, 248, 270–271
    and adolescents, 247–248
    and gender identity disturbance, 269–271
    and infants and toddlers, 48, 72–73
    nurturant behavior in, 202–203

Fathers *(Cont.)*:
  psychoanalytic theory on, 56–58
  summary of role of, 8–9
  television portrayal of, 160
  (See also Parents)
Females:
  chromosome abnormalities in, 18
  media portrayals of, 159–161, 244–245,
    254–257
  prenatal development of, 21–22
  psychoanalytic theory on development of,
    57–58, 61–64
  puberty in, 239–241, 243–246, 260–261
  (See also Daughters; Girls; Masculinized females
    [pseudo-hermaphrodites]; Mothers)
Feminized males (pseudo-hermaphrodites),
  23–25, 27–28
  (See also Gender identity, disturbance of)
Femme Nikita, La (motion picture), 195
5 alpha-reductase deficiency, 27–28
Formal operations stage, 243
Freestyle (television program), 166–168
Friday the 13th (motion picture), 168
Friendships:
  of adolescents, 249–252
  of children:
    and game preferences, 125–126
    gender segregation in, 122
    language used in, 126–128
    play group structure in, 122–125

Game preferences, 125–126
  (See also Play, gender differences in)
Gays and lesbians *(see* Homosexuality)
Gender, definition of, 8
Gender consistency (concept), 97, 101
Gender disturbance *(see* Gender identity,
  disturbance of)
Gender identity:
  with ambiguous sex differentiation, 26–28
  in cogitive-developmental theory:
    behavioral effects of, 96–97, 100–102
    definition of, 91–92
    developmental stages of, 94–100, 113–114
  disturbance of:
    and blended gender roles, 276–277
    diagnosis of, 266–268
    intervention for, 273–276
    in Native American berdaches, 276–277
    overview of, 265
    socialization as a cause of, 269–273
    in transsexualism, 273–274
  and gender-segregated play, 120–121
  of infants, 94–95
  overview of, 11
  peer influence in, 120–121, 130–131
  of preschoolers, 97–101
  in psychoanalytic theory, 55–66
  of toddlers, 95–97, 101
Gender permanence (concepts), 98–100, 113
Gender role, definition of, 4

Gender schemas:
  behavioral effects of, 107–110
  definition of, 92–93, 102
  in-group, out-group bias in, 106–107
  memory effects of, 103–105
  preventing formation of, 111–112
  reasoning effects of, 102–103
  stereotype exaggerations in, 105–106
Gender segregation:
  adult influence on, 131–132
  causes of, 119–121
  effects on mixed-sex interaction, 128–130, 132
  evidence for, 118–119, 121
  and game preferences, 125–126
  and language in friendships, 126–128
  peer influence in, 118–119, 122
  and play group structure, 122–125
  in school-aged children, 121–122
  strategies for change of, 132
  in toddlers and preschoolers, 118–121
Gender stability (concept), 97
Gender stereotypes:
  in adolescents, 243
  and aggression, 188–189, 209, 210
  benefits of, summarized, 5, 283–284
  changes in, 110–112, 285–287
  in children's literature, 170–172
  in descriptions of conception and prenatal
    development, 21–22
  disadvantages of, summarized, 5–6, 284–285
  about infants, 44–45
  and intellectual abilities, 228, 229, 230
  male school teachers' reinforcement of, 139–140
  and nurturant behavior, 203–204, 209–210
  in preschoolers, 101
  and social learning theory, 69
  on television:
    description of, 158–163
    impact of, 163–169
  in toddlers, 96–97, 101
  (See also Gender schemas)
Genetics *(see* Chromosomes)
Genital stage, 55–59
Genitalia:
  ambiguous, in pseudo-hermaphrodites, 22–25
  children's knowledge about, and gender
    identity, 96, 99, 112, 113
  circumsion of, 41, 260–261
  gender-disturbed children's attitude to,
    266–267
  normal prenatal development of, 20, 21
  pubertal effects on, 242
  surgical modifications/corrections to, 24–26,
    274
Girls:
  adolescent friendships of, 249–251
  childhood playgroups of, 123–125
  gender identity disturbance diagnosis in,
    267–268
  (See also Daughters; Females)
Gonad, 20
Groups vs. individuals (statistics), 180–181

Growing Pains (television program), 160

Hand preference, 220, 223
Harrassment (*see* Sexual harrassment)
Helping behavior (altruism), 198–200
Hemispheric specialization, of the brain, 219–223
Hermaphrodites, 22
  (*See also* Pseudo-hermaphroditism [ambiguous
    sexual differentiation])
High schools, influence of, 258
Histogram, 182
Homosexuality:
  adolescent attitudes on, 244, 251, 157
  vs. gender identity disturbance, 273, 275
  of parents, 84–85
  transsexualism, 273–274
  (*See also* Gender identity, disturbance of)
Hormone treatment, 18, 26
Hormones:
  in aggressive behavior, 191–193
  and intellectual abilities, 221–222
  in nurturant behavior, 7, 201–202
  in prenatal development, 20–21, 192, 221–222
  progesterone, in masculinized females, 22
  and puberty, 238, 242
  (*See also* Androgens; Estrogen; Testosterone)
H-Y antigen, 20
Hypothalmus, 219

Id, 52–55
Identity (*see* Gender identity)
Immune system in male prenatal vulnerability, 19
Independence (*see* Dependence vs. independence)
Individuals vs. groups (statistics), 180–181
Infanticide:
  as evidence against "maternal instinct," 202
  for sex selection, 37, 38
Infants:
  activity levels of, 41
  differential treatment of, 42–49
  gender identity of, 94–95
  gender-typed perceptions of, 44–45
  parents' preferences for gender of, 32–40
  perceptual abilities of, 40, 94
  physical development of, 40
  psychoanalytic theory on, 53–54
  social responsiveness of, 46–47
  spatial abilities in, 217
  stress responses of, 47–48
Inferiority, Freud on women's feelings of,
  57–59, 62–63
In-group, out-group bias, 106–107
Instruction, differential treatment in, 137–139
Intellectual abilities:
  biological theory on, 219–223, 232–234, 283
  and chromosome abnormalities, 18, 190
  evidence showing difference in, 214–219
  mathematical ability, 217–219, 222, 223,
    227–232
  overview of, 213

Intellectual abilities (*Cont.*):
  practical significance of differences in, 217,
    230, 233
  socialization theory on, 223–233
  spatial ability, 215–218, 221–223,
    225–227, 233
  strategies for improving girls', 231–232
  verbal abilities, 214–215, 217, 220, 221,
    223–225
International Olympic Committee, 24
Intervention for change:
  in gender identity disturbance, 273–276
  in gender segregation, 132
  in girls' intellectual abilities, 231–232
  in stereotypes, 110–112, 285–287
  in teacher behavior, 112, 152–154
Island of the Blue Dolphins (O'Dell), 170

Junior high schools, influence of, 258–259
Justice, in moral reasoning, 205–206, 208–209

Karyotype, 17
Klinefelter's syndrome, 18

LA Law (television program), 160
Labia:
  in female circumcision, 260–261
  prenatal development of, 21–24
Language:
  sexist, effect of, 173–175
  in speech, 108–110, 126–129
  (*See also* Verbal abilities)
Learning:
  effect of gender schemas on, 105
  in infants, 40
  (*See also* Intellectual abilities; social learning)
Left Hand of Darkness, The (Le Guin), 285
Left-handedness, 220, 222
Lesbians, as parents, 84–85
Libido, 52–54
Little House on the Prairie (Wilder), 173
Little Mermaid, The (motion picture), 9
Love vs. sex, 255

Male dominance:
  in children's literature, 170–171
  in children's television, 161–162
  effect of gender segregation on, 128–130
  school influences on, 151–152
Males:
  chromosome abnormalities in, 18–19
  feminized (pseudo-hermaphrodites),
    23–25, 27–28
  media portrayals of, 159–161, 245, 254–257
  parental preference for, 32–40
  prenatal development of, 20–22, 192
  psychoanalytic theory on development of,
    55–57, 60–61, 64–65
  puberty in, 242–243, 246, 260
  as school teachers, 139–140
  vulnerability of, during prenatal
    development, 19
  (*See also* Boys; Fathers; Male dominance; Sons)

Mary Tyler Moore (television program), 160

Masculinized female (pseudo-hermaphrodites):
  aggressive behavior in, 192–193
  biological development of, 22–23, 26
  intellectual abilities of, 222
  nurturant behavior in, 202
  parental socialization of, 270

Maternal instinct (nurturance), 7, 198, 200–204, 209–210

Mathematical abilities, 217–219, 222, 223, 227–232

Mean (statistics), 179

Media influence:
  on adolescents, 162–163, 244–245, 254–257
  of advertisements, 161, 162, 164, 245
  of motion pictures, 9, 195, 256
  overview of, 9, 157, 175
  on violent behavior, 157–158, 168, 194–195, 256–257
  (*See also* Children's literature; Television)

Memory:
  effect of gender schemas on, 103–105
  of infants, 40

Men (*see* Boys; Fathers; Males; Sons)

Menarche, 239–241, 260, 262

Menopause and nurturant behavior, 202

Menstruation:
  age at menarche, 239, 241, 262
  brain in regulation of, 219
  emotional response to, 239–240, 268
  and gender identity disturbance, 268
  rites of passage associated with, 260

Mental rotation tasks, 216

Miami Vice (television program), 160

Mister Ed (television program), 160

Mister Rogers (television program), 161

Mixed-sex interaction:
  effect of gender segregation on, 128–130, 132
  in romantic relationship rehearsal, 121–122
  (*See also* Romantic relationships; Sexuality)

Morality:
  cognitive theory on, 205–206
  overview of, 204–205, 208–209
  psychoanalytic theory on, 58, 209
  "voice" theory on, 206–208

Mothers:
  absence of, 84
  and adolescents, 248
  differential treatment by, 45–47, 72, 248
  employed, as role models, 80–81
  and infants and toddlers, 45–47, 72
  nurturant behavior in, 7, 198, 200–204, 209–210
  psychoanalytic theory on, 55–58, 59, 60–62
  (*See also* Parents)

Motion pictures, influence of, 9, 195, 256

Mount Holyoke College, 231

MTV, 163, 164

Mullerian ducts, 20, 21

Mullerian inhibiting factor, 20, 22–23

Murphy Brown (television program), 160

Music videos, 163, 164
  (*See also* Rock music)

Mutism, elective, 214

Names, gender-specific:
  effect of, 174
  gender-disturbed children's attitude to, 267
  for infants, 42

Native American berdaches, 276–277

New England Patriots (football team), 188

Newberry Award, 170, 171

Novels, romance, 254–255

Nursery rhymes, 171

Nurturance, 7, 198, 200–204, 209–210

Observational learning, 70, 88
  (*See also* Role models, in social learning theory)

Oedipal stage, 55–57, 65–66, 113

Only children, 86

Oral stage, 53–54

Ovaries, 21–23, 238

Parents:
  absence of 81–84, 248, 270–271
  aggression toward, 187
  and aggressive behavior, 193–194, 196–198
  differential treatment by:
    of adolescents, 247–248
    of infants, 42–49
    of toddlers, 8–9, 69, 72–73, 224
  and gender identity disturbance, 269–272, 275
  gender preferences of, 32–40
  gender-typed perceptions of infants in, 44
  homosexuality of, 84–85
  and intellectual abilities, 223–224, 227
  in preventing gender stereotype formation, 111–112, 286
  and prosocial behavior, 200, 203
  in social learning:
    of achievement, 76–78
    in general, 8–9, 282
    of independence/compliance, 74–78, 247–248
    through play, 8–9, 72–73
  (*See also* Fathers; Mothers)

Paternal instinct, 202–203

Peer influence:
  on adolescents:
    in dating and sexual relationships, 252–257
    in friendships, 249–252
    in rites of passage, 261
    in school behavior, 250–251, 259
  on children:
    gender differences in level of, 130–131
    in gender identity, 120–121, 130–131
    in gender identity disturbance, 271–272
    in gender segregation, 118–119, 122
    overview of, 9, 117–118, 282
    in school, 141, 150–152

Penis:
  in feminized males, 24–25, 27–28

Penis (*Cont.*):
  gender-disturbed children's attitude to,
    266–267
  prenatal development of, 20, 21
Penis envy, Freud on, 57–59, 63, 65
Penis-at-twelve syndrome, 27–28
Perceptual abilities of infants, 40, 94
Permanence, gender (concept), 98–100, 113
Personality differences:
  in altruism, 198–200
  in morality, 58, 204–209
  in nurturance, 7, 198, 200–204, 209–210
  overview of, 177–178, 210–211
  (*See also* Aggression; Psychoanalytic theory,
    Freud's)
Physical development:
  of infants, 40
  at puberty, 238–243
  (*See also* Biological influence; Prenatal
    development)
Play, gender differences in:
  effect on aggression, 188
  Erikson on, 58
  and father absence, 81–82
  in father/infant play, 48
  in game preferences, 125–126
  and gender segregation, 118–122
  and intellectual abilities, 225–226
  parental influence on, 8–9, 72–73
  peer influence on, 118–122
  in rough-and-tumble play, 120, 188
  teachers' influence on, 152–153
  (*See also* Toys, gender-specific)
Play groups, structure of, 122–125
Porky's (motion picture), 256
Positive social deviance, 246
Postconventional reasoning, 206
Preconventional reasoning, 205
Prenatal development:
  and aggressive behavior, 192–193
  chromosomes' role in, 16–20, 22
  of females, 21–22
  gender stereotypes in descriptions of, 21–22
  and intellectual abilities, 221–222
  male vulnerability during, 19
  of males, 20–22, 192
  overview of, 15–16
Preschoolers:
  aggression in, 187–188
  cognitive-developmental theory on, 97–101
  gender identity of, 97–101
  peer influence in gender-segregated play of,
    118–121
  psychoanalytic theory on, 55–59, 65–66
  spatial abilities in, 217
  teachers' influence on, 137
Princess effect, 246
Progesterone, in masculinized females, 22
Prosocial behavior:
  altruism, 198–200
  nurturance, 7, 198, 200–204, 209–210

Prosocial behavior (*Cont.*):
  overview of, 204
Pseudo-hermaphroditism (ambiguous sexual
  differentiation):
  description of, 15, 22–25
  and socialization, 15–16, 23–29
Psychoanalytic theory, Freud's:
  compared to other theories, 87, 113, 114, 209
  evidence for, 64–66
  on female development, 57–59, 61–64
  on male development, 55–57, 60–61, 64–65
  on morality, 58, 209
  overview of, 52–53
  positive contributions of, 59–63
  psychosexual stages in, 53–59
  weaknesses of, 63–64
Pubertal amnesia, 240
Puberty:
  age of, 239, 241, 242
  and aggressive behavior, 193
  cultural rites and ceremonies at, 259–261
  emotional responses to, 239–240, 242, 243,
    245–246, 268
  in feminized males, 24, 25
  gender-disturbed children's response to, 268
  and intellectual abilities, 222–223
  in masculinized females, 23
  physical changes during, 238–243
  (*See also* Adolescents)
Punctuated socialization, 8–11, 282–283

Rambling Rose (motion picture), 256
Rape, 26, 255–256
  (*See also* Sexual abuse/assault; Sexual
    harrassment)
Reading skills, 224
  (*See also* Verbal abilities)
Reasoning:
  and gender schemas, 102–103
  moral, 204–208
  (*See also* Intellectual abilities)
Reinforcement, definition of, 70
Reproductive organs, 20–24, 238
Retaliation vs. attacks, 193
Right-handedness, 220
Risky Business (motion picture), 256
Rites of passage, cultural, 259–261
Rock music, 163, 164, 256–257
Rod and frame task, 216
Role Models:
  and aggressive behavior, 194–195
  in cogitive-developmental theory, 92, 101,
    110, 113
  in social learning theory:
    compared to role models in other theories,
      87, 113
    employed mothers as, 80–81
    general impact of, 70–71, 80
    homosexual parents as, 84–85
    for only children, 86
    and parental absence, 81–84, 248, 270–271

Role Models (*Cont.*):
    representativeness of, 71
    siblings as, 85–87
    on television, 158–163, 194–195
    (*See also* Fathers; Media influences; Mothers)
Romance novels, 254–255
Romantic relationships:
    dating, 249, 252–254
    effect of gender segregation on, 132
    media portrayal of, 159, 162, 254–255,
        256–257
    rehearsed by school-aged children, 121–122
    (*See also* Sexuality)
Rotation tasks, 216

Samples (statistics), 182
SAT (achievement test):
    gender bias in, 224–225, 229–230
    mathematics scores on, 218, 230
    verbal scores on, 215, 224–225
School-aged children (elementary level):
    peer influence on gender segregation of,
        121–122
    social learning of independence/compliance in,
        75–78
    spatial abilities in, 216–217
    (*See also* Schools, influence of; Teachers,
        differential treatment by)
Schools, influence of:
    on adolescents, 257–259
    and male dominance, 151–152
    overview of, 135–136, 154–155
    and peer pressure, 150–151, 250–251, 259
    through textbooks, 172
    (*See also* Teachers, differential treatment by)
Scrotum, 20, 24
Segregation, by gender (*see* Gender segregation)
Selection of sex, 36–38
Self-confidence:
    in academics, 144–150, 174, 227–228, 231
    loss of, in adolescence, 243, 244, 245, 246,
        262
Self-consciousness, in adolescents, 243, 244, 250
Self-control:
    and aggressive behavior, 196
    and father absence, 82
Seminal vescicles, 20
Sesame Street (television program), 161
Sex, definition of, 8
Sex chromosomes (*see* Chromosomes)
Sex constancy task, 98–100
Sex determination (biological process), 16
    (*See also* Sex testing)
Sex hormones (*see* Hormones)
Sex organs, reproductive, 20–24, 238
    (*See also* Genitalia)
Sex preferences of parents, 32–40
Sex reassignment surgery, 24–26, 274
Sex selection, 36–38
Sex testing:
    of athletes, 16–17, 24
    prenatal, for sex selection, 37–38

Sexist language, 173–175
Sex-linked chromosome abnormalities, 17
Sexual abuse/assault:
    by adolescent boys, 255–257
    and Freud's theories, 63–64, 65–66
    media influence in, 256–257
    parents' warnings on, 75
    rape, 26, 255–256
Sexual harrassment, 129–130, 151–152, 188, 256
Sexuality:
    of adolescents, 242, 247, 254–257, 262
    and gender segregation, 121–122
    of girls, and father absence, 83–84
    media influence on, 254–257
    parents' concerns about, 247
    (*See also* Romantic relationships)
She-Ra, Princess of Power (television program), 162
Siblings as role models, 85–87
Single parent homes:
    and gender identity disturbance, 270–271
    influence on adolescent sons, 248
    role models in, 81–84
    television portrayal of, 160
Smurfs (television program), 160
Social advantages/disadvantages of gender:
    and aggressive behavior, 195–196
    and socialization of pseudo-hermaphrodites,
        28, 29
Social class:
    and achievement expectations, 76–77
    and aggressive behavior, 191
    and emotional effects of puberty, 246
Social deviance, positive, 246
Social learning:
    of achievement orientation, 76–78
    of aggression, 7–8, 88, 193–198
    of gender roles in general, 6–7
    of independence/compliance, 74–76, 77–78
    in non-western cultures, 78–79
    of nurturant behavior, 202–203
    observational learning in, 70, 88
        (*See also* Role models, in social learning
         theory)
    play in, 72–73
    theory on:
        compared to other theories, 87, 92, 113
        components of, 70–71
        evaluation of, 87–89
        overview of, 69
        (*See also* Socialization)
Social responsiveness in infants, 46–47
Socialization:
    in gender identity disturbance, 269–273
    in intellectual abilities, 223–233
    of pseudo-hermaphrodites, 15–16, 23–29
    punctuated 8–11, 282–283
    and social advantages/disadvantages of gender,
        28, 29
    summary of gender differences in, 10–11, 282
    (*See also* Role models, in social learning theory;
        Social learning)
Sonograms, 38

Sons:
  as adolescents, 247–248
  effect of father absence on, 81–84
  as infants, 45–48
  parents' preference for, 32–40
  parents' treatment of, 45–48, 247–248
  psychoanalytic theory on development of,
    55–57, 60–61, 64–65
  (*See also* Boys; Males)
Spatial abilities, 215–218, 221–223,
  225–227, 233
Speech, 108–110, 126–129
Spelman College, 231
Spermarche, 242
Sports:
  gender and participation in, 125–126, 226,
    286–287
  and menarche, 241
  sex testing of athletes in, 16–17, 24
  and spatial abilities, 225–226
Stability, gender (concept), 97
Stake-out (motion picture), 256
Standard deviation (statistics), 181–182
Standardized achievement tests (*see* Achievement
  tests)
Star Trek (television program), 160, 174
Statistical methods, 178–187
Stereotypes (*see* Gender stereotypes)
Stress, infants' responses to, 47–48
Success and failure, attributions for, 144–150,
  228–229
Superego, 53, 55, 58
Sure Thing, The (motion picture), 256
Surgery, for sex reassignment, 24–26, 274

Teachers:
  differential treatment by:
    causes of, 140–144, 147
    in classroom management, 136–137,
      141–142
    effect on compliance/independence, 136–137
    effect on self-confidence, 144–150, 259
    in feedback, 144–150
    gender stereotypes in, 139–140,
      142–144, 229
    in instruction, 137–139, 142
    by male teachers, 139–140
    strategies for changing, 152–154
  education of, 154
  in prevention of gender schema formation, 112
Teenage Mutant Ninja Turtles, 157–158
Television:
  advertisements on, 161, 162, 164, 245
  children's programming on, 157–158, 161–162
  children's receptiveness to, 158
  content analysis of, 158–163
  evaluation of impact of, 163–169
  influence on adolescents, 162–163, 245, 254
  level of exposure to, 158
  positive effects of, 169
  reasons for influence of, 158
  and violent behavior, 157–158, 194–195

Terminator 2 (motion picture), 195
Testes, 20, 24
Testosterone:
  in aggressive behavior, 191, 192
  in feminized males, 27
  an intellectual abilities, 222
  in prenatal development, 20, 27, 192, 222
  in pubertal changes, 242
Textbooks, gender stereotypes in, 172
Timing of maturation theory, 222–223
Title IX (Educational Amendments Act), 126
Toddlers:
  aggression in, 187–188
  cognitive-developmental theory on, 95–97, 101
  differential treatment of, by parents, 69, 224
  gender identity of, 95–97, 101
  independence/compliance in, 74–75
  peer influence in gender segregation of,
    118–121
  psychoanalytic theory on, 54
  social learning theory on, 69, 74–75
  verbal ability in, 214
Toxemia, 19
Toys, gender-specific:
  children's response to, 89, 96, 101–102, 108
  for infants, 43–45
  and intellectual abilities, 225–227
  parents' influence in choice of, 72–73
  television advertisements for, 162
  for toddlers, 72–73
Transsexualism, 84–85, 273–274
Trisomy X, 18
Turner's syndrome, 18

Uterus, 20–22

Vagina, 21, 22
Variation within a group (statistics), 181–182
Vas deferens, 20
Verbal abilities, 214–215, 217, 220, 221,
  223–225
Victim blaming, 256
Violent behavior:
  an chromosome abnormalities, 18, 190
  media influence on, 157–158, 168, 194–195
  (*See also* Aggression; Sexual abuse/assault)
Virginity, loss of, 255
Voice, in moral reasoning, 206–208

Water-level task, 216, 222
Weight gain at puberty, 240–241
Who's the Boss (television program), 160
Wolffian ducts, 20
Women (*see* Daughters; Females; Girls; Mothers)
Wonder Woman (television program), 162
Working mothers, 80–81
Wrinkle in Time (L'Engle), 173

XYY males, 18, 190